Violent Offenders

Violent Offenders

Understanding and Assessment

EDITED BY CHRISTINA A. PIETZ

AND

CURTIS A. MATTSON

OXFORD
UNIVERSITY PRESS

Oxford University Press is a department of the University of
Oxford. It furthers the University's objective of excellence in research,
scholarship, and education by publishing worldwide.

Oxford   New York
Auckland   Cape Town   Dar es Salaam   Hong Kong   Karachi
Kuala Lumpur   Madrid   Melbourne   Mexico City   Nairobi
New Delhi   Shanghai   Taipei   Toronto

With offices in
Argentina   Austria   Brazil   Chile   Czech Republic   France   Greece
Guatemala   Hungary   Italy   Japan   Poland   Portugal   Singapore
South Korea   Switzerland   Thailand   Turkey   Ukraine   Vietnam

Oxford is a registered trademark of Oxford University Press
in the UK and certain other countries.

Published in the United States of America by
Oxford University Press
198 Madison Avenue, New York, NY 10016

CIP data is on file at the Library of Congress.
ISBN 978–0–19–991729–7

9 8 7 6 5 4 3 2 1
Printed in the United States of America
on acid-free paper

CONTENTS

SECTION III. Evaluative Approach and Special Considerations

ABOUT THE EDITORS

Dr. Christina A. Pietz earned her PhD from Texas A&M University in 1989. She then completed an internship and postdoctoral fellowship specializing in forensic/correctional psychology. She is board certified in forensic psychology and has worked at the United States Medical Center for Federal Prisoners since 1990. In this capacity, she has completed psychological evaluations for federal courts throughout the United States and testified as an expert witness in federal court, state court, and military court. She has also taught several courses in deviant behavior.

Dr. Curtis A. Mattson earned his PsyD from the Forest Institute of Professional Psychology in 2009. He completed an internship in correctional psychology and a postdoctoral residency with specializations in forensic psychology and personality assessment. Currently, he is a licensed psychologist and professor at the Forest Institute, where he teaches courses in assessment and personality.

CONTRIBUTORS

Kathryn C. Applegate, MS
Department of Psychology
The University of Alabama
Tuscaloosa, Alabama

Ivonne E. Bazerman, PsyD
Federal Bureau of Prisons

Henrik Belfrage, PhD
Department of Social Sciences
Mid Sweden University
Östersund, Sweden

Randy Borum, PsyD
School of Information
University of South Florida
Tampa, Florida

Katherine Bracken-Minor, PhD
Federal Bureau of Prisons

Chad A. Brinkley, PhD, ABPP
United States Medical Center for
Federal Prisoners

David M. Corey, PhD, ABPP
Corey & Stewart, Consulting
Psychologists
Portland, Oregon

Robert L. Denney, PsyD, ABPP
The School of Professional Psychology
at Forest Institute
Springfield, Missouri

Kevin S. Douglas, LLB, PhD
Department of Psychology
Simon Fraser University
Burnaby, Canada
and
Mid Sweden University
Sundsvall, Sweden

Laura E. Drislane, MS
Florida State University
Tallahassee, Florida

Donald Dutton, PhD
Department of Psychology
University of British Columbia
Vancouver, Canada

R. Gregg Dwyer, MD, EdD
Department of Psychiatry and
Behavioral Sciences
Medical University of South
Carolina
Charleston, South Carolina

Rachel Fazio, PsyD
The School of Professional Psychology
at Forest Institute
Springfield, Missouri

Stacey Goldstein, MA
Massachusetts School of Professional
Psychology,
Newton, Massachusetts

Laura S. Guy, PhD
Department of Psychiatry
University of Massachusetts Medical
School
Worcester, Massachusetts

Kathleen M. Heide, PhD
Department of Criminology
University of South Florida
Tampa, Florida

Eric W. Hickey, PhD
California School of Forensic Studies
Alliant International University
Alhambra, California

Christina Karakanta, BA
University of British Columbia
Vancouver, Canada

Robert Kinscherff, PhD, Esq
Massachusetts School of Professional
Psychology
Newton, Massachusetts

Kimberly Larson, JD, PhD
Department of Psychiatry
University of Massachusetts
Medical School
Worcester, Massachusetts

Curtis A. Mattson, PsyD
The School of Professional Psychology
at Forest Institute
Springfield, Missouri

Geoffrey R. McKee, PhD, ABPP
Department of Neuropsychiatry &
Behavioral Sciences
University of South Carolina School
of Medicine
Columbia, South Carolina
and
Department of Psychiatry &
Behavioral Sciences
Medical University of South Carolina
Charleston, South Carolina

Alix M. McLearen, PhD
Federal Bureau of Prisons

Holly A. Miller, PhD
College of Criminal Justice
Sam Houston State University
Huntsville, Texas

David F. Mrad, PhD, ABPP
The School of Professional Psychology
at Forest Institute
Springfield, Missouri

Daniel J. Neller, PsyD, ABPP
Independent practice
Wynne, Arkansas

William Newman, MD
Department of Psychiatry and
Behavioral Sciences
University of California-Davis School
of Medicine
Sacramento, California

Candice L. Odgers, PhD
Sanford School of Public Policy
Duke University
Durham, North Carolina

Christopher J. Patrick, PhD
Department of Clinical Psychology
Florida State University
Tallahassee, Florida

Christina A. Pietz, PhD, ABPP
United States Medical Center for
Federal Prisoners

Gianni Pirelli, PhD
The Center for Evaluation and
Counseling
Parsippany, New Jersey

Philip J. Resnick, MD
Division of Forensic Psychiatry
Case Western Reserve University
School of Medicine
Cleveland, Ohio

Michael A. Russell, MA
Department of Psychology and
Social Behavior
University of California, Irvine
Irvine, California

Melanie Schettler Heto, PsyD
The Persentio Practice
Denver, Colorado

Charles Scott, MD
Department of Psychiatry and
Behavioral Sciences
University of California-Davis
School of Medicine
Sacramento, California

Casey O. Stewart, PsyD, ABPP
Corey & Stewart, Consulting
Psychologists
Portland, Oregon

Terrance J. Taylor, PhD
Department of Criminology &
Criminal Justice
University of Missouri–St. Louis
St. Louis, Missouri

Christie Tetreault, BA
University of British Columbia
Vancouver, Canada

J. Michael Vecchio
Department of Criminal Justice &
Criminology
Loyola University Chicago
Chicago, Illinois

Noah C. Venables, MS
Florida State University
Tallahassee, Florida

Michael J. Vitacco, PhD
Department of Psychiatry
and Health Behavior
Georgia Regents University
Augusta, Georgia

Tina D. Wall, MS
The University of New Orleans
New Orleans, Louisianna

Bethany K. Walters, BS
Alliant International University
Alhambra, California

Katherine White
University of British Columbia
Vancouver, Canada

Dustin B. Wygant, PhD
Department of Psychology
Eastern Kentucky University
Richmond, Kentucky

Patricia A. Zapf, PhD
Department of Psychology
John Jay College of Criminal Justice
The City University of New York
New York, New York

Overview and Correlates of Violence

Psychological Perspectives of Violence

MELANIE SCHETTLER HETO ■

Historically, violence has been an area of considerable interest among psychologists of all camps. Likely as a function of the degree of responsibility that has been placed on the profession to explain and eliminate violence, each orientation of psychology has sought to apply its own tenets to an understanding of such conduct. In cases where a theory has fallen short, a new one has attempted to fill the gaps. The field of psychology has posited innumerable theories, models, and perspectives regarding violence, some with significant empirical support. While there may be no unifying paradigm with which to compare or contrast these perspectives from one another, it does become apparent that the same variables are presented time and time again, although with great variance in the emphasis they are given for their role in violence. For this reason it is likely that models presented within the last 20 years appear to be taking on a more integrated approach to conceptualizing and researching violence. The following chapter, without attempt to analyze or evaluate, offers a glimpse of the variety of psychological viewpoints as they relate to violent offending, whether they have been treated as major or minor to the field. This compilation is by no means exhaustive, but it hopefully contributes to continued generation of thought and understanding of violent behavior.

PSYCHOANALYTIC AND PSYCHODYNAMIC THEORIES OF VIOLENCE

Psychoanalytic and psychodynamic theories of violence are based on understanding how one's past impacts present thoughts, behaviors, and feelings, whether consciously or unconsciously. Therefore, violent behavior is believed to be driven by a person's mental representation of himself or herself or others, by entrenched wishes and motivations, by defensive reactions to trauma or loss, by a learned style for relating to others, or by an affective state.

Freud's psychoanalytic theories described aggression primarily as a function of repressed anger and a subsequent cathartic reaction to that anger. Catharsis is the release or unblocking of negative feelings, which allows for tension reduction. Research has found evidence that anger is at the root of aggressive behavior (Anderson & Bushman, 2002), that the degree of anger is related to the level of aggression, and that an expression of aggression can reduce anger and further aggression (Konečni, 1975). However, nonaggressive acts were also found to decrease anger and subsequent aggression, as well as produce longer term relief (Dollard, Doob, Miller, Mowrer, & Sears, 1939; Konečni, 1975). This remains a commonly held belief in dynamic therapy, and many therapeutic interventions have targeted anger reduction via nonaggressive expression of denied or repressed anger, so as to allow an individual to have diminished need to discharge it.

Freud's later theories emphasized the role of the superego in the inhibition of aggressive impulses. Freud thought that the superego was responsible for the conscience and developed out of the child's vying for his or her parents' affection and ultimately identifying with them both through internalizing parental values and standards (Freud, 1923). Theorists and researchers since then have continued to study such a mechanism's role in the development of morals and values. The father in particular has been held accountable by psychoanalysts for his offspring's potential for violence. Object relations theorists, specifically, believe that without a present attuned parental figure, there can be no internalization of a sophisticated object that provides a model for how to relate to others. As a consequence, violence is relied on as such a method for relating, as it is innate and has not been replaced by higher order defenses in the fatherless child (Bion, 1970; Perelberg, 1999; Winnicott, 1971).

In this way, analytic psychologists also tend to think in terms of the defenses that a person employs to protect himself or herself from ego fracture. The defenses are often qualified in terms of their primitiveness or sophistication. More mature defenses, such as repression, displacement, isolation, intellectualization, or regression, assist an individual in coping with stress without violating the boundaries of reality or social convention. More primitive defenses are necessary when the ego is more fragile. These include projection, splitting, projective identification, denial, and acting out. These defenses are employed to keep emotions altogether warded off from consciousness. As such, they are often acted out, turned into some other feeling, or placed onto someone else. In violent individuals, there is found to be a lack of higher order defenses and an inability to inhibit aggressive urges (Hyatt-Williams, 1998). Similarly, another way for an individual to disown his or her feelings is to identify with the aggressor (A. Freud, 1936/1966). Here, one can escape vulnerability by internalizing the aggression and becoming the source of the menace.

Object relations, more generally, maintained Freud's drive theory and emphasized two primary inborn human drives, libido and aggression, under which all emotions are classified. The experiences that an infant has with primary objects (others) determine how emotions are experienced and developed. Both biological and environmental sources can contribute to the experience of affect, including, for example, cognitive deficits and trauma. According to Kernberg (1992), rage is the primary affect of aggression and is classified with other negative feelings, such as hate, envy, and irritability. In contrast, the libido's primary affect is elation and is categorized with other positive and gratifying feelings. Because an infant is innately driven to seek gratification, such as when feeling close to a loved object, he or she is similarly averse to the pain or frustration caused by separation from that object. Rage follows pain or frustration, and so the source of that pain or frustration is sought to be removed. Violence can enter here as a way to remove the source of rage. Or, when the source of both gratification and rage are the same, such as in the case of an abusive caregiver, Kernberg suggests the two opposing drives come together. The merging of these opposing drives can lead to the characterological disturbance of sadistic pleasure.

John Bowlby (1965) developed his attachment theory out of his study of object relations. He held that prolonged maternal deprivation during early developmental years "stands foremost among the causes of delinquent character development" (p. 41). He believed the deprivation of sustained early attachment led to an "affectionless character" (p. 57). The circumstances that produce such a character, he deemed, included poor opportunity for close attachment in the first 3 years, separation for a period of several months, or changes from one "mother figure" to another.

Bowlby's work has been the source of much continued investigation and empirical support. His construction of the concept of internal working models (IWMs) as unconscious maps of the self and others, which are created through an infant's early caregiving relationships, has been reinforced by sound biological research (Bowlby, 1973, 1980, 1988; Fonagy, Target, Gergely, Allen, & Bateman, 2003). Throughout life, IWMs help one decipher one's own and others' emotional states, serve as a guide to relationship and social experiences, and aid in the process of self-understanding (Bowlby, 1988).

Fonagy and his colleagues have continued to research attachment theory and the concept of an IWM and biological correlates (Fonagy et al., 2003). According to him and his colleagues, the development of mentalization, the ability to understand one's own and others' mental states, is the process that creates IWMs. Mentalization is taught via the attuned and accurately reflected responses of a caregiver, which allows for an individual to become a secure adult (Fonagy et al., 2003). A nonpathological individual with strong mentalization capabilities can regulate his or her emotions, be empathic, and reflect on others' mental states and respond accordingly. As caregivers' behavioral and affective signals are repeated over time, they become expectations in children's minds (Lyons-Ruth & Jacobvitz, 1999). Children learn to behave in novel situations according to the responses they have received in the past. Secure relationships between infants and parents heighten children's receptiveness to their caregivers' socialization incentives. In turn, secure children grow to expect supportive, satisfying interactions with others. When secure children become adults, they carry out relationships in a manner that fosters an environment in which their partners respond according to their positive expectations. Alternatively, the IWMs of insecurely attached children are characterized by distrust and hostility. These children, and later as adults, predict that others will respond to them with negativity, and so behave in a manner that elicits aggression (Fonagy et al., 2003).

Likewise, de Zulueta's (2001) research on trauma and loss provided a similar model to understand aggression. She explained that angry expressions from a baby are intended to reinstate closeness and communicate a need. Loss, enduring disregard for, or abuse of a child's need for connection can promote pathological aggression. Gilligan (1996) supported the notion that violence emerged out of abuse in the early parental relationships in his study of violent inmates. He proposed that rage developed as a response to the shame and humiliation of childhood maltreatment, rejection, or neglect. Indeed, disorganized attachment, a particularly strong form of insecure attachment, is correlated with aggressive behavior (Shaw & Vondra, 1995).

Meloy (2006) also understands violence as pathology of attachment. An individual who has developed maladaptive behaviors may become violent in an attempt to approach or distance oneself from another in order to meet his or her attachment needs. Meloy classifies violence based on whether it is intended for self-preservation or for predation. When violence is in response to fear or anger, and is intended to protect oneself from harm, Meloy called it *affective* violence. When it is not in response to a feeling, but is planned, he considers it to be *predatory* violence. Affective violence is characterized by arousal of the autonomic nervous system; is in response to a perceived threat (internal or external); and is unplanned, reactive, and often impulsive. Predatory violence is meditated and without emotion.

SOCIAL THEORIES ON VIOLENCE

Commonly referred to as the Yale group, Dollard et al. (1939) launched the frustration-aggression model by declaring that aggression is invariably a consequence of frustration. Frustration was defined as the state produced by the interference of the attainment of a goal. When frustration does not lead to aggression, it is thought that some obstacle will prevent the outcome of the aggression or that the predicted consequences to the aggression outweigh the benefits. Additionally, interruptions of the aggressive act were believed to further strengthen the aggression. The model explained that the nature and degree of the aggression are correspondent to how directly the target is related to the frustration. In addition, aggressive acts can be modified or displaced if there is a threat of punishment to the aggressor.

Berkowitz (2008) furthered the study of the frustration-aggression hypothesis. His neoassociationist theory places the responsibility for aggression on negative affect, as opposed to just frustration, and on the automaticity of the behavior, which he asserts can override any available cognition. These uncontrolled and largely unconscious processes create links between constructs in a bonding fashion, which can make associations readily available once a construct is activated. In this way, a situation can produce an uncomfortable, and therefore hostile, reaction simply via the association of a given situation to a social setting that is linked to an original negative experience. The hostile reaction that follows is meant to restore balance, control, or security. Anger is elicited, as opposed to sadness, when the situation is perceived as one that can be changed and the distressing feeling ameliorated (Frijda, 1988).

Berkowitz (2008) explains most violent or aggressive social phenomena with this model. For example, hostility toward minorities is explained by the unconscious activation of stereotypes. Hostile associations are primed, often by media violence, leading one to become aggressive in an ambiguous situation if qualities of the immediate situation have been previously associated with an angering event.

Bandura's (1973) social learning theory of aggression states that individuals can learn from observing others' actions and not be reinforced only by external rewards or aspects of the environment but also by internal states, such as pride, satisfaction, or gratification. Thus, Bandera believed that the principles of conditioning also apply when observing others' learning sequences. In this way, one does not have to persist through a lifetime of trial-and-error learning but can predict consequences and rewards. Observing parents, family members, or television characters; hearing stories or explanations; and gaining information in other ways can produce learning. Social learning was thought by Bandura to be most effective within one's family, subculture, and through television. Findings that children from violent families or communities have higher incidences of violence support the notion of social learning.

Unsurprisingly then, unlike behaviorists, Bandura placed a high value on the cognitive aspects of learning, arguing that learning does not always have to lead to a change in behavior. One has to attend to, retain, be capable of reproducing, and be motivated to attempt a new behavior—as there must be the expectation that it will be reinforced in some way. Social learning theory takes into account one's varied observations, as well as the different ways in which the observation was made, in terms of quantity, rate, or its qualities. The observation then is analyzed based on one's values and the types of incentives or consequences sought (Bandura, 1977).

Bandura and Walters (1959) also explained that while frustration as a result of deprivation of needs "produces an aggression motive," the acts of aggression are modeled and reinforced by the parent. For example, when parents use aggressive punishment, they are modeling the use of aggression for their children. Parents may do this by passively not discouraging such conduct, by behaving aggressively themselves, or by encouraging aggression, for example, by supporting it as self-defense. Likewise, he acknowledged that the lack of modeling an appropriate reaction to frustration, in terms of too little discipline, was equally instrumental in producing frustration and aggressive acts.

Novaco's social behavioral theory explains violent aggression in terms of its functions: *core survival value functions* and *extended social system value functions* (Novaco, 1994). Survival functions include violence for purposes of defense or necessary acquisition of resources. Social system value functions are social-context factors that may influence violence even if they are not directly apparent, such as for social bonding, social ordering and regulation, and expressions of justice, goodness or badness, freedom, or entertainment. Anger, then, is an emotion that can sense threat and mobilize an individual to regulate his or her short- and long-term social needs (Novaco, 1994). Anger is shaped by environment and rooted in one's historical adaptation to environmental demands. Therefore, one may have a higher or lower than normal threshold for the level of threat perceived. The aggressive reaction will be congruent with the degree of threat perceived. Anger regulation is the indicated intervention, so that one can more accurately assess the degree of threat in a given situation and respond with the appropriate level of aggression (Novaco, 1997).

Huesmann (1988) based his script theory or social cognitive information processing model for aggression on the notion that aggressive experiences form patternistic sequences and outcomes in people's minds, to which they return to understand later situations and base their behaviors. Repeated situations and well-rehearsed scripts can produce highly automatized discernments of and reactions to novel situations and people. Scripts are developed via implicit and explicit social reinforcement and punishment, coupled with childhood social learning and experiences. Multiple offshoots of this model are discussed in a later section on integrated models of aggression.

DEVELOPMENTAL PATHS OF VIOLENCE

Developmental theory of aggression finds that "changes in crime and violence are related to age in an orderly way" (Thornberry, 1997, p. 1). Patterns have emerged in the literature that suggested aggressive behavior may fall into one of several independent trajectories, such as lifelong or adolescence limited (Moffitt, 1993). Life-course antisocial individuals are regarded as having psychopathology, and they engage in antisocial conduct at every stage of life. Adolescents with antisocial behavior make up a much larger percentage of those individuals who display violent conduct during their lives. They are thought to be mimicking the life-course antisocial style and reaping some of the rewards before adult maturity kicks in and eclipses those rewards (Moffitt, 2004). Adolescent-limited aggressors show a brief period in their lives of antisocial conduct and generally do not exhibit any such behaviors during childhood or adulthood. Even during adolescence, these youth are inconsistent in their use of antisocial behaviors across contexts and time periods (Moffitt, 1993).

There are also generally predictable patterns that have emerged within these trajectories. For example, there is a progression from less to more serious types of offenses, and such behaviors often begin with impulsive, but not illegal acts. Delinquent conduct during the teenage years may earn some peer approval in a way that it does not when older (Conger & Simons, 1997). The majority of children and adolescents who display criminal behavior stop doing so by early adulthood (Morizot & Le Blanc, 2007). This change in conduct away from aggressive or criminal behavior is generally explained developmentally with one of two concepts: self-control and social control. The self-control perspective posits that as individuals age, they gain greater self-control and are more inhibited (Gottfredson & Hirschi, 1990). The social control model, on the other hand, emphasizes that increased involvement in conventional social roles decreases the likelihood for criminal involvement (Sampson & Laub, 1993).

Kohlberg's stages of moral development (Kohlberg, 1976) were born out of Piaget's stages of moral judgment (Piaget, 1948). He thought the maturation of morality is on a path of progressive cognitive-developmental stages, beginning from an earlier egocentric focus, then to conventional approval seeking, and lastly to early and later stages of conscience development. He believed delinquents to have arrested prior to the existence of an early conscience. It is the social environment that engages the child at various levels of reasoning about morality, challenging him or her to take on new views as his or her intelligence grows.

Agnew's general strain theory (Agnew & Broidy, 1997) states that negative relationships produce negative affect, such as anger, and that crime can alleviate the tension produced by that anger. Crime becomes a lifestyle for individuals who rely on such methods of tension reduction. Aggressive behavior reinvents the cycle, for their behavior pushes others away, prevents them from learning to problem-solve more appropriately, and immerses them further in socially aversive environments. Here, the individual re-creates the negative relationships that produced the negative affect from which he or she initially sought relief, perpetuating the aggressive response.

Sampson and Laub (1993) emphasized the "cumulative disadvantages" that are consequences of criminal behavior and which are believed to force an individual to resort back to aggression. Because the typical sources of social control (school, family, and peers) are powerful deterrents to using violence and are likely to ostracize someone who behaves in that way, an aggressive individual will lose important resources and communities. The authors agreed with Patterson's metaphor of a "cascade" effect of antisocial behavior as a progressive set of reactions to stages of behavior problems (Patterson, 1993). Matsueda and Heimer (1997) instead advocate a symbolic interactionist developmental approach, in which the labeling of an individual as aggressive leads to an internalization of that label, and the associated privileges, thereby perpetuating the aggressive conduct.

PERSONALITY PERSPECTIVES: TRAITS OR DISPOSITIONS OF VIOLENT INDIVIDUALS

The Big Five personality traits (extraversion, agreeableness, conscientiousness, neuroticism, openness), developed by McCrae and Costa (1987), have been applied to aggressive individuals. Agreeableness, in particular, has been found to negatively correlate with individuals who have histories of aggression and violence (Gleason, Jensen-Campbell, & Richardson 2004; Heaven, 1996). Conscientiousness is also negatively related to aggression (Sharpe & Desai, 2001). Together, these two factors, which are associated with disinhibition, are considered a core personality trait central to aggressive individuals. Interpersonal aggression, general externalizing behaviors, and destruction have been related to the personality construct of callousness (Krueger et al., 2002). Other researchers have found callous-unemotional traits are related to conduct problems in children. Furthermore, sensation-seeking behavior, low fearfulness, and low behavioral inhibition are also characteristic of aggressive individuals (Frick & Morris, 2004).

BEHAVIORAL UNDERSTANDING OF VIOLENCE

Behavioral psychologists, as in the estimation of B. F. Skinner (1990), find that the emotional or internal factors pertaining to one's conduct are too unpredictable and variable to be studied. Instead, they find it more scientific to study behaviors within the context of measurable environmental influences. These environmental influences determine one's thoughts, feelings, and actions. Where natural selection explains society-wide behaviorism, operant conditioning explains individual behaviors. In this way, the short-term consequences of aggression present rewards for the aggressor. The immediate gratification of defeating one's opponent and earning the associated winnings is more powerful than the consequences, which are rarely presented immediately following the behavior and thus appear indirect rather than directly related. Bullying, for example, allows one to intimidate a victim into complying with demands, resulting in stolen money or property. A child who throws himself on the ground, kicking and screaming, often gains his parents' attention. The prizes, such as the parents' attention, reinforce the behavior as effective and to be relied upon in the future.

Eysenck and Eysenck (1978) and Eysenck and Gudjonsson (1989) found that individuals who commit criminal and violent behavior are deficient in the emotional reaction (commonly thought of as the conscience), which is learned through classical conditioning. He argues that the construct of the conscience is developed out of learning emotional responses to behaviors. An example, which studies have imitated in a variety of ways, is the scolding that a parent may give a child after an inappropriate action which causes the child to feel uncomfortable. When such an emotional response pattern is poorly conditioned, an individual is more inclined toward antisocial conduct. Specifically, Eysenck (1987) found that antisocial individuals showed low conditioning responses after trials of pairings of conditioned with unconditioned stimuli. Specifically, he found that individuals classified as psychopaths showed poorer conditioning and less anticipatory responding, meaning that they do not show learning reactions or anticipate consequences as others do.

Furthermore, whereas relief from fear and avoidance of punishment are generally reinforcers for individuals to not engage in aggressive or criminal conduct, this is not the case with antisocial individuals. In operant conditioning studies in which individuals are taught a mental puzzle and certain responses were punished or rewarded, Lykken (1957) found that psychopaths learned the pattern as well as others, but they continued to select responses that would knowingly result in punishment (i.e., an electric shock), indicating a decreased sensitivity to punishment. Conversely, there are multiple corresponding findings that antisocial individuals have increased sensitivity to rewards over punishments and are therefore more motivated to seek rewards that are sufficiently arousing to Scerbo et al. (1990). Taken together, such findings indicate that the learning curve for antisocial individuals may be steeper, as they are slower to show conditioning; but when sufficiently rewarded, consistent with their higher arousal level, they attend and learn as well as others (Raine, 1993).

COGNITIVE AND COGNITIVE-BEHAVIORAL MODELS OF VIOLENCE

Cognitive-behavioral theorists agree with pure behaviorists for the most part, but they also find that one's cognitive appraisal of the environment is a key ingredient to the aggressive response. They emphasize that the way in which one reads an environmental trigger plays a significant role in the level of aggression that is expressed (Kassinove & Tafrate, 2006). One's cognitive framework for interpreting triggers is determined by cultural and subcultural experiences as well as previously modeled behaviors. The expression of one's appraisal of the situation, therefore, results in a particular outcome that reinforces the behavior. For example, aggression may be a family's primary method for interacting with one another, leading a child to choose such conduct in a corresponding situation.

The schema model of aggression (Mann & Beech, 2003) explains that developmental experiences lead to an emergence of dysfunctional beliefs, which creates problematic cognitive appraisals of later situations. As in general schema theory, categorical assumptions lead to distorted reflections of social situations. In sexual offenders, the authors found the persistent use of primary schemas of seeing the self as persistently the victim, feeling generally aggrieved, and endorsing entitled beliefs. In addition, they tended to have particular beliefs about control and maintained a generalized disrespect for certain categories of women. Based on these schemas, social situations have to be distorted to comply with such broad-reaching molds.

Ward (2000) extended the concept of schemas to allow for explanation for how they are developed. He theorized that a series of interactions with the environment contributed to developing, testing, and retesting *implicit theories* about people and the world. He believes that one's implicit theories manifest in particular classifications for different types of violence. In his study of sex offenders, for example, he found that abusers maintained overarching beliefs about children as sexual beings, that some individuals are entitled over others, and that the world is a dangerous place in which individuals are subject to predetermined uncontrollable forces. The offenders in his study also believed that types of harm are qualitatively different, and therefore less harmful, than other types. For example, they may say that not using force means that a sexual offense was less harmful to the victim.

BIOLOGICAL UNDERPINNINGS AND ENVIRONMENTAL CORRELATES IN VIOLENT OFFENDERS

The frontal lobe of the brain is probably the most implicated region of the brain across studies in violent individuals. The frontal lobe is generally understood to play a role in inhibiting and controlling emotions and behavior, decision making, problem solving, and abstract reasoning. Emotional awareness and the regulation of feelings are also found to take place in the frontal lobe, as is the planning of one's behavioral responses to those emotions (Davidson, Putnam, & Larson, 2000). Self-control has been repeatedly found to be situated in the prefrontal cortex (Banfeild, Wyland, Macrea, Munte, & Heatherton, 2004). Furthermore, aggression is often found to be a symptom associated with brain lesions in the medial prefrontal cortex (Grafman et al., 1996). Another difference in brain structure between individuals characterized for their aggression is a decrease in the amount of gray matter in the prefrontal cortex (Raine, Lencz, Bihrle, LaCassse, & Colletti, 2000). Gray matter is generally thought to be responsible for transmitting sensory and motor information.

In a similar study, a positron emission tomography (PET) scan revealed that in a group of individuals charged with murder, compared to a control sample, there was less activity in the prefrontal and parietal (primary sensory and abstraction) areas, more activity in the occipital (primary vision) areas, and no difference in their temporal areas (primarily language, emotion, and memory; Raine, Buchsbaum, & La Casse, 1997). These violent offenders also had imbalances in activity between the right and left sides of the amygdala (emotional center), the hippocampus (memory), and the thalamus (alertness, arousal, consciousness), as compared to the controls (Raine et al., 1997). Lesion studies also find involvement of the amygdala and the prefrontal cortex in violence (Seigal & Mirsky, 1990). One study found that the reward center of the brain was activated during certain retaliatory aggressive acts, suggesting that some pleasure is drawn from the act (Krämer, Jansma, Tempelmann, & Munte, 2007).

In meta-analyses, Ortiz and Raine (2004) and Lorber (2004) found that low resting heart rate is significantly related to antisocial, criminal, and violent behavior. The strength of the findings led Raine (2002) to name resting heart rate as likely the best biological correlate of antisocial behavior. The interaction of these biological variables with particular environmental variables creates greater effect sizes for the likelihood of aggression. Such psychosocial variables include ineffective parenting (Oxford, Cavell, & Hughes, 2003), low socioeconomic status, poor parental relationships, or having a teen mother (Farrington, 1997).

Based on twin and adoption studies, it is widely supported that there is a genetic influence on aggression, while environmental factors are key to shaping the genetic development of these qualities (Rhee & Waldman, 2002). Environmental factors known to have a strong relation with violence and antisocial conduct include poverty (Leventhal & Brooks-Gunn, 2000); unemployment, divorce, and low income (Beyers, Bates, Pettit, & Dodge, 2003); childhood domestic violence (Fergusson & Horwood, 1998); childhood physical abuse and corporal punishment (Farrington & Hawkins, 1991; Gershoff, 2002); and peer rejection (Dodge & Pettit, 2003).

INTEGRATED THEORIES OF VIOLENCE

Adriane Raine's sociobiological evolutionary model (1993) described criminal and aggressive conduct as psychopathology that, like most other mental disorders, has a prescribed number of classifying characteristics that occur on a continuum. In this way, crime serves both an individual and social purpose and is buttressed by heritable influences and biological bases. Suggesting a genetic and environmental interaction, there is a higher incidence of aggression and crime when these variables are taken together. Raine argues for the additive nature of environmental factors to account for variations in behaviors. He cites twin and adoption studies to make a case for a genetic influence on antisocial behavior as well as neuroscientific similarities in offenders, which include reduced serotonin, an increased behavioral activity system and an underactive behavioral inhibition system, affective instability, frontal lobe abnormalities, and temporal and limbic dysfunction.

In 1994, Goldstein wrote that the focus in understanding aggression should be on interaction of the person with the environment. He emphasized the social/environmental context of aggression, which can be thought of as opportunity. With his theory of "probabilism," he states that the environment alone does not encourage a behavior but that it reciprocally interacts with a person to propose and reinforce a behavior. He stated that all related individuals contribute to aggressive behavior, criminal and victim alike, together setting the stage for such acts to occur (Goldstein, 1994). He finds support in social identity theory, group conflict theory, and information processing theory to explain the social environmental interaction effect for inducing and sustaining violence.

In a social information-processing model of aggression, Dodge (1990) expound on the steps of information processing that one takes to arrive at a decision about the use of aggression. This problem solving model begins with encoding and interpreting a situation, in which cues taken in are different for every individual and can vary depending on recent and past experiences, values, and fears. Then, there is a process of searching for response alternatives, making a response decision, and enacting the response. Problems with the process, as in individuals who are persistently aggressive, are thought to lie in these people taking in less information to understand the situation and interpreting cues with a more hostile slant (Dodge, 1980; Dodge & Newman, 1981). In addition, aggressive individuals brainstorm fewer alternatives (Richard & Dodge, 1982) and choose more passive or more aggressive responses than may be effective (Dodge, 1986). Dodge (1990) has also described distinctive styles of aggression, used by individuals for different problem-solving purposes. Proactive aggressors use aggression to meet an instrumental need, while reactive aggressors respond to situations in an angry fashion. Those cues form a mental representation used to interpret the other person's intentions. This process is thought to be generally unconscious and often highly automatized. Furthermore, emotional weight can cause an individual to bypass an aggressive response or environmental stimuli, and the model is additive in that experiences continue to shape one's processing (Dodge, 2011).

Anderson and Bushman (2002) developed a multidimensional model (general aggression model) that attempts to account for how one's experiences, cognition, emotions, and arousal interact with a variety of situational variables to produce aggression. The model builds on the concept of knowledge structures (i.e., schemas or scripts; see Huesmann, 1988), which are encoded with certain affective flavors and used to interpret novel situations. Once highly automatized, reactions to events that may resemble in any way one's knowledge structure may or may not actually be relevant to the situation. The model also takes into account the situational (such as media violence, heat, pain, provocation) and personality-based factors (i.e., narcissism, being of the male sex, hostile beliefs) that come into play to produce aggression to influence a person's interpretation of all of the above.

I³ theory (Slotter & Finkel, 2011) is another contemporary integrated model of aggression that accounts for multiple elements that contribute to aggression. Their formula explains how the interaction of instigating triggers, impelling forces, and inhibiting forces generates violence. Instigating triggers occur in the first stage and create the environment that primes an individual to act aggressively. Such triggers may be direct provocation, rejection, or an obstacle to a goal. Forces that may impel aggression may be evolutionary or cultural, personal, relational, or situational. The third stage includes inhibitory forces, which are those that deter an individual from choosing to aggress. When impelling forces overpower inhibitory ones, aggression is the result. When inhibitory forces prevail, aggression is avoided.

CONCLUSION

> To know that we know what we know, and to know that we do not know
> what we do not know, that is true knowledge.
> —Nicolaus Copernicus

The literature review herein illustrates that psychology has made significant advances in understanding, researching, and operationalizing violent behavior. Predominant risk and protective factors have largely been established, and models for the conversion of those factors into violent behaviors have been set forth and investigated. As with most areas of psychological study, it appears that the answer to the question regarding the determinants of violent offending lies not in one variable but in the interaction of many. The advances in psychology's knowledge about the variables involved in violence, then, are compounded by the field's ever-growing capacity for integrating complementary lines of thinking among what may have historically been competing theories. While the field remains limited in forming definitive causes or predictions of violence, its strengths lie in the sheer volume of researchers dedicated to furthering the advances of our psychological ancestors. Nonetheless, we can be certain that what we do not know is still greater than what we know. But through tireless examination, challenge, and re-examination, we can be move toward a greater understanding of the great variable: human behavior.

REFERENCES

Agnew, R. & Broidy, L. (1997). Gender and crime: A general strain theory perspective. *Journal of Research in Crime and Delinquency, 34*(3), 275–306.

Anderson, C., & Bushman, B. (2002). Human aggression. *Annual Review of Psychology, 53*, 27–51.

Bandura, A. (1973). *Aggression: A social learning analysis.* Englewood Cliffs, NJ: Prentice-Hall.

Bandura, A. (1977). *Social learning theory.* New York, NY: General Learning Press.

Banfeild, J., Wyland, C. L., Macrea, C., Munte, T., & Heatherton, T. (2004). The cognitive neuroscience for self-regulation. In R. Baumesister & D. Vohs (Eds.), *Handbook of self-regulation* (pp. 62–83). New York, NY: Guilford Press.

Berkowitz, L. (2008). On the consideration of automatic as well as controlled psychological processes in aggression. *Aggressive Behavior, 34*(2), 117–129.

Beyers, J., Bates, J., Pettit, G., & Dodge, K. (2003). Neighborhood structure, parenting processes, and the development of youths' externalizing behaviors: A multilevel analysis. *American Journal of Community Psychology, 31*, 35–53.

Bion, W. (1970). *Attention and interpretation.* London: Tavistock.

Bowlby, J. (1965). *Child care and the growth of love* (2nd ed.). London, UK: Penguin Books.

Bowlby, J. (1973). *Attachment and loss, Vol. 2. Separation, anxiety, and anger.* London, UK: Penguin Books.

Bowlby, J. (1980). *Attachment and loss, Vol. 3. Loss: Sadness and depression.* New York, NY: Basic Books.

Bowlby, J. (1988). *A secure base: Parent-child attachments and healthy human development.* New York, NY: Basic Books.

Conger, R. D., & Simons, R. L. (1997). Life-course contingencies in the development of adolescent antisocial behavior: A matching law approach. In T. P. Thornberry (Ed.), *Advances in the criminological theory, Vol. 7. Developmental theories of crime and delinquency* (pp. 55–99). New Brunswick, NJ: Transaction Publishers.

Davidson, R. J., Putnam, K. M., & Larson, C. L. (2000). Dysfunction in the neural circuitry of emotion regulation: A possible prelude to violence. *Science, 289*(5479), 591–594.

Dodge, K. A. (1980). Social cognition and children's aggressive behavior. *Child Development, 51*, 162–170.

Dodge, K. A. (1986). A social information processing model of social competence in children. *Minnesota Symposium on Child Psychology, 18*, 77–125.

Dodge, K. A. (1990). Social information processing bases of aggressive behavior in children. *Personality and Social Psychology Bulletin, 16*, 8–22.

Dodge, K. A. (2011). Social information processing patterns as mediators of the interaction between genetic factors and life experiences in the development of aggressive behavior. In P. Shaver & M. Mikulincer (Eds.), *Human aggression and violence: Causes, manifestations, and consequences* (pp. 165–185). Washington, DC: American Psychological Association.

Dodge, K. A., & Newman, J. P. (1981). Biased decision-making processes in aggressive boys. *Journal of Abnormal Psychology, 90*, 375–379.

Dodge, K. A., & Pettit, G. W. (2003). A biopsychosocial model of the development of chronic conduct problems in adolescence. *Developmental Psychology, 39(2),* 349–371.

Dollard, J., Doob, L., Miller, N., Mowrer, O., & Sears, R. (1939). *Frustration and aggression*. New Haven, CT: Yale University Press.

Eysenck, H. J. (1987). Personality theory and problems of criminality. In B. J. McGurk, D. M. Thornton, & M. Williams (Eds.), *Applying psychology to imprisonment: Theory and practice* (pp. 29–58). London, UK: Her Majesty's Stationery Office.

Eysenck, H. J., & Eysenck, S. G. B. (1978). Psychopathy, personality and genetics. In R. D. Hare & D. Schalling (Eds.), *Psychopathic behavior: Approaches to research* (pp. 197–224). New York, NY: Wiley.

Eysenck, H. J., & Gudjonsson, G. H. (1989). *The causes and cures of criminality*. New York, NY: Plenum.

Farrington, D. P. (1997). The relationship between low resting heart rate and violence. In. A. Raine, P. A Brennan, D. P. Farrington, & S. A. Mednick (Eds.), *Biosocial bases of violence* (pp. 89–106). New York, NY: Plenum Press.

Farrington, D. P., & Hawkins, J. D. (1991). Predicting participation, early onset and later persistence in officially recorded offending. *Criminal Behaviour and Mental Health, 1*, 1–33.

Fergusson, D. M., & Horwood, J. L. (1998). Exposure to interpersonal violence in childhood and psychosocial adjustment in young adulthood. *Child Abuse and Neglect, 22*, 339–357.

Fonagy, P., Target, M., Gergely, G., Allen, J. G., & Bateman, A. W. (2003). *Mentalization, affect regulation, and the development of the self*. New York, NY: Other Press.

Freud, A. (1966). The ego and the mechanisms of defense. In *The writings of Anna Freud* (Vol. 2). New York: International Universities Press (original work published 1936).

Freud, S. (1923). *The ego and the id*. New York, NY: W.W. Norton.

Frick, P. J., & Morris, A. S. (2004). Temperament and developmental pathways to severe conduct problems. *Journal of Clinical Child and Adolescent Psychology, 33*, 54–68.

Frijda, N. H. (1988). The laws of emotion. *American Psychologist, 43(5)*, 349–358.

Gershoff, E. T. (2002). Corporal punishment by parents and associated child behaviors and experiences: A meta-analytic and theoretical review. *Psychological Bulletin, 129*, 539–579.

Gilligan, J. (1996). *Violence: Our deadly epidemic and its causes*. New York: Grosset/Putnam.

Gleason, K. A., Jensen-Campbell, L. A., & Richardson, D. (2004). Agreeableness and aggression in adolescence. *Aggressive Behavior, 30*, 43–61.

Goldstein, A. P. (1994). *The ecology of aggression*. New York, NY: Plenum.

Gottfredson, M. R., & Hirschi, T. (1990). *A general theory of crime.* Stanford, CA: Stanford University Press.

Grafman, J., Schwab, K., Warden, D., Pridgen, A., Brown, H. R., & Salazar, A. M. (1996). Frontal lobe injuries, violence, and aggression: A report of the Vietnam Head Injury Study. *Neurology, 46*(5), 1231–1238.

Heaven, P. C. L. (1996). Personality and self-reported delinquency: Analysis of the "Big Five" personality dimensions. *Personality and Individual Differences, 20,* 47–54.

Huesmann, L. R. (1988). An information-processing model for the development of aggression. *Aggressive Behavior, 14,* 13–24.

Hyatt-Williams, A. (1998). *Cruelty, violence and murder: Understanding the criminal mind.* London, UK: Karnac Books.

Lykken, D. T. (1957). A study of anxiety and the sociopathic personality. *Journal of Abnormal and Social Psychology, 55,* 6–10.

Kassinove, H., & Tafrate, R. (2006). Anger related disorders: Basic issues, models, and diagnostic considerations. In E. Feindler (Ed.), *Comparative treatments of anger disorders* (pp. 1–28). New York, NY: Springer.

Kernberg, O. F. (1992). *Aggression in personality disorders and perversions.* New Haven, CT: Yale University Press.

Kohlberg, L. (1976). Moral stages and moralization: The cognitive-developmental approach. In T. Lickona (Ed.), *Moral development and behavior: Theory, research, and social issues* (pp. 31–53). New York, NY: Holt, Rinehart and Winston.

Konečni, V. J. (1975). Annoyance, type and duration of postannoyance activity, and aggression: The "cathartic effect". *Journal of Experimental Psychology, 104,* 76–102.

Krämer, U. M., Jansma, H., Tempelmann, C., & Münte, T. F. (2007). Tit-for-tat: The neural basis of reactive aggression. *NeuroImage, 38,* 203–211.

Krueger, R. F., Hicks, B. M., Patrick, C. J., Carlson, S. R., Iacono, W. G., & McGue, M. (2002). Etiologic connections among substance dependence, antisocial behavior, and personality: Modeling the externalizing spectrum. *Journal of Abnormal Psychology, 111*(3), 411–424.

Leventhal, T., & Brooks-Gunn, J. (2000). The neighborhoods they live in: The effects of neighborhood residence on child and adolescent outcomes. *Psychological Bulletin, 126,* 309–337.

Lorber, M. F. (2004). Psychophysiology of aggression, psychopathy, and conduct problems. A met-analysis. *Psychological Bulletin, 130,* 531–552.

Lyons-Ruth, K., & Jacobvitz, D. (1999). Attachment disorganization: Unresolved loss, relational violence, and lapses in behavioral and attentional strategies. In J. Cassidy & P. Shaver (Eds.), *Handbook of attachment: Theory, research, and clinical applications* (pp. 520–554). New York, NY: Guilford Press.

Mann, R., & Beech, A. R. (2003). Cognitive distortions, schemas and implicit theories. In T. Ward, D. R. Laws, & S. M. Hudson (Eds.), *Sexual deviance: Issues and controversies* (pp. 135–153). London, UK: Sage.

Matsueda, R.L., & Heimer, K. (1997). A symbolic interactionist theory of role-transitions, role-commitments, and delinquency. In T. P. Thornberry (Ed.), *Developmental theories of crime and delinquency* (Vol. 7, pp. 163–213). New Brunswick, NJ: Transaction.

McCrae, R. R., & Costa, P. T. (1987). Validation of the five-factor model of personality across instruments and observers. *Journal of Personality and Social Psychology, 52,* 81–9.0

Meloy, R. (2006). The empirical basis and forensic application of affective and predatory violence. *Australian and New Zealand Journal of Psychiatry, 40,* 539–547.

Moffitt, T. E. (2004). Adolescence-limited and life-course persistent offending: A complementary pair of developmental theories. In T. P. Thornberry (Ed.), *Developmental theories of crime and delinquency* (pp. 11–54). New Brunswick, NJ: Transaction Publishers.

Moffitt, T. T. (1993). "Life-course-persistent" and "adolescence-limited" antisocial behavior: A developmental taxonomy. *Psychological Review, 100,* 674–701.

Morizot, J., & Le Blanc, M. (2007). Behavioral, self, and social control predictors of desistance from crime: A test of launch- and contemporaneous-effect models. *Journal of Contemporary Criminal Justice, 23,* 50–71.

Novaco, R. W. (1994). Anger as a risk factor for violence among the mentally disordered. In J. Monahan & H. Steadman (Eds.), *Violence and mental disorder: Developments in risk assessment* (pp. 21–59). Chicago, IL: University of Chicago Press.

Novaco, R. W. (1997). Remediating anger and aggression with violent offenders. *Legal and Criminological Psychology, 2,* 77–88.

Ortiz, J., & Raine, A. (2004). Heart rate level and antisocial behavior in children and adolescents: A meta-analysis. *Journal of the American Academy of Child and Adolescent Psychiatry, 43,* 154–162.

Oxford, M., Cavell, T. A., & Hughes, J. N. (2003). Callous/unemotional traits moderate the relation between ineffective parenting and child externalizing problems: A partial replication and extension. *Journal of Clinical Child and Adolescent Psychology, 32,* 577–585.

Patterson, G. R. (1993). Orderly change in a stable world: The antisocial trait as a chimera. *Journal of Consulting and Clinical Psychology, 61,* 911–919.

Perelberg, R. J. (1999) A psychoanalytic understanding of violence and suicide: A review of the literature and some new formulations. In R. J. Perelberg (Ed.), *Psychoanalytic understanding of violence and suicide.* London: Routledge and The Institute of Psychoanalysis.

Piaget, J. (1948). *The moral judgment of the child.* New York, NY: Free Press.

Raine, A. (1993). *The psychopathology of crime: Criminal behavior as a clinical disorder.* San Diego, California: Academic Press.

Raine, A. (2002). Biosocial studies of antisocial and violent behavior in children and adults: A review. *Journal of Abnormal Child Psychology, 30,* 311–326.

Raine, A., Buchsbaum, M. S., & La Casse, L. (1997). Brain abnormalities in murderers indicated by positron emission tomography. *Biological Psychiatry, 42,* 495–508.

Raine, A., Lencz, T., Bihrle, S., Lacasse, L., & Colletti, P. (2000). Reduced prefrontal gray matter volume and reduced autonomic activity in antisocial personality disorder. *Archives of General Psychiatry, 57,* 119–127.

Rhee, S. H., & Waldman, I. D. (2002). Genetic and environmental influences on antisocial behavior: A meta-analysis of twin and adoption studies. *Psychological Bulletin, 128*(3), 490–529.

Richard, B. A., & Dodge, K. A. (1982). Social maladjustment and problem solving in school-aged children. *Journal of Consulting and Clinical Psychology, 50,* 226–233.

Sampson, R. J., & Laub, J. H. (1993). *Crime in the making: Pathways and turning points through life.* Cambridge, MA: Harvard University Press.

Sampson, R. J., Raudenbush, S. W., & Earls, F. (1997). Neighborhoods and violent crime: A multilevel study of collective efficacy. *Science, 277*(5328), 918–924.

Scerbo, A., Raine, A., O'Brien, M., Chan, C., Rhee, C., & Smiley, N. (1990). Reward dominance and passive avoidance learning in adolescent psychopaths. *Journal of Abnormal Child Psychology, 18*(4), 451–463.

Seigal, A., & Mirsky, A. F. (1990). *The neurobiology of violence and aggression*. Paper presented at the National Academy of Sciences Conference on the Understanding and Control of Violent Behavior, San Destin, FL.

Sharpe, J. P., & Desai, S. (2001). The revised Neo Personality Inventory and the MMPI-2 Psychopathology Five in the prediction of aggression. *Personality and Individual Differences, 31*(4), 505–518.

Shaw, D. S., & Vondra, J. I. (1995). Infant attachment security and paternal predictors of early behavioral problems: A longitudinal study of low-income families. *Journal of Abnormal Child Psychology, 23*, 335–357.

Skinner, B. F. (1990). Can psychology be a science of the mind? *American Psychologist, 45*, 1206–1210.

Slotter, E. B., & Finkel, E. J. (2011). I3 Theory: Instigating, impelling, and inhibiting factors in aggression. In M. Mikulincer, & P. R. Shaver (Eds.), *Human aggression and violence: Causes, manifestations, and consequences* (pp. 35–52). Washington: American Psychological Association.

Thornberry, T. P. (ed.) (1997). *Developmental theories of crime and delinquency*. New Brunswick, NJ: Transaction Publishers.

Ward, T. (2000). Sexual offenders' cognitive distortions as implicit theories. *Aggression and Violent Behavior, 5*, 491–507.

Winnicott, D. W. (1971). *Playing and reality*. Middlesex, England: Penguin Books.

de Zulueta, F. (2001). Understanding the evolution of psychopathology and violence. *Criminal Behaviour and Mental Health,* 11: S17–S22.

2

Antisocial Behavior Among Children in Poverty

Understanding Environmental Effects in Daily Life

MICHAEL A. RUSSELL AND CANDICE L. ODGERS ■

Children who grow up in poverty are more likely to engage in antisocial behavior—such as aggression, rule-breaking behavior, and delinquency—than children who grow up in better-off circumstances (see reviews by Bradley & Corwyn, 2002; Brooks-Gunn & Duncan, 1997; McLoyd, 1998). The strength and consistency of this relationship have led many to question whether poverty *causes* antisocial development in children, or whether the relationship is better explained by preexisting characteristics shared among children and families who live in poverty (e.g., family history of aggression, personality features, or genetic liability; see Jaffee, Strait, & Odgers, 2012 for a discussion). Answering this question is important for a number of reasons. First, childhood poverty has been shown to predict antisocial behavior at multiple points in the life course. Children from low socioeconomic status (SES) backgrounds are more likely to show chronic aggression during the first 4 years of life (Tremblay et al., 2004), are more likely to engage in serious crime and violence during adolescence (Bjerk, 2007; Elliott & Ageton, 1980; Jarjoura, Triplett, & Brinker, 2002), and are more likely to continue their involvement in antisocial behavior as adults (Fergusson & Horwood, 2002; Lahey et al., 2006; Odgers et al., 2008). Second, child and adolescent antisocial behavior is known to predict a broad range of poor adult outcomes, including physical health problems (Odgers et al., 2007), broad spectrum psychiatric disorder (Kim-Cohen et al., 2003), economic/ occupational difficulties (Moffitt, Caspi, Harrington, & Milne, 2002; Odgers et al., 2008), and involvement in crime and violence (Farrington, 1989; Moffitt, Caspi, Rutter, & Silva, 2001; Theobald & Farrington, 2012). Third, the societal costs associated with antisocial behavior are staggering, as estimates place the aggregate burden of crime in the United States between $1 and $2 trillion *per year* (Anderson, 1999; Ludwig, 2006, 2010).

Taken together, this evidence makes it clear that childhood poverty is a powerful risk factor for the development of antisocial behavior, an important and pressing societal problem. But how does living in poverty increase children's risk for developing antisocial behavior? Theory and research suggest that poverty may be bad for children because low-income youth are embedded in home, school, and neighborhood environments where they are chronically exposed to stressful events in daily life. These stressors include harsh parenting, family turmoil, exposure to violence, low-quality living conditions, and family chaos, to name just a few (Evans, 2004). Exposure to chronic stressors in everyday life results in prolonged activation of the stress response systems, which is thought to impair children's development of self-regulation abilities (e.g., attention and impulse control, delay of gratification, and working memory; Blair & Raver, 2012; Evans & Kim, 2013). Additionally, chronic exposure to aggressive, hostile, or coercive "role" models may train children to engage in aggression themselves via social modeling processes (Patterson, 1982; Patterson, Reid, & Dishion, 1992).

As such, the environment of childhood poverty—particularly the quality of children's everyday experiences—may be a principal source of risk for antisocial development. However, it is challenging to examine the causal effects of poverty on children's antisocial development because obtaining accurate "fly-on-the-wall" measurements of everyday events has been difficult with traditional assessment methods. Thus, there is little evidence on which of these events is most prominent in low-income children's daily lives, which types of stressful events have the most deleterious effects "in the moment," and which children may be the most susceptible to the effects of daily stressors. Given the structural barriers to lifting children out of impoverished conditions, it is imperative that researchers begin to identify factors that could protect children from the adverse effects of poverty-related daily stressors. By doing so, these efforts could have a reasonable shot at improving low-income children's life chances. In this chapter, we discuss how mobile technology can be leveraged to help us characterize the environments of children[1] in poverty and to better understand the effects that these environments may have on the development of antisocial behavior. Because mobile technologies (such as smartphones, tablets, and iPads) provide researchers with enhanced capabilities for assessing social and physical environments, mood, self-regulation, and behavior as people live their everyday lives, these tools seem naturally suited to studying how exposure to relatively minor, yet meaningful stressors in everyday life may increase risk for antisocial behavior among children in poverty.

The chapter is organized into the following sections. In the first section, we discuss the concept of "environment" in children's development and follow with a review of evidence for how the environment of childhood poverty may lead to antisocial behavior problems in children. We focus primarily on the social environment, as the majority of environmental conditions associated with both poverty and antisocial behavior are social in nature (e.g., parental conflict, low parental support, deviant peer affiliation, exposure to violence; cf. Dodge, Coie, & Lynam, 2006; Evans, 2004). Next, we discuss how mobile technologies may help researchers meet the challenges of measuring children's everyday environments and understanding the effects of these environments for children's antisocial behavior. Then, given that not all children exposed to negative environments will develop antisocial behavior, we discuss theory and research suggesting that some children may be more sensitive to their environmental surroundings than others, such that they are at greatest risk when environments are bad but at lowest risk when environments are good (Ellis, Boyce, Belsky, Bakermans-Kranenburg, & van Ijzendoorn, 2011). We conclude with a discussion of future research directions that emerge from our review.

WHAT IS THE ENVIRONMENT OF CHILDHOOD POVERTY?

Imagine a child living in poverty. His home feels crowded; he has little privacy and he feels as though family members are always intruding into his space. His parents are exhausted and short tempered from working long hours, leading to frequent bouts of conflict at home. His school is underfunded and understaffed; his teachers seem constantly stressed and overburdened. He feels pressured to do bad things—like smoking and stealing—by kids at his school. He feels unsafe in his neighborhood, as high levels of crime and disorder characterize the streets surrounding his home. Continuous exposure to these stressful conditions takes its toll over time, as he struggles to keep his focus at school, soothe his seemingly constant anxiety and irritation amid the chaos at home and on the streets, and somehow plan for a future that becomes increasingly uncertain with each passing year.

As this vignette illustrates, the daily lives of children in poverty, are in a word, stressful. Not only do low-income children experience a greater number of major stressful life events (such as parental divorce or residential instability; Attar, Guerra, & Tolan, 1994; Gad & Johnson, 1980; Pryor-Brown, Cowen, Hightower, & Lotyczewski, 1986), but their everyday lives are simply more risky. Their homes, schools, and neighborhoods are more chaotic, unsafe, and conflictual than those of children from middle- to upper-class backgrounds (Evans, 2004). Their daily lives are more likely to be characterized by greater levels of family turmoil, exposure to violence, harsh parenting, low levels of social support, and crowded, chaotic living conditions compared to children who are not poor (Evans, Gonnella, Marcynyszyn, Gentile, & Salpekar, 2005; Grant et al., 2003; Repetti, Taylor, & Seeman, 2002). While an impressive body of research shows that major stressful life events have profound effects on health and antisocial behavior (see, e.g., Attar et al., 1994; Danese et al., 2009; Felitti et al., 1998; Whitfield, Anda, Dube, & Felitti, 2003), evidence from adults suggests that chronic, accumulating exposure to more "mundane" hassles or stressors in everyday life may have effects that are just as strong, if not *stronger* (Almeida, 2005; Kanner, Coyne, Schaefer, & Lazarus, 1981; see review by Odgers & Jaffee, 2013). When combined with evidence that exposure to negative social conditions explains *over 50%* of poverty's effect on child antisocial behavior (Dodge, Pettit, & Bates, 1994), it seems likely that the everyday environment may be a principal source of risk for antisocial behavior in low-income children, as well as an important target for interventions.

HOW CAN WE BETTER CHARACTERIZE AND UNDERSTAND ENVIRONMENTAL EFFECTS?

To obtain a better understanding of how everyday environments affect low-income children's development, it is necessary to start with a clear definition of what is meant by the environment. To this end, it is helpful to consider two complementary perspectives of what environment is. The first invokes the concept of environment as a *context* that consists of the structural and social characteristics of a person's surroundings. The environment-as-context perspective often serves a descriptive function, enhancing knowledge on environment by characterizing the specific exposures faced by individuals across different types of environmental settings, as well as how these exposures are associated with intellectual, behavioral, and physical outcomes. For example, studies that document the characteristics of low-income households (i.e., number of books on the shelf, cleanliness of the home; Bradley, Corwyn, McAdoo, & Coll, 2001), the specific types of daily stressors experienced by adolescents in poverty (Evans, Vermeylen, Barash, Lefkowitz, & Hutt, 2009) or the levels of aircraft noise in metropolitan neighborhoods (Cohen, Krantz, Evans, Stokols, & Kelly, 1981; Haines, Stansfeld, Head, & Job, 2002) provide a better understanding of environment as context.

The second perspective invokes the concept of the environment as a *causal agent*. The environment-as-agent perspective is rooted in behavioral genetics and developmental psychology, and it focuses on determining the causal (read "nongenetic") effects of both measured and unmeasured environmental factors. Studies in this tradition aim to understand whether environments have any effects when children's genes or genetically influenced characteristics are effectively held constant, through natural experiments, twin or adoption designs, and randomized controlled interventions (Moffitt, 2005; Rutter, 2005). This is important to do because prior to Bell's (1968) seminal argument on how children affect their environments (rather than the reverse), few studies had tested the hypothesis that children's genetically influenced characteristics could in truth be the causal agents behind what appeared to be environmental effects. This was followed by convincing arguments, buttressed by behavioral genetic research, that the effect of parental rearing environments was essentially null; children's genetically influenced characteristics were believed to elicit or otherwise account for much of the observed parental rearing effects (Harris, 1995; Scarr, 1992). More recent evidence has shown that parental environments do have potentially causal effects on children's development after all (e.g., Caspi et al., 2004; Jaffee, Caspi, Moffitt, & Taylor, 2004), but the lesson learned here is that in order to determine with any confidence that an effect is environmentally driven, one must first address—and at least partially rule out—preexisting characteristics of children and families that may serve as the primary source of the association between an environmental risk factor and children's behavior (Moffitt, 2005; Rutter, 2005; Rutter, Pickles, Murray, & Eaves, 2001).

DOES POVERTY HAVE AN ENVIRONMENTAL EFFECT ON CHILDREN'S ANTISOCIAL BEHAVIOR?

Jaffee, Strait, and Odgers (2012) reviewed evidence from experimental and quasi-experimental studies that could facilitate causal inferences—including natural experiments, randomized controlled intervention trials, and twin/adoption studies—and found evidence that poverty has effects on children's antisocial behavior that are above and beyond genetic liability or other preexisting child and family characteristics. One of the studies they reviewed was a natural experiment that occurred during an ongoing longitudinal study of the development of psychiatric illness in children (Costello, Compton, Keeler, & Angold, 2003). Four years after the start of the study, a casino opened on a Native American reservation and provided all families in the study with a recurring income supplement that increased in value each year. For some of these families (14%), the income supplements moved them out of poverty, whereas 53% of families remained in poverty despite the supplements and 32% were never poor. Children in families who moved out of poverty showed significant decreases in antisocial behavior during the 4 years following the casino opening. The reduction was so pronounced that, after 4 years of income supplements, children whose families moved out of poverty had levels of antisocial behavior resembling those of the youth who were never poor. Conversely, American Indian children whose families remained poor despite the income supplements did not decrease their antisocial behavior. Because income supplements were delivered to an entire community of Native American families, this study provides a strong natural control for any preexisting characteristics of children and families that may confound the relationship between family income and children's antisocial behavior. As such, this study provides strong evidence that poverty plays a potentially causal role in the development of children's antisocial behavior.

Other studies reviewed by Jaffee and colleagues (2012) relied on quasi-experimental methods to identify whether poverty has environmental effects on children's antisocial behavior. For example, Strohschein (2005), in a study that compared children to themselves across time, showed that children engaged in more antisocial behavior when family income decreased and less antisocial behavior when family income increased. Because this study compares each child's antisocial behavior to that of himself or herself at different points in time, it provides evidence that the effect of poverty on antisocial behavior cannot be explained by factors that remain unchanged, such as sex, ethnicity, and genetic makeup (Allison, 2005). In another quasi-experimental study of over 2,000 twin pairs (50% of twin pairs were monozygotic), Caspi, Taylor, Moffitt, and Plomin (2000) showed that children in socioeconomically deprived neighborhoods had greater emotional and behavioral problems than children living in relatively advantaged neighborhoods, and that neighborhood deprivation had effects on children that were above and beyond the effects of genetic liability—thus evincing an environmentally mediated effect.

HOW POVERTY AFFECTS CHILDREN: THE ROLE OF EVERYDAY EXPERIENCE

Taken together, the aforementioned studies provide evidence that the effect of poverty on children's antisocial behavior is partly explained by environmental factors. These studies have answered the question of *whether* the environment of poverty affects children's antisocial behavior—the next step, therefore, is to determine *how*. In many of the explanations for how poverty affects children's antisocial behavior, the everyday environment takes center stage. In their *risky families model*, Repetti et al. (2002) suggest that everyday family interactions characterized as cold, unsupportive, and neglectful represent an important pathway through which poverty can affect child and adolescent well-being. Similarly, Hertzman and Boyce (2010, p. 331) argue that it is the "mundane, rather than [the] exceptional, exposures" that often have the largest effects by altering children's developmental pathways and leaving lasting imprints on adult outcomes. Predictions such as these have been borne out in studies of adults, which have shown that everyday stressors or "hassles" have stronger effects on physical and mental health than major stressful life events (Almeida, 2005; DeLongis, Coyne, Dakof, Folkman, & Lazarus, 1982). Through their frequent, pervasive, and chronic nature, the effects of daily environmental conditions accumulate with continued exposure, sometimes leading to profound and long-lasting effects on well-being.

A striking example comes from the work of Hart and Risley (1995), who conducted monthly observational visits with 42 families, starting when children were 7–9 months old and ending at 3 years of age. In observed interactions with their parents, children from professional families (high SES) heard an average of 2,153 words an hour, whereas children from working-class families heard 1,251 and children from welfare families heard 616. This difference in language exposure was not inconsequential. By approximately age 3, children from professional families had a vocabulary of around 1,100 words, whereas children from welfare families had less than half; that is, a vocabulary of around 500 words. From their data, Hart and Risley estimated that each year, children in professional families hear 11 million words, whereas children in welfare families hear 3 million. One can clearly see that as the years go by, the gap in language exposure between high- and low-SES children will increase exponentially. Extrapolating to age 4, Hart and Risley estimated that children from welfare families will have heard *32 million* fewer words than children from professional families, which they dubbed *the 30 million word gap* (see Hart & Risley, 2003, p. 8). This ever-increasing gap in language exposure may be expected to produce an ever-increasing gap in cumulative vocabulary and, with it, a substantial decrease in life chances for low-SES children.

The work of Hart and Risley (1995) provides a compelling example of how children's everyday conditions can produce meaningful differences in their developmental outcomes. The accumulating nature of everyday environmental exposures (exposure to language in the Hart and Risley study) may be expected to create ever-widening gaps in academic, behavioral, and physical outcomes for children across socioeconomic strata. In the same way that differential exposure to language led to ever-increasing vocabulary differences among children, it is likely that differential exposure to *stressful events* may produce ever-widening differences in antisocial behavior between low- and high-SES children and thus suggest one reason why antisocial behavior problems are so much more common in low-income youth. The multiple stressors indigenous to poverty, and the reactions these stressors evoke, are central to numerous models describing how poverty affects children's development (McLoyd, 2011). Two prominent examples include family stress (Conger et al., 1992; Elder, 1974) and cumulative stress models (Evans, Kim, Ting, Tesher, & Shannis, 2007), both of which emphasize the damaging effects of repeated stressor exposure and the frequent psychological and physiological reactivity that results. We describe the relevance of these perspectives for low-income children's antisocial behavioral development next.

The Family Stress Model

The family stress model suggests that economic hardship increases children's risk for emotional and behavioral problems by increasing tension, conflict, and hostility in the daily interactions of parents and children. Stress associated with life in poverty compromises parents' ability to respond supportively to their children and often results in more harsh and punitive parenting and family conflict (Bradley et al., 2001; McLoyd, 2011). High levels of family conflict, tension, and hostility increase children's risk for antisocial behavior because the home effectively becomes a training ground in which aggressive, angry, and hostile behavior is modeled, learned, reinforced, and further elaborated (Patterson, 1982; Patterson et al., 1992). The family stress model was originally informed by the classic work of Elder and colleagues (Elder, 1974; Elder, van Nguyen, & Caspi, 1985) following children of the Great Depression. Elder and his colleagues showed that economic hardship had negative effects on parents (primarily fathers), making them more rejecting, indifferent, and less supportive, which in turn had downstream negative effects on children's socioemotional development. Studies since have shown that negative parenting mediates the relationship between economic hardship and children's externalizing or antisocial behavior (Conger, Ge, Elder, Lorenz, & Simons, 1994; Grant et al., 2003).

The Cumulative Stress Model

The cumulative stress model suggests that frequent stressor exposure and prolonged stress reactivity play a key role in the development of socioemotional and behavioral difficulties among children in poverty. This view has been most strongly associated with the work of Gary Evans, who emphasizes the role of poverty-related stress in fostering difficulties in children's self-regulation and in promoting *allostatic load* (Evans & English, 2002; Evans et al., 2007), a physiological marker of wear and tear on bodily systems stemming from frequent activation of the stress response (McEwen, 1998; McEwen & Lasley, 2002). In a study of 8- to 10-year olds, Evans and English (2002) showed that low-income children experience a multitude of environmental stressors, including physical stressors such as higher levels of crowding, noise, and poorer housing quality, as well as psychosocial stressors, including greater levels of family turmoil, family separation, and exposure to violence. For each of the stressors in this study, a child was classified as *exposed* if his or her score was greater than one standard deviation above the sample mean (with the exception of violence, for which any exposure was considered stressful). Not only was exposure to each of these stressors more common in the lives of low- versus middle-income children, but low-income children were also more likely to be exposed to multiple stressors in their lifetime. In fact, 54% of low-income children in the study were exposed to three or more of these stressors in their lifetimes, whereas this was true for only 14% of middle-income children. Multiple-stressor exposure predicted poor psychological outcomes such as impaired self-regulation and poor mental health (including higher conduct problems), as well as poor physiological outcomes such as higher resting blood pressure and higher overnight urinary stress hormone levels (cortisol and epinephrine). Moreover, multiple stressor exposure was shown to mediate the relationship between poverty and children's psychological and physiological outcomes, supporting the idea that exposure to multiple, accumulating stressors may be an important pathway through which poverty increases children's risk for poor psychological outcomes such as antisocial behavior.

NEXT STEPS: CAN MOBILE TECHNOLOGIES HELP IDENTIFY ENVIRONMENTAL EFFECTS ON ANTISOCIAL BEHAVIOR?

Based on this evidence, it seems clear that highly stressful everyday environments play an important role in the development of antisocial behavior for low-income children. A promising strategy for improving the lives of low-income children may be to gain a better understanding of how stressful everyday environments affect low-income children's day-to-day adjustment and risk for antisocial behavior. In doing so, researchers could identify specific environmental factors likely to play a causal role in promoting low-income children's antisocial behavior and thereby inform prevention and intervention efforts aimed at reducing their effects.

However, obtaining accurate and comprehensive measures of children's everyday environments remains a persistent methodological challenge. Although observational studies (e.g., Hart & Risley, 1995; Patterson, 1982; Patterson et al., 1992) provide enormous depth of observation and objectivity in measurement, they cannot well capture the *range* of exposures that a child has in a given day because observers cannot follow the child everywhere he or she goes. Moreover, observational methods by their nature are restricted to measuring observables (i.e., emotional expression, instances of behavior) and may not be well suited toward measuring internal states such as affect and self-regulation, both of which (a) constitute important dimensions of how one reacts to experience and (b) may serve as momentary markers for emotional and behavioral problems or disorders (Larson, Richards, Raffaelli, Ham, & Jewell, 1990; Silk, Steinberg, & Morris, 2003; Whalen, Jamner, Henker, & Delfino, 2001).

Diary methods, also known as experience sampling methodologies (ESMs; Csikszentmihalyi, Larson, & Prescott, 1977) or ecological momentary assessment (EMA; Shiffman, Stone, & Hufford, 2008) strategies, may help researchers better meet the challenge of measuring everyday environments and their effects. Diary methods are assessment strategies that use pagers, handheld computers (Palm pilots), cellular phones, tablets such as the iPad, or paper-and-pencil entries to obtain repeated self-reports on individuals' contexts, social interactions, affect, motivations, self-regulation, and behavior at the tempo of daily life (Bolger, Davis, & Rafaeli, 2003). Because they allow near real-time measurement in people's natural environments, diary measures provide high levels of ecological validity and permit comprehensive reports of context, experience, and well-being. Moreover, diary methods have been effectively used across a wide range of age groups, demonstrating feasibility among children as young as 8 years (Whalen et al., 2009) to adults of oldest old age (Keller-Cohen, Fiori, Toler, & Bybee, 2006). As such, they may be fruitfully applied to measuring relationships between everyday environment and antisocial behavior among low-income children.

Of course, diary methods are not without their limitations. First, these methods often rely solely on self-reports of both exposure and outcome, which may create shared method variance and artificially inflate associations between study variables. Second, the low frequency of severely aggressive or antisocial behaviors may make it difficult to observe environmental effects in daily life. However, researchers may limit assessments to conceptually related but less severe antisocial behaviors, such as bullying, lying, stealing, or vandalism, which are more likely to occur with sufficient frequency at the daily level. Third, because the intensive assessment procedures may become burdensome for children and adolescents, researchers may benefit from designing incentive strategies to keep youth engaged and responsive to diary assessments, especially if the assessments are particularly frequent or the duration of diary data collection is long (see Conner Christensen, Barrett, Bliss-Moreau, Lebo, & Kaschub, 2003 for an excellent review of these and other practical considerations inherent in diary research).

Despite these limitations, however, we believe that diary methods have unique features to contribute to the study of environmental effects on low-income children's antisocial behavior and, as discussed later in this chapter, we believe these methods may be especially promising when combined with the enhanced technological features of mobile phones and other newly emerging technologies. Next, we discuss three potential contributions that diary methods may make in this area. First, by assessing experiences close to when they occur, diary methods allow researchers to better measure the *environment as experienced*, rather than the environment *as remembered*. Second, diary methods allow researchers to appreciate that every child is different. Through repeated measurement of experiences *within* a person, diary methods allow us to appreciate (and measure) the specific constellation of experiences, emotions, behaviors, as well as the unique interrelations between these constructs, *for each child*. Third, the intensive within-person measurement of diary measures allows examinations of within-person processes that may help identify environmental effects. We discuss each of these features in more detail next.

Feature 1: Diary Methods Can Measure the Environment As Experienced, Rather Than As Remembered

The first feature offered by diary methods is the ability to measure the environment *as it is experienced*, because reports of environmental exposures can be obtained within minutes to hours of when the child experiences them. This type of assessment differs from the more typical mode of measurement, which focuses on the *environment as remembered*. Here participants are asked to recall "how much," "how often," or "whether" specific things have happened over a longer time frame, often over the past 6–12 months. The environment-as-remembered measurement strategy is less than ideal if the goal is to accurately measure the routine environmental conditions of a person's daily life. This is because routine experiences are not as easily recalled over long time spans as are unusual events, leaving retrospective reports of daily events more susceptible to heuristic biases that may reduce reporting accuracy (Bradburn, Rips, & Shevell, 1987; Shiffman et al., 2008). This evidence suggests that as time passes, individuals may be increasingly likely to misremember or even forget routine stressful occurrences, leaving researchers with an incomplete understanding of how frequent and impairing these routine stressors can be. Other factors such as the participant's mood at the time of assessment can also affect the accuracy of recall (Shiffman et al., 2008). Diary methods may help researchers to minimize (but not eliminate) retrospective recall biases by shortening the window of recall to minutes or hours, a strategy that has been empirically shown to produce more accurate self-reports (see, e.g., Shiffman, 2009).

One example among low-income children is provided by Evans et al. (2009). Evans and his colleagues used experience sampling methodology (ESM) to obtain hourly reports of daily hassles—minor stressors in everyday life—among both low- and middle-income rural adolescents. The hourly assessment strategy stands in marked contrast to prior research on children's self-reported stressful events, which has typically relied on recall periods ranging from a month to a year (see, e.g., Attar et al., 1994; Compas, Davis, Forsythe, & Wagner, 1987; Kanner, Feldman, Weinberger, & Ford, 1987; Shahar, Henrich, Reiner, & Little, 2003), and because of this, it was able to provide an unprecedented look at the frequency, domain, and content of the daily events that characterize the everyday lives of low- versus middle-income adolescents. For example, Evans and colleagues corroborated prior research findings (e.g., Attar et al., 1994; Gad & Johnson, 1980; Pryor-Brown et al., 1986) by showing that low-income adolescents experienced a greater number of stressful events compared to middle-income adolescents. However, Evans and colleagues provided a more nuanced picture by showing that the source of this difference was primarily in the family context, as negative social interactions (e.g., nagging and activity prohibition from parents), chaotic living conditions, and lack of privacy at home were especially salient stressors for adolescents living in poverty, whereas low- and middle-income adolescents experienced a similar number of stressors in both school and peer domains. In short, the hourly assessment strategy used in this study was able to provide a richer picture of adolescents' daily contexts than had been achieved before, and it allowed for a better understanding of both the similarities and the differences in the daily experiences of low- versus middle-income youths.

In addition to momentary self-reports, the experienced environment can also be measured more objectively through the recording (photo, video, and voice) and global positioning system (GPS) capabilities of the latest generation of mobile devices (i.e., smartphones and tablets). Using these objective features allows researchers to get closer to measuring the *exposome*: the full catalog of an individual's environmental exposures (Borrell, 2011). For example, voice and photo capture on mobile phones is being used to more objectively obtain dietary information from individuals in their everyday lives (see the Food Intake Visual and voice Recognizer or FIVR; Weiss, Stumbo, & Divakaran, 2010). Similarly, mobile phones' photo and video capture capabilities could be used to document the daily contexts and activities of children living in poverty. For example, as part of their daily assessments, youth could be asked to take pictures of "where they are right now" in addition to providing self-reported information about what they are doing. These images could be directly uploaded to the researchers' data files, circumventing privacy and confidentiality concerns. These photos could be coded on dimensions such as disorder (e.g., messiness of the home, quality of housing, vandalism present) and dangerousness (e.g., observer impressions of safety in the home, school, or neighborhood; see Odgers, Caspi, Bates, Sampson, & Moffitt, 2012 for an example of such coding using images from Google Street View). Combined with daily self-reports, these in-the-field photos of contexts could help researchers obtain a richer picture of the types of contexts that children in poverty actually experience in their daily lives.

Similarly, GPS now comes standard on the majority of mobile technologies, and it can provide researchers with another means of acquiring objective measures of children's experienced environments. Using GPS, researchers can get a glimpse of the locations in which children spend their time, as well as the distances they travel in a given day around central locations (such as homes or schools). Wiehe and colleagues (2008) provided evidence that GPS-enabled mobile phones can accurately measure the travel patterns of adolescents in daily life, while at the same time allowing researchers to collect self-reports of adolescents' daily activities. Combined with objective information about the neighborhoods children frequent, researchers could derive a measure of each child's exposure to disordered or dangerous contexts over the course of a day.

Feature 2: Diary Methods Allow Us to Relax the Assumption That Everyone Is the Same

Diary methods allow us to avoid what Conner, Barrett, Tugade, and Tennen (2007) have called the *nomothetic fallacy*: "assuming what is true for the 'average' person is also true for each and every person" (p. 81). The term *nomothetic* was first used by the philosopher Wilhelm Windelband (1894/1998), who broadly dichotomized academic disciplines into (a) those that sought to identify general laws and principles (e.g., natural sciences such as biology) and (b) those that focused on understanding the peculiarities and idiosyncrasies of specific individuals, events, or time periods (e.g., humanities such as history). The former he called *nomothetic*; the latter, *idiographic*. In his book *Personality: A Psychological Interpretation*, Gordon Allport (1937) introduced Windelband's dichotomy to psychologists. Allport suggested that with its nearly exclusive focus on discovering general laws that could apply to everyone, psychology was too entrenched in nomothetic inquiry and should make a greater effort to integrate idiographic inquiry (i.e., case studies or biographies of individual people) into its methodological armamentarium. His argument was that by relying primarily on nomothetic methods to obtain general laws about people, what psychologists were getting in their results described a "hypothetical average" person that in one sense represented everyone and yet in another sense represented no one.

Allport's urging for idiographic inquiry is highly relevant to research on how poverty-related stress influences children's development, because the majority of research in this area has been nomothetic in nature. Nomothetic designs are essentially between-subjects designs, seeking to uncover natural laws about how, for example, poverty-related stress increases risk for antisocial behavior among *all* low-income children. These studies sample large numbers of people, assess them on static measures, and calculate correlations. Thus, nomothetic designs can tell us that among a large sample of children living in poverty, those with higher-than-average daily stressor exposure also typically have higher-than-average levels of antisocial behavior. These designs *cannot* tell us, however, that stress and antisocial behavior are related *within* a person over time. That is, a finding that children with higher-than-average stressor exposure tend to have higher-than-average antisocial behavior (a *between-person effect*) is not the same as a finding that children are more likely to engage in antisocial behavior compared to themselves on high-versus low-stress days (a *within-person effect*; see Bolger & Laurenceau, 2013; Curran & Bauer, 2011; Nesselroade & Ram, 2004 for further discussion of between-versus within-person variability and effects).

In fact, for most psychological processes, between- and within-person effects are likely to be independent, a fact that can be supported on both conceptual and empirical grounds (Bolger & Laurenceau, 2013; Hoffman & Stawski, 2009; Molenaar, 2004; Nezlek, 2001). At a conceptual level, between- and within-person effects are separate entities that most likely result from separate causal processes (Molenaar, 2004; Molenaar & Campbell, 2009). Take aggression as an example. Aggression can vary both between people (in terms of how aggressive each person is on average) and within a person over time (in terms of how much each person's aggression varies day by day). The causal processes explaining between-child differences in children's average levels of aggression are not likely to be the same as those explaining within-child differences in aggression from one day to the next. Why is this so? For one thing, stable factors that differ only between people, such as sex, ethnicity, family history, and genetic makeup, cannot logically explain why a single child was more aggressive on Monday than he was on Tuesday (a within-person effect; see Allison, 2005; Bolger & Laurenceau, 2013). For another, it is seems highly unlikely that a single negative event (such as an argument with a friend) could explain why a child shows a higher mean level of aggression than his peers, whereas this single negative event could easily explain why a single child was more aggressive on one day versus another. At an empirical level, the size, direction, and significance of between- versus within-person effects routinely differ and may even suggest opposite conclusions (see Bolger & Laurenceau, 2013; Nezlek, 2001).

The conceptual and empirical independence of between- and within-person effects makes it clear that we need designs capable of capturing both. Through intensive measurement of children in their natural environments, diary methods represent a "modern idiographic approach" (Conner, Tennen, Fleeson, & Barrett, 2009, p. 292), allowing researchers to better understand both the constellation of environmental exposures as well as the specific environment–behavior relationships that together determine where and with whom each individual child is most like likely to display antisocial or aggressive behavior. These methods are not strictly idiographic, however; aggregating these person-specific results to the group level allows researchers to draw valid group-level inferences that are directly informed by in-depth person-level information (see Nesselroade & Molenaar, 1999, for an example). As such, diary methods allow researchers to answer Allport's call to idiographic arms while still allowing researchers to draw nomothetic inferences. Next, we discuss how diary methods may be applied to study both environments and environmental effects on low-income children's antisocial behavior, in a way that is sensitive to the idiosyncracies of each individual child.

THE STRUCTURE OF EXPOSURE

Although children in poverty, on average, are more likely to experience stressors of all types compared to children not in poverty, each child in poverty is likely to experience his or her own unique constellation of stressors in daily life. For example, some children in low-income circumstances may face stressors that predominantly relate to chaos in their home environments. Others may face stressors relating primarily to neighborhood safety, family conflict, or school bullying. Still others will confront an array of stressors that elude researchers' a priori attempts to neatly categorize them. Combining the intensive time-series measurement of diary studies with empirically driven statistical clustering techniques (i.e., factor and latent class analysis) offers new ways forward for measuring the specific constellation of stressor experiences that characterize each child's daily life.

Cross-sectional research by Seidman et al. (1999) provides an empirical foundation for identifying the constellation of stress exposures unique to each child. Using survey responses, Seidman and colleagues (1999) applied empirical clustering techniques (k-means and hierarchical clustering methods, see Hartigan, 1975; Rapkin & Luke, 1993) to identify different constellations of family and peer social interactions among adolescents in poverty. In both family and peer domains, they identified six clusters of social experience in family and peer groups. Example clusters from the family domain included *dysfunctional* (high hassles, low support, low involvement), *hassling* (high hassles, near average support and involvement), and *enmeshing* (high hassles, low support, high involvement); examples from the peer domain included *rejecting* (high hassles, low acceptance, low involvement and support), *entangling* (high hassles, high involvement and support), and *antisocial-engaging* (high antisocial peer values, high involvement and support). Importantly, membership in these clusters was associated with antisocial behavior in adolescents. In the family domain, adolescents in either the dysfunctional, hassling, or enmeshing clusters showed the highest levels of antisocial behavior. In the peer domain, adolescents in the antisocial-engaging cluster showed the most antisocial behavior.

The clusters identified by Seidman and colleagues (1999) are a grouping of youths who share similar experiences on average. They are not, however, a clustering of *experiences* within each youth. The difference is subtle but important. Empirical clustering of at the *group level* provides the profile, constellation, or factor structure of experiences that best explains the regularities of experiential reports for a group of individuals. It does *not* provide the specific constellation of experiences unique to each *person*. Instead, it takes what may be called a top-down approach, assuming that the group-level solution explains the regularities of experience for each group member. In contrast, by collecting repeated measurements of experience from each person, researchers can employ a *bottom-up* approach, obtaining a profile of experiences unique to each child in the study and then generalizing to the group level by identifying individuals who share similar profiles of experiences. Mapping the regularities of experience for each child in poverty would lead researchers to identify natural clusters of children who can be empirically shown (rather than assumed) to have the same constellation of experiences, and it would lead to stronger group-level inferences regarding the specific constellation of experiences that an actual child in poverty might encounter (see Molenaar & Campbell, 2009; Nesselroade & Molenaar, 1999; Nesselroade & Ram, 2004 for discussion).

The usefulness of the person-based approach has been clearly shown in the emotion literature. For example, in a 90-day diary study, Barrett (1998) obtained university students' reports on their positive and negative emotions three times a day (morning, afternoon, and evening). She then factor analyzed each person's multiple emotion reports separately (a method known as P-technique factor analysis; see Cattell, Cattell, & Rhymer, 1947) and found that some individuals tended to report "clustered" emotional experiences. In other words, when these individuals reported happiness, they were also more likely to report other positive emotions such as joy and cheerfulness *at the same time* (the same was true for negative emotions). Others, however, showed greater differentiation in their real-time emotional reports, such that reports of happiness were less likely to be temporally coupled with other positive emotions (same for negatives as well). These results differ from those obtained using more traditional factor analytic approaches (R-technique; see Cattell, 1952), which would provide information regarding whether a person who reports more happiness on average also reports more joy on average— not whether people experience these emotions at the same time. From this more person-centered approach, Barrett (1998) concluded that a single theory of emotion is unlikely to apply to everyone, as people differed substantially in the complexity of their moment-to-moment (rather than average) emotional experiences. Another study (Carstensen, Pasupathi, Mayr, & Nesselroade, 2000) showed that some adults had a greater tendency to report positive and negative emotions simultaneously in their daily lives than others (which they termed *poignancy*), and that the tendency to experience mixed emotional states was higher among older versus younger adults (age range of the study was 19 to 94 years). Importantly, the type of information gained in the Barrett (1998) and Carstensen et al. (2000) studies can only be obtained through intensive within-person measurement, such as what diary methods can offer (Conner et al., 2009). A similar approach could be fruitfully applied to obtain a more idiosyncratic understanding of the environmental experiences that characterize a day in the life of a child living in poverty.

ENVIRONMENT-BEHAVIOR SIGNATURES

Suppose we find two children who are equal in age, gender, and ethnicity, both of whom have spent their entire lives living in impoverished homes and communities. Suppose we observe these children further and find that they both show high levels of antisocial behavior relative to their same-age peers. Given their similarities, should we assume that these children engage in antisocial behavior for the same reasons and in the same situations? According to personality theorists Walter Mischel and Yuichi Shoda (1995), the answer to this question is "no." It has been clearly shown that even between people who engage in similar levels of behavior on average (such as aggression), there will be important differences between them in terms of *where, with whom*, and *in which situations* each person will engage in aggression.

A classic example comes from a summer treatment camp study of children with self-regulatory and aggressive behavior problems (Shoda, Mischel, & Wright, 1994). Over 6 weeks, these children's behaviors were observed and recorded across a variety of situations. Shoda and colleagues found that children's levels of aggression were not constant across situations, as trait theories of personality would predict. Instead, children's aggression varied greatly across situations. However, Shoda and colleagues found that some situations reliably predicted aggression for some children, but not for others. In other words, some children may reliably show aggression when teased by peers but show no such aggression when scolded by adults. Other children may show the reverse pattern, engaging in aggression when scolded by adults but not when teased by peers. The significance of this finding is perhaps best articulated by Mischel (2004):

> Collectively, the results showed that when closely observed, individuals are characterized by stable, distinctive, and highly meaningful patterns of variability in their actions, thoughts, and feelings across different types of

situations. These *if ... then ...* situation-behavior relationships provide a kind of "behavioral signature of personality" that identifies the individual and maps on to the impressions formed by observers about what they are like. (p. 8)

Evidence for predictable patterns of variability, or behavioral signatures, has been found across numerous independent investigations using a variety of methodologies (Leikas, Lonnqvist, & Verkasalo, 2012; Smith, Shoda, Cumming, & Smoll, 2009; Vansteelandt & Van Mechelen, 1998), including studies using diary methods (e.g., Fournier, Moskowitz, & Zuroff, 2008), which seem naturally poised to answer such questions. Using such methods among children in poverty, researchers could examine the particular environmental exposures or situations that reliably predict antisocial behavior in some children versus others. Using diary measures and multilevel modeling statistical techniques (Raudenbush & Bryk, 2002), a separate effect of each hassle (e.g., family conflict, chaotic home, school stressors) on momentary antisocial behavior can be obtained for each child. The strength of the association between daily hassles and antisocial behavior can be quantified as a regression coefficient for each child. This regression coefficient can then serve as an individual difference variable, characterizing each child's likelihood of engaging in various types of antisocial behaviors (e.g., verbal or physical aggression, anger, and hostility) across these specific situations (see Fleeson, 2007 for an example of this type of approach with personality). As predicted, one may find a group of children who show a strong likelihood of engaging in antisocial behavior when peer hassles are experienced, whereas another group of children shows a strong likelihood of antisocial behavior when parent hassles occur. Using other child or family characteristics, such as the child's previous level of stressful life events, history of antisocial behavior, and parental monitoring, one can then attempt to characterize children who show aggression in response to peer versus parent hassles in daily life.

Feature 3: Diary Methods Allow the Study of Within-Person Processes, Facilitating Causal Inference and Discovery of Environmentally Mediated Effects

Perhaps one of the strongest features of diary methods is their ability to capture processes that occur within a person in response to changing environments. This approach allows the researcher to control for a whole host of characteristics that remain stable over time, measured or unmeasured, by using each person as his or her own control across a range of situations or stressors. This design feature of diary studies gets researchers a step closer to causal inferences about environmental effects because in this within-person framework, stable characteristics such as genetic makeup, biological sex, and ethnicity are effectively held constant (Allison, 2005; Bolger & Laurenceau, 2013).

This within-person focus provides a novel way to facilitate causal inferences regarding the role of stressor exposure in children's antisocial development in a nonexperimental context. If it could be shown that change in stressor exposure correlates with change in antisocial outcomes *within the same child*, this could facilitate causal inferences regarding environmental effects because stable "selection" factors such as genetic makeup, sex, and ethnicity have been held constant. Causal inferences regarding the role of stressors can be further facilitated by adding statistical controls for other potential confounds that do vary over time, such as previous negative mood, sleep quality from the previous night, or even the passage of time itself. Moreover, diary methods allow the estimation of temporal patterns, allowing researchers to test whether stress exposure predicts antisocial behaviors, or vice versa.

A recent example of this type of approach in daily life comes from work by Stadler, Snyder, Horn, Shrout, and Bolger (2012). Using daily diaries in the lives of male-female couples, they found that within-person increases in physical intimacy between partners predicted within-person decreases in self-reported physical symptoms (e.g., headache, upset stomach, back/muscle ache). Stadler and colleagues (2012) further strengthened this result by showing that *previous* increases in physical intimacy (from 2 days ago to yesterday) predicted *current* decreases in physical symptoms (from yesterday to today). They found no evidence for the reverse effect: Previous symptom change did not significantly predict current change in intimacy. All of their models controlled for the effects of elapsed time, following the rationale that this represents a proxy for unmeasured third variables (i.e., fatigue caused by duration of the study; a shared growth process that creates a spurious association between the two variables of interest; see Bolger & Laurenceau, 2013). Taken together, their results provide strong evidence for a causal effect of intimacy on physical symptoms because (a) their focus on within-person change ruled out stable selection factors, (b) they found no evidence for reverse causation, and (c) they statistically controlled for unmeasured time-varying processes that could confound the effects. Although they cannot completely rule out lurking selection effects because physical intimacy was not randomly assigned, the combined use of these methods in a daily life framework nonetheless provides a strong basis for facilitating causal inference.

This within-person process approach could be applied to the question of whether stressful events have environmentally mediated effects on low-income children's antisocial behavior. For instance, by using diary methods to test for the within-person effects of daily stressors on negative affect and aggressive behavior in daily life, each child is used as his or her own "control." If within-person effects are found, they cannot be explained by stable factors that differ between individuals but do not vary over time, such as sex, ethnicity, or genetic makeup. Additionally, information obtained through diary methods can be paired with real-time physiological measures of stress reactivity, such as heart-rate variability, which can now be obtained in children's natural contexts through the newest generation of ambulatory sensors. One of these, the Zephyr Bioharness™ 3,[2] allows real-time remote monitoring of parameters such as heart rate and breathing rate, and can wirelessly stream this information to mobile devices or to the researcher's desktop computer. By synching this information with children's diary reports of stressful events, researchers could obtain a more objective measure stress reactivity that does not rely exclusively on self-report. If daily stressors were found to predict within-person changes in negative affect, antisocial behavior, and physiological stress markers alike, this evidence would provide yet another step toward causal inferences because the effects cannot be explained away by shared method variance. By offering researchers the ability to examine the within-person effects of daily stressors on affect, behavior, and physiology, diary methods allow researchers to get closer to causality regarding whether everyday stressors affect children's antisocial behavior through environmental pathways.

In short, diary methods, delivered through the latest generation of mobile technologies, provide numerous opportunities to improve our current understanding of environmental effects on children's antisocial behavior, while allowing us to appreciate that not every child responds to adversity in the same way. Currently, we are in a unique position to pair the methodological advances offered by diary methods with exciting new theories about why some children may be more reactive to their daily events than others, and whether this increased reactivity can help explain their risk for poor outcomes (such as antisocial behavior) or their receptiveness to targeted intervention efforts. In the next section, we discuss how the within-person power of diary methods can provide novel ways to test theories of person–environment interaction, such as diathesis-stress (Monroe & Simons, 1991) and differential susceptibility (Ellis et al., 2011).

INDIVIDUAL DIFFERENCES IN ENVIRONMENTAL EFFECTS: WHY ARE SOME CHILDREN MORE REACTIVE TO EXPERIENCE THAN OTHERS?

On average, children in poverty are more likely to engage in antisocial behavior than children from higher income backgrounds. Not every child in poverty, however, will engage in antisocial behavior. This fact naturally leads to questions about why some children exposed to high poverty-related stress will develop antisocial behavior and others will not. An exciting idea known as differential susceptibility theory (DST; Ellis et al., 2011) suggests that some children may be, by nature, more sensitive to their environments, both positive and negative, than others. These "sensitive" children may be at greatest risk when environments are chronically stressful but at lowest risk when environments are consistently supportive (Belsky, Bakermans-Kranenburg, & van Ijzendoorn, 2007; Ellis et al., 2011). "Sensitive" or "susceptible" children may be distinguished by genes, physiological parameters, and behavioral phenotypes thought to be under high genetic influence such as early temperaments (Belsky & Pluess, 2009). DST suggests that children with one or more of these sensitivity markers may be more likely to develop negative outcomes (such as antisocial behavior) when exposed to negative contexts (such as disadvantaged homes and neighborhoods), but they may also be more likely to show positive developmental outcomes (i.e., good self-regulation, empathy, prosocial behavior) when exposed to positive contexts (such as supportive home environments and socially cohesive neighborhoods). This is an exciting possibility because it suggests that youth who were previously considered to be highly vulnerable may in fact be more validly considered highly *susceptible* to the good and the bad of whichever environments they are in. As a result, these vulnerable youth may be the ones who will benefit most from targeted interventions.

Here again, diary methods offer a novel and potentially powerful way to test the core assertion of differential susceptibility: that environmental effects are stronger for some children versus others. Differential susceptibility theory falls into a broader class of person-by-environment theories, such as the diathesis-stress model (Monroe & Simons, 1991). The diathesis-stress model suggests that some children possess genetic or temperamental characteristics that make them more vulnerable to bad environments, but not more responsive to good environments, as the differential susceptibility perspective suggests. The majority of research testing person-by-environment interaction theories has tested whether children with *both* an individual sensitivity marker and a negative environment have higher levels of antisocial behavior (for example) than children without the sensitivity marker, negative environment, or either (see, for example, Caspi et al., 2002; Lengua, Wolchik, Sandler, & West, 2000). This type of test is inherently between people, because it compares children to each other on their average levels of antisocial behavior and tests whether children with the most antisocial behavior are more likely to have *both* an individual vulnerability and an environmental risk. A complementary approach to testing person-by-environment theories is to ask whether "sensitive" children are more *reactive* to changing environments. In other words, do sensitive children show more behavior problems in stressful situations compared to themselves in nonstressful situations? This is essentially a within-person question, one which diary methods are well suited to answer. Using a within-person perspective may be particularly important for research on the differential susceptibility theory, because this theory suggests that sensitive children should both be more reactive to negative events *and* more responsive to positive events.

Figure 2.1 illustrates that the use of within-person changes in environments and behaviors could provide strong evidence for whether differential susceptibility operates in the daily lives of youth. As children go through their daily lives, they experience both stressful and positive events. However, some children

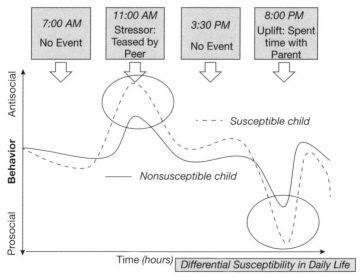

Figure 2.1 A hypothetical illustration of differential susceptibility to the environment in daily life.

will be more sensitive to these events than others. Highly sensitive children (the dashed trajectory in Fig. 2.1) will be more responsive to both stressful and positive events in daily life than typically sensitive children (the solid trajectory). As such, highly sensitive children are predicted to show greater increases in positive outcomes (e.g., prosocial behaviors and positive affect) when experiencing positive events *and* greater increases in negative outcomes (e.g., problem behaviors and negative affect) following negative events, such as daily stressors. Because diary methods allow us to (a) obtain true-to-life or ecologically valid reports of both positive and negative events in daily life, (b) test the effects of these events within each child, and (c) test whether within-person effects are stronger for youth with sensitivity markers, they allow a strong and direct test of the differential susceptibility model's key hypothesis that some children are more sensitive to their environments than others—for better *and* for worse (Belsky et al., 2007).

Which markers may help identify children who are differentially susceptible to environmental effects on behavior? To date, some of the strongest evidence points to the 7-repeat allele of the dopamine receptor D4 gene (*DRD4-7R*), a gene that has been previously associated with novelty/sensation seeking (Laucht, Becker, El-Faddagh, Hohm, & Schmidt, 2005), impulsivity (Congdon, Lesch, & Canli, 2008), anger and delinquency (Dmitrieva, Chen, Greenberger, Ogunseitan, & Ding, 2011), and attention-deificit/hyperactivity disorder (ADHD; Faraone et al., 2005). Rather than being solely a risk allele, the *DRD4-7R* gene may function more like a "plasticity allele," conferring increased sensitivity to whatever environment a child is in (Belsky et al., 2009). This increased sensitivity is thought to provide an evolutionary advantage when environments are positive, which may explain why genes and traits associated with risk have nonetheless been preserved in the human species (Belsky, 2005). In support of this, a recent meta-analysis showed that children with "risky" dopamine genes such as the 7R allele showed *the most* externalizing (or antisocial) behavior in negative rearing environments, but children with these genes in positive rearing environments showed *the least* externalizing behavior (Bakermans-Kranenburg & van Ijzendoorn, 2011).

Particularly compelling support for the *DRD4-7R* gene comes from two experimental studies showing that an intervention designed to promote parent–child attachment was more effective in reducing externalizing behavior problems for children with versus without *DRD4-7R* (Bakermans-Kranenburg, van Ijzendoorn, Mesman, Alink, & Juffer, 2008; Bakermans-Kranenburg, van Ijzendoorn, Pijlman, Mesman, & Juffer, 2008). By conferring increased susceptibility to environmental influence, the *DRD4-7R* gene may identify children who are most sensitive to positive and negative events in their everyday lives. This hypothesis could be tested using diary methods that allow researchers to examine whether daily events have stronger within-person effects on behavior—for better and for worse—among low-income children with versus without the *DRD4-7R* gene. If low-income children with this gene are more sensitive to both positive *and* negative daily events, this evidence may suggest that these children, although at higher risk in their current environments, may be more likely to benefit from intervention strategies targeting the link between daily stressors and antisocial behavior.

FUTURE DIRECTIONS

Diary methods provide tremendous flexibility in the measurement of daily experiences, and their effects, on low-income youth. The most exciting future directions for these methods may lie in their combination with more "traditional" research designs, as well as interventions of known efficacy.

Diary Measurement Bursts: Combining Diary Methods and Longitudinal Designs

Antisocial behavior is a developmental phenomenon. Because of this, longitudinal study designs that follow children over key developmental periods (such as childhood and the transition to adolescence) are necessary in order to truly understand its causes. Although traditional longitudinal designs have provided us with much valuable information about how antisocial behavior develops over years (see e.g., Moffitt et al., 2001; NICHD Early Child Care Research Network, 2004; Sampson & Laub, 2005; Thornberry & Krohn, 2003; Tremblay, 2010), these designs may miss the micro-level processes that affect whether a child will engage in antisocial behavior on one day versus another—such as a provocation from a peer or harsh discipline from a parent (Dodge, 2006; Patterson et al., 1992). Diary methods are especially useful for understanding this type of micro-level change and may be powerfully combined with traditional longitudinal studies to better understand the interaction between short-term and long-term processes in the development of antisocial behavior.

Measurement burst studies embed daily-life measurement bursts into more traditional longitudinal studies that follow people over years (Nesselroade, 1991; Sliwinski, 2008). Despite their potential, these designs have not yet been applied to the study of antisocial behavior. These powerful designs could allow researchers to examine the interplay between short-term processes and long-term changes, and thereby improve our understanding of the causal pathways through which environmental conditions affect antisocial development. For example, measurement burst designs could provide investigators with a means for (a) examining how the relationship between stressor exposure and antisocial behavior changes over time and (b) learning how changes in these micro-level processes feed into developmental "turning points" (Sampson & Laub, 2005), such as desistence or escalation in antisocial behavior during key developmental transitions (such as early adolescence). Moreover, these designs could offer better insight into the *timescale* of environmental effects. For example, with regard to the differential susceptibility hypothesis mentioned earlier, it is not yet known whether "sensitive" children (such as youth with *DRD4-7R*) will be more responsive to environments *in the moment* or whether this sensitivity will only manifest itself over years. In other words, should we expect that a single day of high support will predict less antisocial behavior the next day among youth with the *DRD4-7R* gene? Or does this relationship take years to manifest, such that we will only see larger decreases in antisocial behavior among youth with versus without *DRD4-7R* if they experience a home environment that remains supportive over longer time spans? Through their ability to separate empirically both short- and long-term processes of change, measurement burst designs could provide powerful and unique information regarding the role of environment in low-income children's antisocial development.

Interventions at the Right Time, in the Right Place

Mobile technologies are also providing researchers and health professionals with new opportunities for assessment and intervention among previously hard-to-access, high-risk groups, such as children living in poverty. The movement toward using mobile technologies to administer assessments and deliver intervention has been dubbed *mobile health* (or mHealth) by the National Institutes of Health (National Institutes of Health, 2013) and includes diary measurement techniques such as those described earlier. Among children living in poverty, diary methods could be used to test—and eventually disseminate—message-based interventions focused on fostering positive coping strategies, triggered when youth report experiencing a stressful event. These approaches may offer promise, as evidence suggests that youth who use active coping strategies, such as problem solving, emotion regulation, and positive thinking, may be less likely to display emotional, behavioral, and physical health problems than youth who rely on avoidant coping strategies (Chen & Miller, 2012; Wadsworth, 2012). For example, mobile phone delivery of intervention content could be used as a supplement to cognitive-behavioral therapy (CBT; Beck, 1991), an intervention of known efficacy among youth with antisocial behavior (McCart, Priester, Davies, & Azen, 2006). Mobile devices could be used to reinforce intervention content by sending coping intervention-related messages, reminding children to use positive coping strategies when stressful events occur. In this way, mobile messaging may help clinical professionals with the daunting task of delivering time-tested interventions to high-risk groups, at the times and places they are needed most.

SUMMARY

Children growing up in poverty are at risk for developing antisocial behavior, a significant and costly societal problem. Evidence suggests that the association between poverty and antisocial behavior is consistent with a causal interpretation, and emerging theoretical perspectives argue that the effect of poverty on antisocial development may be driven by the chronically stressful conditions of low-income children's everyday environments. However, accurate measurement of daily events remains a persistent methodological challenge, which limits the field's understanding of causal processes. Diary methods may help by allowing researchers to measure children's everyday experiences, emotion, self-regulation, and behavior as they go through their daily lives, in their natural environments, and in a way that is sensitive to the idiosyncrasies of each individual child. The latest generation of mobile technologies, through their ability to measure within-person change and capture more objective measures of context and physiology, provide added flexibility and can get researchers one step closer to a causal understanding of environmental effects on children's antisocial behavior.

Moreover, these mobile technologies are opening up exciting possibilities for the delivery of intervention to high-risk populations, at the times and places they are needed most. In sum, the stage is set for mobile methods to improve our understanding of environmental effects on children's antisocial behavior and to open up new opportunities for interventions aimed at improving the lives of low-income children and their families.

NOTES

1. Throughout, we use the term *children* to refer to both childhood and adolescence, and to distinguish between the two developmental periods when necessary.
2. Available at http://www.zephyranywhere.com/products/bioharness-3/

REFERENCES

Allison, P. D. (2005). *Fixed effects regressions for longitudinal data using SAS*. Cary, NC: SAS Institute.

Allport, G. W. (1937). *Personality: A psychological interpretation*. New York, NY: Henry Holt.

Almeida, D. M. (2005). Resilience and vulnerability to daily stressors assessed via diary methods. *Current Directions in Psychological Science, 14*, 64–68. doi: 10.1111/j.0963-7214.2005.00336.x

Anderson, D. A. (1999). The aggregate burden of crime. *Journal of Law and Economics, 42*, 611–642. doi: 10.1086/467436

Attar, B. K., Guerra, N. G., & Tolan, P. H. (1994). Neighborhood disadvantage, stressful life events, and adjustment in urban elementary-school-children. *Journal of Clinical Child Psychology, 23*, 391–400. doi: 10.1207/s15374424jccp2304_5

Bakermans-Kranenburg, M. J., & van Ijzendoorn, M. H. (2011). Differential susceptibility to rearing environment depending on dopamine-related genes: New evidence and a meta-analysis. *Development and Psychopathology, 23*, 39–52. doi: 10.1017/s0954579410000635

Bakermans-Kranenburg, M. J., van Ijzendoorn, M. H., Mesman, J., Alink, L. R. A., & Juffer, F. (2008). Effects of an attachment-based intervention on daily cortisol moderated by dopamine receptor D4: A randomized control trial on 1-to 3-year-olds screened for externalizing behavior. *Development and Psychopathology, 20*, 805–820. doi: 10.1017/s0954579408000382

Bakermans-Kranenburg, M. J., van Ijzendoorn, M. H., Pijlman, F. T. A., Mesman, J., & Juffer, F. (2008). Experimental evidence for differential susceptibility: Dopamine D4 receptor polymorphism (DRD4 VNTR) moderates intervention effects on toddlers' externalizing behavior in a randomized controlled trial. *Developmental Psychology, 44*, 293–300. doi: 10.1037/0012-1649.44.1.293

Barrett, L. F. (1998). Discrete emotions or dimensions? The role of valence focus and arousal focus. *Cognition and Emotion, 12*, 579–599. doi: 10.1080/026999398379574

Beck, A. T. (1991). Cognitive therapy: A 30-year retrospective. *American Psychologist, 46*, 368–375. doi: 10.1037//0003-066x.46.4.368

Bell, R. Q. (1968). A reinterpretation of the direction of effects in studies of socialization. *Psychological Review, 75*, 81–95. doi: 10.1037/h0025583

Belsky, J. (2005). Differential susceptibility to rearing influence: An evolutionary hypothesis and some evidence. In B. J. Ellis & D. F. Bjorklund (Eds.), *Origins of the social mind: Evolutionary psychology and child development* (pp. 139–163). New York, NY: Guilford Press.

Belsky, J., Bakermans-Kranenburg, M. J., & van Ijzendoorn, M. H. (2007). For better and for worse: Differential susceptibility to environmental influences. *Current Directions in Psychological Science, 16*, 300–304. doi: 10.1111/j.1467-8721.2007.00525.x

Belsky, J., Jonassaint, C., Pluess, M., Stanton, M., Brummett, B., & Williams, R. (2009). Vulnerability genes or plasticity genes? *Molecular Psychiatry, 14*, 746–754. doi: 10.1038/mp.2009.44

Belsky, J., & Pluess, M. (2009). Beyond diathesis stress: Differential susceptibility to environmental influences. *Psychological Bulletin, 135*, 885–908. doi: 10.1037/a0017376

Bjerk, D. J. (2007). Measuring the relationship between youth criminal participation and household economic resources. *Journal of Quantitative Criminology, 23*, 23–39. doi: 10.1007/s10940-006-9017-8

Blair, C., & Raver, C. C. (2012). Child development in the context of adversity experiential canalization of brain and behavior. *American Psychologist, 67*, 309–318. doi: 10.1037/a0027493

Bolger, N., Davis, A., & Rafaeli, E. (2003). Diary methods: Capturing life as it is lived. *Annual Review of Psychology, 54*, 579–616. doi: 10.1146/annurev. psych.54.101601.145030

Bolger, N., & Laurenceau, J.-P. (2013). *Intensive longtiudinal methods: An introduction to diary and experience sampling research.* New York, NY: Guilford Press.

Borrell, B. (2011). Every bite you take. *Nature, 470*, 320–322.

Bradburn, N. M., Rips, L. J., & Shevell, S. K. (1987). Answering autobiographical questions: The impact of memory and inference on surveys. *Science, 236*, 157–161. doi: 10.1126/science.3563494

Bradley, R. H., & Corwyn, R. F. (2002). Socioeconomic status and child development. *Annual Review of Psychology, 53*, 371–399. doi: 10.1146/annurev. psych.53.100901.135233

Bradley, R. H., Corwyn, R. F., McAdoo, H. P., & Coll, C. G. (2001). The home environments of children in the United States part I: Variations by age, ethnicity, and poverty status. *Child Development, 72*, 1844–1867. doi: 10.1111/1467-8624.t01-1-00382

Brooks-Gunn, J., & Duncan, G. J. (1997). The effects of poverty on children. *The Future of Children, 7*, 55–71.

Carstensen, L. L., Pasupathi, M., Mayr, U., & Nesselroade, J. R. (2000). Emotional experience in everyday life across the adult life span. *Journal of Personality and Social Psychology, 79*, 644–655. doi: 10.1037//0022-3514.79.4.644

Caspi, A., McClay, J., Moffitt, T. E., Mill, J., Martin, J., Craig, I. W., ... Poulton, R. (2002). Role of genotype in the cycle of violence in maltreated children. *Science, 297*, 851–854.

Caspi, A., Moffitt, T. E., Morgan, J., Rutter, M., Taylor, A., Arseneault, L., ... Polo-Tomas, M. (2004). Maternal expressed emotion predicts children's antisocial behavior problems: Using monozygotic-twin differences to identify environmental effects on behavioral development. *Developmental Psychology, 40*, 149–161. doi: 10.1037/0012-1 649.40.20.149

Caspi, A., Taylor, A., Moffitt, T. E., & Plomin, R. (2000). Neighborhood deprivation affects children's mental health: Environmental risks identified in a genetic design. *Psychological Science, 11*, 338–342. doi: 10.1111/1467-9280.00267

Cattell, R. B. (1952). The 3 basic factor-analytic research designs: Their interrelations and derivatives. *Psychological Bulletin, 49*, 499–520. doi: 10.1037/h0054245

Cattell, R. B., Cattell, A. K. S., & Rhymer, R. M. (1947). P-technique demonstrated in determining psychophysiological source traits in a normal individual. *Psychometrika, 12*, 267–288.

Chen, E., & Miller, G. E. (2012). "Shift-and-persist" strategies: Why low socioeconomic status isn't always bad for health. *Perspectives on Psychological Science, 7*, 135–158. doi: 10.1177/1745691612436694

Cohen, S., Krantz, D. S., Evans, G. W., Stokols, D., & Kelly, S. (1981). Aircraft noise and children: Longitudinal and cross-sectional evidence on adaptation to noise and the effectiveness of noise abatement. *Journal of Personality and Social Psychology, 40*, 331–345. doi: 10.1037//0022-3514.40.2.331

Compas, B. E., Davis, G. E., Forsythe, C. J., & Wagner, B. M. (1987). Assessment of major and daily stressful events during adolescence—the adolescent perceived events scale. *Journal of Consulting and Clinical Psychology, 55*, 534–541. doi: 10.1037//0 022-006x.55.4.534

Congdon, E., Lesch, K. P., & Canli, T. (2008). Analysis of DRD4 and DAT polymorphisms and behavioral inhibition in healthy adults: Implications for impulsivity. *American Journal of Medical Genetics Part B-Neuropsychiatric Genetics, 147B*, 27–32. doi: 10.1002/ajmg.b.30557

Conger, R. D., Conger, K. J., Elder, G. H., Lorenz, F. O., Simons, R. L., & Whitbeck, L. B. (1992). A family process model of economic hardship and adjustment of early adolescent boys. *Child Development, 63*, 526–541. doi: 10.1111/j.1467-8624.1992. tb01644.x

Conger, R. D., Ge, X. J., Elder, G. H., Lorenz, F. O., & Simons, R. L. (1994). Economic-stress, coercive family process, and developmental problems of adolescents. *Child Development, 65*, 541–561. doi: 10.1111/j.1467-8624.1994.tb00768.x

Conner Christensen, T., Barrett, L. F., Bliss-Moreau, E., Lebo, K., & Kaschub, C. (2003). A practical guide to experience-sampling procedures. *Journal of Happiness Studies, 4*, 53–78. doi: 10.1023/A:1023609306024

Conner, T. S., Barrett, L. F., Tugade, M. M., & Tennen, H. (2007). Idiographic personality: The theory and practice of experience sampling. In R. W. Robins, R. C. Fraley, & R. F. Krueger (Eds.), *Handbook of research methods in personality psychology* (pp. 79–96). New York, NY: Guilford Press.

Conner, T. S., Tennen, H., Fleeson, W., & Barrett, L. F. (2009). Experience sampling methods: A modern idiographic approach to personality research. *Social and Personality Psychology Compass, 3*, 292–313. doi: 10.1111/j.1751-9004.2009.00170.x

Costello, E. J., Compton, S. N., Keeler, G., & Angold, A. (2003). Relationships between poverty and psychopathology: A natural experiment. *Journal of the American Medical Association, 290*, 2023–2029. doi: 10.1001/jama.290.15.2023

Csikszentmihalyi, M., Larson, R., & Prescott, S. (1977). Ecology of adolescent activity and experience. *Journal of Youth and Adolescence, 6*, 281–294. doi: 10.1007/bf02138940

Curran, P. J., & Bauer, D. J. (2011). The disaggregation of within-person and between-person effects in longitudinal models of change. *Annual Review of Psychology, 62*, 583–619. doi: 10.1146/annurev.psych.093008.100356

Danese, A., Moffitt, T. E., Harrington, H., Milne, B. J., Polanczyk, G., Pariante, C. M., … Caspi, A. (2009). Adverse childhood experiences and adult risk factors for age-related disease depression, inflammation, and clustering of metabolic risk markers. *Archives of Pediatrics and Adolescent Medicine, 163*, 1135–1143.

DeLongis, A., Coyne, J. C., Dakof, G., Folkman, S., & Lazarus, R. S. (1982). Relationship of daily hassles, uplifts, and major life events to health status. *Health Psychology, 1*, 119–136. doi: 10.1037/0278-6133.1.2.119

Dmitrieva, J., Chen, C. S., Greenberger, E., Ogunseitan, O., & Ding, Y. C. (2011). Gender-specific expression of the DRD4 gene on adolescent delinquency, anger and thrill seeking. *Social Cognitive and Affective Neuroscience, 6*, 82–89. doi: 10.1093/scan/nsq020

Dodge, K. A. (2006). Translational science in action: Hostile attributional style and the development of aggressive behavior problems. *Development and Psychopathology, 18*, 791–814. doi: 10.1017/s0954579406060391

Dodge, K. A., Coie, J. D., & Lynam, D. (2006). Aggression and antisocial behavior in youth. In R. M. Lerner & W. Damon (Eds.), *Handbook of child psychology* (pp. 719–786). Hoboken, NJ: Wiley.

Dodge, K. A., Pettit, G. S., & Bates, J. E. (1994). Socialization mediators of the relation between socioeconomic-status and child conduct problems. *Child Development, 65*, 649–665. doi: 10.1111/j.1467-8624.1994.tb00774.x

Elder, G. H. (1974). *Children of the great depression*. Chicago, IL: University of Chicago Press.

Elder, G. H., van Nguyen, T., & Caspi, A. (1985). Linking family hardship to childrens lives. *Child Development, 56*, 361–375. doi: 10.1111/j.1467-8624.1985.tb00112.x

Elliott, D. S., & Ageton, S. S. (1980). Reconciling race and class-differences in self-reported and official estimates of delinquency. *American Sociological Review, 45*, 95–110. doi: 10.2307/2095245

Ellis, B. J., Boyce, W. T., Belsky, J., Bakermans-Kranenburg, M. J., & van Ijzendoorn, M. H. (2011). Differential susceptibility to the environment: An evolutionary-neurodevelopmental theory. *Development and Psychopathology, 23*, 7–28. doi: 10.1017/s0954579410000611

Evans, G. W. (2004). The environment of childhood poverty. *American Psychologist, 59*, 77–92. doi: 10.1037/0003-066x.59.2.77

Evans, G. W., & English, K. (2002). The environment of poverty: Multiple stressor exposure, psychophysiological stress, and socioemotional adjustment. *Child Development, 73*, 1238–1248. doi: Unsp 0009-3920/2002/7304-001710.1111/1467-8624.00469

Evans, G. W., Gonnella, C., Marcynyszyn, L. A., Gentile, L., & Salpekar, N. (2005). The role of chaos in poverty and children's socioemotional adjustment. *Psychological Science, 16*, 560–565. doi: 10.1111/j.0956-7976.2005.01575.x

Evans, G. W., & Kim, P. (2013). Childhood poverty, chronic stress, self-regulation, and coping. *Child Development Perspectives, 7*, 43–48. doi: 10.1111/cdep.12013

Evans, G. W., Kim, P., Ting, A. H., Tesher, H. B., & Shannis, D. (2007). Cumulative risk, maternal responsiveness, and allostatic load among young adolescents. *Developmental Psychology, 43*, 341–351. doi: 10.1037/0012-1649.43.2.341

Evans, G. W., Vermeylen, F. M., Barash, A., Lefkowitz, E. G., & Hutt, R. L. (2009). The experience of stressors and hassles among rural adolescents from low- and middle-income households in the USA. *Children, Youth, and Environments, 19*, 164–175.

Faraone, S. V., Perlis, R. H., Doyle, A. E., Smoller, J. W., Goralnick, J. J., Holmgren, M. A., & Sklar, P. (2005). Molecular genetics of attention-deficit/hyperactivity disorder. *Biological Psychiatry, 57*, 1313–1323. doi: 10.1016/j.biopsych.2004.11.024

Farrington, D. P. (1989). Early predictors of adolescent aggression and adult violence. *Violence and Victims, 4*, 79–100.

Felitti, V. J., Anda, R. F., Nordenberg, D., Williamson, D. F., Spitz, A. M., Edwards, V., … Marks, J. S. (1998). Relationship of childhood abuse and household dysfunction to many of the leading causes of death in adults: The adverse childhood experiences (ACE) study. *American Journal of Preventive Medicine, 14,* 245–258. doi: 10.1016/s0749-3797(98)00017-8

Fergusson, D. M., & Horwood, L. J. (2002). Male and female offending trajectories. *Development and Psychopathology, 14,* 159–177.

Fleeson, W. (2007). Situation-based contingencies underlying trait-content manifestation in behavior. *Journal of Personality, 75,* 825–861. doi: 10.1111/j.1467-6494.2007.00458.x

Fournier, M. A., Moskowitz, D. S., & Zuroff, D. C. (2008). Integrating dispositions, signatures, and the interpersonal domain. *Journal of Personality and Social Psychology, 94,* 531–545. doi: 10.1037/0022-3514.94.3.531

Gad, M. T., & Johnson, J. H. (1980). Correlates of adolescent life stress as related to race, ses, and levels of perceived social support. *Journal of Clinical Child Psychology, 9,* 13–16.

Grant, K. E., Compas, B. E., Stuhlmacher, A. F., Thurm, A. E., McMahon, S. D., & Halpert, J. A. (2003). Stressors and child and adolescent psychopathology: Moving from markers to mechanisms of risk. *Psychological Bulletin, 129,* 447–466. doi: 10.1037/0033-2909.129.3.447

Haines, M. M., Stansfeld, S. A., Head, J., & Job, R. F. S. (2002). Multilevel modelling of aircraft noise on performance tests in schools around Heathrow airport London. *Journal of Epidemiology and Community Health, 56,* 139–144. doi: 10.1136/jech.56.2.139

Harris, J. R. (1995). Where is the childs environment? A group socialization theory of development. *Psychological Review, 102,* 458–489. doi: 10.1037/0033-295x.102.3.458

Hart, B., & Risley, T. R. (1995). *Meaningful differences in the everyday experiences of young American children.* Baltimore, MD: Brookes.

Hart, B., & Risley, T. R. (2003). The early catastrophe: The 30 million word gap by age 3. *American Educator, 27,* 4–9.

Hartigan, J. (1975). *Clustering algortihms.* New York, NY: Wiley.

Hertzman, C., & Boyce, T. (2010). How experience gets under the skin to create gradients in developmental health. *Annual Review of Public Health, 31,* 329–347. doi: 10.1146/annurev.publhealth.012809.103538

Hoffman, L., & Stawski, R. S. (2009). Persons as contexts: Evaluating between-person and within-person effects in longitudinal analysis. *Research in Human Development, 6,* 97–120. doi: 10.1080/15427600902911189

Jaffee, S. R., Caspi, A., Moffitt, T. E., & Taylor, A. (2004). Physical maltreatment victim to antisocial child: Evidence of an environmentally mediated process. *Journal of Abnormal Psychology, 113,* 44–55. doi: 10.1037/0021-843x.113.1.44

Jaffee, S. R., Strait, L. B., & Odgers, C. L. (2012). From correlates to causes: Can quasi-experimental studies and statistical innovations bring us closer to identifying the causes of antisocial behavior? *Psychological Bulletin, 138,* 272–295. doi: 10.1037/a0026020

Jarjoura, G. R., Triplett, R. A., & Brinker, G. P. (2002). Growing up poor: Examining the link between persistent childhood poverty and delinquency. *Journal of Quantitative Criminology, 18,* 159–187. doi: 10.1023/a:1015206715838

Kanner, A. D., Coyne, J. C., Schaefer, C., & Lazarus, R. S. (1981). Comparison of 2 modes of stress measurement daily hassles and uplifts vs. major life events. *Journal of Behavioral Medicine, 4,* 1–40.

Kanner, A. D., Feldman, S. S., Weinberger, D. A., & Ford, M. E. (1987). Uplifts, hassles, and adaptational outcomes in early adolescents. *Journal of Early Adolescence, 7*, 371–394. doi: 10.1177/0272431687074002

Keller-Cohen, D., Fiori, K., Toler, A., & Bybee, D. (2006). Social relations, language and cognition in the 'oldest old'. *Ageing and Society, 26*, 585–605. doi: 10.1017/S0144686X06004910

Kim-Cohen, J., Caspi, A., Moffitt, T. E., Harrington, H., Milne, B. J., & Poulton, R. (2003). Prior juvenile diagnoses in adults with mental disorder: Developmental follow-back of a prospective-longitudinal cohort. *Archives of General Psychiatry, 60*, 709–717. doi: 10.1001/archpsyc.60.7.709

Lahey, B. B., Van Hulle, C. A., Waldman, I. D., Rodgers, J. L., D'Onofrio, B. M., Pedlow, S., ... Keenan, K. (2006). Testing descriptive hypotheses regarding sex differences in the development of conduct problems and delinquency. *Journal of Abnormal Child Psychology, 34*, 737–755. doi: 10.1007/s10802-006-9064-5

Larson, R. W., Richards, M. H., Raffaelli, M., Ham, M., & Jewell, L. (1990). Ecology of depression in late childhood and early adolescence: A profile of daily states and activities. *Journal of Abnormal Psychology, 99*, 92–102. doi: 10.1037/0021-843x.99.1.92

Laucht, M., Becker, K., El-Faddagh, M., Hohm, E., & Schmidt, M. H. (2005). Association of the DRD4 exon III polymorphism with smoking in fifteen-year-olds: A mediating role for novelty seeking? *Journal of the American Academy of Child and Adolescent Psychiatry, 44*, 477–484.

Leikas, S., Lonnqvist, J-E., & Verkasalo, M. (2012). Persons, situations, and behaviors: Consistency and variability of different behaviors in four interpersonal situations. *Journal of Personality and Social Psychology, 103*, 1007–1022. doi: 10.1037/a0030385

Lengua, L. J., Wolchik, S. A., Sandler, I. N., & West, S. G. (2000). The additive and interactive effects of parenting and temperament in predicting adjustment problems of children of divorce. *Journal of Clinical Child Psychology, 29*, 232–244.

Ludwig, J. (2006, September 19). The cost of crime: Understanding the financial and human impact of criminal activity. *Testimony to the US Senate Judiciary Committee*. Retrieved May 2013, from http://www.gpo.gov/fdsys/pkg/CHRG-109shrg42938/html/CHRG-109shrg42938.htm

Ludwig, J. (2010). The costs of crime. *Criminology and Public Policy, 9*, 307–311. doi: 10.1111/j.1745-9133.2010.00628.x

McCart, M. R., Priester, P. E., Davies, W. H., & Azen, R. (2006). Differential effectiveness of behavioral parent-training and cognitive-behavioral therapy for antisocial youth: A meta-analysis. *Journal of Abnormal Child Psychology, 34*, 527–543. doi: 10.1007/s10802-006-9031-1

McEwen, B. S. (1998). Protective and damaging effects of stress mediators. *New England Journal of Medicine, 338*, 171–179.

McEwen, B. S., & Lasley, E. N. (2002). *The end of stress as we know it*. Washington, DC: John Henry Press.

McLoyd, V. C. (1998). Socioeconomic disadvantage and child development. *American Psychologist, 53*, 185–204. doi: 10.1037/0003-066x.53.2.185

McLoyd, V. C. (2011). How money matters for children's socioemotional adjustment: Family processes and parental investment. In G. Carlo, L. J. Crockett, & M. A. Carranza (Eds.), *Health disparities in youth and families: Research and applications* (Vol. 57, pp. 33–72). New York: Springer.

Mischel, W. (2004). Toward an integrative science of the person. *Annual Review of Psychology, 55*, 1–22. doi: 10.1146/annurev.psych.55.042902.130709

Mischel, W., & Shoda, Y. (1995). A cognitive-affective system-theory of personality—reconceptualizing situations, dispositions, dynamics, and invariance in personality structure. *Psychological Review, 102*, 246–268. doi: 10.1037/0033-295x. 102.2.246

Moffitt, T. E. (2005). The new look of behavioral genetics in developmental psychopathology: Gene-environment interplay in antisocial behaviors. *Psychological Bulletin, 131*, 533–554. doi: 10.1037/0033-2909.131.4.533

Moffitt, T. E., Caspi, A., Harrington, H., & Milne, B. J. (2002). Males on the life-course-persistent and adolescence-limited antisocial pathways: Follow-up at age 26 years. *Development and Psychopathology, 14*, 179–207. doi: 10.1017/s0954579402001104

Moffitt, T. E., Caspi, A., Rutter, M., & Silva, P. A. (2001). *Sex differences in antisocial behavior.* Cambridge, UK: Cambridge University Press.

Molenaar, P. C. M. (2004). A manifesto on psychology as idiographic science: Bringing the person back into scientific psychology, this time forever. *Measurement: Interdisciplinary Research and Perspectives, 2*, 201–218. doi: 10.1207/s15366359mea0204_1

Molenaar, P. C. M., & Campbell, C. G. (2009). The new person-specific paradigm in psychology. *Current Directions in Psychological Science, 18*, 112–117. doi: 10.1111/j.1 467-8721.2009.01619.x

Monroe, S. M., & Simons, A. D. (1991). Diathesis stress theories in the context of life stress research—implications for the depressive-disorders. *Psychological Bulletin, 110*, 406–425.

National Institutes of Health. (2013). *mHealth: Mobile health technologies.* Retrieved April 2013, from http://obssr.od.nih.gov/scientific_areas/methodology/mhealth/

Nesselroade, J. R. (1991). The warp and woof of the developmental fabric. In R. Downs, L. Liben, & D. Palermo (Eds.), *Visions of development, the environment, and aesthetics: The legacy of Joachim F. Wohlwill* (pp. 213–240). Hillsdale, NJ: Erlbaum.

Nesselroade, J. R., & Molenaar, P. C. M. (1999). Pooling lagged covariance structures based on short, multivariate time series for dynamic factor analysis. In R. H. Hoyle (Ed.), *Statistical strategies for small sample research* (pp. 223–250). Thousand Oaks, CA: Sage.

Nesselroade, J. R., & Ram, N. (2004). Studying intraindividual variability: What we have learned that will help us understand lives in context. *Research in Human Development, 1*, 9–29.

Nezlek, J. B. (2001). Multilevel random coefficient analyses of event- and interval-contingent data in social and personality psychology research. *Personality and Social Psychology Bulletin, 27*, 771–785. doi: 10.1177/0146167201277001

NICHD Early Child Care Research Network. (2004). Trajectories of physical aggression from toddlerhood to middle childhood: Predictors, correlates, and outcomes In *Monographs of the Society for Research in Child Development* (Vol. 69, pp. vii, 1–143). Boston, MA: Blackwell.

Odgers, C. L., Caspi, A., Bates, C. J., Sampson, R. J., & Moffitt, T. E. (2012). Systematic social observation of children's neighborhoods using google street view: A reliable and cost-effective method. *Journal of Child Psychology and Psychiatry, 53*, 1009–1017. doi: 10.1111/j.1469-7610.2012.02565.x

Odgers, C. L., Caspi, A., Broadbent, J. M., Dickson, N., Hancox, R. J., Harrington, H., ... Moffitt, T. E. (2007). Prediction of differential adult health burden by conduct problem subtypes in males. *Archives of General Psychiatry, 64*, 476–484. doi: 10.1001/archpsyc.64.4.476

Odgers, C. L., & Jaffee, S. R. (2013). Routine versus catastrophic influences on the developing child. *Annual Review of Public Health, 34*, 29–48. doi: 10.1146/annurev-publhealth-031912-114447

Odgers, C. L., Moffitt, T. E., Broadbent, J. M., Dickson, N., Hancox, R. J., Harrington, H., ... Caspi, A. (2008). Female and male antisocial trajectories: From childhood origins to adult outcomes. *Development and Psychopathology, 20*, 673–716. doi: 10.1017/s0954579408000333

Patterson, G. R. (1982). *Coercive family process*. Eugene, OR: Castalia.

Patterson, G. R., Reid, J. B., & Dishion, T. J. (1992). *Antisocial boys*. Eugene, OR: Castalia.

Pryor-Brown, L., Cowen, E. L., Hightower, A. D., & Lotyczewski, B. S. (1986). Demographic differences among children in judging and experiencing specific stressful life events. *Journal of Special Education, 20*, 339–346. doi: 10.1177/002246698602000307

Rapkin, B. D., & Luke, D. A. (1993). Cluster-analysis in community research: Epistemology and practice. *American Journal of Community Psychology, 21*, 247–277. doi: 10.1007/bf00941623

Raudenbush, S. W., & Bryk, A. S. (2002). *Hierarchical linear models: Applications and data analysis methods* (2nd ed.). Thousand Oaks, CA: Sage.

Repetti, R. L., Taylor, S. E., & Seeman, T. E. (2002). Risky families: Family social environments and the mental and physical health of offspring. *Psychological Bulletin, 128*, 330–366. doi: 10.1037//0033-2909.128.2.330

Rutter, M. (2005). Environmentally mediated risks for psychopathology: Research strategies and findings. *Journal of the American Academy of Child and Adolescent Psychiatry, 44*, 3–18. doi: 10.1097/01.chi.0000145374.45992.c9

Rutter, M., Pickles, A., Murray, R., & Eaves, L. (2001). Testing hypotheses on specific environmental causal effects on behavior. *Psychological Bulletin, 127*, 291–324. doi: 1 0.1037//0033-2909.127.3.291

Sampson, R. J., & Laub, J. H. (2005). A life-course view of the development of crime. *Annals of the American Academy of Political and Social Science, 602*, 12–45. doi: 10.1177/0002716205280075

Scarr, S. (1992). Developmental theories for the 1990s: Development and individual-differences. *Child Development, 63*, 1–19. doi: 10.2307/1130897

Seidman, E., Chesir-Teran, D., Friedman, J. L., Yoshikawa, H., Allen, L., Roberts, A., & Aber, J. L. (1999). The risk and protective functions of perceived family and peer microsystems among urban adolescents in poverty. *American Journal of Community Psychology, 27*, 211–237. doi: 10.1023/a:1022835717964

Shahar, G., Henrich, C. C., Reiner, I. C., & Little, T. D. (2003). Development and initial validation of the brief adolescent life event scale (BALES). *Anxiety Stress and Coping, 16*, 119–128. doi: 10.1080/1061580021000057077

Shiffman, S. (2009). How many cigarettes did you smoke? Assessing cigarette consumption by global report, time-line follow-back, and ecological momentary assessment. *Health Psychology, 28*, 519–526. doi: 10.1037/a0015197

Shiffman, S., Stone, A. A., & Hufford, M. R. (2008). Ecological momentary assessment. *Annual Review of Clinical Psychology, 4*, 1–32. doi: 10.1146/annurev.clinpsy.3.022806.091415

Shoda, Y., Mischel, W., & Wright, J. C. (1994). Intraindividual stability in the organization and patterning of behavior—incorporating psychological situations into the idiographic analysis of personality. *Journal of Personality and Social Psychology, 67,* 674–687. doi: 10.1037//0022-3514.67.4.674

Silk, J. S., Steinberg, L., & Morris, A. S. (2003). Adolescents' emotion regulation in daily life: Links to depressive symptoms and problem behavior. *Child Development, 74,* 1869–1880. doi: 10.1046/j.1467-8624.2003.00643.x

Sliwinski, M. J. (2008). Measurement-burst designs for social health research. *Social and Personality Psychology Compass, 2,* 245–261. doi: 10.1111/j.1751-9004.2007.000 43.x

Smith, R. E., Shoda, Y., Cumming, S. P., & Smoll, F. L. (2009). Behavioral signatures at the ballpark: Intraindividual consistency of adults' situation-behavior patterns and their interpersonal consequences. *Journal of Research in Personality, 43,* 187–195. doi: 10.1016/j.jrp.2008.12.006

Stadler, G., Snyder, K. A., Horn, A. B., Shrout, P. E., & Bolger, N. P. (2012). Close relationships and health in daily life: A review and empirical data on intimacy and somatic symptoms. *Psychosomatic Medicine, 74,* 398–409. doi: 10.1097/ PSY.0b013e31825473b8

Strohschein, L. (2005). Household income histories and child mental health trajectories. *Journal of Health and Social Behavior, 46,* 359–375.

Theobald, D., & Farrington, D. P. (2012). Child and adolescent predictors of male intimate partner violence. *Journal of Child Psychology and Psychiatry, 53,* 1242–1249. doi: 10.1111/j.1469-7610.2012.02577.x

Thornberry, T. P., & Krohn, M. D. (Eds.). (2003). *Taking stock of delinquency: An overview of findings from contemporary longitudinal studies.* New York, NY: Kluwer Academic/Plenum.

Tremblay, R. E. (2010). Developmental origins of disruptive behaviour problems: The 'original sin' hypothesis, epigenetics and their consequences for prevention. *Journal of Child Psychology and Psychiatry, 51,* 341–367. doi: 10.1111/j.1469-7610. 2010.02211.x

Tremblay, R. E., Nagin, D. S., Seguin, J. R., Zoccolillo, M., Zelazo, P. D., Boivin, M., … Japel, C. (2004). Physical aggression during early childhood: Trajectories and predictors. *Pediatrics, 114,* e43–e50.

Vansteelandt, K., & Van Mechelen, I. (1998). Individual differences in situation-behavior profiles: A triple typology model. *Journal of Personality and Social Psychology, 75,* 751–765. doi: 10.1037//0022-3514.75.3.751

Wadsworth, M. (2012). Working with low-income families: Lessons learned from basic and applied research on coping with poverty-related stress. *Journal of Contemporary Psychotherapy, 42,* 17–25. doi: 10.1007/s10879-011-9192-2

Weiss, R., Stumbo, P. J., & Divakaran, A. (2010). Automatic food documentation and volume computation using digital imaging and electronic transmission. *Journal of the American Dietetic Association, 110,* 42–44.

Whalen, C. K., Henker, B., Ishikawa, S. S., Floro, J. N., Emmerson, N. A., Johnston, J. A., & Swindle, R. (2009). ADHD and anger contexts: Electronic diary mood reports from mothers and children. *Journal of Pediatric Psychology, 34,* 940–953. doi: 10.1093/ jpepsy/jsn138

Whalen, C. K., Jamner, L. D., Henker, B., & Delfino, R. J. (2001). Smoking and moods in adolescents with depressive and aggressive dispositions: Evidence from surveys and electronic diaries. *Health Psychology, 20,* 99–111. doi: 10.1037//0278-6133.20.2.99

Whitfield, C. L., Anda, R. F., Dube, S. R., & Felitti, V. J. (2003). Violent childhood experiences and the risk of intimate partner violence in adults—assessment in a large health maintenance organization. *Journal of Interpersonal Violence*, *18*, 166–185. doi: 10.1177/0886260502238733

Wiehe, S. E., Carroll, A. E., Liu, G. C., Haberkorn, K. L., Hoch, S. C., Wilson, J. S., & Fortenberry, J. D. (2008). Using GPS-enabled cell phones to track the travel patterns of adolescents. *International Journal of Health Geographics*, *7*. doi: 10.1186/1476-072x-7-22

Windelband, W. (1894/1998). History and natural science [reprinted]. *Theory and Psychology*, *8*, 5–22. doi: 10.1177/0959354398081001

3

Substance Abuse and Violence

CURTIS A. MATTSON AND CHRISTINA A. PIETZ ■

It has been estimated that approximately $67 billion is spent annually in the United States to cope with drug-related problems associated with the effects of crime, lost occupational productivity, foster care, and other social problems; however, the true costs of adult drug and alcohol use are likely beyond any accurate calculation (McLellan et al., 2000; McNichol & Tash, 2001). In 2005, the federal government spent $238.2 billion (9.6% of the total federal budget) on substance abuse and addiction; state governments spent $135.8 billion, while local governments spent a *conservative* $93.8 billion on services related to drug and alcohol use/abuse (National Center on Addiction and Substance Abuse at Columbia University [CASA], 2009). The largest segment of federal and state substance abuse spending, by far, was in the realm of health care ($207.2 billion; 58%). The next largest area of spending was in criminal justice systems, which include jails and prisons ($47.0 billion; 13.1%) (CASA, 2009). Substance-involved parents create a significant social burden through the effects on their children. Research has demonstrated that individuals who come from families where at least one parent abused alcohol or drugs are almost twice as likely to become substance users themselves (CASA, 2010). Some studies have found that almost three quarters of children placed in foster care have been affected by drug and/or alcohol environments; additional research has estimated that 80% of children in foster care (400,540 children during the 2011 fiscal year) had experienced prenatal substance exposure (Dicker & Gordon, 2004; McNichol & Tash, 2001; US Department of Health and Human Services: Administration for Children and Families [ACF], 2012). Furthermore, rates of fetal alcohol syndrome (FAS) are 10 to 15 times higher in foster care than in the general population and are estimated to cost around $2 million per child for special education services and medical and mental health treatment (Astley et al., 2002; Paley & Auerbach, 2010).

Problematic drug and alcohol use also has significant societal implications primarily because it frequently co-occurs with crime and violence. Between 1996 and 2006, the US population increased by approximately 12%; however, the rate of substance-involved adult incarcerations rose by 43% during this same time frame (CASA, 2010). In 2010, the Federal Bureau of Prisons (BOP) had 210,227 inmates within its various facilities (this includes select privately managed facilities with a BOP contract). Within the BOP, those incarcerated with drug-related offenses made up the largest segment of offenders and constituted 51.4% of the inmate population. These drug-related offenders were three times more prevalent than the next largest inmate classification group, who, at 15.3% of the inmate population, had been convicted of crimes involving weapons, explosives, or arson (BOP, 2010). From October 1, 2008, to September 30, 2009, drug-related offenses made up 16.9% of total arrests made by the United States Marshalls, second only to immigration offenses (Motivans, 2012). In 2006, there were over 2.3 million inmates in federal, state, and local jails and 65%, or 1.5 million, met a sufficient number of criteria for a substance abuse or addiction diagnosis (CASA, 2010). There were an additional 458,000 inmates who, despite not meeting criteria for a substance-use-related diagnosis, perpetrated crimes that were considered substance involved (CASA, 2010). On the state level, the number of individuals with drug convictions has increased from 9,000 in 1980 to 107,000 in 1998 (Hora, 2002). More locally, in 1998 an estimated 417,000 jail inmates committed a drug-related offense or engaged in routine substance use, a substantial increase from 261,000 in 1989 (Wilson, 2000). In 2006, approximately 37% of all local, state, and federal inmates were incarcerated with a violent crime as their primary offense; 77.5% of those individuals were substance involved. The most commonly implicated substance was alcohol as reported by 56.6% of all US inmates, including 57.7% of those involved in violent crime (CASA, 2010).

ALCOHOL AND SUBSTANCE USE DISORDERS

Chronic abuse of legal or illicit psychoactive substances can lead to physiological or psychological addiction, which may manifest through a variety of drug-motivated behaviors, including excessive craving, seeking, and consumption. These behaviors are often maintained despite negative consequences that alter or disrupt a person's normal level of functioning (APA, 2000; Leshner, 1997; Volkow, 2004). The nosological system, within the *Diagnostic and Statistical Manual of Mental Disorders* of the American Psychiatric Association (DSM-IV-TR; APA, 2000), broadly classifies problematic use or abuse of substances as substance use disorders (SUDs) with two primary subcategorizations of substance abuse (SA) and substance dependence (SD). However, within this classification system, dependence and abuse are treated as relatively distinct and hierarchical (Hasin, Hatzenbuehler, Keyes, & Ogburn, 2006).

Criteria for SA include recurrent drug use that results in substance-related legal problems, using drugs/alcohol in hazardous situations, and experiencing social and/or interpersonal problems associated with drug use, as well as occupational, academic, or home-living failures (APA, 2000). SA is differentiated from SD by SA's focus on repeat, chronic use rather than on compulsive use, tolerance, or withdrawal. SD (commonly referenced as addiction) is associated with repeated substance use and taking drugs/alcohol despite experiencing problematic physical or psychological consequences (APA, 2000; Hasin et al., 2006). The two primary symptoms of SD are tolerance and withdrawal. Tolerance is defined as the need for larger amounts of a substance in order to gain the same effect or markedly decreased effects with the same amount of the substance. Withdrawal is indicated by changes in physical, cognitive, and behavioral systems that continue after discontinuing substance abuse (APA, 2000). In addition to tolerance and dependence, several other symptoms are associated with drug/alcohol dependence (for a full review, see the *DSM-IV-TR*; APA, 2000). It should be noted that the categorical classification system employed in the *DSM-IV-TR* has come under considerable scrutiny (Widiger & Clark, 2000; Widiger & Samuel, 2005; Wright et al., 2013), and this has been extended to the substance use disorders. Criticism has largely focused on the artificial distinctions between SA/SD and concerns regarding the ordering of various severity indicators and a lack of evidence for intermediate steps between use and addiction (Martin, Chung, Kirisci, & Langenbucher, 2006; O'Brien, 2011; Ray, Kahler, Young, Chelminski, & Zimmerman, 2008; Saha, Chou, & Grant, 2006). The reader is referred to the aforementioned sources for a further review of the critiques related to substance abuse and dependence.

Substance use disorders affect a substantial portion of the general population and the criteria for SA/SD have been shown to be temporally stable (Hasin et al., 2006; Kessler, Chiu, Demler, & Walters, 2005; Kessler et al., 1994; Krueger, Caspi, Moffitt, & Silva, 1998). The Substance Abuse and Mental Health Services Administration (SAMHSA; 2012) reported that 20.6 million individuals, age 12 or older (8% of the entire US population), have met SA or SD criteria at some point over the previous 12 months. Of these, 14.1 million met the criteria for alcohol abuse/dependence alone, 3.9 million for drug abuse/dependence only, and 2.6 million for both drugs and alcohol. Research related to 1-month, 12-month, and lifetime prevalence rates for alcohol dependence, in the general population, have been shown to range from 1.7% (1-month) to 7.9% (lifetime), while drug dependence has shown prevalence estimates, over the same time frame, that range from 0.8% (1-month) to a lifetime rate between 3.5% to 8% (Kessler et al., 2005; Reiger et al., 1990). Of all the illicit substances, cannabis is the most widely used drug in the United States. In 2011, an estimated 5 million individuals, age 12 or older, reported using marijuana on a daily or almost daily basis (300 or more days a year), and lifetime use rates range from 41.2% to 55.9% (Agrawal, Neale, Prescott, & Kendler, 2004; SAMHSA, 2012). Swendsen et al. (2012) examined the substance use patterns of 10,123 adolescents, aged 13 to 18 years, in a nationally representative sample. Findings suggested that approximately 15.1% of adolescents met criteria for lifetime abuse of alcohol, while 16.4% of the older adolescents met criteria for drug abuse. Research specifically related to the abuse of inhalants, a class of substances that are relatively easy to obtain and difficult to track, has indicated that approximately 16% of the eighth graders in the United States report lifetime use. This estimate climbs to almost 40% when considering samples of antisocial youth alone (Howard, Balster, Cottler, Wu, & Vaughn, 2008; Howard & Jenson, 1999).

Alcohol and Substance Use Disorders and the *DSM-5*

With the recent publication of the *DSM-5*, there have been substantial changes in the criteria and methodology used to diagnose an alcohol- or substance-related disorder. In response to the empirical evidence, which questioned the distinction between abuse and dependence, the *DSM-5* now uses the term "substance use disorder" and will be coded on a continuum from mild to severe (APA, 2013; Schuckit, 2012). The term "substance use disorder," according to Schuckit (2012), reflected movement away from the diagnostic schemes of the *DSM-III-R* and *DSM-IV* and a reluctance to use the term "addiction," which can carry multiple meanings and have pejorative undertones. Specific substances will continue to be coded individually (e.g., cocaine use disorder), but most drug classes will be evaluated using the same overarching criteria.

In previous editions of the *DSM*, a diagnosis of abuse could be assigned if only one substance-related symptom was present; however, in the *DSM-5*, a mild substance use disorder will require two to three (out of 11) symptoms (APA, 2013). Furthermore, drug craving is being added as a criterion, while problems with law enforcement are being removed due to concerns about cultural sensitivity and application of the criterion internationally. The *DSM-5* is also moving caffeine use disorder to the section for additional research due to concerns regarding its clinical significance (APA, 2013).

SUBSTANCE ABUSE COMORBIDITY/CO-OCCURRENCE

Before beginning a discussion about the comorbidity/co-occurrence of SUDs, a brief overview of these terms must be offered to clarify the differences between them. In general, co-occurrence simply indicates the number of people who might be expected to exhibit the symptoms of two separate disorders by chance (i.e., expected base rates of the two conditions). Conversely, comorbidity suggests that a correlational association exists between two separate disorders due to a relationship between their symptoms, etiology, or maintenance mechanism (Buitelaar, 2012; Krueger & Markon, 2006; Lilienfeld, Waldman, & Israel, 1994). For a review of the various proposed models related to comorbidity of mental health disorders, the reader is directed to Krueger and Markon (2006).

Substance Use Disorders and Acute Psychopathology

A significant problem related to the understanding of SUDs is the increased prevalence of comorbid disorders spanning the entire spectrum of psychopathology—making etiological identification difficult (Fergusson, Boden, & Horwood, 2011; Iacono, Malone, & McGue, 2008; Kushner, Abrams, & Borchardt, 2000; Ruiz, Douglas, Edens, Nikolova, & Lilienfeld, 2012; Saraceno, Munafo, Heron, Craddock, & van den Bree, 2009). Specifically, research has postulated that at any given time, depending on the identified condition, between 1% and 3% of the general population is affected by the co-occurrence of a mental health and substance use disorder (Jane-Llopis & Matytsina, 2006). However, when considering lifetime comorbidity, these rates are much higher (Kessler et al., 1996; Merikangas et al., 1998). The assessment of SUDs in offender populations is made more complex by the elevated frequencies of comorbid mental health disorders (James & Glaze, 2006), which, when combined with co-occurring substance use, exacerbates the risk for violence (Wallace, Mullen, & Burgess, 2004) and rearrest (Grella, Greenwell, Prendergast, Sacks, & Melnick, 2008). In community samples of individuals diagnosed with SUDs, primary disorders distinguished by impulsivity, disinhibition, and antisocial proclivities are particularly prone to comorbid SUDs and the most commonly co-occurring mental health diagnoses, including mood, anxiety, and antisocial disorders (Armstrong & Costello, 2002; Brady & Sinha, 2005; Kessler et al., 1996, 2006;

Kessler & Wang, 2008; Merikangas et al., 1998; Reiger et al., 1990; Welte, Barnes, Wieczorek, Tidwell, & Parker, 2001). Among individuals diagnosed with alcohol dependence, 26% also had a lifetime comorbid mood disorder, 32% had a lifetime history of anxiety disorders, and 28% to 64% had a lifetime history of adult antisocial behaviors. For those with sufficient indications of drug dependence, nearly 35% met lifetime criteria for a mood disorder, 45% for an anxiety disorder, and 50% for either conduct or antisocial personality disorder (Merikangas et al., 1998).

Substance Use Disorders and Personality Disorder Psychopathology

Research has established individuals with SD can be characterized by externalizing personality traits related to impulsivity and disinhibition (Grant et al., 2004; Sher & Trull, 1994). Specifically, persons with SD have demonstrated lower levels of behavioral constraint (Krueger, Caspi, Moffitt, White, & Stouthamer-Loeber, 1996; Reed, Levin, & Evans, 2012; Verona, Sachs-Ericsson, & Joiner, 2004), psychoticism (Sher, Bartholow, & Wood, 2000), agreeableness and conscientiousness (Trull & Sher, 1994), and higher levels of general sensation seeking (McGue, Slutske, & Iacono, 1999) and novelty seeking/impulsive sensation seeking (Castellanos-Ryan, Rubia, & Conrod, 2011; Finn, Mazas, Justus, & Steinmetz, 2002; Noël et al., 2011; Sher et al., 2000; Zuckerman & Kuhlman, 2000). In addition, the relationships between SD symptoms and externalizing personality traits is linear, with increasing levels of the externalizing traits reported by individuals with SD and the highest levels of these traits being found in individuals with comorbid SD and other externalizing disorders (McGue, Slutske, & Iacono, 1999; McGue, Slutske, Taylor, & Iacono, 1997). Generally, individuals with SD are more likely to be impulsive and disobedient, as well as less able (or willing) to inhibit behavioral impulses when compared to those without SUDs.

Grant and colleagues (2004) found that 39% of individuals considered alcohol dependent and 69% of those diagnosed with drug dependence also met criteria for a comorbid personality disorder—particularly those disorders strongly characterized by affective lability and impulsive behavior. Research suggests that antisocial personality disorder (ASPD) and substance use–related problems occur at a much higher than chance frequency (Krueger et al., 2007). In addition, Reiger et al. (1990) demonstrated that those with an ASPD diagnosis were more likely to meet criteria of SA (29.6 times) and SD (21.1 times) than were those without this diagnostic label. While the association between ASPD and SUDs has been more commonly studied in males, Lewis (2011) found that violent behavior exhibited by incarcerated females with ASPD was associated with both alcohol and opiate dependence. Adolescents exhibiting precursory behaviors related to adult ASPD, namely oppositional defiant disorder (ODD) and conduct disorder (CD), were between 30% and 50% more likely to meet criteria for a comorbid SUD (Brady & Sinha, 2005). Research has also demonstrated that co-occurring CD and alcohol abuse/dependence have been associated with a greater number of adult antisocial behavior problems. However, the relationship between CD and externalized behavior was mediated and exacerbated by the presence of adolescent-onset alcohol abuse (Howard, Finn, Jose, & Gallagher, 2011). White and her colleagues (2001) indicated that increasing severity of adolescent psychopathology, including CD, ODD, and attention-deficit/hyperactivity disorder (ADHD), helped predict higher levels of juvenile alcohol and marijuana use.

In addition, borderline personality disorder (BPD) has been shown to be highly comorbid with SUDs (Grant et al., 2008; Látalová & Praško, 2010; Trull, Sher, Minks-Brown, Durbin, & Burr, 2000). Studies have shown that individuals diagnosed with BPD had increased rates of alcohol and drug use/abuse during adolescence; furthermore, BPD traits and substance use were found to be correlated with a higher order risk factor, rather than simply causal factors of one another (Bornovalova, Hicks, Iacono, & McGue, 2013). Empirical research has also indicated that those with BPD were 5 to 10 times more likely than those without a BPD diagnosis to have a lifetime drug or alcohol dependence diagnosis (Grant et al., 2008; Trull, Waudby, & Sher, 2004).

Substance Use Disorders and Violence

Regardless of the presence or absence of a particular mental health–related diagnostic label, criminal offenders, both male and female, frequently have significantly higher rates of substance use than are found in the general population (Dixon, Howie, & Starling, 2004; Fazel, Bains, & Doll, 2006). In inmates assessed during 2004, substance use at the time of a violent offense (homicide, sexual assault, robbery, and assault) was reported by 27.7% and 24.0% of state and federal inmates, respectively. When considering substance use within the month preceding the offense, these rates rise to 49.6% (state) and 49.1% (federal) of inmates (Mumola & Karberg, 2006). In addition, 8.0% of inmates in local jails (Karberg & James, 2005), 9.8% in state prisons, and 14.8% in federal prisons (Mumola & Karberg, 2006) were convicted of committing a violent offense in order to get money for drugs. The association between drug/alcohol use and violence has been well documented and a wide range of substances, including alcohol, marijuana, cocaine/crack, heroin (and opiate medications), and stimulants (including methamphetamine, anabolic-androgenic steroids, and hallucinogens) have been implicated (Arseneault, Moffitt, Caspi, Taylor, & Silva, 2000; Långström, Sjostedt, & Grann, 2004; Mattson, O'Farrell, Lofgreen, Cunningham, & Murphy, 2012; Mumola & Karberg, 2006; Skårberg, Nyberg, & Engström, 2010; Smith et al., 2012). Additionally, studies have also demonstrated that the relationship between violence and SUDs remains significant even after controlling for a variety of factors, including gender, socioeconomic status (SES), and other Axis I diagnoses (Arseneault et al., 2000).

ETIOLOGICAL ASSOCIATIONS WITH SUBSTANCE USE DISORDERS AND EXTERNALIZING BEHAVIOR

As demonstrated earlier, empirical investigations have consistently demonstrated that many psychological disorders co-occur more frequently than would be expected by chance alone (Kessler et al., 1994, 2005; Kessler & Wang, 2008).

This high rate of co-occurrence has led to extensive examination of structural models of psychopathology, wherein overlap between diagnoses is postulated to be caused by shared underlying liabilities representative of both broad and narrow latent factors (see Krueger, 1999; Krueger et al., 1998; Krueger & Markon, 2006; Vollebergh et al., 2001). One result of these empirical investigations has been the emergence of a well-documented latent phenotype, labeled *externalizing* (see Kendler, Davis, & Kessler, 1997; Krueger et al., 1998), which links factors such as substance use, antisocial behavior, and impulsive and aggressive personality traits on an *Externalizing Spectrum* (Kendler, Prescott, Myers, & Neale, 2003; Krueger et al., 1998, 2002, 2005, 2007). There is a growing body of evidence suggesting that a variety of externalizing behaviors are related to genetic and environmental risk factors. However, research linking substance use to neuropsychological factors associated with the broad externalizing factor, including increased disinhibition, reduced cognitive capacity, and impulsivity, are also proliferating.

Heritability Factors

Early work toward the identification of externalizing liabilities was largely accomplished by analyzing multivariate correlations of observable characteristics of mental disorders among unrelated persons (Krueger, 1999; Krueger et al., 1998; Vollebergh et al., 2001). Pursuant to these findings, continued examination of the externalizing spectrum was extended to related individuals, including families, adoptees, and mono- and dizygotic twins (Cadoret, Troughton, & O'Gorman, 1987; Hicks, Krueger, Iacono, McGue, & Patrick, 2004; King et al., 2009; Krueger et al., 2002).[1]

Recent research has indicated that genetic factors play a substantial role in the development of externalizing disorders, both in adolescence and adulthood. Hicks and his colleagues (2004) demonstrated a general, rather than specific, vulnerability toward the etiology of externalizing behaviors that was highly heritable ($h^2 = 0.80$). These results supported the idea that children inherit a disposition toward general externalizing behavior, which is not specific to the disorder(s) displayed by their parents. However, the researchers also observed disorder-specific risk factors for CD, alcohol dependence, and drug dependence indicating that vulnerability for each condition was partially the result of unique environmental factors. Bornovalova, Hicks, Iacono, and McGue (2010) also found a general, highly inheritable liability that accounted for parent–child transmission of externalizing disorders. Unique environmental effects were detected for each of the examined childhood disruptive disorders, with conduct disorder also demonstrating a significant shared environmental effect. Among adoptees, Cadoret, Troughton, and O'Gorman (1987) found that genetic influences remained highly predictive in regard to the development of externalizing behavior. Specifically, they demonstrated that biological family alcohol use and antisocial behaviors predicted increases in alcohol abuse and the diagnosis of ASPD. However, problematic alcohol use within the adoptive family was also related to increases in alcohol abuse (Cadoret, Troughton, & O'Gorman, 1987). Research by King and her colleagues (2009) indicated that alcohol dependence in the biological family was related to higher levels of behavioral disinhibition in adolescents; however, this association only remained if an adolescent was raised by his or her biological parent(s). In addition, the researchers found evidence of shared environmental risk for behavioral disinhibition among those adolescents that had been adopted and subsequently exposed to parental alcoholism.

Twin studies have also indicated that associations between antisocial behavior disorders and SUDs are heritable and are best accounted for by moderate to large amounts of shared genetic variation (Button et al., 2007; Krueger et al., 2002; Legrand, Keyes, McGue, Iacono, & Krueger, 2008; Slutske et al., 1998; Young, Stallings, Corley, Krauter, & Hewitt, 2000). Slutske et al. (1998) evaluated the relationship between childhood conduct disorder and alcohol dependence among a sample of 2,682 adult twins in Australia. The researchers demonstrated substantial associations between CD and alcohol dependence in both men (OR = 2.8) and women (OR = 9.9), and found that genetic factors accounted "for most of the observed association between the disorders" (Slutske et al., 1998, p. 370). Young and colleagues (2000) found that behavioral disinhibition, a latent phenotype composed of facets related to CD, ADHD, substance experimentation, and novelty seeking, was largely heritable ($a^2 = 0.84$) and not significantly affected by shared environmental factors. Additional research found evidence that genetic influences were primarily responsible for the observed variability within externalizing behaviors among 1,048 sets of 17-year-old twins, with 81% of the variance being accounted for by additive genetic factors and an additional 19% attributable to unique environmental factors (Krueger et al., 2002). Kendler et al. (2003) evaluated genetic and environmental risk factors of common mental disorders with a large sample of same-sex twin pairs. Using the multivariate correlated liabilities model, the researchers were able to assess both common and unique factors believed to increase the risk for each of the common disorders individually. Subsequent results indicated a strong genetic effect for the externalizing liability, associated with alcohol dependence, drug abuse/dependence, adult antisocial behavior, and CD, but also suggested unique genetic and nonshared environmental effects for SUDs. Button et al. (2007) examined the relationship between alcohol (AD) and illicit drug dependence (IDD), and conduct disorder (CD). The researchers reported that "Genetic effects shared in common with CD accounted for approximately 60% of the genetic liability shared by AD and IDD" (p. 51). Furthermore, as the genetic association between AD and IDD was reduced once CD was included in their model, Button and her colleagues (2007) concluded that "the genetic contribution to the comorbidity between AD and IDD was partially explained by the genetic vulnerability they both share in common with CD" (p. 51). Legrand and colleagues (2008) reported that 64% of the variance between substance use and rule-breaking behavior was attributable to heritability factors; however, in rural settings (towns with fewer than 10,000 people), 86% of this variance was related to shared environmental factors. This finding suggests that "certain environments may restrict the expression of particular genetic tendencies" (p. 1347) and supports the "nurture" concept that "environment plays a tremendously important role in development" (Legrand et al., 2008, p. 1347). Hicks, South, DiRago, Iacono, and McGue (2009) examined the gene–environment interplay between externalizing disorders, specifically antisocial behavior and substance use, and environmental risk factors, including academic achievement, life stress, parent–child relationships, and peer affiliation. Findings indicated that, in increasingly adverse environmental conditions, genetic factors became more important in the etiology of externalizing disorders.

Social/Environmental Factors

While existing research has typically found the strongest link between SUDs and externalizing behavior to be genetic, many of these studies have also suggested that shared and unique environmental factors provide moderate contributions toward our understanding of this interaction (Krueger et al., 2002; Legrand et al., 2008; Slutske et al., 1998). However, Hicks et al. (2009) demonstrated a consistent genetic-environment interaction across six different environmental risk factors, which suggested "a general mechanism of environmental influence on external-izing regardless of the particular manifestation of the environmental risk" (p. 645).

INDIVIDUAL/HISTORICAL FACTORS

Elbogen and Johnson (2009) used data from the first and second waves of the National Epidemiologic Survey on Alcohol and Related Conditions (NESARC) to predict violent behavior based on ascertained risk factors. Among the individu-als who engaged in substance-related violence, significant associations (odds ratios in parentheses) related to individual characteristics were found with younger age (5.71), being male (0.28; for females), and having an annual income of less than $20,000 (0.47; for those making more than 20,000). Relevant historical factors included having a parent with a criminal history (1.56), a prior history of violence (2.34), and having been placed in juvenile detention (1.56; Elbogen & Johnson, 2009). Individual-level situational influences, occurring within the 12 months preceding the study, were also associated with the prediction of substance-related violence. These factors included victimization (OR = 1.52), having been fired from a job (1.41), experiencing divorce or separation (2.58), and being unemployed alto-gether (1.46; Elbogen & Johnson, 2009). Family risk factors, including parental substance abuse, low socioeconomic status, minimal behavioral monitoring by the parent(s), and the amount of family conflict, have been implicated as predictive of future substance abuse, risky sexual behavior, and crime—especially in males (Chung, Hawkins, Gilchrist, Hill, & Nagin, 2002; Engels, Vermulst, Dubas, Bot, & Gerris, 2005; Epstein, Hill, Bailey, & Hawkins, 2012; Fergusson, Horwood, & Lynskey, 1995). Keyes, Iacono, and McGue (2007) found that behavioral problems prior to age 14 and environmental risk factors, including parental conflict, lower academic attachment, and exposure to peer deviance, were strongly predictive of SUDs and ASPD at age 18. However, this link was genetically mediated, suggest-ing that individuals with a liability toward externalizing behavior are more likely to come in contact with high-risk environments (Keyes, Iacono, & McGue, 2007).

COMMUNITY-LEVEL FACTORS

Valdez, Kaplan, and Curtis (2007) studied alcohol and drug use, and violent crime in areas of concentrated poverty in urban areas of 24 US cities. They found that social attachments (i.e., marriage) and work-related variables (i.e., education and employment) mediated the relationship between substance use and violence. Additional findings indicated that 3.17% of the community-level variance, not explained by individual factors, was attributable to variations in urban-area female-headed households and those households receiving welfare (Valdez, Kaplan, & Curtis, 2007). Neighborhood disadvantage, as measured by the percentage of residents living below the poverty line, percent of female-headed households, unemployment rate for males, and percentage of families receiving public assistance, has been associated with increased drug use. This relationship was modestly predicted by the presence of greater numbers of negative events, including increased frequency of criminal victimization and tolerance of deviant conduct (Boardman, Finch, Ellison, Williams, & Jackson, 2001). Furthermore, differences between urban and rural environments have been shown to mediate the genetic expression linking substance use and rule-breaking behavior (Legrand et al., 2008).

Neuropsychological Factors

Recent research has indicated that the behavioral tendencies, including substance abuse and aggressive behaviors, found along the externalizing spectrum are marked by facets of disinhibition, including behavioral disconstraint, impulsivity, sensation and novelty seeking, and reduced cognitive capacity (Bogg & Finn, 2010; Finn et al., 2009; Krueger et al., 2007; Patrick, Fowles, & Krueger, 2009). These factors have been associated with neuropsychological deficits often identified through psychological dysregulation linked to neurobehavior disinhibition (ND), executive functioning, and other forms of poor cognitive control (Fishbein, 2000; Kirisci, Tarter, Reynolds, & Vanyukov, 2006; Verdejo-Garcia, Lawrence, & Clark, 2008). Research has demonstrated that ND, an index of behavioral, emotional, and cognitive regulation, is associated with the onset and progression of SUDs and has been shown to discriminate between high and low average risk for development of SUDs in young adult males (Clark, Cornelius, Kirisci, & Tarter, 2005; Kirisci, Vanyukov, & Tarter, 2005; Kirisci et al., 2006; Tarter, Kirisci, Habeych, Reynolds, & Vanyukov, 2004). The link between ND and SUDs is supported by additional findings that early initiation of substance use and increased frequency of drug-related problems are related to impulsivity, even after controlling for parental alcohol use and childhood externalizing disorders (Verdejo-Garcia et al., 2008).

Executive functioning refers to a broad class of processes that include one's ability to engage in goal-directed planning, cognitive flexibility, task initiation, attention maintenance, and inhibition of actions based on situational demands; it involves multiple regions of the brain (prefrontal cortex, basal ganglia, among others) and neurotransmitters (e.g., dopamine, glutamate, aminobutyric acid; Kerns, Nuechterlein, Braver, & Barch, 2008; Miyake et al., 2000). Furthermore, working memory is generally believed to be significantly associated with executive functioning, as information held in short-term memory is then available for manipulation and higher order processing (Miyake et al., 2000). Thoma and his colleagues (2011), in a group of adolescents between the ages of 12 and 18 years, found that increased alcohol use was predictive of poor attention and general executive functioning abilities. More broadly, adolescents using alcohol and/or marijuana with a diagnosis of SA/SD demonstrated lower scores on measures of attention, memory, and processing speed. Inhalant use has also been implicated in problems with verbal and nonverbal processing, behavior, language, and memory among adolescents (Scott & Scott, 2012). Furthermore, adult polysubstance users evidenced reduced performance on neuropsychological measures of processing speed, analogical reasoning, working memory, inhibition, and decision making when compared to non-substance users (Verdejo-Garcia et al., 2010). In regards to specific brain regions, several empirical studies have suggested that disruptions or alterations of prefrontal activity in individuals with substance dependence may be responsible for observed impairments in self-awareness, decision making, attention, motivational arousal, and behavioral control (Goldstein & Volkow, 2011; Rogers & Robbins, 2001). Dysfunction in the prefrontal cortex (PFC) has also been associated with changes in the limbic regions of the brain that are involved in reward sensation and habit formation, thus perpetuating drug use (Goldstein & Volkow, 2002, 2011; Kalivas & Volkow, 2005; Rogers & Robbins, 2001; Volkow, Fowler, & Wang, 2004). Dysregulated cognitive control has been identified as a prominent feature in the expression of increased alcohol consumption and co-occurring manifestations of disinhibition and deficits in cognitive capacity (Iacono et al., 2008). Bogg and his colleagues (2012) demonstrated that poor cognitive control linked behavioral disinhibition, alcohol use, and reduced cognitive capacity via dysregulation in the medial prefrontal cortex (mPFC) in a sample of college students. Individuals with SD also display significant impairments in functions associated with the anterior cingulate cortex (ACC), including poor behavioral inhibition, reduced ability to delay gratification, and an inability to terminate disadvantageous actions despite negative outcomes (Garavan & Stout, 2005; Leeman, Grant, & Potenza, 2009; Moeller et al., 2002; Verdejo-Garcia & Bechara, 2009; Verdejo-Garcia et al., 2008).

TREATMENT FOR SUBSTANCE USE DISORDERS

Despite the clear link between SUDs and multiple negative personal and societal consequences, systematic treatment continues to a relative afterthought because the monetary and structural foundations needed to confront this problem are lacking. In 2005, researchers revealed that federal and state governments spent 96 cents of every drug-related budgetary dollar to help with the effects of illness, crime, and social ills caused by drug abuse and addiction. Only two cents went to substance-related prevention and treatment (CASA, 2009). Attempts to tax licit drug use (alcohol and tobacco) for the purposes of reducing the budgetary deficits have fallen short, as federal and state governments have spent nearly nine dollars to cope with the after-effects of substance use for every dollar made through taxation (CASA, 2009). In addition, public perception is largely focused on substance abuse as a social problem and "pejorative views exist and contribute to policies that would be simply unacceptable if applied to 'real' medical disorders" (Dackis & O'Brien, 2005, p. 1431). These perceptions often limit the availability and funding for addictions treatment both publicly and in our correctional systems, as Dackis and O'Brien (2005) opined, "Even though the United States has a disproportionate number of prisoners, and most have been incarcerated for drug-related crimes, their addiction is seldom treated within the prison walls or, more importantly, after they are released to a drug infested environment" (p. 1432). The Federal Bureau of

Prisons (BOP) has earmarked a significant amount of money solely to fund drug treatment programs and, currently, the BOP offers drug abuse education and substance abuse treatment in each of its 117 institutions, including 63 intensive residential drug abuse programs (RDAPs). Indeed, the proliferation of substance abuse treatment options within the BOP can serve as a reference point for the increased need in programming. In 1990, the BOP treated 5,887 inmates between two substance abuse programs (Drug Education and RDAP); by the end of 2011, a total of 91,854 offenders were receiving one of four substance abuse programming options (Drug Education, Non-Residential, RDAP, and Community Transition; BOP, 2011). In a similar fashion, diversionary substance abuse programs (often referred to as Drug Courts) have also substantially increased in number since their inception in Dade County, Florida, in 1989 (Sanford & Arrigo, 2005); as of June 30, 2012, the National Drug Court Resource Center (2012) indicated there were 2,734 drug courts in operation.

Methods of Treatment

A significant research basis suggests that effective treatments for SUDs are available, although high treatment dropout rates and inconsistent methodologies for tracking long-term outcomes make identification of their true effectiveness difficult. These treatments include psychological, psychosocial, and pharmacological interventions, and they will be reviewed next.

PSYCHOLOGICAL INTERVENTIONS
The most effective treatments for SUDs have been shown to rely on elements indicative of one (or more) of four psychological theories: social learning theory, stress and coping theory, behavioral economics and behavior choice theory, and social control theory (Finney, Wilbourne, & Moos, 2007; Moos, 2007). Within these four theories, Moos (2007) identified common "active ingredients" for effective SUDs treatment, which are demonstrated through social processes; these ingredients include social support, goal direction and structure, alternate rewards to substance abuse, the presence of abstinence-oriented models, and development of self-efficacy through coping skills. These "active ingredients" are thought to increase effectiveness because they not only address problematic alcohol/drug use behavior but also focus on changing an individual's situational context and ability to cope with stressors (Finney et al., 2007; Witkiewitz, Donovan, & Hartzler, 2012). Among treatment modalities containing these "active ingredients," the research base for cognitive-behavioral interventions (both individual and group) has seen the most growth (Carroll & Onken, 2005; Finney et al., 2007).

Recent research on the effectiveness of cognitive-behavioral treatments (CBT) has found that interventions, including contingency management and relapse prevention, are effective with a variety of substances, including alcohol, nicotine, marijuana, cocaine, methamphetamines, and opiates (Dutra et al., 2008; Higgins, Wong, Badger, Ogden, & Dantona, 2000; Lee & Rawson, 2008; Miller & Wilbourne, 2002; Prendergast, Podus, Finney, Greenwell, & Roll, 2006; Rawson et al., 2006; Stephens, Roffman, & Curtin, 2000). In addition to simply treating drug-related behaviors, research has indicated that those with dual diagnoses (SUDs and a co-occurring mental health diagnosis) can be effectively treated using CBT (Carroll et al., 1994; Drake, Mueser, Brunette, & McHugo, 2004; Hunter, Witkiewitz, Watkins, Paddock, & Hepner, 2012). However, research has not consistently demonstrated that a particular set of CBT interventions are most effective or that the length of a certain treatment(s) is of more benefit in terms of abstinence or relapse prevention (Finney et al., 2007; Moyer, Finney, Swearingen, & Vergun, 2002). In addition to CBT-based interventions, motivational approaches (motivational interviewing [MI] and motivational enhancement treatments [MET]) and community reinforcement models have evidenced effectiveness in the treatment of SUDs across a wide variety of substances (Dunn, Deroo, & Rivara, 2001; Finney et al., 2007; Garcia-Fernández et al., 2011; Hettema & Hendricks, 2010; Miller & Rose, 2009; Morgenstern et al., 2012). Copello, Velleman, and Templeton (2005) found that the involvement of family members in treatment can serve dual purposes—increasing treatment engagement in individuals with SUDs and providing social reinforcement of non-drug-abusing behaviors. Furthermore, Garcia-Fernández and her colleagues (2011) demonstrated that the addition of a voucher program increased the effectiveness of a community reinforcement approach (CRA) in cocaine-dependent adult outpatients; the benefits of the voucher program were still evident 6 months post treatment.

Psychosocial Interventions

Self-help or mutual-help groups, such as Alcoholics Anonymous (AA) and Narcotics Anonymous (NA) as well as their variants, are the most widely used and researched psychosocial interventions for SUDs (Groh, Jason, & Keys, 2008). Alcoholics Anonymous first began in 1935 with two members, and within the first 5 years, it was estimated that membership had grown to 1,400 persons meeting in 50 groups (AA, 2012a). As of January 1, 2012, the General Service Office (GSO) of AA estimated that worldwide membership included over 2 million persons, with just over 1.3 million in North America alone (AA, 2012b). Narcotics Anonymous was first established in Los Angeles, California, during the early 1950s as an offshoot of the AA treatment model. As of May 2012, there are an estimated 61,800 weekly meetings in 129 countries (NA, 2012). In a 2008 report, findings from SAMHSA's National Survey on Drug Use and Health (NSDUH) indicated that an average of 5 million persons, age 12 and older, attended a self-help group due to problems with drugs and/or alcohol. Of these, 45.3% attended because of alcohol only, 21.8% attended due to illicit drug use, while 33.0% indicated problems with both drugs and alcohol (SAMHSA, 2008).

These self-/mutual-help groups consist of a 12-step treatment program designed to promote recovery through facilitation of social changes (i.e., decreasing pro-drinking relationships and increasing abstinence models) and development of coping skills, self-efficacy in high-risk situations, and increased abstinence motivation (for a review, see Buckingham, Frings, & Albery, 2013; Kelly, Hoeppner, Stout, & Pagano, 2012; Kelly, Stout, Magill, & Tonigan, 2011; Moos, 2008). Research on AA and related self-/mutual-help groups has indicated that these interventions are at least as effective as other treatments (Kelly, Magill, & Stout, 2009) and, in some cases, have been shown to be more effective in reducing alcohol/drug use and increasing abstinence behavior (Blonigen, Timko, Finney, Moos, & Moos, 2011; Kelly, Hoeppner, et al., 2012). Specific factors, including treatment attendance, social identification and interaction, spirituality/religiosity, reduced negative affect, and decreases in impulsivity, have all been linked to favorable outcomes in self-/mutual-help models (Blonigen et al., 2011; Buckingham et al., 2013; Kelly, Hoeppner, et al., 2012; Kelly, Stout, Magill, Tonigan, & Pagano, 2010; Kelly et al., 2011). However, as reviewed by Miller et al. (2006), several widespread substance abuse interventions continue to be implemented despite little evidence of their efficacy; included in this group are AA attendees who are mandated to attend treatment. This finding appears to highlight the notion that change should be self-regulated based on perceived need (Kelly et al., 2009).

Pharmacological Treatments
Research on pharmacological treatments for SUDs has typically involved medications intended to mimic the effects of a particular substance (as in the case of methadone) or block substance-related effects in the brain (e.g., naltrexone, sertraline, acamprosate; Anton et al., 2006; Oliveto et al., 2012; Vocci, Acri, & Elkashef, 2005). In addition, medication interventions are often evaluated as an adjunct to coadministered psychological and/or psychosocial treatments (Anton et al., 2006; Oliveto et al., 2012) and, as such, effect sizes can be easily misinterpreted (Rösner, Leucht, Lehert, & Soyka, 2008). Indeed, Moos (2007) argues that treatments for SUDs should be part of an empirically supported treatment process—one that combines evidence-based psychological, social, and pharmacological interventions.

Three well-supported pharmacological interventions for the treatment of alcohol use disorders (AUDs) include Naltrexone, Disulfiram, and Acamprosate (Anton et al., 2006; Kelly, Daley, & Douaihy, 2012; Krampe & Ehrenreich, 2010; Miller & Wilbourne, 2002). Acamprosate was approved for use in treating AUDs by the Federal Drug Administration (FDA) in 2004, while Naltrexone has been approved since 1994 and Disulfiram has been used for over 50 years (Krampe & Ehrenreich, 2010; Rösner et al., 2008). A review of available clinical research studies between 2000 and 2008, by Krampe and Ehrenreich (2010), indicated that Disulfiram is a highly effective treatment for alcohol dependence, primarily when integrated into a course of psychological therapy. Indeed, when compared to other pharmacological treatments for alcohol dependence (including Naltrexone and Acamprosate), the effectiveness of Disulfiram was equal to other medications in two trials but superior in a majority of the others (Krampe & Ehrenreich, 2010). Results of a meta-analysis examining both Acamprosate and Naltrexone indicated that the former reduced the risk of drinking after a period of abstinence by 84%, while Naltrexone led to an 88% reduction in risk of heavy drinking among those not considered to be abstinent (Rösner et al., 2008).

Prior studies have suggested that Naltrexone is efficacious in the treatment of heroin dependence, particularly when paired with a therapeutic intervention (Kirchmayer et al., 2002); however, emerging evidence has suggested that this drug is no better than placebo or alternate pharmacotherapies, including benzodiazepines and buprenorphine (Minozzi et al., 2011). Furthermore, Naltrexone has demonstrated little or no efficacy in the treatment of cannabis (Nordstrom & Levin, 2007) or cocaine dependence (de Lima, Soares, Reisser, & Farrell, 2002). Research by Karila and colleagues (2008) and Vocci et al. (2005) indicated that Disulfiram might be efficacious in the treatment of cocaine and/or methamphetamine dependence.

Effective treatment of SUDs using a variety of other pharmacological interventions, including antidepressants (MAO inhibitors and SSRIs), mood stabilizers, dopaminergic agents, and typical and atypical antipsychotics, has been demonstrated in numerous studies, reviews, and meta-analyses (Castells et al., 2007; de Lima et al., 2002; Graves, Rafeyan, Watts, & Napier, 2012; Kelly, Daley, & Douaihy, 2012;[2] Oliveto et al., 2012; Vocci et al., 2005). In general, much of the focus on psychotropic medications as treatment agents has been linked to the belief that they enact changes to (or block) the reward pathways in the brain or alter the saturation or neurotransmitters. Furthermore, researchers have suggested that pharmacological interventions may demonstrate efficacy in the treatment of SUDs due to the effect that they have on symptom frequency and severity of comorbid, non-substance-related disorders (Castells et al., 2007; Kelly, Daley, & Douaihy, 2012; Tiet & Mausbach, 2007).

CONCLUSION

From monetary costs incurred on both societal and individual levels, to the social strain felt by communities and governments, the effects of SUDs are far-reaching indeed. As both a cause and effect of violence, the use of drugs and alcohol impacts nearly every aspect of community living, corrections, and mental health. Alcohol and substance use have been empirically correlated with a phenotypic clustering of symptoms related to other externalizing behaviors, including violence; however, the etiology of such associations can be quite diverse. Both common and unique genetic (heritable) factors, shared and distinctive family situations, neuropsychological sequelae, and the availability of community resources can play a role in the development and maintenance of drug- or alcohol-related problem. A number of therapeutic, psychosocial, and pharmacological treatment approaches have been put forth in order to reduce the negative consequences of substance use. However, interventions emphasizing common mechanisms of change, including social support, goal direction, acceptance of competing, non-substance-involved rewards, the presence of abstinence-oriented models, and development of self-efficacy have been shown to be most beneficial (Moos, 2007). Thus, indications for best practice appear to include a combination of pharmacological intervention and evidence-based psychological treatment to address comorbid disorders while increasing treatment retention. In addition, the intensity and frequency of applied treatments should be informed by the severity of substance-related problems and their impact on other co-occurring disorders (Kelly, Daley, & Douaihy, 2012).

AUTHOR'S NOTE

The opinions expressed in this chapter are those of the authors and do not necessarily represent the opinions of the Federal Bureau of Prisons or the Department of Justice.

NOTES

1. The interested reader is referred to Iacono, Malone, and McGue (2008) and Kreek, Nielsen, Butlelman, and LaForge (2005), among others, for reviews of specific genes and neurotransmitters involved in the acquisition and maintenance of SUDs.

2. See Kelly, Daley, and Douaihy (2012) for a thorough review of pharmacological treatments in patients with comorbid mental health disorders.

REFERENCES

Agrawal, A., Neale, M. C., Prescott, C. A., & Kendler, K. S. (2004). A twin study of early cannabis use and subsequent use and abuse/dependence of other illicit drugs. *Psychological Medicine, 34,* 1227–1237.

Alcoholics Anonymous, General Service Office. (Revised 2012, March 22a). *Estimated worldwide A.A. individual and group membership.* Retrieved March 2013, from http://www.aa.org/en_pdfs/smf-132_en.pdf.

Alcoholics Anonymous, General Service Office. (Revised 2012, March 22b). *Estimates of A.A. groups and members as of January 1, 2012.* Retrieved March 2013, from http://www.aa.org/en_pdfs/smf-53_en.pdf.

American Psychiatric Association (APA). (2000). *Diagnostic and statistical manual of mental disorders* (4th ed., text rev.). Washington, DC: Author.

American Psychiatric Association (APA). (2013). *Substance-related and addictive disorders.* Retrieved on June 2013, from http://www.dsm5.org/Documents/Substance%20Use%20Disorder%20Fact%20Sheet.pdf

Anton, R. F., O'Malley, S. S., Ciraulo, D. A., Cisler, R. A., Couper, D., Donovan, D. M., ... Zweben, A. (2006). Combined pharmacotherapies and behavioral interventions for alcohol dependence: the COMBINE study: A randomized controlled trial. *Journal of the American Medical Association, 295*(17), 2003–2017.

Armstrong, T. D., & Costello, E. J. (2002). Community studies on adolescent substance use, abuse, or dependence and psychiatric comorbidity. *Journal of Consulting and Clinical Psychology, 70*(6), 1224–1239.

Arseneault, L., Moffitt, T. E., Caspi, A., Taylor, P. J., & Silva, P. A. (2000). Mental disorders and violence in a total birth cohort: Results from the Dunedin Study. *Archives of General Psychiatry, 57,* 979–986.

Astley, S. J., Stachowiak, J., Clarren, S. K., & Clausen, C. (2002). Application of the fetal alcohol syndrome facial photographic screening tool in a foster care population. *Journal of Pediatrics, 141*(5), 712–717.

Blonigen, D. M., Timko, C., Finney, J. W., Moos, B. S., & Moos, R. H. (2011). Alcoholics Anonymous attendance, decreases in impulsivity and drinking and psychosocial outcomes over 16 years: Moderated-mediation from a developmental perspective. *Addiction, 106*(12), 2167–2177. doi: 10.1111/j.1360-0443.2011.03522.x

Boardman, J. D., Finch, B. K., Ellison, C. G., Williams, D. R., & Jackson, J. S. (2001). Neighborhood disadvantage, stress, and drug use among adults. *Journal of Health and Social Behavior, 42*(2), 151–165.

Bogg, T., & Finn, P. R. (2010). A self-regulatory model of behavioral disinhibition in late adolescence: Integrating personality traits, externalizing psychopathology, and cognitive capacity. *Journal of Personality, 78*(2), 441–470.

Bogg, T., Fukunaga, R., Finn, P. R., & Brown, J. W. (2012). Cognitive control links alcohol use, trait disinhibition, and reduced cognitive capacity: Evidence for medial prefrontal cortex dysregulation during reward-seeking behavior. *Drug and Alcohol Dependence, 122,* 112–118.

Bornovalova, M. A., Hicks, B. M., Iacono, W. G., & McGue, M. (2010). Familial transmission and heritability of childhood disruptive disorders. *American Journal of Psychiatry, 167*(9), 1066–1074.

Bornovalova, M. A., Hicks, B. M., Iacono, W. G., & McGue, M. (2013). Longitudinal twin study of borderline personality disorder traits and substance use in adolescence: Developmental change, reciprocal effects, and genetic and environmental influences. *Personality Disorders: Theory, Research, and Treatment, 4*(1), 23–32.

Brady, K. T., & Sinha, R. (2005). Co-occurring mental and substance use disorders: The neurobiological effects of chronic stress. *American Journal of Psychiatry, 162*, 1483–1493.

Buckingham, S. A., Frings, D., & Albery, I. P. (2013). Group membership and social identity in addiction recovery. *Psychology of Addictive Behaviors, 27*(4), 1132–1140. doi: 10.1037/a0032480

Buitelaar, J. K. (2012). Understanding comorbidity: From epidemiological designs and model-fitting approaches to systems biology as a new tool. *European Child and Adolescent Psychiatry, 21*(1), 1–3. doi: 10.1007/s00787-011-0236-7

Button, T. M. M., Rhee, S. H., Hewitt, J. K., Young, S. E., Corley, R. P., & Stallings, M. C. (2007). The role of conduct disorder in explaining the comorbidity between alcohol and illicit drug dependence in adolescence. *Drug and Alcohol Dependence, 87*, 46–53.

Cadoret, R. J., Troughton, E. D., & O'Gorman, T. W. (1987). Genetic and environmental factors in alcohol abuse and antisocial personality. *Journal of Studies on Alcohol and Drugs, 48*(1), 1–8.

Carroll, K. M., & Onken, L. S. (2005). Behavioral therapies for drug abuse. *American Journal of Psychiatry, 162*, 1452–1460.

Carroll, K. M., Rounsaville, B. J., Nich, C., Gordon, L. T., Wirtz, P. W., & Gawin, F. (1994). One-year follow-up of psychotherapy and pharmacotherapy for cocaine dependence: Delayed emergence of psychotherapy effects. *Archives of General Psychiatry, 51*(12), 989–997. doi: 10.1001/archpsyc.1994.03950120061010

Castellanos-Ryan, N., Rubia, K., & Conrod, P. J. (2011). Response inhibition and reward response bias mediate the predictive relationships between impulsivity and sensation seeking and common and unique variance in conduct disorder and substance misuse. *Alcoholism: Clinical and Experimental Research, 35*(1), 140–155. doi: 10.1111/j.1530-0277.2010.01331.x

Castells, X., Casas, M., Vidal, X., Bosch, R., Roncero, C., Ramos-Quiroga, J. A., & Capellà, D. (2007). Efficacy of central nervous system stimulant treatment for cocaine dependence: A systematic review and meta-analysis of randomized controlled clinical trials. *Addiction, 102*, 1871–1887. doi: 10.1111/j.1360-0443.2007.01943.x

Chung, I. J., Hawkins, J. D., Gilchrist, L. D., Hill, K. G., & Nagin, D. S. (2002). Identifying and predicting offending trajectories among poor children. *Social Services Review, 76*(4), 663–685.

Clark, D. B., Cornelius, J. R., Kirisci, L., & Tarter, R. E. (2005). Childhood risk categories for adolescent substance involvement: A general liability typology. *Drug and Alcohol Dependence, 77*, 13–21.

Copello, A. G., Velleman, R. D., & Templeton, L. J. (2005). Family interventions in the treatment of alcohol and drug problems. *Drug and Alcohol Review, 24*(4), 369–385. doi: 10.1080/09595230500302356.

Dackis, C., & O'Brien, C. (2005). Neurobiology of addiction: Treatment and public policy ramifications. *Nature Neuroscience, 8*(11), 1431–1436.

de Lima, M. S., Soares, B. G. d. O., Reisser, A. A. P., & Farrell, M. (2002). Pharmacological treatment of cocaine dependence: A systematic review. *Addiction, 97*, 931–949. doi: 10.1046/j.1360-0443.2002.00209.x

Dicker, S., & Gordon, E. (2004). Building bridges for babies in foster care: The babies can't quit wait initiative. *Juvenile and Family Court Journal, 55*(2), 29–41.

Dixon, A., Howie, P., & Starling, J. (2004). Psychopathology in female juvenile offenders. *Journal of Child Psychology and Psychiatry, 45*(6), 1150–1158.

Drake, R. E., Mueser, K. T., Brunette, M. F., & McHugo, G. J. (2004). A review of treatments for people with severe mental illnesses and co-occurring substance use disorders. *Psychiatric Rehabilitation Journal, 27,* 360–374. doi: 10.2975/27.2004. 360.374

Dunn, C., Deroo, L., & Rivara, F. P. (2001). The use of brief interventions adapted from motivational interviewing across behavioral domains: A systematic review. *Addiction, 96*(12), 1725–1742. doi: 10.1080/09652140120089481

Dutra, L., Stathopoulou, G., Basden, S., Leyro, T., Powers, M., & Otto, M. (2008). A meta-analytic review of psychosocial interventions for substance use disorders. *American Journal of Psychiatry, 165*(2), 179–187. doi: 10.1176/appi. ajp.2007.06111851

Elbogen, E. B., & Johnson, S. C. (2009). The intricate link between violence and mental disorder: Results from the National Epidemiologic Survey on Alcohol and Related Conditions. *Archives of General Psychiatry, 66*(2), 152–161.

Engels, R. C., Vermulst, A. A., Dubas, J. S., Bot, S. M., & Gerris, J. (2005). Long-term effects of family functioning and child characteristics on problem drinking in young adulthood. *European Addiction Research, 11,* 32–37.

Epstein, M., Hill, K. G., Bailey, J. A., & Hawkins, J. D. (2012). The effect of general and drug-specific family environments on comorbid and drug-specific problem behavior: A longitudinal examination. *Developmental Psychology, 49*(6), 1151–1164. doi: 10.1037/a0029309

Fazel, S., Bains, P., & Doll, H. (2006). Substance abuse and dependence in prisoners: A systematic review. *Addiction, 101,* 181–191.

Fergusson, D. M., Boden, J. M., & Horwood, L. (2011). Structural models of the comorbidity of internalizing disorders and substance use disorders in a longitudinal birth cohort. *Social Psychiatry and Psychiatric Epidemiology, 46*(10), 933–942. doi: 10.1007/ s00127-010-0268-1

Fergusson, D. M., Horwood, L. J., & Lynskey, M. T. (1995). The prevalence and risk factors associated with abusive or hazardous alcohol consumption in 16-year olds. *Addiction, 90*(7), 935–946.

Finn, P. R., Mazas, C. A., Justus, A. M., & Steinmetz, J. (2002). Early-onset alcoholism with conduct disorder: Go/no go learning deficits, working memory capacity, and personality. *Alcohol: Clinical and Experimental Research, 26,* 186–206.

Finn, P. R., Rickert, M. E., Miller, M. A., Lucas, J., Bogg, T., Bobova, L., & Cantrell, H. (2009). Reduced cognitive ability in alcohol dependence: Examining the role of covarying externalizing psychopathology. *Journal of Abnormal Psychology, 118*(1), 100–116.

Finney, J. W., Wilbourne, P. L., & Moos, R. H. (2007). Psychosocial treatments for substance use disorders. In P. E. Nathan & J. M. Gorman (Eds.), *A guide to treatments that work* (3rd ed., pp. 179–202). New York, NY: Oxford University Press.

Fishbein, D. (2000). Neuropsychological function, drug abuse, and violence: A conceptual framework. *Criminal Justice and Behavior, 27*(2), 139–159. doi: 10.1177/0093854 800027002001

Garavan, H., & Stout, J. C. (2005). Neurocognitive insights into substance abuse. *Trends in Cognitive Sciences, 9,* 195–201.

García-Fernández, G., Secades-Villa, R., García-Rodríguez, O., Álvarez-López, H., Fernández-Hermida, J. R., Fernández-Artamendi, S., & Higgins, S. T. (2011). Long-term benefits of adding incentives to the community reinforcement approach for cocaine dependence. *European Addiction Research*, *17*(3), 139–145. doi: 10.1159/000324848

Goldstein, R. Z., & Volkow, N. D. (2002). Drug addiction and it underlying neuro-biological bases: Neuroimaging evidence for the involvement of the frontal cortex. *American Journal of Psychiatry*, *159*, 1642–1662.

Goldstein, R. Z., & Volkow, N. D. (2011). Dysfunction of the prefrontal cortex in addiction: Neuroimaging findings and clinical implications. *Nature Reviews Neuroscience*, *12*(11), 652–669. doi: 10.1038/nrn3119

Grant, B. F., Chou, S. P., Goldstein, R. B., Huang, B., Stinson, F. S., Saha, T. D., ... Ruan, W. J. (2008). Prevalence, correlates, disability, and comorbidity of *DSM-IV* borderline personality disorder: Results from the Wave 2 National Epidemiologic Survey on Alcohol and Related Conditions. *Journal of Clinical Psychology*, *69*, 533–545.

Grant, B. F., Stinson, F. S., Dawson, D. A., Chou, F. S., Ruan, W. J., & Pickering, R. P. (2004). Co-occurrence of 12-month alcohol and drug use disorders and personality disorders in the United States. *Archives of General Psychiatry*, *61*, 361–368.

Graves, S. M., Rafeyan, R., Watts, J., & Napier, T. C. (2012). Mirtazapine, and mirtazapine-like compounds as possible pharmacotherapy for substance abuse disorders: Evidence from the bench and bedside. *Pharmacology and Therapeutics*, *136*(3), 343–353. doi: http://dx.doi.org/10.1016/j.pharmthera.2012.08.013

Grella, C. E., Greenwell, L., Prendergast, M., Sacks, S., & Melnick, G. (2008). Diagnostic profiles of offenders in substance abuse treatment programs. *Behavioral Sciences and the Law*, *26*, 369–388.

Groh, D. R., Jason, L. A., & Keys, C. B. (2008). Social network variables in Alcoholics Anonymous: A literature review. *Clinical Psychology Review*, *28*(3), 430–450. doi: 10.1016/j.cpr.2007.07.014

Hasin, D., Hatzenbuehler, M. L., Keyes, K., & Ogburn, E. (2006). Substance use disorders: Diagnostic and Statistical Manual of Mental Disorders, fourth edition (DSM-IV) and International Classification of Diseases, tenth edition (ICD-10). *Addiction*, *101*, 59–75.

Hettema, J. E., & Hendricks, P. S. (2010). Motivational interviewing for smoking cessation: A meta-analytic review. *Journal of Consulting and Clinical Psychology*, *78*(6), 868–884. doi: 10.1037/a0021498

Hicks, B. M., Krueger, R. F., Iacono, W. G., McGue, M., & Patrick, C. J. (2004). Family transmission and heritability of externalizing disorders. A twin-family study. *Archives of General Psychiatry*, *61*, 922–928.

Hicks, B. M., South, S. C., DiRago, A. C., Iacono, W. G., & McGue, M. (2009). Environmental adversity and increasing genetic risk for externalizing disorders. *Archives of General Psychiatry*, *66*(6), 640–648.

Higgins, S. T., Wong, C. J., Badger, G. J., Ogden, D. E. H., & Dantona, R. L. (2000). Contingent reinforcement increases cocaine abstinence during outpatient treatment and 1 year of follow-up. *Journal of Consulting and Clinical Psychology*, *68*(1), 64–72.

Hora, P. (2002). A dozen years of Drug Treatment Courts: Uncovering our theoretical foundation and the construction of a mainstream paradigm. *Substance Use and Misuse*, *37*(12-13), 1469–1488.

Howard, M. O., Balster, R. L., Cottler, L. B., Wu, L. T., & Vaughn, M. G. (2008). Inhalant use among incarcerated adolescents in the United States: Prevalence, characteristics, and correlates of use. *Drug and Alcohol Dependence, 93*(3), 197–209.

Howard, M. O., & Jenson, J. (1999). Inhalant use among antisocial youth: Prevalence and correlates. *Addictive Behaviors, 24*(1), 59–74.

Howard, R., Finn, P., Jose, P., & Gallagher, J. (2011). Adolescent-onset alcohol abuse exacerbates the influence of childhood conduct disorder on late adolescent and early adult antisocial behaviour. *Journal of Forensic Psychiatry and Psychology, 23*(1), 7–22.

Hunter, S. B., Witkiewitz, K., Watkins, K. E., Paddock, S. M., & Hepner, K. A. (2012). The moderating effects of group cognitive-behavioral therapy for depression among substance users. *Psychology of Addictive Behaviors, 26*(4), 906–916. doi: 10.1037/a0028158

Iacono, W. G., Malone, S. M., & McGue, M. (2008). Behavioral disinhibition and the development of early-onset addiction: Common and specific influences. *Annual Review of Clinical Psychology, 4,* 325–348.

James, D. J., & Glaze, L. E. (2006). *Bureau of Justice Statistics special report: Mental health problems of prison and jail inmates.* [NCJ 213600]. Washington, DC: US Department of Justice.

Jane-Llopis, E., & Matytsina, I. (2006). Mental health and alcohol, drugs, and tobacco: A review of the comorbidity between mental disorders and the use of alcohol, tobacco, and illicit drugs. *Drug and Alcohol Review, 25,* 515–536.

Kalivas, P. W., & Volkow, N. D. (2005). The neural basis of addiction: A pathology of motivation and choice. *American Journal of Psychiatry, 162,* 1403–1413.

Karberg, J. C., & James, D. J. (2005). *Bureau of Justice Statistics special report: Substance dependence, abuse, and treatment of jail inmates, 2002.* [NCJ 209588]. Washington, DC: Bureau of Justice Statistics, US Department of Justice.

Karila, L., Gorelick, D., Weinstein, A., Noble, F., Benyamina, A., Coscas, S., . . . Lépine, J. P. (2008). New treatments for cocaine dependence: A focused review. *International Journal of Neuropsychopharmacology, 11*(3), 425–438.

Kelly, J. F., Hoeppner, B., Stout, R. L., & Pagano, M. (2012). Determining the relative importance of the mechanisms of behavior change within Alcoholics Anonymous: A multiple mediator analysis. *Addiction, 107*(2), 289–299. doi:10.1111/j.1360-0443.2011.03593.x

Kelly, J. F., Magill, M., & Stout, R. L. (2009). How do people recover from alcohol dependence? A systematic review of the research on mechanisms of behavior change in Alcoholics Anonymous. *Addiction Research and Theory, 17*(3), 236–259. doi: 10.1080/16066350902770458.

Kelly, J. F., Stout, R. L., Magill, M., & Tonigan, J. S. (2011). The role of Alcoholics Anonymous in mobilizing adaptive social network changes: A prospective lagged mediational analysis. *Drug and Alcohol Dependence, 114*(2), 119–126.

Kelly, J. F., Stout, R. L., Magill, M., Tonigan, J., & Pagano, M. E. (2010). Mechanisms of behavior change in alcoholics anonymous: Does Alcoholics Anonymous lead to better alcohol use outcomes by reducing depression symptoms? *Addiction, 105*(4), 626–636. doi: 10.1111/j.1360-0443.2009.02820.x

Kelly, T. M., Daley, D. C., & Douaihy, A. B. (2012). Treatment of substance abusing patients with comorbid psychiatric disorders. *Addictive Behaviors, 37*(1), 11–24. doi: 10.1016/j.addbeh.2011.09.010

Kendler, K. S., Davis, C. G., & Kessler, R. C. (1997). The familial aggregation of common psychiatric and substance use disorders in the National Comorbidity Survey: A family history study. *British Journal of Psychiatry, 170*, 541–548. doi: 10.1192/bjp.170.6.541

Kendler, K. S., Prescott, C. A., Myers, J., & Neale, M. C. (2003). The structure of genetic and environmental risk factors for common psychiatric and substance use disorders in men and women. *Archives of General Psychiatry, 60*, 929–937.

Kerns, J. G., Nuechterlein, K. H., Braver, T. S., & Barch, D. M. (2008). Executive functioning component mechanisms and schizophrenia. *Biological Psychiatry, 64*, 26–33. doi: 10.1016/j.biopsych.2008.04.027

Kessler, R. C., Adler, L., Barkley, R., Biederman, J., Conners, C. K., Demler, O., … Zaslavsky, A. M. (2006). The prevalence and correlates of adult ADHD in the United States: Results from the National Comorbidity Survey Replication. *American Journal of Psychiatry, 163*, 716–723.

Kessler, R. C., Chiu, W. T., Demler, O., & Walters, E. E. (2005). Prevalence, severity, and comorbidity of twelve-month DSM-IV disorders in the National Comorbidity Survey Replication (NCS-R). *Archives of General Psychiatry, 62*, 617–627.

Kessler, R. C., McGonagle, K. A., Zhao, S., Nelson, C. B., Hughes, M., Eshleman, S., … Kendler, K. S. (1994). Lifetime and 12-month prevalence of DSM-III-R psychiatric disorders in the United States. Results from the National Comorbidity Survey. *Archives of General Psychiatry, 52*, 98–119.

Kessler, R. C., Nelson, C. B., McGonagle, K. A., Edlund, M. J., Frank, R. G., & Leaf, P. J. (1996). The epidemiology of co-occurring addictive and mental disorders: Implications for prevention and service utilization. *American Journal of Orthopsychiatry, 66*, 17–31.

Kessler, R. C., & Wang, P. S. (2008). The descriptive epidemiology of commonly occurring mental disorders in the United States. *Annual Review of Public Health, 29*, 115–129.

Keyes, M. A., Iacono, W. G., & McGue, M. (2007). Early onset problem behavior, young adult psychopathology, and contextual risk. *Twin Research and Human Genetics, 10*(1), 45–53.

King, S. M., Keyes, M., Malone, S. M., Elkins, I., Legrand, L. N., Iacono, W. G., & McGue, M. (2009). Parental alcohol dependence and the transmission of adolescent behavioral disinhibition: A study of adoptive and non-adoptive families. *Addiction, 104*(4), 578–586. doi: 10.1111/j.1360-0443.2008.02469.x

Kirchmayer, U., Davoli, M., Verster, A. D., Amato, L., Ferri, M., & Perucci, C. A. (2002). A systematic review on the efficacy of naltrexone maintenance treatment in opioid dependence. *Addiction, 97*, 1241–1249.

Kirisci, L., Tarter, R. E., Reynolds, M., & Vanyukov, M. (2006). Individual differences in childhood neurobehavior disinhibition predict decision to desist substance use during adolescence and substance use disorder in young adulthood: A prospective study. *Addictive Behaviors, 31*, 686–696.

Kirisci, L., Vanyukov, M., & Tarter, R. (2005). Detection of youth at high risk for substance use disorders: A longitudinal study. *Psychology of Addictive Behaviors, 19*, 243–252.

Krampe, H., & Ehrenreich, H. (2010). Supervised disulfiram as adjunct to psychotherapy in alcoholism treatment. *Current Pharmaceutical Design, 16*(19), 2076–2090.

Kreek, M. J., Nielsen, D. A., Butlelman, E. R., & LaForge, K. S. (2005). Genetic influences on impulsivity, risk taking, stress responsivity and vulnerability to drug abuse and addiction. *Nature Neuroscience, 8*, 1450–1457.

Krueger, R. (1999). The structure of common mental disorders. *Archives of General Psychiatry, 107,* 921–926.

Krueger, R. F., Caspi, A., Moffitt, T. E., & Silva, P. A. (1998). The structure and stability of common mental disorders (DSM-III-R): A longitudinal-epidemiological study. *Journal of Abnormal Psychology, 107(2),* 216–227.

Krueger, R. F., Caspi, A., Moffitt, T. E., White, J., & Stouthamer-Loeber, M. (1996). Delay of gratification, psychopathology, and personality: Is low self-control specific to externalizing problems? *Journal of Personality, 64,* 107–129.

Krueger, R. F., Hicks, B. M., Patrick, C. J., Carlson, S. R., Iacono, W. G., & McGue, M. (2002). Etiologic connections among substance dependence, antisocial behavior, and personality: Modeling the externalizing spectrum. *Journal of Abnormal Psychology, 111(3),* 411–474.

Krueger, R. F., & Markon, K. E. (2006). Reinterpreting comorbidity: A model-based approach to understanding and classifying psychopathology. *Annual Review of Clinical Psychology, 2,* 111–133.

Krueger, R. F., Markon, K. E., Patrick, C. J., Benning, S. D., & Kramer, M. D. (2007). Linking antisocial behavior, substance use, and personality: An integrative quantitative model of the adult externalizing spectrum. *Journal of Abnormal Psychology, 116,* 645–666.

Krueger, R. F., Markon, K. E., Patrick, C. J., & Iacono, W.G. (2005). Externalizing psychopathology in adulthood: A dimensional-spectrum conceptualization and its implications for *DSM-V. Journal of Abnormal Psychology, 114(4),* 537–550.

Kushner, M. G., Abrams, K., & Borchardt, C. (2000). The relationship between anxiety disorders and alcohol use disorders: A review of major perspectives and findings. *Clinical Psychology Review, 20,* 149–171.

Långström, N., Sjöstedt, G., & Grann, M. (2004). Psychiatric disorders and recidivism in sexual offenders. *Sexual Abuse: Journal of Research and Treatment, 16(2),* 139–150.

Látalová, K. K., & Praško, J. J. (2010). Aggression in borderline personality disorder. *Psychiatric Quarterly, 81(3),* 239–251. doi: 10.1007/s11126-010-9133-3

Lee, N. K., & Rawson, R. A. (2008). A systematic review of cognitive and behavioural therapies for methamphetamine dependence. *Drug and Alcohol Review, 27(3),* 309–317. doi: 10.1080/09595230801919494

Leeman, R. F., Grant, J. E., & Potenza, M. N. (2009). Behavioral and neurological foundations for the moral and legal implications of intoxication, addictive behaviors and disinhibition. *Behavioral Sciences and the Law, 27(2),* 237–259. doi: 10.1002/bsl.855

Legrand, L. N., Keyes, M., McGue, M., Iacono, W. G., & Krueger, R. F. (2008). Rural environments reduce the genetic influence on adolescent substance use and rule-breaking behavior. *Psychological Medicine, 38,* 1341–1350.

Leshner, A. (1997). Addiction is a brain disease, and it matters. *Science, 278(5335),* 45–47.

Lewis, C. F. (2011). Substance use and violent behavior in women with antisocial personality disorder. *Behavioral Sciences and the Law, 29(5),* 667–676. doi: 10.1002/bsl.1006

Lilienfeld, S. O., Waldman, I. D., & Israel, A. C. (1994). A critical examination of the use of the term and concept of comorbidity in psychopathology research. *Clinical Psychology: Science and Practice, 1,* 71–83.

Martin, C. S., Chung, T., Kirisci, L., & Langenbucher, J. W. (2006). Item Response Theory analysis of diagnostic criteria for alcohol and cannabis use disorders in adolescents: Implications for DSM-V. *Journal of Abnormal Psychology*, *115*, 807–814.

Mattson, R. E., O'Farrell, T. J., Lofgreen, A. M., Cunningham, K., & Murphy, C. M. (2012). The role of illicit substance use in a conceptual model of intimate partner violence in men undergoing treatment for alcoholism. *Psychology of Addictive Behaviors*, *26*(2), 255–264.

McGue, M., Slutske, W., & Iacono, W. G. (1999). Personality and substance use disorders: II. Alcoholism versus drug use disorders. *Journal of Consulting and Clinical Psychology*, *67*, 394–404.

McGue, M., Slutske, W., Taylor, J., & Iacono, W. G. (1997). Personality and substance use disorders: I. Effects of gender and alcoholism subtype. *Alcoholism: Clinical and Experimental Research*, *21*, 513–520.

McLellan, A. T., Lewis, D. C., O'Brien, C. P., & Kleber, H. D. (2000). Drug dependence, a chronic medical illness: Implications for treatment, insurance, and outcomes evaluation. *Journal of the American Medical Association*, *284*, 1689–1695.

McNichol, T., & Tash, C. (2001). Parental substance abuse and the development of children in foster care. *Child Welfare: Journal of Policy, Practice, and Program*, *80*(2), 239–256.

Merikangas, K. R., Mehta, R. L., Molnar, B. E., Walters, E. E., Swendsen, J. D., Aguilar-Gaziola, S., ... Kessler, R. C. (1998). Comorbidity of substance use disorders with mood and anxiety disorders: Results of the International Consortium in Psychiatric Epidemiology. *Addictive Behaviors*, *23*, 893–907.

Miller, W. R., & Rose, G. S. (2009). Toward a theory of motivational interviewing. *American Psychologist*, *64*(6), 527–537. doi:10.1037/a0016830

Miller, W. R., Sorensen, J. L., Selzer, J. A., & Brigham, G. S. (2006). Disseminating evidence-based practices in substance abuse treatment: A review with suggestions. *Journal of Substance Abuse Treatment*, *31*(1), 25–40. doi: 10.1016/j.jsat.2006.03.005

Miller, W. R., & Wilbourne, P. L. (2002). Mesa Grande: A methodological analysis of clinical trials of treatment for alcohol use disorders. *Addiction*, *97*(3), 265–277. doi:10.1046/j.1360-0443.2002.00019.x

Minozzi, S., Amato, L., Vecchi, S., Davoli, M., Kirchmayer, U., & Verster, A. (2011). Oral naltrexone maintenance treatment for opioid dependence. *Cochrane Database of Systematic Reviews*, *4*, CD001333. doi: 10.1002/14651858.CD001333.pub4

Miyake, A., Friedman, N. P., Emerson, M. J., Witzki, A. H., Howerter, A., & Wager, T. D. (2000). The unity and diversity of executive functions and their contributions to complex "frontal lobe" tasks: A latent variable analysis. *Cognitive Psychology*, *41*(1), 49–100.

Moeller, F. G., Dougherty, D. M., Barratt, E. S., Oderinde, B., Mathias, C. W., Harper, R. A., & Swann, A. C. (2002). Increased impulsivity in cocaine dependent subjects independent of antisocial personality disorder and aggression. *Drug and Alcohol Dependence*, *68*, 105–111. doi: 10.1016/S0376-8716(02)00106-0

Moos, R. H. (2007). Theory-based active ingredients of effective treatments for substance use disorders. *Drug and Alcohol Dependence*, *88*(2-3), 109–121.

Moos, R. H. (2008). Active ingredients of substance use-focused self-help groups. *Addiction*, *103*(3), 387–396.

Morgenstern, J., Kuerbis, A., Amrhein, P., Hail, L., Lynch, K., & McKay, J. R. (2012). Motivational interviewing: A pilot test of active ingredients and mechanisms of change. *Psychology of Addictive Behaviors*, *26*(4), 859–869. doi:10.1037/a0029674

Motivans, M. (2012). *Federal justice statistics 2009—Statistical tables.* [NCJ 233464]. Washington, DC: Bureau of Justice Statistics, US Department of Justice.

Moyer, A., Finney, J. W., Swearingen, C. E., & Vergun, P. (2002). Brief interventions for alcohol problems: A meta-analytic review of controlled investigations in treatment-seeking and non-treatment-seeking populations. *Addiction, 97*(3), 279–292. doi: 10.1046/j.1360-0443.2002.00018.x

Mumola, C. J., & Karberg, J. C. (2006). *Bureau of Justice Statistics special report: Drug use and dependence, state and federal prisoners, 2004.* [NCJ 213530]. Washington, DC: Bureau of Justice Statistics, US Department of Justice.

Narcotics Anonymous. (2012, May). *Information about NA.* Retrieved March 2013, from http://na.org/admin/include/spaw2/uploads/pdf/PR/Information_about_NA.pdf.

National Center on Addiction and Substance Abuse (CASA) at Columbia University. (2009). *Shoveling Up II: The impact of substance abuse on federal, state and local budgets.* New York, NY: CASA.

National Center on Addiction and Substance Abuse (CASA) at Columbia University. (2010). *Behind bars II: Substance abuse and America's prison population.* New York, NY: CASA.

National Drug Court Resource Center. (2012). *How many drug courts are there?* Retrieved March 2013, http://ndcrc.org/node/348.

Noël, X., Brevers, D., Bechara, A., Hanak, C., Kornreich, C., Verbanck, P., & Le Bon, O. (2011). Neurocognitive determinants of novelty and sensation-seeking in individuals with alcoholism. *Alcohol and Alcoholism, 46*(4), 407–415. doi: 10.1093/alcalc/agr048

Nordstrom, B. R., & Levin, F. R. (2007). Treatment of cannabis use disorders: A review of the literature. *American Journal on Addictions, 16,* 331–342.

O'Brien, C. (2011). Addiction and dependence in DSM-V. *Addiction, 106*(5), 866–867. doi: 10.1111/j.1360-0443.2010.03144.x

Oliveto, A., Poling, J., Mancino, M. J., Williams, D., Thostenson, J., Pruzinsky, R., … Kosten, T. R. (2012). Sertraline delays relapse in recently abstinent cocaine-dependent patients with depressive symptoms. *Addiction, 107*(1), 131–141. doi: 10.1111/j.1360-0443.2011.03552.x

Paley, B., & Auerbach, B. E. (2010). Children with fetal alcohol spectrum disorders in the dependency court system: Challenges and recommendations. *Journal of Psychiatry and Law, 38,* 507–558.

Patrick, C. J., Fowles, D. C., & Krueger, R. F. (2009). Triarchic conceptualization of psychopathology: Developmental origins of disinhibition, boldness, and meanness. *Development and Psychopathology, 21,* 913–938. doi: 10.1017/S0954579409000492

Prendergast, M., Podus, D., Finney, J., Greenwell, L., & Roll, J. (2006). Contingency management for treatment of substance use disorders: A meta-analysis. *Addiction, 101*(11), 1546–1560. doi:10.1111/j.1360-0443.2006.01581.x

Rawson, R. A., McCann, M. J., Flammino, F., Shoptaw, S., Miotto, K., Reiber, C., & Ling, W. (2006). A comparison of contingency management and cognitive-behavioral approaches for stimulant-dependent individuals. *Addiction, 101*(2), 267–274. doi: 10.1111/j.1360-0443.2006.01312.x

Ray, L. A., Kahler, C., Young, D., Chelminski, I., & Zimmerman, M. (2008). The factor structure and severity of DSM-IV alcohol abuse and dependence symptoms in psychiatric outpatients. *Journal of Studies on Alcohol and Drugs, 69,* 496–499.

Reed, S. C., Levin, F. R., & Evans, S. M. (2012). Alcohol increases impulsivity and abuse liability in heavy drinking women. *Experimental and Clinical Psychopharmacology*, *20*(6), 454–465. doi: 10.1037/a0029087

Reiger, D. A., Farmer, M. E., Rae, D. S., Locke, B. Z., Keith, S. J., Judd, L. L., & Goodwin, F. (1990). Comorbidity of mental disorders with alcohol and other drug abuse. Results from the Epidemiologic Catchment Area (ECA) Study. *Journal of the American Medical Association*, *264*, 2511–2518.

Rogers, R. D., & Robbins, T. W. (2001). Investigating the neurocognitive deficits associated with chronic drug misuse. *Current Opinion in Neurobiology*, *11*(2), 250–257.

Rösner, S., Leucht, S., Lehert, P., & Soyka, M. (2008). Acamprosate supports abstinence, Naltrexone prevents excessive drinking: Evidence from a meta-analysis with unreported outcomes. *Journal of Psychopharmacology*, *22*(1), 11–23. doi: 10.1177/0269881107078308

Ruiz, M. A., Douglas, K. S., Edens, J. F., Nikolova, N. L., & Lilienfeld, S. O. (2012). Co-occurring mental health and substance use problems in offenders: Implications for risk assessment. *Psychological Assessment*, *24*(1), 77–87. doi: 10.1037/a0024623

Saha, T. D., Chou, S. P., & Grant, B. F. (2006). Toward an alcohol use disorder continuum using item response theory: Results from the national epidemiologic survey on alcohol and related conditions. *Psychological Medicine*, *36*, 931–941.

Sanford, J., & Arrigo, B. (2005). Lifting the cover on drug courts: Evaluation findings and policy concerns. *International Journal of Offender Therapy and Comparative Criminology*, *49*(3), 239–259.

Saraceno, L., Munafo, M., Heron, J., Craddock, N., & van den Bree, M. B. M. (2009). Genetic and non-genetic influences on the development of co-occurring alcohol problem use and internalizing symptomatology in adolescence: A review. *Addiction*, *104*, 1100–1121.

Schuckit, M. A. (July 2012). Editor's corner: Editorial in reply to the comments of Griffith Edwards. *Journal of Studies on Alcohol and Drugs*, *73*(4), 521–522.

Scott, K. D., & Scott, A. A. (2012). An examination of information-processing skills among inhalant-using adolescents. *Child: Care, Health and Development*, *38*(3), 412–419. doi:10.1111/j.1365-2214.2011.01277.x

Sher, K. J., Bartholow, B. D., & Wood, M. D. (2000). Personality and substance use disorders: A prospective study. *Journal of Consulting and Clinical Psychology*, *68*, 818–829.

Sher, K. J., & Trull, T. J. (1994). Personality and disinhibitory psychopathology: Alcoholism and antisocial personality disorder. *Journal of Abnormal Psychology*, *103*, 92–102.

Skårberg, K., Nyberg, F., & Engström, I. (2010). Is there an association between the use of anabolic-androgenic steroids and criminality. *European Addiction Research*, *16*, 213–219.

Slutske, W. S., Heath, A. C., Dinwiddie, S. H., Madden, P., Bucholz, K. K., Dunne, M. P., … Martin, N. G. (1998). Common genetic risk factors for conduct disorder and alcohol dependence. *Journal of Abnormal Psychology*, *107*(3), 363–374.

Smith, P. H., Homish, G. G., Leonard, K. E., & Cornelius, J. R. (2012). Intimate partner violence and specific substance use disorders: Findings from the national epidemiologic survey on alcohol and related conditions. *Psychology of Addictive Behaviors*, *26*(2), 236–245.

Stephens, R. S., Roffman, R. A., & Curtin, L. (2000). Comparison of extended versus brief treatments for marijuana use. *Journal of Consulting and Clinical Psychology*, *68*(5), 898–908. doi:10.1037/0022-006X.68.5.898

Swendsen J., Burstein M., Case B., Conway, K. P., Dierker, L., He, J., & Merikangas, K. R. (2012). Use and abuse of alcohol and illicit drugs in US adolescents: Results of the national comorbidity survey–adolescent supplement. *Archives of General Psychiatry*, *69(4)*, 390–398. doi: 10.1001/archgenpsychiatry.2011.1503

Tarter, R. E., Kirisci, L., Habeych, M., Reynolds, M., & Vanyukov, M. (2004). Neurobehavior disinhibition and childhood predisposes boys to substance use disorder by young adulthood: Direct and mediated etiologic pathways. *Drug and Alcohol Dependence*, *73*, 121–132.

Thoma, R. J., Monnig, M. A., Lysne, P. A., Ruhl, D. A., Pommy, J. A., Bogenschutz, M., ... Yeo, R. A. (2011). Adolescent substance abuse: The effects of alcohol and marijuana on neuropsychological performance. *Alcoholism: Clinical and Experimental Research*, *35(1)*, 39–46. doi:10.1111/j.1530-0277.2010.01320.x

Tiet, Q. Q., & Mausbach, B. (2007). Treatments for patients with dual diagnosis: A review. *Alcoholism, Clinical and Experimental Research*, *31*, 513–536.

Trull, T. J., & Sher, K. J. (1994). Relationship between the five-factor model of personality and Axis I disorders in a non-clinical sample. *Journal of Abnormal Psychology*, *103*, 350–360.

Trull, T. J., Sher, K. J., Minks-Brown, C., Durbin, J., & Burr, R. (2000). Borderline personality disorder and substance use disorders: A review and integration. *Clinical Psychology Review*, *20(2)*, 235–253.

Trull, T. J., Waudby, C. J., & Sher, K. J. (2004). Alcohol, tobacco, and drug use disorders and personality disorder symptoms. *Experimental and Clinical Psychopharmacology*, *12(1)*, 65–75.

US Department of Health and Human Services, Administration for Children and Families (ACF). (2012). *The AFCARS report: Preliminary FY 2011 estimates as of July 2012*. Retrieved January 2013, from http://www.acf.hhs.gov/sites/default/files/cb/afcarsreport19.pdf

US Department of Health and Human Services, Substance Abuse and Mental Health Services Administration (SAMHSA). (2012). *Results from the 2011 National Survey on Drug Use and Health: Summary of national findings*. [NSDUH Series H-44, HHS Publication No. (SMA) 12-4713]. Rockville, MD: SAMHSA.

US Department of Health and Human Services, Substance Abuse and Mental Health Services Administration (SAMHSA), Office of Applied Studies. (2008). *The NSDUH Report: Participation in self-help groups for alcohol and illicit drug use: 2006 and 2007*. Rockville, MD: SAMHSA.

US Department of Justice, Federal Bureau of Prisons (BOP). (2010). *State of the bureau: 2010*. Washington, DC: Author.

US Department of Justice, Federal Bureau of Prisons (BOP). (2011). *Annual report on substance abuse treatment programs fiscal year 2011: Report to the Judiciary Committee of the United States Congress*. Washington, DC: Author.

Valdez, A., Kaplan, C. D., & Curtis, R. L. (2007). Aggressive crime, alcohol and drug use, and concentrated poverty in 24 U.S. urban areas. *American Journal of Drug and Alcohol Abuse*, *33*, 595–603.

Verdejo-Garcia, A., & Bechara, A. (2009). A somatic-marker theory of addiction. *Neuropharmacology*, *56*, 48–62.

Verdejo-García, A., del mar Sánchez-Fernández, M., Alonso-Maroto, L., Fernández-Calderón, F., Perales, J. C., Lozano, Ó., & Pérez-García, M. (2010). Impulsivity and executive functions in polysubstance-using rave attenders. *Psychopharmacology*, *210(3)*, 377–392. doi:10.1007/s00213-010-1833-8

Verdejo-Garcia, A., Lawrence, A. J., & Clark, L. (2008). Impulsivity as a vulnerability marker for substance-use disorders: Review of findings from high-risk research, problem gamblers and genetic association studies. *Neuroscience and Biobehavioral Reviews, 32,* 777–810.

Verona, E., Sachs-Ericsson, N., & Joiner, T. E. (2004). Suicide attempts associated with externalizing psychopathology in an epidemiological sample. *American Journal of Psychiatry, 161,* 444–451.

Vocci, F. J., Acri, J., Elkashef, A. (2005). Medication development for addictive disorders: The state of the science. *American Journal of Psychiatry, 162,* 1432–1440.

Volkow, N. (2004). The reality of comorbidity: Depression and drug abuse. *Biological Psychiatry, 56,* 714–717.

Volkow, N. D., Fowler, J. S., & Wang, G. (2004). The addicted human brain viewed in the light of imaging studies: Brain circuits and treatment strategies. *Neuropharmacology, 47,* 3–13.

Vollebergh, W., Iedema, J., Bijl, R., de Graaf, R., Smit, F., & Ormel, J. (2001). The structure and stability of common mental disorders: The NEMESIS study. *Archives of General Psychiatry, 58*(6), 597–603.

Wallace, C., Mullen, P., & Burgess, P. (2004). Criminal offending in schizophrenia over a 25-year period marked by deinstitutionalization and increasing prevalence of comorbid substance use disorders. *American Journal of Psychiatry, 161,* 716–727.

Welte, J., Barnes, G., Wieczorek, W., Tidwell, M., & Parker, J. (2001). Alcohol and gambling pathology among U.S. adults: Prevalence, demographic patterns and comorbidity. *Journal of Studies on Alcohol and Drugs, 62,* 706–712.

White, H. R., Xie, M., Thompson, W., Loeber, R., & Stouthamer-Loeber, M. (2001). Psychopathology as a predictor of adolescent drug use trajectories. *Psychology of Addictive Behaviors, 15*(3), 210–218.

Widiger, T. A., & Clark, L. A. (2000). Toward DSM-V and the classification of psychopathology. *Psychological Bulletin, 126,* 946–963.

Widiger, T. A., & Samuel, D. (2005). Diagnostic categories or dimensions? A question for the *Diagnostic and Statistical Manual of Mental Disorders—fifth edition. Journal of Abnormal Psychology, 114*(4), 494–504.

Wilson, D. (2000). *Drug use, testing, and treatment in jails.* [NCJ 179999]. Washington, DC: Bureau of Justice Statistics Special Report, US Department of Justice.

Witkiewitz, K., Donovan, D. M., & Hartzler, B. (2012). Drink refusal training as part of a combined behavioral intervention: Effectiveness and mechanisms of change. *Journal of Consulting and Clinical Psychology, 80*(3), 440–449. doi: 10.1037/a0026996

Wright, A. C., Krueger, R. F., Hobbs, M. J., Markon, K. E., Eaton, N. R., & Slade, T. (2013). The structure of psychopathology: Toward an expanded quantitative empirical model. *Journal of Abnormal Psychology, 122*(1), 281–294. doi: 10.1037/a0030133

Young, S. E., Stallings, M. C., Corley, R. P., Krauter, K. S., & Hewitt, J. K. (2000). Genetic and environmental influences on behavioral disinhibition. *American Journal of Medical Genetics (Neuropsychiatric Genetics), 96,* 684–695.

Zuckerman, M., & Kuhlman, D. M. (2000). Personality and risk taking: Common biosocial factors. *Journal of Personality, 68*(6), 999–1029.

Major Mental Disorders and Violence

LAURA S. GUY AND KEVIN S. DOUGLAS ▪

For the past several years, interpersonal violence has been among the leading causes of death in the United States. In 2009, the most recent year for which statistics are available, homicide was among the top five causes of death among people 1 to 44 years of age (Heron, 2012). Acts of violence routinely are among the news headlines; when an alleged perpetrator is suspected of having a mental illness, media portrayals often focus on the negative characteristics related to the disorder (Wahl, Wood, & Richards, 2002). Sensational media stories that link violence to mental disorder are harmful not only because they can elicit fear and perpetuate stigma and bias (e.g., Corrigan & O'Shaughnessy, 2007; Corrigan & Penn, 1999; Corrigan et al., 2002; Ferriman, 2000; Owen, 2012; also see Evans-Lacko, Brohan, Mojtabai, & Thornicroft, 2012), but also because they may strengthen misconceptions among the public that mental illness has a strong and inextricable relation with violence (e.g., Pescosolido, Monahan, Link, Stueve, & Kikuzawa, 1999)—a conclusion that cannot be drawn based on the current state of the empirical literature. Given such misperceptions, it perhaps is ironic that individuals with major mental disorder are much more likely to be victims of interpersonal violence or to engage in violence toward themselves than to commit acts of violence against others (e.g., Appleby, Mortensen, Dunn, & Hiroeh, 2001; Hiday, Swartz, Swanson, Borum, & Wagner, 1999; Nicholls, Brink, Desmarais, Webster, & Martin, 2006; Silver, Piquero, Jennings, Piquero, & Leiber, 2011).

In contrast to typical media portrayals, and despite decades of research on the topic, uncertainty persists regarding the precise nature of the association between mental disorder and violence toward others. One thing that is clear, however, is that the issue is a complex one with significant consequences for diverse groups of stakeholders. The presumed connection between mental disorder and violence also has played a defining role in mental health law in this country and abroad. For example, mental health professionals in the United States can be held liable for negligently failing to anticipate and prevent a patient's violence to others (e.g., *Jablonski v. U.S.*, 1983; *Lipari v. Sears Roebuck*, 1980; *Tarasoff v. Board of Regents of the University of California*, 1976). As another example, in contrast to earlier standards for civil commitment that focused on a patient's need for treatment (see, e.g., *O'Connor v. Donaldson*, 1975), current legislation for inpatient and outpatient commitment focuses on dangerousness to others as a result of mental disorder or abnormality (e.g., *Foucha v. Lousiana*, 1992; *Kansas v. Hendricks*, 1997). As such, improving stakeholders' understanding of the magnitude and nature of the association between mental disorder and violence is critical for informing decisions relevant to policy, legislation, and practice. Perhaps most critically, such knowledge is vital for developing and implementing effective risk-reducing intervention strategies and reducing the significant and myriad costs associated with violent behavior.

As this chapter reviews in detail, the available empirical evidence indicates that a subset of individuals with serious mental disorder (SMD) presents an increased risk for behaving violently. Importantly, however, the proportion of violence that this subgroup accounts for is relatively small. In this chapter, we focus on the domains of SMD that have the largest demonstrated associations with violence—psychotic and major affective disorders. It should be noted that other types of psychopathology, such as psychopathic personality disorder and related symptoms on the externalizing spectrum, have substantially more robust associations with violence than psychotic and major affective disorders. However, these and other types of syndromes are addressed in other chapters in this volume (see Chapters 5 and 8). We also briefly discuss risk for violence among individuals with SMD who have comorbid substance abuse disorders; however, substance abuse is focused on more directly in Chapter 3.

EVOLUTIONS IN THE SCIENTIFIC LITERATURE

Over the course of several decades, conclusions about whether mental disorder and violence are related, the magnitude of any such potential association, and the explanatory mechanisms delineating the possible relation have varied widely. Findings from early research on the topic indicated that no demonstrated association between violence and mental disorder had been observed (e.g., Cocozza & Steadman, 1976; Monahan, 1981; Monahan & Steadman, 1983; Steadman & Keveles, 1972; Teplin, 1985). Studies conducted during the 1990s began to challenge this entrenched view, as well-regarded scientists reported findings indicating that, in fact, a small but clinically significant relation existed (Monahan, 1992; Monahan & Steadman, 1994; Mulvey, 1994).

The more recent empirical literature contains many methodologically rigorous studies that continue to yield extremely discrepant findings. A notable characteristic of this body of research—which spans literally hundreds of studies (see, e.g., Douglas, Guy, & Hart, 2009)—is marked divergence in methodological and analytic approaches. Researchers who have drawn conclusions about the magnitude and nature of the relation between mental disorder and violence often have done so after having studied seemingly vastly different entities. For example, the ways in which both mental illness and violence have been defined and measured varies across studies. Researchers also have examined the association between violence and mental disorder using different types of samples and in different settings. In some studies, control or comparison groups are included; other studies have been less rigorous in this regard. Other differences in research designs also are apparent.

These and other key methodological distinctions understandably have contributed to the conflicting conclusions reached about the association between violence and major mental disorder. For example, the importance of considering the role of moderating variables in understanding the magnitude of the association between violence and one type of major mental disorder—psychosis—was demonstrated in a meta-analysis of 166 independent data sets (Douglas et al., 2009). The authors found that the strength of the odds ratio ranged from a meaningful inverse association to a large positive association as a function of the number of moderators present in a given study. Further, roughly 25% of studies showed an inverse association, whereas 25% showed a robust positive association.

In addition, the field lacks consensus regarding whether certain variables should be treated as confounding factors in statistical analyses, thereby thwarting efforts to distill consistent and accurate findings. A researcher's theoretical views about the causal mechanisms underlying the association between mental disorder and violence could contribute to whether she or he treated a variable as a confound (an extraneous variable that was associated with both mental disorder and violence, and which could distort the effects of the relation between those two variables). For example, if a researcher believed that diminished socioeconomic status (SES) is a consequence of mental disorder, as is espoused by the "social drift hypothesis," in which individuals with SMD drift downward in SES as their disorder increasingly interferes with their ability to work, statistically controlling for the effects of SES could distort results about the relation between mental disorder and violence (see Monahan, 1993). On the other hand, if SES is not viewed as being a step in the causal chain between mental disorder and violence, or if downward drift is not a consequence of a mental disorder, then it should not be controlled for statistically (see Rothman, 1986).

As is clear from this brief summary, studying the link between SMD and violence is not a straightforward task. There are intricacies to SMD itself—in terms of symptom mix, disease severity, disease course, and so forth. There are further complicating factors—as alluded to earlier—when SMD is placed in context and evaluated in concert with the numerous other factors that may both influence it and be influenced by it. Deciding whether to control such factors is as much a conceptual issue and decision as it is a methodological one. But it is a decision that may greatly influence both a study's empirical findings, as well as any implications stemming from it. In the remainder of this chapter we will attempt to describe this complicated state of the literature, and highlight the conditions under which SMD is more versus less strongly associated with violence.

EMPIRICAL FINDINGS ON THE ASSOCIATION BETWEEN SERIOUS MENTAL DISORDER AND VIOLENCE

A substantial amount of research has examined rates of violence among psychiatric inpatients or rates of mental disorder among people with histories of known violence. Because such samples by definition comprise relatively more ill or violent individuals, research of this kind typically suffers from selection biases that prevent generalizable findings from being advanced much further than from the types of samples that were under study. Therefore, in this chapter, we focus on meta-analyses and epidemiological studies, which are less likely to be compromised by potential selection biases. In general, research indicates that the association between psychotic or mood disorders and violence is stronger when studied at the symptom, rather than diagnosis, level. In the sections that follow, we review research examining both diagnoses and symptoms of psychotic and mood disorders.

Meta-Analyses

Several meta-analyses have examined the relation between psychosis and violence. Such quantitative syntheses are advantageous in that they can provide a more powerful estimate of the true effect size of the topic under investigation, compared with less precise effect sizes derived from single studies necessarily operating under a particular set of conditions. Of course, the selection criteria followed in a meta-analysis—as with individual studies—directly affect the outcomes reached. Different meta-analyses have produced divergent conclusions. In one such quantitative synthesis, Douglas et al. (2009) investigated the association between psychosis and violence, aggregating 885 effect sizes from 204 studies representing 166 independent data sets. Psychosis was significantly associated with an approximately 49% to 68% increase in the odds of violence relative to the odds of violence in the absence of psychosis, representing a small, but reliable, effect size. Shedding light on why primary research studies have found vastly discrepant results, several methodological variables moderated the association between psychosis and violence. The nature of the comparison group was a key factor: Odds ratios (ORs) were higher when individuals with psychosis were compared with persons without mental disorder (Mdn = 3.68) than when compared with individuals with other mental disorders (Mdn = 1.51). However, odds ratios were significantly greater than chance for both comparisons. In addition, psychosis demonstrated a stronger association with violence when compared with internalizing disorders (e.g., nonpsychotic mood disorders, anxiety disorders; Mdn = 2.15) than when compared with externalizing disorders (e.g., Cluster B personality disorders, substance-related disorders; Mdn = 0.85).

In this meta-analysis, four groups of symptom domains were coded. The median odds ratio for each symptom group was significantly greater than chance: positive (2.32), disorganized (1.85), negative (1.32), and other/unspecified (1.78). The association between violence and positive symptoms was significantly larger than that for negative symptoms. Hallucination and delusional symptoms were significantly different than chance (Mdn OR = 2.31), as were threat/control-override symptoms (Mdn OR = 1.92). As a group, "other" positive symptoms (e.g., bizarre behavior, excitement, suspiciousness, nondelusional or nonhallucinatory paranoia) were significantly different than chance (Mdn OR = 2.37), but these symptoms did not differ from one another. The median odds ratio (1.11) for the 16 studies that reported on paranoid symptoms demonstrated only a trend toward statistical significance.

In a more recent but smaller scale meta-analysis that examined the risk of psychosis (at the diagnostic level) for repeat offending (be it violent or otherwise), Fazel and Yu (2011) aggregated findings from studies that reported on repeat offending among individuals with psychotic disorders (n = 3511) compared with individuals with other psychiatric disorders (n = 5446) and healthy individuals (n = 71,552).

Individuals with psychotic disorders had a modestly higher risk of repeat offending compared with persons without any psychiatric disorders and a similar risk compared with individuals who had other psychiatric disorders. More specifically, compared to individuals without any psychiatric disorder, there was a significantly increased risk of repeat offending among individuals with psychosis (OR = 1.6), although this was based on only four studies. In contrast, there was no association when individuals with other psychiatric disorders were used as the comparison group (OR = 1.0). Importantly, however, there was substantial heterogeneity among effect sizes, indicating that other variables likely affected the strength and/or direction of the association. Focusing on the narrower outcome of violence, Fazel, Gulati, Linsell, Geddes, and Grann (2009) meta-analyzed results of 20 studies. Risk of violence was elevated among individuals with schizophrenia (OR = 5.5, k = 13) and other psychoses (OR = 4.9, k = 7) compared with the general population controls. Comorbid substance use increased the risk (OR = 8.9; k = 11) compared with general population controls.

Highlighting the importance of considering phase of illness, Large and Nielssen (2011) conducted a meta-analysis of nine studies that focused on first episodes of psychosis. Violence of any severity was associated with hostile affect (OR = 3.52) and symptoms of mania (OR = 2.86). More recently, a review of 20 studies indicated that the first episode of psychosis indicated a period of especially elevated risk for violence (Nielssen, Malhi, McGorry, & Large, 2012).

In a meta-analysis of nine studies reporting risk of violence among individuals with bipolar disorder compared with general population controls (Fazel, Lichtenstein, Grann, Goodwin, & Långström, 2010), odds ratios ranged from 2.2 to 8.9. The pooled random-effects crude odds ratio was 4.1 (95% CI, 2.9–5.8). There was high heterogeneity between studies, indicating that moderating variables likely were present.

An often-cited meta-analysis that produced findings that differed from those of the studies reviewed earlier (Bonta, Law, & Hanson, 1998) aggregated results from prospective studies of mentally disordered offenders, most of whom (70%) were diagnosed with schizophrenia. No significant associations between violence (or general recidivism) and psychotic disorders or mood disorders were observed. The weighted correlation between psychosis and violent recidivism, based on 10 studies, was –0.04, although statistically significant heterogeneity was present. Based on three studies, the weighted correlation between mood disorder and violent recidivism was 0.01. Interpretations of findings from this meta-analysis should take into consideration the likelihood that personality characteristics on the externalizing spectrum likely were more prevalent in this sample, as it comprised only offenders, compared to community samples, which may have served to attenuate the relation between psychosis and violence. In addition, it relied on a small number of studies.

Birth Cohort and Epidemiological Studies

Birth cohort and epidemiological research investigations can offer valuable data because of the longitudinal nature of observations over time and avoidance of selection biases. These types of studies tend to be conducted in countries where national registers are used routinely for tracking outcomes of social interest. Whereas some studies focus on the association between different types of mental disorders and vio-lence in the population at large (e.g., Arseneault, Moffitt, Caspi, Taylor, & Silva, 2000), others focus on factors that elevate risk for violence among individuals with certain disorders, such as schizophrenia (e.g., Cannon et al., 2002; Räsänen et al., 1998). Findings from birth cohort samples from numerous countries provide support that a meaningful association exists between mental disorder and violence. Such studies have been conducted, for example, in Australia (Mullen, Burgess, Wallace, Palmer, & Ruschena, 2000), New Zealand (Arseneault et al., 2000), Scandinavia (Brennan, Mednick, & Hodgins, 2000; Hodgins, 1992; Räsänen et al., 1998; Tiihonen, Isohanni, Räsänen, Koiranen, & Moring, 1997), and Israel (Stueve & Link, 1997).

One of the earlier epidemiological studies involving a community sample that answered questions about violence risk, and perhaps the best-known study conducted in the United States, is the Epidemiologic Catchment Area (ECA) study, funded by the National Institute of Mental Health (Swanson, Holzer, Ganju, & Jono, 1990). This cross-sectional survey measured the prevalence rates of mental disorders in a repre-sentative sample of 17,803 people across five cities. A person was considered to have a mental disorder if she or he met the lifetime criteria as defined in the third edition of the *Diagnostic and Statistical Manual of Mental Disorders* (DSM-III, American Psychiatric Association, 1980) for schizophrenia, bipolar disorder, or major depres-sion and had had active symptoms of that disorder within the previous 12 months. Data on self-reported violence that occurred during the previous year were available for a subset of 10,059 people in three of the sites. Violence was measured using the Diagnostic Interview Schedule (DIS; see Robins, Helzer, Croughan, & Ratcliff, 1981), a structured questionnaire for lay interviewers that is computer coded to generate *DSM-III/R* diagnostic categories. Swanson et al. (1990) used five items from the DIS to define violence: (1) hitting or throwing things at a spouse or partner; (2) spank-ing or hitting a child hard enough to cause bruises; (3) fist fighting since age 18 with someone other than a spouse; (4) using a weapon (e.g., stick, knife, or gun) since age 18; and (5) getting into physical fights while drinking. Individuals were assigned to the "violent" group if they answered at least one item positively. It should be noted that because violent behavior was operationalized using the diagnostic sections of the DIS for alcohol abuse and dependence and antisocial personality disorder, defini-tional confounding could obscure clear interpretations of the data.

Among the main findings from the ECA study were that individuals in the com-munity who met diagnostic criteria for a psychiatric disorder were more likely to have reported engaging in violence compared to those who did not meet diagnostic criteria. More specifically, over half of the 368 persons who reported engaging in violence during the preceding year met criteria for a psychiatric disorder compared to 19.6% of persons who reported not acting violently. Stated another way, indi-viduals with one of the three mental disorders—schizophrenia, bipolar disorder, or major depression—were two to three times as likely as people without a disorder to have engaged in violence during the preceding year. Considering lifetime preva-lence of violence, rates were 16% among people with a mental disorder, but only 7% among people without a mental disorder. Another key finding from this land-mark study was that reported rates of violence were highest among individuals with substance abuse disorders (19.2% to 34.7% depending on the category). Persons with alcohol or drug use disorders were more than twice as likely as those with schizophrenia to report having engaged in violent behavior. Results of multivariate regression analyses yielded a significant interaction effect between major mental illness and substance abuse.

In a follow-up study using data from two of the five ECA sites, Swanson (1993) investigated, among other questions, the explanatory role of alcohol abuse in the relation between mental disorder and violence. In this study, people were defined as having been violent ($n = 193$) if they endorsed one of four DIS items: (1) having used a weapon in a fight since age 18, (2) having been in more than one fight in which blows were swapped since age 18, (3) ever having hit or spanked a child hard enough to injure, and (4) among persons who were married or had lived with someone as if married, ever having hit or thrown things at their partner. In this sample, individuals with major mental illnesses who did not have a co-occurring alcohol abuse disorder had an increased risk of violence. However, those with co-occurring mental illness and substance abuse disorders were at even greater risk of violence.

More recently, Elbogen and Johnson (2009) reported on a longitudinal community-based epidemiological data set of 34,653 individuals in the United States. In this sample, lifetime diagnoses of psychotic disorders, bipolar disorder, and major depression at baseline were not statistically associated with violence measured between baseline and follow-up, except among individuals with comorbid substance abuse or dependence (the authors reported extreme skew in cell frequencies, which could have accounted for the lack of statistical significance, as people with schizophrenia did engage in violence about twice as often as those without). Van Dorn, Volavka, and Johnson (2011) used the same dataset but relied on past year diagnoses. They studied a comparison group comprising healthy individuals without diagnoses of SMD and included additional clinically and theoretically relevant covariates in multivariate analyses. These authors reported a modestly sized statistically significant association between SMD and violence in bivariate (OR = 3.55) and multivariate (OR = 1.60) models. Consistent with Elbogen and Johnson's (2009) findings, Van Dorn et al. (2011) also reported a stronger association for co-occurring diagnoses of substance abuse/dependence than for SMD alone.

In a Swedish birth cohort study covering a 13-year period (between 1988 and 2000) that used national hospital and crime registers, Fazel and Grann (2006) observed that individuals diagnosed with psychotic disorders were approximately four times more likely than the general population to have been convicted of a violent crime. The authors further reported, however, that the population-attributable risk fraction, which is the proportion of violent crimes in the whole population that may be attributed to individuals with severe mental illness, was only 5.2%. Nonetheless, at a population level, this still translates to a meaningful number of violent incidents.

Reporting on a Danish birth cohort of more than 358,000 individuals, Brennan et al. (2000) concluded that, after controlling for the potentially confounding factor of low SES, the risk for violent offending for men with schizophrenia was 4.6 times higher than that of the general population. For women, the risk was 23.2 times higher. Earlier publications of birth cohort studies conducted in Europe (e.g., Hodgins, Mednick, Brennan, Schulsinger, & Engberg, 1996; Tiihonen et al., 1997) also provided evidence of significant associations between mental illness and violence. As noted by many authors of the European studies, their findings may not be generalizable to the United States, where crime rates are relatively higher than in most industrialized Western countries. Nonetheless, results of the European studies offer results similar to most studies conducted in the United States.

Primary, Large-Scale Studies

Rigorously completed prevalence studies of mental illness in correctional settings also have the potential to offer valuable information. Fazel and Danesh (2002) conducted a systematic review of psychiatric surveys based on interviews of unselected prison populations on serious mental disorders (psychotic illnesses or major depression within the previous 6 months, or a history of any personality disorder). The authors examined 62 surveys from 12 countries, representing 22,790 prisoners; most (81%) were men. Among the men, 3.7% had psychotic illnesses, 10% had major depression, and 65% had a personality disorder (most frequently, antisocial personality disorder, at 47%). Of the women, 4.0% had psychotic illnesses, 12% major depression, and 42% a personality disorder, including 21% with antisocial personality disorder. Prisoners were several times more likely to have psychosis and major depression, and about 10 times more likely to have antisocial personality disorder, than the general population. Similarly, high rates of mental disorders have been observed among adolescents in detention and correctional facilities (e.g., Fazel, Doll, & Långström, 2008; Vincent, Grisso, Terry, & Banks, 2008).

Baillargeon, Binswanger, Penn, Williams, and Murray (2009) completed a retrospective cohort study comprising all inmates (N = 79, 211) who began serving sentences between September 1, 2006, and August 31, 2007 in any of the 116 state correctional facilities in Texas, the state with the largest prison population. The authors compared the prevalence of having multiple episodes of incarceration during the preceding 6-year period among inmates with any of four types of SMD (major depressive disorder, bipolar disorders, schizophrenia, or nonschizophrenic psychotic disorders). Inmates in all of the disorder groups had substantially increased risks of multiple incarcerations. The greatest increase in risk was observed among individuals with bipolar disorders, who were 3.3 times more likely to have had four or more previous incarcerations compared to inmates without a disorder.

A recent study in the United States of 1,410 patients with schizophrenia receiving treatment at one of 57 mental health sites in 24 states (Swanson et al., 2006) found that positive symptoms of schizophrenia were associated with minor and serious forms of violence, even after controlling for several possible confounds and covariates. High negative psychotic symptoms were significantly associated with *reduced* risk of serious violence. Additional analyses uncovered an interaction effect. Compared to individuals with below-median scores on both positive and negative symptoms, those with above-median positive and below-median negative symptoms had a significantly elevated risk for serious violence (OR = 3.05); those with above-median positive and above-median negative symptoms were not more violent (OR = 0.95); and those with below-median positive and above-median negative symptoms were less violent (OR = 0.12). In addition, interactions were observed for some combinations of symptoms. Risk for serious violence was elevated when delusional thinking co-occurred with suspiciousness/persecutory ideation. Above-median scores on scales assessing general delusions and suspiciousness/persecution elevated risk by a factor of 2.9 for serious violence compared with below-median scores.

In a longitudinal investigation using general population and unaffected sibling controls, Fazel, Lichtenstein, et al. (2010) examined the association between bipolar disorder and violent crime. Studying 3,743 individuals, the authors found evidence of an increased risk for violent crime among disordered individuals; most of the elevated risk was associated with substance abuse comorbidity. However, even among unaffected siblings of individuals with bipolar disorder, increased risk for violent crime was observed, suggesting that shared genetic vulnerability or common elements of the early social environment in families with bipolar disorder are influential to the elevated risk for violence, rather than the presence of bipolar disorder per se.

Threat/control-override (TCO) delusions comprise a subgroup of positive symptoms that has received particular empirical attention. Individuals with TCO symptoms feel threatened and experience their internal controls to be compromised (e.g., believe that their mind is dominated by external forces out of their control and/or believe that forces can insert or remove thoughts from their mind). On the whole, available research suggests that these types of symptoms are associated with an elevated risk for violence (e.g., Hodgins Hiscoke, & Freese, 2003; Link, Monahan, Stueve, & Cullen, 1999; Link & Stueve, 1994; Link, Stueve, & Phelan, 1998; McNiel, Eisner, & Binder, 2003; Stompe, Ortwein-Swoboda, & Schanda, 2004; Stueve & Link, 1997; Swanson, Borum, Swartz, & Monahan, 1996; cf. Appelbaum, Robbins, & Monahan, 2000; Monahan et al., 2001; Skeem et al., 2006). In their meta-analysis, Douglas et al. (2009) found that TCO symptoms were significantly different than chance (Mdn OR = 1.92; Z = 3.09, p = .002).

In a repeated measures evaluation, Hodgins et al. (2003) reported that an increase in TCO symptoms between two assessment periods was associated with a roughly 10-fold increase in risk of violence during the subsequent 6-month period. Studying the distinct types of TCO symptoms separately, Nederlof, Muris, and Hovens (2011) conducted a cross-sectional investigation of 124 inpatients in three psychiatric hospitals in the Netherlands. They reported that the threat component but not the control/override component was correlated with scores on the Dutch version (Meesters, Muris Bosma, Schouten, & Beuving, 1996) of Buss and Perry's (1992) Aggression Questionnaire (after controlling for other known risk factors). The authors concluded that threat ideation and feelings were associated with a possible subsequent defensive response, which could be expressed through aggression, whereas feelings of losing control could be associated with feeling helpless, which could thwart violence.

The Comparative Study of the Prevention of Crime and Violence by Mentally Ill Persons (see Hodgins et al., 2007) also studied TCO delusions, as well as other types of psychotic symptoms. This prospective, repeated measures project studied individuals diagnosed with schizophrenia or schizoaffective disorder who were discharged from civil and forensic psychiatric hospitals in Canada, Finland, Germany, and Sweden. Hodgins et al. (2003) examined the association between violence and symptoms of psychosis, depression, and anxiety measured at the beginning of two 6-month periods among 128 men living in the community. General positive and negative psychotic symptoms were assessed using the Positive and Negative Syndrome Scale (Kay, Fiszbein, & Opler, 1987). TCO symptoms were assessed using the Psychiatric Epidemiology Instrument (see Link & Stueve, 1994). During the first 6 months, severe positive symptoms substantially increased risk for violence (OR = 5.10) after controlling for the presence of a score of 25 or higher on the Psychopathy Checklist-Revised (Hare, 2003) and substance abuse/dependence diagnoses. Significant (adjusted) odds ratios also were found for other clinical conditions, including anxiety (2.01), depression (4.01), and negative psychotic

(2.03) symptoms. During the second 6-month period, several symptoms—and increases in those symptoms—were strongly associated with violence. For example, an increase in TCO symptoms between the first and second assessment increased violence 10-fold (OR adjusted = 10.64). The presence of any positive symptom (OR = 6.51) and an increase in positive symptoms (OR = 2.08) also were associated with violence in the second period. Significant findings also were obtained for anxiety (OR = 3.16), depression (OR = 4.36), and negative psychotic (OR = 2.36) symptoms. In subsequent analyses (Hodgins & Riaz, 2011) using an expanded sample (N = 251), multivariate analyses indicated that risk of violence in the preceding 6 months was increased 2.77 times by each TCO symptom, 1.73 times by each positive symptom, and 1.14 times by each increase of one point on a depression scale.

Coid and colleagues (2013) studied the link between delusions and violence in the year prior to first contact with mental health services among 458 individuals with first episodes of psychosis in inner-city areas in London, England. They investigated 32 specific delusions and four delusional characteristics and their associations with anger during the previous year. Anger stemming from delusions was associated with minor and serious violence even after statistical adjustments. Mixed findings regarding TCO symptoms were observed: Although there was a strong association between serious violence and persecutory delusions (which suggests feeling threatened), delusions of replaced control (indicative of control-override delusions) were not associated with violence. Coid et al. also found support for the predictive validity for serious violence of several specific delusions, even after adjustments for age, gender, ethnicity, comorbid ASPD, and drug use: delusions of being spied on (OR = 2.49), persecutory delusions (OR = 2.33), and delusions of conspiracy (OR = 2.73). When anger due to delusions was modeled as a covariate, these effects were eliminated, suggesting that anger stemming from delusions acted as the primary drive to serious violence. These findings are in line with earlier theorizing that negative affect and threatening perceptions associated with delusions are the key to understanding their link to violence (Junginger, 1996; Junginger & McGuire, 2004; Taylor, 1998).

As noted earlier, high-quality studies have been completed that have yielded conclusions opposite to those of research studies reviewed earlier; that is, major mental disorder does not have a substantial association with violence to others. The MacArthur Violence Risk Assessment Study (Appelbaum et al., 2000; Monahan et al., 2001), which is perhaps the most methodologically rigorous community-based study conducted to date in the United States, provided data consistent with such conclusions. The sample comprised psychiatric patients between the ages of 18 and 40 who had a chart diagnosis of thought or affective disorder, substance abuse, or personality disorder and who were discharged from acute civil inpatient facilities in three states. The researchers used four sources of information to gather data about violence in the community: interviews with patients, interviews with collateral individuals, and arrest and hospital records. Patients and collateral contacts were interviewed twice (every 10 weeks) following the patient's discharge from the hospital. Violence to others in the past 10 weeks was defined to include acts of battery that resulted in physical injury; sexual assaults; assaultive acts that involved use of a weapon; or threats made with a weapon in hand. The investigators found that having a diagnosis of a major mental disorder—especially a diagnosis of schizophrenia—was associated with a statistically significantly lower rate of violence than a diagnosis of a personality or adjustment disorder (although it should be noted that people with paranoid schizophrenia were more likely to not take part in the study). The 1-year prevalence rate of violence was 14.8% for patients with schizophrenia, but 28.5% for patients with depression and 22% for patients with bipolar disorder.

A co-occurring diagnosis of substance abuse was strongly predictive of violence: 31.1% of people who had both a substance abuse disorder and a major mental disorder committed at least one act of violence in a year, compared with 17.9% of people with a psychiatric disorder alone. The highest rate of violence (43%) was among patients with a diagnosis of a personality or adjustment disorder as well as a substance abuse disorder. In a supplement to the larger study (MacArthur Community Violence Risk Study; Steadman et al., 1998) designed to compare the rate of violence among former psychiatric patients with the rate of violence committed by other members of the community, researchers included a stratified random sample of 519 people living in the same neighborhoods in which the discharged patients resided. Discharged patients without diagnoses of alcohol or drug abuse were no more likely to commit violence than were their neighbors who did not have substance abuse problems. The important role of substance use was highlighted in this study, in that the prevalence of violence was higher among people who had symptoms of substance abuse in both the discharged psychiatric patient and nonpatient groups.

Subsequent analyses of data from the MacArthur Violence Risk Assessment Study revealed an association between certain symptoms of mental disorder and violence. Yang, Mulvey, Loughran, and Hanusa (2012) examined affective and positive psychotic symptoms and alcohol use among individuals with a primary diagnosis of depression ($N = 386$) or a psychotic disorder ($N = 201$) in that dataset. Their findings highlighted the importance of considering the association between symptoms and alcohol use within the context of an individual's primary diagnosis when assessing risk for violence to others (measured after 10 weeks). Yang et al. (2012) found that, among individuals with depression, affective symptoms (OR = 1.08) and alcohol use (OR = 2.66) were associated with increased risk for violence. Among individuals with depression but low alcohol use, affective symptoms increased risk of violence (OR = 0.95; despite being less than 1, this odds ratio indicates a positive association; it is negative because "although alcohol use and affective symptoms each increased the risk of violence, together they increased risk less than alcohol alone in this diagnostic group," p. 267). Among those with psychotic disorders, violence was associated only with alcohol use (OR = 1.59); there was no interaction between alcohol use and either type of symptom. Alcohol use and affective symptoms each increased the risk of violence, but together they increased risk less than alcohol use alone.

Initial analyses from the MacArthur Violence Risk Assessment Study indicated that the presence of delusions—including TCO delusions—was not associated with higher rates of violence (Monahan et al., 2001). However, in subsequent analyses, Teasdale, Silver, and Monahan (2006) found significant effects for the threat component and the combined TCO symptom construct among men, but not women. More specifically, the authors reported a significant interaction between gender and threat (OR = 1.55): Men were more likely to be violent when they experienced threat delusions compared with when they did not experience threat delusions, whereas women were less likely to be violent when they experienced threat delusions compared with when they did not. Considering both threat and control-override symptoms concurrently, Teasdale et al. (2006) reported that women were more likely to be violent when they were experiencing a TCO delusion compared with when they were not. However, there was no association between violence and TCO symptoms among men. When control-override delusions were studied independently of the threat component, neither a main effect nor a gender interaction effect was observed. The authors concluded that men may be more likely to respond to threat delusions but less likely to respond to control-override delusions with violence (thereby cancelling out the effect of the combined TCO measure). In other analyses using this data set, associations between violence and command hallucinations to do harm were observed (Monahan et al., 2001). Thus, in this influential study, mental disorder *at the diagnostic level* was not strongly related to violence in the absence of substance use disorders. It did interact with substance use disorders, however. And further, several specific symptoms and symptom features were associated with violence.

PATHWAYS TO VIOLENCE

In what ways could major mental disorder elevate a person's risk for engaging in violence toward others? Research conducted to date offers several promising avenues to explore. Decision theory of violence posits that risk factors can have at least three functional roles regarding one's decision to perpetrate violence. Within this framework, major mental disorder (and the symptoms thereof) could motivate, disinhibit, or destabilize decisions. Broadly, it is possible that major mental disorder could be a cause, correlate, or consequence of violence. For any given individual, major mental disorder may contribute to violence via one or several distinct pathways.

Mental Disorder As a Cause of Violence

Perhaps the most obvious way in which major mental disorder and violence could be associated is via a direct, causal link, although it is likely that only a small proportion of violence committed by people with major mental disorder would occur in this manner. Under this model, certain diagnoses, syndromes, or specific symptoms (most often, positive psychotic symptoms) would lead directly to perpetration of violence.

Several situations could arise in which symptoms of mental disorder could act as a motivator for violence, such that violence is viewed as a rewarding behavior. Junginger (1996) posited that violence stemming from "psychotic action" is more likely when the themes and content of delusions and hallucinations involve violence, and some empirical findings suggest that individuals with psychosis can be motivated to act violently directly by delusions and hallucinations (e.g., Junginger, Parks-Levy, & McGuire, 1998; Taylor et al., 1998). Focusing on the role of TCO symptoms, Link and Stueve (1994; Link, Andrews, & Cullen, 1992) argued that the primary cause of violence among individuals with psychosis is feeling threatened by or losing control to an external force. They advanced the "principle of rationality—within irrationality" (1995, p. 143; see also Thomas & Thomas, 1928, p. 572). That is, if one accepts that an individual perceives her delusional experience to be "real," her actions and beliefs would be logically consistent with one another. As an example of this principle and of major mental disorder acting as a motivator for violence, if an individual with psychosis feels threatened, and when her internal controls are compromised, violence becomes more explicable as a response in service of self-defense or retribution against harmful actions she believes are being directed toward her. Regarding gender differences, Teasdale et al.'s (2006) findings on the TCO delusions-violence link are consistent with the idea that women engage in "tend-and-befriend" coping strategies, rather than violence, in response to threat delusions, whereas men respond with "fight-or-flight" strategies, including violence.

Mental disorder would act as a disinhibitor for an individual if his symptoms made him less likely to be influenced by intrinsic or extrinsic "checks" against violence. For example, severe depression could lead an individual to become so preoccupied with her own problems so as to become less concerned with or aware of the consequences or costs associated with violence. As another example, lack of insight, a common symptom among individuals with psychotic disorders, could lead to devaluing the costs one may perceive to be associated with engaging in violence because the person's understanding of consequences of their behavior could be compromised. Finally, symptoms of mental disorders could act as a destabilizer if they interfered with an individual's ability to monitor and control decision making (e.g., as does emotional dysregulation and many cognitive-related symptoms of psychosis and major mood disorders), such as within the context of managing interpersonal conflicts. Hiday's (1997; see also Hiday, 1995, 2006) theory is relevant to this point; she hypothesized that one of the indirect pathways from severe mental disorder to violence was through bizarre and/or annoying symptoms that could lead to tense situations that, in the context of the other variables, could lead to violence. For example, symptoms that involve an individual acting bizarrely could invite efforts from friends or family members to bring the person's behavior in line with social norms, which could escalate to aggression if the person resisted. Another way in which tense interpersonal encounters could lead to physical aggression is if impairments in thought, behavior, or affect (e.g., extreme hostility, difficult-to-follow speech, labile mood) frustrated individuals experiencing such symptoms or the people with whom they interacted, thereby increasing the likelihood that one or more of the individuals will react violently. Baxter's (1997) notion of the link between psychosis and "disorganized/impulsive" violence and crime would be relevant to this point as well.

Mental Disorder As a Correlate of Violence

Another way in which mental disorder and violence could be related is via associations with other variables. Research on the possible role of such variables has been undertaken from ecological (Silver, Mulvey, & Monahan, 1999), social psychological (Andrews & Bonta, 1994), and criminological (e.g., Silver, 2006) perspectives. As one example, individuals with mental disorder tend to be at least partially dependent on others for financial, social, and/or emotional support

(Estroff, Zimmer, Lachiotte, & Benoit, 1991; Hiday, 1995); such dependency can heighten conflict in relationships that escalates to violence. Relationships with family members or other key people in the social networks of individuals with major mental disorder may lead to physical conflict associated with attempts to provide care, especially if the individual perceives the "help" as being coercive (Monahan et al., 1999; see also Silver, 2006). Some research suggests that mandated interventions provided by a close friend or family member could elicit feelings of anger, fear, or resentment that could escalate to violence (see, e.g., Elbogen et al., 2005).

Another example of a third variable that has been investigated within the context of the mental disorder–violence link is stress—namely, the (in)ability of some individuals with serious mental disorders to cope with stress. Silver and Teasdale (2005) found that the combination of impaired social support and the occurrence of stressful life events such as major changes in living situation, employment, or relationships explained a significant portion of the association between violence and major mental and substance use disorders. In addition, Hiday's (1997) theory regarding the contributory role of stressful social interactions leading to tense interpersonal situations would be relevant here. Related to interpersonal relationships, should such relationships erode or disappear—perhaps because of repeated stressful interactions—the social support that otherwise would have been available to an individual with major mental disorder would disappear, thereby indirectly increasing risk for violence (see, e.g., Silver & Teasdale, 2005).

An important point to make within this section is that mental disorder may be associated with numerous other factors that in turn are associated with violence. Even if the association is "indirect," therefore, it is still crucial in terms of understanding a complex interplay of multiple factors that, in totality, can lead to violence. Such indirect associations are hence still vital to understand in order to manage and ultimately reduce violence (for instance, a well-managed SMD could result in less stress or fewer tense interpersonal situations, and hence a lower probability of violence).

Mental Disorder As a Consequence of Violence

Although likely relatively rare, it is possible that, among individuals who are so predisposed, the stress associated with behaving violently could cause psychiatric decompensation or exacerbate symptoms of a disorder an individual already may be experiencing. Some research evidence supports this possible pathway to violence among civilians (Evans, Ehlers, Mezey, & Clark, 2007) and members of the military (see Elbogen et al., 2010) who developed post-traumatic stress disorder.

IMPLICATIONS AND CONCLUSIONS

Based on the review and discussion herein, a number of concluding points can be made. First, in general, we conclude that there is a small though meaningful connection between SMD and violence. However, this is a very broad level of analysis and hence may not be terribly helpful. Second, the association between SMD and violence is complex. Its strength appears to differ as a function of a number of disorder- and context-related variables. For instance, associations tend to be stronger when people with SMD are compared to people with no disorders at all or to people with internalizing disorders. Relative to externalizing disorders, SMD appears to not *further* elevate the odds of violence. In addition, it appears that certain specific symptom clusters are more important than others in terms of elevating the risk for violence. Positive symptoms, manic symptoms, symptoms involving perceived threat, and those that are associated with anger and other negative affects seem particularly important.

Third, the connection between SMD and violence may be explained through numerous mechanisms—some of which are direct, and some of which are indirect. SMD, by its very nature, tends to impact most areas of a person's functioning (i.e., cognitive, emotional, behavioral, interpersonal, vocational). Hence, it is important to attempt to understand the role of mental disorder in *context*. It does not operate independently of other aspects of a person's life. Therefore, consideration of how it affects other potentially risk-elevating factors (e.g., stress; lack of social support; employment problems) is vital. In a related manner, we make the basic point that risk factors for violence, generally (i.e., those that are important in any sample, disordered or otherwise), are still risk factors for violence among people with SMD (Bonta et al., 1998; Eriksson, Romelsjö, Stenbacka, & Tengström, 2011; Large & Nielssen, 2011; Skeem, Manchak, & Peterson, 2011). This does not reduce the importance that certain features of mental disorder might have in terms of understanding violence, but it just underscores the point that when trying to understand the link between SMD and violence, one simply cannot look only to the disorder itself.

In terms of clinical implications, we would argue that any comprehensive violence risk assessment must consider mental disorder. The evidence base overwhelmingly indicates that, at the very least, it may elevate risk when present. Evaluators should focus on the features of disorder that we have identified earlier but also should consider how SMD impacts an evaluee's other areas of functioning. We would also point out that the mere fact that SMD is present for a given person does not perforce portend ineluctable violence. That is, even if present, it may not be highly relevant for all people. Most contemporary models of violence risk assessment encourage evaluators to determine whether risk factors with support at the nomological level also operate or are relevant at the idiographic level (Douglas, Hart, Webster, & Belfrage, 2013; Hart et al., 2003). The task for the clinician is to determine how SMD might influence risk, and then to take steps to manage that risk (see also Douglas et al., 2014; Douglas, Hart, Groscup, & Litwack, 2013; Guy, Douglas, & Hart, in press).

From a policy perspective, we would argue that agencies and systems that are legally responsible for protecting staff or public safety also must include SMD in their decision-making systems concerning risk. These decisions should take place at entry to a system, within a system (e.g., when considering lower security placements), and upon release from an institution to a community setting. The logic here is the same as it is for individual clinicians—the potential risk-enhancing role to which SMD might give rise needs to be considered, if only to rule it out.

Finally, from a research perspective, there still are numerous topics that warrant consideration. Much has been learned regarding patterns of findings from the meta-analytic studies reviewed earlier. We would recommend more focus on theory-based research questions, such as those posed by Hiday (1997), Junginger (2006), and others. Determining the complex sets of transactions between mental disorder and other life domains will further refine our understanding of the ways in which SMD might play either a direct or indirect role in violence. We also would encourage further work on studying the specific features of SMD itself that are risk enhancing (e.g., types of symptoms; phases of illness). Finally, most research has not paid due attention to the dimensions of violence that might be most influenced by SMD. For instance, we know that family members are more likely to be targeted than are strangers (Estroff et al., 1991; Estroff et al., 1998), and that SMD tends to elevate the risk for both minor and serious forms of violence (e.g., Swanson et al., 2006). However, we have less knowledge about the association between features of SMD and other dimensions of violence, such as motivations, imminence, and goals.

REFERENCES

American Psychiatric Association. (1980). *Diagnostic and statistical manual of mental disorders* (3rd ed.). Washington, DC: Author.

Andrews, D. A., & Bonta, J. (1994). *The psychology of criminal conduct.* Cincinnati: Anderson.

Appelbaum, P. S., Robbins, P. C., & Monahan, J. (2000). Violence and delusions: Data from the MacArthur Violence Risk Assessment Study. *American Journal of Psychiatry, 157,* 566–572.

Appleby, L., Mortensen, P. B., Dunn, G., & Hiroeh, U. (2001). Death by homicide, suicide, and other unnatural causes in people with mental illness: A population-based study. *Lancet, 358,* 2110–2112.

Arseneault, L., Moffitt, T. E., Caspi, A., Taylor, P. J., & Silva, P. A. (2000). Mental disorders and violence in a total birth cohort: Results from the Dunedin study. *Archives of General Psychiatry, 57,* 979–986.

Baillargeon, J., Binswanger, I. A., Penn, J. V., Williams, B. A., & Murray, O. J. (2009). Psychiatric disorders and repeat incarcerations: The revolving prison door. *American Journal of Psychiatry, 166,* 103–109.

Baxter, R. (1997). Violence in schizophrenia and the syndrome of disorganisation. *Criminal Behaviour and Mental Health, 7,* 131–139.

Bonta, J., Law, M., & Hanson, K. (1998). The prediction of criminal and violent recidivism among mentally disordered offenders: A meta-analysis. *Psychological Bulletin, 123,* 123–142.

Brennan, P. A., Mednick, S. A., & Hodgins, S. (2000). Major mental disorders and criminal violence in a Danish birth cohort. *Archives of General Psychiatry, 57,* 494–500.

Buss, A. H., & Perry, M. P. (1992). The aggression questionnaire. *Journal of Personality and Social Psychology, 63,* 452–459.

Cannon, M., Huttunen, M. O., Tanskanen, A. J., Arseneault, L., Jones, P. B., & Murray, R. M. (2002). Perinatal and childhood risk factors for later criminality and violence in schizophrenia: Longitudinal, population-based study. *British Journal of Psychiatry, 180,* 496–501.

Cocozza, J. J., & Steadman, H. J. (1976). The failure of psychiatric predictions of dangerousness: Clear and convincing evidence. *Rutgers Law Review, 29,* 1084–1101.

Coid, J. W., Ullrich, S., Kallis,C., Keers, R., Barker, D., Cowden, F., & Stamps, R. (2013). The relationship between delusions and violence: Findings from the East London first episode psychosis study. *JAMA Psychiatry,* 1-7. doi:10.1001/jamapsychiatry.2013.12.

Corrigan, P.W., & O'Shaughnessy, J.R. (2007). Changing mental illness stigma as it exists in the real world. *Australian Psychologist, 42*, 90–97.

Corrigan, P. W., & Penn, D. L. (1999). Lessons from social psychology on discrediting psychiatric stigma. *American Psychologist, 54*, 765–776.

Corrigan, P. W., Rowan, D., Green, A., Lundin, R., River, P., Uphoff-Wasowski, K., … Kubiak, M. A. (2002). Challenging two mental illness stigmas: Personal responsibility and dangerousness. *Schizophrenia Bulletin, 28*, 293–310.

Douglas, K. S., Guy, L. S., & Hart, S. D. (2009). Psychosis as a risk factor for violence to others: A meta-analysis. *Psychological Bulletin, 135*, 679–706.

Douglas, K. S., Hart, S. D., Groscup, J. L., & Litwack, T. R. (2013). Assessing violence risk. In I. B. Weiner & R. K. Otto (Eds.), *The Handbook of Forensic Psychology, 4th Edition* (pp. 385–441). New York: Wiley.

Douglas, K. S., Hart, S. D., Webster, C. D., Belfrage, H., & Eaves, D. (2013). *HCR-20: Assessing risk for violence, Version 3*. Simon Fraser University, British Columbia, Burnaby.

Douglas, K. S., Hart, S. D., Webster, C. D., Belfrage, H., Guy, L. S., & Wilson, C. M. (2014). Historical-Clinical-Risk Management-20, Version 3 (HCR-20V3): Development and Overview. *International Journal of Forensic Mental Health Services, 13*, 93–108.

Elbogen, E. B., & Johnson, S. C. (2009). The intricate link between violence and mental disorder: Results from the national epidemiologic survey on alcohol and related condition. *Archives of General Psychiatry, 66*, 152–161.

Elbogen, E. B., Swanson, J. W., Swartz, M. S., & Van Dorn, R. (2005). Family representative payeeship and violence risk in severe mental illness. *Law and Human Behavior, 29*, 563–574.

Elbogen, E. B., Fuller, S., Johnson, S. C., Brooks, S., Kinneer, P., Calhoun, P. S., & Beckham, J. C. (2010). Improving risk assessment of violence among military Veterans: An evidence-based approach for clinical decision-making. *Clinical Psychology Review, 30*, 595–607.

Eriksson, A., Romelsjö, A., Stenbacka, M., & Tengström, A. (2011). Early risk factors for criminal offending in schizophrenia: A 35-year longitudinal cohort study. *Social Psychiatry and Psychiatric Epidemiology, 46*, 925–932.

Estroff, S., Zimmer, C., Lachiotte, W., & Benoit, J. (1991). The influence of social networks and social support on violence by persons with serious mental illness. *Hospital and Community Psychiatry, 45*, 669–678.

Estroff, S. E., Swanson, J. W., Lachicotte, W. S., Swartz, M., & Bolduc, M. (1998). Risk reconsidered: Targets of violence in the social networks of people with serious psychiatric disorders. *Social Psychiatry and Psychiatric Epidemiology, 33*, 95–101.

Evans, C., Ehlers A., Mezey G., & Clark, D. M. (2007). Intrusive memories in perpetrators of violent crimes: Emotions and cognitions. *Journal of Consulting and Clinical Psychology, 75*, 134–144.

Evans-Lacko, S., Brohan, E., Mojtabai, R., & Thornicroft, G. (2012). Association between public views of mental illness and self-stigma among individuals with mental illness in 14 European countries. *Psychological Medicine, 42*, 1741–1752.

Fazel, S., & Danesh, J. (2002). Serious mental disorder in 23000 prisoners: A systematic review of 62 surveys. *Lancet, 359*, 545–550.

Fazel, S., & Doll, H., & Långström, N. (2008) Mental disorders among adolescents in juvenile detention and correctional facilities: A systematic review and metaregression analysis of 25 surveys. *Journal of American Academy of Child and Adolescent Psychiatry, 47*, 1010–1019.

Fazel, S., & Grann, M. (2006). The population impact of severe mental illness on violent crime. *American Journal of Psychiatry, 163*, 1397–1403.

Fazel, S., Gulati, G., Linsell, L., Geddes, J. R., & Grann, M. (2009). Schizophrenia and violence: Systematic review and meta-analysis. *PLoS Med, 6*, 8. doi:10.1371/journal. pmed.1000120

Fazel, S., Lichtenstein, P., Grann, M., Goodwin, G. M., & Långström, N. (2010). Bipolar disorder and violent crime: New evidence from population-based longitudinal studies and systematic review. *Archives of General Psychiatry, 67*, 931–938.

Fazel, S., & Yu, R. (2011). Psychotic disorders and repeat offending: Systematic review and meta-analysis. *Schizophrenia Bulletin, 37*, 800–810.

Ferriman, A. (2000). The stigma of schizophrenia. *British Medical Journal, 320*, 522.

Foucha v. Louisiana, 504 U.S. 71 (1992).

Guy, L. S., Hart, S. D., & Douglas, K. S. (in press). Risk assessment and communication. In B. Cutler & P. Zapf (Eds.), *APA handbook of forensic psychology*. Washington, DC: American Psychological Association.

Hare, R. D. (2003). *The Revised Psychopathy Checklist*. Toronto, ON: Multi-Health Systems.

Hart, S. D., Kropp, P. R., Laws, D. R., Klaver, J., Logan, C., & Watt, K. A. (2003). *The risk for sexual violence protocol (RSVP): Structured professional guidelines for assessing risk of sexual violence*. Vancouver, BC: The Mental Health, Law, and Policy Institute, Simon Fraser University, Pacific Psychological Assessment Corporation, British Columbia Institute Against Family Violence.

Heron, M. (2012). Deaths: Leading causes for 2009. *National Vital Statistics Reports, 61*(7). Retreived January 2013, from www.cdc.gov/nchs/data/nvsr/nvsr61/nvsr61_07. pdf.

Hiday, V. A. (1995). The social context of mental illness and violence. *Journal of Health and Social Behavior, 36*, 122–137.

Hiday, V. A. (1997). Understanding the connection between mental illness and violence. *International Journal of Law and Psychiatry, 20*, 399–417.

Hiday, V. A. (2006). Putting community risk in perspective: A look at correlations, causes and controls. *International Journal of Law and Psychiatry, 29*, 316–331.

Hiday, V. A., Swartz, M. S., Swanson, J. W., Borum R., & Wagner, H. R. (1999). Criminal victimization of persons with severe mental illness. *Psychiatric Services, 50*, 62–68.

Hodgins, S. (1992). Mental disorder, intellectual deficiency, and crime. Evidence from a birth cohort. *Archives of General Psychiatry, 49*, 476–483.

Hodgins, S., Hiscoke, U. L., & Freese, R. (2003). The antecedents of aggressive behavior among men with schizophrenia: A prospective investigation of patients in community treatment. *Behavioral Sciences and the Law, 21*, 523–546.

Hodgins, S., Mednick, S. A., Brennan, P. A., Schulsinger, F., & Engberg, M. (1996). Mental disorder and crime. *Archives of General Psychiatry, 53*, 489–496.

Hodgins, S., Muller-Isberner, R., Tiihonen, J., Repo-Tiihonem, E., Eronen, M., Eaves, D., ... Kronstrand, R. (2007). A comparison of general and forensic patients with schizophrenia living in the community. *International Journal of Forensic Mental Health, 6*, 63–75.

Hodgins, S., & Riaz, M. (2011). Violence and phases of illness: Differential risk and predictors. *European Psychiatry, 26*, 518–524.

Jablonski v. U.S., 712 F.2d 391 (9th Cir. 1983).

Junginger, J. (1996). Psychosis and violence: The case for a content analysis of psychotic experience. *Schizophrenia Bulletin, 22*, 91–103.

Junginger, J. (2006). "Stereotypic" delusional offending. *Behavioral Sciences & the Law, 24*, 295–311.

Junginger, J., & McGuire, L. (2004). Psychotic motivation and the paradox of current research on serious mental illness and rates of violence. *Schizophrenia Bulletin, 30*, 21–30.

Junginger, J., Parks-Levy, J., & McGuire, L. (1998). Delusions and symptom-consistent violence. *Psychiatric Services, 49*, 218–220.

Kansas v. Hendricks 521 US 346 (1997).

Kay, S. R., Fiszbein, A., & Opler, L. A. (1987). The positive and negative syndrome scale (PANSS) for schizophrenia. *Schizophrenia Bulletin, 13*, 261–276.

Large, M., & Nielssen, O. (2011). Violence in first-episode psychosis: A systematic review and meta-analysis. *Schizophrenia Research, 125*, 209–220.

Link, B. G., Andrews, H., & Cullen, F. T. (1992). The violent and illegal behavior of mental patients reconsidered. *American Sociological Review, 57*, 275–292.

Link, B. G., Monahan, J., Stueve, A., & Cullen, F. T. (1999). Real in their consequences: A sociological approach to understanding the association between psychotic symptoms and violence. *American Sociological Review, 64*, 316–332.

Link, B. G., & Stueve, A. (1994). Psychotic symptoms and the violent/illegal behavior of mental patients compared to community controls. In J. Monahan & H. J. Steadman (Eds.), *Violence and mental disorder: Developments in risk assessment* (pp. 137–159). Chicago, IL: University of Chicago Press.

Link, B. G., Stueve, A., & Phelan, J. (1998). Psychotic symptoms and violent behaviors: Probing the components of 'threat/control-override' symptoms. *Social Psychiatry and Psychiatric Epidemiology, 33*, S55–SS60.

Lipari v. Sears Roebuck, 497 F.Supp. 185 (1980).

McNiel, D. E., Eisner, J. P., & Binder, R. L. (2003). The relationship between aggressive attributional style and violence by psychiatric patients. *Journal of Consulting and Clinical Psychology, 71*, 399–403.

Meesters, C., Muris, P., Bosma, H., Schouten, E., & Beuving, S. (1996). Psychometric evaluation of the Dutch version of the Aggression Questionnaire. *Behavior Research and Therapy, 34*, 839–843.

Monahan, J. (1981). *Predicting violent behavior: An assessment of clinical techniques.* Beverley Hills, CA: Sage.

Monahan, J. (1992). Mental disorder and violent behavior. *American Psychologist, 47*, 511–521.

Monahan, J. (1993). Mental disorder and violence: Another look. In S. Hodgins (Ed.), *Mental Disorder and Crime* (pp. 287–302). Newbury Park, CA: Sage.

Monahan, J., Lidz, C., Hoge, S., Mulvey, E., Eisenberg, M., Roth, L., ... Bennett, N. (1999). Coercion in the provision of mental health services: The MacArthur studies. In J. Morrissey & J. Monahan (Eds.), *Research in community and mental health, Vol. 10: Coercion in mental health services—international perspectives* (pp. 13–30). Stamford, CT: JAI Press.

Monahan, J., & Steadman, H. J. (1983). Crime and mental disorder: An epidemiological approach. In M. Tonry & N. Morris (Eds.), *Review of research* (pp. 145–189). Chicago, IL: University of Chicago Press.

Monahan, J., & Steadman, H. J. (1994). *Violence and mental disorder: Developments in risk assessment.* Chicago, IL: University of Chicago Press.

Monahan, J., Steadman, H. J., Silver, E., Appelbaum, P. S., Robbins, P. C., Mulvey, E. P., … Banks, S. (2001). *Rethinking risk assessment: The MacArthur study of mental disorder and violence.* New York, NY: Oxford University Press.

Mullen, P. E., Burgess, P., Wallace, C., Palmer, S., & Ruschena, D. (2000). Community care and criminal offending in schizophrenia. *Lancet, 355,* 614–617.

Mulvey, E. P. (1994). Assessing the evidence of a link between mental illness and violence. *Hospital and Community Psychiatry, 45,* 663–668.

Nederlof, A. F., Muris, P., & Hovens, J. E. (2011). Threat/control-override symptoms and emotional reactions to positive symptoms as correlates of aggressive behavior in psychotic patients. *Journal of Nervous and Mental Disease, 199,* 342–347.

Nicholls, T. L., Brink, J., Desmarais, S. L., Webster, C. D., & Martin, M. (2006). The Short Term Assessment of Risk and Treatability (START): A prospective validation study in a forensic psychiatric sample. *Assessment, 13,* 313–327.

Nielssen, O., Malhi, G., McGorry, P., & Large, M. (2012). Overview of violence to self and others during the first episode of psychosis. *Journal of Clinical Psychiatry, 73,* 580–587.

O'Connor v. Donaldson, 422 U. S. 563 (1975).

Owen, P. R. (2012). Portrayals of schizophrenia by entertainment media: A content analysis of contemporary movies. *Psychiatric Services, 63,* 655–659.

Pescosolido, B. A., Monahan, J., Link, B. G., Stueve, A., & Kikuzawa, S. (1999). The public's view of the competence, dangerousness, and need for legal coercion of persons with mental health problems. *American Journal of Public Health, 89,* 1339–1345.

Räsänen, P., Tiihonen, J., Isohanni, M., Rantakallio, P., Lehtonen, J., & Moring, J. (1998) Schizophrenia, alcohol abuse, and violent behavior: A 26-year follow-up study of an unselected birth cohort. *Schizophrenia Bulletin, 24,* 437–441.

Robins, L. N., Helzer, J. E., Croughan, J., & Ratcliff, K. S. (1981). National Institute of Mental Health Diagnostic Interview Schedule: Its history, characteristics, and validity. *Archives of General Psychiatry, 38,* 381–389.

Rothman, K. J. (1986). *Modern epidemiology.* Boston, MA: Little, Brown.

Silver, E. (2006). Understanding the relationship between mental disorder and violence: The need for a criminological perspective. *Law and Human Behavior, 30,* 685–706. doi:10.1007/s10979-006-9018-z

Silver, E., Mulvey, E., & Monahan, J. (1999). Assessing violence risk among discharged psychiatric patients: Toward an ecological approach. *Law and Human Behavior, 23,* 237–255.

Silver, E., Piquero, A., Jennings, W. G., Piquero, N. L., & Leiber, M. (2011). Assessing the violent offending and violent victimization overlap among discharged psychiatric patients. *Law and Human Behavior, 35,* 49–59.

Silver, E., & Teasdale, B. (2005). Mental disorder and violence: An examination of stressful life events and impaired social support. *Social Problems, 52,* 62–78.

Skeem, J. L., Manchak, S., & Peterson, J. K. (2011). Correctional policy for offenders with mental illness: Creating a new paradigm for recidivism research. *Law and Human Behavior, 35,* 110–126. doi: 10.1007/s10979-010-9223-7

Skeem, J. L., Schubert, C., Odgers, C., Mulvey, E. P., Gardner, W., & Lidz, C. (2006). Psychiatric symptoms and community violence among high-risk patients: A test of the relationship at the weekly level. *Journal of Consulting and Clinical Psychology, 74,* 967–979.

Steadman, H. J., & Keveles, G. (1972). The community adjustment and criminal activity of the Baxstrom patients: 1966–1970. *American Journal of Psychiatry, 129,* 304–310.

Steadman, H., Mulvey, E., Monahan, J., Robbins, P., Appelbaum, P., Grisso, T., ... Silver, E. (1998). Violence by people discharged from acute psychiatric inpatient facilities and by others in the same neighborhoods. *Archives of General Psychiatry, 55,* 393–401.

Stompe, T., Ortwein-Swoboda, G., & Schanda, H. (2004). Schizophrenia, delusional symptoms, and violence: The threat/control-override concept reexamined. *Schizophrenia Bulletin, 30,* 31–44.

Stueve, A., & Link, B. G. (1997). Violence and psychiatric disorders: Results from an epidemiological study of young adults in Israel. *Psychiatric Quarterly, 68,* 327–342.

Swanson, J., Borum, R., Swartz, M., & Monahan, J. (1996). Psychotic symptoms and disorders and the risk of violent behavior in the community. *Criminal Behavior and Mental Health, 6,* 309–329.

Swanson, J. W. (1993). Alcohol abuse, mental disorder, and violent behaviour: An epidemiologic inquiry. Special Issue: Alcohol, aggression, and injury. *Alcohol Health and Research World, 17,* 123–132.

Swanson, J. W., Holzer, C. E., Ganju, V. K., & Jono, R. T. (1990). Violence and psychiatric disorder in the community: Evidence from the epidemiologic catchment area surveys. *Hospital and Community Psychiatry, 41,* 761–770.

Swanson, J. W., Swartz, M. S., van Dorn, R. A., Elbogen, E. B., Wagnet, H. R., Rosenheck, R. A., ... Lieberman, J. A. (2006). A national study of violent behavior in persons with schizophrenia. *Archives of General Psychiatry, 63,* 490–499.

Tarasoff v. Board of Regents of the University of California, Cal. 3d 415, 551 P.2d 334, 131 Cal. Rptr. 14 (1976).

Taylor, P. J. (1998). When symptoms of psychosis drive serious violence. *Social Psychiatry and Psychiatric Epidemiology, 33,* S47–S54.

Taylor, P. J., Leese, M., Williams, D., Butwell, M., Daly, R., & Larkin, E. (1998). Mental disorder and violence. A special (high security) hospital study. *British Journal of Psychiatry, 172,* 218–226.

Teasdale, B., Silver, E., & Monahan, J. (2006). Gender, threat/control-override delusions and violence. *Law and Human Behavior, 30,* 649–658.

Teplin, L. A. (1985). The criminality of the mentally ill: A dangerous misconception. *American Journal of Psychiatry, 142,* 593–599.

Thomas, W. I., & Thomas, D. S. (1928). *The child in America: Behavior problems and programs.* New York, NY: Knopf.

Tiihonen, J., Isohanni, M., Räsäsen, P., Koiranen, M., & Moring, J. (1997). Specific major mental disorders and criminality: A 26-year prospective study of the 1966 Northern Finland birth cohort. *American Journal of Psychiatry, 154,* 840–845.

Van Dorn, R., Volavka, J., & Johnson, N. (2011). Mental disorder and violence: Is there a relationship beyond substance use? *Social Psychiatry and Psychiatric Epidemiology, 47,* 487–503. doi: 10.1007/s00127-011-0356-x.

Vincent, G., Grisso, T., Terry, A., & Banks, S. (2008). Gender and race differences in mental health symptoms in juvenile justice: The MAYSI-2 national meta-analysis. *Journal of the American Academy of Child and Adolescent Psychiatry, 47,* 282–290.

Wahl, O. F, Wood, A., & Richards, R. (2002). Newspaper coverage of mental illness: Is it changing? *Psychiatric Rehabilitation Skills, 6,* 9–31.

Yang, S., Mulvey, E. P., Loughran, T. A., & Hanusa, B. H. (2012). Psychiatric symptoms and alcohol use in community violence by persons with a psychotic disorder or depression. *Psychiatric Services, 63,* 262–269.

5

Aggressive Externalizing Disorders

Conduct Disorder, Antisocial Personality Disorder, and Psychopathy

LAURA E. DRISLANE, NOAH C. VENABLES, AND
CHRISTOPHER J. PATRICK ■

Aggressive externalizing disorders, namely conduct disorder (CD), antisocial personality disorder (ASPD), and psychopathic personality (psychopathy), hold strong interest for researchers and practitioners alike due to their chronic nature and costly impact on society. Individuals displaying symptoms of these disorders account for a disproportionate number of crimes (Hare, 2003; Skeem, Polaschek, Patrick, & Lilienfeld, 2011), including violent offenses (Leistico, Salekin, DeCoster, & Rogers, 2008), and are more likely to reoffend than other adjudicated individuals (Corrado, Vincent, Hart, & Cohen, 2004; Douglas, Epstein, & Poythress, 2008; Stockdale, Olver, & Wong, 2010). As such, a clear understanding of this group of disorders is essential for developing effective treatment and prevention programs for curtailing violent victimization.

The objectives of the present chapter are to (1) describe historical and modern perspectives on CD, ASPD, and psychopathy with an emphasis on key empirical findings; (2) discuss how these conditions relate to criminal behavior broadly and violent offending in particular; and (3) provide an integrative framework for understanding similarities and differences among these disorders that helps to clarify the basis of their relations with aggressive deviancy.

HISTORIC PERSPECTIVES ON PSYCHOPATHY AND ANTISOCIALITY

Psychopathy

While ASPD has received disproportionate emphasis in the psychiatric literature in recent decades, due to its inclusion in multiple editions of the field's *Diagnostic and Statistical Manual of Mental Disorders* (*DSM*; APA, 1980, 1987, 1994, 2000, 2013), the concept of ASPD is predated by historical accounts of the condition that came to be known as psychopathy. Early in the 19th century, French physician Philippe

Pinel (1801/1962) applied the term *manie sans delire* ("insanity without delirium") to a somewhat paradoxical condition entailing irrational violent and destructive actions on the part of individuals with seemingly intact reasoning and communication skills. Contemporaries of Pinel (e.g., Pritchard, 1835; Rush, 1812) likewise noted examples of patients who exhibited a profound absence of moral sensibility ("moral insanity") that appeared causally linked to behavioral deviance, including violent and aggressive acts. The term *psychopathic*, however, did not enter the lexicon until 1891, when German psychiatrist J. L. Koch proposed the label "psychopathic inferiority" as an alternative to moral insanity. For Koch, psychopathic inferiorities spanned the range of psychopathologic conditions, including mood and anxiety disorders, schizophrenia, and mental retardation. Subsequently, the scope of the term was narrowed by Emil Kraepelin (1904, 1915), who reserved the label "psychopathic personalities" for persistent conditions considered characterological in nature. Included among these were so-called degenerative personalities, such as chronic liars/swindlers, impulsive criminals, and aimless vagabonds.

American psychiatrist Hervey Cleckley sought to further narrow the scope of the term *psychopathic* and clarify the essential features of the disorder in his seminal monograph, *The Mask of Sanity* (1976). Working with hospital inpatients, Cleckley developed a model of psychopathy as a complex disorder entailing a deep-rooted emotional disturbance concealed by the outward appearance of mental stability. In contrast with other ward patients who appeared visibly disturbed, psychopathic individuals presented as confident, socially poised, and even charming. As reflected in the title of Cleckley's book, it was only through extensive contact with such individuals over time that the nature and extent of their disturbance became evident. As a basis for objective clinical diagnosis, Cleckley highlighted 16 characteristic features of the disorder. Some of these consisted of indicators of chronic behavioral deviance (e.g., unreliability, failure to learn from adverse experience, antisocial acts committed without clear motives, promiscuous sexual behavior); others reflected emotional-interpersonal deficits (e.g., absence of remorse, general poverty of affect, deceptiveness, incapacity for love). Additionally, Cleckley included distinct indicators of resiliency and positive adjustment in his diagnostic criteria for psychopathy, namely, the appearance of charm and good intelligence, a lack of delusions or irrational thinking, absence of nervousness or anxiety, and disinclination toward suicidal acts.

Notably, Cleckley did not characterize psychopathic patients as inherently predatory or cruel. Instead, he considered the harm they caused others to be an unintended consequence of their general lack of emotional sensitivity and social connectedness. As such, along with case descriptions of career criminals, Cleckley included examples of "successful psychopaths," such as businessmen, scholars, and physicians, who displayed many of the same core traits as chronically antisocial individuals, but without engagement in aggressive criminal acts. In contrast, experts working with psychopathic criminal offenders placed greater emphasis on more uniformly pathological features such as viciousness, exploitativeness, and coldness in their definitions of psychopathy. For example, McCord and McCord (1964) identified "lovelessness" (an inability to form close attachments) and "guiltlessness" (absence of remorse) as the core deficits underlying psychopathy. Thus, historic conceptions differ in their relative emphasis on positive adjustment features versus antagonism and Machiavellianism in defining the interpersonal features of psychopathy.

Antisocial Personality Disorder

The historic underpinnings of ASPD, in contrast, can be linked to developments over time in official perspectives on psychiatric classification as embodied in the *DSM*. The first edition of the *DSM* (*DSM-I*; APA, 1952) included a category entitled "sociopathic personality disturbance." Paralleling early usage of the term *psychopathic* (e.g., Koch, Kraeplin), this category encompassed a number of disparate disorders, including addictions, sexual disorders, and antisocial deviance. Among these was "sociopathic personality disturbance: antisocial reaction," which described a prototypical pattern of behavior marked by persistent rule breaking and norm violations. In the second edition of the *DSM* (*DSM-II*; APA, 1968), this condition was renamed "antisocial personality" and was extended to incorporate more trait-like features of psychopathy as described by Cleckley, including unreliability (irresponsibility), callousness, and lack of guilt. Unfortunately, the utility of these diagnostic conceptions was limited, as both *DSM-I* and *DSM-II* relied on prototype descriptions rather than on clearly delineated behavioral criteria for assigning diagnoses, which resulted in poor reliability of diagnostic decisions in both clinical and research settings.

In an effort to mitigate limitations of earlier editions, *DSM-III* (APA, 1980) adopted more explicit, behaviorally oriented criteria for assigning diagnoses. In line with this, the criteria for ASPD in this edition of the *DSM* were strongly influenced by the work of Robins (1966) on developmental aspects of psychopathy (termed "sociopathy" in her writings). In particular, Robins's findings suggested weak discriminability of affective-dispositional characteristics such as lack of remorse or shame, owing to the limited reliability of informant ratings of these characteristics. In consideration of this work, the criteria for ASPD in *DSM-III* focused predominantly on indicators of behavioral deviance, such as truancy, stealing, vandalism, impulsivity, and recklessness, in early and later life. This focus on explicit behavioral indicators dramatically increased reliability of the ASPD diagnosis, but it led some investigators to question its validity, given that the *DSM-III* diagnostic criteria omitted core interpersonal and affective features of psychopathy described by Cleckley and his contemporaries (Frances, 1980; Hare, 1983; Millon, 1981).

In preparation for *DSM-IV*, field trials were conducted to evaluate the incremental validity of incorporating affective and interpersonal traits into the diagnostic criteria for ASPD. Data were collected from four distinct participant samples: psychiatric inpatients, residents of drug treatment centers and homeless shelters, methadone clinic outpatients, and incarcerated offenders. Results from the field trial indicated that affective-interpersonal traits (i.e., lack of empathy, grandiose sense of self-worth, glib interpersonal style) contributed incrementally to prediction of important outcomes in only one of the four samples—the incarcerated offender sample. As such, it was concluded that the evidence was not persuasive enough to warrant this marked shift in the criteria for ASPD. Consequently, the criteria for the disorder in *DSM-IV* remained much the same as they were in *DSM-III/IIIR*, with some minor revisions in the number and wording of items. This decision resulted in persisting concerns about the validity of the ASPD diagnosis as a representation of the classic concept of psychopathy (e.g., Hare & Hart, 1995).

Conduct Disorder

Aggressive and antisocial behaviors were first identified as key elements of child psycho-pathology in the 1940s (e.g., Hewitt & Jenkins, 1946). Following this, researchers sought to characterize different variants or subtypes of antisocial youth. Specifically, much attention was paid to the role of socialization and social bonding in shaping prosocial and antisocial behaviors. So-called undersocialized antisocial youth were described as loners who tended to commit aggressive and assaultive acts alone, and who frequently displayed symptoms of psychological distress (Quay, 1987). In contrast, another subset of children—"socialized" or "group-delinquent" youth—were identified as engaging in both overt and covert antisocial behaviors, despite having formed social connections.

The term *conduct disorder* (CD) was adopted in *DSM-III* as a label for children and adolescents exhibiting antisocial tendencies at clearly nonnormative levels. As with ASPD, the diagnostic features of CD were delineated using explicit behavioral criteria that included covert (e.g., lying, fire-setting) as well as overt (e.g., bullying, weapons use) antisocial acts. *DSM-III* applied liberal rules for making a CD diagnosis, such that the presence of only a small number of relevant features was necessary to warrant a diagnosis. As a result, individuals diagnosed with CD according to *DSM-III* criteria comprised a highly diverse group in terms of symptomatology. To bring some order to this diagnostic heterogeneity, *DSM-III* specified four subcategories of CD delineated on the basis of high versus low socialization crossed with high versus low aggressiveness.

By the 1990s, researchers had moved toward focusing less on the role of socialization processes in the development of early conduct problems, and more on the *age of onset* of such problems. One influential approach formulated by Moffitt (1993) distinguished subgroups of youth with conduct disorder on the basis of age of onset along with persistence. Children who first display antisocial behaviors in puberty—spurred by immaturity—that typically subsides in early adulthood were viewed as comprising an adolescent-limited subtype. In contrast, the much smaller subset of children who display significant symptoms of CD beginning in childhood rather than adolescence were described as a life-course-persistent subtype. For this latter subgroup of CD youth, antisocial behaviors were theorized to arise from neurobiological impairments in combination with exposure to criminogenic environments. The early age of onset (i.e., prior to age 10) of CD symptoms in this latter group was considered prognostic of a more severe, chronic pattern of antisocial behavior throughout the life span. Incorporating this perspective, the fourth edition of the *DSM* included an age of onset specifier for CD in lieu of the socialization-aggression distinction. Notably, the majority of children with an early age of onset of CD symptoms would be classified as both undersocialized and aggressive using the *DSM-III* diagnostic scheme (Hinshaw, Lahey, & Hart, 1993).

MODERN CONCEPTIONS OF AGGRESSIVE EXTERNALIZING DISORDERS

Antisocial Personality Disorder

In line with more recent historic precedent, contemporary diagnostic nosology defines ASPD primarily in terms of observable norm-violating behaviors, rather than more internal affective states or personality traits. Specifically, *DSM-IV-TR*

(2000) states that for an adult to meet criteria for a diagnosis of ASPD, he or she must display a pervasive pattern of disregard for the rights of others since age 15 as displayed by at least three of the following: repeated unlawful behavior, deceptiveness, impulsivity/failure to plan ahead, irritability and aggressiveness, reckless disregard for the safety or self or others, consistent irresponsibility, and lack of remorse. The individual must also have had shown evidence of antisocial behavior in childhood by displaying two or more symptoms of CD (First, Gibbon, Spitzer, Williams, & Benjamin, 1997; see Table 5.1). The prevalence of ASPD in the general community is estimated to be approximately 2%, with base rates of diagnosis considerably higher in men (~3%) than women (~1%; APA, 2000). In forensic settings, the base rate of ASPD is markedly higher—between 50% and 80% (Hare, 2003).

With the exception of items pertaining to remorse and deceptiveness, the diagnostic criteria for ASPD largely reflect behavioral tendencies associated with a highly disinhibited disposition. Indeed, in structural models of common mental disorders, child and adult symptoms of ASPD load onto a common "externalizing" factor with other impulse-control disorders, including alcohol and drug dependence, and traits reflecting impulsivity, sensation seeking, and nonconformity (Krueger, 1999a; Krueger et al., 2002). Further, this common factor is largely genetic in nature, indicating that it reflects an underlying dispositional liability to multiple different disorders. This common liability may in part explain the very high base rate of comorbid substance use disorders in individuals diagnosed with ASPD (~80%; Grant et al., 2004; Kessler & Walters, 2002; Robins & Regier, 1991). Relatedly, the personality correlates of ASPD and substance use disorders are highly similar (Acton, 2003; Lynam, Leukenfeld, & Clayton, 2003): Both are marked by high levels of impulsiveness (as represented by low conscientiousness in the five-factor model [FFM] of personality, or low constraint in Tellegen's [1982] Multidimensional Personality Questionnaire [MPQ] model) along with high aggressiveness (as represented by agreeableness-reversed [also known as antagonism] in the FFM, or the primary trait of aggression in the MPQ; Krueger, 1999b; Trull, 1992).

ASPD is also reliably associated with a number of neurobiological correlates. For example, aggressive forms of ASPD are linked with low levels of the neurotransmitter serotonin (for a review, see Minzenberg & Siever, 2006). Hypoarousal, as indicated by low resting heart rate, is likewise associated with antisocial behavior (Ortiz & Raine, 2004). In fact, low resting heart rate in childhood or adolescence is predictive of adult antisocial deviance (Maliphant, Hume, & Furnham, 1990; Raine & Venables, 1984), suggesting that autonomic hypoarousal may represent a risk factor for the development of impulsive and antisocial behaviors in later life (Raine, 2002). Finally, ASPD is associated with deficits in indices of brain response and in functions related to executive control. In the case of CD and ASPD, a meta-analysis by Morgan and Lilienfeld (2000) yielded robust evidence for deficits in frontal brain function in individuals with these disorders. Deficits in frontal brain function have also been reported in individuals with nonaggressive externalizing problems, including substance use disorders (Iacono, Carlson, & Malone, 2000). Further, ASPD is reliably associated with reductions in amplitude of the P300 brain potential response in so-called oddball task procedures (Bauer, O'Connor, & Hesselbrock, 1994; Iacono, Carlson, Malone, & McGue, 2002). More broadly, reduced P300 brain response amplitude has been shown to operate as

Table 5.1 SUMMARY OF DIAGNOSTIC CRITERIA FOR *DSM-IV* ANTISOCIAL
PERSONALITY DISORDER

Criterion Category	Summary Description of Criterion
A. Adult antisocial behavior (Three or more of the following since age 15):	1. Repeated participation in illegal acts 2. Deceitfulness 3. Impulsiveness or failure to make plans in advance 4. Hostile-aggressive behavior 5. Engagement in actions that endanger self or others 6. Frequent irresponsible behavior 7. Absence of remorse
B. Age criterion	Current age at least 18
C. Evidence of child conduct disorder (three or more of the following before age 15, resulting in impaired social, academic, or occupational function):[a]	*Aggression toward people or animals:* 1. Frequent bullying, threatening, or intimidation of others 2. Frequent initiation of physical fights 3. Use of dangerous weapons 4. Physical cruelty toward people 5. Physical cruelty toward animals 6. Theft involving victim confrontation 7. Forced sexual contact *Destroying property:* 8. Deliberate fire setting with intent to cause damage *Deceptiveness or stealing:* 9. Deliberate destruction of property 10. Breaking/entering (house, building, or vehicle) 11. Frequent lying to acquire things or to avoid duties 12. Nontrivial theft without victim confrontation *Serious rule violations:* 13. Frequent violations of parental curfew, starting before age 13 14. Running away from home 15. Frequent truancy, starting before age 13
D. Comorbidity criterion	Antisocial behavior does not occur exclusively during episodes of schizophrenic or mania.

[a]The *DSM-IV* criteria for conduct disorder require the occurrence of three or more of these behavioral symptoms before age 15. Criterion C for antisocial personality disorder (ASPD) is vague as to the number of child symptoms needing to be met, specifying only "evidence of Conduct Disorder with onset before age 15 years." Some approaches to assessing ASPD, for example the Structured Clinical Interview for *DSM-IV* Axis II Personality Disorders (SCID-II; First et al., 1997), interpret "evidence of" as denoting a lower threshold (i.e., occurrence of two child symptoms, as opposed to three).

SOURCE: Adapted from American Psychiatric Association (2000).

a marker of the general externalizing factor that links differing impulse control disorders (Patrick et al., 2006).

Existing conceptions of ASPD have also been influenced by recent efforts to understand mental disorders in dimensional as opposed to discrete-category terms. Along this line, a supplemental approach to diagnosing personality pathology has been included in the new-released fifth edition of the *DSM* (*DSM-5*; APA, 2013) that conceptualizes personality disorders—including ASPD—in terms of dimensional traits. Within this scheme, ASPD is operationalized in terms of elevations on specific maladaptive traits from domains of disinhibition (i.e., irresponsibility, impulsivity, and risk taking) and antagonism (i.e., manipulativeness, deceitfulness, callousness, and hostility). Extending this formulation, recent work has shown that a more classically psychopathic variant of ASPD can be captured through use of a specifier reflecting low levels of anxiousness and social withdrawal (Strickland et al., 2013).

Conduct Disorder

Currently, the diagnostic criteria for CD (APA, 1994) require the presence of at least three indicators of nonnormative antisocial behavior during childhood or early adolescence. Such behaviors are associated with impairments in family and peer, academic, and personal adjustment domains. While *DSM-IV* cites base rates for CD of 6%–16% in males and 2%–9% in females (APA, 1994), prevalence estimates for CD among children and adolescents in published research studies have ranged widely, from less than 1% to slightly over 10% (e.g., Lahey, Miller, Gordon, & Riley, 1999; Zoccolillo, 1993). As with ASPD, most findings support a much higher base rate of childhood CD in male youth compared to females; however, the gender disparity markedly diminishes by adolescence (Zoccolillo, 1993).

In both children and adolescents, CD shows reliable patterns of comorbidity with other *DSM* disorders and psychosocial deficits. Specifically, the vast majority of children with CD display a history of earlier oppositional defiant disorder (ODD), a less severe constellation of antisocial traits marked by disobedient, hostile, and defiant behavior toward authority figures (Lahey, Loeber, Quay, Frick, & Grimm, 1997; Loeber, Lahey, & Thomas, 1991). Additionally, in clinic-referred samples, the base rate of comorbid ADHD in children diagnosed with conduct disorder is extremely high (50%–80%, Greene et al., 2002; see also Abikoff & Klein, 1992). Comorbid ADHD is also associated with an earlier onset of CD symptomatology (Hinshaw et al., 1993; Loeber, Green, Keenan, & Lahey, 1995; Rutter, Giller, & Hagell, 1998). Further, children diagnosed with CD are at increased risk for academic underachievement (Hinshaw, Heller, & McHale, 1992), problematic substance use (White, Loeber, Stouthamer-Loeber, & Farrington, 1999), and in some cases, higher levels of internalizing (i.e., anxiety and depressive) problems (Loeber, Stouthamer-Loeber, & White, 1999).

VARIANTS OF CONDUCT DISORDER
Recent converging lines of evidence point to systematic heterogeneity in the diagnosis of CD as defined by *DSM* criteria. One relevant body of research consists of factor analytic studies delineating correlated but distinct subfactors (subdimensions)

underlying the symptoms for CD listed within *DSM-IV*. An initial study by Tackett, Krueger, Sawyer, and Graetz (2003) reported evidence for distinguishable subfactors of CD symptomatology reflecting overt (e.g., initiates fights, bullies) versus covert (e.g., stolen without confrontation, run away from home) behavioral tendencies. Based on results of a follow-up study utilizing twin participants (Tackett, Krueger, Iacono, & McGue, 2005), the designation of the two subfactors was modified to "aggressive" versus "rule breaking," and evidence was presented for common as well as distinctive etiologic contributions to each. Subsequent research has supported this distinction and clarified the contributions of genetic and environmental influences to these subfactors. Based on results of a meta-analytic review of behavioral genetic studies, Burt (2009) concluded that the aggressive symptom subfactor is more strongly heritable than the rule-breaking subfactor (estimated contribution of addictive genetic influence = 65% versus 48%), with shared environmental influences contributing to the rule-breaking (estimated contribution = 18%) but not the aggressive subfactor. Extending this work, a recent twin study by Kendler, Aggen, and Patrick (2013) provided evidence for two coherent sources of genetic influence ("genetic factors") contributing to CD symptoms; one genetic factor contributed selectively to aggressive CD symptoms, whereas the other contributed strongly to nonaggressive CD symptoms and, to a lesser degree, to aggressive symptoms.

A second line of research has focused on identifying a distinct subset of CD youth exhibiting salient psychopathic tendencies. Initially, researchers were hopeful that the childhood-onset life-course persistent CD subtype proposed by Moffitt (1993) might identify such a group (Forth & Burke, 1998). While substantial evidence accrued for the presence of this variant of CD (Farrington et al., 2006; Lynne-Landsman, Graber, Nichols, & Botvin, 2011; Moffitt, 2007), questions were raised about the predictive utility of the age of onset specifier more broadly. In Moffitt's own laboratory (Odgers et al., 2008), for example, a third group of youth with conduct disorder (24% of male children) were identified as a displaying a childhood-limited pattern of antisocial behavior.

As an alternative to the age of onset approach for identifying children with a more severe, persistent pattern of antisocial behavior, Lynam (1998) proposed that "fledgling psychopathy" can be effectively identified by the presence of comorbid CD and ADHD in conjunction with an early age of onset of *aggressive* tendencies. However, given the frequent co-occurrence of CD and ADHD, it was unclear to what extent this designated subgroup of youth might differ from the broader array of individuals meeting criteria for CD. In fact, work by Michonski and Sharp (2010) has shown that CD children with comorbid ADHD are no more likely to display the core affective and interpersonal features of psychopathy than children with CD alone.

Another influential line of research has sought to differentiate variants of CD in terms of the presence versus absence of "callous-unemotional" traits (Frick, Lilienfeld, Ellis, Loney, & Silverthorn, 1999; Frick & White, 2008). Findings from this work have led to revisions to the diagnostic criteria for CD in *DSM-5*, such that the diagnosis now includes a callous-unemotional traits specifier (CD with "limited prosocial emotions"). To be assigned this specifier, an individual diagnosed with CD must exhibit at least two of the following features: lack of remorse or guilt, callousness/lack of empathy, shallow or deficient affect, and lack of concern about performance (Frick & Moffitt, 2010). Traits of this sort are viewed as counterparts to the affective features of adult psychopathy, theorized to reflect low anxiousness or fear (Fowles, 1980; Lykken, 1957; Patrick, 1994), or a more generalized emotional deficit (Blair, 2006).

Empirical research has demonstrated that CD children with callous-unemotional traits display greater interpersonal antagonism and aggression, lower negative affectivity, and fewer academic/intellectual impairments than CD children lacking these traits (for reviews, see Frick & White, 2008; Salekin, 2006). After controlling for levels of antisocial behavior, callous-unemotional traits are also related to low anxiety and fear (Frick et al., 1999; Pardini, Lochman, & Powell, 2007) and reduced sensitivity to punishment (for a review, see White & Frick, 2010), and contribute modestly to the prediction of impulsivity and past antisocial behavior (e.g., Pardini, Obradović, & Loeber, 2006; Salekin, Ziegler, Larrea, Anthony, & Bennett, 2003). Additionally, brain imaging studies have revealed that CD youth with high levels of callous-unemotional traits exhibit reduced amygdala activity in the context of fearful face processing relative to CD youth without such traits or control youth (Jones, Laurens, Herba, Barker, & Viding, 2009; Marsh et al., 2008).

Psychopathy

PSYCHOPATHY CHECKLIST-REVISED

The best established measure for diagnosing psychopathy in clinical samples is the Psychopathy Checklist-Revised (PCL-R), developed by Canadian psychologist Robert Hare (1991, 2003) for use with incarcerated offenders. The criterion referent for development of the initial, preliminary version of the PCL (Hare, 1980) was a global rating procedure based on Cleckley's case examples and diagnostic criteria, in which clinicians familiar with the subject's history and behavior assigned a score between 1 and 7 to indicate degree of resemblance to Cleckley's conception of psychopathy (1 = clearly not psychopathic according to Cleckley's description; 7 = clearly psychopathic vis-à-vis Cleckley's description). Items selected for inclusion in the original PCL were those that contributed statistically to differentiation of participants assigned high versus low global ratings, and that cohered together with other candidate items (Hare, 1980).

The current, revised version of the PCL-R (Hare, 1991, 2003) consists of 20 items rated on the basis of information derived from a semistructured interview and review of institutional records (e.g., court and probation reports, criminal records, prison progress logs). Each item is scored on a three-point scale (2 = feature clearly present, 1 = equivocal, 0 = clearly absent) with reference to a detailed narrative description of relevant behavioral indicants. Scores are summed across items to yield a total psychopathy score (range = 0–40), with scores at or above 30 considered indicative of high psychopathy (i.e., a diagnosis of psychopathic personality; Hare, 2003), scores at or below 20 indicative of low psychopathy (nonpsychopathic diagnosis), and scores between 21 and 29 indicative of intermediate levels of psychopathic traits. Research findings indicate the prevalence of psychopathy as defined by the PCL-R in male correctional populations to be between 15% and 25% (Hare, 1998, 2003)—much lower than that for ASPD (i.e., 50%–80%, as discussed earlier), consistent with the idea that psychopathic individuals comprise a distinct subset of persons exhibiting criminal or antisocial behavior (Cleckley, 1976; McCord & McCord, 1964). Given that the PCL-R was created specifically for use in forensic settings, and limited research to date has examined psychopathy as a discrete diagnostic condition in population-representative samples, the prevalence of psychopathy in the community at large is difficult to estimate. Nevertheless, there is a consensus that psychopathy represents a low base-rate phenomenon, with prevalence likely not exceeding 1%–2% in community males (Farrington et al., 2006; Hare, 2003) and presumably lower in community females.

The item set of the PCL-R encompasses both the behavioral deviance (e.g., poor behavioral controls, impulsivity, irresponsibility, criminal versatility) and emotional-interpersonal (e.g., lack of remorse or guilt, shallow affect, callous/lack of empathy) features of psychopathy highlighted by Cleckley; however, resiliency and positive adjustment features included in his classic conception are indexed only indirectly by certain items of the PCL-R, such as Item 1, "glibness/superficial charm" (cf. Hall, Benning, & Patrick, 2004). This presumably reflects the item selection strategy for the PCL-R, which focused on assessing psychopathy as a unitary condition marked by the presence of multiple interrelated indicators. Items pertaining to positive adjustment would not have converged well with the more extensive array of content-relevant indicators reflecting deviancy and maladjustment, and thus they would have been dropped from the inventory (Patrick, 2006).

Although developed to assess psychopathy as a unitary condition, factor analytic work (Cooke & Michie, 2001; Hare et al., 1990; Hare & Neumann, 2006; Harpur, Hare, & Hakstian, 1989) has demonstrated that the PCL-R's 20 items index between two and four distinct symptomatic subdimensions. Most work to date has focused on the subdimensions of the two-factor PCL-R model (Hare et al., 1990), in which Factor 1 encompasses the affective-interpersonal features (e.g., glibness/charm, grandiosity, lying and manipulativeness, shallow affect, lack of remorse) and Factor 2 encompasses the impulsive-antisocial features (e.g., early behavior problems, impulsivity, irresponsibility, poor behavioral controls, lack of long-term goals). Scores on these two PCL-R factors are moderately correlated (~.5; Hare, 1991, 2003) but show divergent patterns of relations with measures of personality and behavior. Specifically, scores on Factor 1 are inversely associated with negative affective tendencies such as trait anxiety, depression, and suicide risk, whereas scores on Factor 2 are associated positively with such variables (Hicks & Patrick, 2006; Verona, Hicks, & Patrick, 2005; Verona, Patrick, & Joiner, 2001). Further, PCL-R Factor 1 scores are associated with high Machiavellianism and narcissism (Harpur et al., 1989; Verona et al., 2001), low empathic tendencies (Hare, 2003), and proneness to instrumental aggressive acts (Patrick, Zempolich, & Levenston, 1997). Scores on Factor 2, on the other hand, show substantially stronger associations with symptoms of CD and ASPD (Hare, 2003; Verona et al., 2001), extent of offense history (Hare, 2003), and reactive aggression (Patrick & Zempolich, 1998; Woodworth & Porter, 2002). Further, symptoms of alcohol and drug dependence are selectively associated with scores on PCL-R Factor 2 (Reardon, Lang, & Patrick, 2002; Smith & Newman, 1990).

ALTERNATIVE SELF-REPORT INVENTORIES

While used widely in correctional and other forensic settings, the PCL-R is not well suited for use with nonoffenders because its items refer extensively to criminal acts and rely upon collateral archival sources for scoring. The PCL-R is also time intensive to administer and score. As alternatives to the PCL-R, a number of self-report inventories have been developed for assessing psychopathy in community as well as forensic samples. The most extensively validated and widely used of these is the Psychopathic Personality Inventory (PPI/PPI-R; Lilienfeld & Andrews, 1996; Lilienfeld & Widows, 2005). The PPI was developed with the goal of assessing psychopathy in terms of dispositional characteristics rather than overt instances of criminal behavior. It contains eight subscales that index distinguishable trait facets of psychopathy, which can be summed to yield a total psychopathy score. As with the PCL-R, factor analytic work has demonstrated a two-factor structure for the PPI subscales (Benning, Patrick, Hicks, Blonigen, & Krueger, 2003). Factor 1, labeled Fearless Dominance, encompasses its Social Potency, Stress Immunity, and Fearlessness subscales. Factor 2, labeled Impulsive Antisociality (or, alternatively, Self-Centered Impulsivity) is defined by the PPI's Impulsive Nonconformity, Blame Externalization, Carefree Nonplanfulness, and Machiavellian Egocentricity subscales. An eighth subscale, Coldheartedness, does not load selectively on either of these higher order factors.

Whereas the two factors of the PCL-R are moderately interrelated, scores on PPI Fearless Dominance and Impulsive Antisociality show minimal association with one another (Benning et al., 2003). These factors display meaningful relations with external criterion measures that parallel those for the PCL-R factors but that diverge more clearly in various instances because of their nonoverlap (Benning, Patrick, Salekin, & Leistico, 2005; Poythress et al., 2010). For example, consistent with Cleckley's conception, scores on Fearless Dominance are positively associated with indices of positive adjustment, such as verbal intelligence and educational attainment, low anxiety and internalizing symptoms, and higher activity and sociability (Benning et al, 2003, 2005; Blonigen et al., 2005; Poythress et al., 2010). In contrast, the Impulsive Antisociality factor of the PPI shows prominent, selective associations with maladaptive clinical outcomes, including aggression, alcohol and drug dependence, features of borderline personality disorder, and suicidal ideation (Patrick, Edens, Poythress, Lilienfeld, & Benning, 2006).

NEUROBIOLOGICAL CORRELATES

As with CD and ASPD, psychopathy is associated with a range of neurobiological correlates. Whereas aggressive forms of ASPD are associated with low resting heart rate (discussed earlier), one of the most consistent findings for overall psychopathy scores is reduced electrodermal (skin conductance) reactivity to aversive cues (for a review, see Lorber, 2004), interpreted as reflecting dispositional fearlessness or weak defensive reactivity (Fowles, 1980; Lykken, 1957; Patrick, 1994). As further evidence for the low-fear hypothesis, highly psychopathic adult offenders fail to show normal potentiation of the startle blink response while viewing aversive pictures (Patrick, 1994; Sutton, Vitale, & Newman, 2002). This lack of fear-potentiated startle has been shown to be associated specifically with Factor 1 of the PCL-R (Vaidyanathan, Hall, Patrick, & Bernat, 2011). Additionally, as mentioned earlier, neuroimaging studies have reported reduced amygdala activation to fearful versus neutral faces in clinic-referred adolescents rated as high in psychopathic features (Jones et al., 2009; Marsh et al., 2008). Findings from neuroimaging studies of adult psychopathic individuals utilizing other types of affective cuing paradigms have been somewhat more mixed (for a review, see Patrick, Venables, & Skeem, 2012).

INTEGRATING ANTISOCIAL AND PSYCHOPATHIC CONCEPTIONS: THE TRIARCHIC MODEL OF PSYCHOPATHY

CD, ASPD, and psychopathy can be viewed as intersecting but distinguishable disorders. A useful point of reference in this regard is the triarchic model of psychopathy (Patrick, Fowles, & Krueger, 2009). Although the model was formulated to reconcile contrasting conceptions of psychopathy in historic and contemporary writings, the symptomatic constructs emphasized in the triarchic model are helpful for clarifying what psychopathy and *DSM* antisocial disorders have in common, as well as what distinguishes them.

The triarchic model defines psychopathy in terms of three distinguishable symptomatic facets—disinhibition, boldness, and meanness—which can be conceived of as the thematic building blocks encompassing alternative conceptions of psychopathy (Drislane, Patrick, & Arsal, 2013). *Disinhibition* reflects poor regulation of emotion and behavior, and it is associated with tendencies toward impulsivity, boredom susceptibility, irresponsibility, mistrust, and rule breaking. From the perspective of the broader psychopathology literature, disinhibition reflects general dispositional proneness to externalizing problems (Venables & Patrick, 2012). By contrast, boldness entails social poise and efficacy, resiliency to stressors, and a tolerance for uncertainty and danger. High levels of boldness are associated with interpersonal dominance and confidence, narcissism, sensation seeking, and low levels of internalizing psychopathology (Benning et al., 2005). Meanness reflects disregard for and exploitation of others (Venables & Patrick, 2012), and it is related conceptually to constructs of callous-unemotionality, coldheartedness, and antagonism. Correlates of meanness include deficient empathy, low social connectedness, emotional insensitivity, and predatory manipulation of others (Drislane et al., 2013).

From the standpoint of the Triarchic model, the constructs indexed in common by CD, ASPD, and psychopathy are disinhibition, and to a lesser extent, meanness. Disinhibition is hypothesized to arise from dysfunction in anterior brain systems (e.g., prefrontal cortex and anterior cingulate cortex) that guide decision making and emotion regulation. Consequently, highly disinhibited individuals tend to act in the present moment, failing to account for future consequences. Tendencies of this kind can contribute directly to criminal or antisocial acts. Symptoms such as truancy, theft (CD), recklessness, failure to plan ahead, consistent irresponsibility (ASPD and psychopathy), boredom proneness, and adult criminal behavior (psychopathy) directly reflect high levels of disinhibition (Krueger, Markon, Patrick, Benning, & Kramer, 2007). Of the three conditions under consideration here—CD, ASPD, and psychopathy—ASPD (its adult symptoms in particular) most strongly reflects high trait disinhibition (Venables, Hall, & Patrick, 2014).

In contrast, CD appears to reflect the confluence of meanness and disinhibition (Venables & Patrick, 2012). Meanness is strongly reflected in symptoms of CD that entail physical intimidation and destructiveness (e.g., bullying, initiation of fights, cruelty to people or animals, deliberate fire setting; Venables & Patrick, 2012). Further, the limited prosocial emotions specifier for CD included in *DSM-5* reflects the affective flattening and social disconnectedness associated with meanness (Drislane et al., 2013). Likewise, meanness is indexed directly by the affective symptoms of PCL-R psychopathy (and to a lesser extent the antisocial facet; Hall et al., 2014) and by the Coldheartedness and Machiavellian Egocentricity subscales of the PPI (Drislane et al., 2013). While the *DSM-IV* criteria for ASPD include fewer symptoms of relevance to meanness (i.e., aggressiveness, lack of remorse), the alternative dimensional conception of ASPD in *DSM-5* includes greater representation of this construct through traits from the domain of antagonism (i.e., callousness, manipulativeness, hostility, deceitfulness; Strickland et al., 2013).

The greatest point of divergence among these three disorders is the extent to which they represent the construct of boldness. This construct is clearly represented in widely used instruments for the assessment of psychopathy. In the PCL-R, boldness is reflected in the interpersonal items of Factor 1, in particular, those dealing with social charm and grandiose sense of self-worth (Hall et al., 2004; Patrick, Hicks, Nichol, & Krueger, 2007). In the PPI, boldness is strongly and directly indexed by subscales associated with the inventory's Fearless Dominance factor (Drislane et al., 2013). Boldness is also clearly represented in other commonly used psychopathy self-report measures developed as counterparts to the PCL-R (Drislane et al., 2012). By contrast, boldness is only weakly related to symptoms of CD and ASPD (Venables et al., 2014), and only as a function of its modest intersection with meanness (cf. Patrick et al., 2009). However, recent work indicates that boldness can be tapped effectively using traits represented in the alternative dimensional conception for *DSM-5* (Strickland et al., 2013), such that a "psychopathic specifier" could be used to designate a distinct variant of ASPD in this new edition of the *DSM*. Further research on the ways in which the distinct constructs of the triarchic model are represented in alternative conceptions of antisocial-externalizing disorders should be helpful in integrating differing bodies of literature and clarifying how and why such disorders link to violent-aggressive behavior.

ASSOCIATIONS WITH AGGRESSION, VIOLENCE, AND CRIMINAL BEHAVIOR

The clinical conditions described in preceding sections—CD, ASPD, and psychopathy—have clear theoretical and empirical ties to aggressive, violent, and criminal behavior. Aggressive features are represented to varying degrees within the *DSM* definitions of CD and ASPD and in the PCL-R criteria for psychopathy, its Factor 2 features in particular. The reliance on aggressive features in diagnosing these disorders complicates the task of determining whether disinhibitory traits are causally linked to aggression, violence, and antisocial behavior, or instead reflect affiliated tendencies in aggression-prone individuals. Before addressing whether disinhibitory tendencies are causally linked to aggression, violence, and crime, we first discuss points of overlap and distinctiveness between *DSM*-defined antisocial disorders and psychopathy.

ANTISOCIALITY AND AGGRESSION
As discussed previously, disorders such as CD, ASPD, and problematic substance use co-occur at high rates (Krueger, 1999a) and are associated in turn with disinhibitory personality traits (i.e., impulsivity, sensation seeking, nonconformity; Krueger et al., 2002). Contemporary models of psychopathology suggest that these antisocial conditions (along with other disruptive disorders, such as ODD and ADHD, and addictive problems, including substance dependence and pathological gambling) represent alternative phenotypic manifestations of an underlying

propensity toward disinhibited behaviors. The common liability factor that connects disorders within this *externalizing spectrum* (Krueger, Markon, Patrick, & Iacono, 2005) is estimated to be highly heritable (>80%; Krueger et al., 2002; Young, Stallings, Corley, Krauter, & Hewitt, 2000) and has important implications for conceptualizing violence, aggression, and antisociality. Whereas the general propensity toward problems of these types appears to be strongly influenced by genes, the specific manner in which this propensity is expressed (e.g., as aggressiveness, alcohol or drug dependency, or reckless risk taking) is determined substantially by environmental influences (Krueger et al., 2002). From this perspective, heightened rates of aggressive behavior associated with CD and ASPD may in part reflect high levels of externalizing proneness, directed toward violent criminal expression as a function of exposure to adverse physical and social experiences.

Consistent with the notion that dispositional factors contribute importantly to the occurrence of aggressive behavior, recent population-based research has conclusively demonstrated that violent offending runs in families. Frisell and colleagues (2011) utilized registry records for the total population of Sweden (over 12.5 million persons) to examine nearly all violent criminal convictions occurring in the country between 1973 and 2004 (violent offenses included homicide, assault, robbery, threats and violence against an officer, gross violation of a person's integrity [sexual assault], unlawful coercion, unlawful threats, kidnapping, illegal confinement, arson, and intimidation). The authors were able to identify full familial pedigrees within the sample, providing for linkage of individuals who committed violent crimes to their full, half, and adoptive siblings, biological and adoptive parents, and grandparents, aunts, uncles, and cousins. Using this design, compelling evidence was found for concordance of violent tendencies between biologically related individuals, with degree of biological relatedness and familial proximity both contributing to the degree of observed concordance. For example, Frisell et al. (2011) reported significantly higher concordance for violent crime between first-degree relatives as compared to more biologically remote relatives. First-degree relatives also evidenced higher concordance for violence than adoptive siblings, who share aspects of their environment but are dissimilar genetically. Additionally, however, evidence was found for higher rates of violent offending in individuals adopted into families with violent histories, and for maternal as compared to paternal half-siblings of individuals with violent histories. Thus, the findings pointed to contributions of constitutional as well as experiential factors to transmission of violent behavior within families.

Elsewhere, Hicks et al. (2004) examined the basis of family transmission of disinhibitory problems, including conduct disorder, adult antisocial behavior, alcohol dependence, and drug dependence, in parents and their biological twin offspring assessed for these disorders. Consistent with prior work, the systematic covariance among these disorders in the twin offspring was found to be substantially (~80%) heritable, confirming the contribution of a common externalizing propensity to these disorders. Additionally, the authors modeled this externalizing factor in the parents of the twins and found that variations in this general propensity accounted almost entirely for parent-to-child transmission of individual externalizing disorders. That is, results indicated that family resemblance for problems entailing antisocial behavior in childhood and/or adulthood and substance-related addictions is attributable to the transmission of a general disinhibitory propensity rather than to transmission of discrete liabilities. Further research will be required to directly establish the role of this heritable externalizing propensity in the family transmission of violent offending. However, when considered in relation to the findings of Frisell et al. (2011), the results reported by Hicks et al. (2004) for child and adult components of ASPD (which include prominent aggressive features) strongly suggest at least some role for heritable disinhibitory tendencies in the transmission of violent tendencies within families.

Also important to consider in this context is the evidence, reviewed earlier, for the role of distinguishable genetic influences contributing to aggressive versus non-aggressive (rule-breaking) subdimensions of antisocial behavior. In parallel with findings for conduct disorder symptoms, a recent twin study by Kendler, Aggen, and Patrick (2012) reported evidence for aggressive and nonaggressive subfactors underlying the adult symptoms of ASPD, with distinguishable genetic sources of influence contributing preferentially to each. Irritability/aggressiveness and disregard for safety of self/others emerged as prominent selective indicators of the aggressive factor, whereas irresponsibility and impulsivity/failure to plan emerged as dominant indicators of the nonaggressive factor. Thus, in addition to paralleling the two distinctive subfactors of CD, these two adult ASPD factors resemble separable callous-aggressive ("meanness") and externalizing proneness ("disinhibition") subdimensions emphasized in historic and contemporary conceptions of psychopathy (Patrick et al., 2009; see also Venables & Patrick, 2012). In conjunction with evidence discussed earlier for CD, these results suggest the possibility of two distinct sources of genetic influence contributing to the systematic family transmission of violent/aggressive behavior—one consisting of a general disinhibitory propensity (cf. Hicks et al., 2004), and the other a more specific disposition entailing agency (i.e., active resource seeking) combined with disaffiliation (i.e., lack of social connectedness; Patrick et al,. 2009).

PSYCHOPATHY AND AGGRESSION

The features that distinguish psychopathy from CD and ASPD have important implications for understanding aggression, violence, and criminality. Whereas CD and ASPD are defined primarily in terms of impulsive, reckless/destructive, aggressive, and illicit behaviors, psychopathy is defined by impulsive-antisocial behavior in the context of distinctive affective-interpersonal features entailing a dominant and forceful social style, manipulativeness, callousness/cruelty, and deficient emotional sensitivity. Structural modeling research indicates that the impulsive-antisocial features of psychopathy reflect externalizing proneness (Patrick, Hicks, Krueger, & Lang, 2005) and account for its robust associations with CD and ASPD, whereas the affective-interpersonal features reflect tendencies distinct from these *DSM*-defined antisocial conditions, and externalizing psychopathology more broadly. In view of these findings, a key question is whether documented predictive relations for PCL-R psychopathy with violent offending and criminal recidivism are accounted for by the externalizing component it has in common with CD and ASPD, or by the affective-interpersonal features that distinguish it from these antisocial conditions.

As reviewed by Kennealy, Skeem, Walters, and Camps (2010), the answer appears to be that PCL-R psychopathy is predictive of violent behavior largely a function of the impulsive-antisocial features encompassed by Factor 2. Using a meta-analytic, regression-based approach in which scores on the two PCL-R factors were evaluated as concurrent predictors, these authors found that the antisocial deviance features associated with PCL-R Factor 2 were substantially predictive of violence (effect size $d = .40$), whereas the affective-interpersonal features associated with Factor 1 were only mildly predictive ($d = .11$). Further analyses were undertaken to examine whether affective-interpersonal (Factor 1) features might interact with impulsive-antisocial (Factor 2) features to predict elevated risk for violence in a nonadditive fashion (cf. Hare & Neumann, 2009). Results indicated that these two components of PCL-R psychopathy do not contribute interactively to violence prediction.

In sum, the findings of Kennealy et al. (2010) indicate that Factor 2 of the PCL-R is markedly predictive of violent behavior, whereas the affective-interpersonal features contribute little beyond this to the prediction of violence. The obvious question raised by these results is why this factor of the PCL-R in particular seems to be predictive of violent behavior. One explanation suggested by material reviewed in the preceding section is that the close relationship of PCL-R Factor 2 to the externalizing liability construct (cf. Patrick et al., 2005) accounts for its robust prediction relationship with aggressive outcomes. Notably, the variance in Factor 2 that overlaps with Factor 1 appears to reflect callous-aggressiveness ("meanness") more so than boldness (Patrick et al., 2007, 2009), and this may (per earlier discussion of the role of callous-aggressive tendencies in the transmission of violence) account in part for the PCL-R's predictive validity with respect to violence. However, an alternative possibility raised by Kennealy et al. (2010) has to do with predictor/criterion overlap. That is, scores on Factor 2 of the PCL-R in part reflect the occurrence of aggressive antisocial behavior in early life (through items reflecting early behavior problems and juvenile delinquency) as well as adulthood (most directly, through the "poor behavioral control" item, which reflects hot temperedness, fighting, and assaultive acts). Since it is well known that past violence predicts future violence, further research is needed to ascertain whether disinhibitory and callous-aggressive tendencies indexed by PCL-R Factor 2 are predictive of violent-aggressive behavior even after controlling for (or omitting) items focusing on past instances of such behavior.

SUMMARY AND FUTURE DIRECTIONS

CD, ASPD, and psychopathy have been widely studied due to their clear relevance to important personal and societal outcomes, including criminal behavior, violence, and recidivism. While the diagnostic criteria for these disorders have shifted over time, CD and ASPD have been defined largely in terms of observable, behavioral indicants of norm violations and aggression. Psychopathy, in contrast, is defined by the presence of persistent impulsive and antisocial behaviors in combination with characterological features entailing impaired emotional sensitivity and social dominance and exploitativeness. A large research literature has elucidated distinct patterns of comorbidity, psychosocial outcomes, and personality and neurobiological correlates for each of these disorders.

Despite these differences, clear overlap also exists among these conditions. From the perspective of the triarchic model of psychopathy, CD, ASPD, and psychopathy share in common the characteristic of disinhibition or general externalizing proneness, and to some degree callous-aggressiveness (meanness). Genetic influences have been shown to contribute both to general disinhibitory tendencies and to callous-aggressive tendencies. Recent research has also produced compelling evidence that violent criminal deviance is transmitted within families. Based on these findings, a plausible hypothesis is that family transmission of violence is causally related, at least in part, to transmission of disinhibitory and callous-aggressive tendencies. This is a question that warrants systematic attention in future research.

In addition, systematic research is needed to evaluate refinements in procedures for diagnosing CD and ASPD in *DSM-5*, which provide for improved coverage of core affective-interpersonal features of psychopathy underrepresented in prior editions of the *DSM*. Specifically, the inclusion of a limited prosocial emotions (callous-unemotional) specifier for CD and an alternative trait-based approach to defining ASPD in *DSM-5* will improve representation of features such as emotional insensitivity, callous disregard, and interpersonal exploitativeness in these disorders—and in the case of ASPD, provide (through supplemental trait assessment) a basis for indexing fearless-dominant tendencies emphasized in influential theories of psychopathy. These important revisions have the potential to resolve some of the major sources of dissatisfaction with the ASPD conception historically and to allow for better integration of findings from research on CD, ASPD, and psychopathy and their relations with violent/aggressive behavior.

ACKNOWLEDGMENTS

Preparation of this chapter was supported by grants MH52384 and MH089727 from the National Institute of Mental Health.

REFERENCES

Abikoff, H., & Klein, R. G. (1992). Attention-deficit hyperactivity disorder and conduct disorder: Comorbidity and implications for treatment. *Journal of Consulting and Clinical Psychology, 60,* 881–892.

Acton, G. S. (2003). Measurement of impulsivity in a hierarchical model of personality traits: Implications for substance use. *Substance Use and Misuse, 38,* 67–83.

American Psychiatric Association. (1952). *Diagnostic and statistical manual of mental disorders.* Washington, DC: Author.

American Psychiatric Association. (1968). *Diagnostic and statistical manual of mental disorders* (2nd ed.). Washington, DC: Author.

American Psychiatric Association. (1980). *Diagnostic and statistical manual of mental disorders* (3rd ed.). Washington, DC: Author.

American Psychiatric Association. (1987). *Diagnostic and statistical manual of mental disorders* (3rd ed., rev.). Washington, DC: Author.

American Psychiatric Association. (1994). *Diagnostic and statistical manual of mental disorders* (4th ed.). Washington, DC: Author.

American Psychiatric Association. (2000). *Diagnostic and statistical manual of mental disorders* (4th ed., text rev.). Washington, DC: Author.

American Psychiatric Association. (2013). *Diagnostic and statistical manual of mental disorders* (5th ed.). Washington, DC: Author.

Bauer, L. O., O'Connor, S., & Hesselbrock, V. M. (1994). Frontal P300 decrements in antisocial personality disorder. *Alcoholism: Clinical and Experimental Research, 18,* 1300–1305.

Benning, S. D., Patrick, C. J., Hicks, B. M., Blonigen, D. M., & Krueger, R. F. (2003). Factor structure of the Psychopathic Personality Inventory: Validity and implications for clinical assessment. *Psychological Assessment, 15,* 340–350.

Benning, S. D., Patrick, C. J., Salekin, R. T., & Leistico, A. R. (2005). Convergent and discriminant validity of psychopathy factors assessed via self-report: A comparison of three instruments. *Assessment, 12,* 270–289.

Blair, R. J. R. (2006). Subcortical brain systems in psychopathy: The amygdala and associated structures. In C. J. Patrick (Ed.), *Handbook of psychopathy* (pp. 296–312). New York, NY: Guilford Press.

Blonigen, D. M., Hicks, B. M., Patrick, C. J., Krueger, R. F., Iacono, W. G., & McGue, M. K. (2005). Psychopathic personality traits: Heritability and genetic overlap with internalizing and externalizing psychopathology. *Psychological Medicine, 35,* 1–12.

Burt, S. A. (2009). Are there meaningful etiological differences within antisocial behavior? Results of a meta-analysis. *Clinical Psychology Review, 29,* 163–178.

Cleckley, H. (1976). *The mask of sanity* (5th ed). St. Louis, MO: Mosby.

Cooke, D. J., & Michie, C. (2001). Refining the construct of psychopathy: Towards a hierarchical model. *Psychological Assessment, 13,* 171–188.

Corrado, R. R., Vincent, G. M., Hart S. D., & Cohen, I. M. (2004). Predictive validity of the Psychopathy Checklist: Youth vrsion for general and violent recidivism. *Behavioral Sciences and the Law, 22,* 5–22.

Douglas, K., Epstein, M., & Poythress, N. (2008). Criminal recidivism among juvenile offenders: Testing the incremental and predictive validity of three measures of psychopathic features. *Law and Human Behavior, 32,* 423–438.

Drislane, L. E., Patrick, C. J., & Arsal, G. (2013). Clarifying the content coverage of differing psychopathy inventories through reference to the Triarchic Psychopathy Measure. *Psychological Assessment.* Advance online publication. doi:10.1037/a0035152

Farrington, D. P., Coid, J. W., Harnett, L., Jolliffe, D., Soteriou, N., Turner, R.., & West, D. J. (2006). *Criminal careers up to the age of 50 and life success up to the age of 48: New findings from the Cambridge Study in Delinquent Development.* London, UK: Home Office.

First, M. B., Gibbon, M., Spitzer, R. L., Williams, J. B. W., & Benjamin, L. S. (1997). *Structured Clinical Interview for DSM-IV axis II personality disorders, (SCID-II).* Washington, DC: American Psychiatric Press.

Forth, A. E., & Burke, H. C. (1998). Psychopathy in adolescence: Assessment, violence, and developmental precursors. In D. J. Cooke, A. E. Forth, & R. D. Hare (Eds.), *Psychopathy: Theory, research, and implications for society* (pp. 205–229). Dordrecht, The Netherlands: Kluwer.

Fowles, D. C. (1980). The three arousal model: Implications of Gray's two-factor learning theory for heart rate, electrodermal activity, and psychopathy. *Psychophysiology, 17,* 87–104.

Frances, A. J. (1980). The DSM-III personality disorders section: A commentary. *American Journal of Psychiatry, 137,* 1050–1054.

Frick, P. J., & Ellis, M. (1999). Callous-unemotional traits and subtypes of conduct disorder. *Clinical Child and Family Psychology Review, 2,* 149–168.

Frick, P. J., Lilienfeld, S. O., Ellis, M., Loney, B., & Silverthorn, P. (1999). The association between anxiety and psychopathy dimensions in children. *Journal of Abnormal Child Psychology, 27*, 383–392.

Frick, P. J., & Moffitt, T. E. (2010). A proposal to the DSM-V childhood disorders and the ADHD and disruptive behavior disorders work groups to include a specifier to the diagnosis of conduct disorder based on the presence of callous-unemotional traits. *American Psychiatric Association.* Retrieved May 2013, from http://www.dsm5.org/Proposed%20Revision%20Attachments/Proposal%20for%20Callous%20and%20Unemotional%20Specifier%20of%20Conduct%20Disorder.pdf.

Frick, P. J., & White, S. F. (2008). The importance of callous-unemotional traits for developmental models of aggressive and antisocial behavior. *Journal of Child Psychology and Psychiatry, 49*, 359–375.

Frisell, T., Lichtenstein, P., & Långström, N. (2011). Violent crime runs in families: A total population study of 12.5 million individuals. *Psychological Medicine, 41*, 97–105.

Grant, B. F., Stinson, F. S., Dawson, D. A., Chou, S. P., Ruan, W. J., & Pickering, R. P. (2004). Co-occurrence of 12-month alcohol and drug use disorders and personality disorders in the United States: Results from the National Epidemiologic Survey on Alcohol and Related Conditions. *Archives of General Psychiatry, 61*, 361–368.

Greene, R. W., Biederman J., Zerwas, S., Monuteaux, M. C., Goring, J. C., & Faraone, S. V. (2002). Psychiatric comorbidity, family dysfunction, and social impairment in referred youth with oppositional defiant disorder. *American Journal of Psychiatry, 159*, 1214–1224.

Hall, J. R., Benning, S. D., & Patrick, C. J. (2004). Criterion-related validity of the three-factor model of psychopathy: Personality, behavior, and adaptive functioning. *Assessment, 11*, 4–16.

Hall, J. R., Drislane, L. E., Patrick, C. J., Morano, M., Lilienfeld, S. O., & Poythress, N. G. (2014). Development and validation of triarchic construct scales from the Psychopathic Personality Inventory. *Psychological Assessment.* Advance online publication. doi: 10.1037/a0035665

Hare, R. D. (1980). A research scale for the assessment of psychopathy in criminal populations. *Personality and Individual Differences, 1*, 111–119.

Hare, R. D. (1983). Diagnosis of antisocial personality disorder in two prison populations. *American Journal of Psychiatry, 140*, 887–890.

Hare, R. D. (1991). *The Hare psychopathy checklist—revised.* Toronto, ON: Multi-Health Systems.

Hare, R. D. (1998). Psychopaths and their nature: Implications for mental health and criminal justice systems. In T. Millon, E. Simonsen, M. Birket-Smith, & R. D. Davis, (Eds.), *Psychopathy: Antisocial, criminal, and violent behavior* (pp. 188–212). New York, NY: Guilford Press.

Hare, R. D. (2003). *The Hare psychopathy checklist—revised* (2nd ed.). Toronto, ON: Multi-Health Systems.

Hare, R. D., Harpur, T. J., Hakstian, A. R., Forth, A. E., Hart, S. D., & Newman, J. P. (1990). The Revised Psychopathy Checklist: Reliability and factor structure. *Psychological Assessment, 2*, 338–341.

Hare, R. D., & Hart, S. D. (1995). Commentary on the DSM-IV antisocial personality disorder field trial. In W. J. Livesley (Ed.), *The DSM-IV personality disorders* (pp. 127–134). New York, NY: Guilford Press.

Hare, R. D., & Neumann, C. N. (2006). The PCL-R assessment of psychopathy: Development, structural properties, and new directions. In C. J. Patrick (Ed.), *Handbook of psychopathy* (pp. 58–88). New York, NY: Guilford Press.

Hare, R. D., & Neumann, C. S. (2009). Psychopathy: Assessment and forensic implications. *Canadian Journal of Psychiatry, 54*(12), 791–802.

Harpur, T. J., Hare, R. D., & Hakstian, R. (1989). A two-factor conceptualization of psychopathy: Construct validity and implications for assessment. *Psychological Assessment, 1,* 6–17.

Hewitt, L. E., & Jenkins, R. L. (1946).*Fundamental patterns of maladjustment: The dynamics of their origin.*Springfield, Ill.: Charles C. Thomas..

Hicks, B. M., Krueger, R. F., Iacono, W. G., McGue, M. K., & Patrick, C. J. (2004). The family transmission and heritability of externalizing disorders. *Archives of General Psychiatry, 61,* 922–928.

Hicks, B. M., & Patrick, C. J. (2006). Psychopathy and negative affectivity: Analyses of suppressor effects reveal distinct relations with trait anxiety, depression, fearfulness, and anger-hostility. *Journal of Abnormal Psychology, 115,* 276–287.

Hinshaw, S. P., Heller, T., & McHale, J. P. (1992). Covert antisocial behavior in boys with attention-deficit hyperactivity disorder: External validation and effects of methylphenidate. *Journal of Consulting and Clinical Psychology, 60,* 274–281.

Hinshaw, S. P., Lahey, B. B., & Hart, E. L. (1993). Issues in taxonomy and comorbidity in the development of conduct disorder. *Development and Psychopathology, 5,* 31–49.

Iacono, W. G., Carlson, S. R., & Malone, S.M. (2000). Identifying a multivariate endophenotype for substance use disorders using psychophysiological measures. *International Journal of Psychophysiology, 1,* 3881–3896

Iacono, W. G., Carlson, S. R., Malone, S. M., & McGue, M. (2002). P3 event-related potential amplitude and risk for disinhibitory disorders in adolescent boys. *Archives of General Psychiatry, 59,* 750–757.

Jones, A. P., Laurens, K. R., Herba, C. M., Barker, G. J., & Viding, E. (2009). Amygdala hypoactivity to fearful faces in boys with conduct problems and callous-unemotional traits. *American Journal of Psychiatry, 166,* 95–102.

Kendler, K. S., Aggen, S. H., & Patrick, C. J. (2012). A multivariate twin study of the DSM-IV criteria for antisocial personality disorder. *Biological Psychiatry, 71,* 247–253.

Kendler, K. S., Aggen, S. H., & Patrick, C. J. (2013). Familial influences on conduct disorder criteria in males reflect two genetic factors and one shared environmental factor: A population-based twin study. *JAMA Psychiatry, 70,* 78–86.

Kennealy, P. J., Skeem, J. L., Walters, G. D., & Camp, J. (2010). Do core interpersonal and affective traits of PCL-R psychopathy interact with antisocial behavior and disinhibition to predict violence? *Psychological Assessment, 22,* 569–580.

Kessler, R. C., & Walters, E. E. (2002). The National Comorbidity Survey. In M. T. Tsuang & M. Tohen (Eds.), *Textbook in psychiatric epidemiology* (2nd ed., pp. 343–362). New York, NY: Wiley.

Koch, J. L. (1891). *Die psychopathischen minderwertigkeiten* [The psychopathic inferiority]. Ravensburg, Germany: Maier.

Kraepelin, E. (1915). *Psychiatrie: Ein lehrbuch* [Psychiatry: A textbook]. (8th ed.). Leipzig, Germany: Barth.

Krueger, R. F. (1999a). The structure of common mental disorders. *Archives of General Psychiatry, 56,* 921–926.

Krueger, R. F. (1999b). Personality traits in late adolescence predict mental disorders in early adulthood: A prospective-epidemiological study. *Journal of Personality, 67,* 39–65.

Krueger, R. F., Hicks, B., Patrick, C. J., Carlson, S., Iacono, W. G., & McGue, M. (2002). Etiologic connections among substance dependence, antisocial behavior, and personality: Modeling the externalizing spectrum. *Journal of Abnormal Psychology, 111,* 411–424.

Krueger, R. F., Markon, K. E., Patrick, C. J., Benning, S. D., & Kramer, M. (2007). Linking antisocial behavior, substance use, and personality: An integrative quantitative model of the adult externalizing spectrum. *Journal of Abnormal Psychology, 116,* 645–666.

Krueger, R. F., Markon, K. E., Patrick, C. J., & Iacono, W. G. (2005). Externalizing psychopathology in adulthood: A dimensional-spectrum conceptualization and its implications for DSM–V. *Journal of Abnormal Psychology, 114,* 537–550.

Lahey, B. B., Loeber, R., Quay, H. C., Frick, P. J., & Grimm, J. (1997). Oppositional defiant disorder and conduct disorder. In T. A. Widiger, A. J. Frances, H. A. Pincus, R. Ross, M. B. First, & W. Davis (Eds.), *DSM-IV sourcebook* (Vol 3, pp 189–209). Washington, DC: American Psychiatric Association.

Lahey, B. B., Miller, T. L., Gordon, R. A., & Riley, A. W. (1999). Developmental epidemiology of the disruptive behavior disorders. In H. C. Quay & A. Hogan (Eds.), *Handbook of the disruptive behavior disorders* (pp. 23–48). New York, NY: Plenum

Leistico, A. R., Salekin, R. T., DeCoster, J., & Rogers, R. (2008). A large-scale meta-analysis relating the Hare measures of psychopathy to antisocial conduct. *Law and Human Behavior, 32,* 28–45.

Lilienfeld, S. O., & Andrews, B. P. (1996). Development and preliminary validation of a self-report measure of psychopathic personality traits in noncriminal populations. *Journal of Personality Assessment, 66,* 488–524.

Lilienfeld, S. O., & Widows, M. R. (2005). *Psychopathic Personality Inventory—Revised (PPI—R) professional manual.* Odessa, FL: Psychological Assessment Resources.

Loeber, R., Green, S. M., Keenan, K., & Lahey, B. B. (1995). Which boys will fare worse? Early predictors of the onset of conduct disorder in a six-year longitudinal study. *Journal of the American Academy of Child and Adolescent Psychiatry, 34,* 499–509.

Loeber, R., Lahey, B. B., & Thomas, C. (1991). Diagnostic conundrum of oppositional defiant disorder and conduct disorder. *Journal of Abnormal Psychology, 100,* 379–390.

Loeber, R., Stouthammer-Loeber, M., & White, H. R. (1999). Developmental aspects of delinquency and internalizing problems and their association with persistent juvenile substance use between ages 7 and 18. *Journal of Clinical Child Psychology, 28,* 322–332.

Lorber, M. F. (2004). Psychophysiology of aggression, psychopathy, and conduct problems: A meta-analysis. *Psychological Bulletin, 130,* 531–552.

Lykken, D. T. (1957). A study of anxiety in the sociopathic personality. *Journal of Abnormal and Clinical Psychology, 55,* 6–10.

Lynam, D. R. (1998). Early identification of the fledgling psychopath: Locating the psychopathic child in the current nomenclature. *Journal of Abnormal Psychology, 107,* 566–575.

Lynam, D. R., Leukefeld, C., & Clayton, R. R. (2003). The contribution of personality to the overlap between antisocial behavior and substance use/misuse. *Aggressive Behavior, 29,* 316–331.

Lynne-Landsman, S. D., Graber, J. A., Nichols, T. R., & Botvin, G. J. (2011). Trajectories of aggression, delinquency, and substance use across middle school among urban, minority adolescents. *Aggressive Behavior, 37,* 161–176.

Maliphant, R., Hume, F., & Furnham, A. (1990). Autonomic nervous system (ANS) activity, personality characteristics and disruptive behaviour in girls. *Journal of Child Psychology and Psychiatry, 31,* 619–628.

Marsh, A. A., Finger, E. C., Mitchell, D. G., Reid, M. E., Sims, C., Kosson, D. S., ... Blair, R. J. (2008). Reduced amygdala response to fearful expressions in children and adolescents with callous-unemotional traits and disruptive behavior disorders. *American Journal of Psychiatry, 165,* 712–720.

McCord, W., & McCord, J. (1964). *The psychopath: An essay on the criminal mind.* Princeton, NJ: Van Nostrand.

Michonski, J. D., & Sharp, C. (2010). Revisiting Lynam's notion of the "fledgling psychopath": Are HIA-CP children truly psychopathic-like? *Child and Adolescent Psychiatry and Mental Health, 4,* 24.

Millon, T. (1981). *Disorders of personality DSM-III: Axis II.* New York, NY: Wiley.

Minzenberg, M. J., & Siever, L. J. (2006). Neurochemistry and pharmacology of psychopathy and related disorders. In C. J. Patrick (Ed.), *Handbook of psychopathy* (pp. 251–277). New York, NY: Guilford Press.

Moffitt, T. E. (1993). Adolescence-limited and life-course-persistent antisocial behavior: A developmental taxonomy. *Psychological Review, 100,* 674–701.

Moffitt, T. E. (2007). A review of research on the taxonomy of life-course persistent versus adolescence-limited antisocial behavior. In D. J. Flannery, A. T. Vazsonyi, & I. D. Waldman (Eds.), *The Cambridge handbook of violent behavior and aggression.* Cambridge, UK: Cambridge University Press.

Morgan, A. B., & Lilienfeld, S. O. (2000). A meta-analytic review of the relation between antisocial behavior and neuropsychological measures of executive function. *Clinical Psychology Review, 20,* 113–136.

Odgers, C. L., Moffitt, T. E., Broadbent, J. M., Dickson, N., Hancox, R. J., Harrington, H., ... Caspi, A. (2008). Female and male antisocial trajectories: From childhood origins to adult outcomes. *Development and Psychopathology, 20,* 673–716.

Ortiz, J., & Raine, A. (2004). Heart rate level and antisocial behavior in children and adolescents: A meta-analysis. *Journal of the American Academy of Child and Adolescent Psychiatry, 43,* 154–162.

Pardini, D. A., Lochman, J. E., & Powell, N. (2007). The development of callous-unemotional traits and anti-social behavior in children: Are there shared or unique predictors? *Journal of Clinical Child and Adolescent Psychology, 36,* 319–333.

Pardini, D. A., Obradović, J., & Loeber, R. (2006). Interpersonal callousness, hyperactivity/impulsivitiy, inattention, and conduct problems as precursors to delinquency persistence in boys: A comparison of three grade-based cohorts. *Journal of Clinical Child and Adolescent Psychology, 35,* 46–59.

Patrick, C. J. (1994). Emotion and psychopathy: Startling new insights. *Psychophysiology, 31,* 319–330.

Patrick, C. J. (2006). Back to the future: Cleckley as a guide to the next generation of psychopathy research. In C. J. Patrick (Ed.), *Handbook of psychopathy* (pp. 605–617). New York, NY: Guilford Press.

Patrick, C. J., Bernat, E., Malone, S. M., Iacono, W. G., Krueger, R. F., & McGue, M. K. (2006). P300 amplitude as an indicator of externalizing in adolescent males. *Psychophysiology, 43,* 84–92.

Patrick, C. J., Edens, J. F., Poythress, N., Lilienfeld, S. O., & Benning, S. D. (2006). Construct validity of the PPI two-factor model with offenders. *Psychological Assessment, 18*, 204–208.

Patrick, C. J., Fowles, D. C., & Krueger, R. F. (2009). Triarchic conceptualization of psychopathy: Developmental origins of disinhibition, boldness, and meanness. *Development and Psychopathology, 21*, 913–938.

Patrick, C. J., Hicks, B. M., Krueger, R. F., & Lang, A. R. (2005). Relations between psychopathy facets and externalizing in a criminal offender sample. *Journal of Personality Disorders, 19*, 339–356.

Patrick, C. J., Hicks, B. M., Nichol, P. E., & Krueger, R. F. (2007). A bifactor approach to modeling the structure of the Psychopathy Checklist-Revised. *Journal of Personality Disorders, 21*, 118–141.

Patrick, C. J., Venables, N. C., & Skeem, J. L. (2012). Psychopathy and brain function: Empirical findings and legal implications. In H. Häkkänen-Nyholm & J. Nyholm (Eds.), *Psychopathy and law: A practitioner's guide* (pp. 39–78). New York, NY: Wiley.

Patrick, C. J., & Zempolich, K. A. (1998). Emotion and aggression in the psychopathic personality. *Aggression and Violent Behavior, 3*, 303–338.

Patrick, C. J., Zempolich, K. A., & Levenston, G. K. (1997). Emotionality and violence in psychopaths: A biosocial analysis. In A. Raine, D. Farrington, P. Brennan, & S. A. Mednick (Eds.), *The biosocial bases of violence* (pp. 145–161). New York: Plenum.

Pinel, P. (1962). *A treatise on insanity.* (D. Davis, Trans.). New York, NY: Hafner. (original work published 1801 as *Traité médico-philosophique sur l'liénation mentale ou la manie [Medico-philosophical treatise on mental alienation or mania]*)

Poythress, N. G., Lilienfeld, S. O., Skeem, J. L., Douglas, K. S., Edens, J. F., Epstein, M., & Patrick, C. J. (2010). Using the PCL-R to help estimate the validity of two self-report measures of psychopathy with offenders. *Assessment, 17*, 206–219.

Pritchard, J. C. (1835). *A treatise on insanity and other disorders affecting the mind.* London, UK: Sherwood, Gilbert & Piper.

Quay, H.C. (1987). Patterns of delinquent behavior. In H. C. Quay (Ed.), *Handbook of juvenile delinquency* (pp. 118–138). New York, NY: Wiley.

Raine, A. (2002). Biosocial studies of antisocial and violent behavior in children and adults: A review. *Journal of Abnormal Child Psychology, 30*(4), 311–326.

Raine, A., & Venables, P. H. (1984). Tonic heart rate level, social class, and antisocial behaviour in adolescents. *Biological Psychology, 18*, 123–132.

Reardon, M. L., Lang, A. R., & Patrick, C. J. (2002). Antisociality and alcohol problems: An evaluation of subtypes, drinking motives, and family history in incarcerated men. *Alcoholism: Clinical and Experimental Research, 26*, 1188–1197.

Robins, L. N. (1966). *Deviant children grown up: A sociological and psychiatric study of sociopathic personality.* Baltimore: Williams & Wilkins.

Robins, L. N., & Regier, D. A. (1991). *Psychiatric disorders in America: The epidemiological catchment area study.* New York, NY: Free Press.

Rush, B. (1812). *Medical inquiries and observations upon the diseases of the mind.* Philadelphia, PA: Kimber & Richardson.

Rutter, M., Giller, H., & Hagell, A. (1998). *Antisocial behaviour in young people.* Cambridge, UK: Cambridge University Press.

Salekin, R. T. (2006). Psychopathy in children and adults: Key issues in conceptualization and assessment. In C. J. Patrick (Ed.), *Handbook of psychopathy* (pp. 389–414). New York, NY: Guilford Press.

Salekin, R. T., Ziegler, T., Larrea, M. A., Anthony, V. L., & Bennett, A. D. (2003). Predicting dangerousness with two Millon Adolescent Clinical Inventory psychopathy scales: The importance of egocentric and callous traits. *Journal of Personality Assessment*, 80, 154–163.

Skeem, J. L., Polaschek, D. L., Patrick, C. J., & Lilienfeld, S. O. (2011). Psychopathic personality: Bridging the gap between scientific evidence and public policy. *Psychological Science in the Public Interest*, 12(3), 95–162.

Smith, S. S., & Newman, J. P. (1990). Alcohol and drug abuse in psychopathic and nonpsychopathic criminal offenders. *Journal of Abnormal Psychology*, 99, 430–439.

Strickland, C. M., Drislane, L. E., Lucy, M. D., Krueger, R. F., & Patrick, C. J. (2013). Representing psychopathy using DSM-5 personality disorder traits. *Assessment*, 20(3), 327–338.

Stockdale, K. C., Olver, M. E., & Wong, S. C. P. (2010). The Psychopathy Checklist: Youth Version and adolescent and adult recidivism: Considerations with respect to gender, ethnicity, and age. *Psychological Assessment*, 22, 768–781.

Sutton, S. K., Vitale, J. E., & Newman, J. P. (2002). Emotion among women with psychopathy during picture perception. *Journal of Abnormal Psychology*, 111, 610–619.

Tackett, J. L., Krueger, R. F., Iacono, W. G., & McGue, M. (2005). Symptom-based subfactors of DSM-defined conduct disorder: Evidence for etiologic distinctions. *Journal of Abnormal Psychology*, 114, 483–487.

Tackett, J. L., Krueger, R. F., Sawyer, M. G., & Graetz, B. W. (2003). Subfactors of DSM-IV conduct disorder: Evidence and connections with syndromes from the child behavior checklist. *Journal of Abnormal Child Psychology*, 31, 647–654.

Tellegen, A. (1982). *Brief manual for the multidimensional personality questionnaire*. Minneapolis, MN: University of Minnesota Press.

Trull, T. J. (1992). DSM-III-R personality disorders and the five-factor model of personality: An empirical comparison. *Journal of Abnormal Psychology*, 101, 553–560.

Vaidyanathan, U., Hall, J. R., Patrick, C. J., & Bernat, E. M. (2011). Clarifying the role of defensive reactivity deficits in psychopathy and antisocial personality using startle reflex methodology. *Journal of Abnormal Psychology*, 12, 253–258.

Venables, N. C., Hall, J. R., & Patrick, C. J. (2014). Differentiating psychopathy from antisocial personality disorder: A triarchic model perspective. *Psychological Medicine*, 44(5), 1005–1013.

Venables, N. C., & Patrick, C. J. (2012). Validity of the Externalizing Spectrum Inventory in a criminal offender sample: Relations with disinhibitory psychopathology, personality, and psychopathic features. *Psychological Assessment*, 24, 88–100.

Verona, E., Hicks, B. M., & Patrick, C. J. (2005). Psychopathy and suicidal behavior in female offenders: Mediating influences of temperament and abuse history. *Journal of Consulting and Clinical Psychology*, 73, 1065–1073.

Verona, E., Patrick, C. J., & Joiner, T. E. (2001). Psychopathy, antisocial personality, and suicide risk. *Journal of Abnormal Psychology*, 110, 462–470.

White, S. F., & Frick, P. J. (2010). Callous-unemotional traits and their importance to causal models of severe antisocial behavior in youth. In R. T. Salekin & D. R. Lynam (Eds.), *Handbook of child and adolescent psychopathy* (pp. 135–155). New York, NY: Guilford Press.

White, H. R., Loeber, R., Stouthamer-Loeber, M., & Farrington, D. P. (1999). Developmental associations between substance use and violence. *Development and Psychopathology*, 11, 785–803

Woodworth, M., & Porter, S. (2002). In cold blood: Characteristics of criminal homicides as a function of psychopathy. *Journal of Abnormal Psychology, 111,* 436–445.

Young, S. E., Stallings, M. C., Corley, R. P., Krauter, K. S., & Hewitt, J. K. (2000). Genetic and environmental influences on behavioral disinhibition. *American Journal of Medical Genetics (Neuropsychiatric Genetics), 96,* 684–695.

Zoccolillo, M. (1993). Gender and the development of conduct disorder. *Development and Psychopathology, 5,* 65–78.

Special Offender Populations

6

Juvenile Homicide

Trends, Correlates, Causal Factors, and Outcomes

KATHLEEN M. HEIDE ■

Murders by youths under 18 years of age have been a matter of serious concern in the United States since the mid-1970s (Heide, 1986). For many years journalistic accounts have depicted juveniles as more dangerous than their predecessors. In 1975, for example, an article appeared in the *New York Times Magazine* section titled "They think I can kill because I'm 14" (Morgan, 1975). The article suggested that society had spawned a new "genetic" strain of child murderer who appeared to kill deliberately, remorselessly, and even joyfully.

An examination of murder arrests provided some evidence for the alarm raised by the media in the 1970s. The Federal Bureau of Investigation analyzes and publishes national data annually on individuals arrested for "murder or nonnegligent homicide" (hereafter referred to as murder or homicide). Arrests of juveniles (defined as individuals under age 18) for murder increased by more than 200% over the period 1960–1975 (FBI, 1976), a percentage that vastly exceeded the number of arrests that could be attributed to age shifts in the US population. During the late 1970s and early 1980s, the involvement of youth in homicide appeared to stabilize and even showed a possible decreasing trend.

The decline in juvenile involvement in murder did not last, however. From the mid-1980s through the mid-1990s, dramatic increases in youths being arrested for homicide and other serious violent crimes (robbery, assault, and rape) were apparent (Heide, 1999). The rise in youth violence was not confined to the United States during this period. England and Wales, Germany, Sweden, the Netherlands, Austria, France, Italy, Denmark, Switzerland, and Poland all reported that violent crimes committed by youths had increased by at least 50% in all of these countries and by more than 100% in most of them (Pfeiffer, 1998; Travis, 1997).

The continuous rise in juveniles arrested for murder in the United States was at near epidemic proportions by 1993 and was particularly alarming because it was occurring during a period when the juvenile population had been declining. Homicide experts feared that murders by youths would increase exponentially in the 21st century because the population under 18 was growing (Ewing, 1990; Fox, 1995, 1996). In contrast to predictions, juvenile arrests for homicide decreased from

1994 through 2000. Since 2000, the percentage involvement of juveniles among homicide arrestees has fluctuated from a high of 10.7% in 2004 to a low of 7.8% in 2011, the latest year for which arrests statistics are available (FBI, 1985–2012). In 2011, 651 of the 8,359 individuals arrested for homicide were under age 18.

Based on a review of US homicide arrests from 1960 to 2011, Zimring concluded that the homicide arrest rates for juveniles and adults in 2011 were "close to 45-year low points" (p. 50). He predicted that "the wide variations observed in the proportion of all homicides that were committed by juveniles are not likely to happen again soon" (Zimring, 2012, p. 48), notwithstanding anticipated demographic changes in the number of juveniles or their racial and ethnic composition. He predicted that juvenile involvement in homicide will follow the trends for adult homicide offenders. He suggested that "perhaps American youth violence has arrived at a 'new normal' after an exciting and peculiar 25-year interlude" (Zimring, 2012, p. 50).

This chapter presents a demographic profile of juveniles arrested for murder in the United States. Thereafter, the clinical literature is reviewed and national studies investigating gender and age differences among juvenile homicide offenders (JHOs) are highlighted. The legal processing of JHOs is discussed with attention to prosecuting and defending young killers. The literature on treatment is summarized along with available follow-up studies. The chapter concludes with a call for action.

JUVENILES ARRESTED FOR MURDER IN THE UNITED STATES

There is no national database of convicted homicide offenders in the United States. The Uniform Crime Report Supplementary Homicide Report (SHR) database is currently the best source of information on total US murders and those arrested for murder or nonnegligent homicide. The SHR offender data set of murder arrests from 1976 to 2007 (Fox & Swatt, 2009) was used to examine offender and offense correlates of JHOs. Examining the characteristics of homicide arrestees over a 32-year time frame gives a more accurate representation of JHOs than relying on 1 year of data.

During this 32-year period, 44,147 youths aged 6 to 17 were arrested for murder. The percentages of juveniles arrested for homicide increased positively with age. As shown in Table 6.1, 88% of JHOs were 15, 16, and 17 years old at the time of arrest. Young teenagers comprised about 10% of JHOs. Less than 2% of juvenile homicide arrestees were aged 12 and under. Juveniles arrested for murder were overwhelmingly male. Only 8% of JHOs were female.

Nearly 98% of homicide arrestees under age 18 were Black or White. The involvement of Black youth among juvenile homicide arrestees (nearly 55%) was disproportionately high given the proportion of the US population that is Black, estimated at about 13%. In contrast, the percentages of juvenile homicide arrestees who were White (about 43%), American Indian and Alaskan Native (less than 1%), and Asian and Pacific Islanders (less than 2%) was disproportionately low given their representation in the population, estimated at 78%, 1.2%, and 5.2%, respectively (US Census Bureau, 2013).

More than 96% of juveniles arrested for murder killed one victim. When one victim was killed, the percentages of juveniles who acted alone were about the same as

Table 6.1 Juvenile Homicide Arrestees, 1976–2007

	Percent
Offender Age (years)	
6–10	.5
11–12	1.4
13	2.8
14	7.3
15	16.5
16	29.1
17	42.4
Total arrests (*n* = 44,147)	100.0
Offender Gender	
Male	91.9
Female	8.1
Total arrests (*n* = 44,088)	100.0
Offender Race	
White	42.6
Black	54.9
American Indian	0.9
Asian and Pacific Islander	1.6
Total arrests (*n* = 43,770)	100.0
Situation	
Single victim/single offender	47.9
Single victim/multiple offender	48.4
Mult victim/single offender	1.3
Mult victim/multiple offender	2.4
Total arrests (*n* = 44,142)	100.0
Region Arrested	
South	37.7
West	25.4
Midwest	21.8
Northeast	15.1
Total arrests (*n* = 44,147)	100.0
Location Arrested	
Large city	59.9
Small city	12.3
Suburban	19.7
Rural	8.2
Total arrests (*n* = 44,147)	100.0
Period Arrested	
1976–1985	27.1
1986–1995	43.9
1996–2007	29.0
Total arrests	100.0

Table 6.2 CIRCUMSTANCES OF JUVENILE HOMICIDE
ARRESTS, 1976–2007

Circumstance	Percent
Crime-related (*n* = 13,280)	
–robbery	19.5
–narcotics laws	4.2
–burglary	1.6
–other felony / crime-related	1.7
–suspected felony	.9
–rape	.8
–other sex offense	.3
–arson	.6
–larceny and auto theft	.6
–Subtotal	30.1
Conflict-related (*n* = 13,655)	
–other arguments	26.0
–arguments over money	2.1
–brawl under alcohol	1.3
–brawl under drugs	.9
–lovers' triangle	.7
–Subtotal	31.0
Gang-related (*n* = 5,548)	
–youth gang killing	11.2
–gangland killing	1.3
–Subtotal	12.5
Other (*n* = 6,462)	
–other (FBI coded)	14.1
–killed by babysitter	.3
–institution killing	.1
–sniper attack	.1
–Subtotal	14.6
Unknown (*n* = 5,202)	11.8
Total (*n* = 44,147)	100.0

Table 6.3 WEAPONS USED BY JUVENILE
HOMICIDE ARRESTEES, 1997–2007

Weapon Used	Percent
Firearm	68.0
Knife	15.5
Personal weapon	5.9
Blunt object	5.6
Other	2.5
Unknown	2.5
Total (*n* = 44,147)	100.0

those who killed with codefendants. Less than 4% of JHOs were arrested for killing multiple victims alone or with accomplices.

Geographical differences in the numbers of JHOs arrested were apparent. The highest percentage of juveniles (nearly 38%) was arrested in the South. Juveniles were arrested in the West (about 26%) and Midwest (nearly 22%) in fairly equivalent proportions. The smallest percentage of JHOs (15%) was arrested in the Northeast.

The largest percentage of youths arrested for murder occurred in large cities (nearly 60%) followed by suburban areas (about 20%). Youths from small cities and rural areas combined comprised the remaining 20% of juvenile homicide arrestees.

When the number of juveniles arrested for murder is examined across three periods, the middle period stands out. Nearly 44% of JHOs arrested for murder during the 32-year time period were arrested from 1986 to 1995. Approximately 27% of JHOs were arrested in the 10-year period preceding this time frame. During the third time period, which is 2 years longer than the first two periods, 29% of JHOs were arrested.

Perusal of Table 6.2 reveals that approximately 31% of JHOs killed during a conflict-related situation. Another 30% were known or suspected to be involved in the commission of a crime when the killing occurred. One out of eight offenders was arrested in relation to a gang-related killing.

As revealed in Table 6.3, more than two thirds of JHOs used firearms as their murder weapons. Nearly 16% used knives. Approximately 6% used personal weapons such as hands and feet, and another 6% used blunt objects. Less than 3% of all juveniles arrested for homicide used other means such as fire, strangulation, asphyxiation, drowning, drugs, poison, pushed out window, or explosives.

THE CLINICAL LITERATURE ON JUVENILE HOMICIDE OFFENDERS

Many researchers and mental health professionals have examined cases of youth killers over the past 70 years (Cornell, 1989; Cornell, Benedek, & Benedek, 1989; Ewing, 1990; Heide, 2003). Research efforts have concentrated largely on children and adolescents involved in murder in the United States, although two large-scale descriptive studies of Canadian youth homicide offenders exist (Meloff & Silverman, 1992; Woodworth, Agar, & Coupland, 2013). Leading authorities on JHOs include Dorothy Otnow Lewis and her colleagues (biopsychological factors of juvenile murderers); Charles Patrick Ewing (clinical and legal factors); Dewey Cornell and colleagues (typology of juvenile murderers); Kathleen Heide (adolescent parricide offenders); Wade Myers (juvenile sexual murderers); Eldra Solomon (biology, childhood trauma, and murder); Dominique Roe-Sepowitz (female juvenile murderers); Rolf Loeber, David Farrington, and colleagues (predictive factors from longitudinal studies of high-risk boys); and Robert Zagar and his colleagues (prospective and retrospective risk factors among homicidal youth).

Most of the available literature on JHOs consists of case reports and studies with small sample sizes. Although some clinical studies have included girls who kill, with few exceptions, the number of females is rarely sufficient to analyze gender differences. Accordingly, most conclusions made about JHOs are actually descriptive of males, particularly those in their teenage years (Heide, Roe-Sepowitz, Solomon, & Chan, 2012).

The term *juvenile* is frequently used interchangeably with *adolescent* in the professional literature on young killers. The two terms are not equivalent, however. Juvenile or minority status is determined by age and is a legislative decision. In the

United States, individuals are legally recognized as adults at age 18 and may then exercise certain rights, such as voting, enlisting in the service, and entering into contracts. *Adolescence*, unlike juvenile status, is based on human development and varies across individuals. It begins with puberty, the period of sexual development, which typically occurs by age 12 but may begin earlier. Adolescence is a turbulent period marked by growth spurts, hormonal changes, enhancement of intellectual abilities and motor skills, and psychological changes. From a biological perspective, adolescence continues through the late teenage years and into the early 20s when the individual becomes a young adult (Solomon, Berg, & Martin, 2011).

Youths who are age 12 and younger are sometimes referred to in the professional literature as *children, preteens*, or *preadolescents* to distinguish them from teenagers or adolescents (see, e.g., Shumaker& McKee, 2001; Shumaker & Prinz, 2000; Sellers & Heide, 2012). Precise definitions are seldom provided because most of these terms have no specific ages associated with them.

The distinction between younger children and older children is an important one and has direct relevance to the involvement of juveniles in homicide (Bender, 1959; Bender & Curran, 1940; Heide, Solomon, Sellers, & Chan, 2011). Younger children, particularly those under age 10, frequently do not completely understand the irreversibility and permanence of death. Younger children often act impulsively and can be induced to participate in homicidal acts by unstable, unscrupulous, or mentally ill parents (Sargent, 1962). Adolescents, in contrast, are more likely to be involved in homicide because of perceived situational demands or the lifestyle that they have embraced (Bender, 1959; Heide, 1992, 1999, 2013; Loeber & Farrington, 2011; Sorrells, 1977; Zenoff & Zients, 1979). In recognition of the importance of maturational differences, this section first reviews the clinical literature on adolescent homicide offenders and younger JHOs separately.

Adolescent Homicide Offenders

Many clinical studies of JHOs exist. Some of these have investigated victim characteristics, including family killings (see, for e.g., Corder, Ball, Haizlip, Rollins, & Beaumont, 1976; Duncan & Duncan, 1971; Evans, McGovern-Kondik, & Peric, 2005; Ewing, 1990, 1997; Heide, 1992, 2013; Kalogerakis, 1971; Rowley, Ewing, & Singer, 1987; Russell, 1986; Sargent, 1962; Wertham, 1941). Others have reported on the social backgrounds (Bailey, 1996a; Cornell, Benedek, & Benedek, 1987; Fenderich, Mackesy-Amiti, Goldstein, Spunt, & Brownstein, 1995; Myers & Scott, 1998) and mental health histories of these offenders (Cornell, Miller, & Benedek 1988; Labelle, Bradford, Bourget, Jones, & Carmichael, 1991; Lewis et al. 1985; Myers, 1994, 2002; Myers & Blashfield, 1997; Myers, Chan, Vo, & Lazarou, 2010; Myers & Kemph, 1990; Myers & Scott 1998; Myers, Scott, Burgess, & Burgess 1995; Roe-Sepowitz, 2007, 2009). Some have examined the alcohol and drug usage of JHOs (Bailey, 1996b; Cornell, Benedek, & Benedek, 1987; Fenderich et al., 1995; Heide, 1999; Myers & Scott, 1998).

A portrait of the typical older male JHO has emerged from many studies. Older boys have been found to have serious mental health problems but were rarely psychotic (Busch, Zagar, Huges, Arbit, & Russell, 1990; Cornell, Miller & Benedek, 1988; Ewing, 1990; Heide, 1999; Labelle et al., 1991; Myers et al., 1995). They were exposed to violence in their homes and in their neighborhoods. They typically had a history of severe abuse and neglect and often experienced other significant trauma in their lives (Darby, Allan, Kashani, Hartke, & Reid, 1998; Heide, 1992, 1999; Heide & Solomon, 2006, 2009; Hughes, Zagar, Busch, Grove, & Arbit, 2009; Lewis et al., 1985; Shumaker & Prinz, 2000; Zagar, Isbell, Busch, & Hughes, 2009). They had histories of drug and/or alcohol abuse (DiCataldo & Everett, 2008; Fenderich et al., 1995; Myers et al., 1995; Myers & Kemph, 1990; Zagar, Isbell, et al., 2009) and also of gang involvement (Busch et al., 1990; Zagar, Isbell, et al., 2009). As a group, they had slightly below average IQs and poor school performance (Heide, 1999; Shumaker & Prinz, 2000; Zagar, Isbell, et al., 2009). Common characteristics found among older male homicide offenders also included poor executive functioning, low social maturity, prior delinquency charges, and prior court contacts (Zagar, Busch, Grove, & Hughes, 2009; Zagar, Isbell, et al., 2009). Most were raised in poverty (Heide, 1999; Zagar, Isbell, et al., 2009).

Loeber, Farrington, and colleagues conducted the first prospective longitudinal study to determine risk factors for later homicide conviction among a sample of 1,507 inner-city boys in Pittsburgh, Pennsylvania. The Pittsburgh Youth Study (PYS) research team gathered official records dating back to childhood and self-report information from the youth, their caretakers, and teachers. Thirty-three of the individuals in the study were convicted of murder within 16 years of the study inception in 1987 (Loeber et al., 2005); the number rose to 37 after 22 years (Loeber & Farrington, 2011). These 37 individuals ranged in age from 15 through 29 at the time of the killing. Nearly 72% were in their teenage years when the killing occurred (Loeber & Farrington, 2011).

Homicide offenders differed significantly from other violent offenders in the PYS in multiple ways. A subset of violence predictors predicted homicide by young men. These included long-term factors (e.g., conduct disorder diagnosis, family on welfare, high risk score) and more proximal risk factors (e.g., carrying a weapon, selling drugs, and peer delinquency) (see Loeber et al., 2005). Farrington, Loeber, and Berg (2012) noted that the most important factors among the cluster of explanatory predictors were environmental and socioeconomic factors rather than individual traits (e.g., callous-unemotional). However, factors from three areas (individual, family, and neighborhood) independently contributed to predicting homicide offenders. These variables included prior delinquent acts (simple assault, weapon carrying, other/conspiracy), having a young mother, and living in a bad neighborhood. Loeber and Farrington (2011) investigated whether there was a dose–response relationship between the number of risk factors and the probability of being convicted of murder. They found that the higher the number of risk factors, the greater the probability of becoming a homicide offender. The false-positive error rate, however, was very high at 87%, indicating that many nonhomicide offenders would be incorrectly identified. While the false-negative error rate was lower at 38%, the data suggested that nearly 4 of 10 homicide offenders would be missed using this prediction method (Loeber & Farrington, 2011).

A portrait of the older female JHO can be tentatively drawn from two studies that had extensive clinical data for both male and female offenders (Roe-Sepowitz, 2007, 2009; Zagar, Isbell, et al., 2009). Roe-Sepowitz found that girls involved in murder typically had serious mental health problems, particularly anxiety and depression. Poor parental supervision was common among female JHOs. As a group, the girls had difficulties managing anger and substance abuse problems if they had tried drugs. They generally had delinquent friends and prior delinquency charges. Their school attendance record, however, was often good. Zagar, Isbell, et al. (2009) found that female JHOs typically had poor executive functioning, low social maturity, prior court contacts, and had been raised in poverty. Both Roe-Sepowitz (2007, 2009) and Zagar, Isbell, and colleagues (2009) reported that a history of family abuse was common in this population.

In their sample of 218 boys and 16 girls arrested for murder, Zagar and his colleagues found only one significant gender difference: Girls were significantly less likely to be involved in gangs than boys. No gender differences were found with respect to race, family composition, physical or sexual abuse, parent/family risk (violent family), physical health, school difficulties, social maturity, executive function, and alcohol and substance abuse. Both male and female JHOs were likely to be poor, to have histories of academic failure and court contacts, to have histories of child maltreatment, low social maturity, compromised executive functioning, and substance abuse (Zagar, Isbell, et al., 2009).

Preadolescent Homicide Offenders

Research on young children who kill was reported more than 70 years ago (Bender & Curran, 1940). Not surprisingly, given its rarity, the literature on young JHOs consists mostly of case studies (Sellers & Heide, 2012). These reports primarily describe individual and social history characteristics of these children. Similar to older JHOs, younger JHOs commonly experienced negative home conditions, such as family violence, child abuse, and heavy drinking by parents (Bender, 1959; Carek & Watson, 1964; Ewing, 1990; Paluszny & McNabb, 1975; Sargent, 1962; Shumaker & Prinz, 2000).

Evidence of epilepsy has been found in this population by some investigators (e.g., Bailey, 1996a; Easson & Steinhilber, 1961; Mouridsen & Tolstrup, 1988; Mukaddes & Topcu, 2006), similar to the literature on institutionalized male adolescent JHOs (Lewis, Pincus, Shanok, & Glaser, 1982), but not by all (Walsh-Brennan, 1977). Only a few cases of children being diagnosed as psychotic or otherwise seriously mentally ill were found in the clinical literature (Sellers & Heide, 2012). Ewing (1990) argued that available evidence suggested that young killers were typically psychologically disturbed and/or abused rather than seriously mentally ill. From their review of the literature, Shumaker and McKee concluded that most killings by young children and preadolescents resulted from a combination of factors, including immaturity, impulsivity, infantile rage, and chance factors. Duncan and Duncan (1971) proposed seven risk factors to account for the involvement of young children in murder. These factors suggested that children with intense hostile reactions, little control of their impulses, limited ability to formulate alternative solutions to problems, and a history of homicidal threats were more at risk for killing, particularly when the intended victim was perceived as provoking the incident and helpless.

Shumaker and Prinz (2000) used case reports from several publications to analyze the JHOs by age groups. They defined children aged 12 and below as "preteens" and children 13 and older as "teenagers." They found that the two groups were similar in many individual risk factors and negative family conditions. They concluded that relative to older JHOs, younger JHOs were more likely to have engaged in cruelty to other children and to have a negative relationship with a male caregiver. They had histories of lying and fire setting, and often drowned or set fire to their victims. Older JHOs, in contrast, were more likely to have experienced unhealthy sexual experiences and to have a history of truancy. They had often ruminated about the murder and used a gun (Sellers & Heide, 2012).

NATIONAL STUDIES OF MALE AND FEMALE JUVENILE HOMICIDE OFFENDERS

Heide and colleagues investigated gender and age differences among JHOs in the United States using national arrest data for three decades. Building on findings suggested by earlier limited studies (Loper & Cornell, 1996; Rowley, Ewing, & Singer, 1987; Snyder & Sickmund, 1999, 2006), this research team used SHR data to further investigate gender differences among US juvenile homicide arrestees in three ways: male and female JHOs, younger versus older male and female JHOs, and male and female JHOs aged 10 and under. Due to the construction of the SHR data set, which records victim offender relationships for only the first victim, the decision was made to restrict analyses to single-victim cases in all three studies. Gender differences were apparent in all age groups tested.

Male and Female Juvenile Homicide Offenders

The first study examined gender differences between 40,361 juveniles arrested for killing one victim during the 30-year period 1976–2005 (Heide et al., 2012). Approximately 92% of JHOs in this sample were male. The profiles of juveniles arrested varied significantly by gender. The typical male JHO was likely to be 16 or 17 years old and to come from a large city. He was about equally likely to act alone or to be involved with others when killing a single victim. The typical female JHO, relative to her male counterpart, was more likely to be under age 16 and almost twice as likely to be age 14 or younger. She was more likely to kill alone than with codefendants.

Girls were significantly more likely than boys to kill younger victims, particularly children age 5 and under. They were significantly more likely to kill female victims, family members, their offspring, and intimate partners. Relative to boys, they were more likely to kill due to conflict rather than as a result of involvement in other crime and to use knives and other weapons. Male JHOs, relative to female JHOs, were significantly more likely to kill strangers, to be involved in gang-related homicides, to use guns, and to have accomplices.

When the 10 variables from the bivariate analyses (victim sex female, victim age under 5, knife, other weapon, conflict, gang, family, intimate, stranger, accomplice) were entered into the regression analysis, they all remained significant. Five of the odds ratios were large. Female juvenile homicide arrestees were nine times more likely than their male counterparts to kill intimate partners, four times more likely to kill children under age 5, and twice as likely to kill female victims and family members. Girls were three times more likely than boys to use knives as their murder weapons (Heide et al., 2012).

Younger (Age 6–12 Years) and Older (Age 13–17 Years) Male and Female Juvenile Homicide Offenders

The second study examined gender differences among young (age 6–12 years) and older (age 13–17 years) using SHR data for the 32-year period 1976–2007. Analysis was restricted to the 42,457 incidents in which juveniles killed one victim. As in the first study, boys comprised approximately 92% of all JHOs. This study found that the relationships identified in the first study with respect to offender gender and victim gender, victim age, victim–offender relationship, murder weapon, and homicide circumstance remained significant when examined within groups of younger and older JHOs. Females in both age groups, relative to their male counterparts, were significantly more likely to kill female victims, younger victims, particularly children under age 5, and family members. (No boys or girls in the younger group were involved in killing offspring; three boys in this group, however, killed intimate partners.) Girls were more likely to be involved in conflict-related homicides and to use knives, personal weapons, and asphyxiation to kill. Males in both age groups, relative to their female counterparts, were significantly more likely to kill male victims, victims aged 14–34 years, and strangers. Boys were more likely to kill during the commission of another crime and to use guns (Heide et al., 2011).

Male and Female Juvenile Homicide Offenders Ages 6–10 Years

The third study is in many ways the most interesting of the three because it is the first and only research effort to examine the victim, offender, and offense characteristics of young children arrested for murder using a large data set (Sellers & Heide, 2012). During the period 1976–2007, 234 children between the ages of 6 and 10 years old were arrested for murder in the United States. Offender gender was available for all but one child arrested. Of these, 88% were males ($n = 205$) and 12% were females ($n = 28$).

This study of young JHOs found, similar to previous studies, that offender gender was significantly related to victim age, weapon used, victim–offender relationship, and homicide circumstance. Relative to their male counterparts, girls under age 11 were significantly more likely to kill younger victims, to use personal weapons and knives, and to be involved in conflict-related homicides. Although girls were more likely to kill female victims, the difference did not reach statistical significance. Boys were significantly more likely to use guns and to kill victims across the age and relationship spectrums. Offender gender and use of accomplices was not significant. When examined within groups of different victim–offender relationship types, however, girls were found to have accomplices significantly more than boys when killing family members (Sellers & Heide, 2012), a relationship also discovered in the first study that investigated gender differences among all JHO arrestees (see Heide et al., 2012).

Given the previous bivariate analyses, seven variables were entered into the regression analysis (personal weapon, knife, other weapon, victim age under 5, victim was a family member, accomplice, and conflict-related homicide). Only two of the seven remained statistically significant (victim age under 5 and knife) and one (family member was a victim) just missed significance at the probability level of .06. Female JHOs under age 11, relative to their male counterparts, were four times more likely to kill victims under age 5 and almost four times more likely to use a knife. Although not technically significant by a slim margin, it is interesting to note that girls were 2.5 times more likely to kill family members than boys (Sellers & Heide, 2012).

Given these findings, profiles of young child killers can be sketched. Young male JHOs were likely to use a firearm to kill. Arson, although not common, was used as a method of killing only by little boys. Boys in this sample tended to kill individuals between the ages of 1 and 13 years old. Although boys had victims from across all age ranges, the oldest victims in this sample (65 to 98 years old) were all killed by boys. Young boys were about equally likely to kill family members (43%) or friends and acquaintances (44%); they killed strangers in less than 13% of cases. Seventy percent of killings committed by boys under age 11 were related to conflict.

Female JHOs were likely to use personal weapons, such as hands or feet, and knives to kill. They were likely to kill children under age 5. Little girls predominantly killed within the family. Girls killed exclusively in conflict-related situations. Unlike their male counterparts, no female JHOs killed strangers, and none were involved in crime-related homicides (Sellers & Heide, 2012).

LEGAL PROCESSING OF JUVENILE HOMICIDE OFFENDERS

In the United States, children involved in homicide may be prosecuted in juvenile court or transferred to adult court depending on state statutes. Many states do not set a *minimum age* for prosecution in juvenile court, permitting the judge to make the decision after considering case law and the competency of the child. Competency at this stage focuses on the child's ability to understand the charges and the possible penalties, assist defense counsel, comprehend the court process, and make decisions related to his or her case (e.g., testify, take a plea to a lesser charge).

There was an irrebuttable presumption under the Common Law of England that children under age 7 did not have the capacity to form criminal intent (Dix, 2010). Hence, they were not held accountable for acts that would otherwise have been criminal. Although many states appear to follow this precedent, North Carolina permits children at age 6 to be prosecuted in juvenile court (McCord, Widom, & Crowell, 2001).

In practice, young children, particularly those 10 and under, are rarely held completely accountable when they kill. Typically, there is the recognition that they acted impulsively and did not comprehend the magnitude of their actions. Accordingly, they are more likely to be referred to social services or mental health agencies for evaluation and treatment (Heide, 2013).

When JHOs are 12 or older, prosecution is common. Depending on the facts of the case, the prosecutor may charge the youth with first- or second-degree murder or voluntary or involuntary manslaughter. First-degree murder is charged when the evidence suggests that the youth premeditated the killing or the killing occurred during the commission of a felony, such as robbery or sexual battery. For example, John would likely be charged with first-degree murder if facts indicated that he decided to kill Jimmy for dating his ex-girlfriend or, if during the course of the robbery of a liquor store, John's codefendant Tommy panicked and shot the clerk behind the counter, killing him. Second-degree murder is a more appropriate charge when the killing does not appear to be willful, deliberate, or intended, but rather resulted from the juvenile's engaging in an act that was imminently dangerous to another person. For example, John would likely be charged with second-degree murder if, while in an enraged state, he fired at his girlfriend's car as she was driving away in an attempt to stop her from leaving him and she was accidentally shot and killed during the incident (Dix, 2010; Heide, 2013).

The prosecutor may decide to file voluntary manslaughter charges if it appears that the killing was committed in response to adequate provocation. In these circumstances, actual or implied intent to kill is not considered present. To support this reduced charge, four elements of adequate provocation must be established. First, the JHO must have killed the victim because of the provocation. Second, the provocation was of a nature that would have caused a reasonable person to lose control. Third, the time between the provocation and the killing must not have been long enough for the passions of a reasonable person to cool. Fourth, the juvenile must not have cooled off between the time the provocation occurred and the killing took place (Dix, 2010; Heide, 2013).

Courts often have not recognized situations that cause many JHOs to become enraged or distressed and to respond violently. For example, young killers on occasion have erupted into lethal violence because of something said to them (e.g, "Get out of my way, motherfucker") or minor batteries (e.g., someone pushed them or bumped into them). They felt "dissed" (disrespected) by these behaviors and felt they had to redress the perceived offense. Traditionally, courts have not considered words, regardless of how insulting or vulgar, to qualify as adequate provocation. Similarly, courts have rarely viewed trivial blows, even if technically constituting a battery, to qualify as sufficient provocation to cause a reasonable person to respond with homicidal violence (Dix, 2010; Heide, 2013).

Involuntary manslaughter charges may be filed in cases when it appears the killing was the result of criminal negligence or occurred during the commission of an unlawful act not amounting to a felony (Dix, 2010). A juvenile was charged with involuntary manslaughter when he admitted that he and the victim were playing around with a gun on a hunting trip and the gun accidentally went off, killing the victim ("Juvenile charged. . .", 2003). In another case, a 17-year-old boy was charged with involuntary manslaughter in connection with a crash caused by his losing control of his car after he made an improper pass that resulted in the death of the driver of the other car (Littrell, 2007).

Most states set the *maximum age* for juvenile court jurisdiction at age 17. All 50 states and the District of Columbia, however, have provisions for transferring juveniles to adult court. These include statutory exclusion from juvenile court jurisdiction for certain offenses such as murder, judicial waiver, prosecutorial discretion, and grand jury indictment (Heide, 2013). In more than 20 states, there is no minimum age at which a child can be transferred to adult court (Gaines & Miller, 2012).

The forum in which a JHO is tried can mean the difference between the juvenile's sentence being calculated in months to his or her serving decades in an adult prison. Up until 2005, juveniles convicted of first-degree murder in the United States could be sentenced to death. In *Roper v. Simmons*, the US Supreme Court held that the death penalty was cruel and unusual punishment under the Eighth Amendment of the US Constitution. In 2010, the US Supreme Court held in *Graham v. Florida* that sentencing juveniles to life without parole in nonhomicide cases, such as robbery and rape, also violated the Eighth Amendment's ban against cruel and unusual punishment. In 2012, the high court went a step further in *Miller v. Alabama* by striking down *mandatory* life without parole sentences for juveniles convicted of first-degree murder. The Court held that trial courts must consider mitigating factors when sentencing juveniles convicted of first-degree murder. One of the primary reasons for the Court's decision in these cases was the recognition that juveniles were developmentally less mature than adult offenders and could potentially be rehabilitated (Heide, 2013).

When a juvenile is arrested for murder, evaluation by a mental health professional (MHP) is needed to assess competency issues and mental status at the time of the crime. Competency issues can apply to any stage of the proceedings and include matters such as competency to waive Miranda rights, to plead guilty, or to forego an insanity defense as well as competency to stand trial. Mental health experts with expertise in criminal cases will likely evaluate whether mental status defenses such as insanity, diminished capacity, or involuntary intoxication apply. In cases when the youth has killed out of fear, the expert will likely look at whether his or her perceptions are consistent with acting in self-defense and whether the battered child defense is applicable by case precedent or state law in the jurisdiction (Heide, Boots, Alldredge, Donerly, & White, 2005). When juveniles appear to have killed due to strong emotion, the clinician will assess whether the defendant was in a state of "extreme emotional disturbance" due to provocation by the victim. A determination of this nature might be helpful in reducing the charge from murder to manslaughter (see Heide, 1999, 2013).

MHPs can also play an invaluable role in helping judges and juries understand the reason that the youth resorted to murder. These factors might include biological, neurological, or psychological factors that put the youth at a higher risk of responding maladaptively at the time of the killing. A history of child maltreatment, mental health problems, drug or alcohol abuse, low maturity, and criminal unsophistication can also be presented as mitigating factors to relevant decision makers (Heide, 2013).

TREATMENT OF THE JUVENILE HOMICIDE OFFENDER

Although many, if not most, JHOs will be released back into society, few receive any type mental health treatment after sentencing. The literature on treating young killers is very limited (Heide, 2013). Hospitalization, although commonly used for very young children, is rarely used for adolescent homicide offenders unless they remain homicidal, appear psychotic, or require intense psychopharmacological management (Hillbrand, Alexandre, Young, & Spitz, 1999; Myers, 1992). Older JHOs, unlike their younger counterparts, are typically viewed as antisocial or impulsive and are likely to be sentenced to secure juvenile commitment programs or, more likely, to adult prisons.

Studies have conclusively shown that juvenile offenders who commit serious crimes, including murder, can be effectively treated and that treatment can reduce reoffending (Heide & Solomon, 2003; Howell, 1995; Howell, Krisberg, Hawkins, & Wilson, 1995; Hubner, 2005; Lipsey, 1992; Lipsey & Wilson, 1999; Lipsey, Wilson, & Cothern, 2002; Texas Youth Commission, 1996, 1997, 2006; Townsend, 2010). Research has also shown that treatment can save money (Caldwell, Vitacco, & Van Rybroek, 2006). Lipsey and colleagues (2002) found that the most effective programs for institutionalized delinquents included teaching family homes, community residential programs, interpersonal skills training, and provision of multiple services. For noninstitutonalized delinquents, the best programs included interpersonal skills training, behavioral programs, individual counseling, and the use of multiple services. Programs that involved family and multisystemic therapy have been shown consistently to be effective in improving individual and family functioning and in reducing recividivism by juvenile offenders (Guerra, Kim, & Boxer, 2008).

One program has shown remarkable results in treating JHOs, the Capital and Serious Violent Offender Program (C&SVOTP) in Giddens, Texas. This program uses social learning, cognitive-behavioral therapy, psychodynamic techniques, and group process to create an intense treatment approach to help youths assume accountability for their behavior, develop empathy for others, learn better coping strategies, and build their strengths. This program has been associated with positive changes in personality of the youths and in reduced recidivism (Heide & Solomon, 1999, 2003, 2013; Texas Youth Commission, 2006; Townsend, 2010).

Vick Agee (1979, 1995), a psychologist who treated violent and emotionally disturbed juvenile offenders for many years and reviewed the literature on empirically validated intervention programs, proposed 11 components to treat juvenile offenders. These components included "(1) effective and extensive assessment using a variety of data sources; (2) comprehensive cognitive behavioral programming or restructuring; (3) prosocial skills training; (4) positive peer communities; (5) anger management; (6) empathy training; (7) clear, firm, and consistent discipline; (8) drug and alcohol abuse counseling and education; (9) transition, including family counseling when appropriate; (10) intensive and extended aftercare; and (11) medication when necessary" (Heide & Solomon, 1999, p. 230). Heide and Solomon (2013) added two additional components: (12) "educational and vocational programs and other activities" that encourage prosocial behaviors and success, and "(13) resolve traumatic experiences with focus on learning to calm the body, regulate emotion, and develop cognitive skills aimed at prosocial decision-making" (p. 322).

These intervention strategies are in agreement with the treatment recommendations made by Susan Bailey, a psychiatrist who evaluated and treated young murderers in England (Bailey, 1996a, 1996b). They are also consistent with the conclusions made by researchers who have evaluated the effectiveness of treatments programs focusing on serious delinquents (Goldstein, 1988, 1993; Guerra, Kim, & Boxer, 2008; Lipsey & Wilson, 1999; Lipsey, Wilson, & Cothern, 2002) and violent juvenile offenders (Boxer & Frick, 2008; Goldstein & Glick, 1987; Lescheid & Cummings, 2002; Tate, Reppucci, & Mulvey, 1995). The 13 treatment components can be tailored to the offender's gender and are well suited to identifying the strengths of JHOs as a means to decrease risks associated with continued violent and criminal behavior. They also incorporate the critical criteria of successful programs identified by Guerra and colleagues (2008): highly structured interventions that link cognitive components to specific skills, provide for family involvement, and address multiple risk factors in varying contexts.

LONG-TERM OUTCOMES OF JUVENILE HOMICIDE OFFENDERS

Follow-up studies of JHOs typically have small sample sizes, which preclude making generalizations to the population of JHOs (Benedek, Cornell, & Staresina, 1989; Liem, 2013). In summarizing the pre-1990 literature on long-term outcomes, Benedek and her colleagues concluded, based largely on clinical reports, that the literature "with few exceptions" was "surprisingly positive" (Benedek et al., 1989). They related that JHOs tended to adjust satisfactorily in prison and in the community and related well to their families. They noted, however, that many of these young offenders killed family members and hypothesized that the outcomes for youth who killed as a result of interpersonal conflict would likely be better than chronic delinquents who killed during the commission of another crime. Extensive follow-up research by Toupin (1993) on adolescent homicide offenders in Canada confirmed that the 23 youth in the conflict group committed significantly fewer offenses, serious offenses, and violent offenses than did the 18 youth in the crime group.

Myers and colleagues (2010) followed up on 11 juvenile sexual homicide offenders. These JHOs would arguably fall into the crime-related group. Six of the 11 recidivated. Of these six, three committed another sexual homicide; the remaining three recidivists committed nonsexual offenses.

In her review of the literature of adolescent parricide offenders, Heide (2013) found mixed outcomes in available case studies. While some adolescents and young adults made successful adjustments when they returned to society (Corder, Ball, Haizlip, Rollins, & Beaumont, 1976; Duncan & Duncan, 1971; Post, 1982; Schlesinger, 1999; Tanay, 1973, 1976), the reports in other cases were mixed (Mack, Scherl, & Macht, 1973; Russell, 1984; Scherl & Mack, 1966). In two cases, juvenile parricide offenders killed again (Anthony, 1973; Reinhardt, 1970). Heide (2013) reported that two of the adolescent parricide offenders she evaluated killed again as adults.

Four studies examined recidivism on groups of JHOs confined in juvenile institutions (Hagan, 1997; Texas Youth Commission, 2006; Trulson, Caudit, Haerle, & De Lisi, 2012; Vries & Liem, 2011). A fifth study investigated recidivism on JHOs sentenced to adult prisons (Heide, Spencer, Thompson, & Solomon, 2001). Four of the five recidivism studies were in the United States; the remaining study by Vries and Liem (2011) took place in the Netherlands. It appeared that intensive treatment was provided in only one of these studies, the Capital and Serious Violent Offender Program (Texas Youth Commission, 2006). Accordingly, the recidivism data from the Texas program are presented after findings from the other four are summarized.

Results from the studies where little or no treatment was provided indicated that JHOs recidivated at high rates (Hagan, 1997; Heide et al., 2001; Trulson et al., 2012; Vries & Liem, 2011). Hagan (1997) compared the recidivism of 20 juveniles convicted of homicide or attempted homicide with 20 juveniles convicted of nonhomicide offenses. Recidivism was nearly the same for the two groups (60% for homicide group and 65% for control group). Thirty-five percent of the 60% of JHOs who recidivated committed crimes against persons; none of these were homicides.

Vries and Liem (2011) followed up on 137 JHOs released from juvenile facilities. The follow-up period ranged from 1 to 16 years. They reported that 81 (59%) of the JHOs recidivated. These 81 recidivists committed 616 offenses or an average of 7.64 per offender. These included two completed homicides, 16 attempted homicides, and 123 other violent offenses. Multivariate analyses found several significant predictors of recidivism. After 5 years, relationship with delinquent friends was clearly the strongest determinant of recidivism, followed by number of previous offenses, age at first arrest, and age at homicide.

Trulson and colleagues (2012) investigated the interrelationship between gang affiliation and commitment for a gang-related murder on the recidivism of serious and violent delinquents. The sample of 1,804 juvenile offenders contained 126 youths incarcerated in juvenile facilities for a gang-related murder and 338 for a non-gang-related homicide. Multivariate analyses found that gang-related homicide offenders, homicide offenders in general, and gang members were more likely to be rearrested for a felony in 3 years than other serious and violent delinquents. Specifically, being a gang-affiliated offender committed for a gang-related murder increased the odds of being arrested for a felony by 89.40%. Being a homicide offender without a gang affiliation or gang-related commitment offense increased the odds of a felony rearrest by 72.10%. Being a gang affiliate also increased the odds of felony rearrest by 28.50% (Trulson, Caudill, Haerle, & De Lisi, 2012).

Recidivism findings of JHOs convicted in adult court and sentenced to adult prison study, similar to those in the juvenile facilities, were high (Heide et al., 2001). Although many received long prison sentences, 73% of these 59 offenders were released from prison during the 15- to 17-year follow-up. Of the 43 JHOs released, 60% were returned to prison, most of them within 3 years, typically for committing new crimes. Three of the 40 individuals released killed again (Heide, 1999).

JHOs sent to the Capital and Serious Violent Offender Treatment Program (C&SVOTP), mentioned earlier, in contrast to JHOs in the four studies reviewed earlier, received extensive residential treatment targeting psychological issues and emotional, social, and cognitive development (see Heide, 1999, 2003, 2013; Texas Youth Commission, 2006; Townsend, 2010). Postrelease outcomes for C&SVOTP participants consistently have been far better than those of untreated control groups when measured in terms of rearrest and reincarceration rates over 1- and 3-year intervals. Highlights of findings from reports over the years indicated that participation in C&SVOTP reduced the likelihood of capital offenders being arrested for a violent crime within a year by 52.9% (Texas Youth Commission, 1996). Relative to their untreated counterparts, treatment participants were 70% and 43% less likely to be reincarcerated within 1-year and 3-year time periods (Heide, 2003). Treatment decreased the probability of being reincarcerated for a felony by 43% and for any offense by 55% (Texas Youth Commission, 2006). The most recent recidivism data, available for participants only, indicted that 13.3% were rearrested, none for a violent offense, and 2.2% were reincarcerated 6 months after release (Texas Juvenile Justice Department, 2011).

CONCLUSIONS

This chapter presented data on arrests of JHOs spanning 50 years. The character-istics of youth under 18 arrested for murder in the United States were examined over a 30-year period. In addition, the literature on JHOs, which covered studies published from 1940 to 2013, was reviewed in terms of psychological, biological, medical, and sociological correlates of adolescents and preadolescents involved in lethal violence. National studies of more than 40,000 juveniles arrested for murder over three decades were summarized in terms of gender differences. Findings from studies on treatment of JHOs and long-term follow-up reports were synthesized.

Several conclusions can be drawn from the statistical analyses and careful review of the literature across several major areas. First, predictions made by homicide forecasters in the 1990s that juvenile arrests would continue to rise to unprece-dented heights were wrong. Evidence suggests that arrests of juveniles for murder, now at a near record low since the 1960s, have stabilized. Americans no longer need to wait in fear for a generation of young superpredators to arrive. The reality is that the bloodbath predicted will not materialize.

Second, to a large extent, juveniles arrested for murder share certain demo-graphic features. Over the 32-year period examined, about 9 out of 10 JHOs were males and 15 to 17 years old. Nearly 6 out of 10 were Black youth and lived in cities. Guns were the weapons used by nearly 7 out of 10 juveniles arrested for murder.

Third, the review of the literature revealed that many studies of JHOs now exist. More important, there are commonalities across studies. Although profiles differ by gender in some ways, one enduring finding across studies old and new is that male and female JHOs commonly have histories of severe childhood maltreat-ment and have endured other forms of significant trauma. Most young killers have mental health difficulties and have been raised in poverty. JHOs as a group have low social maturity and compromised executive functioning, and they abuse sub-stances. Risk factors associated with violent offending, including murder, have been identified. Several predictive factors have been preliminarily identified, paving the way for prevention programs targeted particularly at high-risk youth.

Fourth, despite shared risk factors, studies have shown that male and female JHOs differ across various age groups in identifiable ways. Relative to boys, girls are significantly more likely to kill younger victims, female victims, family members, their own children, and intimate partners. They are also more likely than male JHOs to use knives and weapons other than guns and to kill due to conflict in relationships. Boys, in contrast, are significantly more likely to murder strangers, to use guns, to have accomplices, and to be involved in gang-related homicides. Prevention programs can be developed to take gender differences into account.

Fifth, multiple studies have reported that serious and violent offenders can be effectively treated and can make successful postrelease adjustments. As dis-cussed earlier, one program, the Capital and Serious Violent Offender Program (C&SVOTP) in Giddens, Texas, has shown remarkable success treating juveniles convicted of murder as well as other violent offenses.

Sixth, long-term follow-up studies of convicted juvenile murderers retained in juvenile facilities or housed in adult prisons, although few in number, revealed that JHOs as a group generally had recidivism rates of approximately 60%. It does not appear from reading these studies that treatment was provided to these offenders.

The high recidivism rates of these studies stands in marked contrast to the recidivism rates of participants in the C&SVOTP, where treatment was the critical component of program placement.

The US Supreme Court in *Roper v. Simmons* (2005), *Graham v. Florida* (2010), and *Miller v. Alabama* (2012) recognized the diminished capacity of juvenile offenders. Research has established that the brain does not complete its basic development until age 23–25 years. The last part of the brain to develop is the cerebral cortex, the area of the brain that is critical in evaluating information, making judgments and thoughtful decisions, planning, and organizing responses. The cerebral cortex is the part of the brain that puts the brakes on the limbic system, the emotional part of the brain, allowing individuals to stop and think rather than act impulsively. Adolescents, when confronted with strong feelings, are much more likely than adults to operate from the limbic system. It is much harder for juveniles, when consumed with feelings of jealousy and rage, to stop, think, consider alternatives, and alter their course of action than it is for adults.

As the highest court in the United States recognized, juveniles can change. The essential components of successful intervention have been identified to help JHOs develop into responsible and empathic human beings so that they can make a successful transition back to society. Furthermore, the blueprint is in place to reduce the incidence of juvenile homicide. As noted by Loeber and Farrington (2011), "The time is ripe to adopt a public health approach and embark on risk-focused prevention on a large scale. … Obviously, any program that reduces homicide offenders would also reduce homicide victims. It is crucial to interrupt the intergenerational transmission of crime and violence, and the financial benefits of risk-focused prevention seem very likely to exceed the financial costs" (Loeber & Farrington, 2011, p. 185).

REFERENCES

Agee, V. L. (1979). *Treatment of the violent incorrigible adolescent*. Lexington, MA: Lexington Books.

Agee, V. L. (1995). Managing clinical programs for juvenile delinquents. In B. Glick & A. Goldstein (Eds.), *Managing delinquency programs that work* (pp. 173–186). Laurel, MD: American Correctional Association.

Anthony, E. J. (1973). Editorial comment. In E. J. Anthony & C. Koupernik (Eds.), *The child in his family* (pp. 267–273). New York, NY: Wiley.

Bailey, S. (1996a). Adolescents who murder. *Journal of Adolescence, 19*, 19–39.

Bailey, S. (1996b). Current perspectives on young offenders: aliens or alienated? *Journal of Clinical Forensic Medicine, 3*, 1–7.

Bender, L. (1959). Children and adolescents who have killed. *American Journal of Psychiatry, 116*, 510–513.

Bender, L., & Curran, F.J. (1940). Children and adolescents who kill. *Criminal Psychopathology, 1*, 297–321.

Benedek, E. P., Cornell, D. G., & Staresina, L. (1989). Treatment of the homicidal adolescent. In E. P. Benedek & D. G. Cornell (Eds.), *Juvenile homicide* (pp. 221–247). Washington, DC: American Psychiatric Press.

Boxer, P., & Frick, P.J. (2008). Treatment of violent offenders. In R. D. Hoge, N. G. Guerra, & P. Boxer (Eds.), *Treating the juvenile offender* (pp. 147–170). New York, NY: Guilford Press.

Busch, K., Zagar, R., Hughes, J., Arbit, J., & Russell, R. (1990). Adolescents who kill. *Journal of Clinical Psychology, 46,* 472–485.

Caldwell, M. F., Vitacco, M., & Van Rybroek, G. J. (2006). Are violent delinquents worth treating? A cost-benefit analysis. *Journal of Research in Crime and Delinquency, 43*(2), 148–168.

Carek, D. J., &Watson, A. S. (1964). Treatment of a family involved in fratricide. *Archives of General Psychiatry, 11,* 533–542.

Corder, B., Ball, B., Haizlip, T., Rollins, R., & Beaumont, R. (1976). Adolescent Parricide: A comparison with other adolescent murder. *American Journal of Psychiatry, 133,* 957–961.

Cornell, D., Benedek, E., & Benedek, D. (1987). Characteristics of adolescents charged with homicide: Review of 72 cases. *Behavioral Sciences and the Law, 5,* 11–23.

Cornell, D., Benedek, E., & Benedek, D. (1989). A typology of juvenile homicide offenders. In E. P. Benedek & D. G. Cornell (Eds.), *Juvenile homicide* (p. 59–84). Washington, DC: American Psychiatric Press.

Cornell, D., Miller, C., & Benedek, E. (1988). MMPI profiles of adolescents charged with homicide. *Behavioral Sciences and the Law, 6,* 401–407.

Cornell, D. G. (1989). Causes of juvenile homicide: A review of the literature. In E. P. Benedek & D. G. Cornell (Eds.), *Juvenile homicide* (pp. 3–36). Washington, DC: American Psychiatric Press.

Darby, P. J., Allan, W. D., Kashani, J. H., Hartke, K. L., & Reid, J. C. (1998). Analysis of 112 juveniles who committed homicide: Characteristics and a closer look at family abuse. *Journal of Family Violence, 13*(4), 365–375.

DiCataldo, F., & Everett, M. (2008). Distinguishing juvenile homicide from violent juvenile offending. *International Journal of Offender Therapy and Comparative Criminology, 52,* 158–174.

Dix, G. E. (2010). *Criminal law.* 18 ed. New York: Thomson West.

Duncan, J.W., & Duncan, G.M. (1971). Murder in the family: A study of some homicidal adolescents. *American Journal of Psychiatry, 127,* 1498–1502.

Easson, W. M., & Steinhilber, R. M. (1961). Murderous aggression by children and adolescents. *Archives of General Psychiatry, 4,* 27–35.

Evans, T. M., McGovern-Kondik, M., & Peric, F. (2005). Juvenile parricide: A predictable offense? *Journal of Forensic Psychology Practice, 5,* 31–50.

Ewing, C. P. (1990). *When children kill.* New York, NY: Lexington.

Ewing, C. P. (1997). *Fatal families: The dynamics of intrafamilial homicide.* Thousand Oaks, CA: Sage.

Farrington, D. P., Loeber, R., & Berg, M. (2012). Young men who kill: A prospective longitudinal examination from childhood. *Homicide Studies, 16*(2), 99–128.

Federal Bureau of Investigation. (1976). *Uniform crime reports 1975.* Washington, DC: Government Printing Office.

Federal Bureau of Investigation. (1985–2012). *Uniform crime reports 1984-2011.* Washington, DC: Government Printing Office.

Fenderich, M., Mackesy-Amiti, M., Goldstein, P., Spunt, B., & Brownstein, H. (1995). Substance involvement among juvenile murderers: Comparison with older offenders based on interviews with prison inmates. *International Journal of Addictions, 30,* 1363–1382.

Fox, J. A. (1995, April 11). The dean of death. *USA Today*, p. 1A.

Fox, J. A. (1996). *Trends in juvenile violence*. Washington, DC: US Department of Justice, Bureau of Justice Statistics.

Fox, J. A., & Swatt, M. L. (2009). *Uniform crime reports [United States]: Supplemental homicide reports with multiple imputation, cumulative files 1976-2007* [Computer file]. Ann Arbor, MI: Inter-university Consortium for Political and Social Research. Retrieved May 2014, from http://www.icpsr.umich.edu/icpsrweb/ICPSR/studies/2480 1?q=Uniform+crime+reports+%5BUnited+States%5D%3A+Supplemental+homicide+reports+with+multiple+imputation%2C+cumulative+files+1976-2007&searchSource=icpsr-landing.

Gaines, L. K., & Miller, R. L. (2012). *Criminal justice in action* (6th ed.). Bellmot, CA: Wadsworth, Cengage Learning.

Goldstein, A. P. (1988). *The prepare curriculum*. Champaign, IL: Research Press.

Goldstein, A. P. (1993). Interpersonal skills training interventions. In A. P. Goldstein & R. C. Huff (Eds.), *The gang intervention handbook* (pp. 87–157). Champaign, IL: Research Press.

Goldstein, A. P., & Glick, B. (1987). *Aggression replacement training: A comprehensive intervention for aggressive youth*. Champaign, IL: Research Press.

Graham v. Florida, 560 US ___ (2010). Retrieved May 2014, from http://www.supremecourt.gov/opinions/09pdf/08-7412.pdf.

Guerra, G., Kim, T. E., & Boxer, P. (2008). What works: Best practices with juvenile offenders. In R. D. Hoge, N. G. Guerra, & P. Boxer (Eds.), *Treating the juvenile offender* (pp. 79–102). New York, NY: Guilford Press.

Hagan, M. P. (1997). An analysis of adolescent perpetrators of homicide and attempted homicide upon return to the community. *International Journal of Offender Therapy and Comparative Criminology, 41*(3), 250–259.

Heide, K. M. (1986). A taxonomy of murder: Motivational dynamics behind the homicidal acts of adolescents. *Journal of Justice Issues, 1*, 4–19.

Heide, K. M. (1992). *Why kids kill parents: Child abuse and adolescent homicide*. Columbus: Ohio State University Press.

Heide, K. M. (1999). *Young killers*. Thousand Oaks, CA: Sage.

Heide, K. M. (2003). Youth homicide: A review of the literature and a blueprint for action. *International Journal of Offender Therapy and Comparative Criminology, 47*(1), 6–36.

Heide, K. M. (2013). *Understanding parricide: When sons and daughters kill parents*. New York, NY: Oxford University Press.

Heide, K. M., Boots, D., Alldredge, C., Donerly, B., & White, J. R. (2005). Battered child syndrome: An overview of case law and legislation. *Criminal Law Bulletin, 41*(3), 219–239.

Heide, K. M., Roe-Sepowitz, D., Solomon, E. P., & Chan, H. C. (2012). Male and female juveniles arrested for murder: A comprehensive analysis of U.S. data by offender gender. *International Journal of Offender Therapy and Comparative Criminology, 56*(3), 356–384.

Heide, K. M., & Solomon, E. P. (1999). Treating young killers. In K. M. Heide (Ed.), *Young killers* (pp. 221–238). Thousand Oaks, CA: Sage.

Heide, K. M., & Solomon, E. P. (2003). Treating today's juvenile homicide offenders. *Youth Violence and Juvenile Justice, 1*(1), 5–31.

Heide, K. M., & Solomon, E. P. (2006). Biology, childhood trauma, and murder: Rethinking justice. *International Journal of Law and Psychiatry*, *29*, 220–233.

Heide, K. M., & Solomon, E. P. (2009). Female juvenile murderers: Biological and psychological factors leading to homicide. *International Journal of Law and Psychiatry*, *32*(4), 245–252.

Heide, K. M., & Solomon, E. P. (2013). Treating severely abused parricide offenders. In K. M. Heide, *Understanding parricide* (pp. 317–330). New York, NY: Oxford University Press.

Heide, K. M., Solomon, E. P., Sellers, B. G., & Chan, H. C. (2011). Male and female juvenile homicide offenders: An empirical analysis of U.S. arrests by offender age. *Feminist Criminology*, *6*(1), 3–31.

Heide, K. M., Spencer, E., Thompson, A., & Solomon, E. P. (2001). Who's in, who's out, and who's back: Follow-up data on 59 juveniles incarcerated for murder or attempted murder in the early 1980s. *Behavioral Sciences and the Law*, *19*, 97–108.

Hillbrand, M., Alexandre, J. W., Young, J. L., & Spitz, R. T. (1999). Parricides: Characteristics of offenders and victims, legal factors, and treatment issues. *Aggression and Violent Behavior*, *4*(2), 179–190.

Howell, J. C. (Ed.). (1995, June). *Guide for implementing the comprehensive strategy for serious, violent, and chronic juvenile offenders*. Washington, DC: US Department of Justice, Office of Justice Programs, Office of Juvenile Justice and Delinquency Prevention.

Howell, J. C., Krisberg, B., Hawkins, J. D., & Wilson, J. J. (Eds.). (1995). *A sourcebook: Serious, violent, and chronic juvenile offenders* (pp. 275–277). Thousand Oaks, CA: Sage.

Hubner, J. (2005). *Last chance in Texas*. New York, NY: Random House.

Hughes, J. R., Zagar, R. J., Busch, K. G., Grove, W. M., & Arbit, J. (2009). Looking forward in records of youth abused as children: Risks for homicidal, violent, and delinquent offenses. *Psychological Reports*, *104*, 103–127.

"Juvenile charged with involuntary manslaughter in connection with Sheets' death." (2003, November 19). WRAL.com. Retrieved May 2014, from http://www.wral.com/news/local/story/107735/.

Kalogerakis, M. (1971). Homicide in adolescents: Fantasy and deed. In J. Fawcett (Ed.), *Dynamics of violence* (pp. 93–103). Chicago, IL: American Medical Association.

Labelle, A., Bradford, J. M., Bourget, D., Jones, B., & Carmichael, M. (1991). Adolescent murderers. *Canadian Journal of Psychiatry*, *36*, 583–587.

Lescheid, A. W., & Cummings, A. L. (2002). Youth violence: An overview of predictors, counseling interventions, and future directions. *Canadian Journal of Counseling*, *36*(4), 256–264.

Lewis, D. O., Moy, E., Jackson, L. D., Aaronson, R., Restifo, N., Serra, S., & Simos, A. (1985). Biopsychosocial characteristics of children who later murder: A prospective study. *American Journal of Psychiatry*, *142*, 1161–1166.

Lewis, D. O., Pincus, J., Shanok, S. S., & Glaser, G. H. (1982). Psychomotor epilepsy and violence in a group of incarcerated adolescent boys. *American Journal of Psychiatry*, *139*(7), 882–887.

Liem, M. (2013). Homicide offender recidivism: A review of the literature. *Aggression and Violent Behavior*, *18*, 19–25.

Lipsey, M. W. (1992). Juvenile delinquency treatment: A meta-analytic inquiry into the variability of effects. In T. D. Cook (Ed.), *Meta-analysis for explanation: A casebook* (pp. 83–127). New York, NY: Russell Sage Foundation.

Lipsey, M. W., & Wilson, D. B. (1999). Effective intervention for serious juvenile offenders. In R. Loeber & D. P. Farrington (Eds.), *Serious and violent juvenile offenders* (pp. 313–345). Thousands Oaks, CA: Sage.

Lipsey, M. W., Wilson, D. B., & Cothern, L. (2002). *Effective intervention for serious juvenile offenders*. Washington, DC: US Department of Justice, Office of Juvenile and Delinquency Prevention.

Littrell, W. (2007). Pennington Gap teen charged with involuntary manslaughter waiting to learn fate after fatal crash. *TimesNews*. Retrieved May 2014, from http://www.timesnews.net/article/3723637/pennington-gap-teen-charged-with-involuntary-manslaugher-waiting-to-learn-fate-after-fatal-crash.

Loeber, R., & Farrington, D. (2011). *Young homicide offenders and victims: Development, risk factors and prediction from childhood*. New York, NY: Springer.

Loeber, R., Pardini, D., Homish, D. L., Wei, E. H., Crawford, A. M., Farrington, D. P., ... Rosenfeld, R. (2005). The prediction of violence and homicide in young men. *Journal of Consulting and Clinical Psychology, 73*(6), 1074–1088.

Loper, A., & Cornell, D. (1996). Homicide by juvenile girls. *Journal of Child and Family Studies, 5,* 323–336.

Mack, J. E., Scherl, D. J., & Macht, L. B. (1973). Children who kill their mothers. In E. J. Anthony & C. Koupernik (Eds.), *The child in his family* (pp. 319–332). New York, NY: Wiley.

McCord, J., Widom, C. S., & Crowell, N. A. (2001). *Juvenile crime, juvenile justice*. Washington, DC: National Academy Press.

Meloff, W., & Silverman, R. A. (1992). Canadian kids who kill. *Canadian Journal of Criminology, 34,* 15–34.

Miller v. Alabama, 132 S. Ct. 2455 (2012).

Morgan, T. (1975, January 19). They think I can kill because I'm 14. *New York Times Magazine*, pp. 9–11,16, 21–22,24,26,28,30,32,34.

Mouridsen, S. E., & Tolstrup, K. (1988) Children who kill: A case study of matricide. *Journal of Child Psychology and Psychiatry, 29*(4), 511–515.

Mukaddes, N. M., & Topcu, Z. (2006). Case report: Homicide by a 10-year-old girl with autistic disorder. *Journal of Autism and Developmental Disorders, 36*(4), 471–474.

Myers, W. C. (1992). What treatments do we have for children and adolescents who have killed? *Bulletin of the American Academy of Psychiatry and the Law, 20*(1), 47–58.

Myers, W. C. (1994). Sexual homicide by adolescents. *Journal of the American Academy of Child and Adolescent Psychiatry, 33*(7), 962–969.

Myers, W. C. (2002). *Juvenile sexual homicide*. San Diego, CA: Academic Press.

Myers, W. C., & Blashfield, R. (1997). Psychopathology and personality in juvenile sexual homicide offenders. *Journal of the American Academy of Psychiatry and Law, 25*(4), 497–508.

Myers, W. C., Chan, H. C., Vo, E. J., & Lazarou, E. (2010). Sexual sadism, psychopathy, and recidivism in juvenile sexual murderers. *Journal of Investigative Psychology and Offender Profiling, 7*(1), 49–58.

Myers, W., & Kemph, J. P. (1990). DSM-III-R classification of murderous youth: Help or hindrance? *Journal of Clinical Psychiatry, 51,* 239–242.

Myers, W., & Scott, K. (1998). Psychotic and conduct disorder symptoms in juvenile-emurderers. *Homicide Studies, 2,* 160–175.

Myers, W., Scott, K., Burgess, A., & Burgess, A. (1995). Psychopathology, biopsy-chosocial factors, crime characteristics, and classification of 25 homicidal juveniles. *Journal of the American Academy of Child and Adolescent Psychiatry, 34,* 1483–1489.

Paluszny, M., & McNabb, M. (1975). Therapy of a 6-year-old who committed fratricide. *Journal of American Academy of Child and Adolescent Psychiatry, 14*(2), 319–336.

Pfeiffer, C. (1998). Trends in juvenile violence in European Countries [NIJ Research Preview], Washington, DC: US Department of Justice, Office of Justice Programs.

Post, S. (1982). Adolescent parricide in abusive families. *Child Welfare Journal, 61*(7), 445–455.

Reinhardt, J. M. (1970). *Nothing left but murder.* Lincoln, NE: Johnsen.

Roe-Sepowitz, D. E. (2007). Adolescent female murderers: Characteristics and treatment implications. *American Journal of Orthopsychiatry: Interdisciplinary Perspectives on Mental Health and Social Justice, 77*(3), 489–496.

Roe-Sepowitz, D. E. (2009).Comparing male and female juveniles charged with homicide: Child maltreatment, substance abuse and crime details. *Journal of Interpersonal Violence, 24*(4), 601–617.

Roper v. Simmons, 543 US 551 (2005).

Rowley, J. C., Ewing, C. P., & Singer, S. I. (1987). Juvenile homicide: The need for aninterdisciplinary approach. *Behavioral Sciences and the Law, 5,* 1–10.

Russell, D. H. (1984). A study of juvenile murderers of family members. *International Journal of Offender Therapy and Comparative Criminology, 28*(3), 177–192.

Russell, D. H. (1986). Girls who kill. *International Journal of Offender Therapy and Comparative Criminology, 30,* 171–176.

Sargent, D. (1962). Children who kill: A family conspiracy? *Social Work, 7,* 35–42.

Scherl, D. J., & Mack, J. E. (1966). A study of adolescent matricide. *Journal of the American Academy of Child Psychology, 5*(4), 569–593.

Schlesinger, L. B. (1999). Adolescent sexual matricide following repetitive mother-son incest. *Journal of Forensic Sciences, 44,* 746–749.

Sellers, B. G., & Heide, K. M. (2012). Male and female child murderers: An empirical analysis of U.S. arrest data. *International Journal of Offender Therapy and Comparative Criminology, 56*(5), 691–714.

Shumaker, D. M., & McKee, G. R. (2001). Characteristics of homicidal and violent juveniles. *Violence and Victims,16*(4), 401–409.

Shumaker, D. M., & Prinz, R. (2000). Children who murder: A review. *Clinical Child and Family Psychology Review, 3*(2), 97–115.

Snyder, H. N., & Sickmund, M. (1999). *Juvenile offenders and victims: 1999 national report.* Washington, DC: Office of Juvenile Justice and Delinquency Prevention.

Snyder, H. N., & Sickmund, M. (2006). *Juvenile offenders and victims: 2006 national report.* Washington, DC: US Department of Justice, Office of Justice Programs, Office of Juvenile Justice and Delinquency Prevention.

Solomon, E. P., Berg, L. R., & Martin, D. W. (2011). *Biology* (9th ed.). Belmont, CA: Brooks/Cole/Cengage.

Sorrells, J. M., Jr. (1977). Kids who kill. *Crime and Delinquency, 16,* 152–161.

Tanay, E. (1973). Adolescents who kill parents: Reactive parricide. *Australian and New Zealand Journal of Psychiatry, 7*(4), 263–277.

Tanay, E. (1976). Reactive parricide. *Journal of Forensic Sciences, 21*(2), 76–81.

Tate, D. C., Reppucci, N. D., & Mulvey, E. P. (1995). Violent juvenile delinquents: Treatment effectiveness and implications for future action. *American Psychologist, 50*(9), 777–781.

Texas Juvenile Justice Department. (2011). *Annual review of treatment effectiveness.* Retrieved May 2014, from http://www.tjjd.texas.gov/Docs/Treatment%20 EffectivenessFY2011.pdf

Texas Youth Commission. (1996, December). *Review of treatment programs.* Austin, TX: Author.

Texas Youth Commission. (1997, February 27). *Specialized treatment recidivism effectiveness summary.* Austin, TX: Author.

Texas Youth Commission. (2006, March 24). *Treatment and case management. Capital and serious violent offender treatment program manual.* Austin, TX: Author.

Toupin, J. (1993). Adolescent murderers: Validation of a typology and study of their recidivism. In A. V. Wilson (Ed.), *Homicide: The victim/offender connection* (pp. 135–156). Cincinnati, OH: Anderson.

Townsend, C. K. (2010). 2010 annual review of agency treatment effectiveness. *Texas Youth Commission.* Retrieved from http://www.tjjd.texas.gov/about/Annual_Treatment_Effectiveness_Review2010.pdf

Travis, J. (1997, October 4). *National and comparative perspectives on juvenile violence.* Speech at the 1997 meeting of the International Scientific and Professional Advisory Council of the United Nations Crime Prevention and Criminal Justice Programme, Courmayeur, Italy.

Trulson, C. R., Caudit, J. W., Haerle, D. R., & De Lisi, M. (2012). Cliqued up: The Postincarceration recidivism of young gang-related homicide offenders. *Criminal Justice Review, 37*, 174–190.

US Census Bureau (2013). *State and county QuickFacts.* Retrieved May 2014, from http://quickfacts.census.gov/qfd/states/00000.html.

Vries, A. M., & Liem, M. (2011). Recidivism of juvenile homicide offenders. *Behavioral Sciences and the Law, 29*(4), 483–498.

Walsh-Brennan, K. S. (1977). A socio-psychological investigation of young murderers. *British Journal of Criminology, 17*, 53–63.

Wertham, F. (1941). *Dark legend: A study in murder.* New York, NY: Duell, Sloan, & Pearce.

Woodworth, M., Agar, A. D., & Coupland, R. B. A. (2013). Characteristics of Canadian youth-perpetrated homicides. *Criminal Justice and Behavior.* Advance online publication, doi: 10.1177/0093854813482309

Zagar, R. J., Busch, K. G., Grove, W. M., & Hughes, J. R. (2009). Summary of studies of abused infants and children later homicidal, and homicidal assaulting, later homicidal, and sexual homicidal youth and adults. *Psychological Reports, 104*, 17–45.

Zagar, R. J., Isbell, S. A., Busch, K. G., & Hughes, J. R. (2009). An empirical theory of the development of homicide within victims. *Psychological Reports, 104*, 199–245.

Zenoff, E., & Zeints, A. (1979). Juvenile murderers: Should the punishment fit the crime? *International Journal of Law and Psychiatry, 2*, 53–55.

Zimring, F. E. (2012). *Berkeley Law: From the selected works of Franklin E. Zimring. American youth violence—A cautionary tale.* Retrieved May 2014, from http://works.bepress.com/cgi/viewcontent.cgi?article=1006&context=franklin_zimring.

7

Physically and Sexually Violent Females

GEOFFREY R. MCKEE AND R. GREGG DWYER ∎

The Federal Bureau of Investigation's (FBI) annual Uniform Crime Report (UCR) lists violent offenses as comprising murder and nonnegligent manslaughter, aggravated assault, forcible rape, and robbery (FBI, 2011). The UCR data are drawn from arrests in state and federal jurisdictions, and each incident recorded is based solely on the initial police investigation report instead of postarrest determinations by a court, medical examiner, coroner, jury, or other judicial authority. In 2010, 8,726 law enforcement agencies reported 1,246,248 arrests for violent and other crimes to the FBI's UCR. The estimated number of arrests for violent crimes in 2010 decreased for the fourth consecutive year and was 6.0% lower than in 2009.

Decades of national crime data have consistently indicated that males are arrested at significantly higher rates than females, the "gender gap" in violent and nonviolent offending. However, for all offenses since 2001, arrests of males have declined by 6.8% while the arrests of females have increased 10.5%. For violent crime arrests, the number of males arrested in 2010 declined nearly 12% from 2001, but the number of females arrested increased by almost 1% during the same time period. Among violent offenses, arrests in 2010 of juvenile males and females represented a decrease by 21.8% and 20.1%, respectively, from 2001 (FBI, 2011). Thorough examination of the gender-gap issue in violent crime rates is beyond the scope of this brief chapter; central issues include which databases are used (e.g., UCR versus National Crime Victimization Survey or National Crime Survey data), media exaggeration, and whether females are offending at numerically higher rates or relatively (to male offenders) higher rates as total violent crime arrest rates of males have decreased (Lauritsen, Heimer, & Lynch, 2009; Steffensmeier, Schwartz, Hua, & Ackerman, 2005).

Although males commit violent crimes at much higher rates than females, the magnitude of the gender gap varies greatly with the specific crime: exceedingly divergent in forcible rape cases, but less so in arrests for robbery and familial aggravated assaults. Among familial murder and nonnegligent homicide cases involving parents and preschool child victims, the female-to-male perpetrator rate has been nearly equal for years (Cooper & Smith, 2011; McKee, 2006).

The UCR has defined murder and nonnegligent manslaughter as the willful (nonnegligent) homicide of one human being by another. The category excludes deaths by suicide, negligence, or accident as well as justifiable homicides such as the killing of a felon by a law enforcement officer in the line of duty. Attempted murder or assaults that do not result in a person's death are classified as aggravated assaults as described later. Of the murder cases reported to the FBI in 2010, approximately 11% of those arrested were females, of whom 66 (8.8%) were under age 18 (FBI, 2011).

Aggravated assault is defined in the UCR as an unlawful attack by one person upon another for the purpose of inflicting severe or aggravated bodily injury. The UCR indicates that this violent offense involves the perpetrator's use or threat of a weapon likely to produce death or serious injury. Among the aggravated assault cases reported to the FBI in 2010, 22% of those arrested were females, of whom 6,885 (11.4%) were under age 18. Numerically, more adult and juvenile females were arrested for aggravated assault (60,145 in 2010) than for any other UCR-reported violent crime (FBI, 2011).

Until 2011, the UCR defined forcible rape as the carnal knowledge of a female forcibly and against her will. The definition included attempts and assaults to commit rape by force or threat of force. Sexual acts on a nonfamilial child or adolescent female without force (statutory rape) and other sex offenses (e.g., exhibitionism, possession/distribution of child pornography, prostitution, etc.) were excluded as violent offenses; however, sexual assault of a female victim by a familial offender was categorized as an act of forcible rape, not incest. Sexual attacks on males by male or female perpetrators were counted as aggravated assaults or other sex offenses depending on the circumstances and the extent of injuries to the victim. In 2012, acknowledging that males as well as females are victims of violent sexual assaults, the Department of Justice redefined forcible rape as "the penetration, no matter how slight, of the vagina or anus with any body part or object, or oral penetration by a sex organ of another person, without the consent of the victim" (Justice News, 2012). The data reported within this chapter are based on the UCR's earlier definition of rape because the 2012 UCR report has not yet been completed and distributed. Of the forcible rape cases reported to the FBI in 2010, only 1% of those arrested were females, of whom 28 (24.8%) were under age 18 (FBI, 2011).

The final UCR violent crime category, robbery, is defined as the taking or attempting to take anything of value from the care, custody, or control of a person or persons by force or threat of force of violence and/or by putting the victim in fear. Among the 2010 UCR robbery arrests, dangerous weapons (e.g., firearms, knives, etc.) were used in approximately 60% of the cases. Of the robbery cases reported to the FBI in 2010, more than 12% of those arrested were females, of whom 1,750 (19.4%) were under age 18 (FBI, 2011).

The remainder of this chapter will focus on current descriptions and explanations of females' commission of murder and nonnegligent homicide, the most serious of violent crimes, as well as sexual offending by women and girls. Factors contributing to the development, diagnosis, assessment, and treatment of girls' and women's violence will also be discussed.

MURDER AND NONNEGLIGENT HOMICIDE

The US Department of Justice's Homicide Trends in the United States, 1980–2008 (Cooper & Smith, 2011), comprises the research literature's largest and longest recorded database of murder and nonnegligent homicide offenders' and victims' characteristics. From 1980 to 2008, male and female offenders have consistently differed greatly in many ways: Males were much more likely to commit murder (90% to 11%) under circumstances involving coperpetrators (92% to 8%), drugs (95% to 5%), gangs (98% to 2%), and firearms (92% to 8%), resulting in multiple victims (94% to 6%). Female and male offender homicide rates have been more similar when murder occurred within a family setting (Collins & Nichols, 1999). Homicide by a spouse or ex-spouse has been the most frequent type of familial murder from 1980 (52%) to 2008 (37%); children killed by a parent has been the second-most frequent type of homicide from 15% in 1980 to 25% in 2008 (Cooper & Smith, 2011). Although married or common-law husbands have been up to six times more likely to murder their wives (24% to 4%), when the deceased was a child under 5 years old, fathers (33%) and mothers (30%) had highly similar homicide rates; these extremely vulnerable victims rarely died at the hands of strangers (3%) (Cooper & Smith, 2011).

Spouse/Partner Homicide by Women (Mariticide)

In 2010, 12,996 UCR-reported arrests were made for murder and nonnegligent homicides in the United States; the offender–victim relationship was known in 5,718 (56%) of the cases. Intimate partner homicide (IPH) perpetrated by female and male spouses (including common-law unions) and boyfriend–girlfriend relationships comprised 23.4% of the total arrests, second only to homicides involving acquaintances (47.6%). Male spouses were over five times more likely (10.5%) than female spouses (1.9%) to have been arrested for the offense; boyfriends (8.6%) were arrested 3.7 times more often than girlfriends (2.3%) for IPH. Arguments over money, property, or other matters (59.6%) were by far the most common circumstance in which the homicide occurred; handguns and knives were the most frequently used weapons (Cooper & Smith, 2011).

For decades, female intimate partners have been killed at substantially higher rates than husbands/boyfriends (Paulozzi, Saltzman, Thompson, & Holmgreen, 2001; Rennison & Welchans, 2000). However, while the rates of uxoricide (IPH by male spouse) and mariticide (IPH by female spouse) have decreased over the past 25 years (Campbell, Glass, Sharps, Laughon, & Bloom, 2007), by 2008 IPH arrests of boyfriends and girlfriends had increased since 1980 to be essentially equivalent (48.6%) to spousal murders (46.7%) (Cooper & Smith, 2011).

Uxoricide, and to a much lesser extent mariticide, has been the focus of many researchers over the past four decades. For example, in a recent study of male and female IPH offenders, four risk factors appeared to be precipitants to domestic murder: employment stresses, victim intoxication, self-defense, and alcohol-involved quarrels. The coauthors found that in cases of mariticide, the women's prior abuse victimization was a salient factor (Weizman-Henelius, Matti Gronroos, Putknonen, & Eronen, 2010). The presence of a history of domestic violence between intimate partners, especially following separation or divorce, has been a consistent finding in many studies (Campbell et al. 2007; Farooque, Stout, & Ernst, 2005; Paulozzi et al., 2001) as well as low household income, nonowned residence, urban environment, and young-adult age (Rennison & Welchans, 2000). In a comparative study of heterosexual, gay, and lesbian couples, Mize and Shakelford (2008) found that the

IPH rate for gays was higher than that of heterosexuals or lesbians, but women of both sexual preferences committed more brutal killings than did the male offenders. In a large study of 2,577 IPH cases, Breitman, Shackelford, and Block (2004) found that the partners' age discrepancy—when the male is at least 16 years older than the female or the female is at least 10 years older than the male—is a predictor of heterosexual mariticide and uxoricide.

The most tragic cases of IPH are those that also involve the perpetrator's suicide, intimate partner homicide-suicide (IPHS), and familicide when adult and child family members are killed (Dietz, 1986). Older age in men is a commonly known suicide risk factor. In a study of IPHS cases from 1999 to 2005 of 444 deaths wherein at least one partner was over 60 years old, Salari (2007) found that females were rarely the perpetrator but had often been terrorized prior to being killed. She discovered that only a small proportion of the cases involved suicide pacts or "mercy" killings. In familicide cases, adult males are significantly more likely to kill their spouse and children before committing suicide: In two familicide studies separated by more than 25 years, none of the mothers in either sample committed mariticide before their suicide (Byard, Knight, James, & Gilbert, 1999; Rodenburg, 1971).

Filicide, Infanticide, and Neonaticide

Parental murders of children have occurred for centuries and have been documented in virtually every known society, from advanced industrialized countries to indigenous tribes. Filicide is defined as the killing of any person under age 18; more specifically, neonaticide and infanticide comprise child victims who are hours old and less than 1 year old, respectively (McKee, 2006; Oberman, 2003; Resnick, 1969). Within the United States since 1980, infants and newborns have consistently had the highest homicide victimization rate of all children under age 5 (Cooper & Smith, 2011; Ewigman, Kivlahan, & Land, 1993).

Although filicide has been known to societies throughout history, the scientific study of these horrific acts has been a relatively recent phenomenon of the past 40 years. In the first review of the world's literature of parental filicide, Resnick (1969) discovered only 155 published case reports between 1751 and 1967. He developed the first classification of parental filicide based on the mother's or father's most apparent motive: "altruism" (to relieve a child's prolonged unchanging suffering or anticipated suffering following the parent's suicide), "acute psychosis," "unwanted pregnancy" (neonaticide), "accident," or "revenge" against a spouse/partner. Resnick's (1969, 1970) classification is still the most widely cited model and is the starting point for many subsequent categories in the literature.

Resnick's studies sparked research in numerous countries, including England (d'Orban, 1979; Scott, 1973), Canada (Bourget & Bradford, 1990), Australia (Baker, 1991; Wilczynski, 1997), India (Oberman, 2003), Hong Kong (Cheung, 1986), and Italy (McKee & Bramante, 2010). These studies have found that the reasons for filicide by fathers and mothers are often quite different. For example, Baker's (1991) model of parental filicide specified six major motives: "altruism," "spouse revenge," "jealousy and rejection," "unwanted child," "discipline-related" cases, and "self-defense." She found that her sample's mothers and fathers were not equivalent in their reasons for filicide: "Unwanted" child cases (neonaticides) were only committed by mothers, whereas fathers were the only perpetrators of "spouse revenge," "jealousy/rejection," and "self-defense"—motivated child homicides. Wilczynski (1997) found that some of the 10 categories in her system were more descriptive of fathers or mothers, respectively. Filicides based on "retaliatory" and "jealousy/rejection" almost exclusively involved fathers who were slightly more likely than mothers to kill their child for "disciplinary" motives. Mothers, in contrast, were the parents who most likely committed filicide due to "unwanted child," "Munchausen's by proxy syndrome," or "psychotic" motives.

Other classification systems have focused exclusively on maternal filicides, likely because their motives appear to be more varied, complex, and perplexing than child killings by fathers. The first maternal filicide model was developed by a British psychiatrist based on a sample of mothers incarcerated for child homicide. d'Orban (1979) found their motives could be classified into six groups: "battering," "mentally ill," "neonaticide," "retaliating," "unwanted," and "mercy" killings. More recently, Meyer and Oberman (2001) reviewing national media reports from 1990 to 1999 specified five categories of maternal filicide motives: "ignored pregnancy" (neonaticides), "abuse-related" (excessive physical discipline), "neglect" (negligent supervision), "purposeful" (mental illness, situational distress, and personality disorders), and "assisted/coerced" (forced by partner into coperpetration) homicides.

McKee (2006), based on his individual forensic psychological evaluations of 32 adolescent and adult mothers charged with homicide of their child or children, found five primary motives: "detached mothers" (lack of bonding to the newborn or infant); "abusive/neglectful mothers" (inadequate parenting); "psychotic/depressed mothers" (mental illness); "retaliatory mothers" (rage/revenge for another directed onto the child); and "psychopathic mothers" (self-indulgent maternal exploitation of a child for money, drugs, or attention as in Munchausen by proxy syndrome cases), a new category not previously described in other classification systems. The model was developed to highlight the developmental and longitudinal dimensions of mother–child relationships that end in death.

To further understand the origins and pathways of juvenile and adult mothers who kill their children, the demographic, historical, clinical, victim, and offense characteristics of these violent females are described in the following sections by summarizing the findings of recent research studies.

DEMOGRAPHIC CHARACTERISTICS

The mother's age at the time of her child's death has been one of the most consistently reported statistics in studies of maternal filicide. Most of the research has found that after excluding neonaticide cases, the mothers were typically in their mid-twenties (Bourget & Bradford, 1990; d'Orban, 1979; Spinelli, 2003), but neonaticidal mothers were very young: Overpeck, Brenner, and Trumble (1998) reported that first-time mothers under age 15 were seven times more likely to commit neonaticide or infanticide than new mothers over age 25. Subnormal intellectual functioning has often been found in mothers who committed filicide: McKee and Shea (1998) discovered 5% of their sample was diagnosed with mental retardation, similar to the 4% prevalence found by d'Orban (1979), which is significantly higher than 1% prevalence in the general population. Limited educational achievement has been shown to be a descriptor of mothers who commit child homicide: Overpeck et al. (1998) reported that infants whose mothers did not complete high school were eight times more likely to be killed than the infants of mothers who had completed more than 15 years of school.

Many studies have found that most of the filicidal mothers were married or in an ongoing partnership at the time of the child's death ranging from 52% (Wilczynski, 1997) to 88% (Resnick, 1969). However, if the mother had committed neonaticide, she was unlikely to be married or in a stable relationship: 97% of Meyer and Oberman's (2001) sample of mothers were single. Unmarried status was cited as a risk factor for maternal neonaticide in the research of Cummings, Theis, Miller, and Rivara (1994) as well as Emerick, Foster, and Campbell (1986). Research has indicated that filicidal mothers often come from impoverished situations at the time of their child's death. Investigators have also cited lack of financial resources as a common characteristic of the women who commit filicide or abandon their neonates. For example, McKee and Shea (1998) found that 80% of the mothers in their study had annual incomes of less than $20,000. Meyer and Oberman (2001) discovered that 90% of the mothers who had fatally neglected their child lived below the poverty line. Wilczynski (1997) determined that 61% of the filicidal mothers in her sample reported having housing problems due to financial deficits.

PERSONAL/RELATIONSHIP CHARACTERISTICS

Many studies have shown that the personal histories of mothers who kill their offspring are replete with childhood family crises and victimization. Parental divorce was a common theme: In d'Orban's 1979 study, 57% of the mothers had come from broken homes, compared to 80% of the mothers in McKee and Shea's (1998) sample. Crimmins, Langley, and Brownstein (1997) determined that 64% of the mothers in their sample had come from motherless homes. Filicidal mothers' childhood history of victimization has been a common factor found in many studies. Spinelli (2003) discovered that 53% of the infanticidal mothers she studied were victims of physical and/or sexual abuse. Crimmins et al. (1997) found that 74% of their filicidal mothers had reported a history of serious physical abuse or sexual molestation, which was consistent with Korbin's (1986) finding that 78% of her sample reported a history of childhood physical and/or sexual victimization.

Many studies have reported that filicidal mothers are often in abusive, violent relationships at the time their children are killed. Crimmins et al. (1997) found that 52% of the mothers in their sample were living with an abusive partner; Meyer and Oberman (2001) indicated that 40% of the women in their sample had been abused by their partners. Of the women in McKee and Shea's (1998) study, 43% reported that they were in a violent relationship, and half of those women also described abuse by a former partner.

Generally, filicidal mothers do not have histories of prior legal difficulties before their arrest for killing their child or children. d'Orban (1979) found that 20% of the sample were previously arrested, compared to 5% of the mothers in the sample of McKee and Shea (1998). Holden, Burland, and Lemmen (1996) found that a small minority of their sample of filicidal mothers had been previously charged with crimes by the police.

CLINICAL CHARACTERISTICS

Psychiatric problems within the mothers' biological families appear to occur with higher frequency than in the general population. d'Orban (1979) found that 25% of the sample indicated that one or more of her relatives were mentally ill, compared to 45% of the mothers in the sample of McKee and Shea (1998). Crimmins et al. (1997) showed that in 38% of their cases, the filicidal mother reported that one or more family members suffered from alcoholism and that 7% had serious mental problems. Lewis, Baranoski, Buchanan, and Benedek (1998) indicated that 55% of the women in their sample declared that one or more family members had received psychiatric care. Wilczynski (1997) discovered that 23% of her sample of mothers reported that one or more of their family had previously received psychiatric care and that 7% of the mothers had a family member who had been arrested.

A personal history of mental illness and treatment has been a common finding in many studies of filicidal mothers. In the 1979 study by d'Orban, 41% of the sample had been previously psychiatrically hospitalized. More than 64% of Wilczynski's (1997) sample reported that they had received prior psychiatric treatment, which was comparable to the 60% of filicidal mothers reported by Lewis et al. (1998). Crimmins et al. (1997) found that 59% of their sample had sought mental health care prior to their filicidal acts. Alder and Polk (2001) discovered that the majority of filicidal women in their study had been receiving psychiatric care at the time of their child's death, which was consistent with the findings of Sammons (1987) that 40% of filicidal mothers had been seen by a psychiatrist shortly before committing their crime. Wilczynski (1997) found that 90% of her sample had received at least one psychiatric diagnosis, primarily for depression (68%), suicide attempts (36%), and/or substance abuse (64%). These data were congruent with the study of Crimmins et al. (1997), who discovered that 41% of their sample had one of more prior suicide attempts and 64% had used alcohol or illegal drugs regularly.

VICTIM AND OFFENSE CHARACTERISTICS

Most of the maternal filicide studies have indicated that the mothers' victims are not predominantly male or female. Certain studies, however, have indicated a relationship between victim age and victim gender in child homicides. Among children under age 9, boys are as likely to be killed as girls, but from ages 10 to 18, males are five times more likely to be murdered by their fathers, typically during a domestic dispute (Maguire, Pastore, & Flanagan, 1993). When the perpetrator is the mother, her sons and daughters are equally likely to be victims (Lewis et al., 1998; McKee & Shea, 1998; Resnick, 1969).

The method of killing the child has been found to vary widely depending on the age and vulnerability of the mother's victim. "Hands-on" methods of suffocation or drowning in maternal filicide cases likely occurs because the victims are most often very young children who are incapable of presenting a physical threat to their mothers (Crittenden & Craig, 1990; Meyer & Oberman, 2001). Weapons such as guns or knives are infrequently employed by mothers, as illustrated by 0% of the cases reported by McKee and Shea (1998), 4% of d'Orban's (1979) cases, and only 17% of the cases cited in Resnick's (1969) research. Crittenden and Craig (1990) found a relationship between the victim's age and method of filicide: Neonaticides were committed by suffocation (27%), drowning (22%), or exposure (14%); however, 65% of all children between the ages of 1 month and 5 years died from beatings, and most of the children older than 5 years had been shot or stabbed. Kunz and Bahr (1996) discovered a similar relationship between victim vulnerability (young age) and filicide method: 55% of the victims less than 1 week old had been suffocated, strangled, or drowned, but for victims over 10 years of age, 83% had been either shot or stabbed.

SEXUAL OFFENSES BY WOMEN AND GIRLS

Relative to males and to general female nonsexual offending, research efforts have not focused on females who have sexually offended (Boroughs, 2004; Denov, 2003; Lewis & Stanley, 2000; Peluso & Putman, 1996; Tardif, Auclair, Jacob, & Carpentier, 2004; Tewksbury, 2004; Vandiver & Kercher, 2004). Even when female-perpetrated child sexual abuse has been examined, reactions have been either anger or apathy (Denov, 2003); the literature lacks even an educated estimate for the number of females who have sexually offended—or their personal or offense behavior characteristics—as exists for male offending. The following review is based on the few empirically based studies of females who have offended sexually, which, until recent years, have been composed of very limited sample sizes.

As with males, females who have sexually offended have done so with a variety of etiologies and thus comprise a heterogeneous population. Some frequently identified characteristics have been indicated, but it must be kept in mind that studies are often focused on women (rarely girls) who have sexually offended against children, thus limiting the generalizability of the researchers' results.

Offender Age

The age of female sexual offenders studied varies significantly, but the average is in the thirties. In a Texas study of 471 women on the state's sex offender registry, Vandiver and Kercher (2004) found a range at arrest from 18 to 77 with a mean age of 32 years old. Of the 277 women registered as sex offenders in Indiana and Kentucky during 2004, Tewksbury (2004) had age data that existed for only 40; their average age was 37 years. A study of all of the women (n = 15) charged with sexual assaults who had been referred for competency to stand trial and criminal responsibility assessments in South Carolina from 1987 to 1997 revealed an age range from 13 to 53 with an average age of 28 years old (Lewis & Stanley, 2000). A study of 93 women on the Swedish National Crime Register indicated a mean age of 32 years (Fazel, Sjöstedt, Grann, & Långström, 2010), very similar to the average age of 33 years in a sample of 390 women registered as sex offenders in New York (Sandler & Freeman, 2007) and 30 years in a sample (n = 31) of women sex offender inmates from West Virginia (Johansson-Love & Fremouw, 2009). Among girls who have sexually offended, recent research has indicated an average age of 15 years (Tardif et al., 2004) and 14 years (Matthews, Hunter, & Vuz, 1997), respectively.

Abuse History

Previous victimization is common among females who have sexually offended. Lewis and Stanley (2000) found 80% of the subjects were sexual abuse victims; 80% had been physically abused. The study of Tardif et al. (2005) identified a rate of 62% for sexual abuse and 46% for physical abuse among adults; among girls, the victimization rates were 60% and 40%, respectively. In their study of 111 women, Wijkman, Bijleveld, and Hendriks (2010) found about a third had been victimized. Compared to male sex offenders, and to both female and to male violent offenders, the female sex offender group in the Johansson-Love and Fremouw (2009) study was the most likely to have been sexually victimized. In a comparative study of male and female juvenile sexual offenders, the girls were more likely to have been victimized more aggressively, at a younger age, and by more perpetrators (Matthews et al., 1997).

Psychiatric Diagnoses

A wide variety of findings have documented the presence of psychiatric diagnoses among female sex offenders. Lewis and Stanley's research (2000) found schizophrenia, psychotic disorder not otherwise specified, depressive symptoms, mild mental retardation, borderline intellectual functioning, paranoid personality disorder, borderline personality disorder traits, and dependent personality disorder traits among 67% of their sample having received outpatient psychiatric services; 7% had been inpatients. Another study found depression, anxiety, and posttraumatic stress disorder (PTSD) were common diagnoses among female sexual offenders (Matthews et al., 1997), and other researchers have discovered a rate of 59% for the presence of a mental illness (Wijkman et al., 2010). A comparative study of women and girls who had offended sexually found the adults had often been diagnosed with affective disorders (dysthymia, depression) alone or with concurrent personality disorders (dependent or borderline types), while 87% of the juveniles had received services for "behavioral problems, academic difficulties, and adaptation problems" with diagnoses including learning disorder, attention-deficit/hyperactivity disorder, dysthymic disorder, conduct disorder, and posttraumatic stress disorder (Tardif et al., 2004).

Very recent research (Fazel et al., 2010) found that female sexual offenders were statistically more likely to have been hospitalized psychiatrically and to have been diagnosed with psychotic and substance use disorders in comparison to the general population; however, they found no difference between female sexual and nonsexual violent offenders in terms of psychotic disorders or substance abuse diagnoses.

Victims

When sexual assaults by male or female perpetrators occur, the mental and physical impact on their victims can be horrendous and devastating. Female sexual offenders are more likely than male sexual offenders to have known their victims, been related to their victims, offended with a coperpetrator, and to have had a victim from 11 to 17 years of age (Johansson-Love & Fremouw, 2009). Sandler and Freeman (2007) found an average victim age of 12 years in their sample from New York. In another recent study (Wijkman et al., 2010), victims' mean age was 13 years, 91% were acquaintances, and 50% were family members; over 60% of the female offenders had coperpetrators. Vandiver and Kercher (2004) found that victim gender varied widely among their six offender types: "heterosexual nurturers" (100% male), "noncriminal homosexual offenders" (4% male), "female sexual predators" (60% male), "homosexual criminals" (17% male), "aggressive homosexual offenders" (12% male), and more equal in "young adult child exploiters" of elementary-aged boys and/or girls.

Female Sexual Recidivism

Most sexual offenders, regardless of gender or age, are thought to have low rates of sexual recidivism relative to other types of violent and nonviolent offenders and their offenses. In a Nebraska-based sample of 57 females who had sexually offended, 17.5% had committed a new sexual assault, but their characteristics were not statistically different from the nonrecidivists in the study (Bader, Welsh, & Scalora, 2010). When larger samples are collected or aggregated, female sexual recidivism may be much lower. A meta-analysis of 10 studies with a total of 2,490 offenders found a sexual recidivism rate of less than 3% over an average follow-up of 6.5 years (Cortoni, Hanson, & Coache, 2010). Sandler and Freeman's (2009) recidivism analysis of 1,466 females from New York with sex offenses found a rate of 2.2% based on arrests and 1.9% based on convictions. Overall, however, little is reliably known about female sexual offending recidivism in part because of small sample sizes of perpetrators with similar demographics, geographical and jurisdictional settings, and other empirical criteria.

Most important, as a cautionary note, there are currently no sexual risk assessment instruments with sufficient empirical support for use with adult or adolescent females.

CONSEQUENCES AND IMPACT OF WOMEN'S VIOLENCE

UCR violent crimes are felonies and as such likely lead to prolonged sentences in prison followed by postrelease parole or probation supervision. Clearly, capital punishment is the most serious personal consequence to women who commit murder or nonnegligent homicide. As of January 2010 in the United States, 61 women were confined on death row comprising 1.87% of inmates facing capital punishment. Since the reinstitution of the death penalty in federal and certain states' jurisdictions in 1976, 12 women have been executed (Death Penalty Focus, 2012). Of the women currently on death row, approximately 25% were convicted of mariticide and 20% for filicide; 1 (2%) committed familicide (Strieb, 2010).

In contrast to misdemeanors, felony sentences typically comprise years-long confinement followed by postdischarge supervision on parole or probation. As of June 2009, state and federal prisons housed over 1.6 million adult inmates, a slight increase (0.5%) over the previous year; men were imprisoned at a rate 14 times higher than women. From 2000 to 2009, the proportion of women confined in prison has increased from 6.7% to 7.1% (West, 2010). Of those inmates released from prison over the past decade, females have consistently accounted for 12% of adults on parole, of which, in 2010, 16,000 (15.2%) were under federal jurisdiction and 87,374 (11.9%) under state supervision. At the federal level, considerably fewer women were on probation in 2010—8,154—proportionately more than twice as high (35.9%) as women parolees; among states, the probationer rate (17.5%) was slightly higher than the women's parolee rate (Glaze & Bonczar, 2011).

Approximately two thirds (65.9%) of the women in prison are under age 40 (West, 2010); of those who are mothers, their prolonged confinement likely has a significant and, for some, recurrent negative impact on their children and families.

In the most recent federal and selected-states' study of women's recidivism, 57.6% of female inmates were rearrested within 3 years of their release and 39.9% were reconvicted; 17.3% returned to prison with a new felony sentence (Langan & Levin, 2002). Research has found that a mother's incarceration is correlated to her female (and male) children exhibiting early-onset physical aggression, contact with the criminal justice system, adolescent delinquency, and higher health-risk behaviors (Shlafer, Poehlmann, Donelan-McCall, 2012; Tzoumakis, Lussier, & Corrado, 2012).

NONSEXUAL VIOLENT OFFENSES BY GIRLS

Recent studies have indicated that compared to boys' declining rates, the proportion of juvenile females arrested for violent offenses has increased dramatically over the past 30 years from 11% in 1980, to 18% in 2000, and to 30% in 2004 (Zahn et al., 2008). Researchers have hypothesized that girls may be displaying more violent behavior as indicated by increased arrests for simple assault. However, other factors may include declining arrest rates for boys and policy changes of status offenses, such as "incorrigibility" being charged as a criminal domestic violence or aggravated assault with a mandatory arrest of the alleged daughter-perpetrator: The second most common victim of girls' violence is their mother. Schools' "zero-tolerance" policies wherein student-to-student altercations result in arrests, not in-school suspensions or expulsions, may also be a contributing factor: The most common type of girls' violence is a same-sex assault in self-defense or in response to a verbal insult. Though arrests of girls for simple/other assault have increased, the actual incidence of serious violent offenses (murder, aggravated assault with a weapon, etc.) has not changed substantially over the past two decades (Steffensmeier, Schwartz, Hua, & Ackerman, 2005; Zahn et al., 2008).

Girls have historically engaged in fewer violent offenses when compared to boys. Excluding forcible rape for definitional biases described earlier, in 2010, girls' arrests were proportionately lower than boys for all violent offenses: murder (10.5%), aggravated assault (24.4%), and robbery (10.4%), but they were nearly equal for simple/other assaults (41.2%). From 1980 to 2003, the ratio of simple/other assault to aggravated assault arrests for girls (over 5.0 in 2003) has been higher than the boys' ratio of 3.5 in 2003, validating that adolescent females' violence is substantially less severe than juvenile males (Zahn et al., 2008).

FEMALE VIOLENCE: DEVELOPMENTAL, DIAGNOSTIC, PSYCHOMETRIC, AND TREATMENT ISSUES

Developmental Origins

Childhood and adolescent risk factors of violent behavior in girls (and boys) have been the subject of numerous studies for decades. Economic disadvantage, early exposure to domestic violence, physical and sexual victimization, recurrent family conflict and instability, lack of positive parental supervision, maternal and paternal incarceration, parental substance abuse, and transgenerational antisocial/criminal attitudes have been found to correlate with early-onset physical aggression in children and adolescents (Campbell, Spieker, Vandergrift, Belsky, & Burchinal, 2010; Donovan & Brassard, 2011; Murray & Murray, 2010; Sedlak & Bruce, 2010). In contrast to boys, girls' biological changes with puberty at early ages are frequently coupled with increased conflicts with parents (especially mothers) and premature involvement with older, often sexually active males, early pregnancy decisions (e.g., termination, adoption, single motherhood), and loss of positive peer friendships; that is, girls in gangs are more likely to be violent than other girls (Zahn et al., 2010).

Reviewing the literature of women's pathways to crime, Datchi and O'Neill (2011) have suggested that three overlapping clusters of risk are likely characteristic of juvenile-into-adult female offenders: interpersonal victimization, economic marginalization, and substance abuse. For example, a pathway from interpersonal victimization might evolve as follows: childhood sexual or physical abuse→ (may cause, lead to) physical and emotional traumatic injuries→internalizing (depression/anxiety, low self-esteem) and externalizing (aggression to peers, parents, siblings) symptoms→alcohol and drug abuse as adolescent young-adult coping strategy→loss of educational/vocational opportunities→economic disadvantages→crime to support addiction and children. Research support for females' pathways to crime can be found in the recent work of van Wormer (2010), Tzoumakis et al. (2012), Murray and Murray (2010), Murray, Farrington, and Sekol (2012), and Spieker et al. (2012).

Antisocial Personality Disorder and Conduct Disorder

Antisocial personality disorder (ASPD) is defined by the American Psychiatric Association (2000) as a pervasive pattern of disregard for and violation of the rights of others since age 15, as illustrated by a number of different behaviors, including criminal acts, deceit and repeated lying, impulsivity, repeated physical aggression, reckless disregard for others' safety, repeated failures to honor financial and/or work obligations, and/or lack of remorse for hurting or victimizing others. The individual must be at least 18 years old at the time of diagnosis and must also display, prior to age 15, symptoms of conduct disorder (CD; e.g., aggression to persons or animals, property destruction or theft, and/or serious violations of parental/school rules before age 13, etc.).

Within the general population, ASPD is diagnosed in approximately 3% of males, roughly three times the rate that has been determined in female samples. Among personality disorders found within American culture, ASPD ranks third in prevalence behind obsessive-compulsive and paranoid types (Grant et al., 2004). ASPD is considered to have a chronic course that may abate somewhat by the individual's fourth decade of life.

Because the diagnosis of ASPD requires the presence of certain symptoms prior to and after age 15, a number of researchers have attempted to track the pathway of early childhood behavior problems into adulthood. For example, among an urban sample of late adolescent boys and girls, 29% had at least one contact with the police before age 13 (White & Piquero, 2004). Smith and Farrington (2004) found that across three generations there were continuities of antisocial behavior; that is, antisocial males tended to partner with antisocial females, who in turn tended to produce children with behavior and conduct problems. Foley, Pickles, Rutter, and Gardner (2004) discovered that mothers from stepfather families had higher rates of antisocial personality disorder and alcoholism than mothers from intact families.

In another national study of three-generation households, Black et al. (2002) reported that among adolescent mothers, maternal abuse and clinical depression were significantly associated with childhood externalizing behavior problems characteristic of conduct disorder. In a prospective study of boys and girls followed longitudinally from 12 to 42 months, the interaction between child noncompliance and rejection as a maternal parenting style resulted in significantly higher acting-out patterns among the young children of both genders (Shaw et al., 1998).

Because the diagnosis of ASPD includes many criteria that involve the legal system, significantly higher prevalence rates for both men and women have been found among prison inmates, substance abuse treatment center clients, and forensic hospital patients (Cottler, Price, Compton, & Mager, 1995; Hesselbrock, Meyer, & Keener, 1985; Salekin, Rogers, & Sewell, 1997). For example, in a sample of male and female alcoholics, Hesselbrock et al. (1985) discovered that nearly 50% of the men and 20% of the women met the diagnostic criteria for ASPD. In a study of homeless individuals, North, Smith, and Spitznagel (1993) found ASPD prevalence rates of 25% and 10% for men and women, respectively. Among a sample of cocaine-dependent women, 76% met diagnostic criteria for ASPD (Rutherford, Alterman, Cacciola, & McKay, 1999).

Women and mothers with ASPD are an understudied population, especially within the general community (Cale & Lilienfeld, 2003). Some authors have argued that ASPD has been underdiagnosed in females because the criteria for conduct disorder and ASPD reflect aggressive behavior, which is more characteristic of men than women. For example, in a review of the literature on gender differences in children and adolescents, girls between ages 5 and 13 displayed fewer conduct problems when compared to boys within the same age range; thus, the girls would be much less likely to subsequently qualify for an childhood-onset diagnosis of conduct disorder as a precursor to an adult diagnosis of ASPD (Silverthorn & Frick, 1999). Some authors have suggested that the criteria for borderline personality disorder (instability in interpersonal relationships, self-image, and affect; marked impulsivity) may have more clinical utility for women who engage in violent and criminal behavior (Blonigen, Sullivan, Hicks, & Patrick, 2012; Sprague, Javdani, Sadeh, Newman, & Verona, 2012).

For the newest edition of the APA's *Diagnostic and Statistical Manual of Mental Disorders* (DSM-5), research has focused on the proposed "callous-unemotional" (CU) subtype of conduct disorder in young girls and boys (Frick, 2009; Frick & White, 2008; Pardini, Stepp, Hipwell, Stouthamer-Loeber, & Loeber, 2012). CU traits include lack of guilt, absence of empathy, and callous use of others, which appear to be present in a subsection of adolescents who display patterns of severely aggressive behavior and attitudes. For example, Pardini et al. (2012) examined a community sample of 1,862 girls aged 6 to 8 years in a 6-year longitudinal study of their internalizing/externalizing patterns of problem/conflict resolution, peer relationships, academic achievement, and global impairment ratings. The researchers found that among the girls who developed conduct disorder, those who were initially judged to have higher levels of CU before age 9 years displayed higher levels of externalizing disorder symptoms (e.g., bullying, relational aggression, etc.) during their teenage years. Recently, researchers have developed a promising quantitative assessment of girls' and boys' CU patterns: the Inventory of Callous-Unemotional Traits (Kimonis et al., 2008).

Another approach to the description and classification of antisocial behavior has been the characterization of psychopathy, a term first proposed by Cleckley (1998/1941). Psychopathic individuals have been described along interpersonal, affective-emotional, and behavioral dimensions (Hemphill & Hart, 2003). Interpersonally, such persons often display manipulative, deceitful, and arrogant patterns. Their emotional and affective expressions are highly variable and superficial. Psychopathic individuals have great difficulty developing close, meaningful feelings for others. They do not seem to experience anxiety, guilt, or empathy as others do. Behaviorally, their actions are typically impulsive, sensation seeking, and irresponsible, but they may not necessarily be violent or criminal.

Psychometric Assessment

Over the past 20 years, the clinical, empirical, and psychometric study of psychopathy has been a central feature in the understanding, explanation, prediction, and treatment of antisocial behavior in males and females. A number of peer-reviewed, published psychological tests and/or specialized scales have been developed to assess empirically the presence of psychopathy, including the Hare Psychopathy Checklist-Revised (PCL-R; Hare, 1991), the Antisocial Practices (ASP) content scale of the Minnesota Multiphasic Personality Inventory-2 (MMPI-2; Butcher, Dahlstrom, Graham, Tellegen, & Kaemmer, 1989), the Antisocial Features (ANT) scale of the Personality Assessment Inventory (PAI; Morey, 1991), the Psychopathy Personality Inventory (PPI; Lilienfeld & Andrews, 1996), and its revision, PPI-R (Lilienfeld & Widows, 2005). For juveniles, the Unruly, Oppositional, and Delinquent Predisposition scales of the Millon Adolescent Clinical Inventory (MACI; Millon, 1993) and the Jessness Inventory-Revised (JI-R; Jessness, 2003) have shown promise, as has the Psychopathy Checklist: Youth Version (PCL:YV; Forth, Kosson, & Hare, 2003) for boys, but not for girls (Vincent, Odgers, McCormick, & Corrado, 2008).

Almost all of the research on psychopathy has focused on adult males (Cale & Lilienfeld, 2002; Salekin, Rogers, Ustad, & Sewell, 1998). There have been a few studies involving females and mothers. For example, in a sample of 103 adult female prison inmates assessed with the PCL-R, 15% were able to be categorized as psychopaths using the cutoff score for males recommended by the test's manual (Salekin, Rogers, & Sewell, 1997). The Antisocial (ANT) and Aggression (AGG) scales of the PAI were found to be among the best predictors of future criminal recidivism in a sample of adult female inmates (Salekin et al., 1998). A PPI validation study in a sample of 102 women inmates showed the test had significant correlations with the PCL-R and *DSM-IV* criteria for ASPD (Berardino, Meloy, Sherman, & Jacobs, 2005). In another PPI study of gender differences, men scored significantly higher than women on the following PPI subscales: Machiavellian Egocentricity, Coldheartedness, Fearlessness, Impulsive Nonconformity, Stress Immunity, and Blame Externalization (Lilienfeld & Andrews, 1996).

With the MMPI-2, mothers of children under 2 years old who scored high on the ASP scale were observed to be less understanding and more hostile and harsh in their parenting practices than mothers who scored lower on the scale (Bosquet & Egeland, 2000). In a two-state MMPI-2 profile study of pretrial women charged with filicide, mariticide, or murder of a nonfamily victim, McKee, Shea, Mogy, and Holden (2001) found test scale elevations suggesting mental illness, clinical depression, and antisocial tendencies, respectively, for each group. Noting the sparse literature on psychometric measurement of psychopathy in females, Cale and Lilienfeld (2003) concluded that much work remains to be done before confident conclusions can be drawn.

Interventions and Treatment

Thorough discussion of treatment programs for violent juvenile and adult females is beyond the scope of this chapter. The interested reader is referred to the work of Van Wormer (2010), the National Crime Victims Research and Treatment Center (Saunders, Berliner, & Hanson, 2003), and Kazdin (2002). Research has suggested that persons with antisocial and psychopathic disorders have generally been considered to be very difficult to treat successfully, principally because they experience little guilt or anxiety that might prompt them to seek mental health services (Hemphill & Hart, 2003). Most often, persons with psychopathy and ASPD are involuntarily referred for treatment following involvement with the legal system; as a result, they often have little motivation to change their behavior (Brodsky, 2005). For girls and women, the most successful interventions are "gender sensitive," are implemented when early signs and symptoms are initially observed, and emphasize females' special needs of relationship building, connectedness to their children and family, safety from verbal and sexual threats, overcoming childhood/ adolescent traumas, and access to greater economic autonomy.

This chapter has reviewed the most recent FBI UCR violent felony arrest data perpetrated by adult and adolescent female offenders. Descriptions and explanations of females' commission of murder and nonnegligent homicide, as well as sexual offending, the most serious violent crimes, were highlighted based on current research findings. Personal, family, interpersonal, and environmental factors contributing to the development, diagnosis, assessment, and treatment of girls' and women's violence were also discussed.

REFERENCES

Alder, C., & Polk, K. (2001). *Child victims of homicide*. Cambridge, UK: Cambridge University Press.

American Psychiatric Association. (2000). *Diagnostic and statistical manual of mental disorders* (4th ed., Text rev.). Washington, DC: Author.

Bader, S. M., Welsh, R., & Scalora, M. J. (2010). Recidivism among female child molesters. *Violence and Victims, 25*, 349–362.

Baker, J. (1991). *You can't let your children cry: Filicide in Victoria 1978-1988*. Unpublished Master's thesis, University of Melbourne, Victoria, Australia.

Berardino, S., Meloy, J., Sherman, M., & Jacobs, D. (2005). Validation of the psychopathic personality Inventory on a female inmate sample. *Behavioral Sciences and the Law, 23*(6), 819–836.

Black, M., Papas, M., Hussey, J., Hunter, W., Dubowitz, H., Kotch, J. B., … Schneider, M. (2002). Behavior and development of preschool children born to adolescent mothers: Risk and 3-generation households. *Pediatrics, 109*(4), 573–580.

Blonigen, D., Sullivan, E., Hicks, B., & Patrick, C. (2012). Facets of psychopathy in relation to potentially traumatic events and posttraumatic stress disorder among female prisoners: The mediating role of borderline personality disorder traits. *Personality Disorders, 23*(1), 406–414.

Boroughs, D. (2004). Female sexual abusers of children. *Child and Youth Services Review, 26*, 481–487.

Bosquet, M., & Egeland, B. (2000). Predicting parenting behaviors from antisocial practices content scale scores of the MMPI-2 administered during pregnancy. *Journal of Personality Assessment, 74*(1), 146–162.

Bourget, D., & Bradford, J. M. W. (1990). Homicidal parents. *Canadian Journal of Psyhciatry, 35*, 233–237.

Breitman, N., Shackelford, T., & Block, C. (2004). Couple age discrepancy and risk of intimate partner homicide. *Violence and Victims, 19*(3), 321–342.

Brodsky, S. (2005). Psychotherapy with reluctant and involuntary clients. In G. P. Koocher, J. C. Norcross, & S. S. Hill (Eds.), *Psychologists' desk reference.* (2nd ed., pp. 257–262). New York, NY: Oxford University Press.

Butcher, J. N., Dahlstrom, L., Graham, J. R., Tellegen, A., & Kaemmer, B. (1989). *Minnesota multiphasic personality inventory-2.* Minneapolis: University of Minnesota Press.

Byard, R. W., Knight, D., James, R. A., & Gilbert, J. (1999). Murder-suicides involving children: A 29-year study. *American Journal of Forensic Medicine and Pathology, 20*(4), 323–327.

Cale, E. M., & Lilienfeld, S. O. (2002). Sex differences in psychopathy and antisocial personality disorder: A review and integration. *Clinical Psychology Review, 22*, 1179–1207.

Cale, E. M., & Lilienfeld, S. O. (2003). What every forensic psychologist should know about psychopathic personality. In W. O'Donohoe & E. Levensky (Eds.), *Handbook of forensic psychology: Resource for mental health and legal professionals* (pp. 395–428). San Diego, CA: Elsevier.

Campbell, J., Glass, N., Sharps, P., Laughon, K., & Bloom, T. (2007). Intimate partner homicide: Review and implications of research and policy. *Trauma, Violence and Abuse, 8*(3), 246–269.

Campbell, S., Spieker, S., Vandergrift, N., Belsky, J., & Burchinal, M. (2010). Predictors and sequelae of trajectories of physical aggression in school-age boys and girls. *Development and Psychopathology, 22*(1), 133–150.

Cheung, P. (1986). Maternal filicide in Hong Kong, 1971–1985. *Medicine, Science and the Law, 26*, 185–192.

Cleckley, H. (1998). *The mask of sanity.* St. Louis, MO: Mosby. (original work published in 1941).

Collins, K., & Nichols, C. (1999). A decade of pediatric homicide: A retrospective study at the Medical University of South Carolina. *American Journal of Forensic Medicine and Pathology, 20*(2), 169–172.

Cooper, A., & Smith, E. (2011). Homicide trends in the United States 1980-2008. [NCJ 236018]. Retrieved May 29, 2014 from www.bjs.gov/content/pub/pdf/htus8008.pdf.

Cortoni, F., Hanson R. K., & Coache, M. (2010). The recidivism rates of female sexual offenders are low: A meta-analysis. *Sexual Abuse, 22*(4), 387–401.

Cottler, L. B., Price, R. K., Compton, W. M., & Mager, D. E. (1995). Subtypes of adult antisocial behavior and drug abusers. *Journal of Nervous and Mental Disease, 183*, 154–161.

Crimmins, S., Langley, S., Brownstein, H. H., & Sprunt, B. J. (1997). Convicted women who have killed children: A self-psychology perspective. *Journal of Interpersonal Violence, 12*, 49–69.

Crittenden, P. M., & Craig, S. E. (1990). Developmental trends in the nature of child homicide. *Journal of Interpersonal Violence, 5*, 202–216.

Cummings, P., Theis, M., Mueller, B., & Rivara, F. (1994). Infant injury and death in Washington state, 1981-1990. *Archives of Pediatric and Adolescent Medicine, 148*, 1021–1026.

Datchi, C., & O'Neill, T. (2011). Effective interventions for the management of female offenders. Available from author at: corrine.datchi@shu.edu.

Death Penalty Focus. (2012). Women on death row. Retrieved May 2014, from http://deathpenalty.org/article.php?id=57.

Denov, M. (2003). To a safe place? Victims of sexual abuse by females and their disclosure to professionals. *Child Abuse and Neglect, 27*, 47–61.

d'Orban, P. (1979). Women who kill their children. *British Journal of Psychiatry, 134*, 560–571.

Dietz, P. (1986). Mass, serial, and sensational homicides. *Bulletin of the New York Academy of Medicine, 62*, 477–491.

Donovan, K., & Brassard, M. (2011). Trajectories of maternal verbal aggression across middle school years: Associations with negative view of self and social problems. *Child Abuse and Neglect, 35*(10), 814–830.

Emerick, S. J., Foster, L. R., & Campbell, D. T. (1986). Risk factors for traumatic infant death in Oregon, 1973-1982. *Pediatrics, 77*, 518–522.

Ewigman, B., Kivlahan, C., & Land, G. (1993). The Missouri child fatality study: Underreporting of maltreatment fatalities among children younger than five years of age, 1983-1986. *Pediatrics, 91*, 330–337.

Farooque, R., Stout, R., & Ernst, F. (2005). Heterosexual intimate partner homicide: Review of ten years of clinical experience. *Journal of Forensic Science, 50*(3), 648–651.

Fazel, S., Sjöstedt, G., Grann, M., & Långström, N. (2010). Sexual offending in women and psychiatric disorder: A national case–control study. *Archives of Sexual Behavior, 39*(1), 161–167.

Federal Bureau of Investigation. (2011). Crime in the United States, 2010. Retrieved May 2014, from http://www.fbi,gov/about-us/cjis/ucr/crime-in-the-u.s./2010/tables/.

Forth, A. E., Kosson, D. S., & Hare, R. D. (2003). *Hare psychopathy checklist: Youth version*. Toronto, ON: Multi-Health Systems.

Frick, P. (2009). Extending the construct of psychopathy to youth: Implications for understanding, diagnosing, and treating antisocial children and adolescents. *Canadian Journal of Psyhciatry, 54*(12), 803–812.

Frick, P., & White, S. (2008). Research review: The importance of callous-emotional traits for developmental models of aggressive and antisocial behavior. *Journal of Child Psychology and Psychiatry, 49*(4), 359–375.

Foley, D., Pickles, A., Rutter, M., Gardner, C. O., Maes, H. H., Silberg, J. L., & Eaves, L. J. (2004). Risks for conduct disorder symptoms associated with parental alcoholism in stepfather families versus intact families from a community sample. *Journal of Child Psychology and Psychiatry, 45*(4), 687–696.

Glaze, L., & Bonczar, T. (2011). Probation and parole in the United States, 2010. [NCJ 236019]. Retrieved May 29, 2014 from www.bjs.gov/content/pub/pdf/ppus10.pdf.

Grant, B., Hasin, D., Stinson, F., Dawson, D. A., Chou, S. P., Ruan, W. J., & Pickering, R. P. (2004). Prevalence, correlates, and disability of personality disorders in the United States: Results from the national epidemiologic survey on alcohol and related conditions. *Journal of Clinical Psychology, 65*(7), 948–958.

Hare, R. D. (1991). *The Hare psychopathy checklist-revised.* Toronto, ON: Multi-Health Systems.

Hemphill, J. F. & Hart, S. D. (2003). Forensic and clinical issues in the assessment of psychopathy. In A.M. Goldstein (Ed.), *Handbook of psychology: Vol. 11. Forensic psychology* (pp. 87–107). Hoboken, NJ: Wiley.

Hesselbrock, M., Meyer, R., & Keener, J. (1985). Psychopathology in hospitalized alcoholics. *Archives of General Psychiatry, 42*, 1050–1055.

Holden, C. E., Burland, A. S., & Lemmen, C. A. (1996). Insanity and filicide: Women who murder their children. In E. P. Benedek (Ed.), *Emerging issues in forensic psychiatry: From clinic to courtroom* (pp. 25–34). San Francisco, CA: Jossey-Bass.

Jessness, C. (2003). *Jessness Inventory-Revised: Technical manual.* New York, NY: Multi-Health Systems.

Johansson-Love, J., & Fremouw, W. (2009). Female sex offenders: A controlled comparison of offender and victim/crime characteristics. *Journal of Family Violence, 24*, 367–376.

Justice News. (2012, January 6). Attorney General Eric Holder announces revisions to the Uniform Crime Reports' definition of rape. [Press release]. Retrieved May 29, 2014 from www.justice.gov/opa/pr/2012/January/12-ag-018.html.

Kazdin, A. E. (2002). Psychosocial treatments for conduct disorder in children and adolescents. In P. E. Nathan & J. M. Gordon (Eds.), *A guide to treatments that work.* (2nd ed., pp. 57–85). New York, NY: Oxford University Press.

Kimonis, E., Frick, P., Skeem, J., Marsee, M., Cruise, K., Munoz, L., … Morris, A. (2008). Assessing callous-unemotional traits in adolescent offenders: Validation of the Inventory of Callous-Unemotional Traits. *International Journal of Law and Psychiatry, 31*(3), 241–252.

Korbin, J. E. (1986). Childhood histories of women imprisoned for fatal child maltreatment. *Child Abuse and Neglect, 10*, 331–338.

Kunz, J., & Bahr, S. J. (1996). A profile of parental homicide against children. *Journal of Family Violence, 11*(4), 347–362.

Langan, P., & Levin, D. (2002). Recidivism of prisoners released in 1994. Retrieved May 29, 2014 from www.bjs.gov/content/pub/pdf/rpr94.pdf.

Lauritsen, J., Heimer, K., & Lynch, J. (2009). Trends in the gender gap in violent offending: New evidence from the National Crime Victimization Survey. *Criminology, 47*(2), 361–396.

Lewis, C. F., Baranoski, M. V., Buchanan, J. A., & Benedek, E. P. (1998). Factors associated with weapon use in maternal filicide. *Journal of Forensic Science, 43*(4), 613–618.

Lewis, C. F., & Stanley, C. R. (2000). Women accused of sexual offenses. *Behavioral Sciences and the Law, 18*, 73–81.

Lilienfeld, S. O., & Andrews, B. P. (1996). Development and preliminary validation of a self-report measure of psychopathic personality traits in noncriminal populations. *Journal of Personality Assessment, 66*, 488–524.

Lilienfeld, S. O., & Widows, M. (2005). *Psychopathic Personality Inventory-Revised: Manual.* Lutz, FL: Psychological Assessment Resources.

Maguire, K., Pastore, A., & Flanagan, T. (Eds.). (1993). *Sourcebook of criminal justice statistics 1993.* Washington, DC: US Department of Justice.

Matthews, R., Hunter, J., & Vuz, J. (1997). Juvenile female sexual offenders: Clinical characteristics and treatment issues. *Sexual Abuse, 9*(3), 187–199.

McKee, G. R. (2006). *Why mothers kill: A forensic psychologist's casebook.* New York, NY: Oxford University Press.

McKee, G. R., & Bramante, A. (2010). Maternal filicide and mental illness in Italy: A comparative study. *Journal of Psychiatry and the Law, 38*(3), 271–282.

McKee, G. R., & Shea, S. J. (1998). Maternal filicide: A cross-national comparison. *Journal of Clinical Psychology, 54*(5), 679–687.

McKee, G. R., Shea, S. J., Mogy, R. B., & Holden, C. E. (2001). MMPI-2 profiles of filicidal, mariticidal, and homicidal women. *Journal of Clinical Psychology, 57*(3), 367–374.

Meyer, C. L., & Oberman, M. (2001). *Mothers who kill their children.* New York, NY: New York University Press.

Millon, T. (1993). *Millon Adolescent Clinical Inventory: Manual.* Minneapolis, MN: National Computer Systems.

Mize, K., & Shackelford, T. (2008). Intimate partner homicide methods in heterosexual, gay, and lesbian relationships. *Violence and Victims, 23*(1), 98–114.

Morey, L. C. (1991). *The Personality Assessment Inventory professional manual.* Odessa, FL: Psychological Assessment Resources.

Murray, J., & Murray, L. (2010). Parental incarceration, attachment, and child psychopathology. *Attachment and Human Development, 12*(4), 289–309.

Murray, J., Farrington, D., & Sekol, I. (2012). Children's antisocial behavior, mental health, drug use, and educational performance after parental incarceration: A systematic review and meta-analysis. *Psychology Bulletin, 138*(2), 175–210.

North, C. S., Smith, E. M., & Spitznagel, E. L. (1993). Is antisocial personality a valid diagnosis among the homeless? *American Journal of Psychiatry, 150*, 578–583.

Oberman, M. (2003). Mothers who kill: Cross-cultural patterns in and perspectives on contemporary maternal filicide. *International Journal of Law and Psychiatry, 26*(5), 493–514.

Overpeck, M. D., Brenner, R. A., & Trumble, A. C. (1998). Risk factors for infant homicide in the United States. *New England Journal of Medicine, 339*, 1211–1216.

Pardini, D., Stepp, S., Hipwell, A., Stouthamer-Loeber, M., & Loeber, R. (2012). The clinical utility of the proposed DSM-5 callous-unemotional subtype of conduct disorder in young girls. *Journal of the American Academy of Child and Adolescent Psychiatry, 51*(1), 62–73.

Paulozzi, L., Saltzman, L., Thompson, M., & Holmgreen, P. (2001). Surveillance for homicide among intimate partners—United States, 1981-1998. *Morbidity and Mortality Weekly Reports CDC Surveilance Summary, 50*(3), 1–15.

Peluso, E., & Putnam, N. (1996). Case study: Sexual abuse of boys by females. *Journal of the American Academy of Child and Adolescent Psychiatry, 35*(1), 51–55.

Rennison, C., & Welchans, S. (2000). Intimate partner violence. [NCJ 178247]. Retrieved May 29, 2014 from www.bjs.gov/content/pub/pdf/ipv.pdf.

Resnick, P. J. (1969). Child murder by parents: A psychiatric review of filicide. *American Journal of Psychiatry, 126*(3), 325–334.

Resnick, P. J. (1970). Murder of the newborn: A psychiatric review of neonaticide. *American Journal of Psychiatry, 126*, 1414–1420.

Rodenburg, M. (1971). Child murder by depressed parents. *Canadian Psychiatric Association Journal*, 16(1), 41–48.

Rutherford, M. J., Alterman, A. I., Cacciola, J. S., & McKay, J. R. (1999). Gender differences in the relationship of antisocial personality disorder criteria to Psychopathy Checklist-Revised scores. *Journal of Personality Disorders*, 12, 69–76.

Salari, S. (2007). Patterns of intimate partner homicide suicide in later life: Strategies for prevention. *Clinical Interventions in Aging*, 2(3), 441–452.

Salekin, R. T., Rogers, R., & Sewell, K. W. (1997). Construct validity of psychopathy in a female offender sample: A multitrait—multimethod evaluation. *Journal of Abnormal Psychology*, 106, 576–585.

Salekin, R. T., Rogers, R., Ustad, K. L., & Sewell, K. W. (1998). Psychopathy and recidivism among female inmates. *Law and Human Behavior*, 22, 109–128.

Sammons, R. A. (1987, October). *Psychotic mothers who kill their children*. Paper presented at Institute of Law, Psychiatry, and Public Policy, Charlottesville, VA.

Sandler, J. C., & Freeman, N. J. (2007). Typology of female sex offenders: A test of Vandiver and Kercher. *Sexual Abuse*, 19(2), 73–89.

Saunders, B., Berliner, L., & Hanson, R. (Eds.). (2003). *Child physical and sexual abuse: Guidelines for Treatment (final report: January 15, 2003)*. Charleston, SC: National Crime Victims Research and Treatment Center.

Scott, P. D. (1973). Parents who kill their children. *Medicine, Science and the Law*, 13(3), 120–127.

Sedlak, A., & Bruce, C. (2010). Youth's characteristics and backgrounds. Office of Juvenile Justice and Delinquency Prevention. Retrieved May 2014, from https://www.ncjrs.gov/pdffiles1/ojjdp/227730.pdf.

Shaw, D. S., Winslow, E. B., Owens, E. B. Vondra, J. I., Cohn, J. F., & Bell, R. Q. (1998). The development of early externalizing problems among children from low-income families: A transformational perspective. *Journal of Abnormal Child Psychology*, 26(2), 95–107.

Shlafer, P., Poehlmann, J., & Donelan-McCall, N. (2012). Maternal jail time, conviction, and arrest as predictors of children's 15-year antisocial outcomes in the context of a nurse home visiting program. *Journal of Clinical Child and Adolescent Psychology*, 41(1), 38–52.

Silverthorn, P., & Frick, P. J. (1999). Developmental pathways to antisocial behavior: the delayed-onset pathway in girls. *Development and Psychopathology*, 11, 101–126.

Smith, C. A., & Farrington, D. P. (2004). Continuities in antisocial behavior and parenting across three generations. *Journal of Child Psychology and Psychiatry*, 45(2), 230–247.

Spieker, S., Campbell, S., Vandergrift, N., Pierce, K., Cauffman, E., Susman, E., & Roisman, G. (2012). Relational aggression in middle childhood: Predictors and adolescent outcomes. *Social Development*, 21(2), 354–375.

Spinelli, M. G. (Ed.). (2003). *Infanticide: Psychosocial and legal perspectives on mothers who kill*. Washington, DC: American Psychiatric Association.

Sprague, J., Javdani, S., Sadeh, N., Newman, J., & Verona, E. (2012). Borderline personality disorder as a female phenotypic expression of psychopathy? *Personality Disorders*, 3(2), 127–139.

Steffensmeier, D., Schwartz, J., Hua, Z., & Ackerman, J. (2005). An assessment of recent trends in girls' violence using diverse longitudinal sources: Is the gender gap closing? *Criminology*, 43, 355–405.

Strieb, V. (2010). Death penalty for female offenders, January 1, 1973 through October 21/2010. Retrieved May 2014, from http://www.deathpenaltyinfo.org/documents/femaledeathrow.pdf.

Tardif, M., Auclair, N., Jacob, M., & Carpentier, J. (2004). Sexual abuse perpetrated by adult and juvenile females: An ultimate attempt to resolve a conflict associated with maternal identify. *Child Abuse and Neglect, 29,* 153–167.

Tewksbury, R. (2004). Experiences and attitudes of registered female sex offenders. *Federal Probation, 68*(3), 30–33

Tzoumakis, S., Lussier, P., & Corrado, R. (2012). Female juvenile delinquency, motherhood, and the Intergenerational transmission of aggression and antisocial behavior. *Behavioral Sciences and the Law, 30*(2), 211–237.

Vandiver, D. M., & Kercher, G. (2004). Offender and victim characteristics of registered female sexual offenders in Texas: A proposed typology of female sexual offenders. *Sexual Abuse, 16*(2), 121–137.

Vincent, G. M., Odgers, C. L., McCormick, A. V., & Corrado, R. R. (2008). The PCL:YV and recidivism in male and female juveniles: A follow-up into young adulthood. *International Journal of the Law and Behavior, 31,* 287–296.

Weizmann-Henelius, G., Matti Gronroos, L., Putkonen, H., Eronen, M., Lindberg, N., & Hakkanen-Nyholm, H. (2012). Gender-specific risk factors for intimate partner homicide. *Journal of Interpersonal Violence, 27*(8), 1519–1539.

West, H. (2010). Prison inmates at midyear 2009—Statistical tables. [NCJ 230113]. Retrieved May 29, 2014 from www.bjs.gov/content/pub/pdf/pim09st.pdf.

White, N. A., & Piquero, A. R. (2004). A preliminary empirical test of Silverthorn and Frick's delayed-onset pathway in girls using an urban African-American, U.S.-based sample. *Criminal Behavior and Mental Health, 14*(4), 291–309.

Wijkman, M., Bijleveld, C., & Hendriks, J. (2010). Women don't do such things! Characteristics of female sex offenders and offender types. *Sexual Abuse, 22*(2), 135–156.

Wilczynski, A. (1997). *Child homicide.* London, UK: Greenwich Medical Media.

Zahn, M., Agnew, R., Fishbein, D., Miller, S., Winn, D., Dakoff, G., … Chesney-Lind, M. (2010). *Causes and correlates of girls' delinquency.* Washington, DC: US Department of Justice, Girls Study Group, Office of Juvenile Justice and Delinquency Prevention. Retrieved May 2014, from https://www.ncjrs.gov/pdffiles1/ojjdp/226358.pdf.

Zahn, M., Brumbaugh, S., Steffensmeier, D., Feld, B., Morash, M., Chesney-Lind, M, … Kruttschnitt, C. (2008). *Violence in teenage girls: Trends and context.* Washington, DC: US Department of Justice, Girls Study Group, Office of Juvenile Justice and Delinquency Prevention. Retrieved May 29, 2014 from https://www.ncjrs.gov/pdffiles1/ojjdp/218905.pdf

8

Homicide

A National and Global Perspective

BETHANY K. WALTERS AND ERIC W. HICKEY ■

Homicide, most commonly perceived as murder, is considered by most people to be the ultimate crime. Homicide has many religious and cultural connections, and over the centuries, it appears continuously in textbooks, novels, and other media. The illegal killing of one person can sometimes be far reaching in the types of interdisciplinary investigations needed to help solve the crime, restore justice, and provide a semblance of closure for survivors of the victim's family and friends.

Currently, in Western culture, killing has become such a fascination for public audiences that a media industry dedicated to killing now appears in thousands of movies, weekly shows, and documentaries. Popular shows such as the *CSI* franchise, *Bones, Law & Order*, and countless other fictional series remain permanent fixtures in cable television, in addition to nonfictional shows, including ID, the Investigative Discovery Channel. The public perception of killing, especially due to the influence of relatively rare cases of serial murder, often distorts the actual incidence and frequency of murder in the United States.

Since homicides, however, usually produce identifiable victims, the dead are able to yield quantifiable data in comparison to other crimes, such as rape, in which there is a "dark figure in crime" due to low rates of reporting. The purpose of this chapter is to present an overview of the phenomenon of homicide, including definitions, motivations, trends, victim and offender characteristics, and a view of homicide from a global perspective.

DEFINING HOMICIDE

Homicide is the taking of the life of another person or persons. This includes both illegal and legal killing of another person (Hickey, 2013). Homicides in which killing was not the original intension include voluntary and involuntary manslaughter. Manslaughter is the homicide of another person(s) in which the offender lacks criminal intent or did not have premeditated plans to commit murder (Hickey, 2013). *Voluntary manslaughter* involves the killing of another person(s) without an original intent, such as killing during the heat of passion (Hickey, 2013). In most states this is commonly referred to as second-degree murder. *Involuntary manslaughter*, commonly referred to as negligent homicide or third-degree murder, is when an offender kills another person(s) while committing a nonfelony crime, such as when an offender accidently hits and kills a pedestrian with his or her car while speeding, that is, vehicular manslaughter (Hickey, 2013). *Premeditated homicides* can be legal, such as in the case of legal state executions or during times of war (Hickey, 2013), but, more commonly, *premeditated murder* is the preplanned criminal intent to kill another person (Hickey, 2013).

Definitions of homicide can vary based upon region, county, state, and country. However, a general global definition of homicide as defined by The United Nations Office on Drugs and Crime (UNODC) is the "unlawful death purposefully inflicted on a person by another person" (UNODC, 2011). This definition is consistent with the US definition of premeditated murder, commonly referred to as capital murder, or first-degree murder, and is defined as the offender possessing the criminal intent to willfully kill another person(s) (Dunn, 2012; Federal Bureau of Investigation [FBI], 2012; Hickey, 2013). These types of murders may carry a death penalty in the United States or in a few other countries that still utilize the death sentence. In the United States capital murders may also include felony murder, in which a killing occurs during the commission of a felony crime, regardless of premeditation, as the forethought of violence is presumed during the commission of a crime (Hickey, 2013); for example, during an armed bank robbery a perpetrator accidentally discharges his weapon, striking and killing his accomplice. Felony murder can also apply to an accomplice in a crime in which a homicide is committed, although the accomplice was not directly responsible for the homicide; this is commonly referred to as fourth-degree murder. For the purposes of this chapter, the international definition of homicide will be used as the frame of reference.

Descriptive Homicide Definitions

- Neonaticide: the homicide of a newborn within the first 24 hours of life.
- Infanticide: the homicide of a child more than 1 day old but less than 1 year old.
- Siblicide: the homicide of a sibling.
- Fraticide: the homicide of a brother or sister.
- Prolicide: the homicide of one's own children; also known as filicide or the homicide of a minor child.
- Parricide: the homicide of one's parents or relatives. Specifically, patricide is the homicide of one's father, while matricide is the homicide of one's mother.

HOMICIDE AROUND THE GLOBE

Each year hundreds of thousands of people are murdered worldwide. One function of the United Nations Office on Drugs and Crime (UNODC) is to collect and interpret data on homicides globally from criminal justice and public health records. The most recent data from the UNODC reflect homicides committed in 2010. Keeping in mind that the reporting and recording of crimes occur in different ways in different countries, the estimates must be viewed in the context of being a generally reliable estimation. There were approximately 468,000 homicides committed worldwide in 2010 (UNODC, 2011). When isolating the homicide rates by regions, the following were found: 36% of homicides (170,000) were committed in Africa, 31% (144,000) of homicides were committed in North and South America, 27% (128,000) of homicides were committed in Asia, 5% (25,000) homicides were committed in Europe, and 1% (1,200) were committed in Oceania (UNODC, 2011). Interestingly, not only are the numbers of homicides in Africa and North and South America very high numerically, they are also very high when viewed within the context of their total population; in contrast, compared to the size of their population, Asia and Europe had a low number of homicides (UNODC, 2011). In Africa the homicide rate is at 17.4 per 100,000, and in North and South America the homicide rate is at 15.6 per 100,000 (UNODC, 2011). This is more than double the world average of 6.9 homicides per 100,000 people (UNODC, 2011). Oceania, Europe, and Asia fall well below the world average with 3.5, 3.5, and 3.1 per 100,000, respectively (UNODC, 2011). However, as will be seen later in this discussion when homicide specifically for the United States is reviewed, the rates are significantly lower (FBI, 2012; UNODC, 2011). Indeed, out of 200 surveyed countries the United States ranks in the middle (UNODC, 2011).

In general, homicide rates have been decreasing since the mid-1990s worldwide in many countries, including North America, Europe, and Asia (data trends were not available for Africa); however, in Central America and the Caribbean homicide rates have increased substantially (Dunn, 2012; Hickey, 2013; UNODC, 2011). The UNODC stated that the rise in homicides in Central America is likely directly linked to drug trafficking (UNODC, 2011). In general, the majority of the homicides occurred in developing, third-world countries; rates are almost four times higher in regions with greater disparity between the distributions of wealth (UNODC, 2011). Furthermore, in countries where there has been an increase in a centralized rule of law, homicide rates have decreased, whereas in countries with weaker rules of law, homicide rates have increased (UNODC, 2011). As a general rule, homicide rates tend to be higher in cities with a greater population than in more rural areas (UNODC, 2011). Possibly connected with homicide, those countries that show higher robber rates tend to correlate with higher homicide rates as well (UNODC, 2011).

Homicides need not be committed with a weapon, but many are. In fact, globally, 42%, or 199,000, of the total number of homicides were committed by firearms (UNODC, 2011). Specifically, in North and South America homicide victims were 3.5 times more likely to be killed with a firearm than in Europe (74% vs. 21%, respectively) (UNODC, 2011). However, in Europe a sharp object, such as a knife, was more than twice as likely to be used as the weapon in a homicide when compared to North and South America (36% vs. 16%, respectively) (UNODC, 2011). Interestingly, use of any type of weapon accounted for less than 57% of homicides in Europe but for more than 90% of homicides in North and South America (UNODC, 2011). South America, followed by the Caribbean, Central America, and North America, had the highest percentage of homicides involving firearms, and it is likely due to organized crime being a third variable (UNODC, 2011). The

UNODC points out the relationship between firearms, gangs, and homicide rates, stating that in North and South America more than 25% of homicides were related in some manner to criminal gang activity, as compared to only 5% in Asia and Europe (UNODC, 2011). A relationship has also been demonstrated between homicide and firearm availability (UNODC, 2011).

Based upon regions, mechanisms of homicides can differ vastly. In North and South America 74% of homicides were committed with a firearm, 16% with sharp objects, and 10% by other means, such as strangulation or blunt force trauma (UNODC, 2011). In comparison, in Europe only 21% of homicides were committed with a firearm, whereas 43% used other means, and 36% used sharp objects (UNODC, 2011). The UNODC points out that males in America are six times more likely of being killed by a firearm as opposed to another means of lethality (UNODC, 2011).

GLOBAL HOMICIDE VICTIM CHARACTERISTICS

Globally, young males represent the greatest proportion of homicide victims and offenders (UNODC, 2011). Worldwide, males constitute 90% of the violent offenders in prisons and account for 82% of all homicide victims (UNODC, 2011), whereas women are typically victims of intimate partner and/or family violence (Doerner & Steven, 2005; UNODC, 2011). In North and South America, males account for 90% of homicide victims, whereas females account for 10%. The rates are nearly double that in Africa (81% males, 19% females) and Oceania (80% males, 20% females). In Asia (79% males, 21% females) and Europe (73% males, 27% females) females make up more of the percentage of homicide victims, although a smaller percentage of female homicide victims does not necessarily equate to lower homicide rates of females (UNODC, 2011). In North and South America, gang involvement may explain the large discrepancy in the number of male homicide victims in comparison to female homicide victims (UNODC, 2011). Africa currently has the highest rate of female homicide, although again, males account for more homicide victims in their totality (UNODC, 2011). By comparison, South Africa has an overall homicide rate seven times that of the United States (UNODC, 2011).

In regard to the age of homicide victims, the groups most at risk are young males ages 15–29 years, and the risk of becoming a homicide victim declines with age; homicide rates for men ages 15–29 years is 21.2 homicides per 100,000 people and drops to nearly half, with the rate for men ages 60–69 years at 10.5 homicides per 100,000 people (UNODC, 2011). Explanations for this trend tend to be explained by males' decrease in high-risk activities associated with violence as they age (Doerner & Steven, 2005; Ellis, Beaver, & Wright, 2009; UNODC, 2011; Walsh & Beaver, 2009). Females have a low risk for becoming a homicide victim, which remains fairly consistent throughout the lifetime, with rates remaining between 3 and 4 female homicide victims per 100,000 after the age of 15, which indicates that women's homicides are less likely related to high-risk activities and related more instead to intimate partner incidents (Doerner & Steven, 2005; Ellis et al., 2009; UNODC, 2011; Walsh & Beaver, 2009).

Specifically, in North and South America, males ages 20–24 years, followed by males ages 25–29 years and then 30–34 years made up the largest percentage of homicide victims with 16%, 14%, and 11%, respectively, which trends toward a peak in the structure of male homicide victims (UNODC, 2011). Unlike men, female homicide victims in North and South America peak at ages 20–24 years (2% of homicide victims) and then steadily decline with age (UNODC, 2011). Similar statistics are also seen in South Africa (UNODC, 2011). This trend of increased risk of homicide in young males is considerably smaller in Europe, with males ages 20–24 years accounting for only 5% of homicide victims (versus 16% in North and South America), and decreases with age; female homicide victims show a similar pattern (UNODC, 2011).

Intimate partner and family violence affects females at a greater frequency than males and accounts for a significant proportion of violence against female homicide victims (Doerner & Steven, 2005; UNODC, 2011). In Europe half of all female homicide victims were killed by their intimate partners (35%) or family members (17%). This is a much higher percentage than males, who account for only 5% being killed by their intimate partners and 10% by their family. These trends hold for other countries with rates ranging from 40% to 70% of female homicides resulting from intimate partner and/or family violence in other countries such as the United States, South Africa, Australia, and Canada (UNODC, 2011). In Europe, females account for 77.4% of homicide victims who were killed by either their current or a previous intimate partner (UNODC, 2011). In general, the relative (not absolute) rate of intimate partner/family homicides is higher in countries with lower rates of homicides and a low rate of homicides related to gang/organized crime homicides (UNODC, 2011). Thus, it makes sense that females are more likely to become homicide victims inside the home, while males are more likely to become homicide victims in public places (UNODC, 2011). Countries with lower homicide rates, such as Norway, have more homicides take place in the home of either the victim or offender, highlighting the increased of intimate partner/family homicides, in comparison to countries with higher homicide rates, like Columbia, which have a higher percentage of homicides committed in more public areas and related to organized/gang crimes (UNODC, 2011). The rate of intimate partner/family homicides tends to remain relatively stable over time, regardless of overall homicide trends (UNODC, 2011).

GLOBAL HOMICIDE OFFENDER CHARACTERISTICS

Data on offenders of homicide are limited because not all homicide cases are solved, and results should be interpreted with this limitation in mind; a review of clearance (solved) rates in the United States will be discussed shortly. Homicide offender sex characteristics are similar to that of homicide victim sex characteristics, with over 80% of homicide offenders being male (UNODC, 2011). Specifically, males account for over 90% of the homicide offenders in North and South America (data were not available for Africa) (UNODC, 2011). In the United States, 2 out of every 3 homicides have been a male offender killing a male victim, and every one out of four homicides have been a male offender killing a female victim, while female offenders kill a female victim in only 1 in every 40 homicides (UNODC, 2011). Homicide offenders are more likely to know their victim if the killing takes place in the home, while they are more likely to be unknown to their victims if the killing takes place outside the home and in a more public area (UNODC, 2011).

WORLD HOMICIDE REVIEW

In 2010 almost half a million people were victims of homicide. Homicide rates were higher in developing countries and in countries where there was a large gap between the distributions of wealth. Overall, men, particularly young men, were more likely to be both the victims and offenders of homicides, and the homicides were more likely to be committed in a more public place. Women were more likely to be killed in the home by an intimate partner and/or their family. In general homicide rates have been decreasing since their spike in the 1990s, except for Central America and the Caribbean, which is likely due to drug trafficking and organized/gang activities. Homicide rates still remain high in Africa and North and South America relative to the size of their population, while Europe, Asia, and Oceania have relatively fewer homicides in comparison (UNODC, 2011).

HOMICIDE IN THE UNITED STATES

Information for homicide statistics in the United States is gathered by the Unified Crime Report (UCR), which is analyzed and published by the US Department of Justice under the Federal Bureau of Investigation (FBI). The most recent statistics reflect data collected from the 2013 UCR using 2012 data. Data are collected from law enforcement that chooses to participate in providing supplementary homicide data for each homicide a particular law enforcement agency investigates (Doerner & Steven, 2005). Similar to the international definition of homicide, the FBI's UCR defines murder as "the willful (nonnegligent) killing of one human being by another" (FBI, 2012, p. 1).

The FBI estimates that in 2012 nearly 14,827 persons were homicide victims in America, which when compared to 2011, shows an increase of 1.1% but was still a significant decrease of 10.3% from the homicide rates in 2003 (FBI, 2012). This translates to 4.7 homicides per 100,000 people, which is a 0.4% increase in the national homicide rate from 2011, but again, it was still significantly less when compared to the numbers in 2003 (16.9% decrease) (FBI, 2012). Regionally, 43.6% of all homicides were reported in the South, 21.1% in the Midwest, 21% in the West, and the Northeast had the fewest number of homicides with 14.2% (FBI, 2012).

Similarly to global data, the majority of homicide victims were males (77.7%) (FBI, 2012). Based upon available data, the known race of homicide victims was as follows: 51.1% Black, 46.3% White, and 2.6% classified as "other" (FBI, 2012). Homicides in which there was one victim and one offender accounted for 47.1% of the circumstances of homicides (FBI, 2012). Females who were murdered by someone they knew accounted for 42.7% of female homicides (30.2% of females were killed by someone they knew, such as a boyfriend; 12.5% were killed by family members), and of these 35% were murdered by their significant other (FBI, 2012). For cases in which circumstances surrounding the homicides were known, 40.7%

of homicide victims were killed during fights, while homicides during a felony accounted for 22.5% of homicides (FBI, 2012). Marvin Wolfgang's seminal study on *Patterns in Criminal Homicide* in which he identified common characteristics in many victim-precipitated homicides, including an interpersonal relationship, escalation of disagreements, and alcohol use, still remains relevant today based upon many of the statistics (Doerner & Steven, 2005; Wolfgang, 1958). Homicide offenders consisted of mainly males (89.6%); 53.4% of cases were Black, 44.3% were White, and 2.3% were "other" (FBI, 2012). The majority of homicides involved firearms at 69.4%, with the vast majority involving handguns (71.9%) (FBI, 2012).

American homicide statistics fit well within the global findings, but how does the United States compare to other nations? With an average of 4.7 out of every 100,000 people becoming homicide victims each year, the US homicide rate is significantly lower than most nondeveloped nations—countries such as the Congo (30.8 per 100,000), Cote d'Ivoire (56.9 per 100,000), Jamaica (52.1 per 100,000), and El Salvador (66 per 100,000). However, the US homicide rate is much higher than many other developed nations—Germany (0.8 per 100,000), the United Kingdom and Australia (1.2 per 100,000), Italy (1 per 100,000), China (1.1 per 100,000), and Japan (0.5 per 100,000) (FBI, 2012; UNODC, 2011).

TYPOLOGIES

Humans murder for a variety of different reasons, but usually it is not because the person enjoys killing; rather, there are circumstances surrounding the events that culminate in the homicide. Felony murders typically occur as a result of "something going wrong" during the commission of another crime. Arguments in the heat of passion between lovers can lead to an untimely death, as can a fist fight that gets out of hand at a bar. Douglas, Burgess, Burgess, and Ressler classified homicides into four broad categories: *criminal enterprise*, which includes contract and gang-motivated homicides; *personal cause*, which includes domestic and argument-related homicides; *sexual homicides*, which include sadistic homicides; and *group cause homicides*, which include cult and extremist homicides (Douglas, Burgess, Burgess, & Ressler, 2013).

Homicide offenders, barring involvement in organized/gang-related homicides and sexual homicides, rarely commit multiple murders (Hickey, 2013). However, according to the FBI, any person who commits "the unlawful killing of two or more victims by the same offenders in separate events" is considered a serial killer (Morton & Hilts, 2008). If the offender murders four or more people over a short period of time in a single incident, her or she will be classified as a mass murderer (Morton & Hilts, 2008). Unlike the global trend of homicide rates generally declining, mass murders and serial murders are increasing (Hickey 2013). This, as explained by Hickey, is an artificial construct and can be explained primarily as a function of the lowering of the number of murders to qualify as a serial killer (Hickey, 2013). Currently there is an attempted or completed mass murder, which can include domestic mass murders, once every 7–10 days in the United States (Hickey's personal files). Relative to the number of other types of homicides, mass murders and serial murders are relatively rare (Hickey, 2013). In the United States it has been estimated that there are approximately 20 active serial murderers at any given time (Diamond, 2012), with more than 150+ serial killers apprehended between 2000 and 2011 (Hickey, 2013).

SERIAL AND MASS MURDERERS

According to Hickey (2013), male serial killers account for 76% of all serial killers who killed solo and approximately 84% of serial killers when included in team killings; 57% of offenders were Black, 38% White, 3% Hispanic, and 2% Middle Eastern or East Indian. Male serial killers typically target a specific type of victim (91%), most victims being adults (82%) and strangers (93%) to the offender. Serial murderers have an average of 4.4–5.4 victims before they are apprehended and 46% killed female victims only, 22% killed only male victims, and 78% killed at least one female victim; over 21% of the victims work as prostitutes. The average span an offender kills is 7 years, and 43% involved strangling as a method of homicide while 38% involved shooting, 21% involved stabbing, 19% involved blunt force/beatings, and 4% involved other forms of violence (Hickey, 2013).

Akin to global homicide offenders, female serial murderers account for a relatively small percentage (16%–17%) of serial homicide. Female serial murderers typically prefer to use a less overtly violent means of killing, often employing poison to kill their victims, and are more likely to kill their significant others and/or family members, when compared to male serial murderers. Female serial murderers are also more likely to be part of a team that kills (Hickey, 2013).

The majority of serial murderers possess an average level of intelligence and typically kill within a specific area (74% of male serial murderers) (Hickey, 2013). Most of these homicides have a sexual component, which is linked to the sexual fantasies of the offender; the role of violence in their fantasies, which often includes paraphilia(s), are critical in their progression of homicidal behaviors (Hickey, 2013). While the crimes they commit may be viewed as "crazy" by the public, they are very rarely found criminally insane (2%–3%) (Hickey, 2013). Serial murderers are far more likely to have personality disorders and/or psychopathic tendencies (Hickey, 2013).

In contrast, mass murderers are more likely to suffer from severe psychiatric dysfunction, including severe depression, schizophrenia, and in some cases, psychosis, which may be one of the contributing factors as to why so many commit suicide after they finish their attacks (Hickey, 2013). Unlike serial murderers, sexual gratification is not derived from their killings, but rather the killings are intended to relieve the psychological stress of the offender (Hickey, 2013; White-Hamon, 2000).

Serial murder is not just an American phenomenon. Generally, over the past century there has been a decline in serial murders in European countries, but they have increased in non-European countries (Gorby, 2000). There are many cultural differences in serial murders worldwide that can be attributed to some of the many differences in offender profiles. Globally, males comprise 75% of serial murderers and females comprise 25% (Hickey, 2013). This is a far higher percentage of female serial murderers than in the United States, which only has 16%–17% of female serial murderers and 83%–84% male serial murderers, respectively. Primary motives involving violent sexual fantasies are seen less often in other countries (Hickey, 2013). In Germany, monetary incentives were much more common, and in South

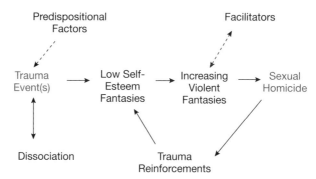

Figure 8.1 Trauma-control model for serial murder (predispositional factors and facilitators may or may not influence the serial killing process). (From Hickey, E. W. [2013]. *Serial murderers and their victims* [6th ed.]. Belmont, CA: Wadsworth. © 2013 South-Western, a part of Cengage Learning, Inc. Reproduced by permission. http://www.cengage.com/permissions)

Africa *muti murders*, in which a murder is committed to collect body parts to be used by a healer in a ceremony to bring the hiring party more financial luck and protection, account for a greater percentage than sexual motivations when compared to American serial murderers (Hickey, 2013; Ulrich, 2000).

To explain the cycle of serial murder committed by male sexual predators, Hickey (2013) developed a trauma-control model (see Fig. 8.1) that displays the process of sexual serial murder. While the model is limited to male sexual predators, this does address many cases of serial murder. The model addresses biological predispositions; early childhood trauma; sexual fantasies; development of paraphilic interests, such as necrophilia, mutilations, and cannibalism; trauma reinforcements; increased violent fantasies; and ultimately serial sexual murder. Larry Hall, a confessed serial killer of 39 women (see Profile 1) is a case best understood using the trauma-control model.

LARRY DEWAYNE HALL, 1980–1994

Larry DeWayne Hall, 50, is currently serving a natural life sentence with no possibility of parole in Butner federal psychiatric prison in North Carolina. Larry has been incarcerated for the past 20 years for the abduction and murder of Jessica Roach, 15, in 1994. Unlike other serial killers, Larry is clearly not comfortable doing interviews. He has very low self-esteem and believes that he is not attractive to women. His fraternal twin brother, Gary, reinforced those feelings of insecurity when they were children. Part Native American, Larry is about 5′5″, stocky, with powerful arms, and has a passion for cars and especially Hemming engines. A man with a high school education, he has only known manual labor. His graying beard, quiet, controlled monotone voice, and nervous half-smile mask the darkness of allegedly one of America's most prolific serial killers of all time. He does not display the typical narcissism so often found in psychopathic serial killers. Larry wants to be liked by everyone, especially the other inmates. More than anything, he fears death for himself. He expresses concern for his aging and ailing mother, who lives in a nursing home, and fears losing her. These are not the characteristics usually seen in serial killers, but then Larry is no stereotypical murderer.

Larry was contacted by investigators regarding the disappearances of several female college students in northern Indiana. Tricia Reitler disappeared from near her dorm at Indiana Wesleyan University in 1993 and has never been found. Anxious to be cooperative, Larry provided a list of 38 names of young women. Except for two names on the list who were prostitutes, all the rest were college students whose whereabouts are unknown. Of course, if Larry is not a serial killer but wanted to implicate himself, he had plenty of time while incarcerated to research these missing persons online. What is compelling to investigators is the fact that Larry was an avid Civil War reenactor, who, with a full Confederate uniform, traveled to many states to participate in these events. He even made it as an extra in the movie *Glory* with Matthew Broderick, about the Civil War. These missing women vanished at approximately the same times Larry was in their area playing soldier. Later Larry added three more names and declared that this one was his "best": Three female college students, all roommates, went out to dinner one evening and upon returning home they went to their separate rooms. They were never seen again, nor was there any sign of struggle.

Larry talks about how he killed women without identifying any specific victims. His preference was to stalk the women while driving his van, abduct them using a knife, and take them out into wooded areas. A few victims voluntarily entered his van, but most required force. The knife was not as effective as he needed because he also had to tie them up once he got them into the van. Eventually he graduated to using starter fluid with ether to render his victims unconscious enough to get them in his van and under his control. Using a belt or rope, he strangled them from behind while they either lay on the ground or stood or sat against a tree. Larry did not like to see his victims die, but he wanted them dead. He then engaged in postmortem mutilation and sex with the corpse. He liked his last victim because she was a prostitute and offered him free sex. He killed her anyway. He claims that most of his victims were buried in wooded areas where the ground is soft or in areas with water. Larry's father was a gravedigger by trade and Larry learned how and where to dig graves with precision. He remembered digging one grave that he never got to use. Larry, a fan of True Detective magazines, was very careful not to leave evidence at the crime scenes.

Larry has always lived in the shadow of his twin brother, Gary. Except for the time he spent with Gary, he was a complete loner and resented women. Some believe that Gary was involved in the killings, but Larry denies any involvement by him. In 2011 CNN aired a 1-hour documentary on the Larry Hall case and interviewed his brother, Gary, for the documentary. Since that time an estrangement has developed between the two brothers. Larry may eventually tell investigators where the bodies are buried, but with each passing year remembering the exact locations becomes more difficult. Of course, Larry fears that if he cooperates he will be convicted of more murders and sentenced to death. He now works as a prison janitor, has no visitors, and spends much of his time researching cars. Larry is still hopeful that he will one day be released.

This is a cold case spanning many years involving one predator (possibly others), who will only go so far to assist investigators. Those assigned to investigate this case are seasoned homicide investigators who have one mission: to bring the bodies home to their families for proper burial.

What do you think? Go online and research this case. If you have any information regarding this case, please contact Detective Sgt. David Ellison of the Indianapolis Police Department: Ph. 317-327-3475.

Source: From Hickey, E. (2013). *Serial murderers and their victims*. Belmont, CA: Wadsworth-Cengage, pp. 424–425.

CRIME SCENE INVESTIGATIONS OF HOMICIDES

The past several years have ushered in tremendous advances in forensic science. Homicide investigators, criminalists (crime lab staff), forensic psychologists, forensic anthropologists, and many others now benefit from the technologies surrounding crime scene investigations as well as the integration of psychosocial and behavioral connections imbedded in and around murder scenes. Crime scenes can reveal a plethora of DNA evidence, hair fibers, mucus, sweat, semen, saliva, hair, fecal material, blood splatters, fingerprints, and other vital information used in resolving a case. Investigators now use *investigative behavioral analysis* to understand motivations for the killing(s), victimology, including victim–offender relationships, and psychological evidence such as the manner in which offenders may pose the bodies of their victims, the staging of crime scenes, and the possible signatures left by sexual predators. Careful scrutiny of a murder scene can often indicate the time of death, body movement, and even the likelihood of future attacks if the offender has yet to be apprehended. Most criminal homicides, because they are domestic, are resolved in relatively short spans of time, while some cases of serial homicide may go unresolved for many years.

CLEARANCE RATES OF HOMICIDES IN THE UNITED STATES

Television shows typically portray all murder investigations as being solved successfully. While the *clearance rates* (meaning an arrest has been made) of homicides are relatively high compared to other types of crimes, the current clearance rates for homicides in the United States is just a little over half, with the UCR reporting that 62.5% of reported homicides were cleared (FBI, 2012). To be cleared, at least one homicide offender must have been arrested, charged with the crime, and turned over to the courts for prosecution (FBI, 2012). Compared to other types of crimes, homicides are more likely to be solved as more resources are utilized in more severe crimes. Increased attention to *cold case files* has brought even more murder cases to resolution. Based upon UCR data, in 2012, 46.8% of all violent crimes were cleared, but only 19% of property crimes were cleared (FBI, 2012). Clearance rates also vary by region; for example, in Los Angeles, California, as many as 60% of all homicides are not prosecuted per year (Hickey, 2013). If a homicide offender is caught and brought to trial, he or she will typically face a sentence of life in prison or, in some states, the death penalty.

THE DEATH PENALTY

Based upon the circumstances of the homicide, offenders can face harsher and more severe sentences or more lenient sentences. Factors that influence sentencing are myriad and are unique to each case. In general, however, aggravating factors that can increase sentence severity can include killing a police officer or torture, while mitigating factors can decrease sentence severity and can include being under duress or not being under the influence of a substance at the time of the offense. In California, for example, to be death eligible, offenders must also be charged with one or more mitigating factors such as being involved in multiple homicides, a drive-by shooting, using armor-piercing bullets, using poisons, lying in wait, or other special circumstances. In the United States, punishment for homicide can include life in prison with or without the possibility of parole, or the penalty of death. Currently there are 32 states with the death penalty as a sentencing option and 18 states with life in prison without the possibility of parole as their most severe penalty; usually the death of the offender is achieved through lethal injection, and the cause of death is listed as a legally sanctioned homicide (DPIC, 2014). Currently Texas executes the majority of those on death row in the United States.

The controversy surrounding the death penalty as being arbitrary, racist, inefficient as a deterrent, and expensive is still hotly debated, although its use continues in the United States and in other countries around the world, such as China, Japan, Egypt, Iran, Syria, and Saudi Arabia, while other countries only have life sentences with parole, such as England and South Africa (DPIC, 2014; Paternoster, Brame, & Bacon, 2008). When comparing the homicide rate to countries that do not have the death penalty, we see that England has far fewer homicides than the United States, although South Africa has slightly more homicides than the United States (UNODC, 2011). The effectiveness of the death penalty cannot be concluded based upon rote comparisons alone, as cultural factors and the implementation of the death penalty factor largely into its effectiveness as a deterrent, and rates of recidivism are not available in all cases.

SUMMARY

Homicide definitions vary, although the concept is universally viewed as the unlawful death that has purposefully been inflicted upon a person by another. Homicide rates have generally declined since the 1990s in most countries of the world except for Central America and the Caribbean, and this is likely due to drug trafficking controlled by gangs/organized crime. Africa and North and South America have more than double the global average homicide rates, while Europe, Asia, and Oceania have nearly half of the global homicide rate average. Young males account for the majority of homicide victims and homicide offenders, and their homicides are likely to occur in more public places. In contrast, female homicide victims are more likely to die by the hands of someone they know in their homes. Depending on region, homicide by firearm may be more or less likely; firearms account for the weapon used in a large proportion of homicides in the United States.

Homicide offenders kill for a variety of reasons, although in the United States victim-precipitated homicides usually include three factors: small disagreements become large arguments, the use of alcohol, and the offender and victim have some sort of interpersonal relationship; that is, they are acquaintances, friends, or family. Unlike general homicides, mass murders and serial murders are slowly increasing in the United States in their frequencies, although these types of crimes are not unique to the United States. Mass murderers commit four or more murders at one time and are at greater risk of suffering from a psychiatric disorder, compared to serial murderers, who kill two or more people on separate occasions. Serial murderers typically have a primary sexual motivation and are not likely to be insane, although most do have personality disorders and higher levels of psychopathy.

Slightly more than half of all homicides in the United States are solved by at least an arrest of the suspected homicide offender, although homicide clearance rates are higher than other crime clearance rates. If a suspect is found guilty of homicide, he or she faces severe legal consequences, which can include life in prison with and without the possibility of parole, and the death penalty, which is currently employed in 32 states in the United States and other countries throughout the world.

FUTURE DIRECTIONS

More research is needed in many areas of homicide. First, efforts to improve the efficiency of gathering and interpreting data will help research to stay as current as humanly possible. Proper record keeping should be encouraged in all countries by various sources, for example, public health records and criminal justice agencies, so that data can be checked and verified against one another. Circumstances surrounding each homicide should be collected and recorded, and if an offender is apprehended, information about the offender and motivations for the homicide should also be collected and recorded in the UNODC database. Research in all areas of homicides, especially global homicide, which takes into account numerous variables, particularly cultural variables, is needed in all areas of homicide research.

REFERENCES

Diamond, D. (2012). Is there a serial killer near you? Retrieved September 2013, from http://www.huffingtonpost.com/diane-dimond/orange-county-serial-killer_b_1222710.html.

Doerner, G. W., & Steven, P. (2005). *Victimology* (4th ed.). Cincinnati, OH: Anderson Publishing

Douglas, J., Burgess, A. W., Burgess, A. G., & Ressler, R. K. (2013). *Crime classification manual: A standard system for investigating and classifying violent crime.* New York, NY: Wiley.

Death Penalty Information Center. (2014). States with and without the death penalty. Retrieved January 2014, from http://www.deathpenaltyinfo.org/states-and-without-death-penalty.

Dunn, G. W. (2012). *Crime in the United States 2012.* Lanham, MD: Bernan Press.

Ellis, L., Beaver, K. M., & Wright, J. (2009). *Handbook of crime correlates.* San Diego, CA: Elsevier.

Federal Bureau of Investigations. (2012). Crime in the United States, 2012. Retrieved December 2013, from http://www.fbi.gov/about-us/cjis/ucr/crime-in-the-u.s/2012/crime-in-the-u.s.-2012/offenses-known-to-law-enforcement/expanded-offense/expandedoffensemain.

Gorby, B. L. (2000). *Serial murder: A cross-national descriptive study.* Fresno: California State University Press.

Hickey, E. W. (2013). *Serial murders and their victims* (6th ed.). Belmont, CA: Wadsworth.

Morton, R. J., & Hilts, M. (2008). *Serial murder: Multi-disciplinary perspectives for investigators.* Washington, DC: US Department of Justice, Federal Bureau of Investigation.

Paternoster, R., Brame, R., & Bacon, S. (2008). *The death penalty: America's experience with capital punishment.* New York, NY: Oxford University Press.

Ulrich, A. (2000). *Morderisches Mirakel* [Murderous miracle]. Berlin, Germany: Der Spiegel.

United Nations Office on Drugs and Crime [UNODC]. (2011). *2011 Global Study on Homicide: Trends, context, data.* New York, NY: Author.

Walsh, A., & Beaver, K. M. (2009). *Biosocial criminology.* New York, NY: Springer.

White-Hamon, L. S. (2000). *Mass murder and attempted mass murder: An examination of the perpetrator with an empirical analysis of typologies.* Fresno: California School of Professional Psychology.

Wolfgang, M. E. (1958). *Patterns in criminal homicide.* Oxford, England: University of Pennsylvania Press.

9

Psychological Factors in Intimate Partner Violence

DONALD DUTTON, CHRISTIE TETREAULT,
CHRISTINA KARAKANTA, AND KATHERINE WHITE ■

For the purposes of this chapter, we focus on physical abuse occurring in heterosexual intimate relationships and review the research on the psychological causes of intimate partner violence (IPV). Formerly called domestic violence (DV), the term *IPV* reflects the fact that intimacy rather than domicile determines the violence. IPV includes the terms wife assault, husband assault, and technically includes physical child abuse, although, in practice, it is rarely used as an alternative to that term. IPV has occurred throughout human history (Davidson, 1977) and across all cultures where attempts have been made to record it (Archer, 2006). Attempts to generate state intervention have included policies as diverse as whipping post legislation (i.e., corporal punishment) for perpetrators (Dutton, 2006) and family visits by social workers (Pleck, 1987). For example, the Puritans thought of abuse against wives, children, and servants as sins. Offenders were publicly ridiculed and required to undergo a religious conversion. Later, other causes of wife abuse were seen as the moral inferiority of men, alcohol use, a male sense of entitlement, or low social class (Dutton, 2006). The 20th century saw a revival in interest in family violence beginning in the 1970s and coinciding with the political momentum for women's rights. This led to the definition of wife assault as a political rather than a psychologically motivated act (e.g., as a way to maintain patriarchy see DeKeseredy, 2011; Dobash & Dobash, 1979) and to emphasize criminal justice approaches to the problem—arrest and incarceration or court-mandated treatment (Dutton, 2006). This view, the gender paradigm (Dutton, 2012; Dutton & Corvo, 2006; Dutton, Corvo, & Hamel, 2009), sees IPV as perpetrated by males only. Until recently, very little had been discussed or researched about husband abuse and female IPV perpetration. Even now there are studies that assume males are the sole perpetrators.

We begin with definitions and incidence studies and then examine psychological features found in perpetrators (e.g., anger, jealousy, substance abuse), personality and personality disorders (PDs) in perpetrators (borderline and antisocial), and characteristics of bilateral IPV. Assessing the incidence or prevalence of IPV has been made largely through surveys—typically victim surveys—but in some cases from self-reports as well (Desmarais, Reeves, Nicholls, Telford, & Fiebert, 2012b). Assessment issues include the definition of abuse—are respondents asked to define it as a crime, or are they asked which specific behaviors have been used by or against them in the context of an intimate conflict. These latter measures use the Conflict Tactics Scale (CTS; Straus, 1979, 1992a). More detail on this scale will be discussed later in the chapter. We note that only methodologically viable, peer-reviewed studies are cited in this review.

Because of the domination of the gender paradigm, rooted in functionalist sociology, psychological profiles of IPV perpetrators have taken a subordinate role as explanatory models (Dutton & Corvo, 2006; Dutton, Hamel, & Aaronson, 2010). The gender paradigm explicitly eschewed psychological explanations in favor of societal norms (patriarchy) and portrayed male–female relationships as explicable sociopolitically. MacKinnon (1989) argued that "sexuality is to feminism what work was to Marxism" (p. 3) and that, hence, only a knowledge of patriarchy sufficed to explain violence towards women. IPV was depicted as a form of such violence; hence, it had a political rather than a psychological explanation. The US Violence Against Women Act was an extension of this view. There are strong empirical arguments against this view; only small minorities of any social or demographic group (including males) commit violence against their intimate partner (Dutton, 2012), and IPV is committed equally by gender (Archer, 2000). That a small group within general demographic categories enacts IPV suggests psychological forces that generate counternormative behavior. IPV is clearly counternormative. In a national survey cited below, Straus, Gelles, and Steinmetz (1980) found that 87% of men, 80% of women, and 85% of couples reported no form of IPV in the year preceding the survey. The majority of couples (86.5% of men, 85% of women, and 84% of couples) reported no potentially injurious IPV. Nor is IPV attitudinally accepted as Simon et al. (2001) found less than 2% of North American men and 1.8% of women agreed with the statement "It's all right to hit your wife/girlfriend to keep her in line." However, 5% of men and 4.4% of women agreed it was acceptable for a woman to hit her husband/boyfriend "to keep him in line." Clearly, more than patriarchal norms and attitudes are at work in the male perpetration of IPV as such violence is statistically perpetrated equally by gender. Although the main focus of research has been on male perpetrators, we report studies on both genders wherever possible.

INCIDENCE OF INTIMATE PARTNER VIOLENCE: THE CONFLICT TACTICS SCALE

The incidence of IPV is typically assessed using the Conflict Tactics Scale (CTS; Straus, 1979; or CTS2; Straus, Hamby, Boney-McCoy, & Sugarman, 1996) that asks respondents which tactics they or their partner use to resolve conflicts. The scale provides rational, verbal-emotional, and physical abuse subscales. The latter is again divided into minor violence (i.e., pushing, shoving, slapping, throwing objects) and severe violence (i.e., kicking, biting, hitting with fist, beating up, using a weapon). The CTS was used in two landmark national surveys by Straus in 1975 (Straus et al., 1980) and 1985 (Straus & Gelles, 1990) and in several cross-national surveys. The CTS is far more sensitive than crime victim surveys (Straus, 1999) because asking respondents how they resolve conflict removes the filter created by requiring them to define physical abuse as criminal. As a result, Straus reported incidence rates as much as 16 times higher in surveys using the CTS compared to those using crime victim definitions. Furthermore, the preponderance of male perpetration disappeared, having been an artifact of the crime victim definition.

Some limitations of the CTS scale are as follows: It does not assess consequences of violence (such as fear or injury), it ignores both the context of (restricted to conflict-related violence) and who initiates the violence, and it does not assess patterns of abuse (chronic abuse or self-defense). Straus (1992a) answered these criticisms, pointing out that the CTS was designed for a one-year period which provided the most accurate recall, and that context and consequences can and should be assessed by other measures. Issues around initiation of IPV and self-defense continue, but some surveys have found that women are more likely to hit first (Bland & Orn, 1986) and to retaliate with violence if hit (Stets & Straus, 1992b). Straus acknowledges that any measure can miss some data but asserts that the data missed through basing the scale on conflict reactions are small. Part of the reason the CTS drew so much criticism is that it revealed equal gender rates of IPV, therefore contradicting the stereotype of the abuser.

Morse (1995) raised the issue of the CTS not assessing repeat violence by examining data from the National Youth Survey (NYS). This survey used a national probability sample (initial $N = 1,725$) of married or cohabiting respondents aged 18–24 and interviewed them every four years until they were 27–33. The author used an eight-item violence measure from the CTS. The NYS found that IPV frequency rates for male perpetrated minor and severe violence (number of separate violent incidents) were 2.6–3.7 and 1.7–2.9 acts (across surveys at different times) respectively. The corresponding rates for females were 4.4–5.3 acts (minor) and 3.6–4.9 acts (severe). Female IPV perpetration was generally repeated more often than male IPV perpetration. Respondents to the NYS indicated that IPV was mutual 47.4% of the time. Of those committing unilateral IPV, about 70% were female and 30% were male. In general, prevalence rates for IPV are higher for younger samples (18–32 years) (Desmarais et al., 2012a) and cohabiting compared to married couples (Stets & Straus, 1992a). A few general characteristics of IPV statistics are worth noting: Severe violence rates are typically about one third of all IPV reported on the CTS (Morse, 1995; Stets & Straus, 1992a), and repeat violence is about two thirds of all reported violence (Feld & Straus, 1990). Also, about half of all reported violence is bilateral (Stets & Straus, 1992a; Whitaker, Haileyesus, Swahn, & Saltzman, 2007). Wife battering describes a relationship where violence is male perpetrated, unilateral, instrumental, repeated, and usually severe (Walker, 2009). To establish rates of stereotypic wife battering, IPV incidence reports have to be subdivided to draw conclusions about severity, unilaterality, or chronicity. Leaving aside instrumentality, which cannot be deduced from incidence data, severe (one third of all), chronic (two thirds of all), and unilateral (half of all) IPV is about 11.0% of all IPV incidence reports (e.g., reported incidence rate $\times \frac{1}{3} \times \frac{2}{3} \times \frac{1}{2}$). Hence, an incidence statistic simply measuring any CTS act against a woman will grossly overestimate wife battering.

Stets and Straus (1989) found that 8.1% of all reports of severe IPV (and 15.6% of all IPV) were for unilateral or preponderant male IPV against nonviolent females. Since only 15% of all married couples in that survey reported any IPV, the wife battering rate in this sample would be .01% (e.g., 15% $\times$ 8.1% or incidence of male/all IPV $\times$ percent of reported IPV); in Whitaker et al. (2007) it was .07%; in Williams and Frieze (2005), .03%; and in Caetano, Vaeth, and Ramisetty-Mikler (2008), .02%. Rates for repeated IPV would be two thirds of these totals. In short, the stereotypic wife battering is relatively rare.

As can be seen from Table 9.1, several large US national surveys found the most common form of IPV to be bilateral, matched for level of severity, followed by female- and then male-perpetrated IPV. Desmarais et al. (2012a) assessed all incidence surveys published from 2001 to 2011. Included in their analysis were 52 large population-based surveys, 36 small community samples, 26 of university students, and 38 of high school students. Summed across all studies, 33.6% of respondents reported victimization in their lifetime, and 19.2% reported it for the year preceding the survey. Past year victimization of IPV was reported by 18% of women and 19.8% of men. Women report much higher rates than men when lifetime measures are taken for perpetration and victimization. Women also report higher past year perpetration rates (28.7% vs. 22.3%) and higher perpetration rates than men report victimization rates. It may be that women have better memories for relationship events than men, or men may be more hesitant to report victimization. Desmarais et al. (2012a) report strong fluctuations in the range of reported prevalence as a function of sample characteristics. For example, a female welfare recipient sample in Illinois reported a 3.5% lifetime victimization prevalence whereas a South African sample reported 99%. Far and away, most studies are conducted in the United States (213 out of 249) with smaller numbers in Canada, Britain, Australia, and New Zealand. Unfortunately, these countries are not representative of the status of women worldwide. Archer (2006) found that women's sociopolitical status (gender empowerment) was inversely related to IPV against women but positively related to IPV by women. As he put it, "both lower levels of women's victimization and higher levels of men's victimization characterize societies with greater female emancipation" (p. 141). Hence, it may not be the case that the relative equality of male and female perpetration rates found in most surveys would be representative worldwide.

PERPETRATOR CHARACTERISTICS

Early Studies

Early studies of psychological characteristics in IPV (male perpetrated) focused on its pathological aspect. An early psychiatric study of note was by Bland and Orn (1986) who presented data from an adult urban random sample ($N = 1,200$). It used the Diagnostic Interview Schedule, which asks 259 questions related to diagnostic criteria from the *DSM-III* and the use of violence. They had a response rate of 80%. The authors reported only three diagnostic categories: antisocial personality disorder (ASPD), major recurrent depression, and alcohol abuse/dependence. For respondents with no diagnosis, the self-reported violence rate was 15.5%. For respondents with any one of the three diagnoses, there was a 54.5% chance of violent behavior (hitting or throwing things at their partner). When alcoholism was combined with either ASPD or depression, or both, the violence rate jumped to

Table 9.1 Past Year Incidence of Intimate Partner Violence in Surveys

		Incidence of IPV Reports[1]	Male more severe[2]	Female more severe[3]	Bilateral
Stets & Straus, 1989	Married	15%	15.6%	36.6%	38.8%
National FV Survey	Cohabiting	35%	12%	34.9%	45.2%
(N = 5,242)					
Whitaker et al. 2007		24%	28.7%	71.3%	49.2%
National Longitudinal Study on Adolescent (18–28) Health (N = 11,370)					
Williams & Frieze, 2005		18.4%	21.6%	28.7%	49%
National Comorbidity Study (N = 3,519)					
Caetano et al., 2008		13%	14.6%	25.6%	59.7%
National Survey of Couples (N = 1,635)					
Morse, 1995		32.4%	16%	30%	47.4%
National Youth Survey 1992 (N = 1,340)					

IPV, intimate partner violence.

[1]The incidence of IPV reports from the total population examined in the survey.

[2]Males engaged in more severe acts of IPV (e.g. male minor, female none; male severe, female none; male severe, female minor). These data indicate percentage of all IPV reports—e.g., of those who reported IPV, 15.6% were Male Only)

[3]Females engaged in more severe acts of IPV (female minor, male none; female severe, male none; female severe, male minor).

80–93%. In terms of initiating the physical aggression, 59% of males and 74% of females said they were the first one to hit or throw things at their partner. The study was largely actuarial (simply counting risk contingencies) and descriptive and did not seek to disentangle IPV from the other diagnoses reported causally.

A thoughtful analysis was presented by Rounsaville (1978) who interviewed 31 female IPV victims about their partners. These women were drawn from emergency rooms and experienced severe and continuous violence. In his sample, 71% of the women had been threatened with death by their partners if they attempted to leave. The partners in his sample had high incidences of alcoholism (45%), prior arrest (58%), imprisonment (35%), and violence outside the relationship (51%). The women described the men as extremely jealous (i.e., prevented them from spending time with female friends). Rounsaville concluded that the key element in abusive relationships was a relational one: The "intense and exclusive dyadic system in which the couple is enmeshed" (p. 20). As he put it, "the most striking phenomenon … was the tenacity of both partners to the relationship in the face of severe abuse sustained by many of the women" (p. 20). He did fall prey to the zeitgeist, however, and assumed all IPV perpetrators were male, based largely on his sample selection. He did not search for male victims in hospital emergency rooms. However, a later study (Mechem, Shofer, Reinhard, Hornig, & Datner, 1999) did just that and found that 13% of all male patients in a Philadelphia emergency room were hospitalized because of injuries sustained from female-perpetrated IPV. Much of the early work on IPV was generalized from women's reports in women's shelters (e.g., Johnson, 1995). These samples are not representative of community samples and differ because of selection factors. Johnson (2008), for example, sees intimate terrorism as male perpetrated. However, broad-based surveys that assessed power motives in perpetrators (Laroche, 2005) or use of other samples (Graham-Kevan & Archer, 2003) indicate that both genders can perpetrate intimate terrorism.

Intimate Partner Violence Perpetrator Traits

A number of factors have been found to be risk markers for IPV in male perpetrators. The reader is reminded that a risk marker simply means that, when it is present, the target behavior's probability is increased; hence, it is similar to correlation, not causation. Meta-analytic studies (e.g., Schumacher et al., 2001; Stith et al., 2004) found the following to be risk markers for wife assault: low socioeconomic status (more risk with a low-income partner), age (more risk with a younger partner), exposure to parental IPV, being a victim of physical child abuse, depression, anger, anxiety, alcohol problems, low self-esteem, personality disorder, stress, and insecure attachment. In addition, Capaldi et al. (2012) reviewed risk factors from a dynamic developmental perspective, examining each partner's developmental history and couples' interaction patterns. This analysis allows features of one member of the couple to be calculated as risk factors for the behavior of the other member and allows risk markers for women to be calculated. We review this latter approach at the end of this chapter. Attitudes condoning violence and traditional sex role ideology had mixed results as risk factors.[1]

Depression in Perpetrators of Intimate Partner Violence

There are numerous studies that investigate depression as an influencing factor in IPV perpetration (and even more in IPV victimization, which is outside the scope of this chapter). Unfortunately, the vast majority of the studies use depression combined with other variables to correlate with IPV perpetration (i.e., weakened internal and social control and alcohol use). Nonetheless, studies generally found moderate effect sizes on the depression–aggression relationship.

Maiuro, Cahn, Vitaliano, Wagner, and Zegree (1988) administered the Beck Depression Inventory (BDI) to four groups of men: Maritally violent; Generally assaultive; Maritally violent and generally assaultive (Mixed); and Non-violent men. Significant differences in BDI scores existed between the four groups, with the highest median score being found among the maritally violent group. Similarly, Julian and McKenry (1993) found that a sample of violent husbands reported more depression than a comparison sample of nonviolent men. In a study of over 10,000 men in the military, Pan, Neidig, and O'Leary (1994) found that men who were physically aggressive toward their partners reported more depressive symptomatology than men who were not.

Cogan and Fennell (2007) conducted two studies ($N = 396$; $N = 298$) with female and male university undergraduates. From Study 1, their results indicated participants who perpetrated violence, both male and female (to partners and nonpartners), scored higher on both sexual depression and general depression. Their second study included female ($n = 138$) and male ($n = 160$) undergraduates who were sexually active in the past year and who completed the CTS2. The participants who were IPV perpetrators scored higher on self-report measures for depressed mood than the nonviolent participants did. In both meta-analyses conducted by Stith et al. (2004) and Schumacher et al. (2001), moderate effect sizes for depression and male-to-female IPV perpetration were discovered. Moreover, for clinical samples, Schumacher et al. (2001) found a stronger effect size ($r = .53$) than in nonclinical samples ($r = .26$) for this link. Capaldi et al. (2012) found depression, as part of a spectrum of internalizing problems, was a stronger risk marker for IPV perpetration by women than by men. Their multivariate analyses indicated that depression might be a risk factor for IPV in women because of its symptoms of irritability and negative affect.

Anger, Hostility, and Intimate Partner Violence

As explainedpreviously, the gender paradigm posited that anger was not a causative feature of IPV in men because IPV was used instrumentally to maintain patriarchy (Dobash & Dobash, 1979; Gondolf, 1988; Johnson, 2008). This belief was used to rally against cognitive-behavioral therapy for court-mandated perpetrators, depicting such treatment as "anger management" (Dutton, 2008). In fact, a consistent finding is that violent husbands experience higher levels of anger and hostility than other men. A landmark set of studies was done by Maiuro and his colleagues (1988) comparing self-report scores on anger and hostility among maritally violent men, generally violent men, and nonviolent men. Each violent group was significantly higher than the nonviolent group on a variety of anger and hostility subscales. In another study, McKenry, Julian, and Gavazzi (1995) recruited aggressive and nonaggressive couples from the community and assessed men's scores on three subscales of a psychiatric symptom checklist: anxiety, hostility, and paranoia. While they found that both hostility and paranoia were positively correlated with the level of husband physical aggression, only hostility was a significant predictor of it. One question that arose in interpreting the data was whether the anger was a cause of the IPV or a consequence of being in a conflicted relationship.

The next few studies controlled for conflicted relationships to tease apart individuals' characteristics from being in a conflicted relationship. Norlander and Eckhardt (2005) conducted a meta-analysis of 33 studies (28 independent samples) of male-to-female IPV to evaluate anger and hostility expression with IPV and quantitatively reviewed how male IPV perpetrators and nonviolent men were distinguishable. In some studies, nonviolent individuals were more likely to articulate statements of annoyance or anger during laboratory anger-arousing activities, suggesting that IPV perpetrators might have problems with emotional labeling. However, male IPV perpetrators—across self-reports, spousal reports, and observations—were higher on anger and hostility compared to nonabusive controls who were also in discordant relationships. They also reported that the more severe the IPV, the higher the anger-hostility levels (comparing low-moderate against moderate-high groups). The authors concluded from their review that it was anger expression that best differentiated abusive from nonabusive men rather than the subjective experience of anger. This was true even when relationship distress was controlled. This finding may seem rather obvious until one considers the common practice of not treating anger in court-mandated groups. Eckhardt, Barbour, and Davison (1998) recruited 88 men who had been married for at least a year and divided these men based on modified self-reported CTS scores. IPV men were categorized as such if they had at least four physically aggressive acts in the past two months (marital discord was controlled). The participants were to articulate their thoughts in response to three scenarios—two of which were designed to arouse anger. Violent men articulated more hostile attribution biases (blaming, perceptions of malevolent intent) and fewer anger-controlling statements. Costa and Babcock (2008) investigated male-to-female violence through an articulated thought anger induction task with 184 couples who were married/cohabitating for six months. Participants were divided into nonviolent or violent based on the partner's reports for the past year. The nonviolent group was further subdivided into distressed or satisfied in their relationship based on their scores on the Dyadic Adjustment Scale. Unexpectedly, overall IPV was not related to the level of power and control, anger, or jealousy articulation. However, the violent group tended to express anger instead of other emotions (i.e., sadness) the nonviolent men expressed. In line with the hypothesis, psychopathology and anger were positively correlated, excluding the interpersonal features of psychopathy (Factor 1 on the PCL). As interpersonal psychopathic features were negatively correlated with anger and jealousy, the authors concluded that men may be IPV perpetrators or violent without showing or experiencing anger. Although this latter group is consistent with gender paradigm profiles, it is statistically rare. The violent group was also the most likely group to engage in both IPV and nonpartner violence.

Murphy, Taft, and Eckhardt (2007) hypothesized IPV men with elevated anger profiles—based on State-Trait Anger Expression Inventory (STAXI) scores—would have elevated levels of physical/emotional IPV perpetration. They cluster analyzed 139 court-mandated male perpetrators and, based on STAXI scores, divided them into three groups: Pathological (problems with all aspects of anger), Low anger control (do not perceive themselves as angry but have difficulty controlling their anger), and Normal anger (no reported problematic anger and composite score fell within the normal range). According to victim reports, Pathological and Low anger control groups had more IPV than the Normal anger group. Also using STAXI scores to measure anger, Taft et al. (2010) reported that those who did not report IPV at baseline and who had a STAXI score greater than one SD above the mean had 71% and 114% higher rates of new incidence of IPV at six- and 12-month follow-ups respectively.

O'Leary et al. (2007) recruited 453 married/cohabitating representative sampled couples who were parenting a -three to seven-year-old biological child of at least one of the parents. They found that anger expression was a direct path to IPV perpetration for males. Interestingly, they did not find significant associations between IPV and experienced anger in either men or women. Counter to the men's results, anger expression in women was not correlated to IPV perpetration. The authors remind the reader that interpretation, in this case of a multivariate model, does not speak to each "variable's importance as a risk factor, rather only to its role in a multivariate model tested with a community sample" (p. 762). In short, results are mixed on the relationship of anger/hostility to IPV.

Schumacher et al. (2001) and Stith et al. (2004) also conducted meta-analytic studies that found anger to be a risk marker for wife assault. Although Schumacher et al. did not compute overall effect sizes for each risk factor, a moderate effect size for anger was established. Stith et al.'s (2004) meta-analysis of 85 peer-reviewed studies also reported similar results for the anger/hostility and IPV perpetration link ($r = .26$). It may seem tautological to relate anger expression to IPV, yet one must consider the political pressure from the gender paradigm against treating anger in court-mandated groups (because the male IPV is viewed as instrumental). About half of all US states with guidelines for court-mandated perpetrators still explicitly outlaw anger management (Norlander & Eckhardt, 2005) because they did not want anger to be an excuse for what they viewed as a conscious choice to abuse.

Intimate Partner Violence and Alcohol/Substance Use/Abuse

Alcohol and substance abuse as factors in IPV have long been established through the literature. However, as the following studies indicate, it is more alcohol/substance abuse per se, not just simply normal consumption, that is more closely linked to IPV perpetration (Kaufman Kantor & Straus, 1992). In a meta-analytic review of 55 studies published between 1980 and 2006 on both male- and female-perpetrated IPV and alcohol use/abuse, Foran and O'Leary (2008) found there was a small to moderate effect size for male perpetrators for the association between alcohol use/abuse and IPV. For female perpetrators of IPV and alcohol use/abuse, they only had a small, yet significant, effect size. Additionally, they reported for men only, both in clinical samples and studies that measured more severe alcohol problems, that abuse/dependence (not just consumption, frequency, or quantity) resulted in a larger association of alcohol and IPV perpetration. Their results are consistent with the Stith et al. (2004) meta-analysis, which found a large effect size for physical IPV perpetration and illicit drug use ($r = .31$) and a moderate effect size for alcohol use ($r = .24$). For men in the Foran and O'Leary (2008) meta-analysis, the overall effect size was .23 (IPV and alcohol) even with a broader inclusion of the type of relationship (divorced, dating). There may be a discrepancy in the results between men and women due to the much smaller number of studies available on women for analysis. Schumacher et al. (2001) reported moderate effect sizes for alcohol abuse ($r = .24$ to .44) while drug dependence showed a strong effect size for clinical samples ($r = .43$ to .65) but a smaller one for community samples ($r = .22$ to .31). Unfortunately, they only investigated male-to-female IPV perpetration.

Fals-Stewart (2003) conducted a longitudinal study to investigate the relationship between alcohol consumption and male-to-female IPV. The author looked at married or cohabiting men who were either entering an IPV treatment program or male IPV perpetrators entering an alcoholism treatment program ($n = 137$ and 135 respectively). On days where alcohol was consumed, the men who were in treatment for IPV were eight times more likely to perpetrate IPV, whereas the men in alcoholism treatment were 11 times more likely. For severe IPV, both groups were 11 times more likely to have consumed alcohol on that day.

Jones and Gondolf (2001) collected data from 308 couples during a one-year longitudinal study (data were collected every three months during that period) with male IPV perpetrators who had completed intake questionnaires at a court-referred batterer intake program in one of four US cities. The male perpetrators' drunkenness (and high frequency of drunkenness) between follow-up intervals indicated a significant risk factor for IPV perpetration recidivism (OR = 3.15–16.3; $p < .005$).

Quigley and Leonard (2000) conducted a three-year longitudinal study with 462 newlywed couples for IPV and alcohol use links. They found a non-heavy-drinking wife and a heavy-drinking husband caused the most husband-wife IPV in the second and third year of marriage. Kessler, Molnar, Feurer, and Appelbaum (2001) assessed data from the National Comorbidity Survey that included married or cohabitating men (n = 1,738) and women (n = 1,799) and investigated premarital/precohabitating history of disorders and their impact on IPV. Male perpetrators of minor IPV were significantly higher on alcohol dependence; while female perpetrators of minor IPV were significantly higher with substance dependence.

In comparing convicted male and female IPV perpetrators (m = 2,254; w = 281) who were sentenced to probation and completed a psychiatric assessment through a local domestic violence center, Henning, Jones, and Holford (2003) noted that male perpetrators were more likely to suffer from substance abuse in adulthood and received previous substance abuse treatment compared to female offenders. Stuart, Moore, Ramsey, and Kahler (2004) divided the 103 women they recruited into either hazardous or nonhazardous drinkers. All of the women in the study had been previously arrested for IPV perpetration and were court-referred to intervention programs for batterers. Those in the hazardous drinking group reported a significantly higher frequency of violence perpetration (physical, sexual, and psychological) against their partners and general violence perpetration compared to the nonhazardous drinking women. Stuart, Moore, Gordon, Ramsey, and Kahler (2006) also found women perpetrators of IPV to have a higher probability of being diagnosed with alcohol or drug dependence (OR = 14.3 and 15.5 respectively). In their review of risk markers for IPV, Capaldi et al. (2012) concluded that, after controlling for other risk factors (age, marital status, parental fighting, and education), current problem drinking was significantly associated with IPV perpetration, although the magnitude of the association was small.

Although there are many studies that demonstrate the association of IPV perpetration and alcohol/substance abuse, there have been mixed and sometimes contradictory results. For example, Cogan and Fennell (2007) found that participants who were generally violent (e.g., towards both nonpartners and partners) had more alcohol misuse and anger than those who were violent towards partners only. The participants who were violent towards partners only did not differ from controls (not abusive to partners or nonpartners). Also, O'Leary et al. (2007) did not find significant associations between IPV and alcohol misuse/abuse or experienced anger in either men or women.

Intimate Partner Violence and Child Abuse
Victimization/Witnessing Abuse

Kalmuss (1984) sampled 2,143 adults (1,183 women) who were either married or cohabiting. The author found rates of IPV increased with childhood maltreatment. For male-to-female aggression, there was a base rate of 1% for males (2% for females) when the person had not experienced aggression in childhood. This rate increased to 3% (4% for women) when they were physically abused by their parents in their teenage years, to 6% (8% for women) when they witnessed physical IPV between their parents, and to 12% (17% for women) when both witnessing and victimization co-occurred. No sex effect was found for witnessing unilateral IPV. Witnessing paternal violence with no maternal retaliation did not increase marital future violence in males disproportionally compared to females.

Widom (1989a) reviewed the literature to examine the claim that violence breeds violence. The majority of the reviewed studies suggested a relationship existed between violence in the family of origin and violence in adult relationships; however, Widom pointed out the fact that these studies had methodological issues. Widom (1989b) addressed many of these methodological issues by utilizing a prospective design study with demographically matched controls for 73.7% of the abuse or neglected children ($n = 667$ and $n = 908$). Widom accessed information about experience of child abuse (frequency/severity) from childhood juvenile court records and adult criminal activity from any law enforcement records. He found that individuals who were abused or neglected in childhood compared to the control group had a greater number of arrests (2.43 vs. 1.41), were younger at first arrest (16.48 vs. 17.29), and were more likely to have five or more offenses (17% vs. 9%). These results support the notion that childhood abuse and neglect may increase the likelihood of adult IPV perpetration; however, not all abused and/or neglected children become violent in adulthood, and not all violent adults were victimized as children.

Dutton and Hart (1992) examined the histories of 604 incarcerated men and found an odds ratio of 2.99 ($p < .001$) between any abuse in childhood and any violence in adulthood. Participants who had experienced physical abuse in childhood were five times more likely (OR = 5.01) to commit physical violence against a family member (either a spouse or other member of the family). Witnessing abuse or abandonment in childhood (considered "other abuse") increased the likelihood of physical abuse and sexual violence against a family member by nearly 3.5 and 4 times respectively. Overall, any type of abuse in childhood (whether the data were examined separately or combined) increased the odds that the person would be either sexually or physically violent against either a stranger or a family member in adulthood. This study used institutional files in order to establish rates of childhood abuse, and it, therefore, may have underestimated child abuse victimization. The authors also found the majority of the incarcerated males (54.6%) that had been violent towards their family as an adult had been victimized as a child within their family of origin.

Ehrensaft et al. (2003) followed 582 youth who had been selected for a larger study examining factors in maternal and childhood health and behavioral factors over a 24-year period. Retrospective self-reports and official records of childhood maltreatment, self-reports of witnessed parent-to-parent IPV, as well as self-reports of adulthood IPV were used in the analysis. The authors found the risk of any violence towards one's partner doubled when the individual had experienced childhood abuse (physical or sexual), and the odds of adult IPV tripled when the individual had witnessed parental IPV as a child. Fang and Corso (2007) examined the childhood and adult experiences of 9,368 individuals (52.2% women) through data collected by the National Longitudinal Study of Adolescent Health, which followed high-school-aged children through adulthood, with three phases of data collection. Participants were asked about their experiences (perpetration and victimization) of violence throughout their life span. They found that childhood maltreatment was linked to both youth violence and IPV perpetration in adulthood. Perpetration, as opposed to victimization of IPV, was more greatly predicted by childhood maltreatment. More specifically, the indirect effects (i.e., youth violence victimization) of this childhood maltreatment were significantly associated with adult IPV. When youth violence was controlled, the authors found that childhood neglect and physical abuse were also direct predictors of adult IPV, but only for females. Childhood sexual abuse was not found to be predictive of adult IPV perpetration for females, but it was the strongest single predictor of male adult IPV perpetration. The study did utilize retrospective reports of childhood maltreatment. Due to this design, it is possible that self-reports of maltreatment may have been underreported.

In a multivariate study reported in more detail below, Godbout, Dutton, Lussier, and Sabourin (2009) examined the relationship of childhood abuse victimization and witnessing abuse to IPV perpetration in a large community sample. Using a structural equation model, they found that early abuse experiences generated attachment issues (abandonment anxiety and intimacy avoidance) in adults which mediated IPV perpetration. The same factor (child abuse victimization) produced IPV perpetration in both males and females; however, the specific form of abuse victimization differed by gender—the main contributor for females was witnessing interparental IPV; while for males, it was parental sexual and psychological abuse victimization.

Post-traumatic Stress Disorder and Intimate Partner Violence

Dutton (1995) examined the relationship between post-traumatic stress disorder (PTSD)-like symptomatology and IPV perpetration in a court-mandated group and demographic controls. The Trauma Symptoms Checklist (TSC-33) and the Million Clinical Multiaxial Inventory (MCMI-II) were used to measure trauma symptoms and any Axis I or II disorders from the *DSM-III-R*. Self-reported anger measures and wife-reported abuse measures assessed the dependent variables of the study. To measure violence or trauma in the participants' family of origin, items on the CTS as well as a Recollections of Parental Treatment (EMBU) retrospective questionnaire were utilized. The men with PTSD-like profiles were more abusive towards their female partners compared to men not exhibiting these symptoms. Early experience factors related to PTSD symptomatology were paternal rejection and paternal physical abuse.

In a study examining the synergistic effects of substance use disorders (SUDs) and PTSD on IPV, Barrett, Mills, and Teeson (2011) recruited 102 participants who self-reported current substance use with a PTSD diagnosis. Participants who had committed a violent crime within the past month had reported more severe PTSD symptoms. The two groups (violent vs. nonviolent) did not differ significantly on the severity of reexperiencing or avoidance symptoms, but those who had committed a violent crime had significantly higher levels of hyperarousal. Individuals who had committed a violent crime also had higher levels of self-reported aggression (Buss & Perry, 1992). The authors suggested that PTSD symptomatology (in particular the hyperarousal symptoms) may act as a mediator between substance use and aggression and may increase the likelihood an individual will commit a violent crime. Unfortunately, this study examined all violent crimes and did not distinguish between the various types. Hughes, Stuart, Gordon, and Moore (2007), on the other hand, found a negative correlation of PTSD symptoms and use of IPV in a court-mandated sample of female perpetrators. They speculated that women with PTSD might withdraw instead of aggress as men do, but more research is needed in this area.

PERSONALITY CONSTELLATIONS, DISORDERS, SUBTYPES OF ABUSERS

Many of the trait risk factors described above may be part of a constellation of chronic, recurring, and problematic perceptions, emotions, and actions that constitute a personality disorder (PD) or pathology. Dutton (1988) argued that repeat offenders had PDs and that three specific forms of PD were most prevalent among wife assaulters: Antisocial, Borderline, and Overcontrolled. Hamberger and Hastings (1991) refined their analysis of court-mandated perpetrators to three groups corresponding to these factors: Schizoid/Borderline, Narcissistic/Antisocial, and Passive/Dependent/Compulsive. Each subgroup scored high on one factor and low on the other two factors. This three-factor solution, or a set of three subtypes of batterers, has been found repeatedly (albeit under different labels) in various studies.

Hamberger, Lohr, Bonge, and Toline (1996) began to report the existence of an expanded non-PD group emerging from their data in 1988. Lohr, Hamberger, and Bonge (1988) cluster-analyzed the eight PD scales on the MCMI-II in a sample of 196 men. This time a cluster was found that showed no elevations on any PD scale (39% of the sample, compared to 12% in the 1986 paper). A second cluster (35%) was termed Negativistic/Avoidant (Overcontrolled), while a third (26%) was labeled Aggressive (Antisocial/Narcissistic/Paranoid). The nondisordered group may be a result of changes in arrest policy or increased unwillingness to report psychopathology.

Hamberger et al.'s (1996) study used a sample of 833 court-referred men but unfortunately relied on self-reports of IPV. Using a two-stage clustering technique, they again obtained three large clusters and three smaller clusters. Cluster 1 was deemed Dependent–Passive Aggressive (Overcontrolled) and composed 18% of the sample. Their average MCMI scale elevations exceeded baseline (>75: clinically present) on the Dependent, Passive Aggressive–Negativistic, and Avoidant subscales. Cluster 2, deemed Instrumental, accounted for 26% of the sample. This group showed elevations of Antisocial or Narcissistic subscales. Cluster 3, deemed no PD, composed 40% of the sample, an increase from the original 12%. The Borderline or

Emotionally Volatile cluster seemed to have disappeared. This could have been due to either of two factors: Increasing self-protectiveness among research participants as criminal justice sanctions increased or increasing arrests of non-PD men who were part of a dyadic violent couple. It is more likely a change in the system of collection than the sample itself resulted in the sudden disappearance of PDs in men in criminal justice samples.

Hart, Dutton, and Newlove (1993) investigated the incidence of PDs in court- and self-referred wife assaulters using the MCMI-II and the Personality Disorder Examination (PDE) structured interview. The PDE results were more modest than the MCMI with a prevalence rate around 50%. The MCMI-II results indicated that 80–90% of the sample (court-referred and self-referred, $N = 85$) met the criteria for some PD. The most frequent PD was what came to be called Negativistic (Passive-Aggressive + Aggressive-Sadistic). Almost 60% of the sample achieved base rate scores equal to 85 or higher, signifying that this particular PD was central and prominent in the psychological makeup of these men. The authors argued that the court-ordered men approximated a random selection of spouse assaulters (compared to self-referred) because the criminal justice system operated somewhat capriciously.

Saunders (1992) cluster analyzed 182 men being assessed for IPV treatment and reported on 13 potential differentiating variables. He too found a trimodal set of patterns described as Family Only (Overcontrolled; 52%), Emotionally Volatile (Impulsive; 17%), and Generally Violent (Instrumental; 26%). The Generally Violent group reported severe abuse victimization as children but low levels of depression and anger. They were violent both within and outside the marriage. The Emotionally Volatile group was the most psychologically abusive and had the highest anger and depression scores. The Family-Only group seemed less violent but harbored deep resentments, had difficulty expressing anger constructively, became anxious and avoidant of conflicts, and had a high level of (sometimes masked) dependency on their partner. This combination could lead to intermittent eruptions of extreme violence.

Murphy, Meyer, and O'Leary (1993) compared batterers, nonviolent men in discordant relationships and well-adjusted men in nonconflicted relationships using the MCMI-II. Each sample contained 24 men. Batterers had significantly higher elevations on Borderline, Nnarcissistic, Aggressive-Sadistic, and Passive-Aggressive PD than nonbatterers. More importantly, desirability scores did not differ among groups although debasement was higher among batterers, possibly reflecting a pervasive remorse about their violence. They found severe physical abuse in the family of origin was related to the presence of psychopathology.

Holtzworth-Munroe and Stuart (1994) reviewed previous studies clustering men involved in IPV, reiterating the tripartite typology of batterers, and again describing instrumental and impulsive batterers. The impulsive batterers (labeled Dysphoric/ Borderline) primarily confined violence to their family, carried out moderate to severe violence, and engaged in sexual and psychological abuse. These batterers were emotionally volatile (as labeled by Saunders, 1992), psychologically distressed, had Borderline and Schizoid PDs, elevated levels of depression, and substance abuse problems. The authors estimated that impulsive batterers made up 25% of the treatment samples. The instrumental cluster (Generally Violent/Antisocial), named after the type of violence they frequently used, engaged in more violence outside the home than the other abusive men, carried out moderate to severe violence, and engaged in psychological and sexual abuse. They may have had ASPD or psychopathy and may have abused alcohol and/or drugs. They also suggested that the instrumental group made up 25% of all batterers in treatment. A third group (Family-Only) appeared to be Overcontrolled and made up 50% of the sample. It is important to note that the authors were not insisting on respondents achieving criteria on a test such as the MCMI to make these determinations.

Holtzworth-Munroe, Meehan, Herron, Rehman, and Stuart (2000) conducted an empirical confirmation of their earlier work, comparing 102 maritally violent men. This time four clusters were observed, the difference being that the Antisocial (Instrumental) cluster was subdivided into two groups, depending on the level of antisocial behavior. The Borderline/Dysphoric group exhibited the highest level of fear of abandonment and had the highest scores on Fearful Attachment and Spouse-Specific Dependency. Their wives reported them to be the most jealous of all groups. They also had significantly higher scores on a self-report of borderline features (the BPO scale) than nonviolent males. Violent men had the highest reports of parental rejection.

Other Aspects: Impulsive versus Instrumental Violence in Intimate Partner Violence

Jacobson et al. (1994) recruited a severely violent sample of couples in which male-perpetrated IPV was occurring. The psychophysiological response of these men was monitored in vivo while they argued with their partners in a laboratory conflict. Two types were obtained. Type 1 batterers demonstrated unexpected heart rate decreases during intimate conflict. They were also more likely to be generally violent and to have scale elevations on the MCMI-II for Antisocial and Aggressive-Sadistic behavior. Type 2 batterers showed psychophysiological increases during intimate conflict. Two types of IPV perpetrator appeared to exist: one with emotion regulation problems and one who appeared cold and psychopathic.

Tweed and Dutton (1998) examined these two groups, which they called Instrumental (Type 1) and Impulsive (Type 2), on a variety of psychological measures. A third group (Overcontrolled) was obtained, but it was too small for analysis. The Instrumentals showed an Antisocial-Narcissistic-Aggressive-Sadistic profile on the MCMI and reported more severe physical violence. The Impulsives also had a high ASPD score (84), but it was accompanied by high scores on Passive-Aggressive, Avoidant, and Borderline PD, higher scores on a measure of Borderline Organization (BPO: a continuum rather than discrete categories), higher chronic anger, and a fearful attachment style on the Relationship Style Questionnaire (RSQ). The Impulsives had difficulties modulating arousal and spiraled out of control in charged, emotionally laden conflicts. The origin of this may be quite "primitive" developmentally. They found the Instrumentals scored higher on Aggressive/Sadistic, Antisocial, and Narcissistic PDs, averaging above the clinically central cutoff score of 85 on the MCMI. While the Instrumentals were self-absorbed and lacking empathy, the Impulsives had problems with self-esteem and assertiveness. In all, the results reinforced the evidence that two main peaks of PD exist for abusive males: Antisocial and Borderline. The former engages in instrumental violence, the latter in impulsive violence. Several researchers have found impulsivity to be a problem for a subgroup of batterers, for instance, Saunders's (1992) emotionally volatile batterers had impulsivity problems.

Edwards, Scott, Yarvis, Paizis, and Panizzon (2003) also found that measures of Borderline and ASPD were significantly correlated with IPV physical aggression in a forensic sample (43 men convicted of IPV and 40 convicted of nonviolent crimes). They hypothesized that a cluster analysis of the scales used would yield two groups of IPV perpetrators, Instrumental and Impulsive, similar to those described by Tweed and Dutton. The Impulsives would have the highest scores for impulsivity, borderline personality, and fearful attachment. This cluster was found and high score correlated with IPV. Also, like Tweed and Dutton, Edwards et al. found high levels of psychopathology and PD in their IPV sample. They concluded that Impulsiveness, Impulsive Aggression, Antisocial, and Borderline PD were significant predictors of IPV.

More recently Capaldi and Kim (2007) have presented a critique of typologies for IPV perpetrators based on studies finding overlap rather than distinct categories and changes in levels of violence over time, inconsistent with a personality explanation. Capaldi and Kim noted that IPV continuity dropped when an IPV perpetrator changes partners, inconsistent with a personality approach. However, while IPV with a new partner changes compared to a same partner group, it still remained at an elevated level compared to no-IPV controls.

Insecure Attachment

Dutton, Saunders, Starzomski, and Bartholomew (1994) assessed adult attachment style (using the RSQ) in a court-mandated group and in controls. Compared to controls, wife assaulters had higher rates on insecure attachment—notably fearful attachment. The authors argued that the fearfulness assaulters experience in intimate relationships manifested as jealousy and anger. Mauricio and Lopez, (2009) and Mauricio, Tein, and Lopez (2007) examined attachment style using the Close Relationships Questionnaire, PD, and abusiveness in a court-mandated sample of 192 men. They used a path model to find that insecure attachment was related to abusiveness through two PDs: Borderline and Antisocial. They argued that the PDs mediated the effects of attachment insecurity on abusiveness. In the more recent study, they performed a latent class analysis to identify subgroups within a court-mandated sample and found associations between subgroup membership and adult attachment orientation. A high-level violence group (most frequent, most severe) comprised the top 40% in a court-ordered group. Membership in this dubious group was predicted by anxious/avoidant attachment and by borderline personality. In the Godbout et al. (2009) multivariate study on a large community sample of couples, insecure attachment mediated the effects of exposure to child abuse on adult IPV perpetration. Within couples, female attachment anxiety was a predictor of both the male's and female's use of IPV.

COMMUNITY AND LONGITUDINAL STUDIES

Longitudinal cohort studies are methodologically the soundest design for study-ing a variety of problem behaviors. The samples are large and representative of an age cohort, not self-selected through their presence in a college, shelter, or a court-mandated group. Hence, the external validity is higher. Also, since the cohort is followed over time, cause-and-effect relationships can be deduced. Unlike snap-shot studies that freeze behavior to a one-time sample and rely on correlations at that time, the protracted longitudinal study can examine effects from a measure taken years before. We will examine the two major peer-cohort longitudinal stud-ies that have been conducted for IPV.

The Concordia Longitudinal Risk Project

The Concordia Longitudinal Risk Project in Montreal used data collected in a longitudinal study of 4,109 French-speaking school children in 1976 (Serbin et al., 2004). The children were categorized into Aggressive and Withdrawn cat-egories using a French version of a systematized peer-rating scale called the Pupil Evaluation Inventory. Extremes in aggression and withdrawal were developed by taking children who scored above the 95th percentile on aggression and below the 75th percentile on withdrawn, yielding in 101 girls and 97 boys (reverse criteria yielded a withdrawn group of 129 girls and 108 boys). Age-matched comparisons were developed by taking children who were average (between the 25th and 75th percentiles) on both aggression and withdrawal. Aggressive children of both sexes had lower IQs and academic achievement and were more physically aggressive dur-ing play than comparison controls.

Girls' aggression was associated with a preference for similarly aggressive male partners. As they approached adolescence, these Aggressive girls had elevated rates of smoking, alcohol, and illicit drug use and still sought out relationships with boys and girls with predelinquent behavioral styles. They had elevated rates of gyneco-logical problems, were more likely to go on birth control sooner, had higher rates of sexually transmitted diseases, and became pregnant sooner. These Aggressive females also had elevated levels of depression and anxiety disorder by late teens. When they married and had children, they became Aggressive mothers (i.e., chil-dren had more visits to hospital emergency rooms for treatment of injuries) and their children had more health risks.

The Dunedin Study

Magdol et al. (1997) followed a birth cohort of 1,037 subjects in Dunedin, New Zealand. The group was studied every two years since its inception for a variety of health, developmental, and behavioral measures. The study on IPV took place when the group was 21, and it was embedded among other questions about mental health issues. Of the original 1,037 individuals, 861 (w = 425) responded and quali-fied because they were in an intimate relationship of at least one month during the previous 12 months. IPV was assessed using the CTS; each respondent reporting for both self and partner. Measures were also reported on the following: socioeconomic status, social ties, substance abuse, criminality, and mental health symptoms (anxiety, depression, mania, and psychosis). They found that both minor and severe physical violence perpetration were higher for women whether self-reported or partner reported. The female severe physical violence perpetration was more than triple that of males (18.6% vs. 5.7%). Based on this same sample, Magdol et al. reported that preexisting characteristics of the women (at age 15) predicted their later choice of an abusive male partner and their own use of violence with that partner apart from the male's violence.

A comprehensive analysis of the Dunedin data was done by Moffitt, Caspi, Rutter, and Silva (2001). Based on the data from the other measures, these authors reported that the following characteristics predicted IPV perpetration in females: Approval of the use of aggression, excessive jealousy and suspiciousness, a tendency to experience intense and rapid emotions, and poor self-control. As we shall see, these are the same characteristics found in male batterers. Moffitt et al. found that antisocial traits measured in females at age 15 made them more likely to be involved in a relationship with an abusive man at 21, and even after controlling for their partners' physical abuse, women were more likely to be IPV perpetrators if they had a history of conduct problems.

The Concordia study and the Dunedin study present clear examinations of the development and independent expression in women of aggression to others—their aggression was not just a reaction to male aggression but developed independently of their male intimate partner's behaviors. The two studies showed the developmental trajectory and the trait character of this aggression. Both studies indicated that these women would select aggressive men and contribute to ongoing intra-couple IPV.

Negative Emotionality

A strong predictor of abusiveness in the Dunedin study was negative emotionality (NEM), which was measured with 49 items from Tellegen's Multidimensional Personality Questionnaire (MPQ) and comprised of strong negative emotions such as anxiety and anger, basic interpersonal mistrust, and an inability to regulate strong emotions. NEM correlated with both antisocial behavior and abusiveness in both males (+.45) and females (+.46). NEM in women measured at age 15 predicted their use of IPV at age 21, controlling for their partner's use of IPV. The abusive personality for males (Dutton, 2007) had a similar profile to NEM in Moffitt et al. (2001): jealousy, impulsivity, rapidly fluctuating emotions, and poor self-control. With the men, these were related to independently assessed borderline traits. These psychological aspects, in fact, are central to definitions of borderline personality, which unfortunately was not formally assessed in the Dunedin women. From the descriptors given by Moffitt et al.; however, it seems that an identical abusive personality existed for male and female IPV perpetrators.

In sum, Moffitt et al.'s study found that antisocial behavior measured in females at age 15 predicted their later use of intimate aggression against male partners at age 21. A woman's conduct problems correlated with her later use of violence against her partner (even with his violence partialled out). It also correlated with his use of violence toward her. Essentially, the pattern of correlations between early conduct problems and later IPV and partners' use of violence was similar for both sexes—the correlations were not significantly different. Moffitt et al. emphasize the importance of puberty as a developmental crossroads for these girls. The authors also made a provocative argument, based on their impressive data set, that males later form two types of antisocial behavior, one against strangers (which may be neurologically based) and another against intimate females; whereas females form only one type of antisocial behavior, against intimate males. The sophisticated path analysis (a statistical method of differentiating independent, moderator, and dependent variables) used on this huge and representative sample gives added weight to their findings. However, the reader is reminded that other studies (i.e., Serbin et al., 2004) found a broader array of antisocial actions by women, including physical abuse of children. Antisocial personality is assessed by both behavioral (crimes) and psychological (lack of empathy and remorse, tendency to lie) criteria.

Ehrensaft et al. (2003) also studied the Dunedin birth cohort, finding that 9% were in clinically abusive relationships—those that required intervention by any professional (e.g., hospital, police, lawyers). More such help exists for women than for men, and they are more likely to use it, so their results may be skewed. However, the authors found comparable rates of violence: 68% of women and 60% of men self-reporting injury. Both male and female perpetrators evidenced signs of personality disturbance. The authors noted, for instance, that the women had "aggressive personalities and/or adolescent conduct disorder" (p. 267). As the authors put it, "these findings counter the assumption that if clinical abuse was ascertained in epidemiological samples, it would be primarily man-to-woman, explained by patriarchy rather than psychopathology" (p. 258).

Ehrensaft, Cohen, and Johnson (2006) followed a randomly selected cohort sample of 543 children over 20 years to test the effects of parenting, exposure to domestic violence between parents (ETDV), maltreatment, adolescent disruptive conduct disorders, and substance abuse disorders on the risk of violence to and from an adult intimate partner. Conduct disorder (CD) was the strongest predictor of perpetration for both sexes, followed by ETDV. In some individuals, CD failed to disappear but developed into a variety of adult PDs. The authors called these personality disorder trajectories. A failure of PDs to diminish from adolescence to adulthood predicted IPV in both sexes. Women with a pattern of distrust, interpersonal avoidance, unusual beliefs, and constricted affect were more likely to assault intimate male partners. This pattern was similar for males.

The US National Youth Survey

The US National Youth Survey (Elliott, Huizinga, & Morse, 1986) used a national probability sample of 1,725 respondents, beginning in 1976, and provided nine waves of data over 17 years. Respondents were interviewed annually using structured, face-to-face, confidential interviews. Violence was measured using the eight-item subscale from the CTS; injury was also assessed. For the years 1983, 1986, 1989, and 1992, female-to-male and severe violence was about double the rate of male-to-female and severe violence.

BORDERLINE PERSONALITY ORGANIZATION AND ASSAULTIVENESS: THE EMPIRICAL STUDIES

In a series of studies, Dutton and his colleagues (1994a, 1994b, 1995, 2007; Dutton, Saunders, Starzomski, & Bartholomew, 1994; Dutton & Starzomski, 1993; Dutton, Starzomski, & Ryan, 1994; Hart et al., 1993) examined personality profiles of assaultive males. The overall strategy of this work was to correlate scores on self-report scales filled out by abusive men in court-mandated treatment groups (as part of an assessment procedure for treatment) with their wives' reports of emotional and physical abuse victimization. Both self- and court-referred men were compared to demographically matched controls. The assessments were completed after three weeks in treatment and after a therapeutic bond was established. It was hoped this would improve validity of the self-reports. Extensive analyses of the men's reporting tendencies were made through the use of several measures of socially desirable responses (see Dutton & Hemphill, 1992; Dutton et al., 1994 for an extensive report on the relationship of social desirability to all self-report scales). Self-reports of the man's anger, jealousy, experience of trauma symptoms, and abusiveness, and his scores on a self-report measure of borderline traits (a BPO Scale) were correlated with reports of the man's abusiveness (both physical and psychological) made by his female partner. Dutton (1994a) found BPO scores to be similar to those for an independent sample of diagnosed borderlines and higher than nonabusive controls. Furthermore, BPO scores were significantly related to chronic anger, jealousy, use of violence, and experience of adult trauma symptoms in the wife assault group. High BPO scorers reported significantly more anger of greater frequency, magnitude, and duration. They also reported greater jealousy and more trauma symptoms, dissociation, anxiety, sleep disturbance, depression, and postsexual abuse trauma. Finally, they reported significantly more abuse (both verbal-symbolic and physical), as measured on the CTS, towards their wives. Analysis of response styles indicated that these associations were not mere disclosure or social desirability effects. The results were corroborated by focusing on wives' reports of abusive treatment by their husbands through the assessment of both physical abuse using the CTS and emotional abuse using a scale that measured two factors called Dominance/Isolation and Emotional Abuse (Dutton & Starzomski, 1993). Strong associations of men's BPO scores with women's reports of male abusiveness were found. A multiple regression indicated that BPO scale scores combined with scores from a self-report for anger accounted for 50% of women's reports of Dominance/Isolation and 35% of Emotional Abuse scores.

Dutton (2007) argued that a personality constellation called the Abusive Personality was indicated by these results. This personality had a borderline center and an insecure attachment style, experienced extreme anger and jealousy in intimate relationships, and was prone to emotional dysregulation and abusiveness. This personality had its origins in early insecure attachment, exposure to IPV in the family of origin, parental shaming, and paternal rejection (Dutton, 1994b; Dutton & Holtzworth-Munroe, 1997; Dutton et al., 1994). The personality constellation was associated with posttreatment recidivism (Dutton, Bodnarchuk, Kropp, Hart, & Ogloff, 1995), leading to an expanded treatment protocol to target its features in a cognitive-behavioral group setting (Dutton, 2003, 2008).

A study of court-ordered female IPV perpetrators (Henning et al., 2003) found that borderline personality was even more prevalent in this group than with male perpetrators although issues with the impact of gender on the diagnosis persist. Clift and Dutton (2011) performed a structural equation analysis on a large ($N = 962$) group of college undergraduate women and found that the abusive personality patterns held for women and predicted self-reports on IPV in dating relationships. Hughes et al. (2007) assessed borderline features in a sample of 103 women arrested for IPV and found that these features mediated the effects of physical abuse victimization in the family of origin on the use of IPV in current adult relationships. The authors described their findings as mirroring Dutton's finding with abusive men. Hines (2008) investigated borderline personality as a predictor of IPV (physical, sexual, and psychological) in 67 universities ($N = 14,154$) around the world, finding that there was a significant relationship between the two that was not moderated by gender.

COUPLES' INTERACTION

Virtually all of the aforementioned studies assessed traits or PDs in individuals, suggesting that these are causative for IPV. However, much of this assumption has been based on the notion of unilateral IPV. In fact, as we saw in the incidence studies above, the most common form of IPV is bilateral. Apart from the survey evidence, studies that showed IPV levels drop with a change in partner (Shortt et al., 2012) also suggest a dyadic aspect to IPV (although the drop is not so great as to rule out trait explanations). Also, work by Serbin (2004), Capaldi, Kim, and Shortt (2004), and Capaldi, Shortt, and Kim (2005) pointed toward assortative mating; that individuals with prior histories of problem behavior, including substance abuse and IPV, combined at a greater than chance level. This may be, as Serbin's work suggests, that these individuals self-selected into marginal subgroups.

Bilaterality suggests a dyadic interaction problem may precede IPV, and several studies have examined this issue (Capaldi et al., 2009; Cordova, Jacobson, Gottman, Rushe, & Cox, 1993; Jacobson et al., 1994; Margolin, John, & Gleberman, 1989; Schumacher & Leonard, 2005). Laboratory studies of couples' interaction typically compare self-identified physically abusive couples with controls. Computerized sequence analysis of in vivo interaction (where a recording is made of identified couples "discussing" an issue in the laboratory) is used to determine the interaction patterns in IPV couples versus conflicted but nonviolent couples. Categories of analysis have included negative voice, gestures, command, etc. Negative reciprocity characterized the IPV couples' sequenced interactions; each member of the couple responding to a negative tone in the other with a more negative tone—a type of coercion trap. Wives in physically abusive couples exhibited greater escalation of negative behaviors during these conflicted discussions (Margolin et al., 1989). Alcohol exacerbated this pattern of negative reciprocity (Leonard & Senchak, 1993; Schumacher & Leonard, 2005). Although this research was focused on male perpetrators, researchers expressed surprise at the levels of aggression shown by female partners (e.g., Cordova et al., 1993). As these authors put it, "the behavior of domestically violent wives does not suggest passivity, docility or surrender. ... rather the women are continuing in conflict engagement" (p. 563). These authors also noted that 50% of the women in their IPV sample (selected because of the males' prior IPV) had used severe violence according to the CTS.

MULTIVARIATE MODELS

O'Leary et al. (2007) examined a number of potentially predictive factors for IPV in a sample of 453 couples, selected through random-digit dialing, and hence, representative of the country's population. Twenty-four demographic and psychological predictors were assessed separately for men and women. No attempts were made to examine male features as predictive of female IPV or vice versa. The authors developed separate models of men and women's aggression without assessing partner aggression as a covariate or separate predictor.

Godbout et al. (2009) examined the relationship of childhood abuse victimization, witnessing abuse, and adult attachment style to IPV perpetration in a community sample of 315 men and 329 women. Using a structural equation model, they found that early abuse experiences generated attachment issues (abandonment anxiety and intimacy avoidance) in adults, which mediated couple IPV perpetration. Factors measured in one member of a couple were predictive of the other member's behavior. For example, female attachment anxiety was a risk factor of both female- and male-perpetrated IPV. Male attachment anxiety was a predictor of female-perpetrated (but not male) IPV. The expression of male IPV did not predict female ratings of marital adjustment. The strongest coefficients to marital adjustment for both sexes were their own score on avoidant attachment (negative related to adjustment).

Capaldi et al. (2012) developed a risk factor analysis for IPV from a couples' interaction perspective called a "dynamic developmental systems" perspective. This approach, rather than just focusing on the presence or absence of IPV, examined risk factors for its emergence, course, and directionality. They examined risk factors for male, female, and couple IPV and through examining studies that had measures of both partners. Therefore, they could say which risk factors in an individual predicted their partners' use of aggression. In general, they found that the same risk factors operated for IPV by men and women. One exception was that internalizing problems, such as depression, was more of a risk factor for women than for men. Shortt et al. (in press) examined the stability of young men's IPV over a 12-year period in the longitudinal (annual assessment from ages 9–32 with couples' data collected between 20 and 32 years of age) Oregon Youth Survey. Men's IPV in their early 20s predicted levels of IPV seven years later. Higher stability was found for men who stayed with the same partner. Levels of IPV decreased from the early 20s to the early 30s. Findings for women were similar, but the sample size was small. The predictability finding is consistent with trait/personality explanations for IPV; the change with partners is consistent with dyadic explanations.

CONCLUSION

In this chapter, we have reviewed psychological features predictive of IPV—anger, depression, alcohol use, PTSD, and exposure to child abuse. The latter seems to impact on the use of IPV in adult relationships through insecure attachment or a PD. We reviewed the growing literature on borderline personality as a risk factor for IPV. These features predict individual use of IPV and may be more predictive in unilateral patterns. However, their precise role in bilateral patterns has yet to be determined. As we showed in Table 9.1, bilateral IPV is the most common form of IPV and its explanation draws on assortative mating couples with commonalities of dysfunction and problems with coercion traps. The less common unilateral IPV, especially when severe, appears to have its origins in child abuse that has crystallized into a PD (Ehrensaft et al., 2006; Godbout et al., 2009). Even when couple violence occurs, individual backgrounds involving parental abuse are apparent (Godbout et al., 2009). IPV is most likely to occur when both members of a couple bring vulnerabilities for IPV to the relationship; the relationship becomes distressed and conflicted, and the partners then reciprocate hostile behavior (Bartholomew, Cobb, & Dutton, in press). The emergence of a coercion trap appears to be the most central problem, and these coercion traps escalate to the use of IPV. Typically these bilateral issues lead to criminal justice intervention, designation of a "primary perpetrator," and a retreat to an individual focus brought about by criminal justice division into perpetrators and victims (see Bartholomew et al., 2012; Capaldi et al., 2009). Many of the psychological risk factors for IPV are symptoms of personality disturbance (anger, anxiety, depression, attachment anxiety) and contribute to unilateral IPV. Little is known about contributors to bilateral IPV or to immersion into coercion traps. This may be the next step in IPV risk analysis.

NOTE

1. Under traditional sex role ideology, Stith et al. (2004) included a study by Dutton (1995) that used the Psychological Maltreatment of Women Inventory, a measure of abuse not ideology. Another two of the four studies they cited for attitudinal acceptance also had dubious measure of attitude (one took a report of females on their husband's attitudes, which were not sexist) (Smith, 1990); the other simply asked abusive and nonabusive men to estimate the likelihood of their being violent in the future and took elevated (and probably accurate) estimates of violent men as measures of "acceptance" (Hanson et al., 1997). Stith et al. (2004) required four independent studies to show an effect before a factor could be considered a risk factor for IPV; hence, by this criterion, attitudinal acceptance was not proven. Also, in a multivariate analysis of partner aggression, O'Leary, Slep, and O'Leary (2007) found that attitudinal acceptance in a community sample did not "account for unique variance in partner aggression" (p. 762).

REFERENCES

Archer, J. (2000). Sex differences in physical aggression to partners: A reply to Frieze (2000), O'Leary (2000), and White, Smith, Koss, and Figueredo (2000). *Psychological Bulletin, 126*(5), 697–702.

Archer, J. (2006). Cross-cultural differences in physical aggression between partners: A social role analysis. *Personality and Social Psychology Review, 10*(2), 133–153.

Barbour, K., & Davison, G. (1998). Articulated thoughts of maritally violent and non-violent men during anger arousal. *Journal of Clinical Psychology, 66*, 259–269.

Bartholomew, K., Cobb, R. J., & Dutton, D. G. (in press). Established and emerging perspectives in the study of violence in intimate relationships. In J. Dovidio & J. A. Simpson (Eds.), *APA Handbook of Personality and Social Psychology, Vol. 3. Interpersonal relationships*. Washington, DC: APA Press.

Barrett, E. L., Mills K. L., & Teeson, M. (2011). Hurt people who hurt people: Violence amongst individuals with comorbid substance use disorder and post-traumatic stress disorder. *Addictive Behaviors, 36*, 721–728.

Bland, R., & Orn, H. (1986). Family violence and psychiatric disorder. *Canadian Journal of Psychiatry, 31*, 129–137.

Buss, A. H., & Perry, M. (1992). The aggression questionnaire. *Journal of Personality and Social Psychology, 63*(3), 452–459.

Caetano, R., Vaeth, P. A. C., & Ramisetty-Milker, S. (2008). Intimate partner violence victim and perpetrator characteristics among couples in the United States. *Journal of Family Violence, 23*, 507–518.

Capaldi, D. M., & Kim, H. K. (2007). Typological approaches to violence in couples: A critique and alternative conceptual approach. *Clinical Psychology Review, 27*(3), 253–265.

Capaldi, D. M., Kim, H. K., & Shortt, J. W. (2004). Women's involvement in aggression in young adult romantic relationships. In M. Putallaz & K. L. Bierman (Eds.), *Aggression, antisocial behavior, and violence among girls* (pp. 223–241). New York, NY: Guilford Press.

Capaldi, D. M., Knoble, N. B., Shortt, J. W., & Kim, H. K. (2012). A systematic review of risk factors for intimate partner violence. *Partner Abuse, 3*(2), 231–280.

Capaldi, D. M., Shortt, J. W., & Kim, H. K. (2005). A life span developmental systems perspective on aggression toward a partner. In W. Pinsof & J. L. Lebow (Eds.), *Family psychology: The art of the science* (pp. 141–168). New York, NY: Oxford University Press.

Capaldi, D. M., Shortt, J. W., Kim, H. K., Wilson, J., Crosby, L., & Tucci, S. (2009). Official incidents of domestic violence: Types, injury and associations with nonofficial couple aggression. *Violence and Victims, 24*(4), 502–519.

Clift, R. J. W., & Dutton, D. G. (2011). The abusive personality in women in dating relationships. *Partner Abuse, 2*(2), 166–188.

Cogan, R., & Fennell, T. (2007). Sexuality and the commission of physical violence to partners and non-partners by men and women. *Journal of Consulting and Clinical Psychology, 75*(6), 960–967.

Cordova, J. V., Jacobson, N. S., Gottman, J. M., Rushe, R., & Cox, G. (1993). Negative reciprocity and communication in couples with a violent husband. *Journal of Abnormal Psychology, 102*(4), 559–564.

Costa, D. M., & Babcock, J. C. (2008). Articulated thoughts of intimate partner abusive men during anger arousal: Correlates with personality disorder features. *Journal of Family Violence, 23*, 395–402.

Davidson, T. (1977). Wife beating: A recurring phenomenon throughout history. In M. Roy (Ed.), *Battered women: A psychosociological study of domestic violence* (pp. 1–23). New York, NY: Van Nostrand.

DeKeseredy, W. S. (2011). Feminist contributions to understanding woman abuse: Myths, controversies and realities. *Aggression and Violent Behavior, 16*(4), 297–302.

Desmarais, S. L., Reeves, K. A., Nicholls, T. L., Telford, R. P., & Fiebert, M. S. (2012a). Prevalence of physical violence in intimate relationships, part 1: Rates of male and female victimization. *Partner Abuse, 3*(2), 140–169.

Desmarais, S. L., Reeves, K. A., Nicholls, T. L., Telford, R. P., & Fiebert, M. S. (2012b). Prevalence of physical violence in intimate relationships, part 2: Rates of male and female perpetration *Partner Abuse, 3*(2), 170–198.

Dobash, R. E., & Dobash, R. P. (1979). *Violence against wives: A case against the patriarchy.* New York, NY: Free Press.

Dutton, D. G. (1988). Profiling wife assaulters: Some evidence for a trimodal analysis. *Violence and Victims, 3*(1), 5–30.

Dutton, D. G. (1994a). Behavioral and affective correlates of borderline personality organization in wife assaulters. *International Journal of Law and Psychiatry, 17*(3), 265–277.

Dutton, D. G. (1994b). The origin and structure of the abusive personality. *Journal of Personality Disorder, 8*(3), 181–191.

Dutton, D. G. (1995). Trauma symptoms and PTSD-like profiles in perpetrators of intimate abuse. *Journal of Traumatic Stress, 8*(2), 299–316.

Dutton, D. G. (2003). Treatment of Assaultiveness. In D. G. Dutton & D. L. Sonkin (Eds.), *Intimate violence: Contemporary treatment approaches* (pp. 7–28.). New York, NY: Haworth Press.

Dutton, D. G. (2006). *Rethinking domestic violence.* Vancouver, BC: UBC Press.

Dutton, D. G. (2007). *The abusive personality* (2nd ed.). New York, NY: Guilford Press.

Dutton, D. G. (2008). Blended behavioral therapy for intimate partner violence. In A. C. Baldry & F. W. Winkel (Ed.), *Intimate partner violence prevention and intervention: The risk assessment and management approach* (pp. 133–146). New York, NY: Nova Press.

Dutton, D. G. (2012). The case against the role of gender in intimate partner violence. *Aggression and Violent Behavior, 17*(1), 99–104.

Dutton, D. G., Bodnarchuk, M., Kropp, R., Hart, S., & Ogloff, J. (1995). *A ten year follow-up of treated and untreated wife assaulters.* Unpublished manuscript, Vancouver, British Columbia.

Dutton, D. G., & Corvo, K. (2006). Transforming a flawed policy: A call to revive psychology and science in domestic violence research and practice. *Aggression and Violent Behavior, 11*(5), 457–483.

Dutton, D. G., Corvo, K. N., & Hamel, J. (2009). The gender paradigm in domestic violence research and practice part II: The information website of the American Bar Association. *Aggression and Violent Behavior, 14*, 30–38.

Dutton, D. G., Hamel, J., & Aaronson, J. (2010). The gender paradigm in family court processes: Re-balancing the scales of justice from biased social science. *Journal of Child Custody, 7*(1), 1–31.

Dutton, D. G., & Hart, S. D. (1992). Evidence for long-term specific effects of childhood abuse and neglect on criminal behavior in men. *International Journal of Offender Therapy and Comparative Criminology, 36*(2), 129–137.

Dutton, D. G., & Hemphill, K. J. (1992). Patterns of socially desirable responding among perpetrators and victims of wife assault. *Violence and Victims, 7*(1), 29–39.

Dutton, D. G., & Holtzworth-Munroe, A. (1997). The role of early trauma in males who assault their wives. In D. Cicchetti & R. Toth (Eds.), *The Rochester Symposium on Development* (pp. 379–402). University of Rochester Press. Rochester, NY.

Dutton, D. G. Saunders, K., Starzomski, A., & Bartholomew, K. (1994). Intimacy-anger and insecure attachment as precursors of abuse in intimate relationships. *Journal of Applied Social Psychology, 24*(15), 1367–1386.

Dutton, D. G., & Starzomski, A. (1993). Borderline personality in perpetrators of psychological and physical abuse. *Violence and Victims, 8*(4), 326–337.

Dutton, D. G., Starzomski, A. J., & Ryan, L. (1994). *Antecedents of abusive personality and abusive behavior in wife assaulters.* Vancouver, British Columbia: Univeristy of British Columbia.

Eckhardt, C., Barbour, K., & Davison, G. (1998). Articulated thoughts of maritally violent and nonviolent men during anger arousal. *Journal of Clinical Psychology, 66*(2), 259–269.

Edwards, D. W., Scott, C. L., Yarvis, R. M., Paizis, C. L., & Panizzon, M. S. (2003). Impulsiveness, impulsive aggression, personality disorder and spousal violence. *Violence and Victims, 18*(1), 3–14.

Ehrensaft, M. K., Cohen, P., Brown, J., Smailes, E., Chen, H., & Johnson, J. G. (2003). Intergenerational transmission of partner violence: A 20-year prospective study. *Journal of Consulting and Clinical Psychology, 71*(4), 741–753.

Ehrensaft, M. K., Cohen, P., & Johnson, J. G. (2006). Development of personality disorder symptoms and the risk of partner violence. *Journal of Abnormal Psychology, 115*(3), 474–483.

Elliott, S., Huizinga, D., & Morse, B. (1986). Self-reported violent offending: A descriptive analysis of juvenile violent offenders and their offending careers. *Journal of Interpersonal Violence, 1*(4), 472–514.

Fals-Stewart, W. (2003). The occurrence of partner physical aggression od days of alcohol consumption: A longitudinal diary study. *Journal of Consulting and Clinical Psychology, 71*(1), 41–52.

Fang, X., & Corso, P. S. (2007). Child maltreatment, youth violence, and intimate partner violence: Developmental relationships. *American Journal of Preventative Medicine, 33*(4), 281–290.

Feld, S. L., & Straus, M. (1990). Escalation and desistance from wife assault in marriage. In M. A. Straus & R. J. Gelles (Eds.), *Physical violence in American families* (pp. 489–502). New Brunswick, NJ: Transaction.

Foran, H. M., & O'Leary, K. D. (2008). Alcohol and intimate partner violence: A meta-analytic review. *Clinical Psychology Review, 28*, 1222–1234.

Godbout, N., Dutton, D. G., Lussier, Y., & Sabourin, S. (2009). Early exposure to violence, domestic violence, attachment representations and martial adjustment. *Personal Relationships, 16*, 365–384.

Gondolf, E. W. (1988). Who are those guys? Toward a behavioral typology of batterers. *Violence and Victims, 3*, 187–203.

Graham-Kevan, N., & Archer, J. (2003). Intimate terrorism and common couple violence: A test of Johnson's predictions in four British samples. *Journal of Interpersonal Violence, 18*(11), 1247–1270.

Hamberger, L. K., & Hastings, J. E. (1991). Personality correlates of men who batter and non-violent men: Some continuities and discontinuities. *Journal of Family Violence, 6*(2), 131–147.

Hamberger, L. K., Lohr, J. M., Bonge, D., & Tolin, D. F. (1996). A large sample empirical typology of male spouse abusers and its relationship to dimensions of abuse. *Violence and Victims, 11*, 277–292.

Hanson, R. K., Cadsky, O., Harris, A., & Lalonde, C. (1997). Correlates of battering among 997 men: Family history, adjustment and attitudinal differences. *Violence and Victims, 12*(3), 191–208.

Hart, S. D., Dutton, D. G., & Newlove, T. (1993). The prevalence of personality disorder among wife assaulters. *Journal of Personality Disorder, 7*(4), 329–341.

Henning, K., Jones, A., & Holford, R. (2003). Treatment needs of women arrested for domestic violence: A comparison with male offenders. *Journal of Interpersonal Violence, 18*(8), 839–856.

Hines, D. A. (2008). Borderline personality traits and intimate partner aggression: An international multisite cross-gender analysis. *Psychology of Women Quarterly, 32,* 290–302.

Holtzworth-Munroe, A., Meehan, J. C., Herron, K., Rehman, U., & Stuart, G. L. (2000). Testing the Holtzworth-Munroe and Stuart (1994) batterer typology. *Journal of Consulting and Clinical Psychology, 68,* 1000–1019.

Holtzworth-Munroe, A., & Stuart, G. L. (1994). Typologies of male batterers: Three sub-types and the differences among them. *Psychological Bulletin, 116*(3), 476–497.

Hughes, F. M., Stuart, G. L., Gordon, K. C., & Moore, T. M. (2007). Predicting the use of aggressive conflict tactics in a sample of women arrested for domestic violence. *Journal of Social and Personal Relationships, 24*(2), 155–176.

Jacobson, N. S., Gottman, J. M., Waltz, J., Rushe, R., Babcock, J., & Holtzworth-Munroe, A. (1994). Affect, verbal content, and psychophysiology in the arguments of couples with a violent husband. *Journal of Consulting And Clinical Psychology, 62*(5), 982–988.

Johnson, M. P. (1995). Patriarchal terrorism and common couple violence: Two forms of violence against women. *Journal of Marriage and the Family, 57,* 283–294.

Johnson, M. P. (2008). *A typology of domestic violence: Intimate terrorism, violent resistance and situational couple violence.* Lebanon, NH: Northeastern University Press.

Jones, A. S., & Gondolf, E. W. (2001). Time-varying risk factors for reassault among batter program participants. *Journal of Family Violence, 16*(4), 345–359.

Julian, T. W., & McKenry, P. C. (1993). Mediators of male violence towards female intimates. *Journal of Family Violence, 8,* 39–56.

Kalmuss, D. S. (1984). The intergenerational transmission of marital aggression. *Journal of Marriage and the Family, 46,* 11–19.

Kaufman Kantor, G., & Straus, M. (1992). The "drunken bum" theory of wife beating. In M. A. Straus & R. J. Gelles (Eds.), *Physical violence in American families* (pp. 203–224). New Brunswick, NJ: Transaction.

Kessler, R. C., Molnar, B. E., Feurer, I. D., & Appelbaum, M. (2001). Patterns and mental health predictors of domestic violence in the United States: Results from the National Comorbidity Survey. *International Journal of Law, 24,* 487–508.

Laroche, D. (2005). *Aspects of the context and consequences of domestic violence— Situational couple violence and intimate terrorism in Canada in 1999.* Quebec City, QB: Government of Quebec.

Leonard, K. E., & Senchak, M. (1993). Alcohol and premarital aggression among newlywed couples. *Journal of Studies on Alcohol, 11,* 96–108.

Lohr, J. M., Hamberger, L. K., & Bonge, D. (1988). The nature of irrational beliefs in different personality clusters of spouse abusers. *Journal of Rational-Emotive and Cognitive-Behavior Therapy, 6,* 273–285.

MacKinnon, C. A. (1989). *Toward a feminist theory of the state.* Cambridge, MA: Harvard University Press.

Magdol, L., Moffitt, T. E., Caspi, A., Newman, D. L., Fagan, J., & Silva, P. A. (1997). Gender differences in partner violence in a birth cohort of 21-year-olds: Bridging the gap between clinical and epidemiological approaches. *Journal of Consulting and Clinical Psychology, 65*(1), 68–78.

Maiuro, R. D., Cahn, T. S., Vitaliano, P. P., Wagner, B. C., & Zegree, J. B. (1988). Anger, hostility and depression in domestically violent versus generally assaultive men and nonviolent control subjects. *Journal of Consulting and Clinical Psychology, 56*(1), 17–23.

Margolin, G., John, R. S., & Gleberman, L. (1989). Affective responses to conflictual discussions in violent and nonviolent couples. *Journal of Consulting and Clinical Psychology, 56*(1), 24–33.

Mauricio, A. M., & Lopez, F. G. (2009). A latent classification of male batterers. *Violence and Victims, 24*(4), 419–438.

Mauricio, A. M., Tein, J. Y., & Lopez, F. G. (2007). Borderline and antisocial personality scores as mediators between attachment and intimate partner violence. *Violence and Victims, 22*(2), 139–157.

McKenry, P. C., Julian, T. W., & Gavazzi, S. M. (1995). Toward a biopsychosocial model of domestic violence. *Journal of Marriage and Family, 57*(2), 307–320.

Mechem, C. C., Shofer, F., Reinhard, S. S., Hornig, S., & Datner, E. (1999). History of domestic violence among male patients presenting to an urban emergency department. *Academic Emergency Medicine, 6*, 786–791.

Moffitt, T. E., Caspi, A., Rutter, M., & Silva, P. A. (2001). *Sex differences in antisocial behavior: Conduct disorder, deliquency, and violence in the Dunedin longitudinal study.* Cambridge, UK: Cambridge University Press.

Morse, B. (1995). Beyond the Conflict Tactics Scale: Assessing gender differences in partner violence. *Violence and Victims, 10*(4), 251–272.

Murphy, C. M., Meyer, S. L., & O'Leary, K. D. (1993). Family origin violence and MCMI-II psychopathology among partner assaultive men. *Violence and Victims, 8*(2), 165–176.

Murphy, C. M., Taft, C. T., & Eckhardt, C. I. (2007). Anger problem profiles among partner violent men: Differences in clinical presentation and treatment outcomes. *Journal of Counseling Psychology, 54*(2), 189–200.

Norlander, B., & Eckhardt, C. (2005). Anger, hostility, and male perpetrators of intimate partner violence: A meta-analytic review. *Psychology Review, 25*, 119–152

O'Leary, K. D., Slep, A., & O'Leary, S. G. (2007). Multivariate models of men's and women's partner aggression. *Journal of Clinical and Consulting Psychology, 75*(5), 752–764.

Pan, H. S., Neidig, P. H., & O'Leary, K. D. (1994). Predicting mild and severe husband-to-wife physical aggression. *Journal of Consulting and Clinical Psychology, 62*(5), 975–981.

Pleck, E. (1987). *Domestic tyranny: The making of American social policy against family violence from colonial times to the present.* New York, NY: Oxford University Press.

Quigley, B. M., & Leonard, K. E. (2000). Alcohol and the continuation of early marital aggression. *Alcoholism: Clinical and Experimental Research, 24*(7), 1003–1010.

Rounsaville, B. (1978). Theories in marital violence: Evidence from a study of battered women. *Victimology, 3*(1-2), 11–31.

Saunders, D. G. (1992). A typology of men who batter: Three types derived from cluster analysis. *American Journal of Orthopsychiatry, 62*(2), 264–275.

Schumacher, J. A., Feldbau-Kohn, S., Smith Slep, A. M., & Heyman, R. E. (2001). Risk factors for male-to-female partner physical abuse. *Aggression and Violent Behavior,* 6(2–3), 281–352.

Schumacher, J. A., & Leonard, K. E. (2005). Husbands' and wives' marital adjustment, verbal aggression, and physical aggression as longitudinal predictors of physical aggression in early marriage. *Journal of Consulting and Clinical Psychology, 73*(1), 28–37.

Serbin, L., Stack, D., De Genna, N., Grunzeweig, N., Temcheff, C. E., Schwartzmann, A. E., & Ledingham, J. (2004). When aggressive girls become mothers: Problems in parenting, health, and development across two generations. In M. Putallaz & K. L. Bierman (Eds.), *Aggression, antisocial behavior and violence among girls* (pp. 262–285). New York, NY: Guilford Press.

Shortt, J. W., Capaldi, D. M., Kim, H. K., Kerr, D. C. R., Owen, L. D., & Feingold, A. (2012). Stability of intimate partner violence by men across 12 years in young adulthood: Effects of relationship transitions. *Prevention Science, 13*(4), 360–369.

Simon, T. R., Anderson, M., Thompson, M. P., Crosby, A. E., Shelley, G., & Sacks, J. J. (2001). Attitudinal acceptance of intimate partner violence among U.S. adults. *Violence and Victims, 16*(2), 115–126.

Smith, M. (1990). Patriarchal ideology and wife beating: A test of feminist hypothesis. *Violence and Victims, 5*(4), 257–273.

Stets, J. E., & Straus, M. A. (1989). The marriage license as a hitting license: A comparison of dating, cohabiting, and married couples. *Journal of Family Violence, 4*(1), 37–54.

Stets, J. E., & Straus, M. A. (1992a). The marriage license as a hitting license: A comparison of assaults in dating, cohabiting and married couples. In M. A. Straus, & R. J. Gelles (Eds.), *Physical violence in American families* (pp. 227–244). New Brunswick, NJ: Transaction.

Stets, J. E., & Straus, M. A. (1992b). Gender differences in reporting marital violence and its medical and psychological consequences. In M. A. Straus & R. J. Gelles (Eds.), *Physical violence in American families* (pp. 151–166). New Brunswick, NJ: Transaction.

Stith, S.M., Smith, D. B., Penn, C. E., Ward, D. B., & Tritt, D. (2004). Intimate partner physical abuse perpetration and victimization risk factors: A meta-analytic review. *Aggression And Violent Behavior, 10*(1), 65–98.

Straus, M. A. (1979). Measuring intrafamily conflict and violence: The conflict tactics scales. *Journal of Marriage and the Family, 41,* 75–88.

Straus, M. A. (1992a). The Conflict Tactics Scale and its critics: An evaluation and new data on validity and reliability. In M. A. Straus & R. J. Gelles (Eds.), *Physical violence in American families* (pp. 49–71). New Brunswick, NJ: Transaction.

Straus, M. A. (1999). The controversy over domestic violence by women: A methodological, theoretical and sociology of science analysis. In X. B. Arriaga & S. Oskamp (Eds.), *Violence in intimate relationships* (pp. 17–44). Thousand Oaks, CA: Sage.

Straus, M. A., & Gelles, R. J. (1990). *Physical violence in American families: Risk factors and adaptations to violence in 8145 families.* New Brunswick, NJ: Transaction.

Straus, M. A., Gelles, R. J., & Steinmetz, S. K. (1980). *Behind closed doors: Violence in the American family.* Garden City, NY: Anchor Press/Doubleday.

Straus, M. A., Hamby, S. L., Boney-McCoy, S., & Sugarman, D. B. (1996). The revised Conflict Tactics Scale (CTS-2): Preliminary psychometric data. *Journal of Family Issues, 17*(3), 283–317.

Stuart, G. L., Moore, T. M., Gordon, K. C., Ramsey, S. E., & Kahler, C. W. (2006). Psychopathology in women arrested for domestic violence. *Journal of Interpersonal Violence, 21*(3), 376–389.

Stuart, G. L., Moore, T. M., Ramsey, S. E., & Kahler, C. W. (2004). Hazardous drinking and relationship violence perpetration and victimization in women arrested for domestic violence. *Journal of Studies on Alcohol, 65,* 46–53.

Tweed, R., & Dutton, D. G. (1998). A comparison of impulsive and instrumental subgroups of batterers. *Violence and Victims, 13*(3), 217–230.

Taft, C. T., O'Farrell, T. J., Doron-LaMarca, S., Panuzio, J., Suvak, M. K., & Gagnon, D. R. (2010). Longitudinal risk factors for intimate partner violence among men in treatment for alcohol use disorders. *Journal of Consulting and Clinical Psyhchology, 78*(6), 924–935.

Walker, L. E. A. (2009). *The battered woman syndrome* (3rd ed.). New York, NY: Springer.

Whitaker, D. J., Haileyesus, T., Swahn, M., & Saltzman, L. (2007). Differences in frequency of violence and reported injury between relationships with reciprocal and nonreciprocal intimate partner violence. *American Journal of Public Health, 97*(5), 941–947.

Widom, C. S. (1989a). Does violence beget violence? A critical examination of the literature. *Psychological Bulletin, 106*(1), 3–28.

Widom, C. S. (1989b). The cycle of violence. *Science, 244,* 160–166.

Williams, S. L., & Frieze, I. H. (2005). Patterns of violent relationships, psychological distress, and marital satisfaction in a national sample of men and women. *Sex Roles, 52,* 771–785.

10

Perpetrators of Sexual Violence

Demographics, Assessments, Interventions

ALIX M. MCLEAREN, IVONNE E. BAZERMAN, AND
KATHERINE BRACKEN-MINOR ■

The commission of a crime with sexual intent is, by nature, an act of violence. In this chapter, we adopt a broad definition of sex offending to include both overt and attempted sexual violence, as well as noncontact offenses. Our reasoning is this: The viewing and distributing of child pornography and similar offenses are crimes that maintain the demand for documenting the sexual exploitation of minors. In addition, there is considerable overlap between contact and noncontact offender populations, and a thorough understanding of their psychological and criminal underpinnings warrants delineation of both their similarities and their differences. Under this inclusive mantel, we also reference spikes in cybercrime, which covers both attempted contact with minors and, most often, child pornography production and distribution.

The chapter opens with detailed definitional and demographic information on those who offend sexually. We then move to a discussion of specific populations among sex offenders, including juveniles and females. As noted, we assert particular emphasis on the trend of sex offending and technology. The Internet has created a new venue for traditional sex crimes (soliciting), a new manifestation of others (e.g., obscene telephone calls morphing into parallel online offenses), and allowed for significant growth and new dimensions of others (child exploitation). Following examination of these types of offenders, we move to coverage of the assessment of sex offenders. In this section, we address current diagnostic controversies, risk prediction, and other measures used to identify and manage sex offenders. Finally, we review the intervention literature as it pertains to sex offender subgroups, including contact and noncontact offenders. We also discuss risk containment in the form of civil commitment programs. The chapter concludes with suggestions for future research, training, and policy initiatives.

GENERAL FACTS AND FIGURES

When sex offending is looked at on the whole, a dramatically spiking trend can be seen in the number of arrests and prosecutions. More detailed examination, however, reveals an overall plateau or even decline in sex crimes that fall under the traditional umbrella of violent crimes (Finkelhor & Jones, 2006; Finkelhor, Turner, Ormrod, & Hamby, 2010). Instead, the record number of recent sex offense convictions owes largely to the rise in technology-based crimes, such as transmission of child pornography over the Internet (Beech, Elliott, Birgden, & Findlater, 2008). In fact, arrests and prosecutions of Internet-related sex crimes, particularly the sharing of child pornography, have skyrocketed as the accessibility of the Internet becomes more and more widespread; this is now the most frequently prosecuted federal sex offense (Motivans & Kyckelhahn, 2007). In a 12-year time span ending in 2006, federal prosecution for these offenses increased by 82% (Motivans & Kycelhan, 2007). The Internet has now become the most utilized method of transmitting images of sexual exploitation. The anonymity it offers, as well as the relative ease of large-scale file sharing offered by peer-to-peer networks, suggests the trends in these crimes will only continue (Laulik, Allam, & Sheridan, 2007; Steel, 2009; Wolak, Finkelhor, & Mitchell, 2011).

While the information presented in the preceding paragraph provides compelling evidence for the need to understand Internet and other forms of indirect sexual victimization, it is not intended to minimize the severity or frequency of violent sexual offending. Foremost, the images traded and collected by those who view child pornography or other sexual violence generally depict real victims. Even if the rates are decreasing, recent figures hold that large numbers of children are sexually victimized annually. Although the exact numbers vary depending on the source data (substantiated claims versus victim reports, for example), a frequently cited figure from 2003 federal government data suggests a victimization rate of 1.2 per 1000 in the United States (Douglas & Finkelhor, 2005). Studies using self-report to determine victimization result in significantly higher estimates, reaching as high as 4.6 per 1000 (Finkelhor, Hammer, & Sedlak, 2004; National Crime Victimization Survey, unpublished data).

In addition to crimes against minors, adults are sexually victimized at high rates as well. One problem in interpreting the figures acquired from these studies is that they may utilize lifetime prevalence reporting. Thus, some adults reporting sexual victimization are identifying a past crime that occurred during their youth. For example, a 2007 study of nearly 10,000 adults found lifetime sexual victimization rates of 10.6% for women and 2.1% for men (Basile, Chen, Lynberg, & Saltzman, 2007). Of note, however, 60.4% and 69.2% of these incidents, respectively, happened before the victim reached adulthood. This same investigation looked at sexual victimization over the preceding year and found rates of unwanted sexual activity of 2.5% (females) and 0.9% (males). Similar and higher sexual victimization rates have been found in other large-sample studies looking more specifically at the crime of rape (Tjaden & Thoennes, 2006). Although the rate of all violent crimes, including rape, reached all-time lows in the recent decade, a high number of victims were still noted (Bureau of Justice Statistics, 2008).

Although it provides contextual relevance, this victim information does not tell us specific information about offenders. For example, from this data we know many people are harmed by sexual crimes, but not how many people are doing the victimizing. The understanding of those who commit sexual offenses is an evolving science that has seen a good deal of recent interest, but much of what we know remains general in nature. One robust finding pertains to the correlation between general and sexual violence. Specifically, research has consistently shown that general criminality or antisocial orientation, including past violence, are predictive of future sex offending (Craig, Browne, Stringer, & Beech, 2005; Hanson & Morton-Bourgon, 2005). Thus, sex offenders are not necessarily a unique population, but rather have significant overlap with the population of those committing general violence. Another commonality is that while both adult and child victims are predominantly female, sexual offenders are overwhelmingly male (Centers for Disease Control, 2006; Snyder, 2000; Tjaden & Thoennes, 2006; US Department of Justice, 2008).

Another generality when it comes to direct victimizers is that they tend to know their victims. Contrary to the idea of "stranger danger," most adult and child victims know their attackers (Bolen & Scannapico, 1999; Finkelhor, Ormrod, & Turner, 2005; Tjaden & Thoennes, 2006). With regard to child victims, their most common abusers are relatives (Briere & Elliot, 2003; Jones, David, & Kathy, 2001), while as many as 40% of adult women and 9% of adult men are sexually assaulted by current or former intimate partners (Tjaden & Theonnes, 2006). Recidivism rates are of questionable accuracy and many crimes go underreported; thus, it is probable that many sex offenders do reoffend but have crimes which are undetected (Bonnar-Kidd, 2010; Hanson, Resnick, Saunders, Kilpatrick, & Best, 1999).

While providing some common threads, the aforementioned information shows that there are few sweeping generalizations that can be made about the entire population of sex offenders. This group is quite heterogeneous (e.g., Deming, 2008; van Wijk, Blokland, Duits, Vermeiren, & Harkink, 2007). With that said, some common factors can be gleaned as sex offender populations are subdivided by criminal or demographic variables.

SEX OFFENDER POPULATIONS

Numerous attempts have been made to develop typologies or offense origin pathways for sex offenders. As of this writing, none have been able to accurately account for the development of noncontact offenders. These efforts are further muddied by the fact that, contrary to popular portrayal, sex offenders often have a diversity of victims and crimes. For example, a person who perpetrates sexual violence may engage in this act a single time but engage in other more general types of violent crimes on a recidivist basis. Similarly, the same offender may engage in child molestation, sexual assault of an adult, and child pornography possession, suggesting varying types of deviance and criminal predilection. Lockmuller, Fisher, and Beech (2008) consider sex offenses to be classifiable into five categories: child abuse, rape, sexual murder, Internet offenses, and exhibitionism. Understanding that no clear-cut taxonomy exists, boundaries between categories are blurred at best, and significant overlap occurs, we adopt a broader view, and in this section explore findings on two primary types of sex offenders: contact and noncontact sex offenders. We then consider two special populations of sex offenders: juvenile and female sex offenders.

Contact Offenders

In the pre-Internet era, a dearth of empirical literature existed about noncontact sex offenders. Instead, sex offenders were viewed as a large, albeit heterogeneous group, and were the subject of a great deal of clinical attention. Nearly all of these individuals were involved in actual or attempted contact offenses, or those more traditionally considered to include violence.

Certainly, sexual offending is not new to the modern era. Breiner (1990) documented the history of child sexual abuse dating back to early Greek cultures, although the behaviors were not generally criminalized. In modern times, sex offending began to be studied as the infamous Jack the Ripper incidents were publicized. Concomitantly, Krafft-Ebing was studying sexuality and published *Psychopathia Sexualis* in 1886 (published in America in 1892). Although some of his opinions and findings have fallen into disfavor as society has progressed, he is often viewed as a pioneer of understanding sexual deviance. He was one of the first to identify, label, and study violent sexual behavior, and he is credited as being the first to use the term "sadism." He defined it as:

> the experience of sexual, pleasurable, sensations (including orgasm) produced by acts of cruelty, bodily punishment afflicted on one's person or when witnessed by others, be they animals or human beings. It may also consist of an innate desire to humiliate, hurt, wound or even destroy others in order, thereby, to create sexual pleasure in oneself. (p. 109)

Krafft-Ebing went on to categorize subtypes of sadistic behavior, to include necrophilia, lust murder, and stabbing as a substitute for sexual penetration. Perhaps surprisingly, research on sadistic rape suggests only 5%–10% of rapists meet full criteria for sexual sadism (Abel, Becker, Cunningham-Rathner, Mittelman, & Rouleu, 1988). Therefore, researchers have investigated other potential rapist typologies.

Multiple rapist typologies have been developed based on motivational, behavioral, and cognitive factors (Groth, 1979; Hazelwood & Burgess, 1987; Knight, 1999; Knight & Prentky, 1990; McCabe & Wauchope, 2005). For instance, Groth's (1979) typology consists of three categories of rapists: anger, power, and sadistic. Rapists motivated by anger are impulsive, forceful, and typically know their victims. Their feelings of rage have built up over time and stem from frustration in multiple domains of their lives, which is then applied to the victim in a purposefully, intensely violent manner, resulting in severe physical injuries and psychological trauma as a result of being forced to perform humiliating sexual acts. This type of rapist uses sex as a weapon, not necessarily with any focus on personal sexual gratification. Groth (1979) estimated that approximately one third of incarcerated rapists fall into this category.

Power rapists use rape as a means of compensating for self-doubt, feelings of incompetence, and insecurity. This type of rapist is more likely to fantasize and plan out the attack. They may use verbal intimidation and threats with a weapon, but they are less likely to use excessive physical violence outside of the act of rape itself. The function of the rape is to capture and control the victim with the underlying dynamic of "reaffirmation of his manhood" (Groth, 1979, p. 28). Groth estimated that this was the more prevalent type of sex offender.

Finally, sadistic rapists are similar to anger rapists in that they use severe physical violence toward their victims, but what distinguishes them is the sexual gratification they receive as a result of these torturous acts (Groth, 1979). They often have low life satisfaction and feel emotionally distant from most people, leaving them with few meaningful relationships. This type of rapist may engage in acts of bondage and torture with their victims. Groth (1979) suggested that approximately 5% of incarcerated sex offenders were of the sadistic type.

Other typologies grew from Groth's (1979) initial theories, including Hazelwood and Burgess's (1987) typology consisting of the power reassurance rapist, the power assertive rapist, the anger retaliatory rapist, and the anger excitation rapist. Knight and Prentky (1990) and Knight (1999) built on these typologies even further through empirical research, leading to nine types of rapists falling under four primary motivations: opportunistic (with high and low social competence types), pervasive anger, sexual gratification (with overtly sadistic versus muted sadistic types, and nonsadistic types with high or low social competence), and vindictiveness (with moderate or low social competence types; see Knight, 1999 for a full description of types). McCabe and Wauchope (2005) point out that rapist typologies currently combine behavioral, motivational, and cognitive factors, and empirical research should move toward validating proposed theories of rapist typologies by examining these domains separately. At this point in the literature, it is unclear whether a detailed versus parsimonious approach to rapist typologies would be most empirically supported or, perhaps more important, most practical in terms of its application to law enforcement needs, assessment, and treatment.

Examination of common psychological disorders in sexually violent samples, including rapists and child molesters, has revealed a variety of results. Swedish researchers investigated psychiatric and neurologic morbidity diagnosed during hospital admissions over a 10-year period prior to the sexual offenses of over 1,200 adult male sex offenders released from Swedish prisons (Långström, Sjöstedt, & Grann, 2004). Results showed that the most commonly diagnosed conditions for rapists were alcohol abuse and dependence (9.3%), drug abuse (3.9%), personality disorders (2.6%), and psychosis (1.7%). Child molesters in this sample had lower rates of psychiatric disorders overall. Psychopathy is also found more often in rapists than in child molesters (Gannon & Ward, 2008; Stinson, Becker, & Tromp, 2005). Finally, rapists are very versatile in their offending, with one study finding that over a third of sex offenders with a history of only offending against adults who reoffended did so against a child, and that they are likely to commit other violent crimes in general (Vess & Skelton, 2010).

Noncontact Offenders

In this section, we essentially focus on individuals with noncontact, Internet-based offenses, specifically the possession and distribution of child pornography, but other noncontact offenses such as exhibitionism are discussed as well. Importantly, contact and noncontact offender populations are not mutually exclusive. Methodological differences have resulted in variation between studies, but it estimated that 12.2% of sex offenders perpetrate crimes in both categories (Seto, Hanson, & Babchishin, 2011).

INTERNET OFFENDERS

Although child pornography and sexual exploitation of children existed prior to the Internet, there has been a significant increase in these criminal acts subsequent to widespread usage of the Internet. Multiple typologies of Internet offenders have been suggested (see Aslan, 2011, for a full review). Internet child pornography offenders have been categorized into individuals that (a) come across child pornography unintentionally or out of curiosity but knowingly download the material and may or may not have a sexual attraction to children; (b) actively seek out child pornography to satisfy sexual desires for children but do not commit contact offenses; (c) initiate online relationships with children and who may use child pornography for purposes of "grooming" them into online and/or in-person sexual contact; and (d) produce and distribute child pornography with the purpose of financial gain, with or without having a sexual interest in children (Krone, 2004; Lanning, 2001). Internet sex offenders that fall into the first two groups (i.e., viewers and collectors of child pornography, hereafter referred to as Internet-only child pornography offenders or ICPOs) are a subgroup that, unlike other sex offenders, are not involved in direct victimization but in a secondary form of victimization. This group of offenders may present differently than contact offenders and likely require special considerations for assessment and treatment.

With regard to demographics of ICPOs versus other contact offenders, results are somewhat mixed. Some studies indicate that ICPOs are typically younger than contact offenders (Elliott, Beech, & Mandelville-Nordin, 2012; Elliott, Beech, Mandeville-Nordin, & Hayes, 2009; Reijnen, Bulten, & Nijman, 2009), but at least one study found contact offenders to be slightly older than ICPOs (Magaletta, Faust, Bickart, & McLearen, 2012). In terms of relationship status, ICPOs are more likely to be single and living alone, and less likely to be divorced, separated, or widowed than contact offenders (Elliott et al., 2012; Reijnen et al., 2009).

A handful of studies have examined the emotional, cognitive, and personality characteristics of ICPOs. Generally, results suggest that ICPOs have socioaffective deficits, including low levels of dominance and warmth, and high levels of depression (Laulik et al., 2007; Magaletta et al., 2012), low levels of assertiveness (Bates & Metcalf, 2007; Elliott et al., 2009), and high emotional loneliness (Bates & Metcalf, 2007). In addition, there is evidence that ICPOs are less likely to have a history of substance abuse and are less likely to exhibit a general criminal lifestyle and antisocial personality traits (Magaletta et al., 2012). In one of the largest studies of ICPOs versus contact offenders and a mixed contact/noncontact offender group (Elliott et al., 2012), the ICPO and mixed offender groups exhibited more victim empathy, fewer pro-offending attitudes, lower levels of assertiveness, a greater likelihood of relating to fictional characters, and less impulsivity compared to contact offenders. Other studies have also found that ICPOs have fewer cognitive distortions and greater empathy than offline offenders (Bates & Metcalf, 2007; Elliott et al., 2009), but some studies have found the opposite (Howitt & Sheldon, 2007). Bates and Metcalf (2007) also found higher levels of socially desirable response styles in Internet sex offenders compared to contact offenders, suggesting that researchers and clinicians alike should take into account the possibility of ICPOs portraying themselves in an overly favorable light.

OTHER NONCONTACT OFFENDERS

Beyond viewing child pornography, other noncontact offenses exist. For instance, exhibitionistic disorder, as defined by the fifth edition of the *Diagnostic and Statistical Manual of Mental Disorders* (*DSM-5*; APA, 2013), consists of having recurrent, intense, sexually arousing fantasies or behaviors of exposing one's genitals to unsuspecting strangers for at least 6 months, and the person must have acted on the urges or experienced clinically significant distress or impairment in social, occupational, or other important areas of functioning. Exhibitionists are typically male (Murphy & Page, 2008), Caucasian (Bader, Schoeneman-Morris, Scalora, & Casady, 2008), and often enter the criminal justice system as a result of these behaviors in their mid-twenties to mid-thirties (Bader et al., 2008; Grant, 2005). This behavior is related to a greater likelihood of having psychiatric comorbidities, decreased life satisfaction, and substance abuse (Långström & Seto, 2006). Similarly, in a study of 202 cases of indecent exposure from the Midwestern United States, it was found that a quarter were suspected to have symptoms of mental illness and a quarter had substance abuse problems (Bader et al., 2008). The authors examined victim characteristics as well and found that 9.2% were under the age of 18, and most of the victims were female. Almost 85% of the individuals charged with indecent exposure had other nonsexual offenses on their records that were mostly nonviolent in nature (e.g., traffic violations, failure-to-appear citations). Finally, results from this study suggest that multiple indecent exposure incidents are associated with subsequent rape or molestation charges (Bader et al., 2008). These results are similar to an earlier study conducted in Australia that showed that although the majority of those arrested for indecent exposure were not considered violent offenders per se, the majority had other offenses on their records, with an average of nine offenses other than indecent exposure for the sample as a whole (Berah & Myers, 1983).

Voyeuristic disorder, or "peeping" as it is often referred to in layman's terms, is another noncontact sex offense. *DSM-5* considers voyeurism to be a period of at least 6 months in which "recurrent, intense sexual arousal" results from watching a nude or disrobing person, and the patient has acted on these sexual urges or experiences resultant impairment from them (p. 686). Unfortunately, there is extremely limited empirical research that has been conducted with this population, and therefore much is unknown of the development and trajectory of voyeurism, as well as its association with other offense behaviors (see Lavin, 2008 for a general overview of theoretical etiology and a critique of related diagnostic issues).

Juvenile Offenders

Over the past 20 to 30 years, there has been a surge of interest in the juvenile sexual offender. Prior to 1970, there were only nine major papers published in the research literature on the adolescent offender (Barbaree, Hudson, & Seto, 1993). While interest in the sexually assaultive behavior of juveniles has an extensive history (Atcheson & Williams, 1954; Cook, 1934; Doshay, 1943; Waggoner & Boyd, 1941), the view of the interpretation of the behavior has transformed over the years. Prior to the 1980s, the prevalent view of criminal sexual behavior committed by juveniles was that of a nuisance value and disregarded the severity of the harm produced (Barbaree et al., 1993; Finkelhor, Ormrod, & Chaffin, 2009). Often, the sexual assaults committed by this age group were not viewed as a problem in and of themselves. Instead, it was a reflection of a more general problem of antisocial behavior. Another factor which contributed to the minimization of the juvenile offenses was the notion that most victims were family members (Becker, 1988). All these factors were enhanced by the fact that these offenders rarely repeated their crimes (Barbaree et al., 1993).

The tendency to minimize the sexual crimes of juveniles has been substantially reduced over the past couple of decades, for a few reasons. First, studies of adult sexual offenders have consistently demonstrated that a large number of adult sexual offenders have admitted to committing some form of sexual offending prior to the age of 18 (Abel, Mittleman, & Becker, 1985). Secondly, the age at which the highest number of sexual assaults is committed by males is age 17 (Shaw, 1999). Lastly, 20% of all rapes, and 30% to 50% of all child molestations are committed by juveniles under 18 years of age (Shaw, 1999).

Early thinking about juvenile sexual offenders was based on what was known about adult offenders, particularly adult pedophiles. They were viewed as young versions of adult sex offenders. However, current clinical characteristics and models emphasize that this prior logic has obscured important motivational, behavioral, and prognostic differences between juvenile and adult sexual offenders. In other words, it overestimated the role of deviant sexual preferences in juvenile sex crimes (Letourneau & Miner, 2005). Since adolescents are still in the developmental process, they have very few fixed ideas or beliefs. They are still very experimental in their behaviors and attitudes as they attempt to develop their personal identities (Rich, 2009). Therefore, recent models are placing emphasis on the diversity of juvenile sexual offenders, their favorable prognosis, which is suggested by their low recidivism rates, and the similarities juvenile sexual offending and juvenile delinquency (Finkelhor et al., 2009).

Sexual offending behavior for juveniles ranges from noncontact sexual behaviors such as obscene phone calls, exhibitionism, voyeurism, and lewd photographs to varying degrees of child molestation involving direct sexual contact (i.e., frottage, fondling, digital penetration, fellatio, sodomy, etc). This exemplifies the diversity and range of severity of the sexual offending behavior of juveniles. Furthermore, research has indicated that in some instances the sexual offending behavior may be related to social and emotional immaturity, curiosity, and experimentation. In other cases, the sexually aggressive acts are but one aspect of a pattern of aggressive/violent acts against others, or a manifestation of severe emotional, behavioral, or developmental psychopathology (Finkelhor et al., 2009). The clinical literature has also revealed teenage and preteen sexual offenders as different offender types: Teenage sexual offenders are predominantly male (more than 90%), whereas a significant number of preteen offenders are female (Silovsky & Niec, 2002). Most offenses described in the clinical literature involve teenage offenders acting alone with young children as victims (Finkelhor et al., 2009).

Although many adult sexual offenders began their histories of sexually abusive behavior as adolescents, the vast majority of research studies indicate that many, if not most, treated juvenile sexual offenders will not become adult sexual offenders (Epperson, Ralston, Fowers, DeWitt, & Gore, 2006; Letourneau & Miner, 2005; Parks & Bard, 2006; Reitzel & Carbonel, 2007). Research has indicated the rates of sexual recidivism for juvenile sexual offenders typically fall somewhere between 7% and 15% (Rich, 2009). Therefore, if some, many, or the majority of adult sexual offenders began as juvenile sexual offenders, it appears most juvenile sexual offenders do not continue as adult sexual offenders. Furthermore, various studies of recidivism among sexually abusive youth make it evident that most juvenile sexual offenders are at far greater risk for engaging in nonsexual criminal behavior than sexual offenses (Letourneau & Miner, 2005). In other words, between 75% and 98% of sexually abusive youth do not engage in any further sexual offenses once apprehended and treated. Nevertheless, a small number of sexual offending juveniles are at an increased risk to progress to adult sexual offenses. To identify those who are more likely to progress to future sexual offending, researchers have developed juvenile-specific actuarial risk assessment tools that have demonstrated some predictive validity, and efforts to enhance these tools are being conducted (Parks & Bard, 2006; Righthand et al., 2006; Worling, 2004).

Due to the heterogeneity of the juvenile sexual offender population, treatment modalities used with adult sexual offenders are not as effective with juveniles (Rich, 2009). Although general components of sex offender interventions will be discussed later in this chapter, here we note a specific treatment approach associated with juvenile sexual offenders. Since the juvenile sexual offender population presents a wide variety of etiologies, comorbidities, and treatment needs, an integrated approach to treatment is recommended (Prentky, Harris, Frizzell, & Righthand, 2000; Rich, 2009; Shaw, 1999). This type of approach should address the emotional, behavioral, and developmental issues that a juvenile sexual offender presents. Treatment must also specifically address the unique needs and resources of the offender and be tailored to these needs. This also includes an inherent decision in treatment planning regarding the level of care required, speaking directly to the need to protect the community from both sexual and nonsexual criminal acts.

Female Offenders

The vast majority of sex offenses, both contact and noncontact, are committed by male offenders. In fact, based on records from an international sample, only 4.6% of sex offenses are perpetrated by women (Cortoni, Hanson, & Coache, 2009). Some authors (Denov, 2003; Vandiver & Walker, 2002) have suggested that the actual number of female sex offenders is underreported due to societal perceptions, failure to address/report crimes with female perpetrators, and other biases leading their offenses to be dealt with unofficially or outside traditional justice settings. As an example, the reader may consider the sensationalism associated with cases of young female teachers who sexually abuse male students, versus similar cases wherein the student is female and the teacher/perpetrator is male. In the case of the female teacher, the student is rarely viewed as a victim, and public perception, sometimes reflected in sentencing, is of a racy rite of passage rather than a sex crime (Bazelon, 2012). Taking that information into account, national data suggest adult females account for 1% of rapes and 6% of other sex offenses (Center for Sex Offender Management, 2007). Juvenile females are represented at slightly higher rates of 3% of forcible rape cases, 5% of other violent sex offenses, and 19% of nonviolent sex offenses. As detailed in the section on juveniles, sex offending among this population is often viewed as both quantitatively and qualitatively different than that perpetrated by adult offenders.

Understanding that those classified as female sex offenders likely are underrepresentative of the true population, the already low number of female sex offenders can be divided into those women who directly offend against victims versus those who act as accessories. Much like drug-related offenses, the involvement of women in sex offending sometimes results from a relationship with a deviant male partner (see Hislop, 2001). In these instances, the female offenders either aid and abet the offender by luring victims or allow for the molestation of a child without alerting authorities. While horrific in nature, these quasi sex offenses do not involve the women engaging in sex acts with minors or nonconsenting partners, nor in producing or collecting deviant stimuli. Relatedly, female sex offender typologies often include a similar category of offenders who do engage in sexual victimization of others but at the behest of a co-offender (Harris, 2010). These women can be further subgrouped into those who act out of fear of violent reprisal from their partner, and those who take a more active role in instigating the abuse. Vandiver (2006) found that women who offend with a partner are more likely to victimize multiple children, their own children, and female children than are women who offend alone.

As this small group is further and further subdivided, what becomes clear is that female sex offenders are a heterogeneous group (e.g., Becker, Hall, & Stinson, 2001). Given these facts, typologies of female sex offenders are more descriptive and less developed than those for their more well-studied male counterparts (Harris, 2010). With that said, certain commonalities can be found in this population. For example, their background often includes a history of physical or sexual victimization, and they have high rates of mental health disorders (Christopher, Lutz-Zois, & Reinhardt, 2007; Faller, 1995; Johansson-Love & Fremouw, 2006; Lewis & Stanley, 2000; Turner, Miller, & Henderson, 2008). In particular, Green and Kaplan (1994) found that personality disorders, depression, posttraumatic stress disorder, and impulse control disorder were common in female sex offenders. More recent research has questioned whether female sex offenders are more disordered than other violent criminals, or simply than members of the general population (Fazel, Sjostedt, Grann, & Langstrom, 2010; Strickland, 2008).

In determining the needs of female sex offenders, stakeholders are often interested in their risk of recidivating. A recent meta-analysis involving nearly 2,500 female offenders found sexual recidivism rates between 1% and 3%, depending on the type of analysis (Cortoni, Hanson, & Coache, 2010). Given these very low rates, as well as the rate at which females sex offend initially, there is no empirically valid risk assessment tool for female sex offenders presently available.

When treatment is warranted, the focus with female offenders should be the same as with male offenders: addressing the exploitative behavior (Cortoni, 2010). With that said, the unique needs of female sex offenders should be taken into account when planning intervention. The aforementioned high rates of mental illness and victimization must also be dealt with so as to prevent their interference in treating the actual sex-offending behaviors (Rousea & Cortoni, 2010). The Center for Sex Offender Management (2007) recommends additional treatment goals such as increasing emotional regulation, promoting independence, reducing self-harm type behaviors, and establishing appropriate, supportive relationships.

ASSESSMENT

In this section, we focus on tools for measuring the treatment needs, pathology levels, and reoffense risks of persons with a history of sex offending. While personality traits associated with different types of sex offenders were previously discussed, here we describe the most common diagnoses associated with sexual violence, as well as methods of assessing sexual deviance with an eye toward intervention needs. We also review actuarial methods for categorizing sex offenders in terms of those most likely to commit additional acts of sexual violence.

Diagnostic Issues

Certainly, the commission of one or several acts of sexual violence can be associated with a variety of mental health disorders. For example, a person with schizophrenia is capable of sexual assault based on delusional ideation. Conversely, a psychiatrically disordered individual can engage in sex offending that is wholly unrelated to nonsexual pathologies. One diagnosis commonly represented in any criminal justice population, including sex offenders, is antisocial personality disorder (ASPD; Fazel, & Danesh, 2002). These exploitative, impulsive, and hedonistic individuals may very well express their traits through the commission of a sex offense, although given the number of persons in correctional settings estimated to have this diagnosis (e.g., Black, Gunter, Loveless, Allen, & Sielini, 2010), it does not appear ASPD is the proximate cause of sex offending more so than it is for any other crime. In fact, Francia et al. (2010) found that nonsexual offenders were more likely to present with antisocial traits than sex offenders, and that within sex-offending groups, rapists had higher levels of antisociality than pedophiles. It appears ASPD may become increasingly common as the risk level of the sex offender increases, however. Levenson (2004) found nearly half of a Florida sample of moderate- to high-risk sex offenders referred for sexual dangerousness commitment met ASPD criteria, while similar findings of 40% were found in an Arizona sample (Becker, Stinson, Tromp, & Messer, 2003). Complicating this picture further, Becker et al. (2003) also noted that individuals in their civil commitment sample were each diagnosed with an average of three disorders. As such, it appears ASPD is often comorbid with other pathologies.

Taxonomically, perpetrators of sexual violence have generally tended to be represented in the diagnostic nomenclature via paraphilias (called paraphilic disorders in *DSM-5*). First introduced in the third edition of the *Diagnostic and Statistical Manual of Mental Disorders* (*DSM-III*; APA, 1980), paraphilias are currently defined as intense and recurrent fantasies, urges, and behaviors involving nonhumans, nonconsenting persons or children, or suffering/humiliation. Like most other diagnoses, criteria also include significant distress or functional impairment. Per *DSM-5* (APA, 2013), these disorders include eight specific syndromes (exhibitionism, frotteurism, fetishism, pedophilia, sexual masochism, sexual sadism, transvestic fetishism, and voyeurism) as well as two more general diagnoses. "Other specified paraphilic disorder" is to be used to denote any of the hundreds of specific paraphilias not included in *DSM-5* that have been identified (see Aggrawal, 2009, for a list). Examples listed in *DSM-5* include telephone scatologia, necrophilia, zoophilia, coprophilia, klismaphila, and urophilia (p. 705). The final diagnostic term is unspecified paraphilic disorder, which replaces the not otherwise specified category in previous editions of the *DSM*.

Among the most researched of the paraphilic disorders, and one of the most clearly linked to sex-offending behavior, is pedophilic disorder, the sexual attraction to prepubescent children. While some sex offenses are opportunistic in nature, many child molesters are persons with a specific, fixed sexual attraction to persons who have not achieved sexual maturity (see Abel et al., 1985). The exact number of persons with pedophilia, like other paraphilias, is hard to quantify, mainly because individuals who engage in the behavior but are not detected are unlikely to pursue treatment, and others may have urges on which they never act (see Seto, 2009). As an example, Ahlers and colleagues (2011) found some form of paraphilic response in over 62% of a male community sample, with 9% having pedophilic arousal. Within convicted sex offender samples, pedophilia is one of the most common diagnoses (Becker et al., 2003). In fact, a fairly robust finding is that greater than one third to as many as one half of those who offend against children are pedophiles (Blanchard, Klassen, Dickey, Kuban, & Blak, 2001; Maletzky & Steinhauser, 2002; Seto & Lalumiere, 2001). Certainly, other paraphilias are commonly found in sex offender populations as well, and many persons meet criteria for multiple paraphilias, as the disorders are commonly comorbid with one another (Abel et al., 1987).

Another diagnosis often seen in forensic settings involving the sex-offending population is that of paraphilia, not otherwise specified. Per *DSM-IV-TR* (2000), individuals with this disorder have a paraphilia that does "not meet criteria for any of the specific categories" (p. 576). As noted, the diagnosis has recently been renamed unspecified paraphilic disorder. One common example of persons with this diagnosis is those who are attracted to minors, but minors who have achieved puberty. Referred to as hebephilia, this disorder was considered for inclusion in some form in the updated edition of the *DSM* (Prentky & Barbaree, 2011). Another application of this category is for those who use force to commit acts of sexual violence. However, the question of whether rape itself is a disorder has engendered significant debate (see later; Abel, Osborn, & Twigg, 1993; McConaghy, 1999). Some express concern that the seriousness of the crime is diminished in attributing it to a mental disorder, and that sexual violence is a manifestation of an antisocial or psychopathic personality (Doren, 2002; Frances & First, 2011). Others point to sexual dangerousness laws (discussed later), which create severe consequences for sex offenders with mental abnormalities (Frances & First, 2011; Hinderlighter, 2011), while yet others have concerns about diagnostic accuracy (Wakefield, 2012; Wollert, 2011). In 2002, Doren proposed criteria for paraphilia, NOS (nonconsent), a syndrome wherein the affected person's paraphilia involves unwilling sexual partners, and which could be characterized by the presence of any of nine observable criteria. These items include arousal to clearly nonconsensual sex acts, repetitive patterns, having an offense history that is almost exclusively sexual, raping when consent was already achieved, raping when being caught is likely, maintaining a "rape kit" of material to perpetrate crimes, having varying types of victims, having both consensual and nonconsensual partners, and raping shortly after a consequence such as arrest. This diagnosis is commonly used by evaluators in civil commitment proceedings and has been accepted by federal and state courts.

Recently, the *DSM* underwent significant revision. Thus, while we felt a discussion of sexual violence was not complete without diagnostic information, we have attempted to focus on the more controversial diagnostic issues. Although much change was discussed throughout the revision process (http://www

.dsm5.org/proposedrevision/Pages/ParaphilicDisorders.aspx), the general categories of paraphilias remained the same as in *DSM-IV-TR*, with the section retitled "Paraphilic Disorders." Expected changes that were ultimately not made included the addition of a hebephilic subtype to the pedophilia diagnosis. This proposed addition could have decreased the misuse or inaccuracy of paraphilia diagnoses, which absent a structured interview, can be difficult to diagnose (Miller, Amenta, & Conroy, 2005). In addition, a variation on the previously discussed paraphilia, NOS (nonconsent) to be called paraphilic coercive disorder, was considered as an area for future research. Finally, a new category, hypersexual disorder, was also proposed for inclusion in this section as an attempt to capture those who are abnormally consumed by sexual fantasies or behaviors.

Nondiagnostic Measures of Sexual Deviancy and Risk

Aside from applying *DSM* diagnoses, other measures of assessing sexual deviancy exist. In fact, given that clinical work with persons who commit sexual violence often involves criminal justice auspices, a concern is the lack of fit between legal and mental health constructs (Witt & Conroy, 2009). As such, while sexual dangerousness proceedings often require diagnostic information, other measures are often used concomitantly and may even carry greater weight in the development of forensic opinions. The measures discussed next are also used to inform treatment, capture risk rates, and otherwise assist in the appropriate management of sex offenders.

Perhaps the hallmark of sexual deviancy evaluation, the penile plethysmography (PPG), is a measure of phallometry. That is, this instrument assesses the level of arousal in males by calculating differences in penis size (tumescence) when a series of different stimuli are presented (see Seto, 2008, for detailed procedural description and administration guidelines). For nearly 50 years, researchers have demonstrated the utility of this method in measuring sexual excitement and differentiating certain sex offenders from each other or from non-sex offenders by presenting images or aural descriptions of sexual acts to those being assessed (Barbaree & Marshall, 1989; Freund, 1965, 1967; Lalumiere, Harris, Rice & Quinsey, 2003; Laws, Hanson, Osborn, & Greenbaum, 2000; Letourneau, 2002; Quinsey & Chaplin, 1988). Purported strengths of PPG instruments are its ability to measure deviant arousal or fantasy that may not be measurable by other means, such as self-report (Terry, 2006). While it can be influenced by dissimulation, there are also procedures that can be used to attenuate this effect (see Quinsey, Harris, Rice, & Cormier, 2006). In addition, Hanson and Bussière (1998) found arousal to children as measured phallometrically to be a very strong predictor of sexual reoffending.

Despite some of the benefits of using the PPG to gain insight into the level of sexual deviance of a particular offender, it has also been widely criticized and appears to be declining in usage (McGrath, Cumming, & Blanchard, 2003). Foremost among these concerns is that of practicality: The equipment can be costly, in terms of material expenses, training requirements, and time spent on administration. Additionally, it is a very invasive procedure when compared to traditional interviews or "pencil-and-paper" tests. Others have raised the issue of poorly validated procedures and the lack of reliable, standardized guidelines for all populations of interest (Fernandez, 2009; Simon & Shouten, 1993). Still others, particularly those engaged in the legal arena, note its infrequent use in important evaluations and its inadmissibility in some court proceedings (Jackson & Hess, 2007; *State v. Spencer*, 1995; *US v. Powers*, 1995).

In sum, despite its weaknesses, phallometry appears to be a useful tool for determining the presence and strength of pedophilic and other deviant arousal in men. Measuring genital arousal in women has been found to be of less utility in determining sexual attraction/preference, due to biological differences in the way women respond to sexual stimuli (see Chivers, 2005; Chivers, Seto, & Blanchard, 2007). An alternative that has generated recent interest is the measure of pupil dilation to determine arousal. There is no research suggesting this method be used to assess criminal behavior or sexual deviancy at present. Neuroimaging may also be a developing method of assessing sexual arousal and deviance. Early results suggest activation in certain brain areas in response to different levels of sexual stimuli (Stoléru et al., 1999), but again, this method is not yet considered appropriate for assessing sexual deviance or predicting sex offending.

Another psychophysiological assessment tool used more for monitoring or for identifying treatment targets than measuring deviance levels is the polygraph. This instrument, which is less physically intrusive than the PPG, measures skin, cardio-vascular, and respiratory responses to questions of interest. Generally, the polygraph is used by nonclinical staff such as probation officers who are monitoring offenders in the community, and in fact the majority of US postrelease monitoring agencies report using it with convicted sex offenders (English, Jones, Pasini-Hill, Patrick, & Cooley-Towell, 2000). Aside from this use, guidelines put forth by the Association for the Treatment of Sexual Abusers (ATSA, 2005) suggest it also can be used to glean information not available to clinicians through self-report methods. For example, understanding the full scope of pathology (deviant fantasies or victim targets) may aid providers in creating appropriate treatment plans. Although research (Grubin & Madsen, 2006) found the polygraph to be 85% accurate with sex offenders and to increase admissions of nonadjudicated offenses (Ahlmeyer, Heil, McKee, & English, 2000), it is criticized on many of the same grounds as the PPG. Specifically, there is limited empirical support for its use, and the potential for significant error (Branaman & Gallagher, 2005) or even fabricated admissions.

Finally, a more traditional assessment approach used with sex offender population is the risk assessment method. As reviewed by Andrews, Bonta, and Wormith (2006), assessment of those in criminal justice settings has evolved alongside an understanding of the Risk-Needs-Responsivity (RNR) model. Although we reference this model here and elsewhere, a full discussion is beyond the scope of this chapter. It is relevant to note that risk assessment in general has reached a threshold wherein static and dynamic risk factors are becoming integrated with criminogenic and noncriminogenic treatment needs to develop services that reduce risk of reoffending (Andrews, Bonta, & Wormith, 2006). Sex offender–specific risk assessment, which has only begun to receive considerable attention recently, is also moving in this direction, but perhaps at a slower pace. We briefly overview sex offender risk assessment tools next.

Most likely because of conflating risk and actual horrors of the crime, there has been extensive public policy focus on sexual dangerousness (Folger, 2008). Thus, for many sex offenders entering treatment or leaving custody, risk assessment is essential, both to determine needs for intervention and monitoring. Although both static and dynamic factors are involved in accurate risk prediction, a great deal of literature has looked at the static factors associated with repeated commission of sex offenses (e.g., Hanson & Bussiere, 1998), and this information has been used to derive common actuarial methods. Generally, results are indicative of two broad factors underlying recidivism of sex offenders: sexual deviance and criminal or antisocial thinking (Doren, 2004; Hanson & Boussiere, 1998; Hanson & Morton-Bourgon, 2005). Additional research has been conducted to explore the interrelation among the individual factors. These investigations have uncovered previously unnamed factors of lifestyle maladjustment, child sexual abuse, persistence, and detached predatory behavior, as well as certain demographic variables (Barbaree et. al., 2006). In studies using the Static-99 instruments, and other common actuarials, three-factor solutions have been found (Brouillette-Alarie, Proulx, Helmus, & Hanson, unpublished data; Roberts, Doren, & Thornton, 2002).

Static-99

Of the actuarial instruments, perhaps the most commonly used is the psychometrically strong Static-99 (Hanson & Thornton, 2000) and its more recent updates, the 99R and 2002 versions (Archer, Buffington-Vollum, Stredny, & Handel, 2006; Jackson & Hess, 2007; McGrath et al., 2003). Meta-analytic findings have determined actuarial approaches in general and the Static-99 instruments in particular to have moderate to large effect size in regard to predictive accuracy (Hanson & Morton-Bourgon, 2009). Specifically, the Static-99 has been validated in international samples, with predictive studies finding respectable AUC findings generally over .70, and significant relationships to reoffending (Barbaree, Seto, Langton, & Peacock, 2001; Beech, Friendship, Erikson, & Hanson, 2002; Endrass, Urbaniok, Held, Vetter, & Rossegger, 2009; Hood, Shute, Feilzer, & Wilcox, 2002; Sjöstedt &Langström, 2001; Stadtland et al., 2006). The instrument also performs as well as or better than others of similar purpose in comparison studies (e.g., Bartosh, Garby, Lewis, & Gray, 2003).

The Static-99 instruments include 10 items, four of which were included on the Rapid Risk Assessment of Sexual Offense Recidivism (RRASOR; Hanson, 1997), one of the earliest sex offender risk assessment instruments. An empirically derived measure of static factors, the instrument is to be used for males who were at least 16 years old at the commission of the most recent sex offense. Between the original and revised version, an adjustment was made in the weighting of the item that measures age at release from most recent sex offense. This change accounts for the infrequent recidivism rates occurring among older sex offenders.

MNSOST

The Minnesota Sex Offender Screening Tool (MNSOST; Epperson, Kaul, & Hesselton, 1998) is a 16-item scale developed by the Minnesota Department of Corrections to be used with inmates and covers a broader range of items than many of the other scales. It is however, more difficult to score than scales like the Static 99 or RRASOR, and it makes assumptions about the availability and nature of sexual offender and chemical dependence treatments that may not apply outside of Minnesota. The items covered are as follows: number of sexual convictions, length of sex offending history, whether the offender was under any supervision when the offense was committed, any sex offense committed in a public place, use or threat of force, multiple acts on a single victim, different age groups of victim, offended against a 13- to 15-year-old and being at least 5 years older than the victim, stranger victims, antisocial behavior as an adolescent, substance abuse, employment history, discipline history while incarcerated, chemical dependency while incarcerated, sex offender treatment while incarcerated, and age at release.

SRA-FV

As noted earlier, static factors alone provide greater accuracy than unstructured clinical judgments with regard to sexual recidivism. However, applying these predictions to an individual requires consideration of acute or changing factors as well. The Structured Risk Assessment (SRA; Thornton, 2002) is a research-guided multistep framework for assessing the risk presented by a sex offender and provides a systematic way of going beyond static risk classification and provides information around dynamic psychological and behavioral domains. The domains are as follows: sexual interests, distorted attitudes, social and emotional functioning, and self-management.

RISK ASSESSMENT OF NONCONTACT OFFENDERS

Despite the considerable emphasis that has been placed on estimating risk of recidivism among sex offenders, these tools generally apply only to contact offenders (i.e., those who either directly victimize or attempt to victimize a real person or fictitious person they believe to be real). Typically, the instruments include items related to victims, which cannot be scored in cases where the sole crime involved the individual possessing child pornography (due to the victimization being indirect). In a recent study, Wakeling, Howard, and Barnett (2011) applied existing instruments, the Risk Matrix 2000 (several versions) and the Offender Group Reconviction Scale-3, to a large sample of sex offenders, including those with no history of contact or attempted contact offending. Results for this segment of the sample produced respectable outcomes, suggesting risk assessment can be done with this population. The authors do note, however, that recidivism rates for this group are comparably low, meaning any risk assessment done on this population can be inherently lacking in accuracy. Further study is needed in this domain so as to identify the small proportion of Internet offenders most likely to recidivate or go on to commit sexually violent acts.

Although all of these measures are generally used for evaluative purposes, the very fact of an assessment occurring suggests the offender has been detected. As such, evaluation is very closely linked to treatment or other criminal justice intervention. We have alluded to using these various types of assessment for treatment as well as management, and it is to those efforts that we now turn.

INTERVENTION

Just as what society has considered sexual deviancy has evolved over time, so has the treatment of sexual deviancy. Early treatment of sex offenders consisted of purely psychodynamic treatment, strictly behavioral approaches such as aversion therapy, in which an individual would receive electrical shock or chemicals to induce vomiting which was paired with a stimulus related to the individual's sexually deviant behavior or fantasy, and highly invasive methods such as surgical castration (Gordon, 2008). Luckily, research on "what works" with regard to sex offender treatment has come a long way, as older forms of treatment (implemented prior to 1980) seem to have little effect on recidivism (Hanson et al., 2002). Here we lay out specific treatment approaches and corresponding studies of treatment efficacy, with the understanding that many treatment programs likely use some combination of two or more of these approaches (McGrath, Cumming, Burchard, Zeoli, & Ellerby, 2010).

Biomedical

The use of biological interventions in an attempt to reduce sexual reoffending has been in practice for many years. For instance, in the late 1960s researchers began investigating the effects of antiandrogens and found that they reduced the offender's ability to have an erection, produce semen, and have an orgasm (e.g., Money, 1970). Yet even early studies acknowledged that medication does not "cure" sex offenders. For instance, in a case study published in 1983, a 25-year-old pedophilic male was treated with medroxyprogesterone acetate for 500 days, and although he exhibited biological changes, such as a decrease in testosterone, the authors noted the patient remained sexually attracted to children (Cordoba & Chapel, 1983). Currently, selective serotonin reuptake inhibitors (SSRIs), a type of antidepressant, are most commonly prescribed, as they aid in the reduction of sexual preoccupation and fantasies while simultaneously helping offenders manage depression (Greenberg & Bradford, 1997; Greenberg, Bradford, Curry, & O'Rourke, 1996; Kafka & Hennen, 2000). The use of antiandrogens is now declining in the United States, perhaps because they are typically more expensive and have more side effects than SSRIs (McGrath et al., 2010), and patients may be more likely to be medication compliant with SSRIs (Fedoroff, 1995).

Cognitive-Behavioral Therapy and Relapse Prevention

Simply put, cognitive-behavioral therapy (CBT) is focused on an individual's thoughts, behaviors, and emotions, and how making changes in one domain can lead to positive changes in another. The vast majority of adult male sex offender programs report working within a CBT model framework, using core treatment targets such as social skills and intimacy development, problem-solving skills, victim empathy and awareness, and emotion regulation skills (McGrath et al., 2010). Meta-analyses provide overwhelming support for a CBT approach in this population for the reduction of sexual and nonsexual recidivism (Grossman, Martis, & Fichtner, 1999; Hanson et al., 2002; Hanson, Bourgon, et al., 2009; Lösel & Schmucker, 2005; Polizzi, MacKenzie, & Hickman, 1999).

Relapse prevention is a form of CBT treatment that has been adapted from the addictions literature (George & Marlatt, 1989; Laws, 1989; Pithers, Marques, Gibat, & Marlatt, 1983). This approach involves teaching offenders about the behavioral chain or cycle that leads one to reoffend (Laws, 1995). The model states that an individual is likely to relapse when there is a lifestyle imbalance (e.g., stressors or obligations outweigh pleasant and rewarding activities). The individual subsequently makes a series of apparently irrelevant decisions (e.g., seemingly trivial decisions that are, in actuality, undermining one's likelihood of success). These decisions ultimately place the offender in a high-risk situation in which one is likely to experience a lapse in self-control for immediate self-gratification purposes. Due to what is referred to as the "abstinence violation effect," the lapse often becomes a full relapse because the abuser believes he is now incapable of abstaining from sexually offending (Laws, 1995). Relapse prevention has historically served as a major framework for sex offender treatment programs, but programs with a singular focus on relapse prevention have decreased over recent years, and it is now typically used as a component of treatment used in conjunction with other strategies (McGrath et al., 2010). This trend is a result of several criticisms of relapse prevention, including its overly simplistic view of the pathway to reoffending (e.g., failing to take into account that many sex offenders reoffend after careful planning as opposed to a sudden lapse in self-control), and its considerable focus on avoidance strategies (Polaschek, 2003). Finally, one of the largest and most methodologically sound studies of relapse prevention found no difference in recidivism rates between those who participated in treatment, those who were offered treatment but refused to participate, and a volunteer control group (Marques, Wiederanders, Day, Nelson, & Ommeron, 2005).

Risk-Need-Responsivity

The risk-need-responsivity (RNR) model of sex offender treatment was created in the 1990s, and the number of sex offender treatment programs operating within this framework continues to grow (Andrews, Bonta, & Hoge, 1990; McGrath et al., 2010). There is a focus on three basic principles in this model. First, the risk principle states that the level of treatment should parallel the offender's level of risk to reoffend. Second, the need principle suggests it is necessary to assess criminogenic needs and target those specific needs in treatment. Third, the responsivity principle states that treatment should be tailored to the offender's learning style, motivation, and strengths. The RNR model has been historically applied successfully with general offenders, including men, women, and juveniles (e.g., Dowden & Andrews, 1999; Vitopoulos, Peterson-Badali, & Skilling, 2012), and results from a recent meta-analysis support the idea that RNR principles reduce sexual recidivism as well (Hanson et al., 2009). However, there are several criticisms of the RNR model for sex offenders, such that "its focus on criminogenic need is a *necessary* by not *sufficient* condition for effective treatment" (Wilson & Yates, 2009, p. 158), the inability of the RNR model to account for an individual client's need as a whole person rather than on the need to reduce risk, and the lack of specific intervention strategies for clinicians to use when applying the RNR model (Wilson & Yates, 2009).

Self-Regulation and Good Lives Models

The self-regulation model (SRM) attempts to fill in the gaps of the RNR and CBT/relapse prevention models. Based in self-regulation theory (Baumeister & Heatherton,

1996), the SRM suggests there are four pathways to reoffending. These four pathways are based on whether an offender's goal is avoid versus approach offending behaviors, and whether there is a passive or active strategy implemented (Kingston, Yates, & Firestone, 2012; Ward & Hudson, 1998). Initial studies provide evidence of validity for these offense pathways for sex offenders, including those with intellectual disabilities (Ford, Rose, & Thrift, 2009; Kingston et al., 2012; Yates & Kingston, 2006).

Incorporated into the self-regulation model is the good lives model (GLM). GLM was developed by Ward and colleagues (Ward, 2007; Ward & Gannon, 2006; Ward & Maruna, 2007; Ward, Yates, & Long, 2006; Yates, Prescott, & Ward, 2010) and is driven by the strengths-based rehabilitation theory (Ward, Yates, & Willis, 2012, p. 95). The treatment has an overarching goal of helping sex offenders develop the skills and resources to live a life that is both socially acceptable and personally meaningful. Offenders are encouraged to learn noncriminogenic methods of attempting to gain what are referred to as "the primary human goods." Ward and colleagues have suggested 11 types of primary goods that are often addressed in treatment: (a) life (e.g., making healthy lifestyle choices), (b) knowledge, (c) excellence in play, (d) excellence in work, (e) excellence in agency (i.e., autonomy and self-directedness), (f) inner peace, (g) friendship, (h) community, (i) spirituality (e.g., finding meaning and purpose in life), (j) happiness, and (k) creativity (Ward & Gannon, 2006). Although the GLM incorporates aspects of the aforementioned psychological treatment modalities, it is altogether a more humanistic approach, placing less of a spotlight on risk management and avoidance-based strategies. Given that SRM and GLM are relatively new, it is unclear how they impact an individual's likelihood of reoffending.

Civil Commitment

Civil commitment was originally designed to confine and treat mentally ill individuals who are considered dangerous to themselves or others (King, 1999). It is important to note that treatment, not punishment, and protection of the public are the functions of commitment. The civil commitment of sexual predators first occurred as a result of the "sexual psychopath laws" that emerged in the 1930s, and by the 1960s these laws were enacted in over half the states. During that time, sex offenses were seen to be the result of mental illness. Because they were "mad, not bad," they were assumed to be amenable to treatment, and treatment at an inpatient facility was argued to be more appropriate than criminal punishment (Lieb, 1996). Illinois, for instance, enacted a statute in 1938 that provides an alternative to criminal prosecution. The statute created a decision tree for the state either to convict and punish an offender through the criminal system or to pursue a civil commitment under this statute. If found to be a sexually dangerous person, the individual is committed to the Department of Corrections until deemed to no longer be dangerous. The statute was found constitutional by the US Supreme Court in 1986 (*Allen v. Illinois*). By the 1980s, these laws by and large had fallen into disfavor as a result of a lack of empirical evidence that the treatment of sex offenders was actually reducing recidivism, and sex offenders were subsequently managed with a focus on punishment in the criminal justice system (McLawsen, Scalora, & Darrow, 2012).

So-called second-generation or second-wave sexual predator commitment laws began in 1990 in Washington State. In 1987 Earl K. Shriner, a man with severe intellectual disabilities and a lengthy criminal record including sexual assault and murder, had finished serving a 10-year sentence for kidnapping and assaulting two young girls. During his imprisonment, officials learned that he intended to continue committing violent acts against children upon his release. However, they were unable to have him detained under the commitment laws of the time, he was released, and subsequently kidnapped and sexually assaulted a young boy. On the heels of the public outrage of this and similar cases, Washington's Community Protection Act of 1990 was enacted, which included harsher sentences and increased supervision of sexual offenders that were released into the community. Importantly, it also contained the "Sexually Violent Predator Statute," which allowed for the civil commitment of convicted offenders found to be sexually violent predators (Lieb & Matson, 2000).

In 1994, the state of Kansas implemented its own Sexually Violent Predator Act, which established the civil commitment of a person who, due to a mental abnormality or personality disorder, would be likely to engage in acts of sexual violence. The state of Kansas filed a petition under the Act to commit Leroy Hendricks, who had an extensive history of sexually molesting children, had a diagnosis of pediphilia, and was scheduled for release from prison. The Kansas Act went into effect shortly before his release, and therefore, the state moved to commit Hendricks. The jury found beyond a reasonable doubt that Hendricks was a sexually violent predator. The Court committed him to the Kansas Secretary of Social and Rehabilitation Services (Grudzinskas et al., 2009). Hendricks appealed and the Kansas Supreme Court found that to commit a person, a state is required by substantive due process to prove by clear and convincing evidence that a person is both mentally ill and dangerous to himself or others (*In re Hendricks*, 1996). The US Supreme Court reversed the Kansas Court (*Kansas v. Hendricks*, 1997). The Court indicated that some additional factor beyond dangerousness, such as mental illness, must coincide with the dangerousness (*Kansas v. Hendricks*, 1997). Once the Supreme Court approved the process of civil commitment for sexually violent predators, numerous state statutes followed.

Similarly, Congress enacted Federal Statute 18 U.S.C. 4248 as part of the Adam Walsh Child Protection and Safety Act of 2006 to protect children from "sexual exploitation and violent crime." Among other things, the Act required all states to maintain consistent databases of identifying information and criminal backgrounds for sex offenders, increased punishment for a variety of sex offenses, placed more guidelines for probation and supervised release, outlawed the trafficking of date rape drugs over the Internet, and eliminated statute of limitations for several sex offenses. Perhaps the most controversial aspect of the Act, however, was the establishment of civil commitment procedures for federal sex offenders who have served out their full sentence. Although this statute was challenged by a group of sex offenders, the US Supreme Court upheld the constitutionality of the civil commitment of these offenders (*United States v. Comstock et al.*, 2010).

In conclusion, there is a need for methodologically sound empirical studies of sex offender treatments. Specifically, future studies should examine the efficacy of individual components of treatments by using dismantling designs, and investigating these treatments in diverse samples is essential. Furthermore, it is clear at this point that treatment can reduce risk but not "cure" offenders. As a result, there is a continued need for long-term monitoring and assessment, such as with ongoing polygraph, with more severe offenders.

Conclusions/Future Directions

Because of the complexities of defining sex offenders and the heterogeneity of this population, we have taken a broad and high-level approach to covering the topic in this chapter. It is our hope that we have accomplished our goal of moving the reader through both the different populations and the different phases from detection to treatment. We conclude with final thoughts on directions needed to more fully understand and manage sex offenders in the areas of training, research, and policy.

With regard to training, one area that comes immediately to mind is to engage the law enforcement and legal communities in a discussion of mental health and science. For example, in the assessment of risk, and therefore in the management and treatment of sexual offenders, the current practice is to rely on official records. Convictions are given more weight than charges, and reports of behavior have little to no weight in many circumstances. Better information in this area may help police and prosecutors understand how their work impacts the accuracy of individual risk assessment, while also improving cross-disciplinary partnering. On a different note, we also highlight the need for specialized training of practitioners working with sexual offenders. Beyond on-the-job experience, it is rare for graduate programs to include curricula focused specifically on diagnosing and managing sex offenders.

Although it sounds trite, more research related to sexual offending is clearly needed. We have a great deal of information about contact offenders, but we need more data on the course and effective interventions for noncontact offenders. We should specifically examine factors leading noncontact offenders to engage in contact such that we can provide early detection and intervention. As noted, we also need more focus on large-scale treatment efficacy evaluation, such that these models can be appropriately implemented both within and outside correctional environs. Finally, we need policy-driven research evaluating the outcomes of sexual dangerousness containment laws.

AUTHOR'S NOTE

The opinions expressed in this chapter are those of the authors and do not necessarily represent the opinions of the Federal Bureau of Prisons or the Department of Justice.

REFERENCES

Abel, G. G., Becker, J. V., Cunningham-Rathner, J., & Mittelman, M. (1988). Multiple paraphilic diagnoses among sex offenders. *Bulletin of the American Academy of Psychiatry and the Law, 16*(2), 153–168.

Abel, G. G., Becker, J. V., Mittelman, M., Cunningham-Rathner, J., Rouleau, J. L., & Murphy, W. D. (1987). Self-reported sex crimes of nonincarcerated paraphiliacs. *Journal of Interpersonal Violence, 2*(1), 3–25. doi:10.1177/088626087002001001

Abel, G. G., Mittleman, M. S., & Becker, J. V. (1985). Sexual offenders: Results of assessment and recommendations for treatment. In M. H. Ben-Aron, S. J. Hucker, & C. D. Webster (Eds.), *Clinical criminology: Current concepts* (pp. 191–205). Toronto, ON: M&M Graphics.

Abel, G. G., Osborn, C. A., & Twigg, D. A. (1993). Sexual assault through the life span: Adult offenders with juvenile histories. In H. E. Barbaree, W. L. Marshall, & S. M. Hudson (Eds.), *The juvenile sex offender* (pp. 104–117). New York, NY: Guilford Press.

Aggrawal, A. (2009). *Forensic and medico-legal aspects of sexual crimes and unusual sexual practices.* Boca Raton, FL: CRC Press.

Ahlers, C. J., Schaefer, G. A., Mundt, I. A., Roll, S., Englert, H., Willich, S. N., & Beier, K. M. (2011). How unusual are the contents of paraphilias? Paraphilia-associated sexual arousal patterns in a community-based sample of men. *Journal of Sexual Medicine, 8*(5), 1362–1370. doi:10.1111/j.1743-6109.2009.01597

Ahlmeyer, S., Heil, P., McKee, B., & English, K. (2000). The impact of polygraphy on admissions of victims and offenses in adult sexual offenders. *Sexual Abuse, 12*(2), 123–138. doi:10.1177/107906320001200204

Allen v. Illinois, 478 U.S. 364, 106 S. Ct. 2988, 92 L. Ed. 2d 296 (1986).

American Psychiatric Association. (1980). *Diagnostic and statistical manual of mental disorders* (3rd ed.). Washington, DC: Author.

American Psychiatric Association. (2000). *Diagnostic and statistical manual of mental disorders* (4th ed., text rev.). Washington, DC: Author.

American Psychiatric Association. (2013). *Diagnostic and statistical manual of mental disorders* (5th ed.). Washington, DC: Author.

Andrews, D. A., Bonta, J., & Hoge, R. D. (1990). Classification for effective rehabilitation: Rediscovering psychology. *Criminal Justice and Behavior, 17*(1), 19–52. doi:10.1177/0093854890017001004

Andrews, D. A., Bonta, J., & Wormith, S. J. (2006). The recent past and near future of risk and/or need assessment. *Crime and Delinquency, 52,* 7–27. doi:10.1177/0011128705281756

Archer, R. P., Buffington-Vollum, J. K., Stredny, R., & Handel, R. W. (2006). A survey of psychological test use patterns among forensic psychologists. *Journal of Personality Assessment, 87*(1), 84–94. doi:10.1207/s15327752jpa8701_07

Aslan, D. (2011). Critically evaluating typologies of internet sex offenders: A psychological perspective. *Journal of Forensic Psychology Practice, 11*(5), 406–431. doi:10.1080/15228932.2011.588925

Association for the Treatment of Sexual Abusers (ATSA), Professional Issues Committee (2005). *Practice standards and guidelines for the evaluation, treatment, and management of adult male sexual abusers.* Beaverton, OR: ATSA.

Atcheson, J. D., & Williams, D. C. (1954). A study of juvenile sex offenders. *American Journal of Psychiatry, 111,* 366–370.

Bader, S. M., Schoeneman-Morris, K. A., Scalora, M. J., & Casady, T. K. (2008). Exhibitionism: Findings from a Midwestern police contact sample. *International Journal of Offender Therapy and Comparative Criminology, 52*(3), 270–279. doi:10.1177/0306624X07307122

Barbaree, H. E., Hudson, S. M., & Seto, M. C. (1993). Sexual assault in society: The role of the juvenile offender. In H. E. Barbaree, W. L. Marshall, & S. M. Hudson (Eds.), *The juvenile sex offender* (pp. 1–24). New York, NY: Guilford Press.

Barbaree, H. E., Langton, C. M., & Peacock, E. J. (2006). The factor structure of static actuarial items: Its relation to prediction. *Sexual Abuse, 18*(2), 207–226. doi:10.1177/107906320601800207

Barbaree, H. E., & Marshall, W. L. (1989). Erectile responses among heterosexual child molesters, father-daughter incest offenders, and matched non-offenders: Five distinct age preference profiles. *Canadian Journal of Behavioural Science, 21*(1), 70–82. doi:10.1037/h0079791

Barbaree, H. E., Seto, M. C., Langton, C. M., & Peacock, E. J. (2001). Evaluating the predictive accuracy of six risk assessment instruments for adult sex offenders. *Criminal Justice and Behavior, 28*(4), 490–521. doi:10.1177/009385480102800406

Bartosh, D. L., Garby, T., Lewis, D., & Gray, S. (2003). Differences in the predictive validity of actuarial risk assessments in relation to sex offender type. *International Journal of Offender Therapy and Comparative Criminology, 47*(4), 422–438. doi:10.1177/0306624X03253850

Basile, K. C., Chen, J., Black, M. C., & Saltzman, L. E. (2007). Prevalence and characteristics of sexual violence victimization among U.S. adults, 2001-2003. *Violence and Victims, 22*(4), 437–448. doi:10.1891/088667007781553955

Bates, A., & Metcalf, C. (2007). A psychometric comparison of internet and non-internet sex offenders from a community treatment sample. *Journal of Sexual Aggression, 13*(1), 11–20. doi:10.1080/13552600701365654

Baumeister, R. F., & Heatherton, T. F. (1996). Self-regulation failure: An overview. *Psychological Inquiry, 7*(1), 1–15. doi:10.1207/s15327965pli0701_1

Bazelon, E. (2012). Not every school boy's fantasy. Slate. Retrieved July 2012, from http://www.slate.com/articles/news_and_politics/crime/2012/05/gabriela_compton_received_lifetime_probation_for_sexually_abusing_two_boys_.html.

Becker, J. V. (1988). Adolescent sex offenders. *Behavior Therapist, 11*, 185–187.

Becker, J. V., Hall, S. R., & Stinson, J. D. (2001). Female sexual offenders: Clinical, legal and policy issues. *Journal of Forensic Psychology Practice, 1*(3), 29–50. doi:10.1300/J158v01n03_02

Becker, J. V., Stinson, J., Tromp, S., & Messer, G. (2003). Characteristics of individuals petitioned for civil commitment. *International Journal of Offender Therapy and Comparative Criminology, 47*(2), 185–195. doi:10.1177/0306624X03251114

Beech, A. R., Elliott, I. A., Birgden, A., & Findlater, D. (2008). The internet and child sexual offending: A criminological review. *Aggression and Violent Behavior, 13*(3), 216–228. doi:10.1016/j.avb.2008.03.007

Beech, A., Friendship, C., Erikson, M., & Hanson, R. K. (2002). The relationship between static and dynamic risk factors and reconviction in a sample of UK child abusers. *Sexual Abuse, 14*(2), 155–167.

Berah, E. F., & Myers, R. G. (1983). The offense records of a sample of convicted exhibitionists. *Bulletin of the American Academy of Psychiatry and the Law, 11*(4), 365–369.

Black, D. W., Gunter, T., Loveless, P., Allen, J., & Sieleni, B. (2010). Antisocial personality disorder in incarcerated offenders: Psychiatric comorbidity and quality of life. *Annals of Clinical Psychiatry, 22*(3), 113–120.

Blanchard, R., Klassen, P., Dickey, R., Kuban, M. E., & Blak, T. (2001). Sensitivity and specificity of the phallometric test for pedophilia in nonadmitting sex offenders. *Psychological Assessment, 13*(1), 118–126. doi:10.1037/1040-3590.13.1.118

Bolen, R. M., & Scannapieco, M. (1999). Prevalence of child sexual abuse: A corrective metanalysis. *Social Service Review, 73*(3), 281–313.

Bonnar-Kidd, K.K. (2010). Sex offender laws and prevention of sexual violence or recidivism. *American Journal of Public Health, 100*(3), 412–419.

Branaman, T. F., & Gallagher, S. N. (2005). Polygraph testing in sex offender treatment: A review of limitations. *American Journal of Forensic Psychology, 23*(1), 45–64.

Breiner, S. J. (1990). *Slaughter of the innocents: Child abuse through the ages and today.* New York, NY: Plenum.

Briere, J., & Elliott, D. M. (2003). Prevalence and psychological sequelae of self-reported childhood physical and sexual abuse in a general population sample of men and women. *Child Abuse and Neglect, 27*(10), 1205–1222. doi:10.1016/j.chiabu.2003.09.008

Bureau of Justice Statistics. (2008). *Bulletin: National crime victimization survey, criminal victimization, 2007.* [NCJ 224390]. Washington, DC: Author. Retrieved November 2012, from http://bjs.ojp.usdoj.gov/content/pub/pdf/cv07.pdf.

Center for Sex Offender Management. (2007). *Female sex offenders.* Retrieved July 2012, from http://www.csom.org/pubs/female_sex_offenders_brief.pdf.

Centers for Disease Control Prevention. (2006). Youth risk behavior surveillance-United States, 2005. *Morbidity and Mortality Weekly Report, 55*, SS-5.

Chivers, M. L. (2005). A brief review and discussion of sex differences in the specificity of sexual arousal. *Sexual and Relationship Therapy, 20*(4), 377–390. doi:10.1080/14681990500238802

Chivers, M. L., Seto, M. C., & Blanchard, R. (2007). Gender and sexual orientation differences in sexual response to sexual activities versus gender of actors in sexual films. *Journal of Personality and Social Psychology, 93*(6), 1108–1121. doi:10.1037/0022-3514.93.6.1108

Christopher, K., Lutz-Zois, C. J., & Reinhardt, A. R. (2007). Female sexual-offenders: Personality pathology as a mediator of the relationship between childhood sexual abuse history and sexual abuse. *Child Abuse and Neglect, 31*(8), 871–883. doi:10.1016/j.chiabu.2007.02.006

Cook, E. B. (1934). Cultural marginality in sexual delinquency. *American Journal of Sociology, 39*, 493–500.

Cordoba, O. A., & Chapel, J. L. (1983). Medroxyprogesterone acetate antiandrogen treatment of hypersexuality in a pedophiliac sex offender. *American Journal of Psychiatry, 140*(8), 1036–1039.

Cortoni, F. (2010). Female sex offenders: A special sub group. In K. Harrison (Ed.), *Dealing with high risk sex offenders in the community: Risk management, treatment, and social responsibilities* (pp.159–173). Devon, UK: Willan.

Cortoni, F., Hanson, R. K., & Coache, M. (2009). Les délinquantes sexuelles: Prévalence et récidive [Female sexual offenders: Prevalence and recidivism]. *Revue international de criminogie et de police technique et scientifique, LXII*, 319–336.

Cortoni, F., Hanson, R., & Coache, M. (2010). The recidivism rates of female sexual offenders are low: A meta-analysis. *Sexual Abuse, 22*(4), 387–401. doi:10.1177/1079063210372142

Craig, L. A., Browne, K. D., Stringer, I., & Beech, A. (2005). Sexual recidivism: A review of static, dynamic and actuarial predictors. *Journal of Sexual Aggression, 11*(1), 65–84. doi:10.1080/13552600410001667733

Deming, A. (2008). Sex offender civil commitment programs: Current practices, characteristics, and resident demographics. *Journal of Psychiatry and Law, 36*(3), 439–461.

Denov, M. S. (2003). The myth of innocence: Sexual scripts and the recognition of child sexual abuse by female perpetrators. *Journal of Sex Research, 40*(3), 303–314. doi:10.1080/00224490309552195

Doren, D. M. (2002). *Evaluating sex offenders: A manual for civil commitments and beyond.* Thousand Oaks, CA: Sage.

Doren, D. M. (2004). Toward a multidimensional model for sexual recidivism risk. *Journal of Interpersonal Violence, 19*(8), 835–856. doi:10.1177/0886260504266882

Doshay, L. (1943). *The boy sex offender and his later career.* New York, NY: Grove & Stratton.

Douglas, E. M., & Finkelhor, D. (2005). Childhood sexual abuse fact sheet. Retrieved May 2014, from http://www.unh.edu/ccrc/factsheet/pdf/CSA-FS20.pdf.

Dowden, C., & Andrews, D. A. (1999). What works for female offenders: A meta-analytic review. *Crime and Delinquency, 45*(4), 438–452. doi:10.1177/0011128799045004002

Elliott, I. A., Beech, A. R., & Mandeville-Norden, R. (2013). The psychological profiles of internet, contact, and mixed internet/contact sex offenders. *Sexual Abuse, 25*(1), 3–20. doi:10.1177/1079063212439426

Elliott, I., Beech, A. R., Mandeville-Norden, R., & Hayes, E. (2009). Psychological profiles of Internet sexual offenders: Comparisons with contact sexual offenders. *Sexual Abuse, 21*(1), 76–92. doi:10.1177/1079063208326929

Endrass, J., Urbaniok, F., Held, L., Vetter, S., & Rossegger, A. (2009). Accuracy of the Static-99 in predicting recidivism in Switzerland. *International Journal of Offender Therapy and Comparative Criminology, 53*(4), 482–490. doi:10.1177/0306624X07312952

English, K., Jones, L., Pasini-Hill, D., Patrick, D., & Cooley-Towell, S. (2000). The value of polygraph testing in sex offender management. *Colorado Department of Public Safety.* Retrieved May 2104, from https://www.ncjrs.gov/pdffiles1/nij/grants/199673.pdf

Epperson, D. L., Kaul, J. D., & Hesselton, D. (1998, October). Final report on the development of the Minnesota sex offender screening tool—Revised (MnSOST-R). Presentation at the Association for the Treatment of Sexual Abusers 17th Annual Conference, Vancouver, BC.

Epperson, D., Ralston, R., Fowers, D., DeWitt, J., & Gore, K.S. (2006). Actuarial risk assessment with juveniles who sexually offend: Development of the Juvenile Sexual Offense Recidivism Risk Assessment Tool-II (JSORRAT-II). In D. S. Prescott (Ed.), *Risk assessment of youth who have sexually abused* (pp. 118–169). Oklahoma City, OK: Wood 'n' Barnes.

Faller, K. (1995). A clinical sample of women who have sexually abused children. *Journal of Child Sexual Abuse, 4*(3), 13–30. doi:10.1300/J070v04n03_02

Fazel, S., & Danesh, J. (2002). Serious mental disorder in 23,000 prisoners: A systematic review of 62 surveys. *Lancet, 359*(9306), 545–550. doi:10.1016/S0140-6736(02)07740-1

Fazel, S., Sjöstedt, G., Grann, M., & Långström, N. (2010). Sexual offending in women and psychiatric disorder: A national case–control study. *Archives of Sexual Behavior, 39*(1), 161–167. doi:10.1007/s10508-008-9375-4

Fedoroff, J. (1995). Antiandrogens vs. serotonergic medications in the treatment of sex offenders: A preliminary compliance study. *Canadian Journal of Human Sexuality, 4*(2), 111–122.

Fernandez, Y. (2009). The standardisation of phallometry. In A. R. Beech, L. A. Craig, & K. D. Browne (Eds.), *Assessment and treatment of sex offenders: A handbook* (pp. 129–143). New York, NY: Wiley.

Finkelhor, D., Hammer, H., & Sedlak, A. J. (2004) *Sexually assaulted children: National estimates and characteristics.* Washington, DC: Office of Juvenile Justice and Delinquency Programs.

Finklehor, D., & Jones, L. (2006). Why have child maltreatment and child victimization declined? *Journal of Social Issues, 62*(4), 685–716. doi:10.1111/j.1540-4560.2006.00483.x

Finkelhor, D., Ormrod, D., & Chaffin, M. (2009). Juveniles who commit sex offenses against minors. *Juvenile Justice Bulletin, December,* 1–11.

Finkelhor, D., Ormrod, R., Turner, H., & Hamby, S. L. (2005). The victimization of children and youth: A comprehensive, national survey. *Child Maltreatment, 10*(1), 5–25. doi:10.1177/1077559504271287

Finkelhor, D., Turner, H., Ormrod, R., & Hamby, S. L. (2010). Trends in childhood violence and abuse exposure: Evidence from 2 national surveys. *Archives of Pediatrics and Adolescent Medicine, 164*(3), 238. doi:10.1001/archpediatrics.2009.283

Ford, H. J., Rose, J., & Thrift, S. (2009). An evaluation of the applicability of the self-regulation model to sexual offenders with intellectual disabilities. *Journal of Forensic Psychiatry and Psychology, 20*(3), 440–457. doi:10.1080/14789940802638317

Frances, A., & First, M. B. (2011). Paraphilia NOS, nonconsent: Not ready for the courtroom. *Journal of the American Academy of Psychiatry and the Law, 39*(4), 555–561.

Francia, C. A., Coolidge, F. L., White, L. A., Segal, D. L., Cahill, B. S., & Estey, J. A. (2010). Personality disorder profiles in incarcerated male rapists and child molesters. *American Journal of Forensic Psychology, 28*(3), 1–14.

Freund, K. (1965). Diagnosing heterosexual pedophilia by means of a test for sexual interest. *Behaviour Research and Therapy, 3*(4), 229–234. doi:10.1016/0005-7967(65)90031-8

Freund, K. (1967). Erotic preference in pedophilia. *Behavior Research and Therapy, 5,* 339–393.

Gannon, T. A., & Ward, T. (2008). Rape: Psychopathology and theory. In D. R. Laws & W. T. O'Donohue (Eds), *Sexual deviance: Theory, assessment, and treatment* (pp. 336–355). New York, NY: Guilford Press.

George, W. H., & Marlatt, G. A. (1989). Introduction. In D. R. Laws (Ed.), *Relapse prevention with sex offenders* (pp. 1–31). New York, NY: Guilford Press.

Gordon, H. (2008). The treatment of paraphilias: A historical perspective. *Criminal Behaviour and Mental Health, 18*(2), 79–87. doi:10.1002/cbm.687

Grant, J. E. (2005). Clinical characteristics and psychiatric comorbidity in males with exhibitionism. *Journal of Clinical Psychiatry, 66*(11), 1367–1371. doi:10.4088/JCP.v66n1104

Green, A. H., & Kaplan, M. S. (1994). Psychiatric impairment and childhood victimization experiences in female child molesters. *Journal of the American Academy of Child and Adolescent Psychiatry, 33*(7), 954–961. doi:10.1097/00004583-199409000-00004

Greenberg, D. M., & Bradford, J. M. W. (1997). Treatment of the paraphilic disorders: A review of the role of selective serotonin reuptake inhibitors. *Sexual Abuse, 9,* 349–360.

Greenberg, D. M., Bradford, J. W., Curry, S., & O'Rourke, A. (1996). A comparison of treatment of paraphilias with three serotonin reuptake inhibitors: A retrospective study. *Bulletin of the American Academy of Psychiatry and the Law, 24*(4), 525–532.

Grossman, L. S., Martis, B., & Fichtner, C. G. (1999). Are sex offenders treatable? A research overview. *Psychiatric Services, 50*(3), 349–361.

Groth, A. N. (1979) *Men who rape: The psychology of the offender.* New York, NY: Plenum Press.

Grubin, D., & Madsen, L. (2006). Accuracy and utility of post-conviction polygraph testing of sex offenders. *British Journal of Psychiatry, 188*(5), 479–483. doi:10.1192/bjp.bp.105.008953

Grudzinskas, A. J., Brodsky, D. J., Zaitchik, M. J., Fedoroff, P., DiCataldo, F., & Clayfield, J. C. (2009). Sexual predator laws and their history. In F. M. Saleh, A. J. Grudzinskas, J. M. Bradford, & D. J. Brodsky (Eds), *Sex offenders: Identification, risk assessment, treatment, and legal issues* (pp. 386–411). Oxford, UK: Oxford University Press.

Hanson, R. K. (1997). *The development of a brief actuarial risk scale for sexual offense recidivism.* [User Report 97-04[. Ottawa, ON: Department of the Solicitor General of Canada.

Hanson, R., Bourgon, G., Helmus, L., & Hodgson, S. (2009). The principles of effective correctional treatment also apply to sexual offenders: A meta-analysis. *Criminal Justice and Behavior, 36*(9), 865–891. doi:10.1177/0093854809338545

Hanson, R., & Bussière, M. T. (1998). Predicting relapse: A meta-analysis of sexual offender recidivism studies. *Journal of Consulting and Clinical Psychology, 66*(2), 348–362. doi:10.1037/0022-006X.66.2.348

Hanson, R. K., Gordon, A., Harris, A. J., Marques, J. K., Murphy, W., Quinsey, V. L., & Seto, M. C. (2002). First report of the collaborative outcome data project on the effectiveness of psychological treatment for sex offenders. *Sex Abuse, 14*, 169–194.

Hanson, R., & Morton-Bourgon, K. E. (2005). The characteristics of persistent sexual offenders: A meta-analysis of recidivism studies. *Journal of Consulting and Clinical Psychology, 73*(6), 1154–1163. doi:10.1037/0022-006X.73.6.1154

Hanson, R., & Morton-Bourgon, K. E. (2009). The accuracy of recidivism risk assessments for sexual offenders: A meta-analysis of 118 prediction studies. *Psychological Assessment, 21*(1), 1–21. doi:10.1037/a0014421

Hanson, R. F., Resnick, H. S., Saunders, B. E., Kilpatrick, D. G., & Best, C. (1999). Factors related to the reporting of childhood rape. *Child Abuse and Neglect, 23*(6), 559–569. doi:10.1016/S0145-2134(99)00028-9

Hanson, R., & Thornton, D. (2000). Improving risk assessments for sex offenders: A comparison of three actuarial scales. *Law and Human Behavior, 24*(1), 119–136. doi:10.1023/A:1005482921333

Harris, D. A. (2010). Theories of female sexual offending. In T. A. Gannon & F. Cortoni (Eds). *Female sexual offenders: Theory, assessment, treatment* (pp. 31–51). West Sussex, UK: Wiley.

Hazelwood, R., & Burgess, A. (1987). *Practical aspects of rape investigation: A multidisciplinary approach.* New York, NY: Elsevier.

Hinderliter, A. C. (2011). Defining paraphilia in DSM-5: Do not disregard grammar. *Journal of Sex and Marital Therapy, 37*(1), 17–31. doi:10.1080/0092623X.2011.533567

Hislop, J. (2001). *Female sex offenders: What therapists, law enforcement, and child protective services need to know.* Ravensdale, WA: Issues Press.

Hood, R., Shute, S., Feilzer, M., & Wilcox, A. (2002). Sex offenders emerging from long-term imprisonment. A study of their long-term reconviction rates and of parole board members' judgments of their risk. *British Journal of Criminology, 42*(2), 371–394. doi:10.1093/bjc/42.2.371

Howitt, D., & Sheldon, K. (2007). The role of cognitive distortions in paedophilic offending: Internet and contact offenders compared. *Psychology, Crime and Law, 13*(5), 469–486. doi:10.1080/10683160601060564

In re Hendricks, 912 P.2d 129 (Kan. 1996).

Jackson, R. L., & Hess, D. T. (2007). Evaluation for civil commitment of sex offenders: A survey of experts. *Sexual Abuse, 19*(4), 425–448.

Johansson-Love, J., & Fremouw, W. (2006). A critique of the female sexual perpetrator research. *Aggression and Violent Behavior, 11*(1), 12–26. doi:10.1016/j.avb.2005.05.001

Jones, L. M., Finkelhor, D., & Kopiec, K. (2001). Why is sexual abuse declining? A survey of state child protection administrators. *Child Abuse and Neglect*, *25*(9), 1139–1158. doi:10.1016/S0145-2134(01)00263-0

Kafka, M. P., & Hennen, J. (2000). Psychostimulant augmentation during treatment with selective serotonin reuptake inhibitors in men with paraphilia-related disorders: A case series. *Journal of Clinical Psychiatry*, *61*(9), 664–670. doi:10.4088/JCP.v61n0912

Kansas v. Hendricks, 521 U.S. 346 (1997).

King, C. A. (1999). Fighting the devil we don't know: Kansas v. Hendricks, a case study exploring the civilization of criminal punishment and its ineffectiveness in preventing child sexual abuse. *William and Mary Law Review*, *40*, 1427–1469.

Kingston, D. A., Yates, P. M., & Firestone, P. (2012). The self-regulation model of sexual offending: Relationship to risk and need. *Law and Human Behavior*, *36*(3), 215–224. doi:10.1037/h0093960

Knight, R. A. (1999). Validation of a typology for rapists. *Journal of Interpersonal Violence*, *14*(3), 303–330. doi:10.1177/088626099014003006

Knight, R. A., & Prentky, R. A. (1990). Classifying sexual offenders: The development and corroboration of taxonomic models. In W. Marshall, D. Laws, & H. Barbaree (Eds.), *The handbook of sexual assault: Issues, theories, and treatment of the offender* (pp. 23–52). New York, NY: Plenum Press.

von Krafft-Ebing, R. R. (1898). *Psychopathia sexualis: A medico-legal study*. (Trans.). Oxford, UK: F. A. Davis.

Krone, T. (2004). A typology of online child pornography offending. *Trends and Issues in Crime and Criminal Justice*, *279*, 1–6.

Lalumière, M. L., Quinsey, V. L., Harris, G. T., Rice, M. E., & Trautrimas, C. (2003). Are rapists differentially aroused by coercive sex in phallometric assessments? *Annals of the New York Academy of Sciences*, *989*(1), 211–224.

Långström, N., & Seto, M. C. (2006). Exhibitionistic and voyeuristic behavior in a Swedish national population survey. *Archives of Sexual Behavior*, *35*(4), 427–435. doi:10.1007/s10508-006-9042-6

Långström, N., Sjöstedt, G., & Grann, M. (2004). Psychiatric disorders and recidivism in sexual offenders. *Sexual Abuse: Journal of Research and Treatment*, *16*(2), 139–150. doi:10.1177/107906320401600204

Lanning, K. V. (2001). Child molesters: A behavioral analysis (4th ed.). Retrieved February 2013, from http://missingkids.com/en_US/publications/NC70.pdf.

Laulik, S., Allam, J., & Sheridan, L. (2007). An investigation into maladaptive personality functioning in Internet sex offenders. *Psychology, Crime and Law*, *13*(5), 523–535. doi:10.1080/10683160701340577

Lavin, M. (2008). Voyeurism: Psychopathology and theory. In Laws, D. R. & W. T. O'Donohue (Eds.), *Sexual deviance: Theory, assessment, and treatment* (pp. 61–75). New York, NY: Guilford Press.

Laws, D. R. (Ed.). (1989). *Relapse prevention with sex offenders*. New York, NY: Guilford Press.

Laws, D. R. (1995). Central elements in relapse prevention procedures with sex offenders. *Psychology, Crime and Law*, *2*(1), 41–53. doi:10.1080/10683169508409763

Laws, D. R., Hanson, R., Osborn, C. A., & Greenbaum, P. E. (2000). Classification of child molesters by plethysmographic assessment of sexual arousal and a self-report measure of sexual preference. *Journal of Interpersonal Violence*, *15*(12), 1297–1312. doi:10.1177/088626000015012004

Letourneau, E. J. (2002). A comparison of objective measures of sexual arousal and interest: Visual reaction time and penile plethysmography. *Sexual Abuse, 14*(3), 207–223. doi:10.1177/107906320201400302

Letourneau, E. J., & Miner, M. H. (2005). Juvenile sex offenders: A case against the legal and clinical status quo. *Sexual Abuse, 17*(3), 293–312. doi:10.1177/107906320501700304

Levenson, J. S. (2004). Sexual predator civil commitment: A comparison of selected and released offenders. *International Journal of Offender Therapy and Comparative Criminology, 48*(6), 638–648. doi:10.1177/0306624X04265089

Lewis, C. F., & Stanley, C. R. (2000). Women accused of sexual offenses. *Behavioral Sciences and the Law, 18*(1), 73–81.

Lieb, R. (1996). Community notification laws: A step toward more effective solutions. *Journal of Interpersonal Violence, 11*(2), 298–300. doi:10.1177/088626096011002013

Lieb, R., & Matson, S. (2000). *Sexual predator commitment laws in the United States.* Olympia: Washington State Institute for Public Policy.

Lockmuller, M., Fisher, D., & Beech, A.R. (2008). Sexual offenders with mental health problems: Epidemiology, assessment, and treatment. In K. Soothill, M. Dolan, & P. Rogers (Eds.), *Handbook of forensic mental health* (pp. 442–475). Devon, UK: Willan.

Lösel, F., & Schmucker, M. (2005). The effectiveness of treatment for sexual offenders: A comprehensive meta-analysis. *Journal of Experimental Criminology, 1*(1), 117–146. doi:10.1007/s11292-004-6466-7

Magaletta, P. R., Faust, E., Bickart, W., & McLearen, A. M. (2012). Exploring clinical and personality characteristics of adult male internet-only child pornography offenders. *International Journal of Offender Therapy and Comparative Criminology.* doi: 10.1177/0306624X12465271 Epub ahead of print.

Maletzky, B. M., & Steinhauser, C. (2002). A 25-year follow-up of cognitive/behavioral therapy with 7,275 sexual offenders. *Behavior Modification, 26*(2), 123–147. doi:10.1177/0145445502026002001

Marques, J. K., Wiederanders, M., Day, D. M., Nelson, C., & van Ommeren, A. (2005). Effects of a relapse prevention program on sexual recidivism: Final results from California's Sex Offender Treatment and Evaluation Project (SOTEP). *Sexual Abuse, 17*(1), 79–107. doi:10.1177/107906320501700108

McCabe, M. P., & Wauchope, M. (2005). Behavioural characteristics of rapists. *Journal of Sexual Aggression, 11*(3), 235–247. doi:10.1080/13552600500272820

McConaghy, N. (1999). Paraphilias. In V. B. Van Hasselt & M. Hersen (Eds.), *Handbook of psychological approaches with violent offenders: Contemporary strategies and issues* (pp. 207–243). New York: Plenum Publishers.

McGrath, R. J., Cumming, G., & Burchard, B. L. (2003). *Current practices and trends in sexual abuser management: The Safer Society 2002 nationwide survey.* Brandon, VT: Safer Society Press.

McGrath, R. J., Cumming, G. F., Burchard, B. L., Zeoli, S., & Ellerby, L. (2010). *Current practices and emerging trends in sexual abuser management.* Brandon, VT: Safer Society Press.

McLawsen, J. E., Scalora, M. J., & Darrow, C. (2012). Civilly committed sex offenders: A description and interstate comparison of populations. *Psychology, Public Policy, and Law, 18*(3), 453–476. doi:10.1037/a0026116

Miller, H. A., Amenta, A. E., & Conroy, M. A. (2005). Sexually violent predator evaluations: Empirical evidence, strategies for professionals, and research directions. *Law and Human Behavior, 29*(1), 29–54. doi: 10.1007/s10979-005-1398-y

Money, J. (1970). Use of an androgen-depleting hormone in the treatment of male sex offenders. *Journal of Sex Research, 6*(3), 165–172. doi:10.1080/00224497009550662

Motivans, M., & Kyckelhahn, T. (2007). *Federal prosecution of child sex exploitation offenders, 2006.* Washington, DC: US Department of Justice, Office of Justice Programs, Bureau of Justice Statistics.

Murphy, W. D., & Page, I. J. (2008). Exhibitionism: Psychopathology and theory. In Laws, D. R. & W. T. O'Donohue (Eds.), *Sexual deviance: Theory, assessment, and treatment* (pp. 61–75). New York, NY: Guilford Press.

Parks, G. A., & Bard, D. E. (2006). Risk factors for adolescent sex offender recidivism: Evaluation of predictive factors and comparison of three groups based upon victim type. *Sexual Abuse, 18*(4), 319–342. doi:10.1177/107906320601800402

Pithers, W. D., Marques, J. K., Gibat, C. C., & Marlatt, G. A. (1983). Relapse prevention with sexual aggressives: A self-control model of treatment and maintenance of change. In J. G. Greer & I. R. Stuart (Eds.), *The sexual aggressor: Current perspectives on treatment* (pp. 214–239). New York, NY: Van Nostrand Reinhold.

Polaschek, D. L. (2003). Relapse prevention, offense process models, and the treatment of sexual offenders. *Professional Psychology: Research and Practice, 34*(4), 361–367. doi:10.1037/0735-7028.34.4.361

Polizzi, D. M., MacKenzie, D., & Hickman, L. J. (1999). What works in adult sex offender treatment? A review of prison and non-prison-based treatment programs. *International Journal of Offender Therapy and Comparative Criminology, 43*(3), 357–374. doi:10.1177/0306624X99433008

Prentky, R., & Barbaree, H. (2011). Commentary: Hebephilia—A would-be paraphilia caught in the twilight zone between prepubescence and adulthood. *Journal of the American Academy of Psychiatry and the Law, 39*(4), 506–510.

Prentky, R., Harris, B., Frizell, K., & Righthand, S. (2000). An actuarial procedure for assessing risk with juvenile sex offenders. *Sexual Abuse, 12*(2), 71–93. doi:10.1177/107906320001200201

Quinsey, V. L., & Chaplin, T. C. (1988). Penile responses of child molesters and normals to descriptions of encounters with children involving sex and violence. *Journal of Interpersonal Violence, 3*(3), 259–274. doi:10.1177/088626088003003001

Quinsey, V. L., Harris, G. T., Rice, M. E., & Cormier, C. A. (2006). *Violent offenders: Appraising and managing risk* (2nd ed.). Washington, DC: American Psychological Association.

Reijnen, L., Bulten, E., & Nijman, H. (2009). Demographic and personality characteristics of internet child pornography downloaders in comparison to other offenders. *Journal of Child Sexual Abuse, 18*(6), 611–622. doi:10.1080/10538710903317232

Reitzel, L. R., & Carbonell, J. L. (2006). The effectiveness of sexual offender treatment for juveniles as measured by recidivism: A meta-analysis. *Sexual Abuse, 18*(4), 401–421. doi:10.1177/107906320601800407

Rich, P. (2009). Understanding the complexities and needs of adolescent sex offenders. In A. R. Beech, A. C. Leam, & K. D. Browne (Eds.), *Assessment and treatment of sex offenders: A handbook* (pp. 432–452). London,UK: Wiley.

Righthand, S., Prentky, R., Knight, R., Carpenter, E., Hecker, J. E., & Nangle, D. (2005). Factor structure and validation of the Juvenile Sex Offender Assessment Protocol (J-SOAP). *Sexual Abuse, 17*(1), 13–30. doi:10.1177/107906320501700103

Roberts, C. F., Doren, D. M., & Thornton, D. (2002). Dimensions associated with assessments of sex offender recidivism risk. *Criminal Justice and Behavior, 29*(5), 569–589. doi:10.1177/009385402236733

Rouseau, M. M., & Cortoni, F. (2010). Mental health needs of female sexual offenders. In T. A. Gannon & F. Cortoni (Eds.), *Female sexual offenders: Theory, assessment, and treatment* (pp. 73–86). Hoboken, NJ: Wiley-Blackwell.

Seto, M. C. (2008). *Pedophilia and sexual offending against children: Theory, assessment, and intervention.* Washington, DC: American Psychological Association.

Seto, M. C. (2009). Pedophilia. *Annual Review of Clinical Psychology, 5,* 391–407.

Seto, M. C., Hanson, R. K., & Babchishin, K. M. (2011). Contact sexual offending by men with online sexual offenses. *Sexual Abuse, 23*(1), 124–145. doi:10.1177/1079063210369013

Seto, M. C., & Lalumiére, M. L. (2001). A brief screening scale to identify pedophilic interests among child molesters. *Sexual Abuse, 13*(1), 15–25. doi:10.1177/107906320101300103

Seto, M. C., & Lalumière, M. L. (2010). What is so special about male adolescent sexual offending? A review and test of explanations through meta-analysis. *Psychological Bulletin, 136*(4), 526–575. doi:10.1037/a0019700

Shaw, J. (1999). *Sexual aggression.* Washington, DC: American Psychiatric Press.

Silovsky, J. F., & Niec, L. (2002). Characteristics of young children with sexual behavior problems: A pilot study. *Child Maltreatment, 7*(3), 187–197. doi:10.1177/1077559502007003002

Simon, W. T., & Shouten, G. W. (1993). The plethysmograph reconsidered: Comments on Barker and Howell. *Bulletin of the American Academy of Psychiatry and the Law, 21*(4), 505–512.

Sjöstedt, G., & Långström, N. (2001). Actuarial assessment of sex offender recidivism risk: A cross-validation of the RRASOR and the Static-99 in Sweden. *Law and Human Behavior, 25*(6), 629–645. doi:10.1023/A:1012758307983

Stadtland, C., Hollweg, M., Kleindienst, N., Dietl, J., Reich, U., & Nedopil, N. (2006). Evaluation of risk assessment instruments for sex offenders. *Der Nervenarzt, 77*(5), 587.

State v. Spencer, 459 S.E.2d 812, 119 N.C. App. 662 (Ct. App. 1995).

Steel, C. (2009). Child pornography in peer-to-peer networks. *Child Abuse and Neglect, 33*(8), 560–568. doi:10.1016/j.chiabu.2008.12.011

Stinson, J. D., Becker, J. V., & Tromp, S. (2005). A preliminary study on findings of psychopathy and affective disorders in adult sex offenders. *International Journal of Law and Psychiatry, 28*(6), 637–649. doi:10.1016/j.ijlp.2004.10.001

Stoléru, S., Grégoire, M., Gérard, D., Decety, J., Lafarge, E., Cinotti, L., ... Comar, D. (1999). Neuroanatomical correlates of visually evoked sexual arousal in human males. *Archives of Sexual Behavior, 28*(1), 1–21. doi:10.1023/A:1018733420467

Strickland, S. M. (2008). Female sex offenders: Exploring issues of personality, trauma, and cognitive distortions. *Journal of Interpersonal Violence, 23*(4), 474–489. doi:10.1177/0886260507312944

Terry, K. (2006). *Sexual offenses and offenders: Theory, practice, and policy.* Belmont, CA: Thompson Wadsworth.

Thornton, D. (2002). Constructing and testing a framework for dynamic risk assessment. *Sexual Abuse, 14,* 137–151.

Tjaden, P., & Thoennes, N. (2006). *Extent, nature, and consequences of rape victimization: Findings from the National Violence against Women Survey.* [NCJ 210346]. Washington, DC: US Department of Justice. Retrieved November 2012, from https://www.ncjrs.gov/pdffiles1/nij/210346.pdf.

Turner, K., Miller, H. A., & Henderson, C. E. (2008). Latent profile analyses of offense and personality characteristics in a sample of incarcerated female sexual offenders. *Criminal Justice and Behavior, 35*(7), 879–894. doi:10.1177/0093854808318922

United States Department of Justice. (2008). *Criminal victimization in the United States, 2006 statistical tables: National Crime Victimization Survey.* [NCJ 223436]. Washington, DC: Author. Retrieved November 2012, from http://bjs.ojp.usdoj.gov/content/pub/pdf/cvus0602.pdf.

US v. Comstock, 130 S. Ct. 1949, 560 U.S., 176 L. Ed. 2d 878 (2010).

US v. Powers, 59 F.3d 1460 (4th Cir. 1995).

van Wijk, A. H., Blokland, A. J., Duits, N. N., Vermeiren, R. R., & Harkink, J. J. (2007). Relating psychiatric disorders, offender and offence characteristics in a sample of adolescent sex offenders and non-sex offenders. *Criminal Behaviour and Mental Health, 17*(1), 15–30. doi:10.1002/cbm.628

Vandiver, D. M. (2006). Female sex offenders: A comparison of solo offenders and co-offenders. *Violence and Victims, 21*(3), 339–354. doi:10.1891/vivi.21.3.339

Vandiver, D. M., & Walker, J. T. (2002). Female sex offenders: An overview and analysis of 40 cases. *Criminal Justice Review, 27*(2), 284–300. doi:10.1177/073401680202700205

Vess, J., & Skelton, A. (2010). Sexual and violent recidivism by offender type and actuarial risk: Reoffending rates for rapists, child molesters and mixed-victim offenders. *Psychology, Crime and Law, 16*(7), 541–554. doi:10.1080/10683160802612908

Vitopoulos, N. A., Peterson-Badali, M., & Skilling, T. A. (2012). The relationship between matching service to criminogenic need and recidivism in male and female youth: Examining the RNR principles in practice. *Criminal Justice and Behavior, 39*(8), 1025–1041. doi:10.1177/0093854812442895

Waggoner, R. W., & Boyd, D. R. (1941). Juvenile aberrant sexual behavior. *American Journal of Orthopsychiatry, 11*, 275–292. doi:10.1111/j.1939-0025.1941.tb05804.x

Wakefield, J. C. (2012). The DSM-5's proposed new categories of sexual disorder: The problem of false positives in sexual diagnosis.*Clinical Social Work Journal, 40*(2), 213–223. doi:10.1007/s10615-011-0353-2

Wakeling, H., Howard, P., & Barnett, G. (2011). Comparing the validity of the RM2000 scales and OGRS3 for predicting recidivism by internet sexual offenders. *Sexual Abuse, 23*(1), 146–168. doi:10.1177/1079063210375974

Ward, T. (2007). On a clear day you can see forever: Integrating values and skills in sex offender treatment. *Journal of Sexual Aggression, 13*(3), 187–201. doi:10.1080/13552600701794036

Ward, T., & Gannon, T. A. (2006). Rehabilitation, etiology, and self-regulation: The comprehensive good lives model of treatment for sexual offenders. *Aggression and Violent Behavior, 11*(1), 77–94. doi:10.1016/j.avb.2005.06.001

Ward, T., & Hudson, S. M. (1998). A model of the relapse process in sexual offenders. *Journal of Interpersonal Violence, 13*(6), 700–725. doi:10.1177/088626098013006003

Ward, T., & Maruna, S. (2007). *Rehabilitation: Beyond the risk paradigm.* London, UK: Routledge.

Ward, T., Yates, P. M., & Long, C. (2006). *The self-regulation model of the offence and relapse process: Vol, 2. Treatment.* Victoria, BC: Pacific Psychological Assessment Corporation.

Ward, T., Yates, P. M., & Willis, G. M. (2012). The good lives model and the risk need responsivity model: A critical response to Andrews, Bonta, and Wormith (2011). *Criminal Justice and Behavior, 39*(1), 94–110. doi:10.1177/0093854811426085

Wilson, R. J., & Yates, P. M. (2009). Effective interventions and the Good Lives Model: Maximizing treatment gains for sexual offenders. *Aggression and Violent Behavior, 14*(3), 157–161. doi:10.1016/j.avb.2009.01.007

Witt, P. H., & Conroy, M. (2009). *Evaluation of sexually violent predators.* New York, NY: Oxford University Press.

Wolak, J., Finkelhor, D., & Mitchell, K. (2011). Child pornography possessors: Trends in offender and case characteristics. *Sexual Abuse, 23*(1), 22–42. doi:10.1177/1079063210372143

Wollert, R. (2011). Paraphilic Coercive Disorder does not belong in DSM-5 for statistical, historical, conceptual, and practical reasons. *Archives of Sexual Behavior, 40*(6), 1097–1098. doi:10.1007/s10508-011-9814-5

Worling, J.R. (2004). The estimate of risk of adolescent sexual offense recidivism (ERASOR): Preliminary psychometric data. *Sexual Abuse, 16*(3), 235–254.

Yates, P. M., & Kingston, D. A. (2006). The Self-Regulation Model of Sexual Offending: The relationship between offence pathways and static and dynamic sexual offence risk. *Sexual Abuse, 18*(3), 259–270. doi:10.1177/107906320601800304

Yates, P. M., Prescott, D., & Ward, T. (2010). *Applying the good lives and self-regulation models to sex offender treatment: A practical guide for clinicians.* Brandon, VT: Safer Society Press.

11

Under the Color of Authority

Police Officers As Violent Offenders

DAVID M. COREY AND CASEY O. STEWART ■

Nearly 800,000 police officers serve in more than 18,000 law enforcement agencies in the United States at the federal, state, county, and municipal levels (Bartol & Bartol, 2004; Bureau of Justice Statistics, 2012). Law enforcement agencies are paramilitary organizations and the job of police officer—a combination of peacekeeper, law enforcer, social worker, and civilian warrior—is substantially different from other occupations. This high-risk profession is demanding, stressful, and dangerous, and those who serve in it function as the gatekeepers of the criminal justice system to maintain social order and protect the public from harm (Scrivner, 1994). To be sure, the police officer's role is "one of the most complex in our society" (Baehr, Furcon, & Froemel, 1968, p. 226; Super, Blau, Wells, & Murdock, 1993).

Police officers are authorized to use force when warranted—a license that, left unbridled, can result in brutal and even fatal consequences. Police officers are the only agents of civil society authorized to use lethal force prior to adjudication, and the exercise of their power "may literally save or destroy individuals" (Carlson & Singer, 1975, p. 2). The discretion they are given about how to enforce the law and by what means they will maintain order and keep the peace is a demanding authority that requires an array of emotional, interpersonal, decisional, and attitudinal competencies (Ones, Viswesvaran, & Dilchert, 2004). Indeed, it is the constant potential for the use of deadly force by a police officer that dominates every police–citizen interaction (Bittner, 1990). This intrinsic feature of policing underlies Klockars's (1985) classic assertion that "[n]o police anywhere has ever existed, nor is it possible to conceive of a genuine police ever existing, that does not claim the right to compel other people forcibly to do something" (pp. 9–10).

Few occupations have been the object of such public attention, controversy, and efforts to predict and alter violent conduct. Headlines and media reports of unwarranted police violence and abuse of power are a major concern of law enforcement agencies and have a significant impact on public trust and officers' ability to police effectively. Indeed, even a single incident of police use of excessive or unnecessary force can alienate communities to the point of civil disorder (Riksheim & Chermak, 1993). Because of the high stakes associated with the occupation, law enforcement personnel are expected to be of strong moral character and psychological resilience, and not to engage in behavior that violates laws or brings disrepute to the employing agency, whether on or off duty.

CLASSIFICATION OF POLICE VIOLENCE

Later in this chapter we discuss the substantial efforts invested in the selection and retention of police officers with high moral character. Partially because of these activities, the incidence of police use of force is low (International Association of Chiefs of Police [IACP], 2001; Lersch & Mieczkowski, 2005); despite them, unlawful police violence persists. Yet any attempt at understanding police violence will first require clarifying what is meant by the term. As with the discussion of other kinds of violence, police violence encompasses a wide swath and diverse mix of behavior. It includes deadly force necessary to protect innocent lives, as well as violence having no other lawful or noble purpose; it encompasses both on-duty and off-duty violence, some of which results from the officer's exploitation of police authority and some that is entirely independent of it. Sorting these highly varied forms of police violence into conceptually coherent clusters may facilitate a sharper understanding of their distinctive risk and protective factors.

Lee and Vaughn (2010) analyzed 86 federal lawsuits alleging the negligent use of deadly force by individual police officers. Among those cases involving liability against the officers, Lee and Vaughn found two categories of violence: (1) use of deadly force against suspects who were surrendering to police authority (including violence that occurs at the conclusion of long and dangerous high-speed chases and foot pursuits, resulting from "adrenalin overload," and violence resulting from "street justice"), and (2) deadly force against uncooperative suspects. This latter group primarily included cases involving (a) overreaction to the behavior of mentally ill or suicidal persons, and (b) overreaction to contemptuous or noncompliant behavior of citizens (see Garner, Maxwell, & Heraux, 2002, for a discussion of the impact of resistance on police use of force).

Fyfe (1986) distinguished between extralegal force, or brutality, and unnecessary police violence. He regarded the former as intentional physical abuse inflicted maliciously and for no legitimate police purpose. This includes instances of violence classified by Lee and Vaughn as "street justice," as well as some of the "abuse of authority" cases resulting from overreaction. In contrast, Fyfe considered unnecessary police violence to result from police incompetence or carelessness rather than malice.

In a study of 1,543 New York City police officers terminated for cause between 1975 and 1996, Kane and White (2009) identified eight categories of career-ending police misconduct, two of which involved violence: (1) assaultive behavior, except for profit-motivated robberies, by off-duty officers, and (2) offenses by on-duty officers that involved "the use of excessive force, psychological abuse, or discrimination based on citizens' membership in a class (i.e., gender, race, ethnicity, or sexual preference)" (p. 745). They reported that 11.6% of the terminations resulted from off-duty assaults and 4.8% from on-duty abuse. Less than one-tenth of 1% of NYPD officers employed during the study period was fired for on-duty abuse.

We propose a police violence classification matrix (see Table 11.1) that combines elements from these research findings and borrows from another common typology of violence that has helped bring an organizing schema to related research. The Occupational Safety and Health Administration (OSHA) and National Institute of Occupational Safety and Health (NIOSH) workplace violence model (University of Iowa Injury Prevention Research Center [UIIPRC], 2001) classifies four types of offenders according to their placement in a 2 x 2 grid: whether they have a relationship with the victim and whether they have a relationship with the business. In the OSHA/NIOSH matrix, for example, Type III workplace violence involves an offender who has both a relationship with the victim and the business (i.e., worker-on-worker violence).

Classifications of police violence that combine extralegal violence and unnecessary or excessive force do little to aid researchers in understanding the risk and protective factors associated with each, inasmuch as excessive and unnecessary force may occur more often as a result of inadequate training or weapon use policies, whereas individual factors may contribute more to extralegal violence. Similarly, models that combine violence carried out in a law enforcement capacity with violence conducted outside of the police role also impede the discovery of the relative influence of individual versus organizational factors. In Table 11.1, we list the kinds of violent offenses associated with each type in our classification schema. In Table 11.2, we give notable examples of each.

Table 11.1 Classification of Police Violence

	Relationship to Police Role	
	Role Dependent	**Role Independent**
Relationship to Antecedent Aggression		
Aggression-Dependent	Type I • Excessive force • Unnecessary force	Type II • Violence occurring in the context of an altercation independent of the officer's occupational role (e.g., domestic violence, bar fights, road rage)
Aggression-Independent	Type III • Street justice • Intimidation • On-duty rape, assault, murder • Sexual exploitation/ assault reliant on police access or authority to find or lure victims	Type IV • Rape, assault, murder, and other extralegal violence independent of the officer's law enforcement role and outside the immediate context of an altercation

Table 11.2 NOTABLE EXAMPLES OF POLICE VIOLENCE CLASSIFICATION

	Relationship to Police Role	
	Role Dependent	**Role Independent**
Relationship to Antecedent Aggression		
Aggression-Dependent	Type I Following a high-speed chase of a vehicle driven by Rodney King, who was legally intoxicated at the time, LAPD officers Laurence Powell, Theodore Briseno, Timothy Wind, and Sgt. Stacey Koon were videotaped repeatedly striking King with their police batons in 1991. A state jury trial acquitted the officers of an assault charge and deadlocked on an excessive force charge, igniting the 1992 Los Angeles riots. Powell and Koon were subsequently convicted on federal charges of violating King's civil rights.	Type II Portland, Oregon, police officers Grant Bailey and Craig Hampton became involved in a dispute with a man while at a downtown club. After the man was thrown out by security, the officers followed him and beat him down in the street in front of more than a dozen witnesses. Both officers were convicted on assault charges.
Aggression-Independent	Type III California Highway Patrol Officer Craig Alan Peyer was convicted of the 1986 murder of college student Cara Knott. Peyer strangled Knott with a rope after he pulled her over in a marked CHP patrol car on an isolated freeway off-ramp and bludgeoned her with his flashlight. Peyer then threw her body off an abandoned bridge.	Type IV Former Tacoma, Washington, police officer Lee Giles was convicted in 2006 of repeatedly performing sex acts against a minor family member over many years, including during his active employment as a police officer.

The first of the two factors in our police violence typology involves the role of *antecedent aggression*, or the aggressive context in which violence unfolds. This factor distinguishes acts of violence that result from an aggressive interaction (e.g., verbal altercation, physical struggle, police chase) from those that occur in isolation from it (e.g., opportunistic and intentional violence). Aggression-dependent acts of violence involve disconstraint or a failure to modulate aggression in response to perceived stress, emotional arousal, or provocation, and they are varyingly referred to as impulsive, predatory, instrumental, reactive, affective, hostile, or proactive aggression (Siever, 2008). In contrast, aggression-independent violence encompasses the kind of extralegal, malicious violence that Fyfe (1986) distinguished from unnecessary force. It occupies its own place on the violence continuum rather than emerging as an unconstrained outgrowth of emotional arousal from antecedent aggression, and it is sometimes termed "premeditated aggression" (Siever, 2008, p. 430).

The second factor in the typology distinguishes acts of violence that depend on the authority or access of the badge in order to carry them out, from those that are independent of the law enforcement role. Some role-dependent violent acts occur in the service of otherwise legitimate objectives, such as the police officer who continues to kick a suspect after he has been handcuffed and is no longer resisting, while others simply exploit and depend upon the power over victims that accompanies the authority of a law enforcement officer. The police crime literature chronicles an ongoing debate on the relative merits of inclusion versus exclusion of an officer's off-duty conduct in criterion variables (Fyfe & Kane, 2006; Kane & White, 2009; Kappeler, Sluder, & Alpert, 1998). In our model, we include both while differentiating violence that implicates some aspect of the officer's occupational authority in carrying them out from violence that is independent of the position. This approach is consistent with the argument by Kane and White (2009) that "absent the abuse of the *police* authority to gain opportunity to commit the crimes, these acts of deviance should not be considered *police* crime" (p. 740).

Type I Police Violence

Type I cases of police violence occur in the context of preceding aggression and in connection with the officer's legitimate law enforcement functions—for example, at the end of a high-speed vehicle pursuit, during a volatile stand-off, or while attempting to handcuff a resistant citizen. Acts of Type I violence involve *excessive force*, that is, the use of more force than necessary to gain compliance in an incident that warrants the use of force, and *unnecessary force*, that is, the use of force prior to citizen resistance, or the continuation of force after resistance has stopped, resulting from emotional disconstraint or "adrenaline overload" (Lee & Vaughn, 2010). Type I offenses may constitute the highest proportion of police officer violence because they occur in the course of an otherwise lawful use of force. They may also be the most preventable through effective policies, training, education, and supervision (Alpert & Dunham, 2010; Bazley, Mieczkowski, & Lersch, 2009; Scrivner, 1994).

Type II Police Violence

Acts of Type II violence are unrelated to the offender's role as a law enforcement officer. Such acts may occur on duty and in full uniform or off duty in civilian clothes. As with Type I violence, they are also characterized by their escalation of violence in reaction to preceding or antecedent aggression. They can result from confrontations with neighbors, spouses, lovers, vendors, and motorists. Domestic assaults and other family violence commonly fall into this category of police violence. Because these incidents frequently occur off duty and result from emotional disconstraint, substance use, particularly alcohol, often plays an aggravating role in Type II violence.

In a study of police officers arrested for criminal offenses in all 50 states and the District of Columbia, Stinson, Liederbach, and Freiburger (2012) examined 2,119 criminal cases involving 1,746 police officers employed by 1,047 nonfederal law enforcement agencies. The authors reported that more than half (53.1%) of the offenses involved officers who were off duty at the time of the incident. Off-duty officers committed 74.7% of the simple assaults and 63.1% of the aggravated assaults by police officers, and 86.5% of all off-duty offenses were related to the consumption of alcohol.

Type III Police Violence

Type III offenses are the most pernicious of all police violence because they are intentional, malicious acts that take place under the color of authority. Some occur ostensibly in the service of legitimate law enforcement objectives, whereas others simply exploit the officer's power and authority to stop and control targeted victims. Street justice or "curbside justice" (Lee & Vaughn, 2010, p. 196) involves extralegal violence by a police officer to accomplish a purpose that he or she perceives as just and appropriate under the circumstances (Hyatt, 2001). It may be retributive or preventive, and while it occurs within the scope of the officer's role as a law enforcement officer, it occurs outside the scope of the law.

Antisocial characteristics of offenders are more clearly associated with Type III than with either Type I or Type II offenses. Police officers who use violence to intimidate or silence potential adverse witnesses, or who sexually assault or exploit women or other victims they encounter in the course of their law enforcement activities, frequently exhibit the glib narcissism that marks the antisocial personality (Sanford & Arrigo, 2007).

Police sexual offenses are a form of Type III violence that exploits police access to potential or targeted victims and their unparalleled power to detain, control, intimidate, and exploit them. Whereas less than 2% of police–citizen encounters result in the use of physical force (Alpert & Dunham, 2010; IACP, 2001), an estimated 19% to 37% of officers engage in some form of sexual misconduct, depending upon whether one credits the estimates of police chiefs (19%) or police officers (37%) (Maher, 2008). Although a substantial portion of these offenses are nonviolent (e.g., officers targeting and pulling over sexually attractive motorists for no law enforcement purpose, engaging in consensual on-duty adult sex) (Walker & Irlbeck, 2003), many others lead to assaults or intimidation and fear. Corey (2010) offered a definition of police sexual misconduct intended to exclude consensual on-duty sex and comparatively benign encounters:

> Police sexual misconduct consists of any behavior by a police officer that exploits the role (including power, authority, access, or other explicit or

attributed features of the position) to commit a sexually violent act, or to initiate or respond to a cue for the apparent purpose of personal sexual gratification, in which a victim would reasonably be expected to experience sexual degradation, exploitation, humiliation, fear, harm, or threat of harm. (p. 33)

This definition derives from an implicit recognition that even a nonviolent sexual act (e.g., an order to disrobe in front of the police officer for no legitimate law enforcement purpose) always carries—at least for the victim—an awareness that violence could follow a refusal to comply. In essence, Type III police sexual misconduct is always a form of violent exploitation, whether or not physical force is present. Stinson et al. (2012) reported that sex offenses were the second most common offense among arrested officers (after assaults), with a slight majority (51.3%) of the crimes occurring on duty.

Type IV Police Violence

In instances of Type IV violence, the offending officer acts outside of his or her role as a law enforcement agent and independent of any antecedent aggression. These acts span the full range of premeditated violence, including some acts of intimate partner and family violence, as well as sexual misconduct that occurs independent of the police role. Stinson et al. (2012) found from their national study that certain sex offenses were committed more often by off-duty officers than on-duty officers, including statutory rape (77.8% of the offenses were committed by off-duty officers), pornography/obscenity offenses (83.3%), online solicitation of a child (93.3%), and incest (100%).

CAUSES OF POLICE VIOLENCE

Any discussion of the causes of police violence must start with the acknowledgment that police officers are selected, in part, for their capacity to use force and are trained regularly on when and how to use it. In discussing the important finding from their national study of police crime, Stinson et al. (2012) noted,

Many of the crimes in our study could be described as cases involving officers who could not distinguish the appropriate and legitimate use of violence within the context of shifts in their duty status—they could not "turn off" the influence of cultural norms that legitimate the use of on-duty violence in cases when they were technically off duty. (p. 155)

Although this provides some foundation for those who would assert that law enforcement officers may be primed for violent action, available statistics indicate that the base rate for police use of force (Types I and III) is between less than 1% (IACP, 2001) and 2% (Alpert & Dunham, 2010) of police–citizen interactions. As Lersch and Mieczkowski (2005) reported in their analysis of violent police–citizen encounters, "one consistent finding remains: violent altercations with citizens are a relatively rare occurrence" (p. 555).

The low incidence of police violence confounds researchers' efforts to identify the risk and protective factors associated with it. In a well-designed empirical study by Cuttler and Muchinsky (2006), the low incidence of specific forms of police misconduct led the authors to aggregate criterion measures into heterogeneous clusters that included counterproductive work behavior as varied as excessive force, sexual misconduct, insubordination, theft, lying, and multiple moving violations (Cuttler & Muchinsky, 2006). Similarly, in a frequently cited meta-analysis conducted by Ones, Viswesvaran, Cullen, Drees, and Langkamp (2003), the low base rate of negative outcome criteria forced the authors to create a single outcome variable consisting of behaviors as diverse as misuse of firearms, inappropriate sexual behavior, and insubordination. Although there is sound methodological justification for aggregating these low-base rate criteria (cf. Marcus & Schuler, 2004), doing so makes it difficult, if not impossible, to ferret out risk and protective factors associated with particular forms of negative employment outcomes in police officers, let alone particular types of police violence. Nevertheless, it is notable that Cuttler and Muchinsky (2006), as well as Ones et al. (2003), found that preemployment personality measures of conscientiousness show a significant correlation with their aggregate negative outcome measures.

An important study of the relationship between the MMPI-2 (administered to police applicants prior to hire) and officers' posthire conduct provides a notable exception to the reliance on aggregate measures (Sellbom, Fischler, & Ben-Porath, 2007). In an examination of the Restructured Clinical scales (Tellegen et al., 2003), Sellbom et al. (2007) found that subclinical elevations on the RC3 scale (indicating cynical beliefs and distrust of others, and correlating with negative interpersonal experiences and feelings of alienation from others) and the RC8 scale (measuring unusual thoughts and perceptions, and correlating with thought disorganization and unrealistic thinking) were significantly correlated with posthire excessive force in a sample of 291 male police officers.

In their review of the empirical correlates of police misconduct, Kane and White (2009) made the important observation, "With the exception of a few recent studies (e.g., Chappell & Piquero, 2004; Kane, 2002), most identified research on police misconduct has been conducted in the absence of rigorous theoretical frameworks. This might be partially because of the difficulty of fully defining the police deviance construct" (p. 741). The largely aggregated and diverse nature of criterion measures in the empirical studies that do exist makes it hard to identify individual risk and protective factors, much less to distinguish individual from organizational ones.

Corey (2010) argued that police violence cannot be adequately understood as a unitary concept, but rather only by examining the risk and protective factors associated with particular types of violence. In an explication of police sexual violence, Corey identified, from his review of the literature, six factors that increase the risk of its occurrence: (1) cognitive distortions, (2) deviant sexual attractions, (3) socioaffective deficits, (4) poor self-regulation, (5) adverse social influences, and (6) decision chain history. The extent to which these risk factors generalize to other forms of police violence has not been sufficiently examined, although several of the factors identified by Corey (2010) have been shown to be associated with police violence (cf. Harris, 2010; Sanford & Arrigo, 2007).

Discussing Type II violence against intimate partners of police officers, Straus and Brooke (2011) reported that these officers "distinguish themselves by using tactics such as abusing power and control, having different public and private behavior, projecting blame, claiming loss of control or anger problems, and minimizing or denying the abuse" (p. 367). They identified the most common traits of these offenders to be (1) a tendency to blame others for their actions, (2) pathological jealousy, (3) dual personality, (4) severe stress reactions, (5) frequent use of sex as an act of aggression, and (6) refusal to believe their actions should have negative consequences. Stinson et al. (2012) reported that more than 40% of the cases in which police committed acts of violence while off duty arose within the context of a domestic relationship, including verbal threats, stalking, destruction of property, and physical assaults causing serious injury. Domestic violence was also the most common offense leading to termination for off-duty misconduct.

One explanation frequently posited for police misconduct is the "rotten apple theory" (Sherman, 1978), which holds that exceptions to the normal pattern of professionalism and prosocial conduct by police officers owe to moral or other deficits in the individual offenders rather than in the police organization or law enforcement system. But Sherman also posited that the pervasiveness and degree of organization associated with police misconduct may point to more structural and environmental causes in specific circumstances. Conceding that some individuals with an authoritarian personality are drawn to police work, Belur (2010) endorsed the "banality of evil" thesis that

> refutes the need for an individualistic theory of some special pathology to explain [police] violence. Instead, it emphasizes the ordinariness of those involved in "evil" practices and argues that "ordinary people are transformed by particular practices in their routine work environments into killers and murderers—they are not dispositionally predisposed towards violence" (Foster, Haupt, & De Beer, 2005, p. 56). (pp. 335–336)

Other studies have reported that a small cohort of officers tended to be much more involved in problem behaviors than others at sustained rates over time (Harris, 2010) and that this small number of individuals account for a disproportionate amount of problems—a finding reached earlier by the Christopher Commission (1991) in its analysis of the Los Angeles Police Department.

Reasons for excessive or unnecessary force (Type I violence) are complex. From a survey of police psychologists, Scrivner (1994) identified five profiles of officers who engage in excessive force: (1) officers with personality disorders; (2) officers with prior trauma exposure; (3) officers who experience early career problems related to impressionability, impulsiveness, low frustration tolerance, and general need for strong supervision; (4) officers with an authoritarian and dominant style who are overly sensitive to challenge and provocation; and (5) officers with personal problems (e.g., relational discord, perceived loss of status) leading to acute distress or destabilization in job functioning.

In a review of the attitudinal typologies of police officers who engage in excessive force (Type I violence) and street justice (Type III violence), Gallo (2011) reported that these officers generally perceive the primary role of police as controlling crime. He described other characteristics common to these offenders:

> They engage an aggressive style of patrol work in which they are rigid rule appliers who enforce all laws from minor types of violations to felonies. They

prefer to make arrests than to handle order-maintenance calls for service. They believe the citizenry hold hostile attitudes toward the police, and are generally suspicious of them. They perceive police department rules and procedures and court decisions as tying their hands and protecting the citizenry, who hate the police, from good street policing. This causes frustration and job dissatisfaction, and stirs emotions. To do their job, they are willing to bend the rules or violate department procedures. The consequences usually involve inappropriate uses of force as street justice or just desserts. (p. 329)

Nevertheless, Gallo concluded that the literature fails to support the existence of "a specific cluster of characteristics, which tend to remain stable over the course of officers' careers, and which relate to excessive force problems on the job" (p. 329). He noted that much of the evidence supporting hypotheses about attitudinal typologies—presumably including his own—is "impressionistic and grounded in unsystematic observations of a few officers" (p. 329).

Ivković (2009) observed that many postscandal police investigative commissions (e.g., Christopher Commission, 1991; Knapp Commission, 1972; Mollen Commission, 1994; Pennsylvania Crime Commission, 1974) and research studies indicate that the problem with police misconduct typically goes beyond individual officers ("rotten apples") to incorporate problems with police departments ("rotten barrels") or their subunits ("rotten branches") (p. 780). She cited the broader factors mediating police misconduct, including the effect of police leadership or administration, official agency rules, recruitment and selection processes, ethics and integrity training, police culture and socialization, supervisors, and internal control systems.

Competing Forces

> *Without integrity, public trust is lost. ...*
> —National Executive Institute, 2010, p. 7

For most police officers, the law enforcement profession is consistent with their personal value system and an extension of a developmental tradition of strong moral or religious values (Miller, 2006). Whereas the psychological suitability of a police officer applicant is statutorily required in only 38 states (Corey & Borum, 2013), all states mandate that a police recruit be evaluated for moral fitness as a condition of certification. This emphasis on moral character is underscored by the "Oath of Honor"[1] (IACP, 2000) taken by police officers at their "swearing in," reinforced by institutional mechanisms (e.g., citizen complaint procedures, internal affairs investigations, citizen review boards), and ultimately maintained by constitutional protections.[2]

The statutory and regulatory mandates for selecting police applicants with good moral character also helps to screen out individuals whose moral or ethical decision making is compromised by attitudinal and impulse control deficits, or by character problems. Evaluating integrity is often state mandated at both the background stage and in the preemployment psychological evaluation. The California

Commission on Peace Officer Standards and Training (2006), for example, requires that California peace officer applicants must be evaluated at both stages for their ability to maintain "high standards of personal conduct [consisting] of attributes such as honesty, impartiality, trustworthiness, and abiding by laws, regulations, and procedures" (POST, 2012, p. 6). Several empirical studies also have identified integrity as an essential competency for successful performance as a police officer (cf. Black, 2000; Sarchione, Cuttler, Muchinsky, & Nelson-Gray, 1998).

This focus on integrity as a prerequisite and an essential element of fitness throughout the course of a police officer's career is an important force behind a relatively low incidence of unlawful violence by police officers, as previously noted. But despite the extensive screening that most law enforcement agencies employ Ben-Porath et al. (2011), some police officers still act violently. This owes in no small part to the prediction errors common to psychological evaluations of all kinds (Melton et al., 2007) but also to the posthire changes in a police officer's functioning sometimes precipitated by the job itself (Gallo, 2008; Scrivner, 1994; Toch, 1995). This latter point was addressed in length by the Christopher Commission (1991) in the wake of the Rodney King beating:

> A critical limitation on initial psychological screening is the fact that police work modifies behavior. An officer's personality may change dramatically after years on the force. Among the many factors that modify a police officer's behavior is the "culture" of police officers, which tends to isolate officers and make them feel set apart from the rest of the world. Fear is also a ubiquitous part of life as a patrol officer. Officers learn they cannot control every situation, and that they are, quite literally, risking their lives every time they stop a car or intervene in a domestic dispute. Officers also may become frustrated and cynical when they learn that even their arrests of obviously guilty suspects may not result in a conviction.

> Facing this fear, frustration, and stress on a daily basis may alter the behavior of even the most well-adjusted officer. ... Thus, some officers may enter the force seemingly well suited psychologically for the job, but may suffer from burnout, alcohol-related problems, anxiety, cynicism, or disenchantment, all of which can result in their having poor control over their impulses and behavior. A person's susceptibility to these behavior-modifying experiences may not be revealed during even the most skilled and sophisticated psychological evaluation process. (p. 114)

The challenge of identifying those police officers who may become violent is complicated by those factors that limit psychologists' ability to predict behavior generally and violence specifically. One of these has to do with an overreliance on individual factors and a de-emphasis on external considerations. Context is essential when assessing risk for violence (Fein, Vossekuil, & Holden, 1995).

Context

In jobs that allow for significant discretion and latitude, personality factors are important (Carlson & Singer, 1975), but environmental and organizational factors may play an especially important role in both risk of, and protection against, police violence (Scrivner, 1994). The culture of law enforcement is characterized by a tight-knit insularity as a function of the cohesion necessary to survive the conditions of the work (Arrigo & Claussen, 2003; Phillips, 2010; Woody, 2005). Such a closed system, with its own values and codes, can breed deviant conformity (Kappeler, Sluder, & Alpert, 2010) and contribute to difficulty in discovering and inspecting norm- and rule-violating behavior within its ranks.

Scrivner (1994), in her examination of the causes for Type I police violence, noted that it has "become clearer that background events in the officer's life, the culture of policing itself, variable police policies on the use of force, and community conditions may all be determinants of excessive force" (p. 4). The size of the agency is a factor as well, with smaller agencies enjoying closer relationships and having an advantage at monitoring and managing behavior, and larger agencies with many commands spread out over broad territory having less capacity to identify the early signs or even a pattern of continuing serious misconduct. Additionally, the demands of the job, including sleep deprivation and fatigue, can exacerbate individual risks.

In Gallo's (2011) analysis of the literature involving excessive force and street justice (Type I and Type III violence), he found "a weak association between police attitudes and behavior" (p. 329). He reported that the evidence instead points to "an occupational context that largely affects police behavior" (p. 329), either through organizational education and modeling or through an interaction of these factors with an officer's preexisting personality.

Terrill and Mastrofski (2002) conducted a field study involving 276 police officers in 3,116 encounters with citizens in Indianapolis and St. Petersburg. They found that officers' decisions to use force were primarily based on legitimate considerations involving citizen characteristics (e.g., resistance, safety considerations). However extralegal factors also differentiated violent from nonviolent encounters, such that "male, nonwhite, poor, and younger suspects were all treated more forcefully, irrespective of their behavior. In addition, encounters involving inexperienced and less-educated officers resulted in increased levels of police force" (p. 215). Notably, Terrill and Mastrofski's study did not attempt to differentiate legal from unlawful (e.g., excessive or unnecessary) force, so the generalizability of their findings to Type I or Type III violence is only speculative.

A number of sociological theories have been posited to explain violent police–citizen encounters (cf. Alpert & Dunham, 2004; Wolfe & Piquero, 2011). Kane (2002) linked the ecological indicators of social disorganization and racial conflict to patterns of police misconduct and argued that in communities characterized by social network and cultural attention, police are most likely to take advantage of misconduct opportunities and residents are least likely to have access to traditional mechanisms of accountability. But opportunity and citizen characteristics alone do not account for differential rates of violence among police officers, as evidenced by the fact that not all police officers patrolling crime-intense neighborhoods and precincts always exhibit a uniform use of force. This reality underlies Toch's (1995) observation that "[h]igh crime rates combined with promiscuous proactivity can lead to higher incident rates than those that would result from more judicious exercises of discretion, given high rates of crime" (p. 100). At least in varying degrees, individual factors—whether alone or in combination with external factors—influence police violence across all types.

MECHANISMS FOR REDUCING RISK

The police violence literature is primarily descriptive and atheoretical (Wolfe & Piquero, 2011), with multiple individual-level correlates noted such as age (Greene, Piquero, Hickman, & Lawton, 2004; McElvain & Kposowa, 2004), gender (Greene et al., 2004; Grennan, 1987; Hickman, Piquero, & Greene, 2000; McElvain & Kposowa, 2004; Sherman, 1975), race (Greene et al., 2004; Hickman, Piquero, & Piquero, 2004; Kane & White, 2009; Rojek & Decker, 2009), education (Kane & White, 2009; Truxillo, Bennett, & Collins, 1998), length of service (Harris, 2010; Hickman et al., 2004; McElvain & Kposowa, 2004; Micucci & Gomme, 2005; Terrill & Mastrofski, 2002), rank (Hickman et al., 2004), prior employment problems (Greene et al., 2004; Kane & White, 2009), and criminal history (Greene et al., 2004; Kane & White, 2009; Mollen Commission, 1994). Other researchers suggest that responsibility for officer misconduct ultimately resides at the organizational level (Ivković, 2005, 2009; King, 2009; Skolnick & Fyfe, 1993). Although this literature provides helpful policy guidance for police agencies,[3] it provides little insight into the risk and protective factors associated with types of police violence classified by aggression and role dependence.

In light of the reactive nature of Type I and Type II violence (Siever, 2008), personality traits and mental conditions that render an individual prone to react impulsively to emotional provocation, arousal, and stress are disqualifying factors in preemployment psychological screening of police applicants (cf. POST, 2012, which specifies Emotional Regulation & Stress Tolerance as a required competency in California law enforcement officers; see also New Hampshire Administrative Rules, Pol 301.07, which defines an "incompatible profile" of a police applicant as including clinical evidence of "(1) [a] lack of impulse control; (2) [a] lack of anger management; [and] (3) [a] propensity for assaultive behavior"). Studies of individual risk factors associated with excessive and unnecessary force (Type I violence) identify age (IACP, 2001; McElvain & Kposowa, 2004) and years of service (Micucci & Gomme, 2005) as negatively correlated with violence risk, but it is unclear whether these factors are simply an artifact of the tendency for police agencies to assign new officers to shifts and beats with the highest likelihood of violent confrontation and tenured officers to supervisory, administrative, and specialized positions (Harris, 2010). Similarly, in their study of terminated NYPD officers, Kane and White (2009) confirmed "much of the conventional wisdom" in finding that

> Young officers who entered the police service with no post-secondary education, records of prior criminality, and prior poor employment; who did not advance in the police organization; who worked in busy patrol assignments; and who accumulated histories of complaints were more likely than others to have ended their careers in involuntary separation. (p. 764)

Here, too, the results do not make clear that the observed relationships are causal or, for example, whether these officers are simply more vulnerable to the internal review and disciplinary process, and their counterparts—the relatively well-educated officers with minimal or no criminal histories who advanced through departmental ranks—were treated with greater deference and lenience. Harris (2010), on the other hand, found that early onset of police deviance was a significant risk factor for prolonged and involved misconduct and argued that the amount of deviance might not be as important as its timing.

In general, the police violence literature suggests that Type I acts involve organizational factors to a substantial degree, as noted in the previous discussion of context. Type I offenses, for example, are reported to occur more frequently in agencies with a "breakdown of division of labor, hierarchy of authority, command and control, and communication" (Lee & Vaughn, 2010, p. 203) and are associated with managerial ambivalence to misconduct, ambiguous policies about misconduct, and poor recruitment and training practices (Ivković, 2005, as cited by Wolfe & Piquero, 2011). The role of the law enforcement organization in managing police violence is underscored by the research of Klockars, Ivković, and Haberfeld (2005), who found from a study of 3,235 officers in 30 US law enforcement agencies that

> [a]n agency's culture of integrity, as defined by clearly understood and implemented policies and rules, may be more important in shaping the ethics of police officers than hiring the "right" people. ... Officers learn to evaluate the seriousness of various types of misconduct by observing their department's behavior in detecting and disciplining it. (p. ii)

In contrast to Type I acts, Type III acts are more likely to be reduced by heightened attention to a combination of individual and environmental factors. The former includes cynicism and related attitudinal predispositions toward citizens that promote victimization (Corey, 2010; Sellbom et al., 2007), peculiar or disorganized thinking (Sellbom et al., 2007), low conscientiousness (Cuttler & Muchinsky, 2006; Ones et al., 2003), and low stress resilience (Siever, 2008). Each of these is commonly targeted in preemployment psychological screening of police officer applicants (cf. POST, 2012, which mandates psychological evaluation of Social Competence, Conscientiousness-Dependability, Impulse Control, Integrity/Ethics, and Decision-Making, among other dimensions).

Environmental factors contributing to Type III violent offenses—at least those involving "street justice" or so-called noble-cause violence involving "a moral commitment to make the world a safer place to live [by] getting bad guys off the street" (Caldero & Crank, 2004, p. 29; see also Cooper, 2012; Crank, Flaherty, & Giacomazzi, 2007)—include associating with peers who favor minor forms of police misconduct, a commitment to the police culture "code of silence" (see Knapp Commission, 1972; Mollen Commission 1994; Skolnick, 2005; Wolfe & Piquero, 2011) and viewing the employing police agency as engaging in unfair and unjust management practices (i.e., organizational injustice; Wolfe & Piquero, 2011). In their study of NYPD officers terminated for serious misconduct, Kane and White (2009) showed that education and training are important protective factors that reduce the risk of serious officer misconduct leading to termination. Those officers with an associate's or bachelor's degree were less likely to be separated than less educated officers, and those who performed well in the academy and during the probationary period were less likely to be fired than those who perform poorly during their early stages of education and training. This finding echoes the conclusions of Terrill and Mastrofski (2002), who found that less educated and less experienced officers were more likely to be involved in each form of force measured in their study.

Type III acts involving sexual misconduct are likely to be best understood in terms of the general literature on adult sexual offenses (Corey, 2011; see also Chapter 10 of this volume). That said, it is important to note that sex crimes as a whole are more often committed by on-duty officers than by their off-duty counterparts (Stinson et al., 2012), notwithstanding the higher incidence of certain kinds of violent sexual offenses by off-duty officers. Nevertheless, as Stinson and his colleagues point out, we know far too little "about how violence may infuse off-duty behavior and the lives of cops *after* the shift is done" (p. 154).

Although Type IV acts of police violence that occur independently of antecedent aggression and the police role may be influenced by the power of the badge and its psychological sequelae, an understanding of its risk and protective factors may be informed less by the police violence literature than by the broader adult violence literature. All acts of police violence, regardless of the type, can be expected to erode public trust in law enforcement, but not all acts of violence carried out by police have an etiology distinct from nonpolice perpetrators of the same offenses (Harris, 2010). Kane and White (2009) made this compelling observation based on their study of fired NYPD officers:

> Although a substantial portion of police misconduct represents administrative nonconformity (similar to nonconformity in other occupational settings) and fits well with organizational theories, a great deal of police misconduct is illegal and can be explained by traditional criminological or justice theories. Furthermore ... with respect to police deviance—perhaps more than other occupations—it is often difficult to distinguish administrative nonconformity from violations of the law: extorting money from drug dealers in exchange for not arresting them is both illegal and administratively impermissible. Thus, criminological theories that might explain criminal police misconduct could also explain some patterns of administrative deviance among officers. (p. 741)

For a fuller understanding of police violence in contexts independent of police roles, see Chapters 3 and 9.

SUMMARY

Violent offenses by police officers pose a serious threat to democratic society even at low incidence rates, and they warrant the substantial efforts invested in preventing, prosecuting, and researching them. Complicating the study of police violence, however, is the heterogeneity of the behaviors included in the concept, ranging from the use of more force than is objectively needed in a police–citizen struggle to deliberate and wholly unjustified assaults on citizens. We have proposed a classification of police violence that considers its relationship to two underlying factors shown in the literature to mediate and differentiate violence: antecedent aggression or arousal (i.e., impulsive vs. premeditated violence) and the police officer's authority over or access to victims (role dependent vs. role independent). In so doing, we suggest that police violence that occurs in the course of high-stress police–citizen encounters belongs to Type I; violence taking place in high-arousal conditions but unrelated to the police officer's role falls into Type II; acts of premeditated violence in which the police officer's authority or access was instrumental in the violence constitute Type III offenses; and Type IV acts encompass premeditated violence independent of police authority or access. We have summarized the available research on police violence within the framework of this typology, and we encourage future research that identifies distinctions in risk and protective factors, whether individual or environmental, across these four types of police violence.

NOTES

1. The *Law Enforcement Oath of Honor* (IACP, 2000) reads, "On my honor, I will never betray my badge, my integrity, my character, or the public trust. I will always have the courage to hold myself and others accountable for our actions. I will always uphold the constitution, my community, and the agency I serve."
2. Section 1983 of the Civil Rights Act of 1871 makes relief, including monetary damages, available to persons whose constitutional rights have been violated by an actor acting under State authority. It is often used by private citizens to redress violations of federally protected rights, frequently against law enforcement agencies and individuals.
3. Among the policy implications cited by Ivković (2009) is the importance of ensuring that efforts are "concentrated at the front end of the police officers' careers with thorough, intense, and complete background checks of applicants. Standards such as no criminal record, no employment disciplinary problems, and certain educational attainment should not only be established, but also be enforced (despite the perceived need, or pressure, from the community to hire police officers rapidly)" (p. 778).

REFERENCES

Alpert, G. P., & Dunham, R. G. (2004). *Understanding police use of force: Officers, suspects, and reciprocity.* New York, NY: Cambridge University Press.

Alpert, G. P., & Dunham, R. G. (2010). Policy and training recommendations related to police use of CEDs: Overview of findings from a comprehensive national study. *Police Quarterly, 13,* 235–259.

Arrigo, B. A., & Claussen, N. (2003). Police corruption and psychological testing: A strategy for preemployment screening. *International Journal of Offender Therapy and Comparative Criminology, 47,* 272–290.

Baehr, M. E., Furcon, J. E., & Froemel, E. C. (1968). *Psychological assessment of patrolman qualifications in relation to field performance.* Washington, DC: U.S. Department of Justice.

Bartol, C. R., & Bartol, A. M. (2004). *Introduction to forensic psychology.* London Oaks: Sage.

Bazley, T. D., Mieczkowski, T., & Lersch, K. M. (2009). Early intervention program criteria. Evaluating officer use of force. *Justice Quarterly, 26,* 107–124.

Belur, J. (2010). Why do the police use deadly force? Explaining police encounters in Mumbai. *British Journal of Criminology, 50,* 320–341.

Ben-Porath, Y. S., Fico, J. M., Hibler, N. S., Inwald, R., Kruml, J., & Roberts, M. R. (2011). Assessing the psychological suitability of candidates for law enforcement positions. *Police Chief, 78*(8), 64–70.

Bittner, E. (1990). The functions of the police in modern society. In E. Bittner, *Aspects of police work* (pp. 120–132). Boston, MA: Northeastern University Press.

Black, J. (2000). Personality testing and police selection. *New Zealand Journal of Psychology, 29,* 2–9.

Bureau of Justice Statistics. (2012). Law enforcement. Retrieved July 2012, from http:// bjs.ojp.usdoj.gov/index.cfm?ty=tp&tid=7.

Carlson, H. M., & Singer, R. D. (1975). Personality and situational factors in evaluation of police departments. In E. Viano (Ed.), *Criminal justice research.* Lexington, MA: D.C. Health.

Chappell, A. T., & Piquero, A. R. (2004). Applying social learning theory to police misconduct. *Deviant Behavior, 25,* 85–108.

Christopher Commission. (1991). *Report of the independent commission on the Los Angeles Police Department.* Los Angeles, CA: Christopher Commission.

Cooper, J. A. (2012). Noble cause corruption as a consequence of role conflict in the police organisation. *Policing and Society, 22*(2), 169–184. doi: 10.1080/10439463.201 1.605132

Corey, D. M. (2010). Police sexual misconduct. In Major Cities Chiefs and Federal Bureau of Investigation, National Executive Institute (Eds.), *Disciplinary trends: Focus on behavior affecting the integrity and effectiveness of the agency* (pp. 31–39). Washington, DC: Major Cities Chiefs and Federal Bureau of Investigation.

Corey, D. M., & Borum, R. (2013). Forensic assessment for high-risk occupations. In R. K. Otto & I. B. Weiner (Eds.), *Forensic psychology* (2nd ed., 246–270). Hoboken, NJ: Wiley.

Cuttler, M. J., & Muchinsky, P. M. (2006). Prediction of law enforcement training performance and dysfunctional job performance with general mental ability, personality and life history variables. *Criminal Justice and Behavior, 33*(1), 3–25.

Fein, R. A., Vossekuil, B., & Holden, G. A. (1995). *Threat assessment: An approach to prevent targeted violence.* [National Institute of Justice Pub. No. 155000]. Washington, DC: US Department of Justice.

Foster, D., Haupt, P., & De Beer, M. (2005). *The theatre of violence: Narratives of protagonists in the South African conflict.* Oxford, UK: James Curry Ltd.

Fyfe, J. J. (1986). The split-second syndrome and other determinants of police violence. In A. T. Campbell & J. J. Gibbs (Eds.), *Violent transactions* (pp. 207–225). Oxford, UK: Basic Blackwell.

Fyfe, J. J., & Kane, R. (2006). *Bad cops: A study of career-ending misconduct among New York City police officers.* [Document No. 215795]. Washington, DC: US Department of Justice, National Institute of Justice.

Garner, J. H., Maxwell, C. D., & Heraux, C. G. (2002). Characteristics associated with the prevalence and severity of force used by the police. *Justice Quarterly, 19*(4), 705–746.

Gallo, F. J. (2008). Police use of force. In B. Cuttler (Ed.), *Encyclopedia of psychology and law* (Vol. 2, pp. 593–596). Newbury Park, CA: Sage.

Gallo, F. J. (2011). Police use of force. In J. Kitaeff (Ed.), *Handbook of police psychology* (pp. 323–344). New York, NY: Routledge.

Greene, J. R., Piquero, A. R., Hickman, M. J., & Lawton, B. A. (2004). *Police integrity and accountability in Philadelphia: Predicting and assessing police misconduct.* Washington, DC: National Institute of Justice.

Grennan, S. A. (1987). Findings on the role of officer gender in violent encounters with citizens. *Journal of Police Science and Administration, 15,* 78–85.

Harris, C. J. (2010). Problem officers? Analyzing problem behavior patterns from a large cohort. *Journal of Criminal Justice, 38,* 216–225.

Hyatt, W. D. (2001). Parameters of police misconduct. In M. J. Palmiotto (Ed.), *Police misconduct: A reader for the 21st century* (pp. 75–99). New York, NY: Prentice Hall.

Hickman, M. J., Piquero, A. R., & Greene, J. R. (2000). Does community policing generate greater numbers and different types of citizen complaints than traditional policing? *Police Quarterly, 3,* 70–84.

Hickman, M. J., Piquero, N. L., & Piquero, A. R. (2004). The validity of Niederhoffer's Cynicism Scale. *Journal of Criminal Justice, 32,* 1–13.

International Association of Chiefs of Police (IACP). (2000, November 15). Ethics training in law enforcement. Resolution adopted at the 107th Annual Conference, San Diego, California. Retrieved July 2012, from http://www.theiacp.org/PoliceServices/ProfessionalAssistance/Ethics/WhatistheLawEnforcementOathofHonor/tabid/150/Default.aspx.

International Association of Chiefs of Police (IACP). (2001). Police use of force in America. Retrieved July 2012, from http://www.theiacp.org/Portals/0/pdfs/Publications/2001useofforce.pdf.

Ivković, S. K. (2005). Police (mis)behavior: A cross-cultural study of corruption seriousness. *Policing, 28*(3), 546–566.

Ivković, S. K. (2009). Rotten apples, rotten branches, and rotten orchards. *Criminology and Public Policy, 8,* 777–785.

Kane, R. J. (2002). The social ecology of police misconduct. *Criminology, 40,* 867–896.

Kane, R. J., & White, M. D. (2009). Bad cops: A study of career-ending misconduct among New York City police officers. *Criminology and Public Policy, 8*(4), 737–769.

Kappeler, V. E., Sluder, R. D., & Alpert, G. P. (1998). *Forces of deviance: Understanding the dark side of policing.* Prospect Heights, IL: Waveland Press.

Kappeler, V. E., Sluder, R. D., & Alpert, G. P. (2010). Breeding deviant conformity: The ideology and culture of police. In R. G. Dunham & G. P. Alpert (Eds.), *Critical issues in policing: Contemporary readings* (6th ed., pp. 265–291). Long Grove, IL: Waveland Press.

King, W. R. (2009). Police officer misconduct as normal accidents: An organizational perspective. *Criminology and Public Policy, 8,* 771–776.

Klockars, C. B. (1985). *The idea of police.* Beverly Hills, CA: Sage.

Klockars, C. B., Ivković, S. K., & Haberfeld, M. R. (2005). *Enhancing police integrity.* Washington, DC: US Department of Justice, National Institute of Justice.

Knapp Commission. (1972). *Report of the New York City Commission to Investigate Allegations of Police Corruption and the City's Anti-Corruption Procedures.* New York, NY: Bar Press.

Lee, H., & Vaughn, M. S. (2010). Organizational factors that contribute to police deadly force liability. *Journal of Criminal Justice, 38,* 193–206.

Lersch, K. M., & Mieczkowski, T. (2005). Violent police behavior: Past, present, and future research directions. *Aggression and Violent Behavior, 10*(5), 552–568.

Maher, T. M. (2008). Police chiefs' views on police sexual misconduct. *Police Practice and Research, 9*(3), 239–250.

Marcus, B., & Schuler, H. (2004). Antecedents of counterproductive behavior at work: A general perspective. *Journal of Applied Psychology, 89*(4), 647–660.

McElvain, J. P., & Kposowa, A. J. (2004). Police officer characteristics and internal affairs investigations for use of force allegations. *Journal of Criminal Justice, 32*, 265–279.

Melton, G. B., Petrila, J., Poythress, N.G., Slobogin, C., Lyons, P. M., & Otto, R. K. (2007). *Psychological evaluations for the courts: A handbook for mental health professionals and lawyers* (3rd ed.). New York, NY: Guilford Press.

Micucci, A. J., & Gomme, I. M. (2005). American police and subcultural support for the use of excessive force. *Journal of Criminal Justice, 33*, 487–500.

Mollen Commission. (1994). *Anatomy of failure, a path for success: The report of the Commission to Investigate Allegations of Police Corruption and the Anti-Corruption Procedures of the New York City Police Department.* New York, NY: City of New York.

New Hampshire Administrative Rules, Police Standards and Training Council, Pol 301.07 (Adopted August 1, 2008).

Ones, D. S., Viswesvaran, C., Cullen, M. J., Drees, S. A., & Langkamp, K. (2003, April). Personality and police officer behaviors: A comprehensive meta-analysis. Paper presented at the 18th Annual Meeting of the Society of Industrial and Organizational Psychology, Orlando, FL.

Ones, D. S., Viswesvaran, C., & Dilchert, S. (2004, November). Personality and police officer work performance: A construct-based, comprehensive meta-analysis and implications for pre-offer screening and psychological evaluations. Paper presented at the Annual Meeting of the International Association of Chiefs of Police (IACP), Los Angeles, CA.

Pennsylvania Crime Commission. (1974). *Report on police corruption and the quality of law enforcement in Philadelphia.* St. Davids, PA: Commonwealth of Pennsylvania, Pennsylvania Crime Commission.

Phillips, S. W. (2010). Police officers' opinions of the use of unnecessary force by other officers. *Police Practice and Research, 11*(3), 197–210.

POST, California Commission on Peace Officer Standards and Training. (2012). http://lib.post.ca.gov/Publications/psychological-traits.pdf. Accessed 7/27/2012.

Riksheim, E. C., & Chermak, S. M. (1993). Causes of police behavior revisited. *Journal of Criminal Justice, 21*, 353–382.

Rojek, J., & Decker, S. H. (2009). Examining racial disparity in the police discipline process. *Police Quarterly, 12*, 388–407.

Sanford, S. J., & Arrigo, B. A. (2007). Policing and psychopathy: The case of Robert Philip Hanssen. *Journal of Forensic Psychology Practice, 7*(3), 1–31.

Sarchione, C. D., Cuttler, M. J., Muchinsky, P. M., & Nelson-Gray, R. O. (1998). Prediction of dysfunctional job behaviors among law enforcement officers. *Journal of Applied Psychology, 83*, 904–912.

Scrivner, E. M. (1994). *The role of police psychology in controlling excessive force.* Washington, DC: National Institute of Justice.

Sellbom, M., Fischler, G. L., & Ben-Porath, Y. S. (2007). Identifying MMPI-2 predictors of police officer integrity and misconduct. *Criminal Justice and Behavior, 34*, 985–1004.

Sherman, L. (1975). An evaluation of policewomen on patrol in a suburban police department. *Journal of Police Science and Administration, 3*, 434–438.

Sherman, L. (1978). *Scandal and reform: Controlling police corruption.* Berkeley: University of California Press.

Siever, L. J. (2008). Neurobiology of aggression and violence. *American Journal of Psychiatry, 165,* 429–442. doi: 10.1176/appi.ajp.2008.07111774

Skolnick, J. H., & Fyfe, J. J. (1993). *Above the law: Police and the excessive use of force.* New York, NY: Free Press.

Stinson, P. M., Liederbach, J., & Freiburger, T. L. (2012). Off-duty and under arrest: A study of crimes perpetuated by off-duty police. *Criminal Justice Policy Review, 23,* 139–163.

Straus, T. K., & Brooke, S. L. (2011). Domestic violence: An analysis of the crime and punishment of intimate partner abuse. In J. Kitaeff (Ed.), *Handbook of police psychology* (pp. 363–382). New York, NY: Routledge.

Super, J. T., Blau, T. H., Wells, C. B., & Murdock, N. H. (1993). Using psychological tests to discriminate between "best" and "least beast" correctional officers. *Journal of Criminal Justice, 21,* 143–150.

Tellegen, A., Ben-Porath, Y. S., McNulty, J. L., Arbisi, P. A., Graham, J. R., & Kaemmer, B. (2003). *The MMPI-2 Restructured Clinical (RC) scales: Development, validation, and interpretation.* Minneapolis: University of Minnesota.

Terrill, W., & Mastrofski, S. D. (2002). Situational and officer-based determinants of police coercion. *Justice Quarterly, 19*(2), 215–248.

Toch, H. (1995). The violence-prone police officer. In W. A. Geller & H. Toch (Eds.), *And justice for all: Understanding and controlling police abuse of force* (pp. 99–112). Washington, DC: Police Executive Research Forum.

Truxillo, D. M., Bennett, S. R., & Collins, M. L. (1998). College education and police job performance: A ten-year study. *Public Personnel Management, 27,* 269–280.

University of Iowa Injury Prevention Research Center (UIIPRC). (2001). *Workplace violence: A report to the nation.* Iowa City: University of Iowa.

Walker, S., & Irlbeck, D. (2003, June). Police sexual abuse of teenage girls: A 2003 update on "driving while female." Police Professionalism Initiative, University of Nebraska, Lincoln.

Wolfe, S. E., & Piquero, A. R. (2011). Organizational justice and police misconduct. *Criminal Justice and Behavior, 38*(4), 332–353.

Woody, R. H. (2005). The police culture: Research implications for psychological services. *Professional Psychology: Research and Practice, 36*(5), 525–529.

12

Institutional Violence Risk

Theory, Assessment, and Management

DANIEL J. NELLER AND MICHAEL J. VITACCO ■

The number of people committed to psychiatric institutions in the United States declined dramatically after the 1960s (Kofman, 2012; Rochefort, 1984). During the decades that followed deinstitutionalization, the number of beds available for psychiatric inpatients in the United States also plummeted (Lamb & Weinberger, 2005). By contrast, the proportion of psychiatric beds appropriated to forensic patients rose (Bloom, Krishnan, & Lockey, 2008; Way, Dvoskin, & Steadman, 1991) so rapidly that many forensic units exceeded their capacities by the mid-1980s (Way, Dvoskin, Steadman, Huguley, & Banks, 1990). Incarceration rates climbed as well (e.g., Blumstein, 2012), and correctional facilities soon housed a high number of severely mentally ill inmates (Hiday & Burns, 2010; for recent prevalence estimates, see Ditton, 1999; James & Glaze, 2006; Magaletta, Diamond, Faust, Daggett, & Camp, 2009). In the aggregate, these trends offer evidence of trans-institutionalism, a phenomenon by which the censuses of the criminal justice and inpatient psychiatric populations inversely relate to, and depend upon, one another (Cummins, 2010; Palermo, Smith, & Liska, 1991).

The phenomenon of trans-institutionalism probably is more complex than a simple inverse relationship between the criminal justice and inpatient psychiatric populations (Lurigio, 2000; Steadman, Monahan, Duffee, Hartstone, & Clark Robbins, 1984). Nevertheless, the apparent constancy of the overall rate of institutionalized persons (Raphael & Stoll, 2010) suggests that society continuously will demand custodial care for a group of individuals who commit deviant acts (Penrose, 1939; cf. Large & Nielssen, 2009). Coupled with the violence potential of prison inmates (Langan & Levin, 2002) and psychiatric patients (Monahan et al., 2001) relative to people in the general population (Elbogen & Johnson, 2009; Fazel & Grann, 2004; Swanson, Holzer, Ganju, & Jono, 1990), this stability of confinement suggests mental health professionals who work in either correctional or psychiatric settings will benefit from studying serious institutional misconduct, irrespective of changes in the rates of confinement of either population alone.

Perhaps contrary to public perception, serious misconduct occurs with relative infrequency in institutional settings. For example, Sorensen, Cunningham, Vigen, and Woods (2011) studied all serious, documented inmate-on-staff assaults that transpired in Texas prisons over a 14-month period. They found an incidence rate of 53 serious assaults per 100,000 inmates. Of these incidents, approximately 5% led to inpatient medical treatment for the victims. The incidence rate of serious inmate-on-staff assaults is lower than the rate of serious inmate-on-inmate assaults, but the latter number nevertheless remains small (e.g., Sorensen & Cunningham, 2010; Stephan & Karberg, 2003). The incidence rate of institutional violence is dramatically lower for its most serious form, homicide: fewer than 5 acts per 100,000 inmates in local jails and state prisons, a figure that is approximately one-tenth of the incidence rate observed in the US general population (Mumola, 2005).

As in correctional facilities, serious acts of violence occur infrequently in psychiatric settings, an observation not limited to institutions in North America. In a study of approximately 3,500 consecutive admissions to an Italian hospital, for instance, researchers identified fewer than 10 acts of serious institutional violence over a span of 7 years (Grassi et al., 2006). Similarities between violence in correctional and psychiatric settings extend to homicide rates. For example, Nielssen and Large (2012) identified all documented homicides that occurred in Australian and New Zealand psychiatric wards between 1985 and 2010. Fewer than a dozen acts of homicide were committed by a total of 10 patients during the 25-year period.

Institutional violence is not only an infrequent event but also a low base-rate phenomenon, as a relatively small group of violent individuals is responsible for most of the assaults that occur in institutional settings (Barlow, Grenyer, & Ilkiw-Lavalle, 2000; Flannery, 2002; Lussier, Verdun-Jones, Deslauriers-Varin, Nicholls, & Brink, 2010; Owen, Tarantello, Jones, & Tennant, 1998). This is supported by research conducted by Harer and Langan (2001), who studied all admissions to US federal prisons from 1991 to 1998. Of the approximately 200,000 inmates housed in the US federal prison system during the study period, approximately 5% committed acts of violence during their first year of admission; less than 1% committed acts of serious violence. The low base rate of physical violence (Gustafson et al., 1998), and of serious violence in particular (Nicholls, Brink, Desmarais, Webster, & Martin, 2006), applies to civil and forensic psychiatric patients as well.

Considered together, these findings indicate serious violence occurs infrequently in institutions, and that which occurs is committed by a small fraction of people confined to those institutions. Yet the costs of institutional violence remain substantial (Flood, Bowers, & Parkin, 2008; Lovell & Jamelka, 1996). Moreover, some evidence indicates institutional violence is positively associated with reoffense following release from confinement (Rice & Harris, 1992; Rice, Quinsey, & Houghton, 1990; cf. Bonta, Law, & Hanson, 1998). Consequently, the study of institutional violence—with the goals of understanding, predicting, and controlling it (e.g., Allport, 1940), and by doing so, possibly reducing community recidivism risk—remains a worthwhile endeavor for researchers and practitioners alike.

This chapter addresses violence committed primarily by adult men while they are confined to correctional or psychiatric settings. We begin with a review of major explanatory models of institutional misconduct and cite empirical findings relevant to each model. Next, we review empirically supported assessment methods, paying particular attention to two instruments designed to assess institutional violence risk. We conclude with an overview of interventions that, at present, offer promise for reducing risk of institutional violence.

EXPLANATORY MODELS

Most available explanations of institutional misconduct are not based on traditional theories of crime (Blevins, Listwan, Cullen, & Jonson, 2010). Rather, the three models most frequently offered to explain institutional misconduct focus on the effects of deprivation, importation, or situational variables. The first of these, the *deprivation* model, commonly is attributed to Clemmer (1940). It focuses on the contribution of losses to an individual's adjustment to confinement. These losses include but are not limited to deprivations of autonomy, heterosexual relationships, liberty, and sense of safety and security (Sykes, 1958; also see Haney, 2006). Accordingly, variables associated with the deprivation model may be operationalized as custody level of an institution, access to visitation from family members, length of confinement, and degree of crowding within a housing unit.

The *importation* model, by contrast, emphasizes the effects of prior experiences and behavior patterns on an individual's adjustment to confinement (Irwin & Cressey, 1962). Its variables include historical, demographic, and dispositional characteristics of confined persons. Finally, the *situational* model emphasizes the role of contextual variables in the occurrence of institutional violence (Roebuck, 1963; Steinke, 1991). Its variables include time and location of violent incidents, seasons in which such incidents occur, the presence or absence of others at the time of violent incidents, and a host of environmental factors.

Each of these three models is supported by research (e.g., Jiang & Fisher-Giorlando, 2002); however, the deprivation model appears to have the least amount of empirical support. Results from experimental designs indicate custody levels have minimal to no effect on institutional misconduct; instead, inmates with similar propensities for misconduct commit rule infractions at similar rates, irrespective of institutional culture and regime (Bench & Allen, 2003; Berecochea & Gibbs, 1991; Berk, Ladd, Graziano, & Baek, 2003; Camp & Gaes, 2005). Access to conjugal visits appears to be unrelated to prison violence (Hensley, Koscheski, & Tewksbury, 2002). Inmates facing long sentences, including sentences of life-without-parole, appear to be no more violent in institutions than inmates serving short sentences (Cunningham & Sorensen, 2006a; Cunningham, Sorensen, & Reidy, 2005; Sorensen & Cunningham, 2010). Finally, neither overcrowding nor the use of large dormitories—each of which would be expected to deprive inmates of privacy and a sense of security—appears to contribute to increased violence in prison settings (Gaes, 1994).

Given the limited empirical support for the deprivation model, at present researchers and practitioners might benefit from focusing mostly on importation (i.e., individual, dispositional, historical) and situational (i.e., context-specific, environmental) variables associated with institutional violence. This two-pronged approach to understanding institutional violence is supported by the results of a quantitative review of 39 prospective studies of predictors of general and violent misconduct in prison settings (Gendreau, Goggin, & Law, 1997). Consistent with more general findings in psychology (Richard, Bond, & Stokes-Zoota, 2003), this meta-analysis supported both individual and situational variables as risk factors; in general, both groups of risk factors explained misconduct with similar levels of magnitude.

The importation model, on its own, is well supported by research that points to the stability of aggression over time (Olweus, 1979) and across contexts: Prison inmates and psychiatric inpatients who engage in acts of institutional violence tend to have a history of general criminality (Ball, Young, Dotson, Brothers, & Robbins, 1994; Drury & DeLisi, 2010; Reidy, Sorensen, & Cunningham, 2012) and community violence (Arango, Barba, Gonzalez-Salvador, & Ordonez, 1999; Barlow et al., 2000; Daffern, Ferguson, Ogloff, Thomson, & Howells, 2007; McNiel & Binder, 1994; Sorensen et al., 2011). They also tend to have a history of having committed violent acts during prior incarcerations (Cunningham & Sorensen, 2007; Drury & DeLisi, 2010) or hospitalizations (Bjorkly, 1995; Steinert, 2002), respectively.

Mental health problems are associated with an increased risk for violence in correctional facilities (Cunningham et al., 2010) and forensic psychiatric hospitals (Hogan & Ennis, 2010). Anger appears to be associated with institutional violence risk among prison inmates and psychiatric inpatients (Doyle & Dolan, 2006; Novaco, 1994; Wang & Diamond, 1999). Psychotic symptoms are related to increased institutional violence risk in samples of prison inmates and civil psychiatric patients (Douglas, Guy, & Hart, 2009); criminal thinking may mediate the relationship (Walters, 2011).

Research has identified personality and behavioral variables associated with violence in institutional settings. These include impulsivity (McDermott, Edens, Quanbeck, Busse, & Scott, 2008; Wang & Diamond, 1999; cf. Ferguson et al., 2005) and antisociality (Mills & Kroner, 2003; Quinsey, Jones, Book, & Barr, 2006). Psychopathy, a personality construct characterized by such features as glibness, superficiality, callousness, lack of remorse, irresponsible lifestyle, and a propensity for antisocial behavior and rule violation (Hare, 1996), is associated with violence and other forms of misconduct within institutional settings (Leistico, Salekin, DeCoster, & Rogers, 2008; cf. Guy, Edens, Anthony, & Douglas, 2005). Among forensic inpatients, a high level of psychopathy has been shown to increase violence risk beyond the effects of such well-established predictors as age and violence history (Gustafson et al., 1998).

A few notable differences in risk factors are observed across correctional and psychiatric settings. Chronically disruptive inmates (Toch & Adams, 2002), including those who engage in institutional violence (Sorensen et al., 2011), tend to be relatively young in age. Inmates who engage in institutional violence tend to belong to racial minority groups (Berg & DeLisi, 2006; Cunningham, Sorensen, Vigen & Woods, 2010). They also tend to be affiliated with security threat groups (Cunningham et al., 2010; Sorensen et al., 2011), even after other variables associated with prison violence are accounted for (Gaes, Wallace, Gilman, Klein-Saffran, & Suppa, 2002). Although young age has been implicated as a risk factor for chronic violence among psychiatric inpatients (Barlow et al., 2000; Flannery, 2002), it enjoys less support for acute violence (e.g., Newton, Elbogen, Brown, Snyder, & Barrick, 2012). Neither race nor security threat group status has been identified consistently as a risk factor for institutional violence among psychiatric inpatients (see, e.g., Bjorkly, 1995). By contrast, mental and emotional states characterized by such features as confusion, irritability, boisterousness, and threatening behavior may signal imminent violence among civil psychiatric inpatients (Abderhalden et al., 2004; Almvik, Woods, & Rasmussen, 2000; Bjorkdahl, Olsson, & Palmstierna, 2005); many of these mental and emotional states have not been consistently identified as violence risk factors in prison settings.

The consistency of many individual-level predictors across settings suggests certain people have a propensity to engage in general criminal and other violent acts irrespective of context or setting. But the differences in predictors observed between settings suggest situational variables cannot be ignored. Gadon, Johnstone, and Cooke (2006) systematically reviewed 48 research findings that measured the relationship between situational factors and institutional violence. They found that, overall, acts of violence were more likely to occur in high-traffic areas of poorly managed institutions. In a study of all US federal prisons in operation in 2007, Bierie (2012) found that staff perceptions of noise, clutter, and cleanliness were associated with serious institutional violence. Other research findings indicate that serious violence in prisons is more likely to occur in cells or corridors than large gathering areas, and it is more likely to be perpetrated by single assailants than groups of assailants (Cunningham et al., 2010). Personal disputes (Cunningham et al., 2010), particularly those involving drug trade, racial issues, homosexual relationships, and arguments over possessions (Gaes, 1994), appear to be associated with violent acts in prisons.

In psychiatric settings, an increase in violence risk is associated with staff members spending a considerable amount of time with patients (Gadon et al., 2006). Violent acts are most likely to occur immediately following a patient's admission (Noble, 1997), ordinarily during day shifts (e.g., Barlow et al., 2000). Acute intoxication, misdirected affection, and denial of services might contribute to increased violence risk in inpatient settings (Flannery, 2002). Poor therapeutic alliance is associated with an increased risk of relatively imminent violence (Quinsey, Jones, et al., 2006). Many violent incidents in psychiatric settings are unprovoked and generally occur while staff members are assisting with activities of daily living or are engaging in limit setting (Almvik et al., 2000). Staff members who exude authoritarian, inflexible attitudes; who communicate poorly; and who fail to address patients' increased anxiety levels may contribute to increased violence risk among psychiatric inpatients (Bjorkly, 2000).

RISK ASSESSMENT

Early research studies indicated clinicians often made inaccurate decisions when assessing violence risk; these findings led to a call for a second generation of research characterized by improved predictor variables, criterion variables, and accuracy indices (Monahan & Steadman, 1994). This second generation of research indicated clinicians assessed violence risk at better-than-chance levels (Mossman, 1994). As in other areas of prediction (Dawes, Faust, & Meehl, 1989; Grove & Meehl, 1996; Grove, Zald, Lebow, Snitz, & Nelson, 2000), risk assessments based on actuarial models were at least as accurate as, and often were more accurate than, risk assessments based on unstructured judgments alone (Ægisdotter et al., 2006; Hanson & Morton-Bourgon, 2009; but see Litwack, 2001).

Among the most widely used (Archer, Buffington-Vollum, Stredney, & Handel, 2006; Jackson & Hess, 2007) and generally accepted (e.g., Lally, 2003) actuarial risk assessment instruments (ARAIs) are the Violence Risk Appraisal Guide (Quinsey, Harris, Rice, & Cormier, 1998, 2006), Sex Offender Risk Appraisal Guide (Quinsey, Harris, et al., 1998, 2006), Rapid Risk Assessment for Sexual Offense

Recidivism (Hanson, 1997), and Static-99 (Hanson & Thornton, 2000). Results from meta-analyses clearly support the validity of scores on these measures for the prediction of community violence (Campbell, French, & Gendreau, 2009; Hanson & Morton-Bourgon, 2009; Singh, Grann, & Fazel, 2011; Yang, Wong, & Coid, 2010), with effect sizes at least as high as those observed in other areas of psychology (cf. Richard et al., 2003). Because factors associated with community recidivism appear to be quite similar to those associated with institutional violence (e.g., Gendreau et al., 1997), one might reasonably deduce that scores on the aforementioned ARAIs are as effective at predicting institutional violence as they are at predicting community violence. Research findings to date indicate such a conclusion would be erroneous.

In a meta-analysis of 88 truly prospective studies, Campbell and her colleagues (2009) found that the weighted correlation between scores on the most extensively validated ARAI and community violence was halved when institutional violence was used as the outcome variable. Similar reductions were observed among other instruments. Overall, for the assessment of violence risk the greatest empirical support was obtained for assessments based on file reviews, static variables, and purely actuarial measures composed of historical factors. Seemingly in contradiction to this trend, however, a structured professional judgment guide ordinarily scored on the basis of a file review and an interview, and comprised of both static and dynamic variables, produced the largest effect size for the prediction of institutional violence.

In the sections that follow, we briefly review instruments commonly used for the assessment for community violence risk that also have empirical support for the assessment of institutional violence risk: the Psychopathy Checklist—Revised (PCL-R; Hare, 2003), the Psychopathy Checklist: Screening Version (PCL:SV; Hart, Cox, & Hare, 1995), and the Historical, Clinical Risk Scheme (HCR-20; Webster, Douglas, Eaves, & Hart, 1997). Then, we discuss empirical support for two measures designed specifically for the assessment of institutional violence risk: the Short Term Assessment of Risk and Treatability (START; Webster, Martin, Brink, Nicholls, & Desmarais, 2009) and the Risk Assessment Scale for Prison (RASP; Cunningham et al., 2005).

Psychopathy Checklist

The revised (Hare, 2003) and screening (Hart et al., 2003) versions of the Psychopathy Checklist (PCL; Hare, 1991) are among the most frequently studied (Campbell et al., 2009; Singh et al., 2011; Yang et al., 2010), used (Archer et al., 2006; Viljoen, McLachlan, & Vincent, 2010), and controversial (Edens & Petrila, 2006) instruments in the area of violence risk assessment. Traditionally, items on these instruments have been shown to load onto one of two factors (Hare, 2003; Hart et al., 1995; cf. Cooke & Michie, 2001; Cooke, Michie, & Hart, 2006; Hall, Benning, & Patrick, 2004). The first factor, characterized by "selfish, callous, and remorseless use of others," reflects such traits and behaviors as glibness, superficiality, callousness, and failure to accept responsibility (Hare, 2003, p. 79). The second factor, which reflects a "chronically, unstable, antisocial, and deviant lifestyle," is marked by such traits and behaviors as poor behavioral controls, impulsivity, irresponsibility, and lack of realistic long-term goals (Hare, 2003, p. 79). Research to date indicates the second factor explains the relationship between psychopathy and violence risk more strongly than the first factor (Leistico et al., 2008; Singh et al., 2011; Walters, 2003; Yang et al., 2010).

Clinicians embraced the PCL instruments as acceptable tools for the assessment of violence risk (e.g., Lally, 2003; Viljoen et al., 2010). It is noted, however, that the early studies that found such a strong relationship between scores on these instruments and risk for violence (Buffington-Vollum, Edens, Johnson, & Johnson, 2002; Hill, Neumann, & Rogers, 2004; Hill, Rogers, & Bickford, 1996) were not supported quite as strongly by some subsequent research (e.g., McDermott et al., 2008). Indeed, in the aforementioned meta-analysis by Campbell et al. (2009), correlations between institutional violence and scores on the PCL/PCL-R and PCL:SV were small- and medium-sized, respectively. Recent studies on the relationship between PCL instruments' scores and institutional violence risk (Vitacco, Gonsalves, Tomony, Smith, & Lishner, 2012; Vitacco, Van Rybroek, et al., 2009) remain generally consistent with this trend. Given the moderate level of empirical support for the relationship between PCL instruments' scores and various antisocial outcomes, clinicians might benefit from using risk and protective factors beyond the PCL instruments when conducting assessments of violence risk (Leistico et al., 2008).

Historical, Clinical Risk Scheme

The HCR-20 (Webster et al., 1997) is a structured professional judgment guide designed to assess violence risk. It stands as one of the most extensively validated (Campbell et al., 2009; Singh et al., 2011; Yang et al., 2010) and widely used (Archer et al., 2006) violence risk assessment tools available, and it has been employed in a variety of psycholegal contexts (Vitacco, Erickson, Kurus, & Apple, 2012). It contains 20 items grouped into three areas: historical (H; 10 items), clinical (C; 5 items), and risk management (R; 5 items).

In their meta-analysis, Campbell et al. (2009) found that scores on the HCR-20 predicted institutional violence more strongly than scores on any other instruments. In addition, they found that the performance of the HCR-20 was consistent across samples. In a separate meta-analysis, Hogan and Ennis (2010) found scores on the C scale, in particular, to be predictive of inpatient violence among forensic psychiatric patients, a finding that has been supported by more recent research (e.g., Vitacco, Gonsalves, et al., 2012). Taken together, these findings are encouraging because the C scale contains variables that might change with intervention. Therefore, at present, clinicians might find the HCR-20 to be quite useful in their assessments of institutional violence risk.

Short-Term Assessment of Risk and Treatability

The START (Webster et al., 2009) is a relatively new instrument designed for use within inpatient forensic, correctional, and outpatient settings. Composed of 20 dynamic variables thought to be related to violence, each item is rated as a strength or vulnerability, and the items are grouped into two scales (strength, risk). The

START's measurement of both risk and protective factors is consistent with a balanced approach to risk assessment (Rogers, 2000).

To date, research on the START (Gray et al., 2011; Nicholls et al., 2006) has supported its use with forensic populations. Nicholls, Petersen, Brink, and Webster (2011) found ease of use of the START, as well as good structural reliability of its scores, in a sample of more than 1,000 forensic psychiatric patients. Chu, Thomas, Ogloff, and Daffern (2011) reported ratings on the risk scale predicted interpersonal violence over a 1-month follow-up period. Notably, low ratings on the strength scale were predictive of negative outcomes, including inpatient violence. In a more recent study (Desmarais, Nicholls, Wilson, & Brink, 2012), START scores added validity to other instruments that might be used in assessments of institutional violence risk (i.e., PCL:SV, HCR-20 H scale). Therefore, at present, the START shows promise as a tool for assessing institutional violence risk.

Risk Assessment Scale for Prison

Cunningham and his colleagues (2005) developed the RASP, an ARAI, by examining predictors of violence in a sample of approximately 2,500 prison inmates housed in a maximum security institution in Missouri. A unique characteristic of the sample was the housing arrangement of the offenders—term-sentenced, life-without-parole, and death-sentenced inmates intermixed with the general prison population. The following variables positively correlated with violent misconduct: prior prison term, property offender, and 6- to 10-year sentence length. The following variables inversely correlated with violence risk: age, education, prior probationary sentence, and either a life or death sentence. The resultant actuarial model was moderately accurate in predicting institutional violence.

The RASP subsequently was revised and extended with additional (and larger) samples of inmates (e.g., Cunningham & Sorensen, 2006b, 2007). Among these revisions was a simplified scoring version constructed from a sample of more than 13,000 Florida inmates, the RASP-Reduce Burgess. Cunningham, Sorensen, Vigen, and Woods (2011) tested the accuracy of scores on various versions of the RASP with a sample of more than 100 former death row inmates in Texas. Versions of the RASP generally performed best when serious assaults, as opposed to potentially violent or less violent infractions, were used as the outcome variable. Particularly noteworthy was the high performance of the RASP-Reduce Burgess. At present, therefore, the RASP appears to be a well-supported tool for the assessment of prison violence risk.

RISK MANAGEMENT

Violence risk management involves efforts to restrict, monitor, and treat individuals in order to reduce their likelihood of violent behavior (Fyfe & Gailey, 2011). Compared to violence risk assessment, less is known about interventions designed to reduce violence risk (Dvoskin & Heilbrun, 2001) or the ways to measure reductions in violence risk (Webster, Douglas, Belfrage, & Link, 2000). Nevertheless, evidence indicates appropriate interventions can lead to significant reductions in institutional misconduct (Gendreau & Keyes, 2001), particularly if both dispositional and situational factors are considered (Cooke, Wozniak, & Johnstone, 2008).

Research shows that violent and nonviolent criminal recidivism (Bonta et al., 1998), as well as violent and nonviolent institutional misconduct (Gendreau et al., 1997), share many of the same predictors. Additionally, research shows that interventions that appear to reduce general recidivism in the community also appear to reduce general misconduct in institutions (French & Gendreau, 2006). It is reasonable to infer, therefore, that much of what we know about the effectiveness of interventions designed to reduce general recidivism in the community might be useful for the reduction of violent acts in institutions.

The effectiveness of correctional treatment has been subjected to more than 60 meta-analyses during the past 25 years (Andrews, 2012). This line of research indicates programs typically have the greatest impact on recidivism when they match program intensity to offender risk level; focus predominantly on criminogenic needs, that is, potentially changeable factors associated with recidivism; and are delivered in a manner well suited for learning styles and abilities of offenders (Andrews & Bonta, 2006). Correctional treatment programs that adhere to these three core principles of risk, need, and responsivity (RNR) are associated not only with reductions in general recidivism but also with reductions in violent recidivism (Dowden & Andrews, 2000).

Adherence to RNR principles is associated with reductions in institutional misconduct. French and Gendreau (2006) quantitatively analyzed nearly 70 studies, involving more than 21,000 inmates and covering a 50-year period. Consistent with meta-analyses of general and violent recidivism, they found that, for the reduction of institutional misconduct, programs of greater duration (i.e., at least 6 months) were more effective than those of shorter duration; programs that targeted at least 3 criminogenic needs were more effective than programs that targeted 2 or fewer criminogenic needs; and programs that employed behavioral interventions were more effective than programs that utilized nonbehavioral interventions. French and Gendreau (2006) also found that programs that isolated treatment participants from the general population were more effective than programs that did not.

Consistent with the risk principle of the RNR model, several authors (e.g., Cooksey, 1999; Edens & Otto, 2001; Gibbons & Katzenbach, 2006) contend that effective risk management begins with objective classification. Indeed, the mere use of a structured risk assessment instrument for classifying offenders has been shown to lead to reductions in institutional violence even when offenders have shown no change on dynamic risk factors (Belfrage, Gransson, & Strand, 2004). Therapies ordinarily effective at reducing recidivism (e.g., group cognitive-behavioral programs; Wilson, Bouffard, & MacKenzie, 2005) may prove ineffective if they fail to consider risk level of participants (Andrews & Dowden, 2006; Lowenkamp, Latessa, & Holsinger, 2006). The provision of intensive interventions to low-risk offenders might even increase recidivism (Andrews, Bonta, & Hoge, 1990), possibly because of disruptions to prosocial networks, reductions in positive opportunities, and influences from negative peers.

Practitioners can objectively classify groups by risk level by utilizing one or more of the instruments covered in this chapter (e.g., HCR-20, RASP). They might further classify groups according to status on individual risk factors, separating for instance, younger and older offenders, and providing early interventions to the former (Craddock, 1996). Just as practitioners might use research to inform their decisions about separating groups, they also might use research to inform decisions about integrating groups. Racial issues, for example, clearly play a role in the perpetration of some acts of institutional violence. Data from more than 70,000 male inmates in Texas suggest efforts to increase racial integration might reduce institutional violence (Worrall & Morris, 2011). Because research indicates inmates facing long sentences are no more dangerous than inmates serving short sentences (Cunningham et al., 2005; Cunningham & Sorensen, 2006a; Sorensen & Cunningham, 2010), the former may be integrated with the latter in an effort to increase programming opportunities to all offenders irrespective of sentence length.

The second core principle of effective correctional treatment involves focusing on risk factors that, when changed, might reduce the likelihood of institutional violence. Douglas and Skeem (2005) identified several such dynamic variables, which may prove to be the most promising targets for violence reduction. These include psychosis, negative affectivity, impulsivity, antisocial attitudes, substance use problems, and interpersonal problems. Heilbrun (2003) identified several interventions that hold the most promise for reducing violence risk. These include psychotropic medication and other clinical services to address symptoms among the mentally ill; anger control training for emotional, impulsive, antisocial offenders; and substance abuse treatment for the chemically dependent.

Several meta-analytic investigations bolster the claims made by Douglas and Skeem (2005) and Heilbrun (2003). Although psychiatric symptoms rarely cause criminal acts (Skeem, Peterson, & Silver, 2011), when they do cause them, psychiatric medications might be as effective at treating symptoms as are medications for other common medical problems (Leucht, Hierl, Kissling, Dold, & Davis, 2012). Olanzapine might be particularly helpful when the goal is the reduction of positive symptoms of psychosis (Leucht, Komossa, et al., 2009). Based on other meta-analytic findings, anger can be effectively reduced with multicomponent therapy, cognitive-behavioral therapy, relaxation-based strategies, and skills training (Saini, 2009). Impulsive behavior might be effectively reduced by contingency management and administration of selective serotonin reuptake inhibitors, mood stabilizers, and B-adrenergic antagonists (Moeller, Barratt, Dougherty, Schmitz, & Swann, 2001).

Employment, vocational, and educational programs effectively reduce recidivism among general offenders (Aos, Miller, & Drake, 2006; cf. Visher, Winterfield, & Coggeshall, 2005). Meta-analyses indicate therapeutic communities are associated with modest reductions in recidivism for drug-involved offenders (Aos et al., 2006; Pearson & Lipton, 1999). Relapse prevention programs are effective as well, particularly when they involve at least two of the following three components: (1) training of significant others, (2) rehearsal of relapse, and (3) development of offense chains (Dowden, Antonowicz, & Andrews, 2003).

Specific characteristics of treatment providers moderate the relationship between service delivery and outcome (Andrews, 2012). A meta-analysis by Dowden and Andrews (2004) showed that staff members have the greatest impact on recidivism when they effectively use authority, provide appropriate modeling and reinforcement, help offenders identify and solve problems, and foster high-quality relationships with offenders. Appropriate training of staff members (Cooke, 2000) in the areas of interviewing, security, and physical management can lead to reductions in institutional violence (Quinsey, 2000).

CONCLUSIONS

History suggests society will continue to demand custodial care for a group of people who commit deviant acts. Most of the people in this group will not commit acts of serious violence while they are housed in institutional settings. Those who do commit acts of violence will tend to have histories of general criminality and violence; they will tend to be young, impulsive, and antisocial; and they will tend to experience anger or possibly mental health problems. Risk assessment instruments, particularly those designed to assess for institutional violence risk, likely will prove helpful in identifying this relatively small fraction of people who present a heightened risk for violence in prisons and psychiatric settings.

The low incidence and base rates of serious violence in institutions pointedly demonstrate the soundness of extant management strategies. Additional strategies might further reduce the incidence and prevalence rates of institutional violence. Separating high- from low-risk individuals—with limited consideration of custody level or sentence length in some circumstances—might be a first step toward reducing institutional violence. Additional steps include the separation of individuals who participate in treatment programs from those who do not; the judicious integration of people from various racial backgrounds; the positioning of well-trained staff members in high-traffic areas; and a commitment to maintaining adequate physical conditions of institutions. Effectiveness in reducing institutional violence likely will be further enhanced by the adoption of empirically supported programs that focus on criminogenic needs, tailored to the learning styles of offenders, and delivered by staff members trained to follow core elements of effective practice.

AUTHOR'S NOTE

Opinions expressed in this chapter do not necessarily represent the views of any institutions, agencies, or departments with which the authors are affiliated.

REFERENCES

Ægisdotter, S., White, M. J., Spengler, P. M., Maugherman, A. S., Anderson, L. A., Cook, R. S., ... Rush, J. D. (2006). The meta-analysis of clinical judgment project: Fifty six years of accumulated research on clinical versus statistical prediction. *Counseling Psychologist, 34,* 341–382.

Abderhalden, C., Needham, I., Miserez, B., Almvik, R., Dassen, T., Haug, H., & Fischer, J. E. (2004). Predicting inpatient violence in acute psychiatric wards using the Broset-Violence-Checklist: A multicentre prospective cohort study. *Journal of Psychiatric and Mental Health Nursing, 11,* 422–427.

Allport, G. (1940). The psychologist's frame of reference. *Psychological Bulletin, 37*(1), 1–28.

Almvik, R., Woods, P., & Rasmussen, K. (2000). The Broset Violence Checklist: Sensitivity, specificity, and interrater reliability. *Journal of Interpersonal Violence*, *15*(12), 1284–1296.

Andrews, D. A. (2012). The Risk-Need-Responsivity Model of correctional assessment and treatment. In J. A. Dvoskin, J. L. Skeem, R. W. Novaco, & K. S. Douglas (Eds.), *Using social science to reduce violent offending* (pp. 127–156). New York, NY: Oxford University Press.

Andrews, D. A., & Bonta, J. (2006). *The psychology of criminal conduct* (4th ed.). Newark, NJ: LexisNexis/Matthew Bender.

Andrews, D. A., Bonta, J., & Hoge, R. D. (1990). Classification for effective rehabilitation: Rediscovering psychology. *Criminal Justice and Behavior*, *17*, 19–52.

Andrews, D., & Dowden, C. (2006). Risk principle of case classification in correctional treatment. *International Journal of Offender Therapy and Comparative Criminology*, *50*(1), 88–100.

Aos, S., Miller, M., & Drake, E. (2006). *Evidence-based adult corrections programs: What works and what does not*. Olympia: Washington State Institute for Public Policy.

Arango, C., Barba, A. C., Gonzalez-Salvador, T., & Ordonez, A. C. (1999). Violence in inpatients with schizophrenia: A prospective study. *Schizophrenia Bulletin*, *25*(3), 493–503.

Archer, R. A., Buffington-Vollum, J. K., Stredny, R. V., & Handel, R. W. (2006). A survey of psychological test use patterns among forensic psychologists. *Journal of Personality Assessment*, *87*(1), 84–94.

Ball, E. M., Young, D., Dotson, L. A., Brothers, L. T., & Robbins, D. (1994). Factors associated with dangerous behavior in forensic inpatients: Results from a pilot study. *Bulletin of the American Academy of Psychiatry and Law*, *22*(4), 605–620.

Barlow, K., Grenyer, B., & Ilkiw-Lavalle, O. (2000). Prevalence and precipitants of aggression in psychiatric inpatient units. *Australian and New Zealand Journal of Psychiatry*, *34*, 967–974.

Belfrage, H., Gransson, G., & Strand, S. (2004). Management of violent behaviour in the correctional system using qualified risk assessments. *Legal and Criminological Psychology*, *9*, 11–22.

Bench, L. L., & Allen, T. D. (2003). Investigating the stigma of prison classification: An experimental design. *Prison Journal*, *83*, 367–382.

Berecochea, J. E., & Gibbs, J. B. (1991). Inmate classification: A correctional program that works? *Evaluation Review*, *15*, 333–363.

Berg, M. T., & DeLisi, M. (2006). The correctional melting pot: Race, ethnicity, citizenship, and prison violence. *Journal of Criminal Justice*, *34*, 631–642.

Berk, R., Ladd, H., Graziano, H., & Baek, J. (2003). A randomized experiment testing inmate classification systems. *Criminology and Public Policy*, *2*, 215–242.

Bierie, D. M. (2012). Is tougher better? The impact of physical prison conditions on inmate violence. *International Journal of Offender Therapy and Comparative Criminology*, *56*(3), 338–355.

Bjorkdahl, A., Olsson, D., & Palmstierna, T. (2005). Nurses' short-term prediction of violence in acute psychiatric intensive care. *Acta Psychiatrica Scandinavica*, *113*, 224–229.

Bjorkly, S. (1995). Prediction of aggression in psychiatric patients: A review of prospective prediction studies. *Clinical Psychology Review*, *15*(6), 475–502.

Bjorkly, S. (2000). High-risk factors for violence. Emerging evidence and its relevance to effective treatment and prevention of violence on psychiatric wards. In S. Hodgins

(Ed.), *Violence among the mentally ill: Effective treatments and management strategies* (pp. 237–250). Dordrecht, The Netherlands: Kluwer Academic.

Blevins, K. R., Listwan, S. J., Cullen, F. T., & Jonson, C. L. (2010). A general strain theory of prison violence and misconduct: An integrated model of inmate behavior. *Journal of Contemporary Criminal Justice, 26*(2), 148–166.

Bloom, J. D., Krishnan, B., & Lockey, C. (2008). The majority of inpatient psychiatric beds should not be appropriated by the forensic system. *Journal of the American Academy of Psychiatry and the Law, 36*, 438–442.

Blumstein, A. (2012). Crime and incarceration in the United States. In J. A. Dvoskin, J. L. Skeem, R. W. Novaco, & K. S. Douglas (Eds.), *Using social science to reduce violent offending* (pp. 3–29). New York, NY: Oxford University Press.

Bonta, J., Law, M., & Hanson, K. (1998). The prediction of criminal and violent recidivism among mentally disordered offenders: A meta-analysis. *Psychological Bulletin, 123*(2), 123–142.

Buffington-Vollum, J., Edens, J. F., Johnson, D. W., & Johnson, J. K. (2002). Psychopathy as a predictor of institutional misbehavior among sex offenders: A prospective replication. *Criminal Justice and Behavior, 29*, 497–511.

Camp, S. D., & Gaes, G. G. (2005). Criminogenic effects of the prison environment on inmate behavior: Some experimental evidence. *Crime and Delinquency, 51*(3), 425–442.

Campbell, M., French, S., & Gendreau, P. (2009). The prediction of violence in adult offenders: A meta-analytic comparison of instruments and methods of assessment. *Criminal Justice and Behavior, 36*, 567–590.

Chu, C., Thomas, S. M., Ogloff, J. P., & Daffern, M. (2011). The predictive validity of the Short-Term Assessment of Risk and Treatability (START) in a secure forensic hospital: Risk factors and strengths. *International Journal of Forensic Mental Health, 10*, 337–345.

Clemmer, D. (1940). *The prison community.* Boston, MA: The Christopher Publishing House.

Cooke, D. J. (2000). Major mental disorder and violence in correctional settings. In S. Hodgins (Ed.), *Violence among the mentally ill: Effective treatments and management strategies* (pp. 291–311–144). Dordrecht, The Netherlands: Kluwer Academic.

Cooke, D. J., & Michie, C. (2001). Refining the construct of psychopathy: Towards a hierarchical model. *Psychological Assessment, 13*, 171–188.

Cooke, D. J., Michie, C., & Hart, S. (2006). Facets of clinical psychopathy: Toward clearer measurement. In C. J. Patrick (Ed.), *Handbook of psychopathy* (pp. 91–106). New York, NY: Guilford Press.

Cooke, D. J., Wozniak, E., & Johnstone, L. (2008). Casting light on prison violence in Scotland: Evaluating the impact of situational risk factors. *Criminal Justice and Behavior, 35*(8), 1065–1078.

Cooksey, M. B. (1999). Custody and security. In P. Carlson & J. Simon Garrett (Eds.), *Prison and jail administration: Practice and theory* (pp. 75–81). Gaithersburg, MD: Aspen.

Craddock, A. (1996). A comparative study of male and female prison misconduct careers. *Prison Journal, 76*(1), 60–80.

Cummins, I. (2010). The relationship between mental institution beds, prison population and crime rate. In *Prison mental health: Vision and reality* (pp. 22–25). London, UK: Royal College of Nursing.

Cunningham, M. D., & Sorensen, J. R. (2006a). Nothing to lose? A comparative examination of prison misconduct rates among life-without-parole and other long-term high-security inmates. *Criminal Justice and Behavior, 33*(6), 683–705.

Cunningham, M. D., & Sorensen, J. R. (2006b). Actuarial models for assessing prison violence risk: Revisions and extension of the Risk Assessment Scale for Prison (RASP). *Assessment, 13*, 253–265.

Cunningham, M. D., & Sorensen, J. R. (2007). Predictive factors for violent misconduct in close custody. *Prison Journal, 87*(2), 241–253.

Cunningham, M. D., & Sorensen, J. R. (2010). Improbable predictions at capital sentencing: Contrasting prison violence outcomes. *Journal of the American Academy of Psychiatry and the Law, 38*(1), 61–72.

Cunningham, M. D., Sorensen, J. R., & Reidy, T. J. (2005). An actuarial model for assessment of prison violence risk among maximum security inmates. *Assessment, 12*(1), 40–49.

Cunningham, M. D., Sorensen, J. R., Vigen, M. P., & Woods, S. O. (2010). Inmate homicides: Killers, victims, motives, and circumstances. *Journal of Criminal Justice, 38*, 348–358.

Cunningham, M. D., Sorensen, J. R., Vigen, M. P., & Woods, S. O. (2011). Correlates and actuarial models of assaultive prison misconduct among violence-predicted capital offenders. *Criminal Justice and Behavior, 38*(1), 5–25.

Daffern, M., Ferguson, M., Ogloff, J., Thomson, L., & Howells, K. (2007). Appropriate treatment targets or products of a demanding environment? The relationship between aggression in a forensic psychiatric hospital with aggressive behaviour preceding admission and violent recidivism. *Psychology, Crime and Law, 13*(5), 431–441.

Dawes, R. M., Faust, D., & Meehl, P. E. (1989). Clinical versus actuarial judgment. *Science, 243*, 1668–1674.

Desmarais, S. L., Nicholls, T. L., Wilson, C. M., & Brink, J. (2012). Using dynamic risk and protective factors to predict inpatient aggression: Reliability and validity of START assessments. *Psychological Assessment, 24*(3), 685–700.

Ditton, P. M. (1999). *Mental health and treatment of inmates and probationers*. [Bureau of Justice Statistics Special Report No. NCJ 174463]. Washington, DC: US Department of Justice.

Douglas, K., Guy, L., & Hart, S. (2009). Psychosis as a risk factor for violence to others: A meta-analysis. *Psychological Bulletin, 135*(5), 679–706.

Douglas, K. S., & Skeem, J. L. (2005). Violence risk assessment: Getting specific about being dynamic. *Psychology, Public Policy, and Law, 11*(3), 347–383.

Dowden, C., & Andrews, D. A. (2000). Effective correctional treatment and violent reoffending. *Canadian Journal of Criminology, 42*, 449–467.

Dowden, C., & Andrews, D. A. (2004). The importance of staff practice in delivering effective correctional treatment: A meta-analytic review of Core Correctional Practice. *International Journal of Offender Therapy and Comparative Criminology, 48*(2), 203–214.

Dowden, C., Antonowicz, D., & Andrews, D. A. (2003). The effectiveness of relapse prevention with offenders: A meta-analysis. *International Journal of Offender Therapy and Comparative Criminology, 47*, 516–528.

Doyle, M., & Dolan, M. (2006). Evaluating the validity of anger regulation problems, interpersonal style, and disturbed mental state for predicting inpatient violence. *Behavioral Sciences and the Law, 24*(6), 783–798.

Drury, A. J., & DeLisi, M. (2010). The past is prologue: Prior adjustment to prison and institutional misconduct. *Prison Journal, 90*(3), 331–352.

Dvoskin, J., & Heilbrun, K. (2001). Risk assessment and release decision-making: Toward resolving the great debate. *Journal of the American Academy of Psychiatry and the Law, 29,* 6–10.

Edens, J. F., & Otto, R. K. (2001). Release decision making and planning. In J. B. Ashford, B. D. Sales, & W. H. Reid (Eds.), *Treating adult and juvenile offenders with special needs* (pp. 335–371). Washington, DC: American Psychological Association.

Edens, J. F., & Petrila, J. (2006). Legal and ethical issues in the assessment and treatment of psychopathy. In C. J. Patrick (Ed.), *Handbook of psychopathy* (pp. 573–588). New York, NY: Guilford Press.

Elbogen, E. B., & Johnson, S. C. (2009). The intricate link between violence and mental disorder: Results from the National Epidemiologic Survey on Alcohol and Related Conditions. *Archives of General Psychiatry, 66*(2), 152–161.

Fazel, S., & Grann, M. (2004). Psychiatric morbidity among homicide offenders: A Swedish population study. *American Journal of Psychiatry, 161*(11), 2129–2131.

Ferguson, C. J., Averill, P. M., Rhoades, H., Rocha, D., Gruber, N., & Gummattira, P. (2005). Social isolation, impulsivity and depression as predictors of aggression in a psychiatric inpatient population. *Psychiatric Quarterly, 76*(2), 123–137.

Flannery, R. B. (2002). Repetitively assaultive psychiatric patients: Review of published findings, 1978-2001. *Psychiatric Quarterly, 73*(3), 229–237.

Flood, C., Bowers, L., & Parkin, D. (2008). Estimating the costs of conflict and containment on adult acute inpatient psychiatric wards. *Nursing Economics, 26*(5), 325–330.

French, S. A., & Gendreau, P. (2006). Reducing prison misconducts: What works! *Criminal Justice and Behavior, 33*(2), 185–218.

Fyfe, I., & Gailey, Y. (2011). The Scottish approach to high-risk offenders: Early answers or further questions. In B. McSherry & P. Keyzer (Eds.), *Dangerous people: Policy, prediction, and practice* (pp. 201–216). New York, NY: Routledge.

Gadon, L., Johnstone, L., & Cooke, D. (2006). Situational variables and institutional violence: A systematic review of the literature. *Clinical Psychology Review, 26,* 515–534.

Gaes, G. G. (1994). Prison crowding research reexamined. *Prison Journal, 74,* 329–363.

Gaes, G. G., Wallace, S., Gilman, E., Klein-Saffran, J., & Suppa, S. (2002). The influence of prison gang affiliation on violence and other prison misconduct. *Prison Journal, 82*(3), 359–385.

Gendreau, P., Goggin, C. E., & Law, M. A. (1997). Predicting prison misconducts. *Criminal Justice and Behavior, 24*(4), 414–431.

Gendreau, P., & Keyes, D. (2001). Making prisons safer and more humane environments. *Canadian Journal of Criminology, 43,* 123–130.

Gibbons, J. J., & Katzenbach, N. (2006). *Confronting confinement: A report of the Commission on Safety and Abuse in America's Prisons.* New York, NY: Vera Institute of Justice.

Grassi, L., Biancosino, B., Marmai, L., Kotrotsiou, V., Zanchi, P., Marangoni, C., … Barbui, C. (2006). Violence in psychiatric units: A 7-year Italian study of persistently assaultive patients. *Social Psychiatry and Psychiatric Epidemiology, 41,* 698–703.

Gray, N. S., Benson, R. T., Craig, R., Davies, H., Fitzgerald, S., Huckle, P., … Snowden, R. J. (2011). The Short-Term Assessment of Risk and Treatability (START): A prospective study of inpatient behavior. *International Journal of Forensic Mental Health, 10,* 305–313.

Grove, W. M., & Meehl, P. E. (1996). Comparative efficiency of informal (subjective, impressionistic) and formal (mechanical, logarithmic) prediction procedures: The clinical-statistical controversy. *Psychology, Public Policy, and Law, 2*, 293–323.

Grove, W. M., Zald, D. H., Lebow, B. S., Snitz, B. E., & Nelson, C. (2000). Clinical versus mechanical prediction: A meta-analysis. *Psychological Assessment, 12*(1), 19–30.

Gustafson, D., Hare, R. D., Hart, S. D., Heilbrun, K., Nunez, C., & White, A. J. (1998). Inpatient and postdischarge aggression in mentally disordered offenders: The role of psychopathy. *Journal of Interpersonal Violence, 13*, 514–527.

Guy, L. S., Edens, J. F., Anthony, C., & Douglas, K. S. (2005). Does psychopathy predict institutional misconduct among adults? A meta-analytic investigation. *Journal of Consulting and Clinical Psychology, 73*, 1056–1064.

Hall, J. R., Benning, S. D., & Patrick, C. J. (2004). Criterion-related validity of the three-factor model of psychopathy: Personality, behavior, and adaptive functioning. *Assessment, 11*(1), 4–16.

Haney, C. (2006). *Reforming punishment: Psychological limits to the pains of imprisonment.* Washington, DC: American Psychological Association.

Hanson, R. K. (1997). *The development of a brief actuarial risk scale for sexual offense recidivism.* Ottawa, ON: Department of the Solicitor General of Canada.

Hanson, R. K., & Morton-Bourgon, K. E. (2009). The accuracy of recidivism risk assessments for sexual offenders: A meta-analysis of 118 prediction studies. *Psychological Assessment, 21*(1), 1–21.

Hanson, R. K., & Thornton, D. (2000). Improving risk assessments for sex offenders: A comparison of three actuarial scales. *Law and Human Behavior, 24*(1), 119–136.

Hare, R. D. (1991). *Technical manual for the Psychopathy Checklist.* North Tonawanda, NY: Multi-Health Systems.

Hare, R. D. (1996). Psychopathy: A clinical construct whose time has come. *Criminal Justice and Behavior, 23*(1), 25–54.

Hare, R. D. (2003). *Technical manual for the Revised Psychopathy Checklist* (2nd ed.). North Tonawanda, NY: Multi-Health Systems.

Harer, M. D., & Langan, N. P. (2001). Gender differences in predictors of prison violence: Assessing the predictive validity of a risk classification system. *Crime and Delinquency, 47*(4), 513–536.

Hart, S. D., Cox, D. N., & Hare, R. D. (1995). *Manual for the Screening Version of the Psychopathy Checklist Revised (PCL:SV).* Toronto, ON: Multi-Health Systems.

Heilbrun, K. (2003). Violence risk: From prediction to management. In D. Carson & R. Bull (Eds.), *Handbook of psychology in legal contexts* (2nd ed., pp. 127–142). Hoboken, NJ: Wiley.

Hensley, C., Koscheski, M., & Tewksbury, R. (2002). Does participation in conjugal visitations reduce prison violence in Mississippi? An exploratory study. *Criminal Justice Review, 27*(1), 52–65.

Hiday, V. A., & Burns, P. J. (2010). Mental illness and the criminal justice system. In T. L. Scheid & T. N. Brown (Eds.), *A handbook for the study of mental health: Social contexts, theories, and systems, second edition* (pp. 478–498). New York, NY: Cambridge University Press.

Hill, C. D., Neumann, C. S., & Rogers, R. (2004). Confirmatory factor analysis of the Psychopathy Checklist: Screening Version in offenders with Axis I disorders. *Psychological Assessment, 16*, 90–95.

Hill, C. D., Rogers, R., & Bickford, M. E. (1996). Predicting aggressive and socially disruptive behavior in a maximum security forensic psychiatric hospital. *Journal of Forensic Sciences, 41,* 56–59.

Hogan, N., & Ennis, L. (2010). Assessing risk for forensic psychiatric inpatient violence: A meta-analysis. *Open Access Journal of Forensic Psychology, 2,* 137–147.

Irwin, J., & Cressey, D. R. (1962). Thieves, convicts, and the inmate culture. *Social Problems, 10*(2), 142–155.

Jackson, R. L., & Hess, D. T. (2007). Evaluation for civil commitment of sex offenders: A survey of experts. *Sexual Abuse, 19,* 425–448.

James, D. J., & Glaze, L. E. (2006). *Mental health problems of prison and jail inmates.* [Bureau of Justice Statistics Special Report No. NCJ 213600]. Washington, DC: US Department of Justice.

Jiang, S., & Fisher-Giorlando, M. (2002). Inmate misconduct: A test of the deprivation, importation, and situational models. *Prison Journal, 82*(3), 335–358.

Kofman, O. L. (2012). *Deinstitutionalization and its discontents: American mental health policy reform.* Unpublished senior thesis, Claremont McKenna College, Claremont, CA.

Lally, S. J. (2003). What tests are acceptable for use in forensic evaluations? A survey of experts. *Professional Psychology: Research and Practice, 34*(5), 491–498.

Lamb, H. R., & Weinberger, L. E. (2005). The shift of psychiatric inpatient care from hospitals to jails and prisons. *Journal of the American Academy of Psychiatry and the Law, 33,* 529–534.

Langan, P. A., & Levin, D. J. (2002). *Recidivism of prisoners released in 1994.* [Bureau of Justice Statistics Special Report No. NCJ 193427]. Washington, DC: US Department of Justice.

Large, M., & Nielssen, O. (2009). The Penrose hypothesis in 2004: Patient and prisoner numbers are positively correlated in low-and-middle income countries but are unrelated in high-income countries. *Psychology and Psychotherapy: Theory, Research and Practice, 82,* 113–119.

Leistico, A. R., Salekin, R. T., DeCoster, J., & Rogers, R. (2008). A large-scale meta-analysis relating the Hare measures of psychopathy to antisocial conduct. *Law and Human Behavior, 32,* 28–45.

Leucht, S., Hierl, S., Kissling, W., Dold, M., & Davis, J. M. (2012). Putting the efficacy of psychiatric and general medicine medication into perspective: Review of meta-analyses. *British Journal of Psychiatry, 200*(2), 97–106.

Leucht, S., Komossa, K., Rummel-Kluge, C, Corves, C., Hunger, K., Schmid, F., … Davis, J. M. (2009). A meta-analysis of head-to-head comparisons of second-generation antipsychotics in the treatment of schizophrenia. *American Journal of Psychiatry, 166,* 152–163.

Litwack, T. R. (2001). Actuarial versus clinical assessments of dangerousness. *Psychology, Public Policy and Law, 7*(2), 409–443.

Lovell, D., & Jamelka, R. (1996). When inmates misbehave: The costs of discipline. *Prison Journal, 76*(2), 165–179.

Lowenkamp, C., Latessa, E., & Holsinger, A. (2006). The risk principle in action: What have we learned from 13,676 offenders and 97 correctional programs? *Crime and Delinquency, 52*(1), 77–93.

Lurigio, A. J. (2000). Persons with serious mental illness in the criminal justice system: Background, prevalence, and principles of care. *Criminal Justice Policy Review, 11*(4), 312–328.

Lussier, P., Verdun-Jones, S., Deslauriers-Varin, N., Nicholls, T., & Brink, J. (2010). Chronic violent patients in an inpatient psychiatric hospital. *Criminal Justice and Behavior*, *37*(1), 5–28.

Magaletta, P. R., Diamond, P. M., Faust, E., Daggett, D. M., & Camp, S. D. (2009). Estimating the mental illness component of service need in corrections: Results from the Mental Health Prevalence Project. *Criminal Justice and Behavior*, *36*(3), 229–244.

McDermott, B. E., Edens, J. F., Quanbeck, C. D., Busse, D., & Scott, C. L. (2008). Examining the role of static and dynamic risk factors in the prediction of inpatient violence: Variable- and person-focused analyses. *Law and Human Behavior*, *32*, 325–338.

McNiel, D. E., & Binder, R. L. (1994). Screening for risk of inpatient violence: Validation of an actuarial tool. *Law and Human Behavior*, *18*, 579–586.

Mills, J. F., & Kroner, D. G. (2003). Antisocial constructs in predicting institutional violence among violent offenders and child molesters. *International Journal of Offender Therapy and Comparative Criminology*, *47*(3), 324–334.

Moeller, F. G., Barratt, E. S., Dougherty, D. M., Schmitz, J. M., & Swann, A. C. (2001). Psychiatric aspects of impulsivity. *American Journal of Psychiatry*, *158*, 1783–1793.

Monahan, J., & Steadman, H. J. (1994). Toward a rejuvenation of risk assessment research. In J. Monahan & H. J. Steadman (Eds.), *Violence and mental disorder: Developments in risk assessment* (pp. 1–17). Chicago, IL: University of Chicago Press.

Monahan, J., Steadman, H. J., Silver, E., Appelbaum, P. S., Robbins, P. C., Mulvey, E. P., … Banks, S. (2001). *Rethinking risk assessment: The MacArthur Study of Mental Disorder and Violence*. New York, NY: Oxford University Press.

Mossman, D. (1994). Assessing predictions of violence: Being accurate about accuracy. *Journal of Consulting and Clinical Psychology*, *62*(4), 783–792.

Mumola, C. J. (2005). *Suicide and homicide in state prisons and local jails*. [Bureau of Justice Statistics Special Report No. NCJ 213006]. Washington, DC: US Department of Justice.

Newton, V. M., Elbogen, E. B., Brown, C. L., Snyder, J., & Barrick, A. L. (2012). Clinical decision-making about inpatient violence risk at admission to a public-sector acute psychiatric hospital. *Journal of the American Academy of Psychiatry and the Law*, *40*, 206–214.

Nielssen, O., & Large, M. M. (2012). Homicide in psychiatric hospitals in Australia and New Zealand. *Psychiatric Services*, *63*(5), 500–503.

Nicholls, T. L., Brink, J., Desmarais, S. L., Webster, C. D., & Martin, M. (2006). The Short-Term Assessment of Treatability (START): A prospective validation study in a forensic psychiatric sample. *Assessment*, *13*, 313–327.

Nicholls, T. L., Petersen, K. L., Brink, J., & Webster, C. (2011). A clinical and risk profile of forensic psychiatric patients: Treatment team STARTs in a Canadian service. *International Journal of Forensic Mental Health*, *10*, 187–199.

Noble, P. (1997). Violence in psychiatric in-patients: Review and clinical implications. *International Review of Psychiatry*, *9*, 207–216.

Novaco, R. (1994). Anger as a risk factor for violence among the mentally disordered. In J. Monahan & H. J. Steadman (Eds.), *Violence and mental disorder: Developments in risk assessment* (pp. 21–60). Chicago, IL: University of Chicago Press.

Olweus, D. (1979). Stability of aggressive reaction patterns in males: A review. *Psychological Bulletin*, *86*(4), 852–875.

Owen, C., Tarantello, C., Jones, M., & Tennant, C. (1998). Repetitively violent patients in psychiatric units. *Psychiatric Services*, *49*(11), 1458–1461.

Palermo, G. B., Smith, M. B., & Liska, F. J. (1991). Jail versus mental hospitals: A social dilemma. *International Journal of Offender Therapy and Comparative Criminology*, 35(2), 97–106.

Pearson, F., & Lipton, D. (1999). A meta-analytic review of the effectiveness of corrections-based treatments for drug abuse. *Prison Journal*, 79(4), 384–410.

Penrose, L. S. (1939). Mental disease and crime: Outline of a comparative study of European statistics. *British Journal of Medical Psychology*, 18, 1–15.

Quinsey, V. L. (2000). Institutional violence among the mentally ill. In S. Hodgins (Ed.), *Violence among the mentally ill: Effective treatments and management strategies* (pp. 213–235). Dordrecht, The Netherlands: Kluwer Academic.

Quinsey, V. L., Harris, G. T., Rice, M. E., & Cormier, C. A. (1998). *Violent offenders: Appraising and managing risk*. Washington, DC: American Psychological Association.

Quinsey, V. L., Harris, G. T., Rice, M. E., & Cormier, C. A. (2006). *Violent offenders: Appraising and managing risk* (2nd ed.). Washington, DC: American Psychological Association.

Quinsey, V. L., Jones, G. B., Book, A. S., & Barr, K. N. (2006). The dynamic prediction of antisocial behavior among forensic psychiatric patients: A prospective field study. *Journal of Interpersonal Violence*, 21(12), 1539–1565.

Raphael, S., & Stoll, M. A. (2010). Assessing the contribution of the deinstitutionalization of the mentally ill to growth in the U.S. incarceration rate. Berkley, CA: Goldman School of Public Policy.

Reidy, T. J., Sorensen, J. R., & Cunningham, M. D. (2012). Community violence to prison assault: A test of the behavioral continuity hypothesis. *Law and Human Behavior*, 36(4), 356–363.

Rice, M. E., & Harris, G. T. (1992). A comparison of criminal recidivism among schizophrenic and nonschizophrenic offenders. *International Journal of Law and Psychiatry*, 15, 397–408.

Rice, M. E., Quinsey, V. L., & Houghton, R. (1990). Predicting treatment outcome and recidivism among patients in a maximum security token economy. *Behavioral Sciences and the Law*, 8, 313–326.

Richard, F. D., Bond, C. F., & Stokes-Zoota, J. J. (2003). One hundred years of social psychology quantitatively described. *Review of General Psychology*, 7(4), 331–363.

Rochefort, D. A. (1984). Origins of the "third psychiatric revolution": The Community Mental Health Centers Act of 1963. *Journal of Health Politics, Policy and Law*, 9(1), 1–30.

Roebuck, J. (1963). A critique of "Thieves, Convicts and the Inmate Culture." *Social Problems*, 11(2), 193–200.

Rogers, R. (2000). The uncritical acceptance of risk assessment in forensic practice. *Law and Human Behavior*, 24, 595–605.

Saini, M. (2009). A meta-analysis of the psychological treatment of anger: Developing guidelines for evidence based practice. *Journal of the American Academy of Psychiatry and the Law*, 37, 473–488.

Singh, J. P., Grann, M., & Fazel, S. (2011). A comparative study of violence risk assessment tools: A systematic review and metaregression analysis of 68 studies involving 25,980 participants. *Clinical Psychology Review*, 31, 499–513.

Skeem, J., Peterson, J., & Silver, E. (2011). Toward research-informed policy for high-risk offenders with severe mental illnesses. In B. McSherry & P. Keyzer (Eds.), *Dangerous people: Policy, prediction, and practice* (pp. 111–121). New York, NY: Routledge.

Sorensen, J. R., & Cunningham, M. D. (2010). Conviction offense and prison violence: A comparative study of murderers and other offenders. *Crime and Delinquency*, *56*(1), 103–125.

Sorensen, J. R., Cunningham, M. D., Vigen, M. P., & Woods, S. O. (2011). Serious assaults on prison staff: A descriptive analysis. *Journal of Criminal Justice*, *39*, 143–150.

Steadman, H. J., Monahan, J., Duffee, B., Hartstone, E., & Clark Robbins, P. (1984). The impact of state mental health deinstitutionalization on United States prison populations, 1968–1978. *Journal of Criminal Law and Criminology*, *75*, 474–490.

Steinert, T. (2002). Prediction of inpatient violence. *Acta Psychiatrica Scandinavica*, *106*, 133–141.

Steinke, P. (1991). Using situational factors to predict types of prison violence. *Journal of Offender Rehabilitation*, *17*(1–2), 119–132.

Stephan, J. J., & Karberg, J. C. (2003). *Census of state and federal correctional facilities, 2000*. [Bureau of Justice Statistics Special Report No. NCJ 198272]. Washington, DC: US Department of Justice.

Swanson, J. W., Holzer, C. E., Ganju, V. K., & Jono, R. T. (1990). Violence and psychiatric disorder in the community: Evidence from the Epidemiologic Catchment Area surveys. *Hospital and Community Psychiatry*, *41*(7), 761–770.

Sykes, G. M. (1958). *The society of captives: A study of a maximum security prison*. Princeton, NJ: Princeton University Press.

Toch, H., & Adams, K. (2002). *Acting out: Maladaptive behavior in confinement*. Washington, DC: American Psychological Association.

Viljoen, J. L., McLachlan, K., & Vincent, G. M. (2010). Assessing violence risk and psychopathy in juvenile and adult offenders: A survey of clinical practices. *Assessment*, *17*(3), 377–395.

Visher, C. A., Winterfield, L., & Coggeshall, M. B. (2005). Ex-offender employment programs and recidivism: A meta-analysis. *Journal of Experimental Criminology*, *1*, 295–315.

Vitacco, M. J., Erickson, S. K., Kurus, S., & Apple, B. N. (2012). The role of the Violence Risk Appraisal Guide and Historical, Clinical, Risk-20 in U.S. courts: A case law survey. *Psychology, Public Policy and Law*, *18*(3), 361–391.

Vitacco, M. J., Gonsalves, V., Tomony, J., Smith, B. R., & Lishner, D. A. (2012). Can standardized measures of risk predict inpatient violence? Combining static and dynamic variables to improve accuracy. *Criminal Justice and Behavior*, *39*, 589–606.

Vitacco, M. J., Van Rybroek, G. J., Rogstad, J. E., Yahr, L. E., Tomony, J. D., & Saewert, E. (2009). Predicting short-term institutional aggression in forensic patients: A multi-trait method for understanding subtypes of aggression. *Law and Human Behavior*, *33*, 308–319.

Walters, G. D. (2003). Predicting institutional adjustment and recidivism with the Psychopathy Checklist factor scores: A meta-analysis. *Law and Human Behavior*, *27*, 541–558.

Walters, G. D. (2011). Criminal thinking as a mediator of the mental illness-prison violence relationship: A path analytic study and causal mediation analysis. *Psychological Services*, *8*, 189–199.

Wang, E. W., & Diamond, P. M. (1999). Empirically identifying factors related to violence risk in corrections. *Behavioral Sciences and the Law*, *17*, 377–389.

Way, B. B., Dvoskin, J. A., & Steadman, H. J. (1991). Forensic psychiatric inpatients served in the United States: Regional and system differences. *Bulletin of the American Academy of Psychiatry and Law*, *19*(4), 405–412.

Way, B. B., Dvoskin, J. A., Steadman, H. J., Huguley, H. C., & Bank, S. (1990). Staffing of forensic inpatient services in the United States. *Hospital and Community Psychiatry, 41*(2), 172–174.

Webster, C. D., Douglas, K. S., Belfrage, H., & Link, B. G. (2000). Capturing change: An approach to managing violence in improving mental health. In S. Hodgins (Ed.), *Violence among the mentally ill: Effective treatments and management strategies* (pp. 119–144). Dordrecht, The Netherlands: Kluwer Academic.

Webster, C. D., Douglas, K. S., Eaves, D., & Hart, S. D. (1997). *HCR-20: Assessing risk for violence (version 2)*. Burnaby, BC: Mental Health, Law, and Policy Institute, Simon Fraser University.

Webster, C. D., Martin, M., Brink, J., Nicholls, T. L., & Desmarais, S. L. (2009). *Manual for the Short-Term Assessment of Risk and Treatability (START), version 1.1*. Port Coquitlam, BC: Mental Health & Addiction Services.

Wilson, D., Bouffard, L., & MacKenzie, D. (2005). A quantitative review of structured, group-oriented, cognitive-behavioral programs for offenders. *Criminal Justice and Behavior, 32*(2), 172–204.

Worrall, J. L., & Morris, R. G. (2011). Inmate custody levels and prison rule violations. *Prison Journal, 91*(2), 131–157.

Yang, M., Wong, S. C., & Coid, J. (2010). The efficacy of violence prediction: A meta-analytic comparison of nine risk assessment tools. *Psychological Bulletin, 136*(5), 740–767.

13

Youth Gangs

An Overview of Key Findings and Directions for the Future

TERRANCE J. TAYLOR AND J. MICHAEL VECCHIO ∎

Youth gangs have received considerable attention by scholars, practitioners, and the general public for quite some time. As of 2009, it was estimated that there were approximately 28,100 youth gangs with 731,000 youth gang members in the United States (Egley & Howell, 2011).[1] Additionally, gangs were found to be present in various locales—large, urban areas; suburban counties; and even rural areas (Egley & Howell, 2011). But how did we get here? What does the "gang problem" actually encompass? Given the enormous public attention focused on the "gang problem," is there any hope for improvement? We think there is reason for hope and attempt to illustrate promising avenues by synthesizing gang research in the current chapter.

It is certainly possible to trace the evolution of gang research. From a research standpoint, we see attention on gangs has waxed and waned over time. Curry and Decker (2003) highlighted four major periods of concerns about youth gangs. The earliest period in the United States was 1870, corresponding with increased immigration into large cities. Additional periods of gang concern occurred in the 1890s and 1920s. Interestingly, the gangs of these early periods died out without formal intervention. The 1960s represented the third period of gang problems in America. This period differed from previous gang "outbreaks" and had a lasting effect.

Interestingly, a review by Bookin-Weiner and Horowitz (1983) highlighted that while gang research was "in favor" and flourished during the 1950s–1960s, it was relatively absent in the 1970s. Indeed, this review led them to question whether gang problems had truly subsided or whether the lack of gang research represented a period when scholars turned their attention to other topics (Bookin-Weiner & Horowitz, 1983).

Gang research made a comeback, though, shortly after Bookin-Weiner and Horowitz (1983) raised their questions. A resurgence of gang activity occurred during the 1980s and 1990s, leading to a new flurry of gang-related research—particularly ethnographies of individual gangs or experiences of a few members or surveys of gang and non-gang-involved youth—that remains relevant today. As will be discussed later, these divergent methodologies often presented very different pictures of gangs and gang membership. It was clear, however, that gangs were still present and gang members were still active.

During the late-1980s through mid-1990s, attention focused on a new *youth violence epidemic* (Cook & Laub, 1998). A flurry of news stories and popular culture (e.g., movies like *Colors* and "gangster rap") began focusing on violence purportedly committed by youth gang members in efforts to establish gang territory. During this period, a new picture emerged, often bolstered by reports by law enforcement officials that new "supergangs" such as the Bloods and Crips were spreading out of Los Angeles, California, to establish satellite drug markets in other areas across the country. The new availability of a cheap, highly potent form of cocaine—named crack—was contemporaneously being sold in poor, inner-city neighborhoods. These were often the neighborhoods where gangs also flourished. Often, the *youth violence epidemic* was attributed to inter-gang battles—often involving firearms—over prime drug-dealing territories. Beginning in the mid-1980s, gangs, violence, and drugs all became almost inextricably linked in the public consciousness and among some researchers (e.g., Blumstein, 1996). This opened the spigot to a number of important uses of federal funds for studying—and hopefully eradicating—the "youth gang problem."

At the tail end of the *youth violence epidemic*, one important new source of information about gangs was institutionalized. Since 1996, the National Youth Gang Survey has collected systematic estimates of law enforcement records of gangs and gang membership on an annual basis. Agency records are by no means perfect, but the systematic collection of data over more than a decade provides a reasonable degree of confidence in the NYGS findings. Findings from the NYGS illustrate three distinct trends in the prevalence of American gangs: (1) there was a steep decrease from the mid-1990s until 2001, (2) an upsurge between 2001 and 2005, and (3) a period of relative stability since 2005 (Egley & Howell, 2011). Although the attention of the nation has turned toward fear of terrorism since 2001, it is clear that gangs remain a pressing issue.

The current chapter provides an overview of what we know about youth gangs and youthful gang members. The focus is on describing the historical evolution of gang research, key findings about gangs and their members, and a direction for future research. Throughout this chapter, efforts to inform effective policy and practice—under the broad umbrella of prevention, intervention, and suppression efforts—are linked to findings of key studies. The hope is that this chapter is useful to academics and practitioners alike.

DEFINITIONAL ISSUES

Like other social phenomena, it is often difficult to precisely define the concept of interest. This is, however, a necessary element of any serious discussion. Thus, we begin by exploring three key definitions:

What is a gang?
What are gang activity and gang crime?
Who is a gang member?

The answers to these three questions are not as straightforward as a casual examination would suggest. These questions are particularly important, however, as they shape the nature and character of what we can refer to as the larger "gang problem."

Equally important is that successful "evidence-based" practices hinge upon accurate definition and measurement.

What Is a Gang?

There is no national uniform definition of what constitutes a "gang." Different jurisdictions use different definitions, making it difficult to succinctly answer the question "What is a gang?" Additionally, scholars have debated the criteria necessary to distinguish a "peer friendship group" from a "gang."

Research on gangs has often relied on five major criteria: (1) a *group* (i.e., more than two people) who (2) is viewed (by themselves and/or others) as being *distinct from other groups*, (3) that have a degree of *permanence*, (4) have methods of *communication* (e.g., signs, symbols, colors), and (5) are *involved in criminal activity*. The most controversial criteria—involvement in criminal activity—is generally thought to be a necessary component to distinguish gangs from more prosocial groups such as Boy/Girl Scouts, fraternity/sorority members, and members of the armed forces. Including this criterion, however, essentially guarantees that gangs will be found to be more involved in crime and delinquency than nongang groups (see Short, 1990).

The National Youth Gang Survey uses the definition of "a group of youths or young adults in your jurisdiction that you or other responsible persons in your agency or community are willing to identify or classify as a 'gang.'" Importantly, their definition excludes motorcycle gangs, hate or ideology groups, and prison gangs because these are more likely to be comprised of adults. Respondents' reports are open to their discretion of different groups being classified as gangs.

The Eurogang Program of Research has provided an alternative definition that has been gaining considerable credence as a definition of a youth street gangs. According to the Eurogang definition, youth street gangs can be defined as "any durable, street oriented youth group whose involvement in illegal activity is part of its group identity" (Klein & Maxson, 2006, p. 4). While the Eurogang Program of Research has led to some very interesting findings, it started slowly. As an aside, rumor has it that there was initial reluctance on the part of Europeans to admit that they had gangs because they were not like those gangs found in Los Angeles or Chicago. The Americans in attendance replied, "Neither do we." This short exchange broke the ice and led to an ongoing partnership between Europeans and Americans in studies of gang issues.

Gang Typologies

Youth gangs are not monolithic. The alleged humorous exchange between the Europeans and Americans contained considerable truth. While there have been several gang typologies proposed dating back to the work of Thrasher (1927), we focus on a more recent typology developed by Maxson and Klein (1995). Their typology was based on law enforcement's reports of the gang with which they were the most familiar. Based on these responses, Maxson and Klein created a typology based on six main criteria: the presence of subgroups, size, age range of members, duration of existence, territoriality, and crime versatility. Based upon these criteria, five types of gangs were identified. A *traditional* gang is the type that most people think about. Traditional gangs are classified as having many members, subgroups based on age or other criteria, a broad age range, existence for a long period of time, territorial claims, and engagement in a wide variety of crime types. Although this is the type of gang that often captures public concern, it is the least common type. The second gang type is known as *neotraditional*. Neotraditional gangs are similar to traditional gangs in terms of subgroups, territory, and crime versatility; they differ, however, in terms of size (they are smaller), age range of members (they may be small or large), and duration (they are around for shorter periods of time). Over time, neotraditional gangs may become traditional gangs. The third gang type is the *compressed* gang. Compressed gangs have no subgroups, are small in size, have narrow age ranges, are in existence for short periods of time, do not claim territory, and are versatile in their criminal activity. It appears that compressed gangs are the most common types of gangs operating in the United States. The fourth type of gang is a *collective* gang. Collective gangs have no subgroups, are medium to large in size, have a medium-to-large age range of members, are around for medium duration, do not claim territory, and are involved in a variety of criminal activity. The final gang type, according to Maxson and Klein, is known as a *speciality* gang. Specialty gangs have no subgroups, have few members, have a narrow age range, are short in duration, claim territory, but specialize in certain types of criminal behavior. The most commonly understood speciality gangs are drug-dealing and/or party gangs.

It is important to understand the type(s) of gang(s) operating in any area. Denying the existence of gangs—a common strategy used by practitioners at early stages of gang identification (Huff, 1998)—can lead to more formalized gang structures. Moreover, policy responses that treat all types of gangs in the same manner can actually lead to more cohesive and/or organized gangs as responses are viewed as a form of threat (discussed in greater detail later). In short, effective antigang strategies should begin with a good understanding of what types of gangs are operating in a given locale, and strategies should be developed to deal with those specific types of gangs.

What Are Gang Activity and Gang Crime?

As is true with defining what constitutes a gang, there are disagreements about what constitutes "gang activity" or "gang crime." From a practical standpoint, different jurisdictions use different definitions. This definitional distinction is present in the two largest American "gang cities." Los Angeles has traditionally used what is known as a "gang-member-based" definition. Accordingly, all crimes that involve a gang member are classified as gang crimes. Conversely, Chicago has traditionally used what is known as a "gang-motivated-based" definition. Under this approach, only crimes that are committed to further the interests of the gangs are recorded as gang crimes. A study by Maxson and Klein (1990) found that the different definitional issues affected the prevalence of gang homicide in each city, but they did not dramatically change the nature of the circumstances associated with the crimes. Thus, Maxson and Klein (1990) argue that different definitions may affect the scope of the gang problem but do little to change the nature of gang problems.

Unfortunately, we have little national-level information about gang crime. Information collected by the Federal Bureau of Investigation's *Uniform Crime Reports, National Incident-Based Reporting System*, and *Supplemental Homicide Reports* provide little guidance as they collect and report information haphazardly. A more systematic recording and reporting of gang crimes in these sources would be incredibly helpful in understanding the nature of criminal activities committed by gang members. This is unlikely to happen anytime soon, however, as these programs are based on local law enforcement data collection practices—many of which do not collect gang information in any systematic fashion (Katz & Webb, 2006).

Who Is a Gang Member?

The simple answer to this question may at first glance seem to be that a gang member is any individual involved in gang activities. This, however, is not sufficient. As we have discussed, it is often difficult to gain consensus on what constitutes "gang activity" or "gang crime." Additionally, such a definition fails to delineate gradations of gang membership.

Esbensen and colleagues (2001) conducted an interesting exercise to demonstrate the importance gang definitions make on the scope and nature of gang problems. Using data collected from nearly 6,000 eighth-grade youth attending public schools in 11 diverse US cities, they employed increasingly restrictive definitions of gang membership to see how they affected the prevalence of gang membership and the characteristics of gang members. The first definition of gang membership was simply the response (affirmative or negative) to the question, "Have you ever been a gang member?" The second definition was similar, consisting of the response, "Are you now in a gang?" Definitions three through five were increasingly restrictive: definition three added gang involvement in *crime/delinquency*,[2] definition four added a degree of *organization*,[3] and definition five added a measure of *embeddedness*.[4] Their findings indicated considerable divergence in the prevalence of gang membership (from 2% of the youth using the most restrictive definition to 17% of the youth using the least restrictive definition). Consistent with expectations, the "core" members of "organized delinquent gangs" had the most antisocial attitudes and most extensive involvement in delinquency. Equally important, however, was the finding that different definitions presented slightly different demographic patterns of gang youth. Contrary to expectations that more restrictive definitions would reveal patterns more in line with studies based on ethnographic methods or police data (e.g., males of minority group status), moving from the least to most restrictive definition, gang members were increasingly female and White. It is important to note, however, that the most salient differences were between those who reported currently being in a gang versus all other definitions. Drawing on these findings, the authors concluded that self-nomination as a current gang member was a valid measure of gang membership.

Similarly, Curry, Decker, and Egley (2002) used a sample of middle-school students in St. Louis, Missouri, to determine how behaviors varied across different gradations of gang membership status. They were interested in (1) gang members, (2) gang affiliates, and (3) nongang youth. Fifteen percent of youth in their study were classified as ever or currently being gang members. Perhaps most important were the findings that a significant proportion of youth (57%) reported some degree of gang involvement,[5] even if they claimed they had never been gang members.

WHAT DO GANG MEMBERS LOOK LIKE?

A considerable amount of research has examined the racial/ethnic characteristics of gang members. What gang members "look like" often depends on which type of research methodology is used. Biographies and journalistic accounts typically portray gang members as racial/ethnic minority youth, of lower socioeconomic status, raised in single-parent families (Esbensen & Tusinski, 2007). Police statistics and ethnographic information typically present a similar characterization. This picture of gang youth is probably not surprising, as gangs are typically comprised of the most marginalized members of society. Indeed, some scholars, such as Vigil (1988), have argued that youth join gangs because they are "multiply marginalized"—they develop problematic self-identities as part of their socialization to the street, often the main source of socialization in the most disadvantaged areas.

Yet the notion that most gang youth come from minority backgrounds is open to debate. Not all minority youth are marginalized, and minority youth are not the only youth to be marginalized.[6] Additionally, an innovative study conducted by Esbensen and Lynskey (2001) examined the race/ethnicity of gang members in a school survey in 11 diverse US cities. Their results indicated that the gang members in each city were of the same background as other residents of the cities examined. In other words, cities with high proportions of Black residents (like Philadelphia, Pennsylvania) had high proportions of Black gang members, cities with high proportions of Hispanic residents (such as Las Cruces, New Mexico) had high proportions of Hispanic gang members, and cities with high proportions of White residents (such as Pocatello, Idaho) had high proportions of White gang members. The point here is not to minimize the experiences of gang members from racial/ethnic minority groups but to highlight that the "picture" of gang membership is not universal across settings.

THE DEVELOPMENT OF GANGS

With the caveat that it is difficult to develop universally valid definitions of gangs, gang activity/crime, and gang membership, we now turn our attention to theories of gang formation. In other words, how and why do gangs develop?

Theories of Gang Development

One may wonder why it is important to explore how gangs develop. After all, we have already seen that gangs have existed for a long period of time. Yet this overshadows the relatively recent upsurge in gang activity in suburban counties, small cities, and rural areas. We argue that it is critically important to understand how gangs develop so that communities that are seeing gang-like behavior can take effective actions to prevent full-scale gang behavior. One of the earliest attempts to understand gangs was written in 1927 by Frederick Thrasher. His book, *The Gang: 1,313 Gangs in Chicago*, is filled with descriptions of gangs operating in Chicago during that time. According to Thrasher (1927), gangs developed as a natural evolution of youth friendship groups. These groups grew up together, engaged in "play fighting," and were ultimately united through conflict.

Although it was conducted nearly a century ago, many of Thrasher's propositions hold true today. First, gangs develop in local settings. It is not uncommon to hear that gang members migrate across the country to search for prime drug dealing territory, but this has received very little empirical support. Maxson (1993, 1998) has conducted the best research on the topic and has consistently reported that migration for establishing drug territory is a "myth" (see also Hagedorn, 1998). In other words, most gangs are "homegrown" and typically neighborhood based. Additionally, these neighborhood-based groups share experiences during their lives and develop strong friendship ties. According to Thrasher, it is when violence or the threat of violence occurs that these groups are likely to transform into gangs.

Klein (1971) discussed the importance of "mythic violence" in fostering gang cohesiveness. Klein argued that actual violence is less common in gang life than commonly believed. What is more common is what he refers to as "mythic violence." Gang members spend a considerable amount of time telling and retelling "war stories" about their experiences with violence. Throughout these discussions, gang members learn to control their fear in the face of violent events when they occur and also to rely on their fellow gang members for protection.

Similarly, Decker (1996) proposes that *threat* of violence is the main factor distinguishing gangs from other youth groups. The sense that violence can occur at any time presents a degree of hyperawareness among gang members. Violence can also be used in initiation rituals, to sanction rule violations, and to enact revenge against rival gang members. Each of these promotes a sense of camaraderie and control within the gang setting. In short, violence is deemed to be the most important factor that differentiates gangs from other delinquent groups.

Risk Factors for Gang Membership

So why do youth join gangs? It is not uncommon for the media or law enforcement personnel to report that gangs recruit members, often in unique ways. For example, social media Web sites such as Facebook, MySpace, Twitter, and YouTube have been implicated in recruiting gang members and facilitating gang activities (National Gang Intelligence Center, 2012). While the jury is still out on the degree to which this is true, research by Scott Decker (2012; Decker & Pyrooz, 2011) calls this into question. His research found that gang members—like others of similar age groups—spent a reasonable amount of time online. However, using the Internet for criminal purposes was rare: 10% of gang members reported harassing someone, 8% attacked someone because of something said or written online, and 7% posted videos of fights on YouTube. Let's keep this in perspective, though: 26% reported illegally downloading software or other digital media. In short, there is little evidence that social networking sites play a critical role in youth gang activity.

It is informative to examine risk factors for gang joining. Klein and Maxson (2006) have conducted the most extensive reviews of risk factors for gang membership. Their study collated findings from 20 studies that identified risk factors in the individual, family, peer, school, and neighborhood domains. Studies included represented a wide range of methodological rigor; they included cross-sectional and longitudinal studies, representative and nonrepresentative samples, and bivariate and multivariate analyses.

Klein and Maxson's (2006) review found that most of the risk factors examined had received "inconclusive" support; additionally, risk factors from the individual, family, and peer domains were more often examined than risk factors in the school or neighborhood domains. Factors to receive the greatest consistent support were negative life events, nondelinquent problem behaviors, and characteristics of peer networks. Delinquent beliefs, parental supervision, and affective dimensions of peer networks were "mostly" supported. Internalizing behaviors, involvement in conventional activities, attitudes toward the future, harsh parenting practices, family deviance, school commitment/educational aspirations, parental attachment, academic achievement, and area crime measures were each classified as "inconclusive." Some other factors received even less support. Self-esteem, poverty, single-parent families, family attachment, unsafe school environment, and criminogenic neighborhood factors were mostly not supported as risk factors for gang joining.

The reasons why youth join gangs appear to be as diverse as gang members themselves. While motivations for joining vary, individuals often note they were either *pulled* or *pushed* into membership. Some discuss being pulled into the gang because of the attractions they believed membership would afford them. Often those that join believe the gang offers the promise of friends, social activities, and ways to make money. Still others feel as if they were pushed into membership; fearing that to not join would lead to harassment or victimization. Within the first evaluation of the Gang Resistance Education and Training program, middle school and high school aged youth indicated that they joined their gang for protection, fun, respect, money, and because a friend was already in the gang (Esbensen et al., 1999; Peterson, Taylor, & Esbensen, 2004). Similar findings have been found in the Rochester Youth Development Study (Thornberry, Krohn, Lizotte, Smith, & Tobin, 2003) as well as other ethnographic research conducted with gang members across the United States (Decker & Van Winkle, 1996; Miller, 2001a, 2001b; Padilla, 1992).

THE EXPERIENCES OF GANG MEMBERS

Most youth—even in the "highest risk" communities—will not become actively involved with gangs. Those who do, however, may find their gang experience to be an important turning point in their lives (Melde & Esbensen, 2011). Periods of gang membership are commonly linked with elevated rates of violence and substance use. The more a youth socializes in the gang context, the greater the amount of time exposed to antisocial norms and behaviors. Additionally, the gang context exposes youth to motivated offenders and lowers capable guardianship. Threats of violence—real or perceived—are also important elements of the "gang lifestyle."

Gang members have been found to be involved in more general delinquent offending, violent offending, and violent victimization than their nongang peers.

Indeed, this is one of the most "robust" of all criminological findings (Thornberry et al., 2003). Yet there are various perspectives as to why this finding holds. We next briefly turn to a discussion of three major perspectives on why the link between gang membership and violence appears so robust.

Selection, Facilitation, and Enhancement Models

There is no question that violence is an important part of gangs. One key question that remains unresolved in the gang literature, however, is whether increased violence is due to individual propensities for violence among gang members, a criminogenic effect of the gang/group context on violence, or a combination of the two. In other words, is there evidence of "selection effects," "facilitation effects," or "enhancement effects?"

Thornberry and colleagues (1993) and Esbensen and Huizinga (1993) were among the first to examine these issues. Using interview data collected from youth residing in high-risk neighborhoods in Rochester, New York (Thornberry, Krohn, Lizotte, & Chard-Wierschem, 1993), and Denver, Colorado (Esbensen & Huizinga, 1993), efforts were made to disentangle *selection, social facilitation*, and *enhancement* models of gangs and violence. Selection models hold that increased rates of gang violence are due to the fact that gang members have an increased propensity to engage in violence, regardless of whether they are in a gang. This model assumes that gang members will be violent offenders, even without being exposed to gangs. No causal relationship between gangs and violence should be observed because gangs are simply collectives of violent individuals. Conversely, social facilitation models suggest that it is the group context of the gang—not individual members' propensity for violence—that is the true culprit. This model hypothesizes that gang members will be involved in no more violence than nongang youth prior to joining a gang or after leaving a gang; periods of gang membership, however, should see higher rates of violence for gang members relative to their nongang peers. The third model, enhancement, may be viewed as a middle ground. This model hypothesizes that gang members may be more violent than nongang members prior to joining and/or after leaving (consistent with the selection model). The greatest divergence, however, should be during periods in which youth are gang involved (consistent with the facilitation model).

Research examining these three models has found more support for the facilitation model than the selection model. That is, it appears that the gang context is responsible for the increased violence exhibited by youth gang members relative to their nongang peers. These differences appear to be linked to two theoretical perspectives: (1) routine activities of youth and (2) the functional utility of violence in gangs.

Routine activity theory suggests that crime—including violence—occurs when motivated offenders encounter suitable targets that lack capable guardianship. In their study of violent victimization among gang and nongang youth, Taylor and colleagues (2008) applied routine activities theory to postulate that gangs provided settings where exposure and proximity to high-risk situations abound. Specifically, gang members were viewed as suitable targets—often having money, drugs, or guns that others desired—or being the targets of retaliatory violence from other gangs (see also Taylor, 2008; Taylor, Peterson, Esbensen, & Freng, 2007). Guardianship is lower for gang members, as they are more likely than nongang members to spend time hanging out with peers without adults present, particularly in situations where drugs and alcohol are available.

Additionally, violence has been found to be *functional* in youth gangs. Specifically, violence—or the *threat* of violence—has been found to increase youth gang solidarity (Decker, 1996; Klein, 1971; Thrasher, 1927). The feeling that violence could erupt at any moment, coupled with the belief that gang youth can only rely on other members of their gang for protection, can increase gang cohesiveness. The threat can be real, perceived, or "mythic," and it is transmitted and reinforced through "war stories" about previous violent confrontations. The perceived aggressors may be members of rival gangs, law enforcement, or anyone viewed as threatening to the gang's existence.

Two studies have examined the importance of Elijah Anderson's (1999) concept of the code of the streets as it relates to gang membership. The first study was conducted by Melde, Taylor, and Esbensen (2009), who sought to determine how fear of violent victimization, perceived risk of violent victimization, and actual violent victimization changed before, during, and after gang membership. The findings illustrated that joining a gang resulted in less fear of victimization, but greater perceived risk and actual victimization among members. The authors concluded that gang members must display "heart" or "nerve" in the face of danger, which is consistent with what Anderson states. In other words, while gang members recognized that they were at increased risk of violent victimization, they also knew that they were supposed to face threats without fear.

A second study examined whether adherence to the code of the street could mediate the link between gang membership and involvement in violent offending and was conducted by Matsuda and colleagues (2013). Their study found that (1) gang membership enhanced belief in violence associated with the code of the streets, and (2) these beliefs in the use of violence to gain and maintain respects was, indeed, a significant mediator of the relationship between gang membership and violence. In short, these authors found that gang members' belief in the elements of street code–related violence was a primary reason why gang membership is associated with increased violence.

Time of Entry and Exit

Surveys and interviews of youth have found a promising fact: Most youth gang members are gang involved for a relatively short duration. Results from longitudinal studies of youth conducted in Rochester, New York (Thornberry et al., 2003); Denver, Colorado (Esbensen & Huizinga, 1993); Seattle, Washington (Gordon et al., 2004); and a host of other US cities (Esbensen, Peterson, Taylor, & Freng, 2010; Thornberry, Huizinga, & Loeber, 2004) have found that gang youth are active members for approximately 1 year or less. The fact that gang membership is far from a permanent condition provides considerable reason for optimism among those who are striving to get current gang members out of their gangs.

What About Girls in Gangs?

The connection between gender and gangs has been a hotly debated issue. The first issue is the representation of girls within youth gangs. Official estimates garnered from police place the percentage of gang members who are female at 10% or less (National Youth Gang Center, 2009). Estimates gathered through self-reports, however, indicate that girls comprise somewhere between 30% and 50% of all gang members (Bjerregaard & Smith, 1993; Esbensen & Huizinga, 1993; Esbensen & Lynskey, 2001).

In addition to disagreements concerning estimates of the percentage of gang members who are female, there is also debate as to the degree to which female gang members are involved in gang-related delinquent and violent activities. Traditionally, girl gang members were viewed as being only peripherally involved in gang-related crime. Esbensen and colleagues' (1999) review of the literature indicated that most research had classified gang girls as "tomboys" or "sex objects" (see also Peterson, 2012). In short, girls in gangs traditionally have not been viewed as being as serious a problem as boys in gangs.

More recent research on girls in gangs, however, has called into question the results from earlier research. Data from self-report surveys reported by Esbensen and Winfree (1998), for example, indicate that gang girls are more involved in delinquency and violence than are nongang girls and nongang boys (but not to the degree of male gang members). Additionally, ethnographic work reported by Jody Miller (2001a, 2001b) confirms that female gang members are involved in delinquency and violence to a greater degree than that suggested by earlier research. Also consistent with prior findings, Miller found that girl gang members were found to be less involved in these activities than were gang boys. Miller's work suggested that these differential levels of involvement in delinquency and violence were due to norms about appropriate gender roles. Girls' lesser involvement was due to two different processes. On the one hand, girls were able to play on gender roles to avoid the most serious types of offending. On the other hand, boys often used gender roles to prevent girls from being involved in the most serious types of offending. In short, gender plays an important role in the experiences and behaviors of youth gang members.

Exiting Gangs

Gang membership is predominately a fleeting youth experience. Several longitudinal youth studies (e.g., the Denver Youth Study, Pittsburgh Youth Study, Rochester Youth Development Study, and the Seattle Social Development Project) have demonstrated that membership typically peaks around early to mid-adolescence (around age 14), and most gang joiners leave within 1 year or less (Gordon et al., 2004; Thornberry et al., 2003). These findings suggests that for many individuals, gang affiliation is as transitory an experience as is involvement in other nongang adolescent youth groups (Decker & Curry, 2000; Warr, 2002). On the whole, relatively little is known about who gang leavers are as well as why and how they desist from their gang. What has been established is that (1) they do leave (again, typically after approximately 1 year of participation), (2) desistance is motivated by a range of factors, and (3) members most commonly leave their gang through informal means with little or no consequences.

With almost all members eventually leaving their gang, this raises questions about the timing of desistance. Specifically, the questions of what the primary motivations for leaving are and, to some degree, who are the youth who are more likely to leave earlier than others? While research has found disproportionate involvement of minority youth in gangs, the likelihood of desisting from gang involvement is relatively consistent across different racial and ethnic groups (Thornberry et al., 2003). However, gang leaving does appear to be strongly influenced by one important demographic characteristic: gender. Females both join and leave their gang at an earlier age than do their male counterparts (Esbensen & Huizinga, 1993; Thornberry et al., 2003). Beyond demographic characteristics, members who are less embedded in their gang (e.g., peripheral or fringe members compared to core members) are more apt to leave their gang more quickly and with fewer repercussions (Horowitz, 1983; Thornberry et al., 2003; Vigil, 1988).

So why then do gang members leave their gang? Most of what is known about gang leavers is based on ethnographic research conducted with current and former gang members. Overall, this research has found that former members indicate the importance of a wide variety of factors in their decision to leave. What's more, the desire to leave the gang can either build gradually over time or can be abruptly sparked by a particularly salient experience.

While protection is one of the most commonly found motivations for joining a gang, exposure to violence and victimization is a paradoxically common factor that motivates gang desistance. Decker and Lauritsen's (2002) research with current and former members in St. Louis, Missouri, found exposure to violence to be one of the most discussed motivators for gang desistance (see also Decker & Van Winkle, 1996; Peterson, 2012; Pyrooz & Decker, 2011). Their work demonstrated that some members were motivated by a single and severe violent victimization while others were gradually worn down by an accumulation of violent experiences throughout their period of affiliation (see also Vigil, 1988). For these former members, direct and vicarious experiences with violence, as well as a desire to prevent future victimization, directly motivated their desire to leave the gang.

Other members have left their gang because of other gang and life experiences. This includes growing disinterested in gang activities and other members, growing interest in nongang peers and other prosocial activities, and moving to a new school or city (Decker & Lauritsen, 2002; Peterson, 2012; Vigil, 1988). Research with older members has found that experiences like graduating high school, getting a good job, having a child, and getting married motivated other members to leave their gang (Decker & Lauristen, 2002; Hagedorn & Devitt, 1999; Vigil, 1988). For many, these experiences not only motivated a desire to leave gang life behind them but also further spurred changes in peer group composition and interactions with former gang acquaintances.

Once a gang member feels as if he or she wants to leave the gang, the popular myth is that the member must undergo a formal and often violent exit ritual or ceremony. This may often include committing a crime (e.g., killing your own mother or a rival gang member), undergoing a violent jumping or beating out ritual, or being formally blessed out by the gang's leader. While tales of these violent and organized means of leaving the gang are often echoed across active gang members, former members seldom discuss engaging in any of these ceremonial processes of leaving. So how then do most gang members leave their gang? Most research has instead found that gang members leave through more informal means (Decker & Lauritsen, 2002; Peterson, 2012; Pyrooz & Decker, 2011). This mostly includes a gradual or abrupt reduction in time spent with former gang associates as well as an increase in time spent with other nongang individuals.

Former members often experience a variety of consequences following their change in gang status. While some gang leavers may find themselves—as well as their close friends and family members—the focus of threats or acts of violence from their former gang associates (Decker & Lauritsen, 2002), recent research by Pyrooz and Decker (2011) demonstrated that leavers are most likely to face threats or acts of violence from rival gangs as well as continued police scrutiny because their "leaver" status is not recognized or acknowledged by others. However, leaving the gang does not lead to only negative consequences. In their research with middle school gang youth, Melde and Esbensen (2011) demonstrated notable increases in prosocial attitudes and involvement with nongang prosocial peers following gang desistance. What is more, dramatic reductions in individual involvement in crime as well as experiences with violent victimization are commonly witnessed following gang leaving (Decker & Van Winkle, 1996; Peterson et al., 2004).

In their research with the Rochester Youth Development Study, Thornberry and colleagues (2003) demonstrated that gang affiliation—for any length of time—can, however, have long-lasting deleterious consequences (e.g., arrest in adulthood, early parenthood, and unstable employment) across the lives of members. While those who had the longest length or duration of gang membership experienced the greatest number of long-term consequences, those with shorter periods of membership experienced far fewer negative outcomes. This is a hopeful finding for practitioners and policy makers, demonstrating that reducing the amount of time an individual spends in a gang can yield a meaningful reduction in negative long-term outcomes.

Given gang members increased exposure to violent victimization, one of the most promising points for intervention is immediately following a violent incident. Decker and Lauritsen (2002) assert that intervention services that are provided shortly after the violent incident and away from the influence of gang associates—often within a hospital emergency room, police station, or in a family setting—have the greatest likelihood of success. For example, Cure Violence in Chicago—formally Operation CeaseFire—has used this approach by dispatching volunteers to hospital emergency rooms to speak with victims of violence as well as referring them to a variety of services (e.g., support services as well as educational and job placement services) (see CeaseFire Chicago, 2009).

ANTIGANG STRATEGIES

Antigang programs typically take one of three forms: *prevention, intervention,* or *suppression.* "Prevention" efforts are aimed at stopping gang membership before it occurs. In other words, youth are targeted before they join gangs. The second strategy is known as "intervention." Intervention efforts are aimed at getting gang members out of gangs. The final strategy is known as "suppression." Like intervention efforts, suppression efforts target youth after they join gangs.

Prevention

There are many efforts aimed at preventing youth from joining gangs, but there are few research studies examining the effectiveness of prevention efforts. One example of a gang prevention program that has been extensively studied and found to prevent gang membership is known as the Gang Resistance Education and Training (G.R.E.A.T.) program. This program is catalogued as a primary prevention program, meaning it targets all youth. The main part of the program consists of a standardized, 13-lesson curriculum targeting sixth- or seventh-grade students.[7] The G.R.E.A.T. program is delivered in a classroom setting by uniformed law-enforcement officers who have received extensive training in the program.

Evaluation efforts have provided mixed support for the G.R.E.A.T. program. Results from an early cross-sectional study of approximately 6,000 eighth graders attending public schools in 11 diverse US cities indicated that students who had received the G.R.E.A.T. program were less likely to be gang members, to be less involved in delinquent behavior, to hold fewer delinquent attitudes and associations, and to hold more prosocial attitudes than youth who had not received the G.R.E.A.T. program (Esbensen & Osgood, 1999). A more rigorous longitudinal panel study of approximately 3,600 youth attending public schools in six diverse cities, however, reported less favorable results. Youth who had the G.R.E.A.T. program reported more prosocial attitudes and less prodelinquent attitudes than students who had not participated in the G.R.E.A.T. program, but the differences took approximately 2 years to emerge; equally important, there were no differences between the two groups in terms of gang membership or involvement in delinquent offending (Esbensen et al., 2001).

It should be noted that the G.R.E.A.T. program underwent considerable revision based primarily on the results of these two earlier evaluations. A more recent experimental panel study of the "revised" G.R.E.A.T. program found that the revisions paid off: Youth who completed the G.R.E.A.T. program were less likely than youth without the G.R.E.A.T. program to report gang membership; no differences, however, were found in terms of involvement in violence (Esbensen et al., 2012). Still, G.R.E.A.T. remains an example of an antigang primary prevention program.

Intervention

Gang intervention efforts, broadly speaking, are those that deal with active gang members in ways that encourage them to desist or at least reduce their level of gang participation. Intervention efforts have had a long history of use in the United States and include individual, group, and community-focused approaches. Intervention programs often rely on individual and group counseling; the use of outreach workers, including former gang members; providing alternative opportunities for members; and neighborhood violence reduction efforts. One notable approach uses detached street workers employed to assist gang members in finding legitimate opportunities based upon their needs as well as reducing sources of gang cohesion. According to Klein (1971), programs such as the Midcity Project in Boston (1954–1957), the Chicago Youth Development Project (1960–1965), and the Group Guidance Project and Ladino Hills Program (1961–1965) provide perhaps the "purist" examples.

While intervention programs temporarily fell out of popular favor, Spergel (1995) demonstrated a resurgence of renewed national use beginning around the late 1980s. One recent intervention effort that was evaluated by Spergel and colleagues (2006) and deemed *effective* is the Building Resources for the Intervention and Deterrence of Gang Engagement (BRIDGE) program in Riverside, California. The program relied on an intervention team (which included police officers, probation and parole officers, outreach workers, and social service provides) to develop and implement individual treatment plans for gang youth. Spergel and colleagues (2006) demonstrated that involvement in the BRIDGE program reduced the likelihood of arrest for drug offenses as well as involvement in serious and nonserious violent offenses.

Another recent example is the Boys and Girls Club Gang Intervention through Targeted Outreach (GITTO) program. The program targets "wannabe" and active gang youth between the ages of 10 to 17 years and recruits them for the GITTO intervention program. Through Boys and Girls Club membership, the program focuses on providing gang youth improvement across five core areas: individual character development; educational development; health and life skills; the arts; and sports, fitness, and recreation. Similar to the Boys and Girls Club Gang Prevention through Targeted Outreach program—which has been evaluated and identified as an *effective* prevention program (Arbreton & McClanahan, 2002; Spergel, Wa, & Sosa, 2006)—the GITTO program has been endorsed by the National Gang Center as a *promising* program based on the positive outcomes of youth involved in the program. These include reductions in involvement in gang-related behavior, reduced contact with the juvenile justice system, and improvements in positive school engagement (Howell, 2010).

Suppression

Suppression efforts aimed at youth gangs also have a long history. These techniques typically involve intensive "crackdowns" or "roundups" by law enforcement officers against gang members. Perhaps the most widely known efforts have been found in Los Angeles, with the Community Resources Against Street Hoodlums (CRASH) unit. Such suppression efforts typically involve law enforcement officers saturating areas with a heavy gang presence to make large numbers of arrests for any and all offenses possible.

While suppression techniques present a visible effort by law enforcement that provides the public with a sense that police are "doing something" to eradicate the gang problem, this approach is fraught with problems. Klein (1995) has argued that such efforts are particularly ineffective in dealing with gangs. For one thing, gang members are rounded up but only spend a short time in police custody before being released. This undermines the severity element of deterrence-based strategies. The fact that these efforts are carried out only occasionally also undermines the certainty element of deterrent-based strategies. In short, there is little reason to believe that suppression-based strategies are successful at eradicating gang problems.

CONCLUSION

The current chapter has explored the literature regarding youth gangs. We began with a discussion of what constitutes a gang, gang member, and gang crime. Next we turned our attention to theoretical explanations of how gangs develop and what makes members join. The specific role of violence in both gang development and gang member joining was highlighted. We then turned to a discussion of what gang life is like, again with an emphasis on the role of violence. This transitioned into a discussion of theoretical perspectives of selection, facilitation, and enhancement of crime and violence since gang membership is a transitory state. While we were unable to cover all relevant topics related to youth gangs, we hope that this overview provides discussion (and perhaps even controversy) related to media and law enforcement perspectives of youth gangs and their activities.

We concluded with a discussion of two key factors: gang desistance and programs designed to facilitate desistance. Our conclusion that gangs often desist "naturally"—that is, without official intervention—may be somewhat surprising to the uninitiated. Yet the growing body of literature on gang desistance suggests that youth often simply "age out" or "burn out" of the gang lifestyle. The role of violence in desistance, however, cannot be understated, though. Research has found that one of the most important times to intervene in the lives of gang youth to try to get them out of gangs is shortly following a violent event affecting them, a friend, or a family member (Decker & Lauritsen, 2002). We conclude with a brief discussion on effective (and ineffective) gang prevention, intervention, and suppression strategies.

In summary, violence and gangs often go "hand in hand." This postulate presents some sense of optimism. First, as gang members are high-rate violent offenders, efforts to reduce gang membership should result in a corresponding decrease in violent activity. Second, violence—or the threat of violence—presents a functional purpose for gang cohesiveness. While challenging, reducing the degree of violence—real or perceived—in the gang context has the potential of reducing gang cohesiveness. Finally, intervening shortly after a serious violent offense occurs can be an effective time to start helping youth out of gangs.

NOTES

1. This chapter is focused on what we know about youth gangs. When relevant, we will make reference to adult gangs. Given the divergent findings of studies of youth and adult gang characteristics, activities, and risk factors for involvement, however, it is important to limit the scope of the discussion.

2. *Crime/delinquency* was a measure indicating whether the respondent's gang was involved in at least one of the following: getting in fights with other gangs, stealing things, robbing other people, stealing cars, selling marijuana, selling other illegal drugs, or damaging property.

3. *Organization* was a measure indicating whether the respondent's gang had initiation rites, established leaders, or symbols or colors.

4. *Embeddedness* was a measure indicating whether the respondent considered himself or herself a "core" or "peripheral" member of the gang.

5. Gang involvement was indicated by responses to questions about having friends in gangs, wearing gang colors, hanging out with gang members, or flashing gang signs.

6. Note Wilson's (1987) work highlighting the rise of an upwardly mobile Black middle class during the 1970s and 1980s.

7. The program also has a less often used elementary school component, family training component, and summer component.

REFERENCES

Arbreton, A. J. A., & McClanahan, W. S. (2002). *Targeted outreach: Boys and Girls Clubs of America's approach to gang prevention and intervention.* Philadelphia, PA: Public/ Private Ventures.

Anderson, E. (1999). *Code of the street: Decency, violence, and the moral life of the inner city.* New York, NY: W. W. Norton.

Blumstein, A. (1996). *Youth gangs, guns, and illicit drug markets. National Institute of Justice research preview.* Washington, DC: US Department of Justice, National Institute of Justice.

Bookin-Wiener, H., & Horowitz, R. (1983). The end of the youth gang: Fad or fact? *Criminology, 21,* 585–602.

Bjerregaard, B., & Smith, C. (1993). Gender differences in gang participation, delinquency, and substance use. *Journal of Quantitative Criminology, 9,* 329–355.

CeaseFire Chicago. (2009). Hospital emergency room responses. Retrieved July 2009, from http://www.ceasefirechicago.org/ER_response.shtml.

Cook, P. J., & Laub, J. H. (1998). The unprecedented epidemic in youth violence. In M. Tonry & M. H. Moore (Eds.), *Youth violence, crime and justice: A review of research* (Vol. 24, pp. 27–64). Chicago, IL: University of Chicago Press.

Curry, G. D., & Decker, S. H. (2003). *Confronting gangs: Crime and community.* Los Angeles, CA: Roxbury.

Curry, G. D., Decker, S. H., & Egley, A., Jr. (2002). Gang involvement and delinquency in a middle school population. *Justice Quarterly, 19,* 275–292.

Decker, S. H. (1996). Collective and normative features of gang violence. *Justice Quarterly, 13,* 243–264.

Decker, S. H. (2012). The criminal and routine activities of gang members online. Paper presented at the 11th Youth Violence Prevention Conference. St. Louis, MO: University of Missouri—St. Louis.

Decker, S. H., & Curry, G. D. (2000). Addressing key features of gang membership: Measuring the involvement of young members. *Journal of Criminal Justice, 28,* 473–482.

Decker, S. H, & Lauritsen, J. L. (2002). Leaving the gang. In C. R. Huff (Ed.), *Gangs in America* (Vol. 3, pp. 51–57). Thousand Oaks, CA: Sage.

Decker, S. H., & Pyrooz, D. C. (2011). *Leaving the gang: Logging off and moving on.* Council on Foreign Relations Press.

Decker, S. H., & Van Winkle, B. (1996). *Life in the gang: Family, friends, and violence.* New York, NY: Cambridge University Press.

Egley, A., & Howell, J. C. (2011). *Highlights of the 2009 National Youth Gang Survey. Juvenile Justice Fact Sheet.* Washington, DC: U.S. Department of Justice, Office of Juvenile Justice and Delinquency Prevention.

Esbensen, F.-A., & Deschenes, E. P. (1998). A multisite examination of youth gang membership: Does gender matter? *Criminology, 36,* 799–828.

Esbensen, F.-A., Deschenses, E. P., & Winfree, L. T., Jr. (1999). Differences between gang girls and gang boys: Results from a multi-site survey. *Youth and Society, 31,* 27–53.

Esbensen, F.-A., & Huizinga, D. (1993). Gangs, drugs, and delinquency in a survey of urban youth. *Criminology, 31,* 565–589.

Esbensen, F.-A., & Lynskey, D. (2001). Young gang members in a school survey. In M. W. Klein, H-J. Kerner, C. L. Maxson, & E. G. M. Weitekamp (Eds.), *The Eurogang paradox: Street gangs and youth groups in the U.S. and Europe* (pp. 93–114). The Hague, The Netherlands: Kluwer.

Esbensen, F.-A., & Osgood, D. W. (1999). Gang resistance education and training (G.R.E.A.T.): Results from the National Evaluation. *Journal of Research in Crime and Delinquency, 36,* 194–225.

Esbensen, F.-A., Peterson, D., Taylor, T. J., & Freng, A. (2010). *Youth violence: Understanding the role of sex, race/ethnicity, and gang membership.* Philadelphia, PA: Temple University Press.

Esbensen, F.-A., Peterson, D., Taylor, T. J., Osgood, D. W., Carson, D. C., & Matsuda, K. N. (2012). Evaluation and evolution of the Gang Resistance Education and Training (G.R.E.A.T.) program. *Journal of School Violence, 12,* 53–70.

Esbensen, F.-A., & Tusinski, K. (2007). Youth gangs in the print media. *Journal of Criminal Justice and Popular Culture, 14,* 21–38.

Esbensen, F.-A., Winfree, L. T., Jr., He, N., & Taylor, T. J. (2001). Youth gangs and definitional issues: When is a gang a gang, and why does it matter? *Crime and Delinquency, 47,* 105–130.

Esbensen, F.-A., & Winfree, L. T., Jr. (1998). Race and gender differences between gang and non-gang youth: Results from a multi-site survey. *Justice Quarterly, 15,* 505–526.

Gordon, R. A., Lahey, B. B., Kawai, E., Loeber, R., Stouthamer-Loeber, M., & Farrington, D. P. (2004). Antisocial behavior and youth gang membership: Selection and socialization. *Criminology, 42,* 55–88.

Hagedorn, J. M. (1998). Gang violence in the postindustrial era. In M. Tonry & M. H. Moore (Eds.), *Youth violence, crime and justice: A review of research* (Vol. 24, pp. 365–419). Chicago, IL: University of Chicago Press.

Hagedorn, J. M., & Devitt, M. L. (1999). Fighting females: The social construction of the female gang. In M. Chesney-Lind & J. M. Hagedorn (Eds.), *Female gangs in America: Essays on girls, gangs and gender* (pp. 256–276). Chicago, IL: Lakeview Press.

Horowitz, R. (1983). *Honor and the American dream: Culture and identity in a Chicano community.* New Brunswick, NJ: Rutgers University Press.

Howell, J. C. (2010). *Gang prevention: An overview of research and programs. Juvenile Justice bulletin.* Washington, DC: US Department of Justice, Office of Juvenile Justice and Delinquency Prevention.

Huff, C. R. (1998). *Comparing the criminal behavior of youth gangs and at-risk youths. National Insitute of Justice research in brief.* Washington, DC: US Department of Justice, Office of Justice Programs, National Institute of Justice.

Katz, C. M., & Webb, V. J. (2006). *Policing gangs in America.* New York, NY: Cambridge University Press.

Klein, M. W. (1971). *Street gangs and street workers.* Englewood Cliffs, NJ: Prentice Hall.

Klein, M. W. (1995). *The American street gang: It's nature, prevalence, and control.* New York, NY: Oxford University Press.

Klein, M. W., & Maxson, C. L. (2006). *Street gang patterns and policies.* New York, NY: Oxford University Press.

Matsuda, K. N., Melde, C., Taylor, T. J., Freng, A., & Esbensen, F.-A. (2013). Gang membership and adherence to the 'code of the streets'. *Justice Quarterly, 30,* 440–468.

Maxson, C. L. (1993). Investigating gang migration: Contextual issues for intervention. *Gang Journal, 1,* 1–8.

Maxson, C. L. (1998). *Gang members on the move.* Washington, DC: National Institute of Justice.

Maxson, C. L, & Klein, M. W. (1990). Street gang violence: Twice as great, or half as great? In C. R. Huff (Ed.), *Gangs in America.* Newbury Park, CA: Sage.

Maxson, C. L, & Klein, M. W. (1995). Investigating gang structures. *Journal of Gang Research, 3,* 33–40.

Melde, C., & Esbensen, F-A. (2011). Gang membership as a turning point in the life course. *Criminology, 49,* 513–552.

Melde, C., Taylor, T. J., & Esbensen, F-A. (2009). "I got your back": Examining the protective function of gang membership in adolescence. *Criminology, 47,* 565–594.

Miller, J. (2001a). *One of the guys: Girls, gangs and gender.* New York, NY: Oxford University Press.

Miller, J. (2001b). Young women's involvement in gangs in the United States: An overview. In M. W. Klein, H-J. Kerner, C. L. Maxson, & E. G. M. Weitekamp (Eds.), *The Eurogang paradox: Street gangs and youth groups in the U.S. and Europe* (pp. 115–132). The Hague, The Netherlands: Kluwer.

National Gang Intelligence Center. (2012). *2011 National Gang Threat Assessment—emerging trends.* Washington, DC: US Department of Justice.

National Youth Gang Center. (2009). National Youth Gang Survey Analysis. Retrieved May 2014, from http://www.nationalgangcenter.gov/Survey-Analysis.

Padilla, F. M. (1992). *The gang as an American enterprise.* New Brunswick, NJ: Rutgers University Press.

Peterson, D. (2012). Girlfriends, gun-holds, and ghetto-rats? Moving beyond narrow views of girls in gangs. In S. Miller, L. D. Leve, & P. K. Kerig (Eds.), *Delinquent girls: Contexts, relationships, and adaptation* (pp. 71–84). New York, NY: Springer.

Peterson, D., Taylor, T. J., & Esbensen, F-A. (2004). Gang membership and violent victimization. *Justice Quarterly, 21,* 793–815.

Pyrooz, D. C., & Decker, S. H. (2011). Motives and methods for leaving the gang: Understanding the process of gang desistance. *Journal of Criminal Justice, 39,* 417–425.

Short, J. F. (1990). New wine in old bottles? In C. R. Huff (Ed.), *Gangs in America,* (pp. 223–239). Newbury Park, CA: Sage.

Spergel, I. A. (1995). *The youth gang problem.* New York, NY: Oxford University Press.

Spergel, I. A., Wa, K. M., & Sosa, R. V. (2006). The comprehensive, community-wide, gang program model: Success and failure. In J. F. Short & L. A. Hughes (Eds.), *Studying youth gangs* (pp. 203–224). Lanham, MD: AltaMira Press.

Taylor, T. J. (2008). "The boulevard ain't safe for your kids. . .": Youth gang membership and violent victimization. *Journal of Contemporary Criminal Justice, 24*, 125–136.

Taylor, T. J., Freng, A., Esbensen, F-A., & Peterson, D. (2008). Youth gang membership and serious violent victimization: The importance of lifestyles and routine activities. *Journal of Interpersonal Violence, 23*, 1441–1464.

Taylor, T. J., Peterson, D., Esbensen, F-A., & Freng, A. (2007). Gang membership as a risk factor for adolescent violent victimization. *Journal of Research in Crime and Delinquency, 44*, 351–380.

Thrasher, F. M. (1927). *The gang: A study of 1,313 gangs in Chicago.* Chicago, IL: University of Chicago Press.

Thornberry, T. P., Huizinga, D., & Loeber, R. (2004). The causes and correlates studies: Findings and policy implications. *Juvenile Justice, 9*, 3–19.

Thornberry, T. P., Krohn, M. D., Lizotte, A. J., & Chard-Wierschem, D. (1993). The role of juvenile gangs in facilitating delinquent behavior. *Journal of Research in Crime and Delinquency, 30*, 55–87.

Thornberry, T. P., Krohn, M. D., Lizotte, A. J., Smith, C. A., & Tobin, K. (2003). *Gangs and delinquency in a developmental perspective.* New York, NY: Cambridge University Press.

Vigil, J. D. (1988). *Barrio gangs: Street life and identity in Southern California.* Austin, TX: University of Texas Press.

Warr, M. (2002). *Companions in crime: The social aspects of criminal conduct.* New York, NY: Cambridge University Press.

Wilson, W. J. (1987). *The truly disadvantaged: The inner city, the underclass, and public policy.* Chicago, IL: University of Chicago Press.

14

Understanding Terrorists

RANDY BORUM ■

After the Soviet Union dissolved in 1991, the focus of global security shifted from a Cold War standoff between two superpowers to a diffuse proliferation of violent nonstate actors, often operating in lawless or unstable spaces. For some of these nonstate actors, terrorism became the tactic of choice (Buzan, 2006; Enders & Sandler, 1999). The ability to instill fear in a population gave these actors leverage against the vastly superior military and economic power of nations (Ben-Yehuda & Levin-Banchik, 2010).

Terrorism is certainly not a new tactic, but its form and appearance have changed over time (Mello, 2010; Neumann, 2009; Pfahl-Traughber, 2011). Throughout the first decade of the 21st century, terrorism was widely regarded as one of the most significant contemporary threats to global security. While scholars and politicians talked endlessly about the problem of terrorism, few could even agree on how to define it (Schmid & Jongman, 1988).

WHAT IS A TERRORIST?

What is terrorism and who is a terrorist? Some would argue that those questions are objectively unanswerable; that "one man's terrorist is another man's freedom fighter" (Ganor, 2002; Garrison, 2004). More than a hundred formal definitions of *terrorism* have been proposed (Schmid & Jongman, 1988). Most involve some description of the *behavior* (from threat to actual force), of the *actor* (not acting as a representative of a nation or its military), of the *target* (typically civilian noncombatants), and of the *motivation* (e.g., to further a political, religious, or ideological cause). But small differences in definitions can mean big changes in classification. While not claiming the "truth" of this conceptualization, the term *terrorism* is used here to refer to *acts of violence (as opposed to threats or more general coercion) intentionally perpetrated on civilian noncombatants with the goal of furthering some ideological, religious, or political objective* (Borum, 2004). This chapter will focus on the offenders—those who perpetrate terrorism—the terrorists themselves.

WHY TERRORISM?

The question that has dominated much of the scholarly and public discourse on terrorists is "Why?" Why would someone intentionally harm or kill third parties (civilians) to further his or her cause? (Crenshaw, 1986; Helmus, 2009; Horgan, 2005; Hudson, 1999; Victoroff, 2005). Acts of terrorism are relatively uncommon, often horrific, and sometimes self-destructive. They seem to defy easy explanation. The fact is that there are many different answers to the "why" question. And those answers can vary from person to person or change for any given person over time. Reasons and explanations also may differ between the group level (i.e., Why would groups choose terrorism as a tactic?) (Pape, 2005) and the individual level (i.e., Why would a person commit such an act?) (Crenshaw, 1988). As other chapters in this volume will attest, no single psychological theory has emerged to satisfactorily explain all types of violence. Terrorism is a distinct form of violence. It is most often deliberate (not impulsive), strategic, and instrumental; it is linked to and justified by ideological (e.g., political, religious) objectives and most often involves a group or multiple actors/supporters (Crenshaw, 1986, 1988; Laqueur, 2003). These issues all add complexity to the construction of terrorism as a form of violence and challenge the emergence of a unifying explanatory theory.

ARE TERRORISTS CRAZY?

Because terrorism is so unusual and so horrific, it is sometimes assumed that terrorists' aberrant behavior must be driven by some type of mental or personality abnormality (Schmid & Jongman, 1988). For most terrorists and most types of terrorism, however, the evidence suggests otherwise. Forty years of research on the relationship between psychopathology and terrorism has been nearly unanimous in its conclusion that mental illness and abnormality are typically not critical factors in explaining terrorist behavior (Borum, 2004; Crenshaw, 1992; Horgan, 2008; Ruby, 2002; Silke, 1998; Victoroff, 2005). Studies have found that the prevalence of mental illness among samples of incarcerated terrorists is as low as or lower than in the general population (Ruby, 2002; Victoroff, 2005). Moreover, although terrorists often commit heinous acts, they would rarely be considered prototypical psychopaths (Silke, 1998; Victoroff, 2005).[1] Terrorists often are willing to sacrifice themselves for principles and form attachments to other people who share them. Psychopaths typically do not (Elliott, 1992; Martens, 2004).

Research to date has neither found, nor come close to finding, any constellation of characteristics resembling a "terrorist personality," or a psychological profile of the terrorist (Horgan, 2003). Though there is no terrorist personality type, it does appear that certain conditions and characteristics can create greater vulnerability to involvement in violent extremism (Horgan, 2008). Vulnerabilities may be viewed as "factors that point to some people having a greater openness to increased engagement than others" (Horgan, 2005, p. 101). Rather than being simple causes, these vulnerabilities may be leveraged as possible sources of motivation or as mechanisms for acquiring or hardening one's militant ideology. Three commonly occurring vulnerabilities are (1) perceived injustice/humiliation; (2) need for identity; and (3) need for belonging (Borum, 2004).

Perceived injustice and humiliation have a long history of being linked to violence generally and terrorism specifically. In the mid-1970s, Hacker (1980) concluded that "remediable injustice is the basic motivation for terrorism" (p. 148).

An individual's search or struggle for identity may draw him or her to extremist or terrorist organizations in a variety of ways. The absolutist, Manichaean, "black and white" nature of most extremist ideologies is often attractive to those who feel overwhelmed by the complexity and stress of navigating a complicated world. It is sometimes easier for an individual to define his or her identity simply through group membership, or identification with a cause, rather than struggle with a quest for personal meaning (Taylor & Louis, 2004). Many prospective terrorists do find a sense of meaning in their "cause," but many also find a sense of belonging, connectedness, and affiliation. Crenshaw (1988) argues that "for the individuals who become active terrorists—the initial attraction is often to the group, or community of believers, rather than to an abstract ideology or to violence" (p. 59). Vulnerabilities may make the individual more open to engagement with violent extremist groups, but those vulnerable conditions are typically not sufficient, by themselves, to create a terrorist.

HOW DO PEOPLE BECOME INVOLVED IN TERRORISM?

Instead of just asking why people become terrorists, it is useful to consider *how* they become involved as well. Involvement is probably best understood as a process, rather than as an event. As McCormick (2003) points out, terrorism involvement is rarely "the product of a single decision, but the end result of a dialectical process that gradually pushes an individual toward a commitment to violence over time" (McCormick, 2003, p. 492). For an individual, the process is often framed as comprising phases of becoming, engaging (in terrorism), and disengaging. Motivations may be different at each stage, and not even necessarily related to each other. At the group/organization level, the corresponding processes are recruitment, mobilization, and demobilization.

Radicalization

The pathways in and through terrorism are much more varied than one might expect. In recent years, many people have used the term "radicalization" to refer generically to the process of becoming a terrorist. But "radicalization" in this narrow sense may be somewhat misleading (Borum, 2011a; Githens-Mazer, 2012). Radicalizing connotes a transformative process of change by which people adopt an extreme, violent ideology—and that ideology ultimately leads them to violent action (Bhui, Dinos, & Jones, 2012). That is certainly one pathway into terrorism involvement, but it is not the only one. Neither "radicalization" nor grievances alone are typically sufficient to cause an individual to engage in terrorism (Bartlett & Miller, 2012; Borum, 2011b; Horgan, 2008).

Ideology

Though ideas or ideologies sometimes drive behavior, behaviors also affect ideas and ideologies (Drake, 1998). Some people attach to a grievance because they adhere to a particular ideology, but others gravitate toward an ideology because they hold a particular grievance. The same is true for group affiliation. Some join a group because they support a shared ideology, but others develop an ideological commitment because of their group affiliation. The strength of a person's conviction and commitment to a cause may precede his or her willingness to participate in violence, but participating in violence may also strengthen a person's conviction and commitment to a cause (Borum, 2011b).

Motivation

Terrorists often have complex and diverse sets of motivations and reasons for their activity (Borum, 2011a, 2011b, 2011c; King & Taylor, 2011). Different people are vulnerable or drawn to violent ideologies and groups for different reasons at different times (Bokhari, Hegghammer, Lia, Nesser, & Tønnessen, 2006; Friedland, 1992; Horgan, 2008; see Borum, 2011a, 2011b, 2011c, for reviews).

HOW DO PEOPLE COME TO ADHERE TO A VIOLENT IDEOLOGY?

The ways that people come to join, engage, and disengage with violent ideologies and actors will vary (Horgan, 2008). There is no universal progression, but there are a couple of conceptual models that describe a generic sequence of stages, events, or issues that might apply across and within group types. Some focus more on the individual, others focus more on the group process, and most include a blend of driving/motivating factors and disinhibiting factors or processes. One approach to understanding the "terrorist mindset" describes how grievances and vulnerabilities are transformed into hatred of a target group and how hatred is transformed—for some—into a justification or impetus for violence (Borum, 2003). The model was not developed as a formal social science theory but as a heuristic for thinking about the process. The starting point is when some unsatisfying event, condition, or grievance (e.g., It's not right) is framed as being unjust (e.g., It's not fair). The injustice is blamed on a target policy, person, or nation (e.g., It's your fault). The responsible party is then vilified—often demonized—(e.g., You're evil), which both drives aggression and disinhibits moral objections.

A similar approach uses a "staircase" metaphor (Moghaddam, 2005) to describe progressions toward terrorism involvement. In the staircase model, a person's feelings of discontent and perceived deprivation nudge him or her initially onto a path to terrorism, though fewer people ascend to each successive level. When an individual's attempts to alleviate his or her discontent and improve her or his situation are unsuccessful, this often leads to feelings of frustration and aggression, which are displaced onto some perceived causal agent, who is then regarded as an enemy. As anger toward that enemy builds, it is possible to increasingly sympathize with the justifications for violence and with the terrorist groups that act against the enemy. Some sympathizers may eventually join an extremist group, organization, or movement that advocates for, and perhaps engages in, terrorist violence. At the top of the staircase are those who have joined, overcome barriers to violent action, and actually commit a terrorist act (Moghaddam, 2005).

Social movement theory (SMT) offers an approach that focuses more on group-level processes to understanding terrorism (Della Porta, 1995). Applying SMT to a Western-based militant jihadist group (Al-Muhajiroun), Wiktorowicz (2003, 2005) observed that "joining the jihad" and becoming a terrorist, for most, were processes that evolved over time. The process of "becoming" typically involved various mechanisms of persuasion occurring in ongoing transactions between the recruit and the members (Wiktorowicz, 2005). His SMT-based model has four key components. A breakdown at any stage can divert the individual from a path to joining or ultimately participating. Wiktorowicz describes those stages as follows:

1. *Cognitive opening*—an individual becomes receptive to the possibility of new ideas and worldviews.
2. *Religious seeking*—the individual seeks meaning through a religious idiom.
3. *Frame alignment*—the public representation proffered by the radical group makes sense to the seeker and attracts his or her initial interest.
4. *Socialization*—the individual experiences religious lessons and activities that facilitate indoctrination and identity-construction. The latter process often includes ideological precepts that tie the individual's self-interest to the risky activism of the movement. (Wiktorowicz, 2005)

A second, group-oriented approach uses a general framework of political radicalization, based on social psychological principles. McCauley and Moskalenko (2008) identified key mechanisms of radicalization that can operate at the individual, group, and mass-public levels. They view radicalization as "[i]ncreasing extremity of beliefs, feelings, and behaviors in directions that increasingly justify intergroup violence and demand sacrifice in defense of the ingroup" (McCauley & Moskalenko, 2008, p. 416). They believe the following mechanisms are most often prominent:

- *Extremity shift in like-minded groups—group polarization*: a dynamic based on the social psychological principle of "group polarization," that the "average" opinions of group members tend to become more extreme as they attempt to negotiate consensus.
- *Social reality power of isolated groups—the multiplier*: a dynamic based on numerous social psychological studies showing when groups are isolated and experiencing conditions of threat, their levels of cohesiveness and perceived interdependence increase, which also enhances member compliance.
- *Group radicalization in competition for the same base of support— outbidding*: a dynamic based on intergroup competition, in which groups who are more radical or more extreme may be perceived as more

committed or devout, which may make them more attractive to potential members and supporters.

- *Activist radicalization in competition with state power—condensation*: a dynamic by which the pressures and adversity of state opposition to a radical group cause less committed members to drop out, with only the most active remaining. Radicalism and commitment among those remaining members tend to intensify.
- *Group radicalization from within-group competition—fissioning*: a dynamic based on the observation that divisive tensions often cause factions to develop within ideologically based groups. Sometimes these factions evolve into "splinter" groups that compete (and sometimes fight) with one another in an escalating battle of extremity.

WHAT ARE THE ROLES OF IDEOLOGY AND "MINDSET"?

An ideology is a common and broadly agreed-upon set of rules to which an individual subscribes and which help to regulate and determine behavior. While ideologies that support terrorism differ greatly from one another, many appear to serve some common *functions*:

- They provide a set of beliefs that guide and justify a series of behavioral mandates.
- Those beliefs must be inviolable and must be neither questionable nor questioned.
- The behaviors must be goal directed and seen as serving some cause or meaningful objective.

A related question is whether common *structures* or patterns might exist across violent extremist ideologies, even when the content of the beliefs is dramatically different (Borum, 2004). One simplistic approach, developed more as a teaching tool than as a social science theory, reviewed a range of violent ideologies from across the religious and political spectra. Four common, overarching characteristics of these ideologies are summarized with the acronym PATH (Borum, 2011d):

- *Polarized*: the essence of which is an "us versus them" mindset, or what some would regard as ingroup–outgroup conflict.
- *Absolutist*: the beliefs are regarded as truth in the absolute sense, sometimes supported by sacred authority. This squelches questioning, critical thinking, and dissent. It also adds moral authority to framing us versus them as a competition between good and bad (or evil).
- *Threat oriented*: external threat causes ingroups to cohere. Good leaders know this intuitively, if not from reading social psychological research. They persistently remind adherents that the "us" is at risk from the "them." Because the "us" is seen as being good or right in the absolute sense, this works not only to promote internal cohesion but also external opposition.

- *Hateful*: hate energizes violent action. It allows principled opposition to impel direct action. It also facilitates various mechanisms of moral disengagement—such as dehumanization—which erode the social and psychological barriers to engaging in violence that one believes are justified (an important point, since many more people endorse the justification for extremist violence than actually commit such acts).

A more systematic and empirically driven approach to understanding the terrorist mindset has been led by Gerard Saucier—a social psychologist at University of Oregon—and his international team of colleagues (Saucier, Akers, Shen-Miller, Knežević, & Stankov, 2009). Saucier and colleagues began with a rationally derived "working model of the major components of the militant-extremist mind-set," then collected books and Web-based material from a diverse range of militant-extremist individuals or groups (religious, social, and political) to see how often certain themes appeared (Saucier et al., 2009, p. 258). The team identified 16 prominent, recurring themes that they judged to be characteristic of a militant-extremist mindset. Each of these 16 themes was found to occur in three or more groups (Saucier et al., 2009, p. 259).

1. The necessity of unconventional and extreme measures
2. Use of tactics that function to absolve one of responsibility for the bad consequences of the violence one is advocating or carrying out
3. Prominent mixtures of military terminology into areas of discourse where it is otherwise rarely found
4. Perception that the ability of the group to reach its rightful position is being tragically obstructed
5. Glorifying the past, in reference to one's group
6. Utopianizing. There is frequently reference to concepts of a future paradise, or at least "the promise of a long and glorious future."
7. Catastrophizing. There is a perception that great calamities either have occurred, are occurring, or will occur.
8. Anticipation of supernatural intervention: miraculous powers attributed to one's side, miraculous events coming to help one's side, or commands coming from supernatural entities
9. A felt imperative to annihilate (exterminate, crush, destroy) evil and/or purify the world entirely from evil
10. Glorification of dying for the cause
11. Duty and obligation to kill, or to make offensive war
12. Machiavellianism in service of the "sacred." This theme involves the belief that those with the right (i.e., true) beliefs and values are entitled to use immoral ends if necessary to assure the success of their cause.
13. An elevation of intolerance, vengeance, and warlikeness into virtues (or nearly so), including, in some cases, the ascribing of such militant dispositions to supernatural entities
14. Dehumanizing or demonizing of opponents
15. The modern world as a disaster. Among militant extremists, there is commonly a perception that modernity, including the consumer society

and even instances of successful economic progress, is actually a disaster for humanity.

16. Civil government as illegitimate

These are the thematic elements that militant-extremist groups appear to use to craft a "narrative" for their ideologies. Saucier and colleagues offer the following description of how these themes might cohere in a narrative:

> We (i.e., our group, however defined) have a glorious past, but modernity has been disastrous, bringing on a great catastrophe in which we are tragically obstructed from reaching our rightful place, obstructed by an illegitimate civil government and/or by an enemy so evil that it does not even deserve to be called human. This intolerable situation calls for vengeance. Extreme measures are required; indeed, any means will be justified for realizing our sacred end. We must think in military terms to annihilate this evil and purify the world of it. It is a duty to kill the perpetrators of evil, and we cannot be blamed for carrying out this violence. Those who sacrifice themselves in our cause will attain glory, and supernatural powers should come to our aid in this struggle. In the end, we will bring our people to a new world that is a paradise. (Saucier et al., 2009, p. 265)

Though their research is based primarily on written documents and secondary sources, the work of Saucier and colleagues stands out in a field where empirical research is all too uncommon.

HOW DO GROUPS CONTRIBUTE TO TERRORISM INVOLVEMENT?

Recruitment

While some militants enter in as seekers, others are strategically sought out. This is the process of recruitment. Surprisingly little research or analysis has been conducted on terrorist recruitment (Daly & Gerwehr, 2006; Faria & Arce, 2005, 2012). Some debate even exists among contemporary scholars about what qualifies as recruitment activity. Many people "enlist" in a militant cause because they want to join. In studies of militant Islamist groups, nearly 90% "join the jihad" through friendship and kinship (Sageman, 2004). Traditional recruitment—as the military does with a dedicated budget and personnel—may not be terrorists' modus operandi. It is almost beyond question, though, that militants seek new supporters, activists, and members and that they engage in active efforts to influence others to adopt their point of view. That is arguably just a broader conceptualization of recruitment.

Social movement scholars have studied activist recruitment for decades. One of the prevailing concepts is that when members of the movement look to recruit others, they operate as "rational prospectors" (Brady, Schlozman, & Verba, 1999). They want to be efficient and effective, so they seek to identify those most likely to agree, if asked, to act effectively to further the cause. Brady and colleagues (1999)

"conceive of the recruitment process as having two stages: (1) rational prospectors use information to find likely targets; (2) after locating them, recruiters offer
information on participatory opportunities and deploy inducements to persuade
recruits to say 'yes'" (p. 154). Central to both tasks is the existence and strength of
relationships. Understanding relationships among potential prospects is critical to
understanding recruitment networks.

Mobilization

Ideology, by itself, is generally not sufficient to create a terrorist. Not all extremist
ideologies facilitate violence, nor are all extremists violent. Getting people to *act* in
service of a cause, not just to espouse a set of beliefs or maintain nominal allegiance
to a group, is a process that social movement theorists call mobilization (Zald &
McCarthy, 1987).

People and structures within a movement mobilize others by increasing their
perceived benefits (e.g., sense of belonging, personal meaning, and approval of god/
others) and minimizing and manipulating the perceived costs (Munger, 2006).
There are common barriers and disincentives to engaging in violence, including
how we think that others will judge our behavior as well as how we judge ourselves.
To mitigate these barriers, extremist groups will often use levers of psychological
and social influence. The barriers can be manipulated externally (i.e., effects of
the group or social environment) or internally (i.e., making an internal cognitive
adjustment about how to perceive the environment or situation).

Facilitating Violence

Four external influences operate to minimize disincentives (psychological costs) to
high-risk (violent) activism: diffusion of responsibility, deindividuation, obedience,
and social identity. Diffusion of responsibility is a social-psychological phenomenon
by which individuals feel less responsible (or less culpable) for transgressive behavior when they commit it either in the presence of or on behalf of a group (Darley
& Latane, 1968; Guerin, 2012). Deindividuation is a state or situation in which
the focus of judgment is on a collective rather than on an individual (Zimbardo,
1969). This reduces an individual's inhibition or restraint either by reducing his or
her self-awareness or by facilitating conformity to situation-specific norms (Silke,
2003). Obedience to authority is another phenomenon that diminishes personal
responsibility because the actor transfers his or her moral agency from self to the
authority (Blass, 1999; Milgram, 1974). Finally, social identities (Tajfel & Turner,
1986)—the ways in which we view ourselves in relation to social groups or categories—can also weaken individual responsibility by boosting the salience of group
norms (Cikara, Botvinick, & Fiske, 2011; Muldoon, Schmid, & Downes, 2009).

Internal influences that mitigate disincentives typically involve modifying
self-appraisals (Leidner, Castano, Zaiser, & Giner-Sorolla, 2010). As adults, most
people have developed a basic capacity to control their behavior and regulate their
actions. Their internal moral code typically guides their choices. If a person violates
his or her own moral code, he or she may make negative judgments or attributions

about himself or herself (Bandura, 1990, 2004). Psychologist Albert Bandura notes, however, that these self-sanctions can be selectively "activated and disengaged" to facilitate behavior that a person's moral code would otherwise inhibit. Bandura describes this process of breaking down barriers as "moral disengagement," which can operate through a variety of processes.

One way to remove the barrier of self-sanction is to change the way you interpret events so that they justify the act (moral justification). Terrorists typically have some type of justification for their action, whether it is personally construed or derived from the group's ideology (Leidner & Castano, 2012; Leidner et al., 2010). A second mechanism is "blaming the victim," since targeting aggression at people who have caused harm or are considered blameworthy or deserving of retribution is more morally acceptable. Another mechanism of moral disengagement is for the actor to dehumanize the way he or she views the victim (Bastian, Denson, & Haslam, 2013). Della Porta (1992), for example, describes how Italian "militants justified their use of political violence by depersonalizing their victims, defined in the documents of the underground groups as 'tools of the system' and later as 'pigs' or 'watch dogs.'"

ARE LONE OFFENDERS DIFFERENT THAN OTHER TERRORISTS?

In recent years, there has been increasing concern about lone offender attacks, but the phenomenon of solo or lone offender terrorism is certainly not new. In the latter part of the 19th century, Russian (and some European) anarchists were inciting individual attacks and direct actions as a way to bring attention to their cause (Iviansky, 1977). Attacks by unaffiliated individuals have been a feature of terrorism in the United States for many decades, comprising about 6.5% of known terrorist attacks there between 1970 and 2007 (NC-START, 2010). In fact, an analysis from the National Consortium for the Study of Terrorism and Responses to Terrorism (NC-START) suggests that the 1995 Oklahoma City Bombing marked a shift in American terrorism toward more individual attackers. Their report notes that:

> since 1995, a much higher percentage of terrorist attacks in the United States have been conducted by unaffiliated individuals, rather than by organized groups. In the period 1995 (post-Oklahoma City) through 2007, 43 out of 131 incidents with attributed perpetrators were committed by individuals—**33% of all attacks** in the United States in this period. (NC-START, 2010, p. 2) (emphasis in original)

A variety of terms and definitions have been used within the past decade to characterize the phenomenon of lone offender terrorism. Popular use of the term "lone wolf" as it applies to terrorist-type attacks appears to have its origins in American White supremacist movements in the 1990s. The term has been criticized, however, because it carries the potential to glorify or to imbue an image of power to attackers who are otherwise powerless and often ineffectual.

Deciding what should qualify as a "lone offender" attack is more complicated than it might seem at first. A range of definitions has emerged (Borum, Fein, & Vossekuil, 2012; COT, 2007; Pantucci, 2011; Schmid & Jongman, 1988; van der Heide, 20011). Some definitions indicate the attacker must act alone; others allow for an accomplice. Some completely exclude cases in which there is any evidence of contact with an extremist group. Still others exclude them only when the attack is "group involved." Some definitions stick to the narrow traditional requirement of political/social/ideological motivations, whereas others allow for a fuzzy blend of personal and ideological motivations.

Dimensions of an Attack

Analyzing cases by their features (using a dimensional approach), rather than by their types, might lead to a better case conceptualization. Three possible dimensions for this type of analysis have been proposed: loneness, direction, and motivation (Borum et al., 2012). Loneness describes the extent to which the offender/ attacker initiated, planned, prepared for, and executed the attack without assistance from any other person. It is the dimension of planning and acting alone, characterizing the independence of activity. This dimension would include the nature and degree of the suspect's contacts with other extremists or accomplices, as well as others' "roles," and the nature and degree of their involvement with the suspect or with the attack. Support from others might include both material (typically involving goods or services) and expressive (typically involving social or emotional transactions that facilitate or amplify a permissive environment) types.

Direction, the second dimension, refers to nature and extent of the attacker's independence and autonomy in all decisions across the spectrum of attack-related activity from idea to action. It describes not only influences but also the extent to which issues of whether, whom, when, or how to attack were "directed" by others.

Finally, motivation describes the extent to which the attack is significantly driven by a political, social, or ideologically based grievance, not solely by revenge or some other personal motive. Motivation is of interest, in part because a subject's motives for an attack are usually related to the target he or she selects, and it is possibly the most difficult of the three dimensions to discern (Artiga, n.d.). As COT (2007) noted, "[a]ssigning purposes and motivations to individual acts of terror is inherently subjective and open to considerable interpretation."

Mental Illness

A number of recent case studies and observations suggest that mental health issues tend to occur more often and more prominently among lone offenders than among other terrorists (COT, 2007; Fein & Vossekuil, 1999; Gill, Horgan, & Deckert, 2014; Spaaij, 2010). A recent study by Gruenewald et al. (2013) found "mental illness" to be one of only a handful of factors that reliably distinguished lone offenders from other extremist homicide offenders.

Based on news reports and other open-source documents, Gill et al. (2014) also found that nearly one third (31%) of the 119 lone-actor terrorists they studied had a history of mental health problems. A systematic study of the thinking and behavior of all 83 individuals known to have attacked, or approached to attack, a prominent public official or public figure in the United States since 1949 (Fein & Vossekuil, 1999) found nearly two thirds (61%) had been evaluated or treated by a mental health professional; almost half (44%) had a history of serious depression or despair. More than 40% (43%) were known to be delusional at the time of the principal attack/approach incident, and one in five had a history of auditory hallucinations.

In 2012, reporter Mark Follman, Gavin Aronsen, and Deanna Pan (2013) from *Mother Jones* magazine reviewed open-source information from 63 firearm-related mass murders (all by lone shooters) occurring in the United States since 1982 and found evidence of mental health problems in two thirds (65%) of the cases.

Just because the offender has identifiable psychological problems, however, does not mean that the diagnostic label or disorder fully accounts for his thinking, motives, and behavior. People with mental illnesses and personality disorders often can plan and execute bad behaviors just as well as those who do not have a diagnosis (Fein & Vossekuil, 1999). Several researchers have noted that whether a lone offender is organized may be more important than any mental disorder that an offender may have (Borum, 2013).

A person's level of personal organization includes his or her ability to engage in goal-directed behavior and to act on his or her intentions. The cognitive organizational skills necessary for goal-directed behavior involve *thinking logically* (i.e., that anticipated consequences reasonably follow from anticipation action); *coherence* (i.e., the ability to connect together different ideas and elements of thought to formulate an overarching concept or plan); *consistency* (i.e., that the assumptions, premises, and anticipated actions are "internally consistent"—that they do not conflict or directly contradict one another); and finally, *control* (i.e., capacity for self-regulation to monitor, inhibit, and intentionally execute specific cognitive, emotional, and behavioral functions) (Borum, 2013).

CONCLUSION

In the second decade of the 21st century, terrorism remains among the most serious global security concerns. Behavioral scientists have often attempted to explain why people engage in terrorism, but the reasons and mechanisms by which people become involved, stay involved, and sometimes leave terrorism are diverse and dynamic. No "terrorist personality" type has been identified, nor has any accurate, useful profile been developed. Mental illness, in most cases, is not a significant driving factor, though recent studies show that psychological problems may be more common among "lone offender" terrorists. Group dynamics can strongly influence the process of terrorism involvement and a person's attachment to a violent ideology. But those influences work both ways. Some join a group because they support a shared ideology, but others develop or strengthen an ideological commitment because of their group affiliation. By better understanding the human dynamics of terrorism and of the terrorists, perhaps more effective actions can be taken to manage the threat.

NOTE

1. Psychopaths are persons who possess both a pervasive and persistent history of antisocial behavior and severe, endogenous emotional/affective deficits such as callousness and lack of empathy and remorse.

REFERENCES

Artiga, V. (n.d.) Lone wolf terrorism: What we need to know and what we need to do. *Homeland Security News. Tak Response.* Retrieved from http://www.takresponse. com/index/homeland-security/lone-wolf_terrorism.html

Bandura, A. (1990). Mechanisms of moral disengagement. In W. Reich (Ed.), *Origins of terrorism: Psychologies, ideologies, theologies, states of mind* (pp. 161–191). Cambridge, UK: Cambridge University Press.

Bandura, A. (2004). The origins and consequences of moral disengagement: A social learning perspective. In F. M. Moghaddam & A. J. Marsella (Eds.), *Understanding terrorism: Psychosocial roots, consequences, and interventions.* Washington, DC: American Psychological Association.

Bartlett, J., & Miller, C. (2012). The edge of violence: Towards telling the difference between violent and non-violent radicalization. *Terrorism and Political Violence, 24*(1), 1–21.

Bastian, B., Denson, T. F., & Haslam, N. (2013). The roles of dehumanization and moral outrage in retributive justice. *PloS One, 8*(4), e61842.

Ben-Yehuda, H., & Levin-Banchik, L. (2010). The dangers of terror in world politics: International terror crises, 1918–2006. *Studies in Conflict and Terrorism, 34*(1), 31–46.

Bhui, K. S., Dinos, S., & Jones, E. (2012). Psychological process and pathways to radicalization. *Journal of Bioterrorism and Biodefense,* S5, 003.

Blass, T. (1999). The Milgram Paradigm after 35 years: Some things we now know about obedience to authority. *Journal of Applied Social Psychology, 29*(5), 955–978.

Bokhari, L., Hegghammer, T., Lia, B., Nesser, P., & Tønnessen, T. (2006, March 15). Paths to global jihad: Radicalisation and recruitment to terror networks. [FFI/RAPPORT-2006/00935]. Proceedings from a FFI Seminar, Oslo. Kjeller, Norway: Norwegian Defense Research Establishment.

Borum, R. (2003). Understanding the terrorist mind-set. *FBI Law Enforcement Bulletin, 72*(July), 7–10.

Borum, R. (2004). *Psychology of terrorism.* Tampa: University of South Florida.

Borum, R. (2011a). Rethinking radicalization. *Journal of Strategic Security, 4*(4), 1–6.

Borum, R. (2011b). Radicalization and involvement in violent extremism I: A review of definitions and applications of social science theories. *Journal of Strategic Security, 4*(4), 7–36.

Borum, R. (2011c). Radicalization and involvement in violent extremism II: A review of conceptual models and empirical research. *Journal of Strategic Security, 4*(4), 37–62.

Borum, R. (2011d). Understanding terrorist psychology. In A. Silke (Ed.), *The psychology of counter-terrorism* (pp. 19–33). New York, NY: Routledge.

Borum, R. (2013). Informing lone-offender investigations. *Criminology and Public Policy, 12*(1), 103–112.

Borum, R., Fein, R., & Vossekuil, B. (2012). Dimensions of lone offender terrorism. *Aggression and Violent Behavior, 17,* 389–396.

Brady, H., Schlozman, K., & Verba, S. (1999). Prospecting for participants: Rational expectations and the recruitment of political activists. *American Political Science Review, 93,* 153–168.

Buzan, B. (2006). Will the 'global war on terrorism' be the new Cold War? *International Affairs, 82*(6), 1101–1118.

Cikara, M., Botvinick, M. M., & Fiske, S. T. (2011). Us versus them social identity shapes neural responses to intergroup competition and harm. *Psychological science, 22*(3), 306–313.

COT (Ed.). (2007, July). Lone-wolf terrorism. [Case study for Work Package 3 'Citizens and governance in a knowledge-based society']. Retrieved from http://www.transna tionalterrorism.eu/tekst/publications/Lone-Wolf%20Terrorism.pdf

Crenshaw, M. (1986). The psychology of political terrorism. In M.G. Hermann (Ed.), *Political psychology: Contemporary problems and issues* (pp. 379–413). London, UK: Josey-Bass.

Crenshaw, M. (1988). The subjective reality of the terrorist: Ideological and psychological factors in terrorism. In R. O. Slater & M. Stohl (Eds.), *Current perspectives in international terrorism*. Basingstoke, UK: Macmillan.

Crenshaw, M. (1992). How terrorists think: What psychology can contribute to understanding terrorism. In L. Howard (Ed.), *Terrorism: Roots, impact, responses* (pp. 71–80). London, UK: Praeger.

Daly, S., & Gerwehr, S (2006). Al-Qaida: Terrorist selection and recruitment. In D. Kamien (Ed.), *The McGraw-Hill homeland security handbook* (pp. 73–89). New York, NY: McGraw-Hill.

Darley, J. M., & Latane, B. (1968). Bystander intervention in emergencies: Diffusion of responsibility. *Journal of Personality and Social Psychology, 8*, 377–383.

Della Porta, D. (1992). Political socialization in left-wing underground organisations: Biographies of Italian and German militants. *International Social Movement Research, 4*, 259–290.

Della Porta, D. (1995). *Social movements, political violence and the state.* Cambridge, UK: Cambridge University Press.

Drake, C. J. M. (1998). The role of ideology in terrorists' target selection. *Terrorism and Political Violence, 10*(2), 53–85.

Elliott, C. (1992). Diagnosing blame: Responsibility and the psychopath. *Journal of Medicine and Philosophy, 17*(2), 199–214.

Enders, W., & Sandler, T. (1999). Transnational terrorism in the post–Cold War era. *International Studies Quarterly, 43*(1), 145–167.

Faria, J. R., & Arce, D. (2012). Counterterrorism and its impact on terror support and recruitment: Accounting for backlash. *Defence and Peace Economics, 23*(5), 431–445.

Faria, J. R., & Arce, D. G. (2005). Terror support and recruitment. *Defence and Peace Economics, 16*(4), 263–273.

Fein, R. A., & Vossekuil, B. (1999). Assassination in the United States: An operational study of recent assassins, attackers, and near-lethal approachers. *Journal of Forensic Sciences, 50*, 321–333.

Follman, M., Aronsen, G., & Pan, D. (2013, December 28). US Mass Shootings, 1982–2012: Data from Mother Jones' investigation. Mother Jones. Retrieved May 2013 from http://motherjones.com/politics/2012/12/mass-shootings-mother-jones-full-data.

Friedland, N. (1992). Becoming a terrorist: Social, and individual antecedents. In L. Howard (Ed.), *Terrorism: Roots, impacts, responses* (pp. 81–93). New York, NY: Praeger.

Ganor, B. (2002). Defining terrorism: Is one man's terrorist another man's freedom fighter? *Police Practice and Research, 3*(4), 287–304.

Garrison, A. H. (2004). Defining terrorism: Philosophy of the bomb, propaganda by deed and change through fear and violence. *Criminal Justice Studies, 17*(3), 259–279.

Gill, P., Horgan, J., & Deckert, P. (2014). Bombing alone: Tracing the motivations and antecedent behaviors of lone-actor terrorists. *Journal of Forensic Sciences, 59*(2), 425–435.

Githens-Mazer, J. (2012). The rhetoric and reality: Radicalization and political discourse. *International Political Science Review, 33*(5), 556–567.

Gruenewald, J., Chermak, S., & Freilich, J. D. (2013). Distinguishing "loner" attacks from other domestic extremist violence. *Criminology and Public Policy, 12*(1), 65–91.

Guerin, B. (2012). Diffusion of responsibility. In D. Christie (Ed.), *Encyclopedia of peace psychology.* Chichester, UK: Wiley-Blackwell.

Hacker, F. J. (1980). Terror and terrorism: Modern growth industry and mass entertainment. *Studies in Conflict & Terrorism, 4*(1–4), 143–159.

Helmus, T. (2009), Why and how some people become terrorists. In P. K. Davis & K. Cragin (Eds.), *Social science for counterterrorism: Putting the pieces together* (pp. 71–111). Santa Monica, CA: RAND Corporation.

Horgan, J. (2003). The search for the terrorist personality. In A. Silke (Ed.), *Terrorists, victims, and society: Psychological perspectives on terrorism and its consequence* (pp. 3–27). London, UK: John Wiley.

Horgan, J. (2005). *The psychology of terrorism.* London, UK: Routledge.

Horgan, J. (2008). From profiles to pathways and roots to routes: Perspectives from psychology on radicalization into terrorism.' *Annals of the American Association of Political and Social Sciences, 618,* 80–94.

Hudson, R. (1999). *The sociology and psychology of terrorism: Who becomes a terrorist and why?* Washington, DC: Library of Congress, Federal Research Division.

Iviansky, Z. (1977). Individual terror: Concept and typology. *Journal of Contemporary History, 12,* 45.

King, M., & Taylor, D. M. (2011). The radicalization of homegrown jihadists: A review of theoretical models and social psychological evidence. *Terrorism and Political Violence, 23*(4), 602–622.

Laqueur, W. (2003). *No end to war: Terrorism in the twenty-first century.* New York, NY: Continuum.

Leidner, B., & Castano, E. (2012). Morality shifting in the context of intergroup violence. *European Journal of Social Psychology, 42*(1), 82–91.

Leidner, B., Castano, E., Zaiser, E., & Giner-Sorolla, R. (2010). Ingroup glorification, moral disengagement, and justice in the context of collective violence. *Personality and Social Psychology Bulletin, 36*(8), 1115–1129.

Martens, W. (2004). Terrorist with antisocial personality disorder. *Journal of Forensic Psychology Practice, 4,* 45–56.

McCauley, C., & Moskalenko, S. (2008). Mechanisms of political radicalization: Pathways toward terrorism. *Terrorism and Political Violence, 20*(3), 415–433.

McCormick, G. H. (2003). Terrorist decision making. *Annual Review of Political Science, 6*(1), 473–507.

Mello, P. A. (2010). Review article: In search of new wars: The debate about a transformation of war. *European Journal of International Relations, 16*(2), 297–309.

Milgram, S. (1974). *Obedience to authority: An experimental view*. New York, NY: Harper & Row.

Moghaddam, F. M. (2005). The staircase to terrorism: A psychological explanation. *American Psychologist, 60*, 161–169.

Muldoon, O. T., Schmid, K., & Downes, C. (2009). Political violence and psychological well-being: The role of social identity. *Applied Psychology, 58*(1), 129–145.

Munger, M. (2006). Preference modification vs. incentive manipulation as tools of terrorist recruitment: The role of culture. *Public Choice, 128*, 131-146.

National Consortium for the Study of Terrorism and Responses to Terrorism (START). (2010, April 16). *Background report: On the fifteenth anniversary of the Oklahoma City bombing*. College Park, MD: National Consortium for the Study of Terrorism and Responses to Terrorism.

Neumann, P. (2009). *Old and new terrorism. Late modernity, globalization and the transformation of political violence*. Cambridge, UK: Polity Press.

Pantucci, R. (2011, March). *A typology of lone wolves: Preliminary analysis of lone Islamist terrorists*. London, UK: International Centre for the Study of Radicalisation and Political Violence (ICSR).

Pape, R. (2005). *Dying to win: The strategic logic of suicide terrorism*. New York, NY: Random House Digital.

Pfahl-Traughber, A. (2011). Potential risks of politically motivated violence-A comparative analysis of old and new terrorism. *Siak-Journal for Police Science and Practice, International Edition, 1*, 79-87.

Ruby, C. (2002). Are terrorists mentally deranged? *Analyses of Social Issues and Public Policy, 2*, 15–26.

Sageman, M. (2004). *Understanding terror networks*. Philadelphia: University of Pennsylvania Press.

Saucier, G., Akers, L., Shen-Miller, S., Knežević, G., & Stankov, L. (2009). Patterns of thinking in militant extremism. *Perspectives on Psychological Science, 4*(3), 256–271.

Schmid, A., & Jongman, A. (1988). *Political terrorism: A new guide to actors, authors, concepts, data bases, theories, and literature*. New Brunswick, NJ: Transaction.

Silke, A. (1998). Cheshire-Cat logic: The recurring theme of terrorist abnormality in psychological research. *Psychology, Crime and Law, 41*, 51–69.

Silke, A. (2003). Deindividuation, anonymity and violence: Findings from Northern Ireland. *Journal of Social Psychology, 143/4*, 493–499.

Spaaij, R. (2010). The enigma of lone wolf terrorism: An assessment. *Studies in Conflict and Terrorism, 33*, 854–870.

Tajfel, H., & Turner, J. C. (1986). The social identity theory of inter-group behaviour. In S. Worchel & L. W. Austin (Eds.), *Psychology of intergroup relations*. Chicago, IL: Nelson-Hall.

Taylor, D. M., & Louis, W. (2004). Terrorism and the quest for identity. In F. Moghaddam & A. Marsella (Eds.), *Understanding terrorism: Psychosocial roots, consequences, and interventions* (pp. 169–185). Washington, DC: American Psychological Association.

van der Heide, L. (2011, August 15). Individual terrorism: Indicators of lone operators. Master thesis in International Relations, University of Utrecht. Retrieved from: http://igitur-archive.library.uu.nl/student-theses/2011-0902-202354/UUindex.html

Victoroff, J. (2005). The mind of the terrorist: A review and critique of psychological approaches. *Journal of Conflict Resolution, 49*, 3–42.

Wiktorowicz, Q. (Ed.). (2003). *Islamic activism: A social movement theory approach.* Bloomington: Indiana University Press.

Wiktorowicz, Q. (2005). *Radical Islam rising: Muslim extremism in the West.* Lanham, MD: Rowman & Littlefield.

Zald, M., & McCarthy, J. (1987). *Social movements in an organizational society.* New Brunswick, NJ: Transaction.

Zimbardo, P. G. (1969). The human choice: Individuation, reason, and order versus deindividuation, impulse, and chaos. *Nebraska Symposium on Motivation, 17,* 237–307.

Evaluative Approach and Special Considerations

15

Legal, Clinical, and Scientific Foundations of Violence Risk Assessment

DAVID F. MRAD AND DANIEL J. NELLER ■

The assessment of violence risk is a common task among forensic practitioners. Such assessments, in one form or another, occur in a variety of criminal and civil contexts. Formal violence risk assessments, ones in which assessing violence risk is a main and explicit goal, occur in traditional and sexual predator civil commitment and release proceedings, pretrial bond hearings, parole decisions, and criminal sentencing proceedings, especially in capital cases. A practitioner who does not engage in these activities might nonetheless routinely conduct informal violence risk assessments each time he or she allows a client or patient to leave his or her office or emergency room. Thus, the need for training in violence risk assessment is virtually universal for clinical practitioners.

Arguably, no area of forensic mental health has developed more in the past three decades, both in terms of practice and research, than violence risk assessment. The impetus for this growth was a now classic monograph by Monahan (1981), describing the state of the field, recommending more thorough approaches, and challenging others to improve the quality of the research. Although Monahan may have ignited three decades of advancing research, the legal arena of the times provided the fuel that kindled the fire.

LEGAL FOUNDATIONS OF RISK ASSESSMENT

As Heilbrun (2009) indicated, there is no single meaningful legal standard related to risk assessment; this is because standards vary for different legal questions. In fact, Heilbrun also noted that at least half of the 20 volumes in the current *Best Practices in Forensic Mental Health Assessment* series (Heilbrun, Grisso, & Goldstein, 2009) deal with some aspect of risk assessment. There are, however, some landmark decisions that have necessitated or supported the clinical practice of risk assessment.

In 1975, the US Supreme Court in *O'Connor v. Donaldson* held that substantive due process required that "nondangerous" individuals, who could live safely in the community with the willing assistance of others, could not be deprived of liberty by involuntary psychiatric hospitalization. The effect of that decision was to nullify statutes allowing civil commitment on the basis of mental illness alone. Subsequently, determinations of dangerousness would be necessary to justify involuntary civil commitment.

A year later, the Supreme Court of California established a new duty for psychotherapists whose patients posed a risk of harm to third parties (*Tarasoff v. The Regents of the University of California*, 1976). In that now famous decision, the court held that therapists had a duty to protect identifiable third parties when they "determine, or under applicable professional standards reasonably should have determined, that a patient poses a serious danger of violence to others" (p. 439). Apart from the requirement that therapists break confidentiality to comply with this ruling, perhaps the most controversial aspect was the expectation that reasonable therapists should be able to determine when a patient poses a serious risk of danger.

Particularly given the state of predictive knowledge at that time, the expectation that all reasonable therapists should be able to predict violence was anything but reasonable. In fact, in his separate opinion, Judge Mosk concurred that psychotherapists had a duty to protect when they determined a patient posed a danger; however, in reference to applying that duty to situations in which the therapist "should have" been able to predict violence, he wrote, "The majority's expansion of that rule will take us from the world of reality into the wonderland of clairvoyance" (p. 452).

Despite Judge Mosk's caveat, several states subsequently adopted some version of the *Tarasoff* duty, either by statute or case law. Those versions differ greatly in defining when the duty is triggered and how it must be discharged (by warning or protecting); however, they all establish some requirement that therapists recognize when their clients pose a risk of danger to someone else in order to take some action.

In 1983, the US Supreme Court decided a pair of cases that further clarified the Court's thinking on establishing dangerousness and predicting violence. In *Barefoot v. Estelle* (1983), the Court addressed the issue of whether a psychiatrist who had not examined a defendant could testify about risk of future violence based on hypothetical questions. In accordance with Texas law, jurors, in the penalty phase of a capital case, were required to decide whether a defendant convicted of murder would pose a risk of future harm to others. Although the principal issue in this case was the admissibility of testimony based on hypotheticals, the American Psychiatric Association filed an *amicus* brief contending that psychiatrists could not accurately, and therefore should not, offer opinions on future dangerousness.

In its holding, the Court identified numerous instances in both criminal and civil proceedings in which estimations of violence risk were essential and routinely made. It concluded that there was no reason to believe psychiatrists were uniquely unqualified to offer opinions that were routinely drawn by judges and parole boards. The Court stated, "The suggestion that no psychiatrist's testimony may be presented with respect to a defendant's future dangerousness is somewhat like asking us to disinvent the wheel" (*Barefoot v. Estelle*, p. 896).

In reaching its opinion in *Barefoot*, the Court pointed out that neither side contended clinicians were always wrong when predicting future violence, just usually wrong. It seems that the Court's reasoning in this case was based on the principle of necessity. The legal system requires and depends on risk assessments; therefore, someone must be capable of doing them, and mental health professionals should not be regarded as unsuited for the task.

The other important case decided in 1983 was that of a young man in the District of Columbia who was adjudicated not guilty by reason of insanity for an attempted theft of a jacket (*Jones v. U.S.*, 1983). Jones challenged the D.C. law that allowed for indefinite commitment, arguing that he should not be detained any longer than the sentence he could have received if convicted of the crime, or at least his continued commitment should be subject to a different burden and standard of proof after that time period. The Court denied his appeal, reasoning that his commitment was for treatment of his mental illness and dangerousness and was not subject to the limitations of commitments for punishment.

More important, for the issue of violence risk assessment, the Court clarified its view on the type of evidence needed to establish risk. Recognizing that a defendant who pleads not guilty by reason of insanity is acknowledging commission of the underlying criminal act, the majority held, "The fact that a person has been found, beyond a reasonable doubt, to have committed a criminal act *certainly indicates dangerousness*" (p. 364; emphasis added). Although many mental health professionals might have believed that only criminal acts of violence were indicative of dangerousness, the Court also stated, "This Court never has held that 'violence,' however that term might be defined, is a prerequisite for a constitutional commitment" (p. 365). Thus, the Court made clear that an act of actual violence was not a necessary element to justify a commitment based on mental illness and dangerousness.

An additional case, *Foucha v. Louisiana* (1992), sheds light on the constitutional requirements for managing a potentially dangerous person. The petitioner in the case, Foucha, committed violent acts while possibly experiencing a substance-induced psychosis. He was acquitted by reason of insanity and then civilly committed. According to Louisiana law, insanity acquittees could be released from commitment only after they proved they were no longer dangerous. The practitioners who evaluated Foucha following his commitment described him as antisocial and possibly paranoid, but they agreed he was no longer psychotic and was "in 'good shape' mentally" (p. 75). Nonetheless, one of the practitioners expressed discomfort in opining Foucha would be safe for release. The Court ruled the Louisiana law unconstitutional because it permitted continued commitment on the basis of dangerousness without a finding of present mental disorder. According to several commentators (e.g., Conroy & Murrie, 2007; Heilbrun, 2009), Foucha demonstrates the Court's willingness to make distinctions based on what it views as the underlying causes of an individual's violence risk rather than on violence risk alone. These distinctions may prove important in jurisdictions that require a nexus between violence risk and mental disease or defect.

These cases demonstrate some important principles in understanding the expectations and requirements of the legal system regarding risk assessment. The courts expect violence predictions to be made in a number of contexts, and they believe that mental health professionals are capable of making them. The legal system may attach specific meanings to the term "dangerous" that may not be consistent with the typical thinking of practitioners. Finally, the legal system does not treat all risks the same and may determine dispositions based on the underlying contributors to risk.

CLINICAL AND SCIENTIFIC FOUNDATIONS OF RISK ASSESSMENT

The use of a model is a fundamental principle of forensic mental health assessment (Heilbrun, 2001; Heilbrun et al., 2009; Heilbrun, Marczyk, & DeMatteo, 2002). Several such models are available for the assessment of violence risk (e.g., Conroy & Murrie, 2007; Heilbrun, 2009; Mills, Kroner, & Morgan, 2011; also see Witt & Conroy, 2009). These models share common themes, yet we find the one developed by Conroy and Murrie (2007) to be particularly useful because it is general enough to apply across most situations that demand assessments of violence risk.

In their model, Conroy and Murrie contend the following components are essential to violence risk assessment: defining the question, considering base rate and normative data, considering empirically supported risk and protective factors, considering idiographic risk factors, communicating results, and linking risk assessment to risk management. In the sections that follow, we discuss the importance of defining the question; we address base rate issues; we review findings relevant to assessment methods and instruments; and we list common risk factors. Then, we provide a brief overview of findings relevant to risk communication and risk management.

Defining the Question

Practitioners may easily overlook or make incorrect assumptions about the first of these components, defining the question. As Conroy and Murrie indicate, practitioners should be concerned about and clarify, at least, the type of violence that is at issue, the time period for which the assessment is being made, and whether the specific cause for the violence is relevant. For instance, two relevant federal statutes define the type of violence at issue as "substantial risk of bodily injury to another or serious damage to the property of another" (Title 18 U.S. Code, Sections 4243 and 4246). Those same statutes do not specify a timeframe. The risk is not limited to imminent danger. The statutes do, however, specify that the risk be the result of a mental disease or defect.

Attending to Base Rates

Just as practitioners might fail to adequately define the referral question, so too might they neglect base rates. Yet the base rate (BR) arguably is the single most important piece of data available for the assessment of recidivism risk (Furby, Weinrott, & Blackshaw, 1989; Monahan, 1981). Applied to violence risk assessment, it is the proportion of people who violently recidivate; sometimes referred to as a priori probability, it represents a probability estimate before any procedures have been applied. Generally, it is good practice to consider BR data in light of the true- and false-positive rates (TPR, FPR) of the classification method (Haynes, Smith, & Hunsley, 2011).[1]

Recidivism BRs are unstable for several reasons (e.g., Blumstein & Larson, 1971). These include but are not limited to varying operational definitions of recidivism (e.g., self-report, rearrest, reconviction, reincarceration); lengths of follow-up periods (e.g., 2 months, 25 years); contexts in which the outcome is expected to occur (e.g., institution, community); types of offender populations under study (e.g., psychiatric inpatients, child sexual abusers); and rates of jurisdictional apprehension and reporting.

Local BRs are preferred when available (e.g., Meehl & Rosen, 1955). When local BRs are unavailable, in many contexts practitioners may discern reasonable estimates from epidemiological studies, well-controlled studies with large samples, and meta-analytic investigations. From these data, practitioners might reasonably deduce that approximately 2%–3% of people in the general population commit at least one violent act over a period of 1–3 years (Elbogen & Johnson, 2009; Swanson Holzer, Ganju, & Jono, 1990). They might conclude that 10%–15% of sexual offenders sexually recidivate over a period of 4–6 years (Hanson & Bussiere, 1998; Hanson & Morton-Bourgon, 2005), and that more than 20% of released prison inmates commit at least one new violent offense within 3 years (Langan & Levin, 2002). Finally, they might estimate that nearly 30% of psychiatric patients commit at least one violent act within 1 year of discharge (Monahan et al., 2001).

The importance of attending to BRs cannot be overstated (e.g., Arkes, 1981; Elwood, 1993a, 1993b; Gigerenzer, 2002). To illustrate, consider the assessment of an examinee drawn from a population that has a 7-year violent recidivism BR of 2%. For our purposes, assume the practitioner employs a highly accurate assessment instrument, the sensitivity (TPR) and specificity (1-FPR) of which are each .90. This means the assessment instrument correctly classifies 90% of violent recidivists as violent recidivists, and it correctly classifies 90% of the nonrecidivists as nonrecidivists. If the examinee "hits" on the instrument, the probability that he or she will violently recidivate barely exceeds 15%. If the same examinee had been assessed with the same instrument but drawn from a population in which the BR of violent recidivism were 30%, then his or her likelihood of violent recidivism would have risen to nearly 80%. (See Fig. 15.1.) This illustration underscores the importance of attending to BRs when conducting violence risk assessments, even when highly accurate assessment instruments are used.[2]

Assessment Methods and Instruments

The use of multiple sources and methods is a fundamental principle of forensic mental health assessment (Heilbrun, 2001; Heilbrun et al., 2002, 2009). This principle applies to violence risk assessment as well (e.g., Conroy & Murrie, 2007; Heilbrun, 2009). Of available sources and methods, interviews might provide no more than limited information in the context of violence risk assessment; indeed, in some circumstances interview data might even decrease the accuracy of risk assessments that are based exclusively on file reviews (Campbell, French, & Gendreau, 2009) or actuarial models (Grove & Meehl, 1996; Grove, Zald, Lebow, Snitz, & Nelson, 2000).

A variety of assessment methods are available for the assessment of violence risk. Broadly, these include unstructured clinical judgment (UCJ), actuarial assessment, and structured professional judgment (SPJ). In UCJ, the examiner combines data in his or her head, ordinarily without guidance from empirical studies or a formal assessment tool (Dawes, Faust, & Meehl, 1989). By contrast, actuarial methods typically provide explicit criteria for data collection and scoring, and

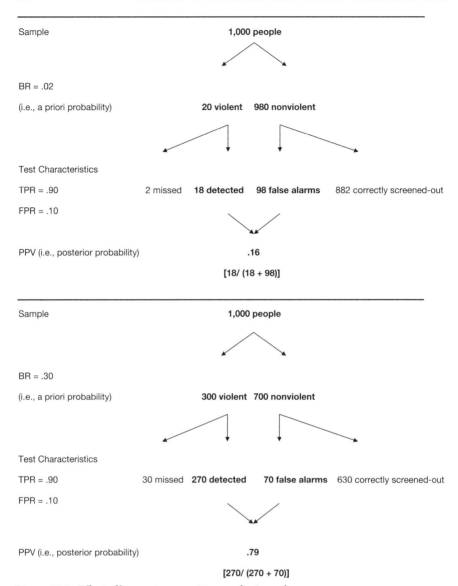

Figure 15.1 Effect of base rate on positive predictive value.

they ordinarily offer a probability estimate based on the combination of those data. Like actuarial methods, SPJ methods offer explicit criteria for data collection and scoring; the combination and weighting of those data are left to the practitioner, however, and ordinarily no numerical probability estimate is generated (see Chapter 17, this volume).

Research indicates UCJ is associated with better-than-chance performance, with the accuracy of short-term predictions measuring about as high as long-term predictions (Mossman, 1994). The American Psychological Association (2011) nevertheless has cautioned against UCJ-based violence risk assessments when alternative methods are available. Indeed, some commentators have asserted that the use of UCJ-based risk assessments may be unethical in some circumstances (e.g., Grisso, 2009).

The superiority of actuarial assessment methods over UCJ is supported by more than a half-century of research conducted across a wide range of disciplines and tasks (Grove & Meehl, 1996; Grove et al., 2000). This superiority holds true across mental health classification decisions in general (Ægisdotter et al., 2006) and in the context of violence risk assessment in particular (Hanson & Morton-Bourgon, 2009; Hilton, Harris, & Rice, 2006; Mossman, 1994; but see Litwack, 2001).

Among the most widely used (Archer, Buffington-Vollum, Stredney, & Handel, 2006; Jackson & Hess, 2007; Viljoen, McLachlan, & Vincent, 2010) actuarial risk assessment instruments (ARAIs) are the Violence Risk Appraisal Guide (VRAG; Quinsey, Harris, Rice, & Cormier, 1998, 2006), Sex Offender Risk Appraisal Guide (SORAG; Quinsey et al., 1998, 2006), Rapid Risk Assessment for Sexual Offense Recidivism (RRASOR; Hanson, 1997), and Static-99 (Hanson & Thornton, 2000). Quantitative reviews support the validity of these measures for the assessment of violence risk (Campbell et al., 2009; Hanson & Morton-Bourgon, 2009; Singh, Grann, & Fazel, 2011; Yang, Wong, & Coid, 2010), with effect sizes at least as high as those observed in several other areas of psychology (cf. Richard, Bond, & Stokes-Zoota, 2003). These measures appear to be more accurate when applied to samples that closely match the demographics of the original validation samples than when applied to samples of different demographic characteristics (Singh et al., 2011).

As a group, ARAIs appear to be more accurate than SPJ guides for the assessment of sexual-specific violence risk (Hanson & Morton-Bourgon, 2009). By contrast, available research suggests they appear to be no more accurate than SPJ methods for the assessment of nonsexual violence risk (Campbell et al., 2009; Singh et al., 2011; Yang et al., 2010). SPJ guides typically are developed from extensive literature reviews; this might make them applicable to a broader range of populations than ARAIs, which typically are calibrated on single samples.

An SPJ guide, the Historical, Clinical Risk Assessment Scheme (HCR-20; Webster, Douglas, Eaves, & Hart, 1997), is perhaps the most frequently used risk assessment tool among forensic psychologists (Archer et al., 2006; Viljoen et al., 2010). It also is among the most extensively validated SPJ guides available for the assessment of violence risk (Singh et al., 2011). Its practitioner-discerned categorical risk ratings (e.g., low, moderate, high) appear to lack a high level of interrater reliability (Douglas & Reeves, 2010). Nevertheless, some research (Douglas, Yoemans, & Boer, 2005) indicates these ratings have the potential to add validity to actuarial measures used alone.

Empirically Supported Risk Factors

Notwithstanding their widespread use and empirical validity, structured measures cannot be applied in all circumstances. Therefore, practitioners might add structure to their judgments by considering factors that have been validated across several different populations, using large, well-controlled studies, epidemiological data, or meta-analyses. Risk factors that have been associated with violent behavior across multiple groups—the general population (Elbogen & Johnson, 2009), civil

Table 15.1 RISK FACTORS ACROSS
MULTIPLE POPULATIONS

Young age
History of violence
History of nonviolent crime
History of juvenile delinquency
Substance use problems
Relationship or family problems
Personality disorder

psychiatric patients (Monahan et al., 2001), mentally disordered offenders (Bonta, Law, & Hanson, 1998), and sexual offenders (Hanson & Bussiere, 1998; Hanson & Morton-Bourgon, 2005)—might be useful in these circumstances.

Factors that have been validated as predictors in at least three of the four studies listed earlier are presented in Table 15.1. In addition to the risk factors listed in the table, it is worth noting that psychosis has been found to increase risk for violence in studies sampling the general population, civil (but not forensic) psychiatric patients, and correctional inmates (Douglas, Guy, & Hart, 2009). Also noteworthy is the finding that substance abuse appears to moderate the magnitude of the relationship between severe mental illness and violence (Elbogen & Johnson, 2009; Fazel, Langstrom, Hjern, Grann, & Lichtenstein, 2009; Swanson et al., 1990).

RISK COMMUNICATION AND RISK MANAGEMENT

Practitioners report a preference for using nonnumerical terms when communicating about violence risk (Heilbrun, O'Neill, Strohman, Bowman, & Philipson, 2000; Heilbrun, Philipson, Berman, & Warren, 1999). Indeed, in a review of 91 forensic reports, Grann and Pallvick (2002) identified 56 nonnumerical terms that practitioners used to describe risk. Practitioners lack agreement about the meaning of these terms (Hilton, Carter, Harris, & Sharpe, 2008). They also make less accurate decisions when using them than when using numerical communication formats (Hilton, Harris, Rawson, & Beach, 2005). By contrast, the addition of numerical to nonnumerical communication formats may help consumers of forensic reports make more informed decisions about violence risk (Kwartner, Lyons, & Boccaccini, 2006). When feasible, therefore, practitioners might enhance the quality of their risk communication by including numerical estimates (National Research Council, 1989).

The quality of risk communication might be enhanced further if practitioners offer risk management strategies when appropriate (Dvoskin & Heilbrun, 2001). Programs that adhere to the principles of the risk-needs-responsivity (RNR) model deserve attention in this regard, as they appear to be more effective at reducing violent recidivism than programs that do not adhere to the model (Dowden & Andrews, 2000). Briefly, RNR-consistent programs apply the most intensive interventions to the highest risk cases; address potentially changeable factors associated with recidivism risk; and utilize treatment models based on social learning and other behavioral principles (Andrews, 2012; Andrews & Bonta, 2006). The most promising interventions for reducing violence risk include but are not limited to specialized case management, vocational and interpersonal skills training, anger control training, substance abuse treatment, family interventions and social support, and housing assistance (Heilbrun, 2003).

CONCLUSION

The recent history of violence risk assessment has included dramatic changes in the legal requirements and uses of such assessments, the empirical research available to support the assessment process, the methods and instruments available to practitioners, and the degree of sophistication in which assessment results are communicated.

Although some controversies regarding violence risk assessment remain, such as the relative accuracy of actuarial predictions versus structured professional judgment, there is now a much more detailed literature and greater consensus about risk assessment among clinicians than there was in 1981 when Monahan first called the field to task. Other chapters in this volume provide additional information intended to help practitioners make informed decisions about the assessment and management of violence risk.

AUTHOR'S NOTE

Opinions expressed in this chapter do not necessarily represent the views of any institutions, agencies, or departments with which the authors are affiliated.

NOTES

1. The TPR is the proportion of subjects with the condition that is correctly detected by the classification method. The FPR is the proportion of subjects that does not have the condition but is incorrectly classified as having it.
2. For a discussion of a method to estimate local BRs, see papers by Frederick and his colleagues (Frederick & Bowden, 2009a, 2009b; Neller & Frederick, 2013).

REFERENCES

Ægisdotter, S., White, M. J., Spengler, P., Maugherman, A., Anderson, L., Cook, R., … Rush, J. D. (2006). The meta- analysis of clinical judgment project: Fifty six years of accumulated research on clinical versus statistical prediction. *Counseling Psychologist, 34*, 341–382.

American Psychological Association. (2011). *Brief for amicicuriae: American Psychological Association and Texas Psychological Association in support of petition for a writ of certiorari*. Washington, DC: Author.

Andrews, D. A. (2012). The Risk-Need-Responsivity Model of correctional assessment and treatment. In J. A. Dvoskin, J. L. Skeem, R. W. Novaco, & K. S. Douglas (Eds.), *Using social science to reduce violent offending* (pp. 127–156). New York, NY: Oxford University Press.

Andrews, D. A., & Bonta, J. (2006). *The psychology of criminal conduct* (4th ed.). Newark, NJ: LexisNexis/Matthew Bender.

Archer, R. A., Buffington-Vollum, J. K., Stredny, R. V., & Handel, R. W. (2006). A survey of psychological test use patterns among forensic psychologists. *Journal of Personality Assessment, 87*(1), 84–94.

Arkes, H. R. (1981). Impediments to accurate clinical judgment and possible ways to minimize their impact. *Journal of Consulting and Clinical Psychology, 49*(3), 323–330.

Barefoot v. Estelle 463 U.S. 880, 103 S. Ct. 3383 (1983).

Blumstein, A., & Larson, R. C. (1971). Problems in modeling and measuring recidivism. *Journal of Research in Crime and Delinquency, 8*(2), 124–132.

Campbell, M., French, S., & Gendreau, P. (2009). The prediction of violence in adult offenders: A meta-analytic comparison of instruments and methods of assessment. *Criminal Justice and Behavior, 36*, 567–590.

Conroy, M. A., & Murrie, D. C. (2007). *Forensic assessment of violence risk: A guide for risk assessment and risk management.* Hoboken, NJ: Wiley.

Dawes, R. M., Faust, D., & Meehl, P. E. (1989). Clinical versus actuarial judgment. *Science, 243*, 1668–1674.

Douglas, K., Guy, L., & Hart, S. (2009). Psychosis as a risk factor for violence to others: A meta-analysis. *Psychological Bulletin, 135*(5), 679–706.

Douglas, K., & Reeves, K. (2010). Historical-Clinical-Risk Management-20 (HCR-20) Violence Risk Assessment Scheme: Rationale, application, and empirical overview. In R. Otto & K. Douglas (Eds.), *Handbook of violence risk assessment* (pp. 147–185). New York, NY: Routledge.

Douglas, K., Yoemans, M., & Boer, D. (2005). Comparative validity analysis of multiple measures of violence risk in a sample of criminal offenders. *Criminal Justice and Behavior, 32*(5), 479–510.

Dowden, C., & Andrews, D. (2000). Effective correctional treatment and violent reoffending: A meta-analysis. *Canadian Journal of Criminology, 42*(4), 449–467.

Dvoskin, J., & Heilbrun, K. (2001). Risk assessment and release decision-making: Toward resolving the great debate. *Journal of the American Academy of Psychiatry and the Law, 29*, 6–10.

Elbogen, E., & Johnson, S. C. (2009). The intricate link between violence and mental disorder: Results from the National Epidemiologic Survey on Alcohol and Related Conditions. *Archives of General Psychiatry, 66*(2), 152–161.

Elwood, R. W. (1993a). Clinical determinations and neuropsychological tests: An appeal to Bayes' Theorem. *Clinical Neuropsychologist, 7*(2), 224–233.

Elwood, R. W. (1993b). Psychological tests and clinical determinations: Beginning to address the base rate problem. *Clinical Psychology Review, 13*, 409–419.

Fazel, S., Langstrom, N., Hjern, A., Grann, M., & Lichtenstein, P. (2009). Schizophrenia, substance abuse, and violent crime. *Journal of the American Medical Association, 31*(19), 2016–2023.

Foucha v. Louisiana 504 U.S. 71 (1992).

Frederick, R., & Bowden, S. (2009a). The test validation summary. *Assessment, 16*, 215–236.

Frederick, R., & Bowden, S. (2009b). Using the test validation summary to explore constructs in symptom validity tests. *Journal of Head Trauma Rehabilitation, 24*, 105–122.

Furby, L., Weinrott, M., & Blackshaw, L. (1989). Sex offender recidivism: A review. *Psychological Bulletin, 105*(1), 3–30.

Gigerenzer, G. (2002). *Calculated risks: How to know when numbers deceive you.* New York, NY: Simon & Schuster.

Grann, M., & Pallvick, A. (2002). An empirical investigation of written risk communication in forensic psychiatric evaluations. *Psychology, Crime and Law, 8,* 113–130.

Grisso, T. (2009). Foreword. In J. Andrade (ed.), *Handbook of violence risk assessment and treatment: New approaches for mental health professionals.* New York: Springer, p. xv–xvii.

Grove, W. M., & Meehl, P. E. (1996). Comparative efficiency of informal (subjective, impressionistic) and formal (mechanical, lgorithmic) prediction procedures: The clinical-statistical controversy. *Psychology, Public Policy, and Law, 2,* 293–323.

Grove, W. M., Zald, D. H., Lebow, B. S., Snitz, B. E., & Nelson, C. (2000). Clinical versus mechanical prediction: A meta-analysis. *Psychological Assessment, 12*(1), 19–30.

Hanson, R. K. (1997). *The development of a brief actuarial risk scale for sexual offense recidivism.* Ottawa, ON: Department of the Solicitor General of Canada.

Hanson, R. K., & Bussiere, M. T. (1998). Predicting relapse: A meta-analysis of sexual offender recidivism studies. *Journal of Consulting and Clinical Psychology, 66,* 348–362.

Hanson, R. K., & Morton-Bourgon, K. E. (2005). The accuracy of recidivism risk assessments for sexual offenders: A meta-analysis of 118 prediction studies. *Psychological Assessment, 21*(1), 1–21.

Hanson, R. K., & Thornton, D. (2000). Improving risk assessments for sex offenders: A comparison of three actuarial scales. *Law and Human Behavior, 24*(1), 119–136.

Haynes, S., Smith, G., & Hunsley, J. (2011). *Scientific foundations of clinical assessment.* New York, NY: Routledge.

Heilbrun, K. (2001). *Principles of forensic mental health assessment.* New York, NY: Kluwer Academic/Plenum.

Heilbrun, K. (2003). Violence risk: From prediction to management. In D. Carson & R. Bull (Eds.), *Handbook of psychology in legal contexts* (2nd ed., pp. 127–142). Chichester, UK: Wiley.

Heilbrun, K. (2009). *Evaluation for risk of violence in adults.* New York, NY: Oxford University Press.

Heilbrun, K., Grisso, T., & Goldstein, A. M. (2009). *Foundations of forensic mental health assessment.* New York, NY: Oxford University Press.

Heilbrun, K., Marczyk, G. R., & DeMatteo, D. (2002). *Forensic mental health assessment: A casebook.* New York, NY: Oxford University Press.

Heilbrun, K., O'Neill, M. L., Strohman, L. K., Bowman, Q., & Philipson, J. (2000). Expert approaches to communicating violence risk. *Law and Human Behavior, 24*(1), 137–147.

Heilbrun, K., Philipson, J., Berman, L., & Warren, J. (1999). Risk communication: Clinicians' reported approaches and perceived values. *Journal of the American Academy of Psychiatry and Law, 27,* 397–406.

Hilton, N. Z., Carter, A., Harris, G., & Sharpe, A. (2008). Does using nonnumerical terms to describe risk aid violence risk communication? Clinician agreement and decision making. *Journal of Interpersonal Violence, 23*(2), 171–188.

Hilton, N. Z., Harris, G. T., Rawson, K., & Beach, C. A. (2005). Communicating violence risk information to forensic decision makers. *Criminal Justice and Behavior, 32*(1), 97–116.

Hilton, N., Harris, G., & Rice, M. (2006). Sixty-six years of research on the clinical versus actuarial prediction of violence. *Counseling Psychologist, 34*(3), 400–409.

Jackson, R. L., & Hess, D. T. (2007). Evaluation for civil commitment of sex offenders: A survey of experts. *Sexual Abuse, 19*, 425–448.

Jones v. United States 463 U.S. 354 (1983).

Kwartner, P. P., Lyons, P. M., & Boccaccini, M. T. (2006). Judges' risk communication preference in risk for future violence cases. *International Journal of Forensic Mental Health, 5*(2), 185–194.

Langan, P. A., & Levin, D. J. (2002). *Recidivism of prisoners released in 1994.* [Bureau of Justice Statistics Special Report No. NCJ 193427]. Washington, DC: US Department of Justice.

Litwack, T. R. (2001). Actuarial versus clinical assessments of dangerousness. *Psychology, Public Policy and Law, 7*(2), 409–443.

Meehl, P., & Rosen, A. (1955). Antecedent probability and the efficiency of psychometric signs, patterns or cutting scores. *Psychological Bulletin, 52*, 194–216.

Mills, J. F., Kroner, D. G., & Morgan, R. D. (2011). *Clinician's guide to violence risk assessment.* New York, NY: Guilford Press.

Monahan, J. (1981). *Predicting violent behavior: An assessment of clinical techniques.* Beverly Hills, CA: Sage.

Monahan, J., Steadman, H. J., Silver, E., Appelbaum, P. S., Robbins, P. C., Mulvey, E. P., ... Banks, S. (2001). *Rethinking risk assessment: The MacArthur Study of Mental Disorder and Violence.* New York, NY: Oxford University Press.

Mossman, D. (1994). Assessing predictions of violence: Being accurate about accuracy. *Journal of Consulting and Clinical Psychology, 62*(4), 783–792.

Neller, D. J., & Frederick, R. I. (2013). Classification accuracy of actuarial risk assessment instruments. *Behavioral Sciences and the Law, 31*(1), 141–153.

O'Connor v. Donaldson 422 U.S. 563 (1975).

Quinsey, V. L., Harris, G. T., Rice, M. E., & Cormier, C. A. (1998). *Violent offenders: Appraising and managing risk.* Washington, DC: American Psychological Association.

Quinsey, V. L., Harris, G. T., Rice, M. E., & Cormier, C. A. (2006). *Violent offenders: Appraising and managing risk* (2nd ed.). Washington, DC: American Psychological Association.

Richard, F. D., Bond, C. F., & Stokes-Zoota, J. J. (2003). One hundred years of social psychology quantitatively described. *Review of General Psychology, 7*(4), 331–363.

Singh, J. P., Grann, M., & Fazel, S. (2011). A comparative study of violence risk assessment tools: A systematic review and metaregression analysis of 68 studies involving 25,980 participants. *Clinical Psychology Review, 31*, 499–513.

Swanson, J. W., Holzer, C. E., Ganju, V. K., & Jono, R. T. (1990). Violence and psychiatric disorder in the community: Evidence from the epidemiologic catchment area surveys. *Hospital and Community Psychiatry, 41*(7), 761–770.

Tarasoff v. The Regents of the University of California 551 P.2d 334 (1976).

Viljoen, J. L., McLachlan, K., & Vincent, G. M. (2010). Assessing violence risk and psychopathy in juvenile and adult offenders: A survey of clinical practices. *Assessment, 17*(3), 377–395.

Webster, C. D., Douglas, K. S., Eaves, D., & Hart, S. D. (1997). *HCR-20: Assessing risk for violence, version 2*. Burnaby, BC: Mental Health, Law, and Policy Institute.

Witt, P., & Conroy, M. A. (2009). *Evaluation of sexually violent predators*. New York, NY: Oxford University Press.

Yang, M., Wong, S., & Coid, J. (2010). The efficacy of violence prediction: A meta-analytic comparison of nine risk assessment tools. *Psychological Bulletin, 136*(5), 740–767.

16

Use of Assessment Measures for the Evaluation of Future Risk

CHAD A. BRINKLEY ■

Mental health professionals are frequently asked to assess future risk in a variety of contexts (Conroy & Murrie, 2007). For example, practicing clinicians are often required to determine whether a patient is at risk to commit suicide or engage in self-harm behaviors. In other contexts, forensic evaluators are routinely asked to determine whether a defendant is likely to engage in violence or commit a future sexual crime. Typically, the evaluator's assessment of risk forms the primary basis for determining whether an individual needs to be hospitalized or committed to a secure facility for treatment (Dempster, 2003; Slovic, Monahan, Hart, & McNeil, 2000).

Evaluators assessing risk need to be sensitive to the potential consequences of inaccurate judgments. Working to balance the sensitivity and specificity of risk assessments is essential since there are significant consequences associated with errors in the judgment of future risk (Miller & Brodsky, 2011). An inaccurate assessment of high risk for violence could result in an unnecessary civil commitment and a significant loss of liberty for the affected individual. In contrast, an inaccurate assessment of low risk for violence may allow a potentially dangerous individual to assault, murder, or sexually molest someone. Rarely do errors in judgment in a psychological evaluation have such significant consequences for both individual rights and public safety. Given the risks associated with such errors, mental health experts have a vested interest in utilizing the best validated assessment methods for preventing both under- and overprediction of risk (Conroy & Murrie, 2007; Miller & Brodsky, 2011).

Prior research has demonstrated that mental health experts are not always good at assessing future risk (Dawes, Faust, & Meehl, 1989). In some studies, clinicians were found to be no better than lay people, and sometimes worse than chance, when they attempted to predict risk for future violence (Ennis & Litwack, 1974; Monahan, 1981). Despite evidence that clinical judgment concerning future risk can be very poor, some experts have testified in court that they could be 100% certain about a particular individual's risk for future violence (*Barefoot v. Estelle*, 1983).

Such confidence in the face of questionable accuracy leads some experts to suggest that offering predictions of future violence may be unethical (Grisso & Applebaum,

1992). In 1983, the American Psychiatric Association went so far as to issue an amicus brief arguing that courts should not allow psychiatric testimony regarding risk for violence because psychiatrists were unable to make such predictions with any accuracy. The US Supreme Court's responses, however, made it clear that courts would continue to rely on the opinions of mental health experts: "The suggestion that no psychiatrist's testimony may be presented with respect to a defendant's testimony is somewhat like asking us to dis-invent the wheel" (*Barefoot v. Estelle*, 1983, p. 19). Subsequent legal standards confirmed that psychologists and psychiatrists would be required to provide expert opinions regarding future risk for the purposes of determining when to initiate or end a civil commitment—even if the accuracy of those opinions might be questionable (American Bar Association, 1989).

Psychologists responded by working diligently to develop improved methods for the assessment of risk (Hanson, 2005). What they discovered is that the poor accuracy of clinically based risk assessments can likely be attributed to factors such as failure to consider the impact of base rates on predictions of behavior and focusing on idiosyncratic rather than empirically validated risk factors (Miller & Brodsky, 2011). Subsequent research has demonstrated that evaluators can improve their assessment of future risk by utilizing structured, empirically derived, and theoretically based tools that help them identify and systematically consider relevant risk factors (Campbell, French, & Gendreau, 2009; Lidz, Mulvey, & Gardner, 1993). Despite the growing empirical literature regarding the usefulness of risk assessment tools, research suggests that some evaluators rarely use them (Boothby & Clements, 2000). Given that risk assessments are high-stakes evaluations, why would an evaluator not use a potentially helpful tool?

There is much controversy regarding the use of risk assessment instruments in the existing literature (Heilbrun, Douglas, & Yasuhara, 2009). Some researchers have argued that evaluators should use only actuarial methods, while others have suggested that structured professional judgment tools are better (Campbell et al., 2009). As such, it may be unclear to an evaluator which of these tools may be more helpful. In other cases, experts have suggested that the potential prejudicial effects of utilizing some measures may outweigh their probative value—an argument that the measure should not be utilized for risk assessment evaluations (Edens, 2006). Finally, some evaluators may feel uncomfortable utilizing risk assessment tools because they are unfamiliar with them, lack the necessary training to utilize them, or have questions about what the results on such assessment tools may mean.

The purpose of the present chapter is to provide a helpful summary that may help evaluators make good decisions about using and interpreting risk assessment instruments as well as presenting the results in reports and testimony. What follows is a brief description of the different kinds of risk assessment measures and guidelines for evaluators to determine which (if any) assessment tool may be most helpful to them. The chapter will then turn to a discussion about how to interpret and present results of risk assessment instruments.

TYPES OF RISK ASSESSMENT TOOLS

Since the 1980s, a number of assessment measures have been published to assist evaluators trying to assess future risk (Campbell et al., 2009; Hanson, 2005). The various measures can be classified into four general groups based on their characteristics. These groups include unstructured clinical judgment (UCJ), first-generation actuarial assessments (FGAs), second-generation actuarial assessments (SGs), and structured professional judgment (SPJ) measures. Although it is a personality measure rather than a risk assessment instrument per se, the Psychopathy Checklist Revised (PCL-R) considers special consideration, given that it is frequently used by evaluators to assess future risk (Hart, 1998). The following is a brief description of each type of instrument. A complete review of all available risk assessment instruments is beyond the scope of this chapter, but specific descriptions of a few particular measures that exemplify each type of approach are included.

Unstructured Clinical Judgment

Unstructured clinical judgment (UCJ) generally refers to assessments where the evaluator's final assessment of risk is based on an unsystematic, idiographic analysis in which no risk assessment tools were used. A UCJ-based evaluation may or may not include explicit consideration of empirically validated risk factors. Research has consistently demonstrated that UCJ assessments are prone to error (Grove, Zald, Lebow, Snitz, & Nelson, 2000) and generally less accurate than either actuarial or SPJ assessments (Monahan, 2002; Mossman, 1994). As such, UCJ is generally not recommended as an approach to risk assessment (Doren, 2002; Monahan, 2002). There are, however, times when UCJ is the only viable option. In situations where UCJ is utilized, clinicians should still make an effort to systematically consider the known empirically validated risk factors, and they should always acknowledge the limitations of their clinical judgments (Conroy & Murrie, 2007).

First-Generation Actuarial Assessments

Actuarial assessments utilize a statistical formula as a decision-making tool. The formula for first-generation actuarial assessment (FGA) instruments is typically created by using research to identify a set of specific variables that are empirically associated with violent behavior in a known sample. Since items are selected empirically rather than rationally, the item's relation to violence risk assessment and implication for risk management is not always clear (Bonta, 2002). FGA instruments are typically composed only of items measuring static risk factors (Andrews & Bonta, 2006; Campbell et al., 2009).

Evaluators using actuarial tools typically obtain information about which of the identified risk variables apply to the specific individual they are assessing. Those data are then entered into the statistical formula. The results of the formula provide an estimate of how many characteristics the individual shares with members of the sample group who were known to become violent. The greater the number of shared characteristics, the higher the score on the actuarial assessment, and the higher the probability that the individual will engage in future violence.

Actuarial assessments are widely used for assessing future risk in a variety of fields, including medicine, insurance, and criminal justice. Studies have shown that actuarial assessments routinely provide better estimates of future risk than clinical judgments in different contexts, including parole decisions (Grove & Meehl, 1996). Research has consistently demonstrated that FGAs generally have moderate predictive validity (Campbell et al., 2009). As such, some authors have argued that all assessments of future risk should be based on unmodified actuarial assessments (Quinsey, Harris, Rice, & Cormier, 2006). Others, however, have argued that relying only on actuarial data and excluding potentially important ideographic data is problematic (Heilbrun et al., 2009).

The potential advantages and limitations of utilizing an actuarial approach to risk assessment have been described in detail elsewhere (Conroy & Murrie, 2007; Monahan, 2003; Quinsey et al., 2006), but a brief summary follows. In terms of potential advantages, actuarial assessments (1) make decision making objective, uniform, and consistent; (2) have a rational basis justifying their use; (3) make it clear which risk factors have been considered in an evaluation; (4) make it clear how risk factors have been weighted; and (5) typically account for base rates of violence better than clinical judgment (Loza & Dahilwal, 1997).

Potential limitations of FGA instruments include the following: (1) reliance on only static risk factors limits the ability of FGAs to measure changes in risk due to dynamic factors; (2) failure to consider dynamic risk factors limits the ability of FGAs to inform risk management strategies (Andrews, Bonta, & Hoge, 1990); (3) FGAs do not account for rare or ideographic risk factors that may be highly predictive of violence for a particular person (Monahan, 2001, 2003); (4) FGAs generate specific estimates of future risk for individuals based on group data which may be easily misinterpreted (Heilbrun, Dvoskin, Hart, & McNeil, 1999; Heilbrun et al., 2009); (5) the risk estimates generated by FGAs are less precise when used for individuals who are increasingly different from the sample that was used to validate the initial measure (Monahan, 2001); (6) actuarial measures may not be available for all cases where a risk assessment is required (i.e., there is no available actuarial assessment to evaluate risk for female sex offenders; Conroy & Murrie, 2007; Doren, 2002).

One of the most widely used FGA instruments is the Violence Risk Appraisal Guide (VRAG; Quinsey et al., 2006). The VRAG is a 12-item instrument used to assess an offender's risk to commit a violent crime within 10 years of returning to the community. Each item represents a different historical risk factor that has been demonstrated by research to predict future violent behavior. All 12 risk factors are considered static in that each is highly unlikely to improve over time. Each item is weighted based on how predictive of future violence it is. VRAG scores range from –11 to +32 with higher scores indicating a higher risk of violent recidivism. It has been found to be a reliable measure with higher scores on the VRAG being associated with higher rates of violent recidivism in a variety of samples (Quinsey et al., 2006).

Second-Generation Actuarial Assessments

Like FGA instruments, second-generation actuarial assessment (SGA) measures are created by identifying empirically validated risk factors for future violence. As such, SGAs share many of the strengths of FGAs, and higher scores on SGAs are consistently associated with higher future risk (Campbell et al., 2009). Unlike FGAs, the items for SGAs are typically selected rationally (based on theories of recidivism) rather than through strict statistical means (Andrews & Bonta, 2006). As such, SGAs tend to have more face validity than FGAs, and the results are arguably easier to interpret. SGA measures also include dynamic risk factors. As such, they are better capable of assessing changes in risk over time and informing risk management strategies than FGAs (Douglas & Skeem, 2005; Heilbrun, 1997). Although SGAs address many of the limitations associated with FGAs, they still do not account for rare, unusual, or ideographic risk factors that may play a unique role in a given individual's risk for violence.

Perhaps the best example of an SGA measure is the Levels of Service Inventory Revised (LSI-R; Andrews & Bonta, 1995). The LSI-R consists of 54 items that were selected based on a review of the recidivism literature, discussions with parole officers, and a consideration of broad social learning theory. The measure utilizes both static and dynamic risk factors to generate an estimate of a person's risk for general short-term recidivism. The measure can also be used to identify treatment goals for minimizing future risk. Scores on the measure range from 0 to 162, and higher scores are consistently associated with higher recidivism rates (Campbell et al., 2009).

Structured Professional Judgment

Structured professional judgment (SPJ) is a systematic approach to risk assessment that relies on consideration of empirical/rational risk factors to ground clinical opinions and minimize bias typically associated with UCJ. The method acknowledges that there are rare or unusual factors that may influence risk for particular individuals but are difficult or impossible to codify in an actuarial assessment (Monahan, 2003). It is difficult to know how to account for such risk factors without utilizing some form of clinical judgment. As such, SPJ methods endorse the use of clinical judgment to make final determinations of risk based on all relevant risk factors—static, dynamic, and idiographic (Webster, Douglas, Eaves, & Hart, 1997).

SPJ measures require evaluators to determine whether several empirically validated risk factors are present or absent in a specific individual at a specific time. That evaluation typically results in a score on an assessment instrument. Although higher scores on SPJ instruments are generally associated with higher risk for violence, SPJ encourages evaluators not to base risk assessments on total scores (Douglas, Cox, & Webster, 1999; Webster et al., 1997). Instead, evaluators using SPJ instruments can identify a person as being at high risk if one particularly salient risk factor is present (e.g., a current and specific plan to murder someone). Conversely, individuals who have several historical risk factors may be deemed to be at moderate or even low risk if they have few dynamic risk factors and have a well-considered plan for managing their risk for future violence. As such, SPJ risk assessments are typically characterized in terms of level of estimated risk (high, medium, or low) rather than by a numerical score on an assessment instrument. Evaluators using SPJ assessments are encouraged to identify specific dynamic risk factors that can be targeted for change as part of a risk management/reduction plan (Douglas, Webster, Eaves, Hart, & Ogloff, 2001).

SPJ has several strengths as an approach to risk assessment (Douglas et al., 2001): (1) SPJ utilizes a logical, rational approach to decision making that minimizes potential bias; (2) reliance on empirical risk factors makes the evaluation of future risk more objective; (3) the inclusion of dynamic risk factors makes it easier to evaluate changes in risk over time and provide specific advice for risk management/reduction strategies; and (4) SPJ allows the evaluator the freedom to consider potentially important ideographic risk factors.

Potential criticisms of SPJ instruments include the following: (1) SPJ relies on the evaluator to account for the impact of base rates on assessment of violence—something even well-trained evaluators have difficulties with (Miller & Brodsky, 2011); (2) results of SPJ instruments may be more difficult to explain since individuals with similar scores may be judged to have different levels of future risk; and (3) SPJ evaluations require the use of clinical judgment and are, arguably, less objective than actuarial assessments—some experts have argued that modifying any actuarial assessment with clinical judgment reduces the accuracy of the evaluation (Quinsey et al., 2006). Recent research, however, has consistently demonstrated that SPJ assessments are as accurate as actuarial measures for assessing future risk (Campbell et al., 2009; Heilbrun et al., 2009).

Perhaps the most widely used SPJ instrument is the Historical-Clinical-Risk-20 (HCR-20; Webster et al., 1997). The HCR-20 was developed as way of formalizing risk assessment decisions and generating risk management plans for correctional systems. The HCR-20 has ten items that measure historical/static risk factors, five items that measure current/dynamic/clinical factors, and five risk items to examine specifically how the person's risk for violence may be impacted by placement in a specific setting.

The HCR-20 can be scored numerically and scores on the HCR-20 range from 0 to 40. The authors, however, emphasize that the instrument is designed to provide a guide for thinking about how to weight risk factors rather than simply relying on specific scores to make risk judgments. Ratings of the individual risk factors identified on the HCR-20 are based on data collected during clinical interviews as well as collateral information from other data sources such as files.

Existing peer-reviewed data support the HCR-20's usefulness in risk prediction. Specifically, scores on the HCR-20 have been found to have modest but significant correlations with past violence (.44), with the VRAG (.54), and with violence observed in an inpatient setting (.30). HCR-20 scores have also been shown to be predictive of several measures of community violence, readmission to forensic hospitals, and subsequent psychiatric hospitalizations (Douglas et al., 2001). Risk decisions made using the HCR-20 have been found to predictive of violent recidivism in various samples (Campbell et al., 2009; Douglas et al., 2001; Heilbrun et al., 2009). For more information about the HCR-20 and SPJ assessments, see Chapter 17 in this volume.

The Psychopathy Checklist Revised

Standard psychological instruments are generally not recommended for use in risk assessment evaluations since they were not validated for assessing risk (Conroy & Murrie, 2007). There is, however, one exception to this rule. The Psychopathy Checklist Revised (PCL-R; Hare, 2003) was originally constructed to be a measure of a personality. Research, however, has demonstrated that higher PCL-R scores are predictive of both general and violent recidivism in a variety of samples (Hemphill, Hare, & Wong, 1998). As such, the PCL-R has been described as a "forensically relevant instrument" because it "measures a construct that, although not specifically psycho-legal in nature, may be pertinent to consider in relation to various legal questions" (Edens & Petrila, 2006; p. 575). A survey of American Board of Forensic Psychology diplomats found that the majority believed that it was either acceptable or recommended to use the PCL-R as part of a risk assessment evaluation (Lally, 2003). It is noteworthy that the PCL-R is utilized as a subcomponent of two frequently used risk assessment measures—the VRAG and the HCR-20 (Dolan & Doyle, 2000).

The PCL-R is a 20-item instrument designed to measure negative interpersonal style (glibness/superficial charm, grandiose sense of self-worth, pathological lying, conning/manipulation), limited affect (lack of remorse, shallow affect, callousness, failure to accept responsibility), deviant lifestyle (need for stimulation, poor long-term planning, impulsivity, irresponsibility, living off others), and antisocial behavior (poor behavior controls, early behavioral problems, criminal activity). PCL-R scores are determined based on information obtained from both clinical interviews and review of collateral file information. PCL-R scores range from 0 to 40. Scores below 20 are generally considered indicative of a distinct lack of psychopathic traits. Scores of 30 or more are generally considered indicative of the presence of significant psychopathic traits.

As noted previously, higher scores on this instrument have been found to be associated with higher risk for revocation of parole, revocation of mandatory supervision, being unlawfully at large, and general recidivism (Hare, 2003). Published data have shown that PCL-R scores provide significant improvement in the prediction of violent recidivism over simple chance or the use of historical risk variables by themselves (Hemphill et al., 1998). Research has demonstrated that the PCL-R can be rated reliably by properly trained evaluators (Hare, 2003).

Although the PCL-R can be a useful risk assessment tool, some concerns have been raised about using the measure (Edens & Petrilia, 2006; Hart, 1998). These criticisms include the following: (1) individuals with high PCL-R scores are at risk of being labeled as "psychopaths," which may have an unnecessarily prejudicial effect on legal decision making (Edens, Colwell, Desforges, & Fernandez, 2005); (2) there is some evidence to suggest that the reliability of the PCL-R may be lower in legal/adversarial contexts than in research contexts (Edens, 2006); (3) although there is good evidence that PCL-R scores predict risk in community settings, the ability of PCL-R scores to predict institutional violence is not as clear (Hare, 2003); (4) although there is good evidence that PCL-R scores are predictive of risk for adult males, the ability of PCL-R scores to predict risk in other groups (i.e., adult females) is less clear (Falkenbach, 2008; Vitale & Newman, 2001).

CRITERIA FOR SELECTION OF A RISK ASSESSMENT INSTRUMENT

Given the wide variety of risk assessment tools that are available, how should evaluators decide which instruments to utilize for an evaluation? One means of answering this question is to ask a series of more specific questions about the nature of the risk assessment at hand. The answers to the following questions will likely help evaluators identify and select risk assessment measures that are best suited to their purposes (Conroy & Murrie, 2007; Doren, 2002).

What Kind of Risk Are You Trying to Assess?

Not all instruments were designed to assess the same kinds of risk. For example, the VRAG was designed to assess risk for future violent offenses (Quinsey et al., 2006) while the LSI-R was designed to assess general recidivism (Andrews & Bonta, 1995). There are other measures, such as the Static-99-R (Harris, Phenix, Hanson, & Thornton, 2003), which have been designed specifically to assess risk for future sexual offenses. Evaluators should select instruments that measure the kind of risk they are trying to assess. For example, someone tasked with assessing risk for future sexual offenses would be better off using the Static-99-R than the LSI-R (Doren, 2002).

How Imminent Is the Risk You Are Trying to Assess?

Different instruments have been validated for assessing risk in different time frames. The VRAG, for example, assesses future risk over an extended period of time (7–10 years; Quinsey et al., 2006), whereas the HCR-20 was designed to assess risk in the short term (up to about 12 months; Webster et al., 1997). The time frame where someone may be at risk matters, and this can impact the type of instrument an evaluator would want to utilize. For example, the VRAG may not be useful for assessing risk if you are assessing someone for civil commitment and the statute in question requires an individual to be at "imminent" risk of violence. In contrast, the results of the VRAG may be meaningful in jurisdictions where the only question is whether someone is significantly likely to commit a violent act at some time in the future.

How Reliable Is the Instrument?

In order for an assessment instrument to be useful, it must be reliable. If two evaluators working independently who have access to the same information reach different conclusions using the same measure (i.e., low interrater reliability), then the measure is of questionable utility. Actuarial measures tend to have higher interrater reliability ratings than measures that rely on clinical judgment, but existing research reveals that the interrater reliability for most widely used risk assessment measures is quite high: VRAG (.90; Quinsey et al., 2006), HCR-20 (.76–.96; Webster et al., 1997), LSI-R (.92; Andrews & Bonta, 1995), and PCL-R (.85–.95; Hare, 2003). Measures that assess only static risk factors should have high test-retest reliability, whereas scores on measures that assess dynamic factors can be expected to change over time.

Evaluators should keep in mind that reliability estimates obtained in research settings are likely to be higher than reliability observed in actual legal-adversarial contexts (Edens, 2006). Such differences in reliability can be accounted for by a variety of different factors, including (but not limited to) (1) evaluator bias, (2) deviation from standardized administration or scoring procedures, and (3) different evaluators having access to different information.

The following are some recommendations for helping evaluators minimize bias and maximize reliability when using risk assessment instruments (Conroy & Murrie, 2007; Doren, 2002): (1) evaluators are encouraged to only use measures that they have been properly trained to use; (2) all evaluators, even experienced ones, should be careful to adhere to standardized procedures for utilizing the instrument; (3) when scoring individual items on a risk assessment measure, evaluators should explicitly consider all evidence (both for and against) endorsing each item for a particular individual; (4) evaluators should keep detailed notes documenting their reasons for assigning specific scores on each instrument that they use. Such notes may prove useful for helping a trier of fact understand why one evaluator's scores on a given assessment instrument differ from another evaluator's.

What Is the Instrument's Predictive Validity?

Evaluators should only utilize assessment instruments that have been well validated for predicting some form of risk. Most widely utilized measures have data indicating that higher scores on the instrument are associated with some outcome of interest (i.e., general recidivism, violent recidivism, sexual recidivism, or suicide). Ideally, that data should be from well-controlled, prospective studies (Doren, 2002).

There has been much debate in the literature about what kinds of risk assessment measures should be used (SPJ, FGA, SGA, etc). A recent meta-analysis indicates that most of the widely used instruments (VRAG, HCR-20, LSI-R) have comparable effect sizes for assessing risk (Campbell et al., 2009). In that same study, however, the results indicated that some types of instruments demonstrated slight advantages for specific types of assessments. For example, instruments utilizing dynamic risk factors were better at predicting violent recidivism, whereas FGA instruments and static risk factors were better predictors of institutional violence.

Was the Instrument Validated for the Kind of Person Being Assessed?

In general, the ability of a measure to identify accurately a person's future risk is dependent on how similar the individual being evaluated is to the sample that was used to validate the instrument. The more a particular person differs from the validation sample, the more error is introduced into the assessment and the less valid scores on the instrument are likely to be. Some instruments, such as the PCL-R, have been cross-validated in a variety of samples (Hare, 2003) and there is an extensive literature regarding how the measure functions in those different samples (Cooke, 1998). Evaluators should make efforts to examine which samples the various risk assessment measures have been validated for prior to selecting tools. When evaluators are interpreting and reporting risk assessment results, they should take caution to identify such potential sources of error (Heilbrun, Douglas, & Yasuhara, 2009). There may be some cases where no risk assessment instruments have been validated for assessing a particular type of individual or kind of risk. In these cases, UCJ tempered by a consideration of known empirically validated risk factors may be the only available option (Conroy & Murrie, 2007).

How Much Collateral Information Is Available?

As with any type of forensic evaluation, individuals conducting risk assessments should make efforts to obtain collateral information (Melton, Petrilia, Poythress, & Slobogin, 2007). In some cases, however, collateral information may be limited. Some instruments, such as the PCL-R, can only be used if "sufficient" collateral records are available (Hare, 2003). Other instruments, like the VRAG, cannot be scored if the evaluator is unable to discover some of the information required to rate the individual items (Quinsey et al., 2006). As such, the amount and type of information available to the evaluator may limit the types of assessment instruments that can be utilized for a particular evaluation.

Is a Particular Instrument Required by Statute?

Some jurisdictions require that particular instruments be utilized for risk assessments (Doren, 2002). For example, sexual predator evaluations in some states require use of the PCL-R. If a particular instrument is required by statute, then the evaluator must either utilize that instrument or explain why it was not possible to do so.

INTERPRETATION AND PRESENTATION OF RESULTS

When an evaluator utilizes a risk assessment instrument, the results require interpretation. Interpretation, even of actuarial instruments, involves clinical judgment (Dvoskin & Heilbrun, 2001). Such judgments can be influenced by poor understanding of the statistical properties of the risk assessment instrument, failure to account for the impact of base rates, or personal bias (Miller & Brodsky, 2011). The evaluator's interpretations can have significant impact on legal outcomes such as release decisions, jury verdicts, and sentencing (Dolores & Redding, 2009; Dvoskin & Heilbrun, 2001). As such, evaluators should utilize caution when interpreting and reporting results. What follows is a brief discussion of the factors influencing interpretation and some advice for reporting risk assessment results.

How Statistics Influence Interpretations of High and Low Risk

If a given measure is going to be used to classify individuals as being either high or low risk, evaluators need to understand how to use the measure so as to minimize the number of misclassifications. When making such decisions, evaluators will need to consider information about how using different cut scores on the measure will impact the rates of false positives (identifying nonviolent people as being at high risk) and false negatives (identifying violent people as being low risk).

Both types of errors have potentially significant consequences for personal freedom and public safety (Miller & Brodsky, 2011). Unfortunately, it is difficult to minimize both kinds of error simultaneously since each is related to cutting scores in a different way. In general, using lower cut scores minimizes the chance that a dangerous person will be declared low risk, but it increases the chance that a non dangerous person will be declared high risk. In contrast, using higher cutting scores minimizes the chance that a nondangerous individual will be declared high risk, but it increases the chance that a dangerous person will be declared low risk.

One statistical measure that can help evaluators compare cut scores is the receiver operating curve (ROC). The ROC is a graphical means of looking at how changing cut scores influences the number of false positives and false negatives. The ROC can be used to determine what cut score is optimal for minimizing both types of errors. If evaluators are more concerned about one type of error, however, the ROC can also be used to determine the effects of selecting higher or lower cut scores.

Impact of Base Rates on Interpretation of Risk Assessment Results

Simply put, the base rate of violence can be defined as the number of people in the relevant sample who will be violent compared to the total number of people in the sample. Base rates are difficult to calculate because they (1) differ by the type of outcome (i.e., violence, sexual offending, general recidivism); (2) vary by method of detection (i.e., self-report, arrests, convictions); and (3) can change over time (Conroy & Murrie, 2007). Knowing base rates is important for assessing risk because it influences how accurate the assessment can be (Doren, 2002; Monahan, 1981). Events with low base rates (like violence) are generally difficult to predict positively because they are relatively rare. Winning the lottery, for example, has a very low base rate, so it is difficult to predict when someone will win, but it is relatively easy to predict that someone will not win. Low base rates for violence mean that it is extremely difficult to predict accurately when someone will be violent in the future. This is one reason why experts currently recommend focusing on risk assessment and management rather than risk prediction (Douglas et al., 1999; Heilbrun, 1997; Monahan, 2003).

Clinical Judgment and Interpretation of Risk

Once evaluators are aware of how base rates and differing cut scores influence the accuracy of their assessments, they must make a decision about how to actually use scores on the instrument to classify particular individuals as low, moderate, or high risk. This is, by necessity, a clinical decision since only the evaluator can determine which kind of error it is more important to minimize. Evaluators must determine whether it is preferable to use lower cutting scores to minimize unnecessary confinement of nondangerous people or higher cutting scores to minimize the risk of releasing a dangerous individual.

Evaluators may also be required to take into consideration information that is not inherent in the risk assessment results. Risk assessment instruments typically address how likely someone may be to engage in future violence. They do not, however, address other potentially important aspects of violence such as severity or imminence—factors that should play an important role in the assessment of risk (Conroy & Murrie, 2007; Dvoskin & Heilbrun, 2001). For example, an individual with a low likelihood of offending (say 20%–40%) may be determined to be at "high risk" if the crime he or she is at risk of committing would be murdering his or her spouse in the next 24 hours. In contrast, someone with a high likelihood of offending (say 60%–80%) may be deemed to be at "low risk" if the crime he or she is at risk of committing is shoplifting sometime in the next 10 years.

When using clinical judgment to interpret risk assessment results, evaluators should be cautious. Evaluators should be aware of their personal biases (i.e., personal feelings about particular types of offenders) and make efforts to limit their influence when interpreting risk assessment results. Evaluators should also try to limit the potential influence of outside forces (i.e., influence from attorneys or employers who hired the evaluator) on interpretation of results (Miller & Brodsky, 2011).

Reconciling Differential Results

If an evaluator uses multiple risk assessment measures, it is possible to obtain differential results about an individual's future risk. When such differences occur, the burden is on the evaluator to explain them. Typically, such differential results are due to differences in what the instruments measure or the types of variables that they utilize to assess likelihood for future risk. For example, the VRAG utilizes only static risk factors and is designed to predict violence (Quinsey et al., 2006), whereas the LSI-R includes dynamic risk factors and predicts general recidivism (Andrews & Bonta, 1995). Thus, an individual with few historical risk factors and no history of violence who is at risk for general offending would likely score low on the VRAG but may score moderately on the LSI-R. In such cases, clinical judgment aided by a thorough understanding of the risk assessment measures being utilized will allow an evaluator to interpret and explain differential results in reports and testimony.

Presentation of Risk Assessment Results

Research on risk communication has been reviewed in detail elsewhere (Conroy & Murrie, 2007; Heilbrun et al., 2000). What follows is a brief summary of relevant findings that evaluators should keep in mind when determining how to present the results of risk assessments in reports or testimony: (1) information about future risk is only valuable if it can be understood and utilized by legal and clinical decision makers (Heilbrun et al., 1999); (2) information about future risk may be more easily understood if it is communicated categorically (low, medium, or high) rather than in terms of frequency or probability (Monahan & Steadman, 1996); (3) risk for future violence is generally judged to be greater if it is communicated in terms of frequency estimates (30 out of 100) rather than probability estimates (30%; Slovic et al., 2000); (4) clinicians generally prefer risk communication strategies that identify relevant risk factors and suggest strategies for risk management over information about specific probability estimates of future risk (Heilbrun et al., 2004); (5) judges tend to prefer categorical estimates of future risk over probability estimates of future risk (Kwartner, Lyons, & Boccaccini, 2006); (6) if probability estimates of future risk are utilized, the evaluator should acknowledge the limits of drawing conclusions about an individual's risk for future violence based on group data and should make efforts to clarify the associated margins for error (Heilbrun et al., 2009).

Based on the existing literature, Conroy and Murrie (2007) proposed specific guidelines for communication of risk assessment results. Salient points that relate to the interpretation and presentation of results on risk assessment instruments include the following: (1) clearly describe the instruments used, their properties, and the interpretation procedure used to arrive at the estimate of future risk in language that is easily understood by lay people; (2) present all relevant data regarding risk factors but avoid including data that may be distracting or irrelevant to the risk assessment decision; (3) consider the implications of presenting risk information in different ways (by category, frequency, or probability) and consider using multiple approaches to make the results of risk assessments clear; (4) clarify how context may influence results on risk assessment instruments (i.e., will the individual be at higher risk for violence in the community without supervision or in a highly supervised group home?); (5) acknowledge the limits of confidence in the risk assessment results and include information that quantifies such limits (i.e., confidence intervals, error ranges, etc); (6) consider discussing explicitly how risk factors identified on instruments can be controlled or minimized via specific risk management plans (see also Doren, 2002; Douglas et al., 1999).

EXAMPLES OF GOOD AND POOR RISK COMMUNICATION STRATEGIES
The following are brief examples of efforts to communicate the results on the VRAG.

> Example 1: *The VRAG was administered to Mr. X to evaluate his risk for future violence. Mr. X's VRAG score was +12, placing him in the sixth highest of nine risk categories. This score suggests that Mr. X.'s risk for engaging in future violence is 44%.*

This is an example of poor practice because it (1) provides no explanation of the measure or the basis for making an estimate of future risk using the instrument; (2) makes unwarranted conclusions about an individual's future risk based on group data; (3) includes no information about how error may impact the results; (4) uses only probabilistic means to report results about future risk; and (5) includes no specific details about the factors that place the subject at risk or how those factors might be managed.

> Example 2: *The VRAG is an actuarial instrument used to assess an offender's risk to commit a violent crime within 10 years of returning to the community. Each item represents a different historical risk factor that has been demonstrated by research to predict future violent behavior. All 12 risk factors are considered static in that each is highly unlikely to improve over time. Each item is weighted based on how predictive of future violence it is. VRAG scores range*

from −11 to +32 with higher scores indicating a higher risk of violent recidivism. It has been found to be a reliable measure with higher scores on the VRAG being associated with higher rates of violent recidivism in a variety of samples (Quinsey et al., 2006). It should be noted, however, that it is difficult to make precise predictions about an individual's risk for future violence based on group data (Heilbrun et al., 2009). The VRAG also does not account for dynamic risk factors or risk factors that may be specific to the individual. As such, it provides only an estimate of future risk and cannot be used to see how an individual's risk for violence may change over time.

Mr. X's VRAG score was +12, placing him in the sixth highest of nine risk categories. Specific factors indicating that Mr. X may be at higher risk for future violence include his inappropriate behavior in elementary school, the fact that he has never married, the fact that he didn't live with both parents until at least age 16, his criminal history, his failure on prior conditional release, and his prior diagnosis of antisocial personality disorder. One possible protective factor for Mr. X, as identified by the VRAG, was his advanced age at the time of the index offense.

In the standardization sample of 600 criminal offenders, 44% of inmates with similar risk factors committed a violent offense after 7 years and 58% committed a violent offense after 10 years of being released from confinement. Based on data from the standardization sample, individuals with similar risk factors are estimated to be at a moderate risk of committing a violent offense within 10 years of release (estimated risk for committing a new violent offense between 48.4% and 68.2% once error estimates have been considered).

Example 2 adheres more closely to the guidelines proposed by Conroy and Murrie (2007) in that it (1) provides a clear description of the VRAG and the basis for using it to assess future risk; (2) clearly discusses the limitations of the measure and the interpretations of the results; (3) provides information about how error rates impact estimates of future violence; (4) avoids making overly precise predictions about future risk for an individual based on group data; and (5) discusses explicitly the specific risk and possible protective factors identified by the instrument. Example 2 does not provide specific risk management recommendations because the VRAG's focus on static risk factors means it does not assess dynamic risk factors that would make targets for change.

CONCLUSIONS AND RECOMMENDATIONS

In this chapter, several different approaches to risk assessment have been reviewed, including actuarial assessment, SPJ, and UCJ. The various strengths and weaknesses of these approaches have been identified so evaluators can make informed choices about which approach to use for any given assessment. Although UCJ has generally been found to be unreliable and prone to bias, there are situations where it must be used because no empirically validated risk assessment measures are yet available (i.e., assessing future risk for female sex offenders). Evaluators should utilize risk assessment instruments only when the measure has good empirical support, the clinician has been properly trained to use the instrument, and the probative value of the instrument outweighs any potential prejudicial impact. Evaluators should always be cautious about how opinions about risk are presented, as these may have significant influence on critical legal decisions. Whether using instruments or UCJ, it is important to explicitly state the limitations of risk judgments. Evaluators should strive to address different elements of risk for violence (severity, imminence, frequency) rather than just focusing on the likelihood of future offenses. Finally, good assessments of future risk should be utilized to provide suggestions for effective risk management plans.

AUTHOR'S NOTE

The views expressed in this chapter are those of the authors only and do not represent the policies or opinions of the Federal Bureau of Prisons or the Department of Justice.

REFERENCES

American Bar Association. (1989). *Criminal justice mental health standards*. Chicago, IL: Author.

Andrews, D., & Bonta, J. (1995). *LSI-R: The Level of Service Inventory-Revised*. Toronto, ON: Multi-Health Systems.

Andrews, D., & Bonta, J. (2006). *The psychology of criminal conduct* (4th ed.). Cincinnati, OH: Anderson.

Andrews, D., Bonta, J., & Hoge, (1990). Classification for effective rehabilitation: Rediscovering psychology. *Criminal Justice and Behavior, 17*, 19–52.

Barefoot v. Estelle, 463 U.S. 880 (1983).

Bonta, J. (2002). Offender risk assessment: Guidelines for selection and use. *Criminal Justice and Behavior, 29*, 355–379.

Boothby, J. L., & Clements, C. B. (2000). A national survey of correctional psychologists. *Criminal Justice and Behavior, 27*, 715–731.

Campbell, M. A, French, S., & Gendreau, P. (2009). The prediction of violence in adult offenders: A meta-analytic comparison of instruments and methods of assessment. *Criminal Justice and Behavior, 36*, 567–590.

Conroy, M. A., & Murrie, D. C. (2007). *Forensic assessment of violence risk*. Hoboken, NJ: Wiley.

Cooke, D. J. (1998). Psychopathy across cultures. In D. J. Cooke, A. E. Forth, & R. D. Hare (Eds.), *Psychopathy: Theory, research, and implications for society* (pp. 13–45). Dordrecht, The Netherlands: Kluwer Academic.

Dawes, R., Faust, D., & Meehl, P. (1989). Clinical versus actuarial judgment. *Science, 243*, 1668–1674.

Dolores, J. C., & Redding, R. E. (2009). The effects of different forms of risk communicating on judicial decision making. *International Journal of Forensic Mental Health, 8*, 142–146.

Dempster, R. J. (2003). Issues in the assessment, communication, and management of risk for violence. In W. T. O'Donohue & E. R. Levensku (Eds.), *The handbook of forensic psychology: Resource for mental health and legal professionals.* San Diego, CA: Elsevier Academic Press.

Dolan, M., & Doyle, M. (2000). Violence risk prediction: Clinical and actuarial measures and the role of the Psychopathy Checklist. *British Journal of Psychiatry, 177*(4), 303–311.

Doren, D. M. (2002). *Evaluating sex offenders: A manual for civil commitments and beyond.* Thousand Oaks, CA: Sage.

Douglas, K. S., Cox, D. N., & Webster, C. D. (1999). Violence risk assessment: Science and practice. *Legal and Criminological Psychology, 4,* 149–184.

Douglas, K. S., & Skeem, J. (2005). Violence risk assessment: Getting specific about being dynamic. *Psychology, Public Policy, and Law, 11,* 347–383.

Douglas, K. S., Webster, C. D., Hart, S. D., Eaves, D., & Ogloff, J. R. P. (Eds.). (2001). *HCR-20: Violence risk management companion guide.* Vancouver, BC/Tampa, FL: Mental Health, Law, and Policy Institute, Simon Frasier University and Department of Mental Health Law & Policy, University of South Florida.

Dvoskin, J. A., & Heilbrun, K. (2001). Risk assessment and release decision-making: Toward resolving the great debate. *Journal of American Academy of Psychiatry and the Law, 29,* 6–10.

Edens, J. F. (2006). Unresolved controversies concerning psychopathy: Implications for clinical and forensic decision making. *Professional Psychology: Research and Practice, 37*(1), 59–65.

Edens, J. F., Colwell, L. H., Desforges, D. M., & Fernandez, M. A. (2005). The impact of mental health evidence on the support for capital punishment: Are defendants labeled psychopathic more deserving of death? *Behavioral Sciences and the Law, 23,* 603–625.

Edens, J. F., & Petrila, J. (2006). Legal and ethical issues in the assessment and treatment of psychopathy. In C. Patrick (Ed.), *Handbook of psychopathy* (pp. 573–588). New York, NY: Guilford Press.

Ennis, B., & Litwack, T. (1974). Psychiatry and the presumption of expertise: Flipping coins in the courtroom. *California Law Review, 62,* 693–752.

Falkenbach, D. M. (2008). Psychopathy and the assessment of violence in women. *Journal of Forensic Psychology Practice, 8,* 212–224.

Grisso, T., & Applebaum, P. S. (1992). Is it unethical to offer predictions of future violence? *Law and Human Behavior, 16,* 621–633.

Grove, W. M., Zald, D. H., Lebow, B. S., Snitz, B. E., & Nelson, C. (2000). Clinical vs. mechanical prediction: A meta-analysis. *Psychological Assessment, 12,* 19–30.

Hanson, R. T. (2005). Twenty years of progress in violence risk assessment. *Journal of Interpersonal Violence, 20,* 212–217.

Hare, R. D. (2003). *The Hare Psychopathy Checklist—Revised* (2nd ed.). Toronto, ON: Multi-Health Systems.

Harris, A., Phenix, A., Hanson, R. K., & Thornton, D. (2003). *Static-99 coding rules revised.* Retrieved July 18, 2014, from http://www.static99.org/pdfdocs/static-99-coding-rules_e.pdf

Hart, S. D. (1998). The role of psychopathy in assessing risk for violence: Conceptual and methodological issues. *Legal Criminology and Psychology, 3,* 123–140.

Heilbrun, K. (1997). Prediction versus management models relevant to risk assessment: The importance of legal decision making context. *Law and Human Behavior, 21,* 347–359.

Heilbrun, K., Douglas, K. S., & Yashuhara, K. (2009). Violence risk assessment: Core controversies. In J. L. Skeem, K. S. Douglas, & S. O. Lilienfeld (Eds.), *Psychological science in the courtroom: Consesus and controversy.* New York, NY: Guilford Press.

Heilbrun, K., Dvoskin, J., Hart, S. D., & McNiel, D. (1999). Violence risk communication: Implications for research, policy, and practice. *Health, Risk, and Society, 1,* 91–106.

Heilbrun, K., O'Neill, M. L., Stevens, T. N., Strohman, L. K., Bowman, Q., & Lo, Y. (2004). Assessing normative approaches to communicating violence risk: A national survey of psychologists. *Behavioral Sciences and the Law, 22,* 187–196.

Heilbrun, K., O'Neill, M. L., Strohman, L. K., Bowman, Q., & Philipson, J. (2000). Expert approaches to communicating violence risk. *Law and Human Behavior, 24,* 137–148.

Hemphill, J. F., Hare, R. D., & Wong, S. (1998). Psychopathy and recidivism: A review. *Legal and Criminological Psychology, 3,* 141–172.

Kwartner, P. K., Lyons, P. M., & Boccaccini, M. T. (2006). Judges' risk communication preferences in risk for future violence cases. *International Journal of Forensic Mental Health, 5,* 185–194.

Lally, S. J. (2003). What tests are acceptable for use in forensic evaluations? A survey of experts. *Professional Psychology: Research and Practice, 34,* 491–498.

Lidz, C., Mulvey, E., & Gardner, W. (1993). The accuracy of predictions of violence to others. *Journal of American Medical Association, 269,* 1007–1011.

Loza, W., & Dhaliwal, G. K. (1997). Psychometric evaluation of the Risk Appraisal Guide (RAG): A tool for assessing violent recidivism. *Journal of Interpersonal Violence, 12*(6), 779–793.

Melton, G., Petrilia, J., Poythress, N., & Slobogin, C. (2007). *Psychological evaluations for the courts: A handbook for mental health professionals and lawyers* (3rd ed.). New York, NY: Guilford Press.

Miller, S. L., & Brodsky, S. L. (2011). Risky business: Addressing the consequences of predicting violence. *Journal of American Academy of Psychiatry and the Law, 39,* 396–401.

Monahan, J. (1981). *The clinical prediction of violent behavior.* Rockville, MD: US Department of Health and Human Services.

Monahan, J. (2002). The scientific status of research on clinical and actuarial predictions of violence. In D. Faigman, D. Kaye, M. Saks, & J. Sanders (Eds.), *Modern scientific evidence: The law and science of expert testimony* (2nd ed., pp. 423–445). St. Paul, MN: West.

Monahan, J. (2003). Violence risk assessment. In A. M. Goldstein & I. B. Weiner (Eds.), *Handbook of psychology, Vol. 11. Forensic psychology* (pp. 527–540). Hoboken, NJ: Wiley.

Monahan, J., Steadman, H. J., Silver, E., Applebaum, P. S., Robbins, P. C., Mulvey, E. P., … Banks, S. (2001). *Rethinking risk assessment—The Macarthur Study of Mental Disorder and Violence.* New York, NY: Oxford University Press.

Mossman, D. (1994). Assessing predictions of violence: Being accurate about accuracy. *Journal of Consulting and Clinical Psychology, 62,* 783–792.

Quinsey, V. L., Harris, G. T., Rice, M. E., & Cormier, C. A. (2006). *Violent offenders: Appraising and managing risk* (2nd ed.). Washington, DC: American Psychological Association.

Slovic, P., Monahan, J., & MacGregor, D. (2000). Violence risk assessment and risk communication: The effects of using actual cases, providing instruction, and employing probability versus frequency formats. *Law and Human Behavior, 24,* 271–296.

Vitale, J. E., & Newman, J. P. (2001). Using the Psychopathy Checklist-Revised with female samples: Reliability, validity, and implications for clinical utility. *Clinical Psychology: Science and Practice, 8,* 117–132.

Webster, C. D., Douglas, K. S., Eaves, D., & Hart, S. D. (1997). *HCR-20: Assessing the risk for violence (Version 2).* Vancouver, BC: Simon Fraser University, Mental Health, Law, and Policy Institute.

17

The Structured Professional Judgment Approach to Violence Risk Assessment and Management

Why It Is Useful, How to Use It, and Its Empirical Support

KEVIN S. DOUGLAS AND HENRIK BELFRAGE ■

In numerous clinical and legal contexts, professionals from numerous fields must determine whether any of the people under their care or charge pose undue risks for violence. This is true in correctional settings, psychiatric settings, forensic settings, and policing settings. This chapter will describe the basic features of one approach to making such decisions—the structured professional judgment (SPJ) approach. We will contrast it to the actuarial approach; describe its features that are common across specific SPJ instruments; review its research base; and describe its use in practice.

In a recent survey by Singh (2013) of 2,135 clinicians across 44 different countries, the HCR-20 (Historical, Clinical, Risk Management-20; Webster, Eaves, Douglas, & Wintrup, 1995, for Version 1; Webster, Douglas, Eaves, & Hart, 1997 for Version 2; Douglas, Hart, Webster, & Belfrage, 2013 for Version 3)—one of the earliest developed SPJ instruments—was the most commonly used violence risk assessment instrument. This popularity may stem from the fact that it, and all other SPJ instruments, strive to be clinically helpful, as well as scientifically grounded. This dual goal of clinical usefulness and scientific grounding has been a mainstay of the SPJ approach for two decades. For instance, in one of the earliest instantiations of the SPJ approach—the first version of the HCR-20—Webster, Eaves, Douglas and Wintrup (1995, p. v) wrote:

> The great challenge in what remains of the 1990s is to integrate the almost separate worlds of research on the prediction of violence and the clinical practice

of assessment. At present the two domains scarcely intersect. Researchers keep writing papers, publishing books, and even receiving awards from prestigious organizations but their labours find no root in clinical practice.

We and our colleagues have been working for the past two decades to bring these two domains closer together and to provide empirically grounded guidelines to clinicians and other professionals to help them do their jobs. Since the mid-1990s, the SPJ model has developed from a nascent, interesting idea, to a widely used and heavily researched model. Singh's (2013) research indicates that its uptake is widespread internationally.

The SPJ model presumes professional expertise—the SPJ model cannot work without it. It is intended to provide a lens through which professionals can weigh and evaluate risk-relevant information and ultimately make sensible decisions. This is in drastic and stark contrast to some actuarial approaches that view clinicians as detrimental to the risk assessment process and hold that they should be removed from the decision-making process altogether. As the authors of the Violence Risk Appraisal Guide (VRAG), wrote: "What we are advising is not the addition of actuarial methods to existing practice, but rather the complete replacement of existing practice with actuarial methods" (Quinsey, Harris, Rice, & Cormier, 1998, p. 171; see also Quinsey, Harris, Rice, & Cormier, 2006, p. 182).

These two quotations summarize one of the key differences between actuarial and SPJ approaches. Orthodox actuarial approaches, as represented by the VRAG, eschew the role of professionals. SPJ approaches, on the other hand, rely on the expertise of professionals. In the next section we will describe some of the features of both the unstructured clinical approach, as well as the actuarial approach, that led to the development of the SPJ approach. After that, we will review some of the core features of the SPJ approach, review its empirical basis, and describe how to use it.

APPROACHES TO RISK ASSESSMENT

Although unstructured risk assessments are still commonly used, their validity and reliability have been demonstrated to be inferior to structured approaches, and hence they will not be considered further here. As described by Meehl (1954), unstructured prediction lacks rules for the weighting or consideration of risk factors. In fact, this characteristic of unstructured prediction led to the development of structured approaches—both actuarial and structured professional judgment (SPJ). We do note, however, that the *use* of clinical judgment and discretion within a structured model remains vital. We will elaborate upon this point in our description of the SPJ approach later.

In part, SPJ arose out of perceived weaknesses not only with unstructured clinical approaches but also actuarial approaches. The actuarial approach is "a formal method" that "uses an equation, a formula, a graph, or an actuarial table to arrive at a probability, or expected value, of some outcome" (Grove & Meehl, 1996, p. 294). Such procedures use replicable rules for integrating risk factors, which themselves are chosen because they are predictive of violence.

Actuarial prediction methods improve upon unstructured approaches in terms of predictive validity and tend to be rated reliably. However, in our view they have some shortcomings. For example, predictive properties of actuarial methods can be sample dependent. Often such instruments are developed on single samples and may not be cross-validated on independent samples prior to use (i.e., Violence Risk Appraisal Guide [VRAG]; Quinsey, Harris, Rice, & Cormier, 2006; cf. Classification of Violence Risk [COVR; Monahan et al., 2005]). Being optimized on unique samples means that precise probability estimates may not generalize to new samples. Blair, Marcus, and Boccaccini (2008) demonstrated in a meta-analysis that effect sizes from several commonly used actuarial instruments shrank between validation and cross-validation samples, especially if the cross-validation studies were conducted by authors not involved in developing the instruments.

Reliance on single (or even a few) samples also can result in the exclusion of important risk factors that just happened either to not be measured in the development sample or were not predictive in that particular sample. For instance, the Static-99, a widely used actuarial instrument for sexual violence risk assessment, omits sexual deviation, despite its being associated with sexual violence in many studies (Laws & O'Donohue, 2008). It is not on the Static-99 simply because it was not measured in the derivation research. Further, if a variable was not measured reliably, it might not make it through the statistical selection procedures, despite having been shown to predict violence in other samples. From a true actuarial perspective, this means that such variables should not be considered by evaluators. Such problems threaten the comprehensiveness of risk assessments and may increase the risk that evaluators miss important risk-relevant information.

Many actuarial procedures weight individual risk factors, again based on their performance in (typically) a single sample. This process presumes that such factors should be weighted the same, relative to other risk factors, in all other samples and applications, and that such risk factors are comparably important for all persons.

Grann and Långström (2007) tested different weighting procedures in a sample of 404 Swedish forensic psychiatric patients. Using the risk factors from the H scale of the HCR-20, they observed *worse* prediction upon cross-validation for more complex weighting procedures. Equal weighting of risk factors outperformed four weighting methods. Mills, Jones, and Kroner (2005) evaluated whether categorical probability estimates from two common actuarial instruments—the VRAG and the *Level of Service Inventory-Revised* (LSI-R; Andrews & Bonta, 1995)—generalized beyond their derivation samples. In their view, the "results of this study do not support the generalizability of the original probabilities associated with the prediction bins, although the LSI-R bins performed much better than the VRAG bins" and "this study does not support the use of the initial validation probability bins of either instrument with our sample" (p. 579).

Further, actuarial instruments tend not to include dynamic risk factors, which are the most important to target in terms of risk management. As we discuss next, SPJ instruments include treatment-relevant factors and include recommendations for using these to track risk-relevant progress over time.

STRUCTURED PROFESSIONAL JUDGMENT

The SPJ approach to risk assessment strives to provide comprehensive risk assessment procedures for professionals to assess, monitor, and manage risk for violence. By "comprehensive," we mean that most important risk factors are included on SPJ instruments (i.e., they are not sample specific or dependent), and a thorough set of professional guidelines is included with each specific instrument. There are numerous SPJ instruments, but the conceptual bases of each are essentially the same. Examples of major SPJ instruments are provided in Table 17.1. Next we describe common features of SPJ instruments.

Method of Item Selection

All SPJ instruments use logical or rational item selection methods to select their risk factors. The purpose of this approach is to select risk factors with broad support across the scientific and professional literatures. This method avoids sample-dependence issues discussed earlier. As such, SPJ instruments tend to have high content validity. As a recent example, in the development of the HCR-20 Version 3 (Douglas et al., 2013), we first commissioned a 300-page report on literature supportive of HCR-20 Version 2 (Webster et al., 1997) risk factors (Guy & Wilson, 2007) so we could determine whether any of them were in need of revision or omission, and whether any new risk factors should be added. We also included as an electronic appendix to Version 3 a thorough literature review for each V3 risk factor—roughly 2,000–3,000 words per risk factor (Guy et al., 2014). As such, the rationale for the selection of the risk factors is manifestly clear, and together the risk factors provide comprehensive coverage of risk-relevant factors.

Nonnumeric Categorical Risk Communication

In part due to the difficulty of deriving instruments with stable numeric probability estimates, SPJ instruments do not use numeric cutoffs or algorithms to produce probability or frequency estimates of risk. One of the allowable circumstances when using SPJ approaches is that people with few risk factors may be considered high risk, and people with many risk factors may be considered low risk. Generally, the more risk factors, the greater the risk. However, professionals must be free to exercise discretion when this typical premise does not hold true. For example, if a person has a history of violence in the context of paranoid delusions and when making threats to kill others, these three risk factors alone may compel a conclusion of high risk, despite the fact that they would produce a low "score" on a given instrument. To arrive at a decision of low, moderate, or high, clinicians consider the number and relevance of risk factors that are present in a given case, and the degree and intensity of management required to mitigate risk. This process will be described in greater detail later in the chapter. Further, as we review later, research evidence suggests that this decision-making process predicts violence as well as or better than actuarial approaches.

Table 17.1 SELECT STRUCTURED PROFESSIONAL JUDGMENT VIOLENCE RISK ASSESSMENT INSTRUMENTS

Instrument	Intended Application	No. of Items
HCR-20 Version 2 (Historical-Clinical-Risk Management-20; Webster et al., 1997)	Violence among adult males or females	20
HCR-20 Version 3 (Douglas et al., 2013)	Violence among adult males or females	20
SARA (Spousal Assault Risk Assessment Guide; Kropp et al., 1999)	Violence against a current or former intimate partner by a man or a woman	20
START (Short-term Assessment of Risk and Treatability; Webster et al., 2009)	Short-term violence by adult psychiatric inpatients	20
SVR-20 (Sexual Violence Risk-20; Boer et al., 1997)	Sexual violence among male adults with histories of sexual violence	20
RSVP (Risk for Sexual Violence Protocol; Hart et al., 2003)	Sexual violence among male adults with histories of sexual violence	22
SAVRY (Structured Assessment of Violence Risk Among Youth; Borum et al., 2003)	Violence among adolescents	30
EARL-20B, Version 2 (Early Assessment Risk List for Boys, EARL-20B, Version 2; Augimeri et al., 2001)	Antisocial and violent behavior in boys under 12	22
ERASOR (Estimate of Risk of Adolescent Sexual Offense Recidivism, Version 2.0; Worling & Curwen, 2001)	Sexual violence among adolescents with histories of sexual violence	25
SAPROF (SAPROF. Guidelines for the assessment of protective factors for violence risk, 2nd Edition; de Vogel et al., 2012)	Violence amongst adults; to be used in conjunction with HCR-20 or SVR-20	17

NOTE: This listing of risk assessment instruments is not intended to be exhaustive but to provide a sampling of commonly used and researched instruments.

Weighting of Risk Factors

The SPJ approach recommends that professionals not only consider the presence of specified risk factors but also their relevance in the individual case. For this reason, risk factors are not "preweighted" according to their performance in a given sample, as is typical of most actuarial instruments. Rather, upon considering the manifestation and relevance of risk factors for a given patient, client, or offender, the professional deems which are most important in the given case to understand violence. Risk factors are not equally relevant to all people. For example, for some people substance use problems could be highly predictive of violence, and for others, they may not be. Professionals must have the discretion to make this decision. In our view, this optimizes the bridge between the nomothetic and idiographic levels of analysis, or between science and practice. That is, evaluators first consider the nomothetic evidence base, represented by the preselected, empirically supported, and operationally defined risk factors contained on a given SPJ instrument. Then, they determine how said risk factors "play out" at the individual case level.

Relevance to Treatment and Risk Management

All SPJ violence risk instruments are intended to assist professionals in managing risk and, when applicable, in designing treatment and intervention plans to do so. As such, all SPJ instruments include *dynamic risk factors*, or risk factors that can change over time. Although not a design feature, most actuarial instruments do not feature dynamic risk as an important element, which limits their utility in risk reduction (Douglas & Skeem, 2005). More recent SPJ instruments include greater focus on issues of formulation and scenario planning, as we will review later.

RESEARCH EVALUATION

There are now literally hundreds of studies on SPJ measures and hundreds on actuarial measures as well. Therefore, reviewing single studies is impractical and runs the risk of selectivity as well. For that reason we will focus to some extent on meta-analytic evaluations.

Meta-Analytic Evaluations

Campbell, French, and Gendreau (2009) meta-analyzed 88 studies from between 1980 and 2006. Given this date range, some instruments included are now obsolete, and much of the last decade of research is not included. Most analyses focused on *general* recidivism among adults, although some focused on violent recidivism. They were able to evaluate some specific measures if there were enough studies to do so: HCR-20, PCL-R (*Psychopathy Checklist-Revised*; Hare, 1991; 2003), Statistical Information on Recidivism (SIR; Nuffield, 1982), the VRAG, and the Level of Service family of instruments, which includes the original *Level of Supervision Inventory* (LSI; Andrews, 1982) and its revisions, the LSI-R and the *Level of Service/Case Management Inventory* (LS/CMI; Andrews, Bonta, & Wormith, 2004). In general, no instrument clearly outperformed others, as confidence intervals overlapped between them. The range of effect sizes (Zr) for institutional violence was .08 to .28, and for violent recidivism, from .22 to .32. Instruments that contained dynamic risk factors produced larger effect sizes than those without.

In a meta-analysis of 118 sex offender risk assessment studies, Hanson and Morton-Bourgon (2009) concluded that actuarial assessments were more accurate than unstructured clinical judgments. SPJ measures were found to be intermediate. However, only six SPJ studies were included. In fact, an SPJ measure, the SVR-20

(*Sexual Violence Risk—20*; Boer, Hart, Kropp, & Webster, 1997), produced the largest effect sizes, although based on only three studies. Given the small number of SPJ instruments included, it does not appear prudent to conclude one way or the other how SPJ performed relative to actuarial measures.

Two meta-analyses have evaluated risk assessment instruments for young offenders. Olver, Stockdale, and Wormith (2009) compared the *Hare Psychopathy Checklist-Revised: Youth Version* (PCL:YV; Forth, Kosson, & Hare, 2003), the *Structured Assessment of Violence Risk in Youth* (SAVRY; Borum, Bartel, & Forth, 2003), and the *Youth Level of Service/Case Management Inventory* (YLS/CMI; Hoge & Andrews, 2002) in 44 studies. (Note that the PCL:YV is not a risk assessment instrument per se, but it is often included in risk assessments and risk assessment research.) The measures performed comparably to one another. For the SAVRY, effect sizes (with sexual recidivism removed—none of the instrument predicted this well) ranged from .30 to .38, for the YLS/CMI, from .26 to .32, and for the PCL:YV, .16 to .28. Another such meta-analysis, focusing solely on youth sexual recidivism (Viljoen, Mordell, & Beneteau, 2012), also reported no meaningful differences between actuarial and SPJ instruments.

Yang, Wong, and Coid (2010) were able to make some comparative conclusions about risk assessment instruments concerning their ability to add incremental validity over and above the PCL-R. They analyzed nine instruments across 28 recent studies (1999–2008) and tested whether they could add incrementally to the PCL-R. Although there were few differences between instruments, only two were able to add incrementally to the PCL-R: the HCR-20 and the Offender Group Reconviction Scale (OGRS; Copas & Marshall, 1998). However, there were only 2 studies of the OGRS that permitted this comparison, compared to 16 for the HCR-20.

Another meta-analysis compared the HCR-20 and PCL-R (Guy, Douglas, & Hendry, 2010). Across 34 samples that contained both instruments, the authors found comparable univariate effect sizes for both instruments (AUCs = .69 for both). The HCR-20's predictive validity was not diminished when its psychopathy item was removed (AUC = .71). Based on meta-analytic logistic regression using seven raw data sets, the HCR-20 (with its psychopathy item removed) added unique, incremental validity to the PCL-R. The PCL-R did not add incrementally to the HCR-20.

Singh, Grann, and Fazel (2011) evaluated nine instruments across 88 samples based on studies between 1995 and 2008. They used a "binning" strategy whereby they used the categorical risk systems that most instruments contain, be they actuarial or nonnumeric. For 27 SPJ studies, 22 such "bins" were based on the nonnumeric judgments of low, moderate, or high risk (collapsed into either low/moderate or moderate/high). Although there were 88 studies included, instrument-specific analyses were typically based on fewer than 10 studies, and no more than 12. The SAVRY (an SPJ instrument) produced the largest effect size, whereas the Level of Service and PCL measures produced the smallest. They also reported that measures designed to predict violence, as opposed to those designed to predict general recidivism, did better. In a related meta-analysis that overlapped in terms of samples included, Fazel, Singh, Doll, and Grann (2012) reported a similar finding, in that instruments designed for the assessment of *violence* risk as opposed to *crime* risk generally, produced meaningfully larger effect sizes. This was regardless of whether they were actuarial or SPJ in design.

Because most published meta-analyses rely on a small number of studies for measure-specific analyses, or even for SPJ versus actuarial comparisons, we review one dissertation that was comprehensive in terms of its coverage of SPJ studies and SPJ-actuarial comparisons. Guy (2008) evaluated 113 SPJ disseminations. When actuarial instruments were included in the disseminations, she compared these to the SPJ instruments. She also determined that the performance of SPJ instruments did not differ as a function of several important potential moderators: gender, geographic locale (Europe versus North America), age (adult versus adolescent), legal setting (civil, forensic, correctional, mixed/other), context (institution versus community), method (file versus file + interview), or authorship (whether authors or translators were involved in the validation research).

The nonnumeric summary risk ratings of low, moderate, or high risk were more strongly associated with violence than were the sums of risk factors on SPJ instruments (i.e., if one were to total up scores for the instruments). Based on all coded effect sizes, SPJ summary risk ratings produced larger effect sizes (AUC = .68) than actuarial instruments (AUC = .62). Based on a single effect size per study, SPJ summary risk ratings (AUC = .69) and actuarial instruments (.67) were comparably associated with violence.

In general, then, based on the meta-analytic research, SPJ instruments and their summary risk ratings are at least as strongly associated with violence as are actuarial instruments, or the PCL instruments. Some studies have focused in more detail on the summary risk ratings that SPJ instruments rely upon. We review these next.

Focus on Summary Risk Ratings

As described earlier, one of the distinctive features of the SPJ approach is that it relies on a nonnumeric, categorical risk communication method. We have identified 34 published studies that have evaluated the predictive validity of these judgments (Arbach-Lucioni, Andres-Pueyo, Pomarol, & Gomar-Sones, 2011; Belfrage et al., 2012; Braithwaite, Charette, Crocker, & Reyes, 2010; Catchpole & Gretton, 2003; de Vogel & de Ruiter, 2005, 2006; de Vogel, de Ruiter, Hildebrand, Bos, & van de Ven, 2004; de Vogel, de Ruiter, van Beek, & Mead, 2004; de Vries Robbé, de Vogel, & de Spa, 2011; Desmarais, Nicholls, Wilson, & Brink, 2012; Dolan & Rennie, 2008; Douglas, Ogloff, & Hart, 2003; Douglas, Yeomans, & Boer, 2005; Enebrink, Långström, & Gumpert, 2006; Gammelgård, Koivisto, Eronen, & Kaltiala-Heino, 2008; Jovanović, Toševski, Ivković, Damjanović, & Gašić, 2009; Kropp & Hart, 2000; Langton, Hogue, Daffern, Mannion, & Howells, 2009; Lodewijks, de Ruiter, & Doreleijers, 2008; Lodewijks, Doreleijers, & de Ruiter, 2008; Lodewijks, Doreleijers, de Ruiter, & Borum, 2008; Meyers & Schmidt, 2008; Neves, Goncalves, & Palma-Oliveira, 2011; Nonstad et al., 2010; Pedersen, Rasmussen, & Elsass, 2010; Penney, Lee, & Moretti, 2010; Rajlic & Gretton, 2010; Schaap, Lammers, & de Vogel, 2009; Schmidt, Campbell, & Houlding, 2011; Sjöstedt & Långström, 2002; van den Brink, Hooijschuur, van Os, Savenije, & Wiersma, 2010; Verbrugge, Goodman-Delahunty, & Frize, 2011; Viljoen et al., 2008; Vincent, Chapman, & Cook, 2011).

For research purposes, it is possible to simply assign scores of 0 (low risk), 1 (moderate risk), or 2 (high risk) to these ratings and evaluate the extent to which they are associated with future violence. The vast majority of these 34 studies (30, or 88%) found that they were significantly predictive of violence. Further, in half of these studies, the incremental validity of summary risk ratings was tested (against the total of summing the instruments' risk factors—an actuarial procedure, against actuarial measures, or against PCL measures). Such studies test whether adding summary risk ratings to a multivariate model adds unique predictive variance. Incremental validity was observed in 15 of 17 studies. The same incremental validity effect has been found with the newly revised HCR-20 Version 3 (Strub, Douglas, & Nicholls, in press).

Dynamic Risk and Risk Reduction

One of the important assumptions of the SPJ approach is that changeable risk factors for violence should be targeted for intervention. More basic still is the assumption that there exists a set of risk factors that indeed change, and when they change, such changes are associated with violence. Generally, from the broad mental health and intervention fields, it is well established that numerous constructs (i.e., anger; stress; psychotic symptoms; substance use problems) are sensitive to change (see Douglas & Skeem, 2005, for a review). These assumptions, as they pertain to SPJ instruments, have now been tested in a number of samples.

Using the HCR-20 with 150 forensic psychiatric patients, Belfrage and Douglas (2002) showed that several of the C and R items, as well as the sums of C and R factors, decreased over the course of forensic treatment. Similarly, Douglas and Belfrage (2001) reported that C scale items (which, when summed for research purposes, can range from 0 to 10), dropped on average three points between admission to and discharge from a psychiatric hospital.

Michel et al. (2013) used the C and R scale items in a mixed sample of civil and forensic psychiatric patients to evaluate not only the change in the items but also whether the change was related to violence. The sample included 248 participants followed postrelease into the community for 24 months and evaluated every 4 months. They reported that 6 of the 10 individual items not only showed change, but that this change was associated with violence. That is, when these risk factors increased, so did violence, and when they decreased, so too did violence.

Douglas, Strand, and Belfrage (2011) reported that, in a sample of 174 forensic psychiatric inpatients who were reevaluated four times (roughly every 6 months), changes in the C scale scores were associated with corresponding changes in violence within the institution. Using a cluster-based approach, they also reported that there were distinct groupings of patients who demonstrated very different patterns of change. Similarly, the rates of violence across follow-up periods tended to shadow the changes. Blanchard (2013; see also Blanchard & Douglas, 2014) reported similar findings regarding the C and R scale for community violence amongst civil psychiatric patients and offenders.

de Vries Robbé, de Vogel, Douglas, and Nijman (in press) evaluated whether the HCR-20 and a measure of protective factors (the SAPROF) changed over the course of forensic treatment in the Netherlands and, if so, whether this change was related to later, postdischarge violence. Using a pseudo-prospective design with 108 discharged forensic patients, pre-post changes in the HCR-20 C and R factors, and in the SAPROF factors, were associated with future violence. That is, people whose risk factors decreased and whose protective factors increased were at lower risk for recidivism after discharge.

Belfrage et al. (2012) evaluated the use of the SARA by Swedish police in 429 cases of domestic violence. Officers evaluated each case using the SARA, and ratings of low, moderate, and high risk were made. Then, officers determined their risk management strategies. The authors coded whether the risk management strategies themselves could be considered of high or low intensity. They found that there was a risk reduction effect for high-risk cases if high-intensity risk management strategies were employed, but not if low-intensity strategies were employed. Further, in low-risk cases, if high-intensity strategies were employed, there was a risk-enhancing effect. This study provides good support for how the SPJ model is intended to be used in practice—decisions of high risk should lead to more intensive risk management strategies so as to reduce future violence. Lower risk cases do not need such intensive intervention.

Although additional research on such topics is still necessary, it is fair to conclude the following about the SPJ model: (a) both the risk factors and summary risk ratings are associated with violence; (b) SPJ measures and summary risk ratings are as strong or more strongly associated with violence compared to actuarial approaches; (c) dynamic risk factors on SPJ measures are sensitive to change; (d) changes on SPJ dynamic risk factors are associated with violence; and (e) there is emerging evidence that linking SPJ-identified high-risk cases to high-intensity management results in lower observed future violence. In the next main section we will present an overview of the decision-making steps in the SPJ model.

CLINICAL DECISION MAKING USING THE STRUCTURED PROFESSIONAL JUDGMENT APPROACH

One of the decided advantages of the SPJ approach—in addition to its strong empirical support—is its high relevance to the individual decisions that professionals must make about violence risk. That is, estimating the level or risk that a person poses is but one step in the assessment approach. Professionals are often confronted with myriad other decisions pertaining to risk management, risk monitoring, treatment, and so forth. As such, one of the primary goals of SPJ is to foster solid decision making about violence risk and the management thereof. The earliest SPJ instruments, such as the HCR-20 Version 1 (Webster et al., 1995) and the SARA (Kropp et al., 1994/1999), focused on the specification of the most important risk factors that should be considered in any given evaluation. Since that time, the SPJ field has developed considerably in terms of the conceptual underpinnings intended to guide the risk assessment task (for a thorough review of this developmental process, see the introductory chapter of the most recent SPJ measure—HCR-20 Version 3 [Douglas et al., 2013]).

Current SPJ conceptualizations of the risk assessment and management process delineate seven steps. Building on measures such as the *Risk for Sexual*

Table 17.2 STEPS IN THE STRUCTURED PROFESSIONAL
JUDGMENT DECISION-MAKING PROCESS AS
EMBODIED BY THE HCR-20 VERSION 3

Step	Task
1.	Case information
2.	Presence of risk factors
3.	Relevance of risk factors
4.	Risk formulation
5.	Risk scenarios
6.	Management strategies
7.	Conclusory opinions

Violence Protocol (RSVP; Hart et al., 2003) and the *Stalking Assessment Manual* (SAM; Kropp, Hart, & Lyon, 2008), and as both embodied in and exemplified by the HCR-20 Version 3, these steps are portrayed in Table 17.2 and will be briefly reviewed next.

Step 1: Case Information

Evaluators should use whatever means necessary to collect all information relevant to violence and risk. Generally, we recommend that, at a minimum, evaluators conduct a thorough review of available file information (police; health and mental health; correctional; nursing; etc), as well as conduct interviews with the evaluee. It may be desirable in some cases to interview treating professionals, family members, and victims. Sources of information should be documented, as should the person's history of violence and violent ideation.

Step 2: Presence of Risk Factors

Next, evaluators rate whether the specified risk factors on the SPJ instrument are present, not present, or possibly/partially present. Most SPJ instruments use this three-level rating system. In rare cases, evaluators might have to omit the rating if there is simply no reliable information upon which to make a decision. As all SPJ measures include risk factors that are dynamic, evaluators will also need to decide when to reevaluate these (if they are working in a context in which they will have continuing oversight of a case). The HCR-20 V3 manual provides detailed instructions on determining reevaluation windows.

As an example of one set of SPJ risk factors, the items of the HCR-20 V3 are presented in Table 17.3. For all SPJ instruments, if an evaluator is of the opinion that a case-specific risk factor is not captured by the preset risk factors, she or he may specify it as an "other consideration," so long as strong rationale is provided for its risk-enhancing nature.

Table 17.3 RISK FACTORS ON THE HCR-20 VERSION 3

Historical Scale (History of Problems With ...)

H1. Violence
   a. As a child (12 years and under)
   b. As an adolescent (13–17 years)
   c. As an adult (18 years and over)
H2. Other antisocial behavior
   a. As a child (12 years and under)
   b. As an adolescent (13–17 years)
   c. As an adult (18 years and over)
H3. Relationships
   a. Intimate
   b. Nonintimate
H4. Employment
H5. Substance use
H6. Major mental disorder
   a. Psychotic disorder
   b. Major mood disorder
   c. Other major mental disorders
H7. Personality disorder
   a. Antisocial, psychopathic, and dissocial
   b. Other personality disorders
H8. Traumatic experiences
   a. Victimization/trauma
   b. Adverse childrearing experiences
H9. Violent attitudes
H10. Treatment or supervision response

Clinical Scale (Recent Problems With ...)

C1. Insight
   a. Mental disorder
   b. Violence risk
   c. Need for treatment
C2. Violent ideation or intent
C3. Symptoms of major mental disorder
   a. Psychotic disorder
   b. Major mood disorder
   c. Other major mental disorders
C4. Instability
   a. Affective
   b. Behavioral
   c. Cognitive
C5. Treatment or supervision response
   a. Compliance
   b. Responsiveness

(Continued)

Table 17.3 (CONTINUED)

Risk Management Scale (Future Problems With ...)

R1. Professional services and plans

R2. Living situation

R3. Personal support

R4. Treatment or supervision response

    a. Compliance

    b. Responsiveness

R5. Stress or coping

Step 3: Relevance of Risk Factors

Once the presence of risk factors has been determined, evaluators should then consider the case-specific relevance of risk factors. As discussed earlier, not all risk factors are equally relevant to all persons' risk for violence. According to the HCR-20 V3 (p. 51), a risk factor can be considered to be "relevant" at the individual level if it:

1. Was a material contribution to past violence
2. Is likely to influence the person's decision to act in a violent manner in the future
3. Is likely to impair the individual's capacity to employ nonviolent problem-solving techniques or to engage in nonviolent or nonconfrontational interpersonal relations
4. Is crucial or critical to manage this factor in order to mitigate risk

Step 4: Risk Formulation

The purpose of risk formulation is to reduce the number of risk-relevant pieces of information by integrating risk factors in a meaningful way. In essence, the purpose is to derive an individual theory of violence—*why* might this person be violent? There are various approaches, both pragmatically and theoretically based. For instance, one could identify clusters of risk factors that are inextricably linked to one another for the case at hand. As an example, consider a person who was severely abused, and as a result of this he or she later had difficulties in relationships, in garnering social support, and in trusting authority figures. He or she might perhaps also have turned to substances to deal with emotional problems and might even have developed a personality disorder. The "root cause" of this cluster of risk factors, all of which are linked to one another, is abuse. The purpose is to condense a larger set of risk factors into a smaller set of workable, sensible units.

As Hart and Logan (2011) have discussed, formulation can be theory based as well. For example, one might draw from social learning theory or from the good lives model (Ward, 2002; Ward & Laws, 2010). The "four P" model (Weerasekera, 1996) might also be of help, in which evaluators identify predisposing, precipitating, perpetuating, and protective factors.

Step 5: Risk Scenarios

As described by Hart and Logan (2011) and by the HCR-20 V3 manual, scenario planning has been used for decades in other fields, such as military, health care, and finance. Its main purpose is to identify, based on one's formulation (and hence based on ratings of the presence and relevance of risk factors, and the nature of past violence), realistic areas of future concern. It is a method that allows the evaluator to speculate, in an informed way, about what *might* happen in the future. It encourages evaluators to derive a small number of scenarios (usually, three to five), and then to identify the warning signs that a given scenario might unfold, and, perhaps most important, what management strategies might prevent it. It can be useful to think about different types of scenarios, including a repeat scenario (the person will do something she or he has already done in the past), a twist scenario (the person will commit a related but slightly different type of violence), a worst-case scenario (severity of violence will escalate), and a best-case scenario (severity of violence will decrease).

Step 6: Management Strategies

Based on all previous steps, the necessary risk management strategies will have become clearer. As a general principle, no important (i.e., relevant) risk factor should be left unaddressed by the risk management strategy. Further, higher risk cases should receive more intensive risk management efforts, be they of a correctional or mental health nature. As described in the HCR-20 V3 manual, risk management can take various forms, including supervision, monitoring, treatment, and victim safety planning. We will return to victim safety planning momentarily, as it is a relatively specialized form of management of particular relevance to targeted forms of violence in which specific victims might be identifiable.

Step 7: Conclusory Opinions

The final step consists of summarizing one's judgments and recommendations. As described earlier, the SPJ approach uses summary risk ratings of low, moderate, and high risk. These can also be thought of as case prioritization ratings—those rated high risk are at highest priority to receive available treatment resources and repeated monitoring and assessment. A rating of "high risk" means that, *generally*, there are a large number of risk factors that are present and relevant (although recall from our previous discussion that a person can be considered high risk based on a small number of risk factors), and that there is an urgent need to develop a risk management plan. Typically, high risk also means that a high level of intervention is necessary to mitigate risk. As reviewed earlier, summary risk ratings perform as well as or better than numeric and actuarial approaches in terms of forecasting who will be violent in the future. We also recommend that evaluators make summary risk ratings for imminent violence and serious physical violence, and set a date for case review.

FOCUS ON TARGETED VIOLENCE AND VICTIM SAFETY

As mentioned under Step 6, one of the possible risk management strategies is victim safety planning. This option is particularly relevant in contexts involving targeted violence, such as stalking, intimate partner violence, and honor-based violence. We highlight this particular form of risk assessment in addition to our review of SPJ in general because it can involve some different dynamics and decisions.

In cases of targeted violence, contrary to the most common scenario in the assessment of general violence in forensic and correctional institutions, we know who the perpetrators and the probable victims are. This has some implications for how risk assessment methods are developed and used in practice. Among other things, risk assessment tools in the context of targeted violence can incorporate more context-specific risk factors and, maybe most important, also analyze vulnerability factors among victims. The latter helps the assessor to get a broad picture of the case, in order to work out the best possible case-specific preventive actions.

Intimate Partner Violence

Intimate partner violence (IPV), particularly the abuse of women perpetrated by men, is a societal problem of pandemic proportions (e.g., Garcia-Moreno, Jansen, Ellsberg, Heise, & Watts, 2006). Furthermore, victimization surveys show that approximately 10%–15% of people aged 15 years or older report that they have been stalked in a way that caused them to fear for their safety or the safety of someone known to them (see Kropp et al., 2008). Perpetrators are often the former intimate partners of victims, but in other cases they are family members, acquaintances (e.g., friends or coworkers), or even complete strangers.

The use of victim vulnerability factors (vv factors) when assessing risk for targeted violence has shown to be very important in recent years research, both in the context of spousal assault (e.g., Belfrage & Strand, 2008), stalking (e.g., Belfrage & Strand, 2008), and honor-based violence (Belfrage et al., 2012). Thus, vv factors are now incorporated in most of the SPJ tools of various types of targeted violence, for example, the B-SAFER (Kropp, Hart & Belfrage, 2010), the SAM (Kropp et al., 2008), and the PATRIARCH (Belfrage, 2005).

Probably the most common SPJ tool in this context, and also the oldest, is the SARA (Kropp et al., 1994, 1999). A more recent instrument, commonly used in law enforcement and social authorities, is the short version of the SARA; the B-SAFER (Kropp, Hart, & Belfrage, 2005, 2010). Originally, the SARA was developed for use by clinicians. However, in recent years, there has been a growing awareness that other, nonclinician, professional groups could benefit from SPJ measures when performing risk assessments. This is particularly the case among police all over the world, who every day perform risk assessments and make decisions about what protective actions to take in cases of spousal assault. The majority of these assessments and decisions are still not based on any evidence-based and structured approaches, but it has become more common that SPJ tools have been implemented within law enforcement worldwide. In Sweden, for example, use of the B-SAFER is mandatory for the police to use as a base for risk assessments in cases of spousal assault.

The B-SAFER was constructed through statistical analyses of existing data sets to identify possible redundancy among the original 20 SARA risk factors (Cooke, 2003) and tested in various settings within law enforcement. A comprehensive test was performed within the Swedish police, reported in Belfrage (2008). (The whole process of developing the B-SAFER is closely described in Kropp [2008] and Kropp and Hart [2010].) In addition to its 10 risk factors, the B-SAFER has five vv factors: inconsistent behavior/attitude; extreme fear; inadequate access to resources; unsafe living situation; and personal problems. It is important to point out that the inclusion of vv factors in no way places blame on people for being victimized. However, there are interventions that can be implemented with potential victims to reduce their risk of being victimized.

Stalking

Stalking may be defined as *unwanted and repeated communication, contact, or other conduct that deliberately or recklessly causes people to experience reasonable fear or concern for their safety or the safety of others known to them* (see Kropp et al., 2008). This definition includes manifest stalking, as well as attempts or conspiracies to commit stalking. There are just two risk tools available in this context, both with a SPJ approach. These two devices seem to be complementary. One is commonly used by law enforcement (the SAM, *Stalking Assessment and Management*, by Kropp et al., 2008), while the other is more designed for use by clinicians (the SRP, *Stalking Risk Profile*, by MacKenzie et al., 2009).

The SRP focuses on five domains of factors: the relationship between stalker and victim, the type of motivation driving the stalking, the stalker's risk profile, the victim's risk profile, and the legal and mental health context of the stalking, while the SAM focuses on three domains: the nature of stalking, perpetrator risk factors, and—as with the B-SAFER—victim vulnerability factors. The SAM has 10 such vv factors, some of which are essentially the same as the B-SAFER factors. The SAM vv factors are as follows: inconsistent behavior toward perpetrator; inconsistent attitude toward perpetrator; inadequate access to resources; unsafe living situation; problems caring for dependents; intimate relationship problems; nonintimate relationship problems; distressed; substance use problems; and employment and financial problems.

As with the B-SAFER, the primary purpose of including vv factors is to provide further avenues for risk reduction, so as to implement victim safety planning. The fact that intimate partner violence and stalking often include identifiable victims, and perpetrators and victims who are known to one another, creates distinct characteristics to these types of violence but also unique opportunities for risk reduction. That is, not only can interventions be aimed at the perpetrator but help can also be provided to potential victims.

Honor-Based Violence

Honor-based violence is usually defined as violence or threats of violence toward a family member (most often a woman or girl) due to the belief of the perpetrators that the victim has brought dishonor upon the family (Belfrage et al., 2012).

A more formal definition is "actual, attempted or threatened physical harm, including forced marriages, with honor as the motive" (Belfrage, 2005). The perceived dishonor is most often the result of one of the following behaviors, or the suspicion of such behaviors: (a) dressing in a manner unacceptable to the family or community, (b) wanting to terminate or prevent an arranged marriage or desiring to marry by own choice, (c) engaging in sexual acts outside marriage, or even due to a nonsexual relationship perceived as inappropriate, or (d) engaging in homosexual acts (e.g., Chesler, 2009).

According to the United Nations, approximately 5,000 women and girls lose their lives—most at the hands of family members—in honor killings around the world each year (http://www.unfpa.org). The problem seems to be particularly confined to the Palestinian territories, the Kurdish regions of Turkey and Iraq, and majority Muslim countries in the Balkans, Bangladesh, Egypt, and Afghanistan. However, studies suggest that honor killing is accelerating in North America and may correlate with the numbers of first-generation immigrants (Chesler, 2009). In Europe, there are also cases reported from all countries, where Great Britain seems to have the highest number of honor killings—approximately one every month (Foreign & Commonwealth Office, 2004).

Undoubtedly, there are few other crimes that are as complicated to investigate and understand as honor-based crimes. Law enforcement is usually dealing with criminals who mostly work alone and regularly engage in criminal activity. But when dealing with honor-based criminality, the planning and execution often involve multiple family members, most of whom do not have personality disorders, major mental disorders, or past criminality. They can include mothers, sisters, brothers, male cousins, uncles, and grandfathers. Their honor-based violence may be considered moral and necessary by many of the people in their social networks and families. And if a woman or a girl escapes such an execution, the extended family/clan often will continue to search for her to kill her. Since whole families, and sometimes even social communities, are involved, investigations often have to be carried out pan-nationally, involving many authorities and sometimes several countries. Thus, traditional risk instruments with traditional risk factors do not necessary help us here. This context is a very clear example of the importance of having various risk instruments for various contexts.

The PATRIARCH is the only SPJ instrument to deal with honor-based violence, and it too considers victim vulnerability factors. It consists of risk factors that are a mix of traditional risk factors with strong support in previous research on targeted violence (violent threats or thoughts, previous violent acts, escalation, and personal problems) and factors more specifically directed at honor-based violence (previous honor-based violence, attitudes that support honor-based violence, arranged marriages or engagements, high degree of insult, origin from an area with known subcultural values, and lack of cultural integration). Its vv factors were drawn from the B-SAFER.

We wished to highlight these three forms of violence because they present unique challenges in terms of assessment and management. Often there is a direct link between perpetrator and victim. Indeed, there may be a singular focus on the victim. We also wished to highlight these forms of violence because they represent the most common contexts in which nonclinical professionals (i.e., police officers) might benefit from the SPJ approach. Indeed, Belfrage et al.'s (2012) study showed that police use of one of these SPJ instruments led to a reduction of recidivistic intimate partner violence. Finally, we sought to illustrate that not all assessment procedures should stop with the assessment of the perpetrator. Indeed, in the contexts covered in this section, they must not.

CONCLUSION

Over the past two decades, the SPJ approach to violence risk assessment and management has grown remarkably. The first SPJ instruments—the HCR-20 and SARA—were developed concurrently and published within a few months of each other. Since then, research has proliferated: There are roughly 200 disseminations on the HCR-20 *alone*. It has been translated into 20 languages and used or evaluated in at least 35 countries. There are SPJ instruments for a variety of forms of violence. We have learned in a quick 20 years that this approach "works" as well as or better than any alternatives; that it can be used to track changes in risk over time because its risk factors are demonstrably dynamic; that professionals' judgments, when exercised in an SPJ context, are as or more accurate than actuarial prediction; and that changes in risk factors—purposive or otherwise—are associated with corresponding changes in violence. In future research we hope that some of the newer features of the SPJ approach (i.e., relevance, formulation, and scenario planning) receive a good amount of evaluation as well.

REFERENCES

Andrews, D. A. (1982). *The Level of Supervision Inventory (LSI): The first follow-up*. Toronto: Ontario Ministry of Correctional Services.

Andrews, D. A., & Bonta, J. (1995). *Level of Service Inventory-Revised*. Toronto, ON: Multi-Health Systems.

Andrews, D. A., Bonta, J., & Wormith, S. J. (2004). *The Level of Service/Case Management Inventory (LS/CMI)*. Toronto, ON: Multi-Health Systems.

Arbach-Lucioni, K., Andres-Pueyo, A., Pomarol-Clotet, E., & Gomar-Sones, J. (2011) Predicting violence in psychiatric inpatients: A prospective study with the HCR-20 violence risk assessment scheme. *Journal of Forensic Psychiatry and Psychology, 22*, 203–222.

Belfrage, H. (2005). PATRIARCH. Checklist for the assessment of risk for patriarchal violence with honor as motive. Sundsvall Forensic Psychiatric Hospital. Retrieved May 2014, from http://www.lvn.se/rpk.

Belfrage, H. (2008). Police-based structured spousal violence risk assessment: The process of developing a police version of the SARA. In A. C. Baldry & F. W. Winkel (Eds.), *Intimate partner violence prevention and intervention: The risk assessment and management approach* (pp. 33–44). Hauppauge, NY: Nova Science.

Belfrage, H., & Douglas, K. S. (2002). Treatment effects on forensic psychiatric patients measured with the HCR-20 violence risk assessment scheme. *International Journal of Forensic Mental Health, 1*, 25–36.

Belfrage, H., & Strand, S. (2008). Structured spousal violence risk assessment: Combining risk factors and victim vulnerability factors. *International Journal of Forensic Mental Health, 7*, 39–46.

Belfrage, H., Strand, S., Storey, J. E., Gibas, A. L., Kropp, P. R., & Hart, S. D. (2012). Assessment and management of risk for intimate partner violence by police officers using the Spousal Assault Risk Assessment guide (SARA). *Law and Human Behavior*, *36*(1), 60–67.

Blair, P. R., Marcus, D. K., & Boccaccini, M. T. (2008). Is there an allegiance effect for assessment instruments? Actuarial risk assessment as an exemplar. *Clinical Psychology: Science and Practice*, *15*, 346–360.

Blanchard, A. J. E. (2013). Dynamic risk factors in violence risk assessment: A multiple time-point evaluation of the HCR-20 and START. Unpublished Master's thesis, Simon Fraser University, Burnaby, British Columbia.

Blanchard, A. J. E. (2014, March). Dynamic risk: A prospective repeated measures examination of the HCR-20 and START. Paper presented at the annual convention of the American Psychology-Law Society, New Orleans, LA.

Boer, D. P., Hart, S. D., Kropp, P. R., & Webster, C. D. (1997). *Manual for the Sexual Violence Risk—20: Professional guidelines for assessing risk of sexual violence.* Vancouver: British Columbia Institute Against Family Violence, and Mental Health, Law, and Policy Institute, Simon Fraser University.

Braithwaite, E., Charette, Y., Crocker, A. G., & Reyes, A. (2010). The predictive validity of clinical ratings of the Short-Term Assessment of Risk and Treatability (START). *International Journal of Forensic Mental Health*, *9*, 271–281.

Campbell, M. A., French, S., & Gendreau, P. (2009). The prediction of violence in adult offenders: A meta-analytic comparison of instruments and methods of assessment. *Criminal Justice and Behavior*, *36*, 567–590.

Catchpole, R. E. H., & Gretton, H. M. (2003). The predictive validity of risk assessment with violent young offenders: A 1-year examination of criminal outcome. *Criminal Justice and Behavior*, *30*, 688–708.

Chesler, P. (2009). Are honor killings simply domestic violence? *Middle East Quarterly*, *Spring 2009*, 61–69.

Cooke, D. (2003, April). Content-related validity of the SARA: A psychometric evaluation. Presentation at the 3rd Annual Conference of the International Association of Forensic Mental Health Services, Miami, FL.

Copas, J., & Marshall, P. (1998). The Offender Group Reconviction Scale: The statistical reconviction score for use by probation officers. *Journal of the Royal Statistical Society*, *47C*, 159–171.

de Vogel, V., & de Ruiter, C. (2005). The HCR-20 in personality disordered female offenders: A comparison with a matched sample of males. *Clinical Psychology and Psychotherapy*, *12*, 226–240.

de Vogel, V., & de Ruiter, C. (2006). Structured professional judgment of violence risk in forensic clinical practice: A prospective study into the predictive validity of the Dutch HCR-20. *Psychology, Crime and Law*, *12*, 321–336.

de Vogel, V., de Ruiter, C., Hildebrand, M., Bos, B., & van de Ven, P. (2004). Type of discharge and risk of recidivism measured by the HCR-20: A retrospective study in a Dutch sample of treated forensic psychiatric patients. *International Journal of Forensic Mental Health*, *3*, 149–165.

de Vogel, V., de Ruiter, C., van Beek, D., & Mead, G. (2004). Predictive validity of the SVR-20 and Static 99 in a Dutch sample of treated sex offenders. *Law and Human Behavior*, *28*, 235–251.

de Vries Robbé, M., de Vogel, V., & de Spa, E. (2011). Protective factors for violence risk in forensic psychiatric patients: A retrospective validation study of the SAPROF. *International Journal of Forensic Mental Health*, *10*, 178–186.

de Vries Robbé, M., de Vogel, V., & Douglas, K. S., & Nijman, H. L. I. (in press). Changes in dynamic risk and protective factors for violence during inpatient forensic psychiatric treatment: Predicting reductions in post-discharge community recidivism. Law and Human Behavior.

Desmarais, S. L., Nicholls, T., Wilson, C. M., & Brink, J. (2012). Reliability and validity of the Short-Term Assessment of Risk and Treatability (START) in assessing risk for inpatient aggression. *Psychological Assessment*, *24*, 685–700.

Dolan, M. C., & Rennie, C. E. (2008). The Structured Assessment of Violence Risk in Youth as a predictor of recidivism in a United Kingdom cohort of adolescent offenders with conduct disorder. *Psychological Assessment*, *20*, 35–46.

Douglas, K. S., & Belfrage, H. (2001). Use of the HCR-20 in violence risk management: Implementation and clinical practice. In K. S. Douglas, C. D. Webster, S. D. Hart, D. Eaves, & J. R. P. Ogloff (Eds.), *HCR-20: Violence risk management companion guide* (pp. 41–58). Burnaby, BC: Mental Health, Law, and Policy Institute, Simon Fraser University.

Douglas, K. S., Hart, S. D., Webster, C. D., & Belfrage, H. (2013). *Historical Clinical Risk Management 20 (Version 3) violence risk assessment guidelines* (HCR-20 V3). Burnaby, BC: Mental Health, Law, and Policy Institute, Simon Fraser University.

Douglas, K. D., Ogloff, J. R. P., & Hart, S. D. (2003). Evaluation of a model of violence risk assessment among forensic psychiatric patients. *Psychiatric Services*, *54*, 1372–1379.

Douglas, K. S., & Skeem, J. L. (2005). Violence risk assessment: Getting specific about being dynamic. *Psychology, Public Policy, and Law*, *11*, 347–383.

Douglas, K. S., Strand, S., & Belfrage, H. (2011, June). *Dynamic risk: Evaluating the nature and predictive validity of change on the Clinical and Risk Management scales of the HCR-20*. Paper presented at the annual convention of the International Association of Forensic Mental Health Services, Barcelona, Spain.

Douglas, K. S., Yeomans, M., & Boer, D. P. (2005). Comparative validity analysis of multiple measures of violence risk in a sample of criminal offenders. *Criminal Justice and Behavior*, *32*, 479–510.

Enebrink, P., Långström, N., & Gumpert, C. H. (2006). Predicting aggressive and disruptive behavior in referred 6- to 12-year-old boys: Predictive validation of the EARL-20B risk/needs checklist. *Assessment*, *13*, 356–367.

Fazel, S., Singh J. P., Doll, H., & Grann, M. (2012). Use of risk assessment instruments to predict violence and antisocial behaviour in 73 samples involving 24,827 people: Systematic review and meta-analysis. *British Medical Journal*, *345*, e4692.

Forth, A. E., Kosson, D. S., & Hare, R. D. (2003). *The Hare Psychopathy Checklist-Revised: Youth Version*. Toronto, ON: Multi-Health Systems.

Foreign & Commonwealth Office. (2004). *Young people and vulnerable adults facing forced marriage. Practice guidance for social workers*. London, UK: Author.

Gammelgård, M., Koivisto, A., Eronen, M., & Kaltiala-Heino, R. (2008). The predictive validity of the Structured Assessment of Violence Risk in Youth (SAVRY) among institutionalised adolescents. *Journal of Forensic Psychiatry and Psychology*, *19*, 352–370.

Garcia-Moreno, C., Jansen, H., Ellsberg, M., Heise, L., & Watts, C. H. (2006). Prevalence of intimate partner violence: Findings from the WHO multi-country study on women's health and domestic violence. *Lancet, 368*, 1260–1269.

Grann, M., & Långström, N. (2007). Actuarial assessment of violence risk: To weigh or not to weigh? *Criminal Justice and Behavior, 34*, 22–36.

Grove, W. M., & Meehl, P. E. (1996). Comparative efficiency of informal (subjective, impressionistic) and formal (mechanical, algorithmic) prediction procedures: The clinical-statistical controversy. *Psychology, Public Policy, and Law, 2*, 293–323.

Guy, L. S. (2008). *Performance indicators of the structured professional judgement approach for assessing risk for violence to others: A meta-analytic survey.* Unpublished Ph.D. dissertation, Simon Fraser University, Burnaby, British Columbia.

Guy, L. S., Douglas, K. S., & Hendry, M. (2010). The role of psychopathic personality disorder in violence risk assessments using the HCR-20. *Journal of Personality Disorders, 24*, 551–580.

Guy, L. S., & Wilson, C. M. (2007). *Empirical support for the HCR-20: A critical analysis of the violence literature.* [HCR-20 Violence Risk Assessment White Paper Series, #2]. Burnaby, BC: Mental Health, Law, & Policy Institute, Simon Fraser University.

Guy, L. S., Wilson, C. M., Douglas, K. S., Hart, S. D., Webster, C. D., & Belfrage, H. (2014). *HCR-20 Version 3: Item-by-item summary of violence literature.* [HCR-20 Violence Risk Assessment White Paper Series, #3]. Burnaby, BC: Mental Health, Law, & Policy Institute, Simon Fraser University.

Hanson, R. K., & Morton-Bourgon, K. E. (2009). The accuracy of recidivism risk assessments for sexual offenders: A meta-analysis of 118 prediction studies. *Psychological Assessment, 21*, 1–21.

Hare, R. (1991). *The Hare Psychopathy Checklist-Revised.* Toronto, ON: Multi-Health Systems.

Hare, R. (2003). *The Hare Psychopathy Checklist-Revised* [2nd ed.]. Toronto, ON: Multi-Health Systems.

Hart, S. D., & Logan, C. (2011). Formulation of violence risk using evidence-based assessments: The structured professional judgment approach. In P. Sturmey & M. McMurran (Eds.), *Forensic case formulation* (pp. 83–106). Chichester, UK: Wiley-Blackwell.

Hoge, R. D., & Andrews, D. A. (2002). *Youth Level of Service/Case Management Inventory: User's manual.* Toronto, ON: Multi-Health Systems.

Jovanović, A. A., Toševski, D. L., Ivković, M., Damjanović, A., & Gašić, M. J. (2009). [Predicting Violence in veterans with posttraumatic stress disorder]. *Vojnosanitetski Pregled: Military Medical and Pharmaceutical Journal of Serbia and Montenegro, 66*, 13–21.

Kropp, P. R., Hart, S. D., Webster, C. D., & Eaves, D. (1994/1999). *Spousal Assault Risk Assessment guide user's manual.* Toronto, ON: Multi-Health Systems/British Columbia Institute on Family Violence.

Kropp, P. R., Hart, S. D., Lyon, D. R., & Storey, J. E. (2011). The development and validation of the guidelines for stalking assessment and management. *Behavioral Sciences and the Law, 29*(2), 302–316.

Kropp, P. R. (2008). The development of the SARA and the B-SAFER. In A. C. Baldry & F. W. Winkel (Eds.), *Intimate partner violence prevention and intervention: The risk assessment and management approach* (pp. 19–32). Hauppauge, NY: Nova Science.

Kropp, P. R., & Gibas, A. (2010). The spousal assault risk assessment guide (SARA). In R. K. Otto & K. S. Douglas (Eds.), *Handbook of violence risk assessment* (pp. 227–250). New York, NY: Routledge.

Kropp, P. R., & Hart, S. D. (2000). The Spousal Assault Risk Assessment (SARA) guide: Reliability and validity in adult male offenders. *Law and Human Behavior, 24*, 101–118.

Kropp, P. R., & Hart, S. D (2010). *The reliability, validity, and utility of the Brief Spousal Assault Form for the Evaluation of Risk (B-SAFER) as a domestic violence risk assessment tool for use by police*. Victoria, BC: Ministry of Public Safety and Solicitor General.

Kropp, P. R., Hart, S. D., & Belfrage, H. (2010). *Brief Spousal Assault Form for the Evaluation of Risk (B-SAFER), Version 2: User manual*. Vancouver, BC: Proactive Resolutions.

Kropp, P. R., Hart, S. D., & Lyon, D. R. (2008). *Stalking assessment and management*. Vancouver, BC: Proactive Resolutions.

Langton, C. M., Hogue, T. E., Daffern, M., Mannion, A., & Howells, K. (2009). Prediction of institutional aggression among personality disordered forensic patients using actuarial and structured clinical risk assessment tools: Prospective evaluation of the HCR-20, VRS, Static-99, and Risk Matrix 2000. *Psychology, Crime and Law, 15*, 635–659.

Laws, D. R., & O'Donohue, W. T. (2008). *Sexual deviance: Theory, assessment, and treatment*. New York, NY: Guilford Press.

Lodewijks, H. P. B., de Ruiter, C., & Doreleijers, T. A. H. (2008). Gender differences in violent outcome and risk assessment in adolescent offenders after residential treatment. *International Journal of Forensic Mental Health, 7*, 133–146.

Lodewijks, H. P. B., Doreleijers, T. A. H., & de Ruiter, C. (2008). SAVRY risk assessment in relation to sentencing and subsequent recidivism in a Dutch sample of violent juvenile offenders. *Criminal Justice and Behavior, 35*, 696–709.

Lodewijks, H. P. B., Doreleijers, T. A. H., de Ruiter, C., & Borum, R. (2008). Predictive validity of the Structured Assessment of Violence in Youth (SAVRY) during residential treatment. *International Journal of Law and Psychiatry, 31*, 263–271.

MacKenzie, R. D., McEwan, T. E., Pathé, M. T., James, D. V., Ogloff, J. R. P., & Mullen, P. E. (2009). *Stalking risk profile: Guidelines for the assessment and management of stalkers*. Melbourne, Australia: StalkInc. and the Centre for Forensic Behavioural Science, School of Psychology and Psychiatry, Monash University.

Meehl, P. E. (1954). *Clinical versus statistical prediction: A theoretical analysis and a review of the evidence*. Minneapolis: University of Minnesota Press.

Meyers, J. R., & Schmidt, F. (2008). Predictive validity of the Structured Assessment for Violence Risk in Youth (SAVRY) with juvenile offenders. *Criminal Justice and Behavior, 35*, 344–355.

Michel, S. F., Riaz, M., Webster, C., Hart, S. D., Levander, S., Müller-Isberner, R., … Hodgins, S. (2013). Using the HCR-20 to predict aggressive behavior among men with schizophrenia living in the community: Accuracy of prediction, general and forensic settings, and dynamic risk factors. *International Journal of Forensic Mental Health, 12*, 1–13.

Mills, J. F., Jones, M. N., & Kroner, D. G. (2005). An examination of the generalizability of the LSI-R and VRAG probability bins. *Criminal Justice and Behavior, 32*, 565–585.

Monahan, J., Steadman, H., Appelbaum, P., Grisso, T., Mulvey, E., Roth, L., ... Silver, E. (2005). *The classification of violence risk*. Lutz, FL: Psychological Assessment Resources.

Neves, A. C., Goncalves, R. A., & Palma-Oliveira, J. M. (2011). Assessing risk for violent and general recidivism: A study of the HCR-20 and the PCL-R with a non-clinical sample of Portuguese offenders. *International Journal of Forensic Mental Health, 10,* 137–149.

Nonstad, K., Nesset, M. B., Kroppan, E., Pedersen, T. W., Nöttestad, J. A., Almvik, R., & Palmstierna, T. (2010). Predictive validity and other psychometric properties of the Short-Term Assessment of Risk and Treatability (START) in a Norwegian high secure hospital. *International Journal of Forensic Mental Health, 9,* 294–299.

Nuffield, J. (1982). *Parole decision-making in Canada*. Ottawa, ON: Communication Division, Solicitor General of Canada.

Olver, M., Stockdale, K., & Wormith, J. (2009). Risk assessment with young offenders: A meta-analysis of three assessment measures. *Criminal Justice and Behavior, 36,* 329–353.

Ogloff, J. R. P. (2001). Professional, legal, and ethical issues in violence risk management. In K. S. Douglas, C. D. Webster, D. Eaves, S. D. Hart, & J. R. P. Ogloff (Eds.), *The HCR-20 violence risk management companion manual* (pp. 59–71). Burnaby, BC: Mental Health, Law, and Policy Institute, Simon Fraser University.

Pedersen, L., Rasmussen, K., & Elsass, P. (2010). Risk assessment: The value of structured professional judgments. *International Journal of Forensic Mental Health, 9,* 74–81.

Penney, S. R., Lee, Z., & Moretti, M. M. (2010). Gender differences in risk factors for violence: An examination of the predictive validity of the Structured Assessment of Violence Risk in Youth. *Aggressive Behavior, 36*(6), 390–404.

Quinsey, V. L., Harris, G. T., Rice, M. E., & Cormier, C. A. (1998). *Violent offenders: Appraising and managing risk*. Washington, DC: American Psychological Association.

Quinsey, V. L., Harris, G. T., Rice, M. E., & Cormier, C. (2006). *Violent offenders: Appraising and managing risk* (2nd ed). Washington, DC: American Psychological Association.

Rajlic, G., & Gretton, H. (2010). An examination of two sexual recidivism risk measures in adolescent offenders. *Criminal Justice and Behavior, 37,* 1066–1085.

Schaap, G., Lammers, S., & de Vogel, V. (2009). Risk assessment in female forensic psychiatric patients: A quasi-prospective study into the validity of the HCR-20 and PCL-R. *Journal of Forensic Psychiatry and Psychology, 20,* 354–365.

Schmidt, F., Campbell, M. A., & Houlding, C. (2011). Comparative analyses of the YLS/CMI, SAVRY, and PCL:YV in adolescent offenders: A 10-year follow-up into adulthood. *Youth Violence and Juvenile Justice, 9,* 23–42.

Singh, J. P. (2013, March). *The international risk survey (IRiS) project: Perspectives on the practical application of violence risk assessment tools*. Paper presented at the Annual Conference of the American Psychology-Law Society, Portland, OR.

Singh, J. P., Grann, M., & Fazel, S. (2011). A comparative study of violence risk assessment tools: A systematic review and metaregression analysis of 68 studies involving 25,980 participants. *Clinical Psychology Review, 31,* 499–513.

Sjöstedt, G., & Långström, N. (2002). Assessment of risk for criminal recidivism among rapists: A comparison of four different measures. *Psychology, Crime and Law, 8,* 25–40.

Strub, D. S., Douglas, K. S., & Nicholls, T. L. (in press). The validity of Version 3 of the HCR-20 violence risk assessment scheme amongst offenders and civil psychiatric patients. *International Journal of Forensic Mental Health*.

van den Brink, R. H. S., Hooijschuur, A., van Os, T. W. D. P., Savenije, W., & Wiersma, D. (2010). Routine violence risk assessment in community forensic mental health-care. *Behavioral Sciences and the Law, 28*, 396–410.

Verbrugge, H. M., Goodman-Delahunty, J., & Frize, M. C. J. (2011). Risk assessment in intellectually disabled offenders: Validation of the suggested ID supplement to the HCR-20. *International Journal of Forensic Mental Health, 10*, 83–91.

Viljoen, J. L., Mordell, S., & Beneteau, J. L. (2012). Prediction of adolescent sexual reof-fending: A meta-analysis of the J-SOAP-II, ERASOR, J-SORRAT-II, and Static-99. *Law and Human Behavior, 36*, 423–438.

Viljoen, J. L., Scalora, M., Cuadra, L., Bader, S., Chávez, V., Ullman, D., & Lawrence, L. (2008). Assessing risk for violence in adolescents who have sexually offended: A comparison of the J-SOAP-II, J-SORRAT-II, and SAVRY. *Criminal Justice and Behavior, 35*, 5–23.

Vincent, G. M., Chapman, J., & Cook, N. (2011). Predictive validity of the SAVRY, racial differences, and the contribution of needs factors. *Criminal Justice and Behavior, 38*, 42–62.

Ward, T. (2002). The management of risk and the design of good lives. *Australian Psychologist, 37*, 172–179.

Ward, T., & Laws, R. (2010). Desistence from sex offending: Motivating change, enriching practice. *International Journal of Forensic Mental Health, 9*, 11–23.

Webster, C. D., Douglas, K. S., Eaves, D., & Hart, S. D. (1997). *The HCR-20 scheme: The assessment of dangerousness and risk, version 2.* Burnaby, BC: Mental Health, Law, and Policy Institute, Simon Fraser University.

Webster, C. D., Eaves, D., Douglas, K. S., & Wintrup, A. (1995). *The HCR-20 scheme: The assessment of dangerousness and risk.* Burnaby, BC: Simon Fraser University and Forensic Psychiatric Services Commission of British Columbia.

Weerasekera, P. (1996). *Multiperspective case formulation: A step towards treatment integration.* Malabar, FL: Krieger.

Yang, M., Wong, S. C. P., & Coid, J. (2010). The efficacy of violence prediction: A meta-analytic comparison of nine risk assessment tools. *Psychological Bulletin, 136*, 740–767.

18

Assessing Facets of Personality and Psychopathology in Violent Offenders

DUSTIN B. WYGANT, KATHRYN C. APPLEGATE, AND TINA D. WALL ∎

As a research subject, Lecter has proven most disappointing. He's simply impenetrable to psychological testing. Rorschach, Thematic Apperception … he folds them into origami.

—Dr. Chilton reflects on Hannibal Lecter in *Red Dragon* (2002)

Violence has been around for as long as people have existed, and humans have been both horrified by and marveled at the lengths at which violent individuals have gone. In considering the causes of violence, much debate has contrasted internal versus external causes (i.e., the person versus the situation). Sociologists and criminologists often identify various societal factors such as poverty and social stratification as the cause of crime (including violent crime) (Gottfredson & Hirschi, 1990; Shaw & Mckay, 1942; Sutherland, 1960). As mental health professionals, we can only devote so much attention to these societal factors as explanatory (and perhaps mitigating factors) in our encounters with violent individuals. Our work is more focused on understanding the psychological makeup of the violent individual, often with the aim of explaining previous behavior or predicting future behavior.

This chapter will specifically examine the assessment of psychological constructs related to violence that are useful to consider when conducting a violence risk assessment. We will focus on four measures of psychopathology and personality: the Minnesota Multiphasic Personality Inventory-2 (MMPI-2; Butcher et al., 2001), MMPI-2 Restructured Form (MMPI-2-RF; Ben-Porath & Tellegen, 2008/2011), Personality Assessment Inventory (PAI; Morey, 2007), and the Psychopathic Personality Inventory-Revised (PPI-R; Lilienfeld & Widows, 2005).

These four measures were selected for several reasons. First, each utilizes self-report methods, thus affording an ease of administration, scoring, and interpretation. Administration and scoring can be performed by a trained technician or support staff (or in some cases by computer), thus freeing up the clinician for other duties. Second, all four measures contain embedded response bias indicators (i.e., "validity scales") that can be used to appraise how the examinee approached the test. With the exception of the PPI-R, the remaining three tests' validity scales have been extensively examined and found effective in identifying various forms of response bias (Rogers, Sewell, Martin, & Vitacco, 2003; Sellbom & Bagby, 2008; Sellbom, Toomey, Wygant, Kucharski, & Duncan, 2010; Wygant et al., 2009, 2011). Third, these measures were selected because of their extensive empirical validation and popularity by clinical and forensic practitioners in a variety of settings, including the assessment of violence risk. Indeed, surveys have found these measures to be the most widely used self-report measures of personality and psychopathology in forensic and correctional settings (Archer, Buffington-Vollum, Stredny, & Handel, 2006; Lally, 2003; Viljoen, McLachlan, & Vincent, 2010).

Rather than provide an extensive discussion of test interpretation for the MMPI-2, MMPI-2-RF, PAI, and PPI-R, which is covered in detail by the tests' respective manuals and interpretative texts (e.g., Ben-Porath, 2012; Blais, Baity, & Hopwood, 2010; Graham, 2011; Morey, 2003), the current chapter will provide only a brief description of the measures and instead discuss their particular utility in the assessment of violence risk as well as review any research that has directly examined the measure in the assessment of violence risk. Additionally, we will discuss in general how such measures can be incorporated into violence risk assessments. We will conclude with a case example.

REVIEW OF SELF-REPORT PERSONALITY AND PSYCHOPATHOLOGY MEASURES

Minnesota Multiphasic Personality Inventory-2 (MMPI-2)

The Minnesota Multiphasic Personality Inventory-2 (MMPI-2) is a 567-item self-report measure that assesses a broad range of personality traits, psychopathological symptoms, and behavioral proclivities (Butcher et al., 2001) and is a revision to the original MMPI, developed in the 1940s (Hathaway & McKinley, 1943). The MMPI-2 comprises 9 Validity Scales, 10 Clinical Scales (with 31 subscales), 9 Restructured Clinical (RC) Scales, 15 Content Scales (with 28 Content Component Scales), 15 Supplementary Scales, and 5 Personality Psychopathology Five (PSY-5) Scales. The test can be used with individuals aged 18 years and older and is available in several different languages. The MMPI-2 manual (Butcher et al., 2001) and subsequent reviews (Graham, 2011) provide extensive psychometric information about the test.

One of the primary means by which the MMPI-2 can be utilized in risk assessment is its measurement of various personality and psychopathological characteristics. In this regard, the MMPI-2 (as an extension of the original MMPI) is unsurpassed in terms of empirical validation (Graham, 2011). The test has numerous measures of both internalizing and externalizing psychopathology, as well as measures of thought disorder, pathological personality traits, various attitudes, and behavioral tendencies. Specific links between psychopathological constructs assessed by the MMPI-2 and violence risk will be discussed later in the chapter.

The original clinically substantive measures of the MMPI were the Clinical Scales, which were developed by Hathaway and McKinley (1943) through empirical keying. This approach involved the comparison of item responses between various clinical groups and nonpathological "normal" individuals who were primarily comprised of visitors to the University of Minnesota Hospitals. Graham (2011) provides a good discussion of the development of each Clinical Scale. While these scales were the mainstay of MMPI research and interpretation for many years, they were not without their limitations. Indeed, the empirical keying methodology employed in their development produced highly intercorrelated, heterogeneous measures that were generally saturated with a single "distress" factor, which contributes to their relatively weak discriminant validity (Tellegen et al., 2003). The interpretative challenges posed by this situation were addressed to some degree by configural interpretation (i.e., Code-Types), subscales (e.g., Harris & Lingoes, 1955), content-based scales, and various supplementary scales.

Given the immense research base on the MMPI Clinical Scales, the MMPI-2 Restandardization Committee kept the scales fairly intact for the MMPI-2. While this allowed for continuity in terms of the research on the original scales, it also maintained some of the psychometric challenges posed by the scales. Tellegen and colleagues (2003) sought to address these limitations with the development of the Restructured Clinical (RC) scales. The RC scales were developed by constructing a *Demoralization* (RCd) scale as a measure of general dysphoric mood through a factor analysis of Clinical Scales 2 and 7. After removing the variance attributed to demoralization from the remaining Clinical Scales with factor analysis, Tellegen and company identified the "core" components of each scale independent of this common distress factor. Ben-Porath (2012) and Tellegen, Ben-Porath, and Sellbom (2009) provide extensive reviews of the RC scales' development and subsequent validation across a variety of clinical contexts. It is the opinion of these authors that the RC scales offer a substantial psychometric improvement over the Clinical Scales in interpretability and clinical utility.

Given the extent of research on the MMPI and MMPI-2, there is surprisingly little research that has directly examined the ability of the test to predict violence. Megargee and his colleagues (1979, 2001) developed a configural-based system of classifying inmates with the MMPI and MMPI-2 Clinical Scales based on their analysis of over 1,300 federal inmates administered the MMPI between 1970 and 1972. Several of the offender groups they identified through cluster analysis exhibited significantly higher rates of recidivism after release, while others engaged in higher rates of institutional violence.

Sellbom and colleagues (2008) examined the ability of the RC scales to predict violent recidivism among domestic violence offenders undergoing intervention for battering. They found that *Antisocial Behaviors* (RC4) and *Hypomanic Activation* (RC9) were able to predict treatment failure and recidivism above and beyond historical (e.g., criminal history, substance abuse) and demographic (e.g., age) variables. Indeed, offenders scoring above 65T on either RC4 of RC9 were at approximately 60%–70% greater risk to recidivate compared to those without elevations on these scales.

Assessing Psychopathy With the MMPI-2

Psychopathy is widely recognized as a robust predictor of criminal behavior, recidivism, violent behavior, and sexual aggression (Hare, 1996; Hare & Neumann, 2006; Salekin, Rogers, & Sewell, 1996). One of the strengths of personality measures such as the MMPI-2 is its ability to assess this important construct. While Scale 4 from the original MMPI, *Psychopathic Deviate* (Pd), was developed to assess psychopathy (McKinley & Hathaway, 1944), numerous studies have subsequently shown that the scale fails to adequately load onto various measures of the construct (e.g., Hare & Cox, 1978; Harpur, Hare, & Flakstian, 1989; Lykken, 1957). Pd is highly correlated with negative emotionality, limiting the scale's ability to capture various elements of psychopathy, particularly in line with Cleckley's (1941) conceptualization (Lilienfeld, 1994). Two-point codetypes involving scale 4, such as 4-6/6-4 or 4-9/9-4, have been linked to higher levels of anger and antisocial personality traits, respectively.

The Content Scale *Antisocial Practices* (APS) was added to the MMPI-2 to provide a more direct assessment of antisocial attitudes and behaviors. Lilienfeld (1996) found that ASP exhibited incremental validity over Pd in assessing global ratings of psychopathy and measures of externalizing behavior but noted that it still failed to capture low levels of trait anxiety and stress resiliency.

Sellbom and colleagues (2005, 2007) illustrated particular utility in the assessment of psychopathy using the RC scales. In their 2007 study, Sellbom, Ben-Porath, and Stafford showed that RC4 outperformed ASP and Pd in predicting scores on the PCL Screening Version (PCL-SV; Hart, Cox, & Hare, 1995) as well as behavioral criteria associated with psychopathy. Sellbom, Ben-Porath, Lilienfeld, Patrick, and Graham (2005) showed similar findings in terms of RC4 outperforming Pd in capturing the socially deviant components of psychopathy. They also illustrated potential for scores on *Low Positive Emotions* (RC2) and *Dysfunctional Negative Emotions* (RC7) to assess the affective and interpersonal components of psychopathy. Taken together, these two studies illustrate that the heterogeneous nature of psychopathy (e.g., fearlessness, callousness, impulsivity) is best construed by elevations on RC4 and *Hypomanic Activation* (RC9), coupled with low scores on RC2 and RC7.

One final set of scales on the MMPI-2 bears mentioning in its ability to capture relevant personality factors is the Personality Psychopathology Five (PSY-5). The PSY-5 (Harkness & McNulty, 1994) is a dimensional model of personality pathology developed in consideration of both diagnostic criteria and "normal" descriptions of personality in order to capture a broad range of personality traits. PSY-5 scales were developed for the MMPI-2 (Harkness, McNulty, & Ben-Porath, 1995). They include *Aggressiveness* (AGGR), which measures interpersonal dominance, grandiosity, and proclivity toward using instrumental aggression. *Psychoticism* (PSYC) captures one's proneness to disconnection from reality. *Disconstraint* (DISC) measures behavioral disinhibition, impulsivity, and sensation seeking. *Neuroticism/Negative Emotionality* (NEGE) captures one's disposition to experience a broad range of negative emotional experiences. Finally, *Introversion/Low Positive Emotionality* (INTR) captures introverted social detachment as well as low hedonic capacity. Harkness and colleagues (2012) provide an extensive review of the development and validation of the PSY-5 model and scales. Interestingly, the PSY-5 scales map conceptually on the personality domains proposed for the *DSM-5* conceptualization of personality disorders (see Skodol et al., 2011), thus lending diagnostic utility for the scales with the release of the *DSM-5*. The PSY-5 scales have been found to capture symptoms of antisocial personality disorder and psychopathy (Bagby, Sellbom, Costa, & Widiger, 2008; Marion & Sellbom, 2011; Sellbom, Ben-Porath, & Stafford, 2007; Sellbom, Ben-Porath, Lilienfeld, Patrick, & Graham, 2005; Wygant, Sellbom, Graham, & Schenk, 2006; Wygant & Sellbom, 2012), in particular DISC and AGGR, coupled with low levels of NEGE.

MMPI-2 RESTRUCTURED FORM (MMPI-2-RF)

The MMPI-2- Restructured Form developed by Ben-Porath and Tellegen was released in 2008. The restructuring of the Clinical Scales (described earlier) was the initial step in the development of the MMPI-2-RF. Ben-Porath and Tellegen wanted to augment the RC scales with additional scales to capture numerous clinical constructs in line with contemporary conceptualizations of personality and psychopathology. The test has 51 scales in total, organized into 9 validity scales, 3 Higher Order scales (*Emotional/Internalizing Dysfunction, Thought Dysfunction*, and *Behavioral/Externalizing Dysfunction*), 9 RC scales, 23 Specific Problems scales (arranged by various content that include Somatic/Cognitive, Internalizing, Externalizing, and Interpersonal problems), 2 interest scales, and restructured variants of the PSY-5 scales. Tellegen and Ben-Porath (2008/2011), along with Ben-Porath (2012), provide extensive description of the test's empirical validation.

Assessing Psychopathy With the MMPI-2-RF

The RC scales provide the backbone for the test's clinical interpretation. The MMPI-2-RF RC scales are comprised of the same items as their MMPI-2 counterparts. Consequently, the two previous studies by Sellbom and colleagues (2005, 2007) that examined the utility of the MMPI-2 RC scales in the assessment of psychopathy apply as well to the MMPI-2-RF. In addition, several studies have specifically examined the MMPI-2-RF's ability to assess psychopathy. Sellbom and colleagues (2012) developed regression-based estimates of three indices from the Psychopathic Personality Inventory (PPI; Lilienfeld & Andrews, 1996), specifically *Total Psychopathy* (a global rating of the construct), *Fearless-Dominance*, and *Impulsive-Antisociality*. These regression-based indices of the PPI incorporated the RC scales as well as six Specific Problems scales (*Behavior Restricting Fears, Multiple Specific Fears, Interpersonal Passivity, Social Avoidance, Shyness,* and *Disaffiliativeness*). Utilizing correctional, forensic, undergraduate, and community mental health samples, these authors found that the indices generally exhibited a conceptually expected pattern of associations with the PCL-SV; psychopathy-related traits such as narcissism, empathy, sensation seeking, antisociality, and impulsivity; and therapist ratings of antisociality and aggression.

    Rock, Sellbom, Ben-Porath, and Salekin (2013) examined the MMPI-2-RF psychopathy-based indices (Sellbom et al., 2012) in a sample of convicted males undergoing domestic violence batterers' treatment. They found that the *Total*

Psychopathy and *Impulsive-Antisociality* indices were significantly associated with treatment failure and recidivism at 1-year follow-up. Moreover, the *Fearless-Dominance* index positively moderated the association between *Impulsive-Antisociality* and treatment failure such that individuals high on *Fearless-Dominance* who also exhibited a proclivity toward *Impulsive-Antisociality* were at an especially high risk of treatment failure. Mattson, Powers, Halfaker, Akeson, and Ben-Porath (2012) also examined treatment failure, specifically in a drug court treatment program, and found that individuals elevated on MMPI-2-RF measures of externalizing problems were at an increased risk for failing to complete the program.

Kastner, Sellbom, and Lilienfeld (2012) illustrated associations between various MMPI-2-RF scales and the PPI in a correctional and college student sample. In particular, *Fearless Dominance* exhibited moderated to large positive associations with *Aggressiveness* (AGGR-r) and negatively with *Social Avoidance* (SAV), *Shyness* (SHY), *Multiple Specific Fears* (MSF), *Neuroticism/Negative Emotionality* (NEGE-r), and *Stress/Worry* (STW). *Impulsive Antisociality* exhibited moderate to large associations with *Aggression* (AGG), *Disconstraint* (DISC-r), RC4, *Juvenile Conduct Problems* (JCP), and *Substance Abuse* (SUB).

Wygant and Sellbom (2012) examined the MMPI-2-RF PSY-5 in relation to psychopathy as indexed by the PCL-SV in a sample of individuals undergoing forensic psychological evaluations. AGGR-r was strongly associated with the PCL-SV global measure of psychopathy, as well as both parts and the four facets of the PCL-SV. DISC-r was preferentially associated with the behavioral facets of psychopathy, whereas low NEGE-r was related to the affective characteristics of the construct.

PERSONALITY ASSESSMENT INVENTORY (PAI)

The Personality Assessment Inventory (PAI) is a 344-item self-report item measure that was developed to evaluate a broad range of personality factors and psychopathological symptoms, including internalizing and externalizing psychopathology, thought dysfunction, and pathological personality traits (Morey, 2007). The PAI comprises 22 scales in total, organized into validity scales, clinical scales (most with 3–4 subscales), treatment consideration scales, and interpersonal scales. The test was designed and standardized for individuals aged 18 years and older and is available in seven different languages. The PAI manual (Morey, 2007) provides extensive psychometric information about the test.

Assessing Psychopathy and Antisocial Personality Disorder With the PAI

The PAI has several scales that can assess the different facets of psychopathy (see Table 18.1), which was previously discussed as an important risk assessment factor. Most notably, Morey (2007) developed the *Antisocial Features* (ANT) scale to specifically assess features that are pertinent to the constructs of antisocial personality disorder and psychopathy. ANT includes three subscales that assess both the personality (e.g., egocentricity, need for stimulation) and behavioral features (e.g., criminal behavior) of psychopathy (Morey, 2007).

Numerous studies have examined the utility of the PAI in the assessment of psychopathy. The majority of this research has found ANT to be highly associated with the behavioral aspects of psychopathy. However, ANT has not fared as well in capturing the affective/interpersonal qualities of psychopathy (Benning, Patrick, Blonigen, Hicks, & Iacono, 2005; Edens, Hart, Johnson, Johnson, & Olver, 2000; Kucharski, Petitt, Toomey, & Duncan, 2008; Morey & Quigley, 2002). Even ANT-E, which was designed to specifically address these aspects, was more highly correlated with Factor 2 (behavioral deviance) of the Psychopathy Checklist-Revised (PCL-R; Hare, 1991, 2003) and PCL-SV than Factor 1 (affective/interpersonal) (Edens et al., 2000).

Douglas and colleagues (2007) found additional PAI scales (other than ANT) associated with the PCL-R. While still focused primarily on Factor 2, the PAI contains scales that measure aspects of psychopathy such as dominant interpersonal style, suspiciousness and hostility, drug use, and low anxiety (see Table 18.1). In addition, while only exhibiting a moderate relationship, these researchers found *Dominance* (DOM) to be significantly correlated with Factor 1 of the PCL-R.

In addition to ANT, Morey and Quigley (2002) showed that incarcerated inmates might also show elevations on DRG and lower scores on scales measuring suicidal ideation (SUI) and internalizing indicators, such as *Somatic Complaints* (SOM), *Anxiety* (ANX), *Anxiety-Related Disorders* (ARD), and *Depression* (DEP).

Risk Assessment With the PAI

Several scales and indices are included in the PAI to assess aggression and violence. The *Aggression* (AGG) scale was designed to assess a person's potential toward aggression and includes three subscales that assess aggressive attitudes, and verbal and physical aggression. The PAI also includes the *Violence Potential Index* (VPI), which is a supplementary index that includes 20 PAI scales and configuration markers to enhance the PAI's ability in risk assessment (Morey, 1996).

Numerous studies have examined the PAI's ability to predict violence risk. Boccaccini and colleagues (2010) examined the utility of the VPI and AGG, ANT, and DOM scales in predicting recidivism rates among a sample of sex offenders screened for civil commitment as sexually violent predators. While all of the PAI measures predicted recidivism to some degree, AGG emerged as the strongest general predictor of recidivism (which included nonviolent recidivism), and DOM was the best predictor of sexually violent recidivism, although the authors noted that the scale was likely limited in predicting sexual violence.

Skopp, Edens, and Ruiz (2007) found that ANT was the best predictor of general and aggressive misbehavior among a sample of female prisoners. Furthermore, they found that the VPI moderately correlated with general and aggressive infractions. Newberry and Shuker (2012) found similar findings in their sample of male prisoners. Importantly, they found that both ANT and ANT-A were significant predictors of an inmate's risk of reconviction. Caperton, Edens, and Johnson (2004) found the VPI, AGG, and ANT to be good predictors of major infractions in a sample of incarcerated men, with ANT emerging as the best predictor. Finally, Crawford and colleagues (2007) found that AGG was a significant indicator of problematic

Assessment Measure/Scales

Potential Violence Risk Factor	MMPI-2	MMPI-2-RF	PAI	PPI-R
Antisocial/Psychopathic Personality Traits				
Fearlessness	FRS (-)	MSF (-)	ANX (-), ARD-O (-)	F
Narcissism/grandiosity	RC9, AGGR	RC9, SFD (-), AGGR-r	MAN-G	SOI
Aggression	RC9, AGGR	RC9, AGG, AGGR-r	AGG, VPI	
Interpersonal dominance/social potency	RC2 (-), INTR (-)	RC2 (-), IPP (-), SHY (-)	DOM	SOI
Impulsivity	RC4, ASP,DISC	BXD, RC4, DISC-r	ANT, ANT-S, BOR, BOR-S	CN, RN
Anger	ANG	ANP	AGG, WRM (-)	
Criminal behavior/history	RC4, ASP	RC4, JCP	ANT	
Low trait anxiety	RC7 (-), NEGE (-)	RC7 (-), NEGE-r (-)	ANX (-) ANX-C (-), ANX-P (-)	STI
Callousness			ANT-E, WRM (-)	ME, C
Blame externalization	ASP			BE
Psychosis/Thought Disorder				
Paranoia/suspiciousness	RC6, BIZ	RC6	PAR, PAR-H, PAR-P	
Hallucinations	RC8, BIZ	RC8	SCZ	
Substance Abuse	RC4, AAS	RC4, SUB	ALC, DRG	

NOTE.. Low scores on these scales are denoted by (-). MMPI-2 scales: FRS = Fears, RC9 = Hypomanic Activation, AGGR = Aggressiveness, RC2 = Low Positive Emotions, RC4 = Antisocial Behavior, ASP = Antisocial Practices, DISC = Disconstraint, ANG = Anger, RC7 = Dysfunctional Negative Emotions, NEGE = Negative Emotionality/Neuroticism, RC6 = Ideas of Persecution, BIZ = Bizarre Mentations. RC8 = Aberrant Experiences, AAS = Addiction Acknowledgement Scale. MMPI-2-RF scales: MSF = Multiple Specific Fears, SFD = Self-Doubt, AGGR-r = Aggressiveness-Revised, AGG = Aggression, IPP = Interpersonal Passivity, SHY = Shyness, BXD = Behavioral/Externalizing Dysfunction, DISC-r = Disconstraint-Revised, ANP = Anger Proneness, JCP = Juvenile Conduct Problems, NEGE-r = Negative Emotionality/Neuroticism-Revised, SUB = Substance Abuse. PAI scales: ANX = Anxiety, ARD-O = Anxiety Related Disorders–Obsessive-Compulsive, MAN-G = Mania-Grandiosity, AGG = Aggression, VPI = Violence Potential Index, DOM = Dominance, ANT = Antisocial Features, ANT-S = Antisocial Features–Stimulus-Seeking, BOR = Borderline Features, BOR-S = Borderline Features–Self-Harm, WRM = Warmth, ANX-C = Anxiety-Cognitive, ANX-P = Anxiety–Physiological, ANT-E = Antisocial Features–Egocentricity. PPI-R scales: F = Fearlessness, SOI = Social Influence, CN = Carefree Nonplanfulness, RN = Rebellious Nonconformity, STI = Stress Immunity, ME = Machiavellian Egocentricity, C = Coldheartedness, BE = Blame Externalization.

hostility and aggression in a sample of veterans suffering from posttraumatic stress disorder (PTSD). In addition, the VPI exhibited moderate to strong associations with measures of anger, violence, and hostility.

PSYCHOPATHIC PERSONALITY INVENTORY-REVISED (PPI-R)

General Description and Development

The Psychopathic Personality Inventory (PPI; Lilienfeld & Andrews, 1996) was originally developed to create a relatively brief, yet comprehensive self-report measure of psychopathic personality traits that could be used in both correctional and noncorrectional settings. The PPI was developed to represent the core personality traits associated with Cleckley (1941) and others' conceptions of psychopathy without items explicitly referencing criminal behavior and has been extensively validated in undergraduate, community, and correctional settings (see Lilienfeld & Andrews, 1996, for a thorough review of the PPI development).

The Psychopathic Personality Inventory-Revised (PPI-R; Lilienfeld & Widows, 2005) is a revised version of the PPI. The 154-item inventory is commercially available and incorporates the same basic design and structure of the PPI; however, it includes normative references via community and correctional norms. Research has established the psychometric similarity of the PPI and PPI-R (Ray, Weir, Poythress, & Richelm, 2011). Thus, empirical findings on the PPI can reasonably be generalized to the PPI-R. The PPI-R manual (Lilienfeld & Widows, 2005) contains extensive information regarding its basic psychometric properties.

The PPI-R includes eight content scales that capture various component traits of psychopathy. Several studies have identified two higher order factors among the PPI/PPI-R's eight primary scales utilizing factor-analytic approaches. Benning and colleagues (2005) labeled the first factor *Fearless Dominance*, which consists of three scales (*Social Potency, Fearlessness*, and *Stress Immunity*). This factor assesses social dominance, manipulativeness, ability to remain calm in stressful situations, as well as the lack of anticipatory fear. The second factor, labeled by Benning and colleagues (2005) as *Impulsive Antisociality*, was later referred to as *Self-Centered Impulsivity* in the PPI-R, and consists of four scales (*Machiavellian Egocentricity, Rebellious Nonconformity, Blame Externalization*, and *Carefree Nonplanfulness*). This factor measures self-centered and reckless tendencies, impulsivity, and a proneness to blame others. The remaining PPI-R scale, *Coldheartedness*, represents callousness and a lack of guilt or empathy, and did not load onto *Fearless Dominance* or *Self-Centered Impulsivity* and was assigned as a third factor on the PPI-R. To aid its use in forensic evaluations, the PPI-R includes a measure of response consistency and over- and underreporting. However, as indicated earlier, these scales have yet to undergo independent empirical investigation. Consequently, caution should be utilized in relying on these scales solely to assess response bias.

While the PPI/PPI-R has amassed an impressive amount of empirical research since the mid-1990s (see and Lilienfeld & Fowler, 2006, for an empirical review), much of this research has focused on the construct validity of the measure rather than examining the clinical utility of PPI-R in forensic and risk assessment evaluations.

UTILITY OF THE PPI-R IN ASSESSING PSYCHOPATHY

Interpretation of the PPI-R is based on a dimensional conceptualization of psychopathy. Unlike the PCL-R, there is not an ideal cutoff for classifying an individual as psychopathic. Rather, the PPI-R Total Score should be understood as reflecting one's standing on a global range of psychopathy, with higher scores indicating the presence of more psychopathic traits. However, the strength of the PPI-R lies in the examination of its Content scales (organized into the three factors that were just discussed), as this focused level of interpretation affords the clinician with the particular psychopathic traits endorsed by the individual.

When interpreting PPI-R factors, it is noteworthy to consider that *Fearless Dominance* and *Self-Centered Impulsivity* factors only moderately correspond to the two-factor structure of the PCL-R (e.g., Berardino, Meloy, Sherman, & Jacobs, 2005; Copestake, Gray, & Snowden, 2011).

USE IN VIOLENCE RISK ASSESSMENT

Because the PPI-R assesses psychopathic personality traits, it can be a useful assessment to implement in appraising one's risk of violence. Examining the factor structure of the PPI-R in relation to a range of internalizing and externalizing psychopathology, Edens and McDermott (2010) found that *Self-Centered Impulsivity* (SCI) was positively related to both impulsivity and anger. SCI was also moderately associated with scores on the Violence Risk Appraisal Guide (VRAG; Quinsey, Harris, Rice, & Cormier, 1998) and the Historical-Clinical-Risk Mangement-20 (HCR-20; Webster, Douglas, Eaves, & Hart, 1997). Another study found that SCI was associated with a variety of externalizing behaviors, including substance use, antisocial behavior, intimate partner violence, and gambling (Jones & Miller, 2012). Kruh and colleagues (2005) examined a sample of insanity acquittees and found that the PPI and the PCL-SV accounted for approximately the same amount of variance in past violence. In particular, the PPI was better at predicting self-reported violent acts, whereas the PCL-SV better predicted officially documented incidents of violence.

ROLE OF PERSONALITY AND PSYCHOPATHOLOGY MEASURES IN VIOLENCE RISK EVALUATIONS

The assessment of violence risk has focused on the identification and use of static and dynamic risk factors (Douglas & Skeem, 2005). Static factors are those that include historical (including demographic) variables that have been empirically linked to violence risk, such as age at first offense and criminal history, among others. Dynamic factors, on the other hand, are those factors that are current, clinically oriented, and potentially subject to change under various circumstances. Examples of dynamic risk factors include presence of mental illness, substance abuse, and poor anger management. As such, dynamic variables are inevitably focused on in clinical risk assessment. A thorough review of static and dynamic risk factors is beyond the scope of this chapter. The interested reader is directed to Conroy and

Murrie (2007) and several chapters in the current text (Chapters 15–17) for a more complete discussion of static and dynamic risk factors.

While broadband measures of personality and psychopathology are likely to be limited in the direct prediction of violence risk, they can nevertheless play an important role in assessing risk in a peripheral manner. While there has been some research that directly examines the predictive ability of personality measures in assessing violence outcomes (e.g., Boccaccini, Murrie, Hawes, Simpler, & Johnson, 2010; Rock, Sellbom, Ben-Porath, & Salekin, 2013; Sellbom, Ben-Porath, Baum, Erez, & Gregory, 2008), the major utility of these measures in violence risk assessment is their ability to assess psychological variables empirically related to risk of violence. Each of the four measures we reviewed in this chapter has been empirically found to capture constituent personality traits of psychopathy (e.g., impulsivity, egocentricity, fearlessness). Moreover, the first three measures are omnibus measures of psychopathology that can assess (among other things) symptoms of thought disorder (e.g., paranoid ideation), affective states associated with violence (e.g., anger), substance abuse, and negative attitudes, which constitute potential ideographic risk factors. These variables can also be incorporated in treatment and intervention, as the assessor works with the criminal justice system to move from risk assessment to risk management. Table 18.1 provides a list of potential risk factors and the scales on these measures that we recommend using to assess them.

It is advisable to administer self-report personality and psychopathology measures prior to performing a clinical interview. However, discussing the role of psychological testing up front generally elicits greater cooperation from the client. It is important to note, that good clinical and ethical practice requires that clients are informed of evaluation procedures and provide consent before they begin the testing and interviews.

Self-report measures of personality and psychopathology can assist the clinician through (1) formulation of diagnostic impressions, particularly as they pertain to psychopathic traits and other relevant clinical risk factors; (2) assessment of possible symptom distortion on the validity scales; (3) formulation of impressions about how to approach the client during the evaluation; (4) incorporation of test results into risk-specific measures, such as the HCR-20; and (5) planning for risk management strategies. Each of these points will be discussed further in more detail.

Formulating Diagnostic Impressions

The self-report measures we review in this chapter were designed to assess personality and psychopathology. Consequently, their primary utility in violence risk evaluations is aiding in the formulation of diagnostic impressions. While there are some diagnostic variables inherently related to violence risk (e.g., psychopathy), more often than not, particular psychiatric diagnoses will be relevant on a case-by-case basis. For instance, while psychosis is generally considered, by the public, to be associated with violence (Penn & Martin, 1998), the empirical evidence on the link between psychosis and violence is mixed (see Douglas & Skeem, 2005). Douglas and Skeem (2005) provide a useful conceptualization of dynamic risk factors, such as psychosis, and discuss ways in which these factors might be related to violence. They noted, in particular, that the experience of persecutory ideations can lead to negative emotions and prompt the individual to act on them. Three of the measures we discuss include well-validated measures of paranoid ideation: *Ideas of Persecution* (RC6) on the MMPI-2 and MMPI-2-RF and *Paranoia* (PAR) on the PAI. Scores on these scales can be used to assess symptoms of paranoia and integrated with other clinical information (e.g., interviews, records) to determine their potential link to violence in a particular case.

Douglas and Skeem (2005) identified impulsivity as a dynamic risk factor, which can be assessed on the MMPI-2 with *Disconstraint* (DISC, DISC-r on the MMPI-2-RF), *Behavioral/ Externalizing Dysfunction* (BXD) on the MMPI-2-RF, *Antisocial Features* (ANT) on the PAI, and *Carefree Nonplanfulness* (CN) on the PPI-R. These authors also included negative affectivity (anger and general dysphoric mood) as another risk factor, which can be assessed via *Dysfunctional Negative Emotions* (RC7) and the *Anger* Content scale (ANG) on the MMPI-2, RC7 and *Anger Proneness* on the MMPI-2-RF, and the *Aggression* (AGG) scale on the PAI. Antisocial attitudes and substance use problems were also noted by Douglas and Skeem (2005) as dynamic risk factors, both of which can be assessed via self-report measures, such as the *Antisocial Attitudes* (ASP1), *Antisocial Behavior* (RC4), Addiction Admission Scale (AAS) on the MMPI-2; RC4, *Juvenile Conduct Problems* (JCP), and *Substance Abuse* (SUB) on the MMPI-2-RF; and *Antisocial Features* (ANT), and *Alcohol Problems* (ALC) and *Drug Problems* (DRG) on the PAI.

We pointed out earlier how each of the measures discussed in this chapter have shown utility in capturing psychopathic traits, particularly the PPI-R, which was developed specifically for this task.

Assessment of Possible Symptom Distortion

Forensic evaluations (including violence risk assessment) potentially place the evaluee at odds with the assessor. Indeed, risk assessments often take place within the context of litigious and adversarial settings. Moreover, the stakes are often very high for the individual being evaluated (e.g., civil liberties in a civil commitment hearing, return to work in a fitness-for-duty evaluation). The client might view the mental health professional (rightfully so) as an agent of the criminal justice system. Consequently, it is not uncommon for clients to exhibit varying degrees of cooperation. Lack of cooperation can include dissimulation of psychiatric symptoms (either over- or underreporting). Chapter 19 is devoted to this topic, as well as Rogers's (2008) handbook on malingering. Each of the four measures we review in this chapter includes embedded validity scales to detect various threats to response bias and dissimulation. Administering these measures prior to the clinical interview (as discussed earlier) can provide the clinician information concerning the openness of the client to discuss psychiatric symptoms. This can impact the clinician's approach with the client during the clinical interview, which is the topic of our next section.

Formulating Impressions About How to Approach the Client During the Evaluation

Administering self-report measures of personality and psychopathology (particularly prior to a clinical interview) can provide the clinician with a *starting point* in planning an effective clinical interview. Initiatives in behavioral health care are increasingly curtailing clinical procedures and face-to-face client contact time, making effective use of our limited time important. Reviewing psychological test results prior to performing a clinical interview can identify potential target areas of inquiry, perhaps even shortening the interview by making it more efficient. In effect, these measures can serve as screening tools. For example, a valid PAI profile with distinct elevations on externalizing scales, such as *Antisocial Features* (ANT) and *Aggression* (AGG), but within normal limits scores on scales assessing internalizing psychopathology, such as *Depression* (DEP), *Anxiety* (ANX), and *Anxiety-Related Disorders* (ARD), suggests that less time can be planned (and devoted) to covering internalizing problems during the interview.

Forensic interviewing is inherently difficult, given the stakes and the often vying agendas of those involved. Consequently, the ability to tailor one's approach to a client in a clinical interview can be crucial in establishing effective rapport and thus obtaining useful and credible information. Psychological test results can play a role in assisting the clinician in formulating an approach for interacting with the client. For instance, low scores on the MMPI-2-RF *Interpersonal Passivity* (IPP) scale or elevations on the PAI *Dominance* (DOM) scale can alert the clinician to a potentially difficult interactional style with the client, thus allowing him or her to plan accordingly. Underreporting indicators on these measures may suggest an unsophisticated guarded or defensive stance (as well as poor psychological insight) that might not be as directly apparent during a clinical interview. Scales reflecting emotional turmoil, such as *Demoralization* (RCd) on the MMPI-2 and MMPI-2-RF, might prompt the clinician to take a more gentle approach in the clinical interview. Conversely, elevations on scales reflecting grandiose narcissism, such as *Hypomanic Activation* (RC9) on the MMPI-2 and MMPI-2-RF, or *Mania-Grandiosity* (MAN-G) on the PAI, can suggest that a deferential approach (e.g., "stroking the ego") might influence the client to volunteer useful information in the interview.

Incorporate Test Results Into Risk-Specific Measures

Risk-specific measures generally fall into two categories. The first includes actuarial methods, which calculate risk scores based on empirically identified static variables (e.g., age of perpetrator, history of violence or delinquency). Examples of such measures include the Static-99 (Hanson & Thornton, 1999), Violence Risk Appraisal Guide (VRAG; Quinsey et al., 1998), and Sex Offender Risk Appraisal Guide (SORAG; Quinsey et al., 1998). The other category of risk assessment instruments is labeled structured professional judgment (SPJ) guides. These measures provide the clinician with systematic variables that should be considered during the assessment, such as presence of mental illness or history of violence. Rather than quantitatively arriving at risk score, SPJ measures often provide a categorical descriptor of risk (e.g., low, moderate, high). We wanted to touch on how personality and psychopathology measures can be incorporated in SJP measures. We will use the HCR-20 as an example. The HCR-20 indicates that psychological test results can be considered in formulating ratings. It should be noted that psychological tests can be used to support ratings on SJP measures (in a confirmatory manner), or they can be used to formulate hypotheses about an individual (in an exploratory manner). Either way, it is contingent upon the clinician to substantiate psychological test findings with other sources of information, such as a clinical interview or records. Psychological test results should never be used as the sole source of information in formulating ratings on SJP measures.

The HCR-20 can be used with civil and forensic psychiatric clients as well as criminal offenders. This measure provides the clinician with 20 risk-relevant factors, divided into 10 *Historical* variables (static), as well as 5 current, dynamic *Clinical* variables and 5 *Risk Management* items that the assessor should consider to mitigate future risk of violence. Several items in the *Historical* and *Clinical* sections bear relevance to constructs captured by the self-report measures we review in this chapter. In the *Historical* section, *Substance Use Problems* (H5) requires the clinician to rate (0, 1, 2) whether the client has misused substances in the past. This, of course, needs to be extensively evaluated in records and during a clinical interview. However, scales such as *Substance Abuse* (SUB) on the MMPI-2-RF and *Alcohol Problems* (ALC) and *Drug Problems* (DRG) on the PAI can certainly aid the assessment of substance misuse. *Major Mental Illness* (H6) requires the clinician to identify the historical presence of psychopathology that disturbs thought and affect, such as psychosis and mania. While tests such as the MMPI-2, MMPI-2-RF, and PAI do not differentiate between current and historical mental illness, elevations on scales reflective of severe psychopathology can obviously be used in forming an impression about this item. The historical presence of a personality disorder is rated in H7. The authors of the HCR-20 specifically mention antisocial and borderline personality disorder as particularly relevant in the assessment of violence risk. The PAI contains scales directly assessing features of these two personality disorders, *Antisocial Features* (ANT) and *Borderline Features* (BOR). With the MMPI-2 and MMPI-2-RF, the PSY-5 scales assess a dimensional model of personality psychopathology. While the MMPI-2 and MMPI-2-RF do not contain single scales to capture particular personality disorders, configurations of the PSY-5 scales have shown utility in assessing personality disorders (Bagby et al., 2008; Wygant et al., 2006). For instance, Wygant and colleagues (2006) found that borderline personality disorder was associated with elevations on *Psychoticism* (PSYC) and Neuroticism/Negative Emotionality (NEGE), whereas antisocial personality disorder was associated with elevations on *Aggressiveness* (AGGR) and *Disconstraint* (DISC).

Information from psychological testing relates to four of the five *Clinical* items on the HCR-20. *Lack of Insight* (C1) pertains to the client's awareness of factors such as mental illness and violence potential. Comparison of psychological test results (particularly valid test results as indicated by validity scales) and information gathered from records and the clinical interview might reveal discrepancies reflective of poor insight. To illustrate, consider this example from one of the first author's risk assessments. In this particular case, the court requested a risk assessment on an individual charged with violating a protective order against his estranged wife following a previous conviction of aggravated menacing. The defendant experienced a traumatic brain injury (to his frontal region) in an automobile accident approximately 6 months prior to his arrest in the matter. As part of the evaluation, the defendant was administered a battery of neuropsychological tests. Results indicated general cognitive dysfunction with particular deficits in planning and response inhibition. He produced a valid, nondefensive MMPI-2-RF in which his score on *Cognitive Complaints* (COG) was 40T (raw score 0). The discrepancy was supported in the clinical interview, during which the defendant denied any cognitive difficulties or limitations. His profound lack of insight into how the automobile accident affected his general functioning, particularly his judgment and impulse control, represented a significant risk factor that the court took into consideration from a management perspective.

Negative Attitudes (C2) requires the clinician to examine various negatively oriented attitudes that might relate to violence. The HCR-20 manual lists (among others) antisocial, procriminal, attitudes about violence and its impact on others (e.g., callousness), and general sense of optimism versus pessimism. As indicated earlier, *Antisocial Attitudes* (ASP1) and *Antisocial Behavior* (RC4) on the MMPI-2 (RC4 also on the MMPI-2-RF) and *Antisocial Features* (ANT) on the PAI all assess variants of antisocial attitudes, as well as *Rebellious Nonconformity* (RN) on the PPI-R. Callousness and lack of empathy are captured by *Antisocial Features-Egocentricity* (ANT-E) on the PAI and *Coldheartedness* on the PPI-R. Pessimism and hopelessness are captured by *Demoralization* (RCd) on the MMPI-2 and MMPI-2-RF, *Hopelessness/Helplessness* (HLP) on the MMPI-2-RF, and *Depression-Cognitive* (DEP-C) on the PAI. It should be noted that this dysphoric mood state does not in and of itself relate to violence risk, but on an ideographic basis, it might lead an individual to feelings of resignation and apathy.

As indicated earlier, psychological test results cannot generally be used to differentiate active versus historical symptoms of mental illness. In effect, most self-report measures of psychopathology include items worded in the present and past tense. Moreover, the four self-report measures we review do not specify a time context (e.g., *in the past month*) for the examinee to consider in responding to the items. Consequently, elevations on psychopathology scales need to be reviewed during the clinical interview to determine whether they reflect current or historical symptoms. As such, the same guidelines discussed for H6 (*Major Mental Illness*) can be applied to C3 (*Active Symptoms of Major Mental Illness*).

Finally, the HCR-20 identified *Impulsivity* (C4) as a *Clinical* risk variable. The authors of the HCR-20 specify that impulsivity includes affective instability as well as behavioral problems with impulse control. Scales reflecting behavioral indicators of impulsivity include the aforementioned Disconstraint (DISC/DISC-r) on the MMPI-2 and MMPI-2-RF, Behavioral/Externalizing Dysfunction (BXD) on the MMPI-2-RF, *Antisocial Features* (ANT) on the PAI, and *Carefree Nonplanfulness* (CN) on the PPI-R. Emotional instability is captured by *Dysfunctional Negative Emotions* (RC7) and the *Anger* Content scale (ANG) on the MMPI-2, RC7 and *Anger Proneness* on the MMPI-2-RF, and the *Aggression* (AGG) scale on the PAI.

Planning for Risk Management Strategies

Taking into account the impressions that these self-report measures can provide about diagnosis, test-taking approach, and potential for risk, one can plan intervention strategies to help reduce or manage the chance of future violence. Constructs assessed by tests like the MMPI-2, MMPI-2-RF, and the PAI can provide targets for intervention through psychiatric treatment. If an individual's profile is suggestive of a severe mental illness or emotional problems such as poor anger control, interventions can take the form of psychiatric referrals for medication, individual psychotherapy to improve emotional stability, or anger management. Identifying specific interventions and client needs will give professionals the best possibility of success. We will illustrate this with a case example in the next section of the chapter.

CASE EXAMPLE

Case Background

Mr. Smith[1] is a 36-year-old, single, Caucasian male who was referred for a psychological evaluation by the court to aid in risk management. His most recent conviction was domestic violence and violation of protective order (both third-degree felonies) against Sharon, his live-in girlfriend at the time, whom he believed had killed his mother. He had been sentenced to 3 years of incarceration but was granted judicial release after 1 year and placed in a reentry-based court program.

Mr. Smith was born and raised by his mother, whom he described as "emotionally abusive" and had no contact with his biological father. His mother maintained relationships with predominantly physically abusive individuals (including violence toward him). Mr. Smith had frequent suspensions and expulsions from school for insubordination and fighting. He was placed in special education classes before dropping out in middle school. His employment record was limited, and he was unemployed at the time of his arrest.

Mr. Smith began dating Sharon, whom he described as a "drug seeker," 3 years prior to the evaluation. He was convicted of domestic violence against her in the first year of their relationship and once again 1 year later, ending their relationship.

Mr. Smith reported regular use of alcohol, marijuana, and powdered cocaine when he was not incarcerated. He failed residential drug treatment on two occasions and had twice been psychiatrically hospitalized for suicidal ideation. He was prescribed antidepressant medication and a sleep aid.

With regard to his mental status, Mr. Smith was guarded throughout the interview. Despite denying imminent intent to harm Sharon, he acknowledged feeling angry toward her for "killing my mother" and devoted considerable time talking about her in an obsessive manner. He described odd and paranoid thoughts throughout the interview, such as beliefs that others tried to poison him in the past and that a radio communicated with him on several occasions. Mr. Smith described his mood as depressed, yet he denied any current suicidal and homicidal ideation.

Mr. Smith had several juvenile offenses that included robbery, truancy, and possession of marijuana. As an adult, he was convicted of 36 misdemeanor offenses and 16 additional contempt of court charges. Felony convictions included theft and his most recent convictions for domestic violence and violation of protective order. Mr. Smith's mother died while he was in jail awaiting his court proceedings. He became obsessed with the belief that Sharon killed her, noting that she was with her when she died. An autopsy report indicated she died of natural causes, but Mr. Smith remained unconvinced, believing that it was part of a conspiracy to deny him justice in the matter.

Psychological Test Results

Mr. Smith's psychological test results[2] are presented in Table 18.2. He produced a valid MMPI-2-RF profile.[3] His results are characterized by *Emotional/Internalizing Dysfunction* (71), *Thought Dysfunction* (77), and *Behavioral/Externalizing Dysfunction* (84), which reflect significant psychological disturbance.

Demoralization (75) and *Dysfunctional Negative Emotions* (73) indicate significant dissatisfaction with his life and depressed and anxious mood, which, coupled with his score on *Stress/Worry* (73), suggests that he has intense pessimism and poor resources for coping with stress. This is important to consider from a risk management perspective. Moreover, his scores on *Low Positive Emotions* (80) and *Disaffiliativeness* (78) suggest strong levels of anhedonia and alienation, which can be reflective of depression and negative symptoms of schizophrenia.

In addition to depression and anxiety, Mr. Smith's MMPI-2-RF results reflect significant thought dysfunction in the form of auditory or visual hallucinations (*Aberrant Experiences* = 76) and delusions of a persecutory nature (*Ideas of Persecution* = 80). He is highly suspicious of the motivations of others and guarded and untrusting in relationships (*Cynicism* = 70).

With regard to externalizing concerns, Mr. Smith's MMPI-2-RF results reflect a general proclivity toward impulsive, disconstrained behavior (*Disconstraint* = 82). Research has shown that individuals with similar scores have histories of antisocial behavior, find it difficult to conform to societal norms, and have problems with authority figures (*Antisocial Behaviors* = 82, *Juvenile Conduct Problems* = 77). Mr. Smith also endorsed items that suggest abuse of alcohol or drugs (*Substance Abuse* = 85).

Interpersonally, Mr. Smith's scores on *Aggression* (79) and *Aggressiveness* (78) suggest a proclivity toward antagonistic instrumental aggression, which is likely influenced by low frustration tolerance, impatience, and anger (*Anger Proneness* = 80).

Even though Mr. Smith's PCL-R *Total Score* was 27, below the traditional cutoff for classification as a psychopath, his high score on Factor 2 and specifically on Facet 4: *Antisocial* score have been linked to risk for violence (Walters, 2010). Mr. Smith's *Total Score* (47) on the PPI-R does not indicate a markedly elevated level of psychopathy, although his *Self-Centered Impulsivity* factor score (65) is one and a half standard deviations above the mean in the offender normative group. Overall, his PPI-R profile is indicative of an individual who has a reckless deviance of societal norms (*Rebellious Nonconformity* = 63), a nonchalant lack of forethought and planning (*Carefree Nonplanfulness* = 63), and failure to accept responsibility for his actions (*Blame Externalization* = 66).

Recommendations and Risk Management

Based on the records, interview, and psychological test scores, Mr. Smith was diagnosed with paranoid schizophrenia, polysubstance dependence, and antisocial personality disorder, and he was characterized as a high-risk individual. Risk factors include (1) history of violence against women that has not been reduced by incarceration or protective orders; (2) severe mental illness characterized by internalizing

Table 18.2 CASE EXAMPLE TEST SCORES

MMPI-2 Restructured Form

Validity Scales	
Variable Response Inconsistency (VRIN-r)	53
True Response Inconsistency (TRIN-r)	57
Infrequent Responses (F-r)	79
Infrequent Psychopathology Responses (Fp-r)	59
Infrequent Somatic Responses (Fs)	50
Symptom Validity (FBS-r)	48
Response Bias Scale (RBS)	46
Uncommon Virtues (L-r)	47
Adjustment Validity (K-r)	42
Higher Order Scales	
Emotional/Internalizing Dysfunction (EID)	71
Thought Dysfunction (THD)	77
Behavioral/Externalizing Dysfunction (BXD)	84
Restructured Clinical Scales	
Demoralization (RCd)	75
Somatic Complaints (RC1)	47
Low Positive Emotions (RC2)	80
Cynicism (RC3)	70
Antisocial Behavior (RC4)	82
Ideas of Persecution (RC6)	80
Dysfunctional Negative Emotions (RC7)	73
Aberrant Experiences (RC8)	76
Hypomanic Activation (RC9)	74
Somatic/Cognitive Scales	
Malaise (MLS)	63
Gastrointestinal Complaints (GIC)	46
Head Pain Complaints (HPC)	53
Neurological Complaints (NUC)	59

Externalizing Scales	
Juvenile Conduct Problems (JCP)	77
Substance Abuse (SUB)	85
Aggression (AGG)	79
Activation (ACT)	44
Interpersonal Scales	
Family Problems (FML)	68
Interpersonal Passivity (IPP)	39
Social Avoidance (SAV)	65
Shyness (SHY)	57
Disaffiliativeness (DSF)	78
Interest Scales	
Aesthetic-Literary Interest (AES)	39
Mechanical-Physical Interests (MEC)	52
Personality Psychopathology Five Scales	
Aggressiveness (AGGR-r)	78
Psychoticism (PSYC-r)	69
Disconstraint (DISC-R)	82
Negative Emotionality/Neuroticism (NEGE-r)	73
Introversion/Low Positive Emotions (INTR-r)	70
Psychopathy Checklist-Revised[a]	
Total Score	27 (56T)
Factor 1: Interpersonal/Affective	10 (54T)
Facet 1: Interpersonal	4 (52T)
Facet 2: Affective	6 (56T)
Factor 2: Social Deviance	17 (61T)
Facet 3: Lifestyle	8 (58T)
Facet 4: Antisocial	9 (62T)

(Continued)

Table 18.2 (CONTINUED)

Cognitive Complaints (COG)	64
Internalizing Scales	
Suicidal/Death Ideation (SUI)	45
Helplessness/Hopelessness (HLP)	60
Self-Doubt (SFD)	56
Inefficacy (NFC)	43
Stress/Worry (STW)	73
Anxiety (AXY)	70
Anger Proneness (ANP)	80
Behavior-Restricting Fears (BRF)	56
Multiple Specific Fears (MSF)	51

Psychopathic Personality Inventory-Revised[b]

Total Score	47
Fearless Dominance (FD)	40
Social Influence (SOI)	44
Fearlessness (F)	47
Stress Immunity (STI)	40
Self-Centered Impulsivity (SCI)	65
Machiavellian Egocentricity (ME)	55
Blame Externalization (BE)	66
Carefree Nonplanfulness (CN)	63
Rebellious Nonconformity (RN)	63
Coldheartedness (C)	54

[a]PCL-R T-scores based on Male Offender Norms (Hare, 2003).

[b]PPI-R T-scores based on correctional norms (Lilienfeld & Widows, 2005).

and externalizing symptoms and thought dysfunction in the form of intense, obsessive paranoid delusions in reference to his victim; (3) poor coping skills and anger management; and (4) history of unsuccessfully treated substance abuse.

The evaluator in the case (DBW) recommended to the court that Mr. Smith be subjected to intensive supervision throughout the re-entry court program. Specifically, he recommended Mr. Smith remain in a halfway house to increase daily monitoring, maintain compliance with his psychiatric medication (along with a referral to determine the appropriateness of antipsychotic medication), and mental health counseling to monitor his mental status and improve his coping skills and anger management. Additionally, it was recommended that Mr. Smith abstain from drugs and alcohol (monitored by frequent and random drug screens) and complete drug and alcohol treatment. Finally, it was recommended that he have no contact with the victim and that she be made aware of his transition back into community by court officials or law enforcement.

Case Outcome

While in the re-entry court program, the court generally followed the assessment recommendations. Mr. Smith was placed in a 180-day residential substance abuse treatment program, but he failed out of it after he was arrested for occupying a drug premise. Consequently, he was terminated from the re-entry court program and was sent back to prison for 1 year. Shortly after his release, Mr. Smith was arrested again for felonious domestic violence against the same victim while on parole. He was sentenced to 1 year in prison and 3 years of parole. At the time this chapter was written, Mr. Smith was listed as a parole violator at large.

CONCLUSION

We hope we have provided some useful information about the ways in which self-report measures of personality and psychopathology can be meaningfully incorporated into violence risk assessments. While these instruments are likely to take a peripheral role in these types of evaluations, they can nevertheless provide useful information, particularly in the scope of identifying relevant psychopathological and personality variables, such as psychopathy, as well providing useful information to plan and strategize client contact during clinical interviews. Moreover, these measures can provide objective data that can be incorporated into ratings on structured professional judgment instruments such as the HCR-20. Future research should continue to examine and identify ways to effectively incorporate these types of measures in violence risk evaluations.

NOTES

1. Note that aspects of the case have been modified to protect the client and victim's anonymity.
2. T-scores for the various test score scales are presented in parentheses.

3. Interpretative statements throughout come from the MMPI-2-RF manual (Ben-Porath & Tellegen, 2008/2011), which are based on extensive initial empirical examination by Tellegen and Ben-Porath (2008/2011), in addition to summaries of MMPI-2-RF peer-reviewed literature provided by Graham (2011) and Ben-Porath (2012).

REFERENCES

Archer, R. P., Buffington-Vollum, J. K., Stredny, R. V., & Handel, R. W. (2006). A survey of psychological test use patterns among forensic psychologists. *Journal of Personality Assessment, 87*, 84–94.

Bagby, R., Sellbom, M., Costa, P., & Widiger, T. (2008). Predicting Diagnostic and Statistical Manual of Mental Disorders-IV personality disorders with the five-factor model of personality and the personality psychopathology five. *Personality and Mental Health, 2*, 55–69.

Ben-Porath, Y. S. (2012). *Interpreting the MMPI-2-RF*. Minneapolis: University of Minnesota Press.

Ben-Porath, Y. S., & Tellegen, A. (2008/2011). *Minnesota Multiphasic Personality Inventory-2 Restructured Form: Manual for administration, scoring, and interpretation*. Minneapolis: University of Minnesota Press.

Benning, S. D., Patrick, C. J., Blonigen, D. M., Hicks, B. M., & Iacono, W. G. (2005). Estimating facets of psychopathy from normal personality traits: A step toward community epidemiological investigations. *Assessment, 12*, 3–18.

Berardino, S. D., Meloy, J. R., Sherman, M., & Jacobs, D. (2005). Validation of the Psychopathic Personality Inventory on a female inmate sample. *Behavioral Sciences and the Law, 23*, 819–836.

Blais, M. A., Baity, M. R., & Hopwood, C. J. (2010). *Clinical applications of the Personality Assessment Inventory*. New York, NY: Routledge.

Boccaccini, M. T., Murrie, D. C., Hawes, S. W., Simpler, A., & Johnson, J. (2010). Predicting recidivism with the Personality Assessment Inventory in a sample of sex offenders screened for civil commitment as sexually violent predators. *Psychological Assessment, 22*, 142–148.

Butcher, J. N., Graham, J. R., Ben-Porath, Y. S., Tellegen, A., Dahlstrom, W. G., & Kaemmer, B. (2001). *MMPI-2 (Minnesota Multiphasic Personality Inventory-2):Manual for administration, scoring, and interpretation, revised edition*. Minneapolis: University of Minnesota Press.

Caperton, J. D., Edens, J. F., & Johnson, J. K. (2004). Predicting sex offender institutional adjustment and treatment compliance using the Personality Assessment Inventory. *Psychological Assessment, 16*, 187–191.

Cleckley, H. (1941). *The mask of sanity*. St. Louis, MO: Mosby.

Conroy, M. A., & Murrie, D. C. (2007). *Forensic assessment of violence risk: A guide for risk assessment and risk management*. Hoboken, NJ: Wiley.

Copestake, S., Gray, N. S., & Snowden, R. J. (2011). A comparison of a self-report measure of psychopathy with the psychopathy checklist-revised in a UK sample of offenders. *Journal of Forensic Psychiatry and Psychology, 22*, 169–182.

Crawford, E. F., Calhoun, P. S., Braxton, L. E., & Beckham, J. C. (2007). Validity of the Personality Assessment Inventory Aggression Scales and Violence Potential Index in veterans with PTSD. *Journal of Personality Assessment, 88*, 90–98.

De Laurentiis, D. (Producer), & Ratner, B. (Director). (2002). *Red dragon* [Motion picture]. United States: Metro-Goldwyn-Mayer.

Douglas, K. S., Guy, L. S., Edens, J. F., Boer, D. P., & Hamilton, J. (2007). The Personality Assessment Inventory as a proxy for the Psychopathy Checklist-Revised: Testing the incremental validity and cross-sample robustness of the antisocial features scale. *Assessment, 14,* 255–269.

Douglas, K. S., & Skeem, J. L. (2005). Violence risk assessment: Getting specific about being dynamic. *Psychology, Public Policy, And Law, 11,* 347–383.

Edens, J. F., Hart, S. D., Johnson, D. W., Johnson, J. K., & Olver, M. E. (2000). Use of the Personality Assessment Inventory to assess psychopathy in offender populations. *Psychological Assessment, 12,* 132–139.

Edens, J. F., & McDermott, B. E. (2010). Examining the construct validity of the Psychopathic Personality Inventory-Revised: Preferential correlates of fearless dominance and self-centered impulsivity. *Psychological Assessment, 22,* 32–42.

Gottfredson, M., & Hirschi, T. (1990). *A general theory of crime.* Stanford, CA: Stanford University Press.

Graham, J. R. (2011). *MMPI-2: Assessing personality and psychopathology* (5th ed.). New York, NY: Oxford University Press.

Hanson, R. K., & Thornton, D. (1999). *Static–99: Improving actuarial risk assessments for sex offenders.* [User Rep. No. 1999–02]. Ottawa, ON: Department of the Solicitor General of Canada.

Hare, R. D. (1991). *The Hare Psychopathy Checklist—Revised.* Toronto, ON: Multi-Health Systems.

Hare, R. D. (1996). Psychopathy: A clinical construct whose time has come. *Criminal Justice and Behavior, 23,* 25–54.

Hare, R. D. (2003). *The Psychopathy Checklist—Revised manual* (2nd ed.). Toronto, ON: Multi-Health Systems.

Hare, R. D., & Cox, D. N. (1978). Clinical and empirical conceptions of psychopathy, and the selection of subjects for research. In R. D. Hare & D. Schalling (Eds.), *Psychopathic behaviour: Approaches to research* (pp. 1–21). Chichester, UK: Wiley.

Hare, R. D., & Neumann, C. S. (2006). The PCL-R assessment of psychopathy: Development, structural properties, and new directions. In C. J. Patrick (Ed.), *Handbook of psychopathy* (pp. 58–90). New York, NY: Guilford Press.

Harkness, A. R., Finn, J. A., McNulty, J. L., & Shields, S. M. (2012). The Personality Psychopathology-Five (PSY-5): Recent constructive replication and assessment literature review. *Psychological Assessment, 24,* 432–443.

Harkness, A. R., & McNulty, J. L. (1994). The personality psychopathology five (PSY-5): Issue from the pages of a diagnostic manual instead of a dictionary. In S. Strack & M. Lorr (Eds.), *Differentiating normal and abnormal personality* (pp. 291–315). New York, NY: Springer.

Harkness, A. R., McNulty, J. L., & Ben-Porath, Y. S. (1995). The Personality Psychopathology Five (PSY-5): Constructs and MMPI-2 scales. *Psychological Assessment, 7,* 104–114.

Harpur, T. J., Hare, R. D., & Flakstian, A. R. (1989). Two-factor conceptualization of psychopathy: Construct validity and assessment implications. *Psychological Assessment, 1,* 6–17.

Harris, R., & Lingoes, J. (1955). *Subscales for the Minnesota Multiphasic Personality Inventory.* Mimeographed materials, The Langley Porter Clinic.

Hart, S. D., Cox, D. N., & Hare, R. D. (1995). *The Hare Psychopathy Checklist: Screening Version* (PCL- SV). Toronto, ON: Multi-Health Systems.

Hathaway, S. R., & McKinley, J. C. (1943). *The Minnesota Multiphasic Personality Inventory manual.* New York, NY: Psychological Corporation.

Jones, S., & Miller, J. D. (2012). Brief report: Psychopathic traits and externalizing behaviors: A comparison of self- and informant reports in the statistical prediction of externalizing behaviors. *Psychological Assessment, 24,* 255–260.

Kastner, R. M., Sellbom, M., & Lilienfeld, S. O. (2012). A comparison of the psychometric properties of the Psychopathic Personality Inventory full-length and short-form versions. *Psychological Assessment, 24,* 261–267.

Kucharski, L., Petitt, A. N., Toomey, J., & Duncan, S. (2008). The utility of the Personality Assessment Inventory in the assessment of psychopathy. *Journal of Forensic Psychology Practice, 8,* 344–357.

Kruh, I. P., Whittemore, K., Arnaut, G. L. Y., Manley, J., Gage, B., & Gagliardi, G. J. (2005). The concurrent validity of the psychopathic personality inventory and its relative association with past violence in a sample of insanity acquittees. *International Journal of Forensic Mental Health, 4,* 135–145.

Lally, S. J. (2003). What tests are acceptable for use in forensic evaluations? A survey of experts. *Professional Psychology: Research and Practice, 34,* 491–498.

Lilienfeld, S. O. (1994). Conceptual problems in the assessment of psychopathy. *Clinical Psychology Review, 14,* 17–38.

Lilienfeld, S. O. (1996). The MMPI—2 Antisocial Practices Content Scale: Construct validity and comparison with the Psychopathic Deviate Scale. *Psychological Assessment, 8,* 281–293.

Lilienfeld, S. O., & Andrews, B. P. (1996). Development and preliminary validation of a self report measure of psychopathic personality traits in noncriminal populations. *Journal of Personality Assessment, 66,* 488–524.

Lilienfeld, S. O., & Fowler, K. A. (2006). The self-report assessment of psychopathy: Problems, pitfalls, and promises. In C. J. Patrick (Ed.), *Handbook of psychopathy* (pp. 107–132). New York, NY: Guilford Press.

Lilienfeld, S. O., & Widows, M. R. (2005). *Psychopathic Personality Inventory-Revised (PPI-R) professional manual.* Odessa, FL: Psychological Assessment Resources.

Lykken, D. T. (1957). A study of anxiety in the sociopathic personality. *Journal of Abnormal and Social Psychology, 55,* 6–10.

Marion, B. E., & Sellbom, M. (2011). An examination of gender-moderated test bias on the Levenson self-report psychopathy scale. *Journal of Personality Assessment, 93,* 235–243.

Mattson, C., Powers, B., Halfaker, D., Akeson, S., & Ben-Porath, Y. S. (2012). Predicting drug court treatment completion using the MMPI-2-RF. *Psychological Assessment, 24,* 937–943.

McKinley, J., & Hathaway, S. R. (1944). The MMPI: Hysteria, hypomania, and psychopathic deviate. *Journal of Applied Psychology, 28,* 153–174.

Megargee, E. I., Bohn, M. J., Meyer, J. E., Jr., & Sink, F. (1979). *Classifying criminal offenders: A new system based on the MMPI.* Beverly Hills, CA: Sage.

Megargee, E. I., Carbonell, J. L., Bohn, M. J., & Sliger, G. L. (2001). *Classifying criminal offenders with the MMPI-2: The Megargee System.* Minneapolis: University of Minnesota Press.

Morey, L. C. (2003). *Essentials of PAI assessment.* Hoboken, NJ: Wiley.

Morey, L. C. (2007). *The Personality Assessment Inventory: Professional manual* (2nd ed.). Odessa, FL: Psychological Assessment Resources.

Morey, L. C., & Quigley, B. D. (2002). The use of the Personality Assessment Inventory (PAI) in assessing offenders. *International Journal of Offender Therapy and Comparative Criminology, 46*, 333–349.

Newberry, M., & Shuker, R. (2012). Personality Assessment Inventory (PAI) profiles of offenders and their relationship to institutional misconduct and risk of reconviction. *Journal of Personality Assessment, 94*(6), 586–592. doi: 10.1080/00223891.2012.669220

Penn, D. L., & Martin, J. (1998). The stigma of severe mental illness: Some potential solutions for a recalcitrant problem. *Psychiatric Quarterly, 69*, 235–247.

Quinsey, V. L., Harris, G. T., Rice, M. E., & Cormier, C. A. (1998). *Violent offenders: Appraising and managing risk.* Washington, DC: American Psychological Association.

Ray, J. V., Weir, J. W., Poythress, N. G., & Richelm, A. (2011). Correspondence between the psychopathic personality inventory and the psychopathic personality inventory-revised: A look at self-reported personality traits. *Criminal Justice and Behavior, 38*, 375–385.

Rock, R. C., Sellbom, M., Ben-Porath, Y. S., & Salekin, R. T. (2013). Concurrent and predictive validity of psychopathy in a batterers intervention sample. *Law and Human Behavior, 37*(3), 145–154.

Rogers, R. (2008). *Clinical assessment of malingering and deception* (3rd ed.). New York, NY: Guilford Press.

Rogers, R., Sewell, K. W., Martin, M. A., & Vitacco, M. J. (2003). Detection of feigned mental disorders: A meta-analysis of the MMPI-2 and malingering. *Assessment, 10*, 160–177.

Salekin, R. T., Rogers, R., & Sewell, K. W. (1996). A review and meta-analysis of the Psychopathy Checklist and Psychopathy Checklist-Revised: Predictive validity of dangerousness. *Clinical Psychology, 3*, 203–215.

Sellbom, M., & Bagby, R. M. (2008). Response styles on multi-scale inventories. In R. Rogers (Ed.), *Clinical assessment of malingering and deception* (3rd ed.). New York, NY: Guilford Press.

Sellbom, M., Ben-Porath, Y. S., Baum, L. J., Erez, E., & Gregory, C. (2008). Empirical correlates of the MMPI-2 Restructured Clinical (RC) Scales in a batterers intervention program. *Journal of Personality Assessment, 90*, 129–135.

Sellbom, M., Ben-Porath, Y. S., Lilienfeld, S. O., Patrick, C. J., & Graham, J. R. (2005). Assessing Psychopathic Personality Traits with the MMPI-2. *Journal of Personality Assessment, 85*, 334–343.

Sellbom, M., Ben-Porath, Y. S., Patrick, C. J., Wygant, D. B., Gartland, D. M., & Stafford, K. P. (2012). Development and construct validation of MMPI-2-RF measures assessing global psychopathy, fearless-dominance, and impulsive-antisociality. *Personality Disorders: Theory, Research, and Treatment, 3*, 17–38.

Sellbom, M., Ben-Porath, Y. S., & Stafford, K. P. (2007). A comparison of measures of psychopathic deviance in a forensic setting. *Psychological Assessment, 19*, 430–436.

Sellbom, M., Toomey, J. A., Wygant, D. B., Kucharski, L. T., & Duncan, S. A. (2010). Utility of the MMPI-2-RF (Restructured Form) Validity Scales in detecting malingering in a criminal forensic setting: A known-groups design. *Psychological Assessment, 22*, 22–31.

Shaw, C. R., & Mckay, H. D. (1942). *Juvenile delinquency and urban areas.* Chicago, IL: University of Chicago Press.

Skodol, A. E., Bender, D. S., Morey, L. C., Clark, L. A., Oldham, J. M., Alarcon, R. D., … Siever, L. J. (2011). Personality disorder types proposed for DSM-5. *Journal of Personality Disorders, 25*, 136–169.

Skopp, N. A., Edens, J. F., & Ruiz, M. A. (2007). Risk factors for institutional misconduct among incarcerated women: An examination of the criterion-related validity of the Personality Assessment Inventory. *Journal of Personality Assessment, 88*, 106–117.

Sutherland, E. H. (1960). *Principles of criminology* (6th ed.). Philadelphia, PA: Lippincott.

Tellegen, A., & Ben-Porath, Y. S. (2008/2011). *MMPI-2-RF (Minnesota Multiphasic Personality Inventory-2 restructured form): Technical manual.* Minneapolis: University of Minnesota Press.

Tellegen, A., Ben-Porath, Y. S., McNulty, J. L., Arbisi, P. A., Graham, J. R., & Kaemmer, B. (2003). *MMPI-2 Restructured Clinical (RC) Scales: Development, validation, and interpretation.* Minneapolis: University of Minnesota Press.

Tellegen, A., Ben-Porath, Y. S., & Sellbom, M. (2009). Construct validity of the MMPI-2-Restructured Clinical (RC) Scales: Reply to Rouse, Greene, Butcher, Nichols, & Williams. *Journal of Personality Assessment, 91*, 211–221.

Viljoen, J. L., McLachlan, K., & Vincent, G. (2010). Assessing violence risk and psychopathy in adolescent and adult offenders: A survey of clinical practices. *Assessment, 17*, 377–395.

Walters, G. D. (2010). Violence risk assessment and facet 4 of the psychopathy checklist: Predicting institutional and community aggression in two forensic samples. *Assessment, 17*, 259–268.

Webster, C. D., Douglas, K. S., Eaves, D., & Hart, S. D. (1997). *HCR–20: Assessing risk for violence* (Version 2).Vancouver, BC: Mental Health, Law, and Policy Institute, Simon Fraser University.

Wygant, D. B., Anderson, J. L., Sellbom, M., Rapier, J. L., Allgeier, L. M., & Granacher, R. P. (2011). Association of the MMPI-2 Restructured Form (MMPI-2-RF) validity scales with structured malingering criteria. *Psychological Injury and Law, 4*, 13–23.

Wygant, D. B., Ben-Porath, Y. S., Arbisi, P. A., Berry, D. T. R., Freeman, D. B., & Heilbronner, R. L. (2009). Examination of the MMPI-2 Restructured Form (MMPI-2-RF) validity scales in civil forensic settings: Findings from simulation and known group samples. *Archives of Clinical Neuropsychology, 24*, 671–680.

Wygant, D. B., & Sellbom, M. (2012). Viewing psychopathy from the perspective of the Personality Psychopathology Five Model: Implications for DSM-5. *Journal of Personality Disorders, 26*, 717–726.

Wygant, D. B., Sellbom, M., Graham, J. R., & Schenk, P. W. (2006). Incremental validity of the MMPI-2 PSY-5 scales in assessing self-reported personality disorder criteria. *Assessment, 13*, 178–186.

19

Assessing Malingering in Violent Offenders

HOLLY A. MILLER ■

Malingering is the feigning of a disorder or symptoms of a disorder for some external incentive. Violent offenders, and defendants of all types, have motives to create an impression that they are more mentally disturbed than they actually are. There are numerous situations in which violent offenders may be assessed for possible malingered mental illness within the criminal justice system. Circumstances may include evaluations for competency to stand trial, insanity, capital sentencing, competency for execution, and any "in-house" prison evaluation for possible cell moves, psychotropic medication, or prison transfer.

Although base rates for malingered mental illness may vary according to the specific situation, actual base rates are challenging to assess due to the difficulty in having a true or "known-groups" malingering diagnoses in forensic contexts and because both physicians and psychologists are trained to accept what their clients report to them at face value. However, during the last couple of decades, as assessment has become more refined, exaggerated mental illness symptoms are much more likely to be considered, discussed, and assessed.

This chapter will present the current research on malingering base rates, motivation for feigning mental disorder, the relationship between malingering and psychopathy, detection strategies, and performance of the most commonly utilized malingering assessments with offender populations.

DEFINING MALINGERING AND BASE RATES

Malingering is listed as a V Code in the *Diagnostic and Statistical Manual of Mental Disorders*, fourth edition, text revision (*DSM-IV-TR*) and used to describe problems that "may be the focus of clinical attention." The V Code of Malingering is described as the "intentional production of false or grossly exaggerated physical or psychological symptoms, motivated by external incentives" such as evading criminal prosecution or obtaining drugs (American Psychiatric Association, 2000, p. 739). A malingering diagnosis requires more than minor exaggerations of symptoms or a possible external incentive. The feigned symptomology must be grossly exaggerated symptoms with a certain external motivation and gain for the client. Additionally, comparable to other V Codes and possible foci of clinical attention, the *DSM* provides no formal inclusion or exclusion criteria similar to the majority of diagnoses. Alternatively, the *DSM* provides a list of screening items that are listed to raise suspicion of malingering. These include a medicolegal context, discrepancy between claimed disability and objective findings, lack of cooperation or treatment compliance, and antisocial personality disorder.

As Rogers (2008) notes, the context, uncooperativeness, and antisocial personality disorder do not make for effective screens for malingering because these are all very common and would include large numbers of false-positive diagnoses. Thus, these items do not aid the evaluator or clinician in effectively making a malingering determination. Unfortunately, poorly trained evaluators continue to utilize these screening items to "diagnose" malingering at the cost of calamitous results for four out five forensic clients being inaccurately labeled as a malingerer (Rogers, 2008).

The extent to which forensic clients, including violent offenders, malinger mental illness remains unknown, but research attempting to examine accurate base rates indicates that it can be a significant problem in several criminal justice contexts. Although research has reported marked variations in malingering base rates across forensic settings (SD = 14%; Rogers, Salekin, Sewell, Goldstein, & Leonard, 1998), if malingering is assessed in every forensic situation base rates remain a significant concern (10%–30%; Rogers, 2008). Additionally, in both high-stakes situations (i.e., insanity evaluations) and forensic contexts where malingering screens such as the Miller Forensic Assessment of Symptoms Test (M-FAST) are utilized, base rates can surpass 50% (Rogers, 2008).

The best estimates of malingering base rates have come from two large surveys of forensic experts in the field (Rogers, Salekin, Sewell, Goldstein, & Leonard, 1998; Rogers, Sewell, & Goldstein, 1994). These survey results did produce fairly consistent estimates for forensic/offender evaluations with a range between 15.7% and 17.4%, but they should not serve as firm base rates of malingered mental illness. Base rates vary widely depending upon the population, circumstances, referral source, and even the evaluator themselves.

MOTIVATION FOR MALINGERING/EXAGGERATION IN OFFENDER POPULATIONS

Rogers et al. (1994, 1998) have proposed three explanatory models for malingered mental illness in offender populations, including pathogenic, criminological, and adaptational. The pathogenic model suggests that malingering is a symptomatic sign of psychological decompensation where the offender is attempting to control his or her genuine impairment by feigning impairment. This model conceptualizes that an underlying mental disorder is motivating the malingering. However, research (Rogers et al., 1998) has indicated that this model is not commonly represented in forensic and offender settings.

The criminological model of malingering, the model of the *DSM*, suggests that malingering is typically an antisocial act that is committed by antisocial persons. Because this model relies on common rather than distinguishing factors (e.g., uncooperative, antisocial background) this model results in too many false-positive malingering diagnoses and is not useful with offender populations even as a screening measure. For example, rates of antisocial personality disorder in correctional environments are said to range from approximately 50% to 80% (Huss, 2009; Moran, 1999). If an evaluator suspects malingering of all those individuals with this diagnosis and the actual base rate is around 15%, there is an unacceptable level of false positives even as a screening procedure.

The adaptational model proposes that the malingerer is motivated by common sense or rational choice. Here the offender attempts to engage in a cost-benefit analysis and chooses to malinger psychological symptoms in an effort to best deal with his or her situation in the difficult and adversarial conditions found in jails, prisons, and courtrooms. Penalties for unsuccessful malingering are often severe, ranging from cessation of mental health services to the death penalty or life in prison. Survey research with forensic evaluators has indicated that the adaptational model is prototypical of offenders (Rogers et al., 1998).

Walters (2006) argues that the models proposed earlier include seven motives for malingering of psychiatric symptoms in offender populations. The seven motives include compensation, avoidance, separation, relocation, entitlement, attention, and amusement. Some offenders will malinger mental illness in order to receive financial gain through disability payments, Supplemental Security Income (SSI) from the Social Security Administration, or through the government if an offender is litigating civil rights violations. Offenders, especially violent offenders, will sometimes malinger mental illness in an attempt to avoid consequences of their behavior (i.e., long prison sentences or the death penalty). The avoidance may take place at several points during the judicial process, including faking competency to stand trial, feigning responsibility as not guilty by reason of insanity, or in an attempt to get back into the courtroom to receive a reduced sentence or clemency.

As assaults (physical and sexual) are common within the prison system, offenders may attempt to separate themselves from predation by feigning a mental illness (Miller & McCoy, 2013). Because myths that people with severe mental illness are unpredictable and dangerous still persist, mental illness feigners may believe that they will be left alone from predators in prison or receive a transfer to a prison that is considered safer or less threatening, receive a single cell, or be housed in segregation. Similar to the motive of separation, offenders may feign a mental disorder in an attempt to be relocated to a forensic hospital or medical wing rather than the general prison population. Often forensic hospitals and medical centers are seen as more pleasant, less severe in conditions, and will result in fewer threats/assaults from other offenders. Similarly, offenders may malinger mental illness as they see that it may entitle them to privileges otherwise not afforded. These privileges may be release from a prison job or receiving medication that could be sold to other offenders or used to get high rather than to treat psychological symptoms.

Finally, offenders may malinger mental illness to gain attention or for their own amusement (Walters, 2006). Some offenders may enjoy the attention they receive when reporting psychological distress. They may be able to miss prison work in order to be seen by medical or psychological services and receive desired attention and care. Offenders may also malinger for their own pleasure when seemingly they confuse or deceive a clinician. This brings us to the next topic: the relationship between psychopathy and malingering.

RELATIONSHIP BETWEEN PSYCHOPATHY/ANTISOCIAL
PERSONALITY DISORDER AND MALINGERING

As stated previously, the *DSM-IV-TR* (American Psychiatric Association, 2000) defines malingering as the intentional production of fake or grossly exaggerated physical or psychological symptoms, motivated by external incentives. The *DSM* also provides additional circumstances where clinicians should suspect malingering when any combination of these is present: medicolegal context, discrepancy between self-report and objective findings, lack of cooperation during the evaluation, and the presence of antisocial personality disorder. Thus, from the diagnostic criteria there is an assumption of relationship between antisocial personality (or psychopathy) and the probability of malingered mental illness. The assumption here is that offenders with antisocial personality or psychopathy will be more likely to malinger mental illness. An additional assumption about offenders with antisocial personality or psychopathy is that they will be more effective in their ability to lie and less likely to be detected in their feigning of mental illness.

Personality disorders are defined by chronic, maladaptive patterns of thoughts, feelings, and behaviors. Lying or deceptive behaviors are common behaviors for many of the personality disorders (especially Cluster B syndromes), although the primary personality disorder associated with lying and deception is antisocial personality disorder which is marked by voluntary, conscious, and manipulative lying. According to epidemiological surveys with inmate samples, the prevalence of antisocial personality disorder is reported to be between 50% and 80% (Huss, 2009; Moran, 1999).

Psychopathy is a disorder that is associated with antisocial personality disorder and, generally, is a set of personality and behavioral symptoms. These symptoms include affective-interpersonal features (e.g., superficial, callous, lack of remorse) and antisocial behaviors such as impulsiveness, sensation seeking, and lying. Psychopathic individuals are significantly more likely to engage in criminal behavior beginning at a young age, and they are disproportionally responsible for large rates of violent crime and violent recidivism (Andrews, Bonta, & Wormith, 2006; Hare & Neumann, 2008; Leistico, Salekin, DeCoster, & Rogers, 2008; Walters, 2003). Because individuals who have high levels of psychopathy are more likely to be involved in crime and violent crime, they are likely to be involved in a forensic evaluation, whether it is an evaluation for competency to stand trial or an evaluation for mediation within prison.

One of the major concerns with individuals who have antisocial personality disorder or psychopathy (or both) is that they may be more likely to exaggerate, distort, or feign information or symptoms because of their manipulative and deceptive interpersonal style. In addition, both antisocial personality disorder and psychopathic individuals have characteristics of grandiosity and entitlement that may make them attempt to obtain unwarranted resources or gains (e.g., medication, money). Because of these characteristics and concerns about both individuals with antisocial personality disorder and psychopathy, these disorders are considered a red flag for possible malingering in forensic evaluations. Although research has indicated that individuals with these disorders are more likely to be deceptive, whether this translates into individuals with these disorders as more likely to malinger is a question for study.

Empirical findings reporting the actual incidence of malingering among individuals with antisocial personality disorder or psychopathy or the frequency of psychopathy and antisocial personality disorder among malingerers is sparse. Early research has found both a relationship between symptom exaggeration and high psychopathy levels (Gacono, Meloy, Sheppard, Speth, & Roske, 1995; Heinze & Vess, 2005; Sierless, 1984) and that the majority of psychopaths do not malinger mental illness with their feigning secondary to environmental factors (Poythress, Edens, & Watkins, 2001; Rogers, 1997). Heinze and Vess (2005) examined the relationship between malingering diagnosis, MMPI-2 validity scales, and PCL-R psychopathy scores with 392 forensic inpatient males and found that psychopathy had a reliable (although modest) but clinically meaningful relationship with malingering. The authors concluded that although most psychopaths may not malinger mental illness, inpatient forensic males with high levels of psychopathy are related to a greater likelihood of malingering.

Kucharski and his colleagues, in two studies (2004, 2006), found that criminal defendants scoring high on antisocial personality disorder and psychopathy also scored high on measures of malingered mental illness. However, in each study, results indicated that high proportions of defendants diagnosed with antisocial personality disorder and psychopathy did not show any evidence of exaggeration, lending both of these diagnoses to be poor discriminators of malingered mental illness. Both investigations demonstrated that antisocial personality disorder and psychopathy were poor predictors of malingered mental illness with criminal defendants. Similar conclusions, with divergent results, were presented by Pierson et al. (2011). In their examination of criminal defendants, Pierson et al. (2011) utilized the SCID-II and the SIRS to diagnose antisocial personality disorder and malingering, respectively, and found no relationship between the two constructs. Forensic psychiatric patients with antisocial personality disorder were no more likely to malinger than those without antisocial personality disorder. These studies concur and suggest that diagnoses of antisocial personality disorder and psychopathy do not meaningfully aid in the evaluation of malingering.

Although this modest set of studies indicate that the diagnoses of antisocial personality disorder and psychopathy alone do not assist the evaluator in the determination of malingered mental illness, the question remains whether individuals diagnosed with these disorders are more successful at malingering (not detected) when they do attempt to feign mental illness symptoms. Heinze and Vess (2005), in their sample of almost 400 forensic inpatients, suggested that "the psychopath's malingering may be less detectable by the MMPI-2 validity scales" (p. 46) when the patients in their study with high psychopathy levels scored lower on validity scales of the MMPI-2 than the nonpsychopaths. This finding coincides with early studies that indicated that the MMPI was susceptible to manipulation by psychopaths (Lawton, 1963; Lawton & Kleban, 1965).

Contrary to the majority of previous studies examining whether individuals with antisocial personality disorder or psychopathy are more likely to effectively malinger mental illness, several studies have presented opposing results. Cogburn (1993), in an experimental design, reported that psychopaths were no more likely to avoid detection of malingering. Similar to Cogburn's dissertation, Poythress, Edens, and Watkins (2001) found that prison inmates diagnosed with psychopathy were no more likely to avoid detection of malingering than nonpsychopathic inmates.

Additional studies (Book, Holden, Starzyk, Wasylkiw, & Edwards, 2006; MacNeil & Holden, 2006) indicate that psychopathy is not associated with the ability to successfully malinger. Lastly, the most recent examinations concur; individuals with the diagnoses antisocial personality disorder and/or psychopathy are not more adept at evading detection of malingered mental illness than individuals without these disorders (Marion et al., 2012; Pierson, Rosenfeld, Green, & Belfi, 2011).

In summary, the relationship between the disorders that are more associated with criminal and violent behavior, antisocial personality disorder and psychopathy, with malingered mental illness indicate that although these individuals may be more likely to deceive, they are not more likely to attempt to malinger mental illness. Additionally, the preponderance of current evidence suggests that offenders with antisocial personality disorder and psychopathy are not more likely to avoid detection when they do in fact attempt to malinger. These results are similar to the results indicating that psychopaths are no more likely to avoid deception detection on the polygraph (Patrick & Iacono, 1989; Raskin & Hare, 1978).

DETECTION STRATEGIES

Rogers (2008) defines detection strategies as a standardized method that is conceptually based and empirically validated for systematically differentiating malingering (in this case) from honest responding. Detection strategies focused on a specific response style have proven to be the most effective. For example, the strategy should focus on assessing exaggeration of symptoms rather than an absence of defensive responding. Detection strategies should also assess specific domains of symptoms. The majority of malingered symptoms include mental disorder, cognitive impairment, and medical conditions. For the purposes of this chapter, the domain of mental disorder malingering is of importance. Rogers (1984, 2008) and Miller (2001) have outlined several validated detection strategies of malingered mental illness. These strategies will be outlined next.

One of the detection strategies for malingered mental disorder that has produced the largest effect sizes is the assessment of rare symptoms. For example, a Cohen's d of 2.48 on the Negative Impression Management (NIM) scale of the Personality Assessment Inventory (PAI) has been reported (Blanchard, McGrath, Pogge, & Khadivi, 2003), indicating the scale's ability to distinguish between feigners and honest responders. This strategy asks the offender about extremely rare symptoms that are infrequently (e.g., <5%) endorsed by individuals who have a bona fide mental disorder. Malingerers are often detected because they will report several of these extremely rare symptoms. Several psychological assessment tools (described in more detail in the next section) employ this detection strategy. Besides the NIM scale on the PAI, the Rare Symptoms scale on the Structured Interview of Reported Symptoms (SIRS; Rogers, 1992) and the Unusual Hallucination scale of the Miller Forensic Assessment of Symptoms Test (M-FAST; Miller, 2001) utilize this robust strategy. An example of an extremely rare symptom is hearing music; hallucinations of hearing music are rare among individuals with schizophrenia (Fischer, Marchie, & Norris, 2004).

Similar to extremely rare symptoms, assessing quasi-rare mental disorder symptoms has been utilized as a detection strategy. This strategy also has produced large to very large effect sizes but also may produce more false positives because patients with severe disorders often endorse these severe symptoms (Rogers, 2008). For example, the symptoms on the quasi-rare symptoms assessed on the F scale on the MMPI-2 are often endorsed by individuals who have schizophrenia. Thus, elevations of quasi-rare symptom assessments are often confounded by genuine pathology in forensic psychiatric settings. Similar to rare and quasi-rare symptom detection strategies are improbably symptom assessment detection strategies. This strategy is an extreme variant of rare symptoms where additional improbable or preposterous symptom items are asked of the offender. Because these symptoms are so absurd, few explanations besides malingering make sense. However, because these symptoms are so extreme, more sophisticated malingerers will not endorse such symptoms.

One of the detection strategies that are more resistant to coaching and preparation is the rare symptom combination strategy. This strategy assesses symptom combinations that are rarely endorsed together in bona fide patient populations. Malingering offenders often endorse a wide variety of symptoms that are infrequent pairs or combinations of true symptom profiles. For example, a malingerer may endorse symptoms of schizophrenia and a sleep disorder. Examples on assessment tools include the Rare Combinations scale of the M-FAST and the Symptom Combinations on the SIRS. Malingerers often also endorse a large proportion of symptoms within and across various diagnoses as well as a large number of severe symptoms. The detection strategy utilized to detect large proportions of symptoms is the indiscriminant symptom endorsement strategy, while the symptom severity strategy is used to assess a wide array of psychological problems with extreme severity. Examples are found on the M-FAST scale of Extreme Symptomatology.

Another malingering detection strategy that produces large effect sizes is the strategy of reported versus observed symptoms (Guy & Miller, 2004; Miller, 2001; Rogers, 2008; Rogers, Sewell, & Gillard, 2010). This strategy assesses marked discrepancies between symptoms the offender is reporting and what is actually being observed by the evaluator or other staff that work closely with the offender. For example, an offender may endorse that he or she runs and hides from imaginary people every 15 minutes when this behavior has not been observed. This detection strategy is utilized on both the M-FAST and the SIRS with reported effect sizes (Cohen's d) ranging between 1.08 and 2.82 (Guy & Miller, 2004; Rogers et al., 2010).

Lastly, the detection strategy of erroneous stereotypes is sometimes utilized to assess whether an offender is endorsing common misconceptions about mental illness. For example, it is false to believe that people with severe mental illness have low self-esteem or constant tremors. If an offender endorses numerous inaccurate symptoms or stereotypes of mental illness, it can be an effective detection strategy. However, most malingering scales or measures do not include many of these types of items. One good example of the utilization of this strategy is found on the MMPI-2 Ds scale. The Gough (1954) Dissimulation (Ds) scale consists of items that represent erroneous stereotypes of neuroticism that are rarely endorsed by bona fide patients.

THE ASSESSMENT OF MALINGERING IN OFFENDER POPULATIONS

As noted by the examples provided in the previous section, there are several scales on clinical assessments as well as specific malingering assessment tools that are utilized in the detection of malingered mental illness with offender populations. Most of these assessments either include scales that assess detection strategies (e.g., F scale on the MMPI-2) or, if it is a malingering-specific instrument, only include scales that assess malingering detection strategies (e.g., M-FAST). The following section will outline the utility of the most commonly utilized tools in the assessment of malingered mental disorders with offender populations.

General Personality and Psychopathology Inventories

Minnesota Multiphasic Personality Inventory-2 (MMPI-2)

The MMPI-2 (Butcher et al., 2001) is a personality inventory that includes several validity scales that have been researched extensively and utilized to assess and screen for malingering and other response styles. The validity scales that are most utilized to assess symptom exaggeration are the Infrequency scales and include the F scale, F Back scale (Fb), Symptom Validity scale (FBS), Infrequency Psychopathology scale (Fp), the Ds and Ds-r, and the Criminal Offender Infrequency (Fc) scale. Two meta-analytic studies support the use of the infrequency scales of the MMPI-2 for the assessment of malingering (Rogers, Sewell, & Salekin, 1994; Rogers, Sewell, Martin, & Vitacco, 2003).

Although several infrequency scales are available on the MMPI-2 for the detection of exaggeration, the F and Fb scales are often also elevated by bona fide psychiatric patients found in forensic hospital settings, where more violent offenders are assessed. Thus, these infrequency scales may not provide the best discrimination that is warranted in this forensic setting. Because of the potential confound with genuine symptoms, Arbisi and Ben Porath (1995) developed the Fp scale by including items that were only endorsed by less than 20% of hospitalized psychiatric patients. Although support of the effectiveness of the Fp scale to detect malingering has been mixed, the majority of the work (including the meta-analyses) indicates evidence to support use as a detection strategy. Megargee (2004) posited, and also demonstrated by research findings, that as a result of deviant backgrounds and unusual life circumstances, offenders have a tendency to elevate the Fp scale even when answering honestly. Following this research, Megargee developed the Criminal Offender Infrequency (Fc) scale, which consists of items that were endorsed by less than 16% of the 852 offenders in Megargee's 2004 study and less than 15% of the MMPI-2 normative sample. The Fc scale contains 51 items, of which 48 items overlap with the F, Fb, or Fp scales. Recent research examining the utility of the Fc scale has supported its utility with criminal defendants and forensic patients, both of which are likely to include more violent offenders attempting to malinger (Barber-Rioja, Zottoli, Kuckarski, & Duncan, 2009; Gassen, Pietz, Spray, & Denney, 2007).

Since Megargee specifically developed the Fc scale for use with a criminal population, Glassen et al. (2007) examined the Fc scale's utility with incarcerated male sample. The authors found that although the Fc scale did not produce the largest area under the curve (AUC), the cutoff of Fc b 14 (Megargee, 2004, suggested cut score of b15) was the most accurate at differentiating malingerers from honest responders. This cut score performed better than any other of the MMPI-2 exaggeration/malingering indicators. Similar to these findings, Barber-Rioja et al. (2009)

examined the utility of the Fc scale among criminal defendants and found the Fc scale performed better than the Fp and Fb scales of the MMPI-2.

The MMPI-2 scales that utilize Rogers et al.'s (2003) erroneous stereotypes malingering detection strategy include the Symptom Validity scale (FBS), Gough's Dissimulation scale (Ds), and an abbreviated version of Ds, the Dissimulation-Revised scale (Ds-r). Although these scales were developed to assess personal-injury litigants (FBS) or feigned neurotic symptoms (Ds and Ds-r), these MMPI-2 scales have been found to be effective at malingering detection with offender and violent offender populations (e.g., Gassen, Pietz, Spray, & Denney, 2007). For example, Nelson, Sweet, and Demakis (2006) completed a meta-analysis comparing the validity indicators on MMPI-2 in only forensic offender situations and found the FBS to have the largest effect size (0.96) and to perform as well or better than the other validity indicators included in the studies on forensic offenders.

In summary, the MMPI-2 validity indicators overall have demonstrated their effectiveness at discriminating between honest responders and individuals attempting to malinger mental disorder. Each of the scales varies in effectiveness and effect size depending on the setting and base rate of malingering. Thus, different cut scores are often recommended by researchers. Additionally, the detection scales specifically designed to assess exaggeration in criminal populations seem to perform better with general and violent offenders.

PERSONALITY ASSESSMENT INVENTORY (PAI; MOREY, 1991)

The PAI is another multiscale personality inventory that has become popular in forensic settings (Archer et al., 2006). Although the PAI lacks the extensive research on the utility of the validity scales to detect symptom exaggeration and malingering, especially in offender samples, the PAI has a lower reading level (fourth grade) than the MMPI-2 and also has multiple indicators of feigning that utilize the specific detection strategies.

The PAI scales that were designed specifically to detect malingering are the Negative Impression Management (NIM), Malingering Index (MAL), and the Rogers Discriminant Function (RDF) scales. The NIM consists of nine items that utilize the rare symptoms or infrequency detection strategy. The MAL is based on the endorsement of eight characteristics across the NIM and other PAI clinical scales that are more associated with feigners than bona fide patients. The MAL utilizes the unlikely patterns or rare combinations detection strategy. The RDF is a discriminant function index comprised of items from 20 of the PAI scales that best differentiate simulators from honest responders. Similar to the MAL, the RDF utilizes the unlikely patterns or rare combinations detection strategy. Recent critical review and meta-analysis studies (Hawes & Boccaccini, 2009; Rogers, 2008; Sellbom & Bagby, 2008) highlight some of the strengths and weaknesses of the PAI indicators for the assessment of malingering.

Although results of several PAI simulation studies show promising results for the utility of the malingering assessment scales (e.g., Baity, Siefert, Chambers, & Blais, 2007; Edens, Poythress, & Watkins-Clay, 2007; Rogers, Wolsen, & Ross, 2012; Sullivan & King, 2010), the results are less impressive among the known group comparison studies (e.g., Edens et al., 2007; Kucharski et al., 2007; Rogers et al., 1998). Approximately 15 studies have examined the utility of the PAI malingering indicators within known-group settings such as forensic hospitals or psychiatric correctional inmates. Although results are modest for the NIM and MAL scales as malingering indicators, several authors suggest utilizing these scales as a screen to be combined with other malingering assessment tools (Rogers, 2008; Rogers et al., 1998; Rogers & Granacher, 2011). Additionally, although the RDF functioned very well as a discriminator between simulators and honest responders, the RDF has not functioned well in known-group samples and, at this time, should not be utilized in the detection of malingering with offender populations.

Specific Measures of Malingering

MILLER FORENSIC ASSESSMENT OF SYMPTOMS TEST (M-FAST; MILLER, 2001)

The M-FAST is a 25-item brief structured interview that was developed to screen for malingered mental illness in forensic settings (Guy & Miller, 2004; Miller, 2001, 2004, 2005). The screen was rationally derived from the empirical detection strategies explained previously in this chapter and then items were tested and chosen through simulation studies and known groups in psychiatric facilities or prison. Since the development of the M-FAST, it has been validated in several forensic and nonforensic settings.

The M-FAST is comprised of seven scales (or detection strategies): Reported versus Observed (RO) Symptoms, Extreme Symptomatology (ES), Rare Combinations (RC), Unusual Hallucinations (UH), Unusual Symptoms Course (USC), Negative Image (NI), and Suggestibility (S). The 25 items included on the M-FAST are scored by strategy and then summed. Miller (2001) suggests a cut score of 6 to produce the most effective utility of the screen, as this cut score minimizes false negatives and allows a modest number of false positives for further evaluation. The M-FAST is intended for use with adults in the assessment of malingered general psychopathology. To date, no research has examined the utility of the M-FAST to detect malingering in adolescent populations.

The M-FAST has been validated in several different populations, including prison inmates with property, drug, and violence offenses (Guy & Miller, 2004); forensic inpatients who had charges ranging from theft to homicide (Miller, 2001, 2004); forensic/competency to stand trial defendants (Jackson, Rogers, & Sewell, 2005); acute psychiatric inpatients (Veazey, Hays, Wagner, & Miller, 2005); and personal injury (Alwes et al., 2008). The M-FAST has yielded sound scale characteristics in the original studies as well as in subsequent research with researchers other than the author. The internal consistency of the total score has been consistently reported as high (e.g., .91) and the classification accuracy good for the intended screening purpose. Effect sizes for the M-FAST total score are consistently very large, ranging from 1.47 to 3.32, providing excellent evidence of discriminant validity.

In summary, the M-FAST has demonstrated sound scale characteristics across several studies and settings. It was developed and first assessed with a sample of forensic psychiatric patients where much of the sample had engaged in violent behavior. The total score is the most effective and produces the largest effect sizes in differentiating malingerers from bona fide patients. Its brevity and ease of administration and scoring make this measure an attractive screening tool in general, as well with violent offender populations.

Structured Inventory of Malingered Symptomatology (SIMS; Widows & Smith, 2005)

The SIMS is a 75-item self-report true/false screening instrument for the detection of malingered psychopathology and cognitive impairment. The SIMS has five subscales: affective disorders (AF), amnestic disorders (AM), low intelligence (LI), neurological impairment (N), and psychosis (P). Each subscale contains 15 items designed to identify the malingering of that particular type of disability. The total score is calculated by summing the raw scores from all five scales, and a total cut score of b14 is suggested by the authors to be indicative of possible malingering. Similar to the M-FAST, the SIMS is a screen that should be utilized with other tools to confirm a diagnosis of malingering.

SIMS research includes both simulation and known group designs. In the known group studies, the SIMS was assessed in correctional and civil forensic populations. Internal consistency of the SIMS total score and scales is reported as high across samples, and it is very effective at retaining potential malingerers for further assessment with a low false-positive rate (Alwes, Clark, Berry, & Granacher, 2006; Heinze & Purisch, 2001; Smith, 2008). SIMS research has indicated impressive effect sizes (ranging from 1.09 to 3.52) for malingered mental illness and moderate effective sizes for the malingering of cognitive impairment. Rogers, Hinds, and Sewell (1996) sought to extend the utility of the SIMS to adolescence, but the psychometric properties were not promising in this initial study. Much further validation with adolescent samples is warranted before the SIMS can be utilized with that population.

Overall, the SIMS has demonstrated sound utility as a screen for malingered mental illness. The relatively low reading level (5.3) makes the measure useful in many forensic populations. Additionally, the SIMS is developing validation support in offender populations.

Structured Interview of Reported Symptoms-2 (SIRS-2: Rogers et al., 2010)

The first version of the SIRS was published in 1992 and became the most validated malingering assessment measure to date. Although the SIRS was recently revised, the eight primary scales remained intact, thus retaining previous validity results. The SIRS (and SIRS-2) is a structured interview consisting of 172 items that form the eight primary scales developed from empirically supported detection strategies: Rare Symptoms (RS); Symptom Combinations (SC); Improbable or Absurd Symptoms (IA); Blatant Symptoms (BL); Subtle Symptoms (SU); Selectivity of Symptoms (SEL); Severity of Symptoms (SEV); and Reported vs. Observed Symptoms (RO). Additionally, both versions of the SIRS include supplementary scales used for clinical description (e.g., Direct Appraisal on Honesty; Overly Specified Symptoms). Classification of malingering on the SIRS is reported as probable if three or more of the primary scales are scored in the probable (or definite) range of malingering. This classification was established to minimize the number of false positives.

SIRS research has produced good to excellent internal consistency and reliability estimates (i.e., .77–.92) with an average interrater reliability of .99 (Rogers, 2008). Decades of validity research on the SIRS have established the measure as a valid tool in the assessment of malingered mental illness. Studies with criminal forensic samples have generally produced large effect sizes (ranging from 1.24 to 3.37) for the SIRS primary scales.

In summary, the SIRS is the most widely validated and utilized measure to assess malingered mental illness. Decades of research with forensic populations indicate that the SIRS is an effective measure in the detection of malingering with offenders and violent offenders.

Base Rates and Suggested Cut Score Caution

Since malingering, unlike psychological disorders, is by definition a volitional act, the rate at which offenders malinger varies from setting to setting, depending on, among other things, the defendant's perception of the cost/benefit ratio of attempting to feign. The base rate of malingering in a forensic hospital where competency restoration is the focus is probably considerably higher than a prison sex offender treatment program. Additionally, as stated previously, depending on the population and the tool utilized to assess malingering, base rates are variable. Therefore, a cutoff score (i.e., total score on the M-FAST or F-scale of the MMPI-2) that may be useful in the assessment of malingering in one context may lead to highly misleading results in another where the base rate for malingering is much higher or lower than the first. For example, some authors have suggested using different cut scores depending on the population (Graham, Watts, & Timbrook, 1991) or report different effectiveness depending on assessing offenders or bona fide patient populations (Hawes & Boccaccini, 2009; Kucharski & Duncan, 2007).

Being cautious about cut score utilization is also important as the effectiveness of cut scores depends also upon the purpose of the evaluation. Cut scores used for screening purposes may not be the same as those used to obtain the highest overall classification accuracy. As previously stated in the M-FAST section, the cut score that provides the lowest rate of false negatives (NPP) is appropriate for a screen, but not for diagnosis. Sellbom and Bagby (2008) reported, in their review of the PAI, that a cut score of greater or equal to 77 on the NIM scale was ideal for screening purposes, but the cut score of greater or equal to 110 was most effective for predicting a strong likelihood of malingering.

CONCLUSION

In the assessment of violent offenders there are several circumstances where malingered mental illness may be of concern. The adaptational model of malingering suggests that feigning mental disorder may be some offenders' best alternative for their circumstances. Although malingering base rates vary substantially by context, the rates are reported to be consistently high enough to consider malingering in most forensic evaluations. Decades of previous research have provided several empirical detection strategies for malingering assessment. Additionally, most of these strategies are found both on commonly utilized assessments of personality and psychopathology as well as measures specifically designed to assess malingered mental illness. Currently, the forensic evaluator has many resources to effectively screen and assess for malingering in violent offender populations.

REFERENCES

Alwes, Y. R., Clark, J. A., Berry, D. T. R., & Granacher, R. P. (2008). Screening for feigning in a civil forensic setting. *Journal of Clinical and Experimental Neuropsychology*, *30*, 1–8.

American Psychiatric Association. (2000). *Diagnostic and statistical manual of mental disorders* (4th ed., text rev.). Washington, DC: Author.

Andrews, D. A., Bonta, J., & Wormith, J. S. (2006). The recent past and near future of risk and/or need assessment. *Crime and Delinquency*, *52*(1), 7–27.

Arbisi, P. A., & Ben-Porath, Y. S. (1995). An MMPI-2 infrequent response scale for use with psychopathology scale F(p). *Psychological Assessment*, *7*, 424–431.

Archer, R. P., Buffington-Vollum, J. K., Stredny, R. V., & Handel, R. W. (2006). A survey of psychological test use patterns among forensic psychologists. *Journal of Personality Assessment*, *87*, 84–94.

Baity, M. R., Siefert, C. J., Chambers, A., & Blais, M. A. (2007). Deceptiveness on the PAI: A study of naïve faking with psychiatric inpatients. *Journal of Personality Assessment*, *88*, 16–24.

Barber-Rioja, V., Zottoli, T. M., Kucharski, L. T., & Duncan, S. (2009). The utility of the MMPI-2 criminal offender infrequency (Fc) scale in the detection of malingering in criminal defendants. *International Journal of Forensic Mental Health*, *8*, 16–24.

Blanchard, D. D., McGrath, R. E., Pogge, D. L., & Khadivi, A. (2003). A comparison of the PAI and MMPI-2 as predictors of faking bad in college students. *Journal of Personality Assessment*, *80*, 197–205.

Book, A. S., Holden, R. R., Starzyk, K. B., Wasylkiw, L., & Edwards, M. J. (2006). Psychopathic traits and experimentally induced deception in self-report assessment. *Personality and Individual Differences*, *41*, 601–608.

Butcher, J. N., Graham, J. R., Ben-Porath, Y. S., Tellegen, A., & Dahlstrom, G. W. (2001). *Minnesota Multiphasic Personality Inventory-2 (MMPI-2): Manual for administration and scoring*. Minneapolis: University of Minnesota Press.

Cogburn, R. A. K. (1993). *A study of psychopathy and its relation to success in interpersonal deception*. Unpublished Ph.D. dissertation, University of Oregon, Eugene.

Edens, J. F., Poythress, N. G., & Watkins-Clay, M. M. (2007). Detection of malingering in psychiatric unit and general population prison inmates: A comparison of the PAI, SIMS, and SIRS. *Journal of Personality Assessment*, *88*, 33–42.

Fischer, L., & Marchie, A., & Norris, M. (2004). Musical and auditory hallucinations: A spectrum. *Psychiatry and Clinical Neurosciences*, *58*, 96–98.

Gacono, C. B., Meloy, J. R., Sheppard, K., Speth, E., & Roske, A. (1995). A clinical investigation of malingering and psychopathy in hospitalized insanity acquittees. *Bulletin of the American Academy of Psychiatry and Law*, *23*, 387–397.

Gassen, M. D., Pietz, C. A., Spray, B. J., & Denney, R. L. (2007). Accuracy of Megargee's criminal offender infrequency (Fc) scale in detecting malingering among forensic examinees. *Criminal Justice and Behavior*, *34*, 493–504.

Gough, H. G. (1954). Some common misconceptions about neuroticism. *Journal of Consulting Psychology*, *18*, 287–292.

Graham, J. R., Watts, D., & Timbrook, R. E. (1991). Detecting fake-good and fake-bad MMPI-2 profiles. *Journal of Personality Assessment*, *57*, 264–277.

Guy, L., & Miller, H. A. (2004). Screening for malingered psychopathology in a correctional setting: Utility of the Miller-Forensic Assessment of Symptoms Test (M-FAST). *Criminal Justice and Behavior*, *31*, 695–716.

Hare, R. D., & Neumann, C. S. (2008). Psychopathy as a clinical and empirical construct. *Annual Review of Clinical Psychology, 4*, 217–246.

Hawes, S. W., & Boccaccini, M. T. (2009). Detection of overreporting of psychopathology on the personality assessment inventory: A meta-analytic review. *Psychological Assessment, 21*, 112–124.

Heinze, M. C., & Purisch, A. D. (2001). Beneath the mask: Use of psychological tests to detect and subtype malingering in criminal defendants. *Journal of Forensic Psychology Practice, 1*, 23–52.

Heinze, M. C., & Vess, J. (2005). The relationship among malingering, psychopathy, and the MMPI-2 validity scales in maximum security forensic psychiatric inpatients. *Journal of Forensic Psychology Practice, 5*, 35–53.

Huss, M. T. (2009). *Forensic psychology: Research, clinical practice, and applications.* West Sussex, UK: Wiley-Blackwell.

Jackson, R. L., Rogers, R., & Sewell, K. W. (2005). Forensic applications of the Miller Forensic Assessment of Symptoms Test (M-FAST): Screening for feigned disorders in competency to stand trial evaluations. *Law and Human Behavior, 29*, 199–210.

Kucharski, T. L., & Duncan, S. (2007). Differentiation of mentally ill criminal defendants from malingerers on the MMPI-2 and PAI. *American Journal of Forensic Psychology, 25*, 21–42.

Kucharski, T. L., Duncan, S., Egan, S. S., & Falkenback, D. M. (2006). Psychopathy and malingering of psychiatric disorder in criminal defendants. *Behavioral Sciences and the Law, 24*, 633–644.

Kucharski, T. L., Falkenback, D. M., & Duncan, S. (2004, October). Antisocial personality disorder and malingering. Presented at the Annual Meeting of the American Academy of Psychiatry and Law, Phoenix, AZ.

Lawton, M. P. (1963). Deliberate faking on the psychopathic deviate scale of the MMPI. *Journal of Clinical Psychology, 19*, 327–330.

Lawton, M. P., & Kleban, M. H. (1965). Prisoners' faking on the MMPI. *Journal of Clinical Psychology, 21*, 269–271.

Leistico, A. R., Salekin, R. T., DeCoster, J., & Rogers, R. (2008). A large-scale meta-analysis relating the Hare measures of psychopathy to antisocial conduct. *Law and Human Behavior, 32*, 28–45.

MacNeil, B. M., & Holden, R. R. (2006). Psychopathy and the detection of deception on self-report inventories of personality. *Personality and Individual Differences, 41*, 641–651.

Marion, B. E., Selbom, M., Salekin, R. T., Toomey, J. A., Kucharski, L. T., & Duncan, S. (2012). An examination of the association between psychopathy and dissimulation using the MMPI-2-RF validity scales. *Law and Human Behavior.* Advance online publication. doi: 10.1037/lhb0000008

Megargee, E. I. (2004, May). Development and initial validation of an MMPI-2 infrequency scale (Fc) for use with criminal offenders. Paper presented at the 39th Annual Symposium on Recent Developments on the MMPI-2/MMPI-A, Minneapolis, Minnesota.

Miller, H. A. (2001). *M-FAST: Miller Forensic Assessment of Symptoms Test Professional Manual.* Odessa, FL: Psychological Assessment Resources.

Miller, H. A. (2004). Examining the use of the M-FAST with criminal defendants incompetent to stand trial. *International Journal of Offender and Comparative Criminology, 48*, 268–280.

Miller, H. A. (2005). The Miller-Forensic Assessment of Symptoms Test (M-FAST): Test generalizability and utility across race, literacy, and clinical opinion. *Criminal Justice and Behavior, 32,* 591–611.

Miller, H. A., & McCoy, L. (2013). Special needs offenders in correctional institutions: Inmates under protective custody. In L. Gideon (Ed.) *Special needs offenders in correctional institutions* (pp. 259–283). Los Angeles, CA: Sage.

Moran, P. (1999). The epidemiology of antisocial personality disorder. *Social Psychiatric Epidemiology, 34,* 231–242.

Morey, L. C. (1991). *Personality Assessment Inventory.* Odessa, FL: Psychological Assessment Resources.

Nelson, N. W., Sweet, J. J., & Demakis, G. J. (2006). Meta-analysis of the MMPI-2 Fake Bad Scale: Utility in forensic practice. *Clinical Neuropsychologist, 20,* 39–58.

Patrick, C. J., & Iacono, W. G. (1989). Psychopathy, threat, and polygraph accuracy. *Journal of Applied Psychology, 74,* 347–355.

Pierson, A. M., Rosenfeld, B., Green, D., & Belfi, B. (2011). Investigating the relationship between antisocial personality disorder and malingering. *Criminal Justice and Behavior, 38,* 146–156.

Poythress, N. G., Edens, J. F., & Watkins, M. M. (2001). The relationship between psychopathic personality features and malingering symptoms of major mental illness. *Law and Human Behavior, 25,* 567–582.

Raskin, D. C., & Hare, R. D. (1978). Psychopathy and detection of deception in a prison population. *Psychophysiology, 15,* 126–136.

Rogers, R. (1984). Towards an empirical model of malingering and deception. *Behavioral Sciences and the Law, 2,* 93–112.

Rogers, R. (1992). *Structured interview of reported symptoms.* Odessa, FL: Psychological Assessment Resources.

Rogers, R. (Ed.). (1997). *Clinical assessment of malingering and deception* (2nd ed.). New York, NY: Guilford Press.

Rogers, R. (2008). Detection strategies for malingering and defensiveness. In R. Rogers (Ed.) *Clinical assessment of malingering and deception* (3rd ed., pp. 14–35). New York, NY: Guilford Press.

Rogers, R., & Granacher, R. P. (2011). Conceptualization and assessment of malingering. In E. Y. Drogin, F. M. Dattilio, R. L. Sadoff, & T. G. Gutheil (Eds.), *Handbook of forensic assessment: Psychological and psychiatric perspectives* (pp. xx–xx). Hoboken, NJ: Wiley.

Rogers, R., Hinds, J. D., & Sewell, K. W. (1996). Feigning psychopathology among adolescent offenders: Validation of the SIRS, MMPI-A, and SIMS. *Journal of Personality Assessment, 67,* 244–257.

Rogers, R., Salekin, R. T., Sewell, K. W., Goldstein, A., & Leonard, K. (1998). A comparison of forensic and nonforensic malingerers: A prototypical analysis of explanatory models. *Law and Human Behavior, 22,* 353–367.

Rogers, R., Sewell, K. W., & Gillard, N. (2010). *Structured Interview of Reported Symptoms-2 (SIRS-2) and professional manual.* Odessa, FL: Psychological Assessment Resources.

Rogers, R., Sewell, K. W., & Goldstein, A. (1994). Explanatory models of malingering: A prototypical analysis. *Law and Human Behavior, 18,* 543–552.

Rogers, R., Sewell, K. W., & Martin, M. A., & Vitacco, M. J. (2003). Detection of feigned mental disorders: A meta-analysis of the MMPI-2 and malingering *Assessment, 10,* 160–177.

Rogers, R., Sewell, K. W., & Salekin, R. T. (1994). A meta-analysis of malingering on the MMPI-2. *Assessment, 1*, 227–237.

Rogers, R., Woslen, N. D., & Ross, C. N. (2012). The detection of feigned disabilities: The effectiveness of the PAI in a traumatized inpatient sample. *Assessment, 19*, 77–88.

Sellbom, M., & Bagby, R. M. (2008). Response styles on multiscale inventories. In R. Rogers (Ed.), *Clinical assessment of malingering and deception* (3rd ed., pp. 182–206). New York, NY: Guilford Press.

Sierless, F. S. (1984). Correlates of malingering. *Behavioral Sciences and the Law, 2*, 113–118.

Smith, G. P. (2008). Brief screening measures for the detection of feigned psychopathology. In R. Rogers (Ed.), *Clinical assessment of malingering and deception* (3rd ed., pp. 329–339). New York NY: Guilford Press.

Sullivan, K., & King, J. (2010). Detecting faked psychopathology: A comparison of the tests to detect malingered psychopathology using a simulation design. *Psychiatry Research, 176*, 75–81.

Veazey, C. H., Hays, J. R., Wagner, A. L., & Miller, H. A. (2005). Validity of the Miller Forensic Assessment of Symptoms Test in psychiatric patients. *Psychological Reports, 96*, 771–774.

Walters, G. D. (2003). Predicting institutional adjustment and recidivism with the Psychopathy Checklist factor scores: A meta-analysis. *Law and Human Behavior, 27*, 541–558.

Walters, G. D. (2006). Coping with malingering and exaggeration of psychiatric symptomatology in offender populations. *American Journal of Forensic Psychology, 24*, 21–40.

Widows, M., & Smith, G. P. (2005). *Structured Inventory of Malingered Symptomatology (SIMS) and professional manual*. Odessa, FL: Psychological Assessment Resources.

20

Assessment of Neurophysiological and Neuropsychological Bases for Violence

RACHEL FAZIO AND ROBERT L. DENNEY ■

Violence can be broadly defined as an act of physical aggression against another person with the intent to harm (Meloy, 2006). Typically, this definition of violence is dichotomized into two types of aggression: affective and predatory. The etiology of affective aggression includes strong emotions of anger or fear. It is accompanied by arousal of the autonomic nervous system and is impulsive or reactive to that situation at hand (Meloy, 2006). Predatory violence is preplanned aggression that from an evolutionary standpoint is necessary for survival, as in hunting, for example. In both of these types of violence, the perpetrator is awake, alert, and cognitively aware of what is happening. From a neurological standpoint, however, there may be a third type of violence: incidental violence. Incidental violence can be thought of as violence that is a by-product of the neurobiological processes underlying a number of neurological conditions. While in a strict sense one could categorize it as affective violence due to its obvious lack of *malice aforethought*, the perpetrators of incidental violence are often not aware, in a true sense, of the environment around them and their own actions. In this chapter, we will briefly review the potential neurophysiological foundations of violence, including neuroanatomy, neurotransmitters, hormones, genetics, and dietary influences, as well as specific neuropathologies and neuropsychological assessment methods potentially pertaining to violence.

PREDATORY AND AFFECTIVE VIOLENCE

A vast body of literature exists regarding the various neurophysiological bases of affective and predatory aggression in animals, particularly rats and cats, although some studies have focused on nonhuman primates as well (see McEllistrem, 2004, for a review). While support exists for a spectrum of violent behaviors from affective to predatory in humans, there is also criticism that the neurophysiology of animal models does not carry over to humans. While animal aggression, particularly predatory aggression, nearly always targets other species, these types of aggression in humans often represent an intraspecies attack, potentially implicating different neurophysiological etiologies (Blair, Peschardt, Budhani, Mitchell, & Pine, 2006). Differences in brain morphology are also important; the presence of a large frontal neocortex in humans adds an additional feature of aggression regulation not present in lower animals (McEllistrem, 2004).

Despite these criticisms, evidence supports potential different neurophysiological origins of predatory and affective violence in humans. Much of this research has been framed in the context of psychopathy, which may be considered the most severe manifestation of predatory aggression in humans. Too often, however, aggression has been treated as a unitary construct, making the literature difficult to interpret (Blair et al., 2006). Due to this frequent lack of specificity in human research, our discussion of the neurobiological bases of aggression will take on a more general scope, although we will discuss the different neurophysiological mechanisms underlying affective and predatory aggression when specific information avails itself.

NEUROANATOMY IN BRIEF

A number of structures are implicated in the neuroanatomy of violence, including various components of the prefrontal cortex, such as the medial frontal cortex, orbitofrontal cortex, and dorsolateral prefrontal cortex. The amygdalae have also been thoroughly scrutinized due to their primary role in various forms of aggression in animal models. Additionally, the insula and hypothalamus may have roles. Here we will briefly review each area in order to familiarize the reader with basic structural functions.

FRONTAL LOBES

Medial Frontal Cortex

The supplementary motor area and anterior cingulate cortex comprise the medial frontal cortex (Cummings & Miller, 2007). The anterior cingulate cortex is technically a paralimbic structure with neural circuits pairing it strongly with the dorsolateral prefrontal cortex (Kaufer, 2007). It is a center for the brain to integrate attention with motivation, and emotion with autonomic functioning and motoric activity (Kaufer, 2007). Damage to the anterior cingulate will result in apathy. This apathy can manifest as motoric, cognitive, affective, emotional, or motivational apathy. In other words, the person may show any and all of the following: reduced gesturing or speech, impaired deduction, decreased curiosity, impaired prosody, masked facies, social withdrawal, lack of enthusiasm, and poor initiation or maintenance of activities (Cummings & Miller, 2007).

Orbitofrontal Cortex

Social convention originates in the orbitofrontal cortex, especially on the right side. Those with damage to this area may be disinhibited, have poor judgment, make decisions impulsively, show little concern for the consequences of their behavior, and lack empathy (Cummings & Miller, 2007). Those who evidence these behaviors have been entitled "pseudopsychopathic" and sometimes commit minor crimes, although physical violence is less common.

Dorsolateral Prefrontal Cortex

The dorsolateral prefrontal cortex is home to what are generally thought of as executive functions, although "executive functions" is a broad term and involves areas throughout the brain. These functions include responding to the environment effectively, making plans, self-monitoring behavior, inhibition, and incorporating feedback to successfully achieve one's goal (Cummings & Miller, 2007).

KEY LIMBIC SYSTEM STRUCTURES

Hypothalamus

The hypothalamus is located right below the thalamus, which is the brain's main "switchboard" for transferring information throughout the brain. The hypothalamus is an important link between the nervous and endocrine systems as well as regulating the body's homeostatic functions, exerting autonomic control, and participating in regulation of the limbic system (Blumenfeld, 2002). Most pertinent to the discussion of violence, the connections between the hypothalamus and amygdala are believed to be the mechanism by which emotions cause autonomic arousal, such as piloerection (Blumenfeld, 2002). The hypothalamus also has connections to the hippocampus, the limbic structure perhaps most important for learning, and the periaqueductal gray matter, which has been implicated in aggression in animals.

A number of case studies have been published regarding the use of deep brain stimulation (DBS) of the posterior hypothalamus for the control of intractably aggressive behavior. Each has shown favorable outcomes for the patient(s) after a follow-up of 1 year or more (Franzini, Marras, Ferroli, Bugiani, & Broggi, 2005; Hernando, Pastor, Pedrosa, Peña, & Sola, 2008). While historically this area was surgically destroyed, DBS offers the advantage of being relatively nonpermanent if unfavorable side effects are generated; on this same note, the parameters of the stimulation can also be adjusted and individualized to the patient as needed (Hernando et al., 2008).

Amygdala

The amygdala helps regulate emotions and drives, particularly the emotions of anxiety, fear, and anger (Blumenfeld, 2002). In addition to being connected with the hypothalamus, it also has reciprocal connections with the medial orbitofrontal cortex and the cingulate cortex. Furthermore, there are reciprocal connections between the amygdala and hippocampus, which is how our memories achieve emotional valence. It also receives input from the olfactory system (Blumenfeld, 2002).

Numerous animal studies as well as the tragic case of Charles Whitman (University of Texas tower shooter) in 1966 implicate the involvement of the hypothalamus and amygdala in generating violence. Whitman was found to have a fast-growing tumor in the hypothalamus that was judged to be pressing on the amygdala and possibly contributing to a growing irrational hostility, paranoia, and rage (Leestma, 2005). Ultimately, he took the lives of many, and notes he left behind suggested he had little rationale for the behavior (Whitman, 1966).

Early researchers were enthusiastic about the role of the amygdala in the etiology of violent behavior. This led to a large series of amygdalotomies being performed starting in the 1960s. Unfortunately, the results were mixed (Mpakopoulou., Gatos, Brotis, Paterakis, & Fountas, 2008). To date, there have been data from over 500 stereotactic amygdalotomies published in the literature. A recent review of 13 studies examined the success rates of the various case series in alleviating aggressive and violent behavior. Improvement rates ranged from 28% to 100%, although the definition of improvement was not always thoroughly explained. Similarly, follow-up intervals were variable, and not all were stated. While the operation had a high complication rate (up to 42%), the mortality rate was low (Mpakopoulou et al., 2008). The high variability across all facets of these studies likely has to do with the surgical and anesthetic technology at the time in combination with the limited neuroimaging available. The amygdala has 23 distinct nuclei; more accurate targeting of specific nuclei may produce more successful outcomes should this procedure be performed again in the future (Mpakopoulou et al., 2008).

THE ROLE OF NEUROTRANSMITTERS

Unfortunately, little is known about the role of neurotransmitters in violent behavior, with the exception of serotonin, which has been widely studied. At this point in time, all we can say about dopamine is that there appears to be a positive correlation between dopamine and violence (Beaver, 2010). The relationships between GABA and norepinephrine and violence are unclear. On a more general note, we can say that lower levels of monoamine oxidase (MAO)—which is an enzyme that metabolizes serotonin, dopamine, norepinephrine, and perhaps other neurotransmitters—are associated with higher levels of violence (Beaver, 2010). Low levels of MAO have been associated with increased criminality, impulsivity, hyperactivity, sensation seeking, substance abuse, and psychopathy. MAO levels are primarily determined by genetics (Beaver, 2010); therefore, the relationship between MAO and violence will be discussed further in that section.

Serotonin

A plethora of studies have linked low serotonin levels to impulsive violence, whether toward self or others. The dietary precursor of serotonin is tryptophan. Therefore, dietary deficiencies, abnormalities of the metabolism of tryptophan into serotonin, or other deviations from the normal manufacture and effective use of serotonin could all be implicated in impulsive violence (Tiihonen et al., 2001). While tryptophan depletion has been implicated in impulsive violence, conversely, a number of studies have shown that violent male criminals have increased plasma levels of free l-tryptophan (Soderstrom et al., 2004; Tiihonen et al., 2001). Essentially, it is postulated this may mean there is low serotonin use in the brain, indicating less need for the tryptophan, and therefore higher plasma levels of tryptophan rather than lower (Tiihonen et al., 2001).

While this relationship is gaining support in more observational, naturalistic studies, findings from experimental studies have been more equivocal. One study used dietary manipulations to deplete participants' tryptophan before having them participate in an aggression-provoking task (Krämer, Riba, Richter, & Münte, 2011). They found tryptophan depletion actually reduced aggressive behavior in subjects with low trait aggressiveness and had no effect on aggressive behavior in subjects with higher trait aggressiveness.

Concerning serotonin itself, given the current state of technology, the measurement of serotonin in various parts of the brain cannot be directly assessed. Rather, the utilization of serotonin across the whole brain has largely been measured by assessing the serotonin metabolite 5-HIAA in the cerebrospinal fluid (CSF). A meta-analysis of 20 studies concerning 5-HIAA levels and antisocial behavior (including violence toward persons and property) found that subjects who evidenced antisocial behavior had nearly a half a standard deviation lower 5-HIAA levels than those without antisocial behavior (Moore, Scarpa, & Raine, 2002). This effect was even stronger in men, those who abused alcohol, and particularly those less than 30 years of age. This finding is interesting as it may be one reason antisocial behavior in general tends to decline as age increases (Moore et al., 2002).

In line with this postulate that increased serotonin may therefore decrease violence, Butler et al. (2010) conducted an open-label trial of sertraline in impulsively violent men. While it was a small trial with only 20 individuals completing the study, self-reported assault was decreased by 51% in those participants. They reported a 35% decrease in impulsivity. Several participants noted improved relationships with family and friends, and all asked to be continued on the medication at the completion of the 3-month trial (Butler et al., 2010). This indicates selective serotonin reuptake inhibitors may help reduce impulsive violence in those with enough insight to appreciate their effects and have no, or tolerable, side effects.

Alternately, serotonin is not the only factor responsible for violence. One study performed a longitudinal follow-up of a group of boys who were physically aggressive but discontinued their aggressive behavior as adolescents (Booij et al., 2010). As adults 21 years later, those who demonstrated aggression as children had significantly lower serotonin synthesis in their orbitofrontal cortex when compared to control subjects who were not aggressive as children. Therefore, the authors argue that while serotonin levels may predispose an individual to aggression, intervening developmental and environmental factors may preclude its expression (Booij et al., 2010). From these results, we can conclude the relationship between tryptophan, serotonin, and violence is neither simple nor linear. This area of study is still young, however, and the nature of these relationships should soon be elucidated.

HORMONAL INFLUENCES

The relationship between testosterone and aggression in lower mammals is well understood due to the ease of experimental manipulation. Studies concerning how testosterone relates to violence in humans have been less definitive. Indeed, most studies of adult males have not shown a relationship between plasma testosterone and aggressiveness (Giammanco, Tabacchi, Giammanco, Di Majo, & La Guardia, 2005). While some of the equivocality of the relationship between testosterone and aggression in humans can be explained by various methodological limitations, a potentially more causative factor is the difference in brain morphology between humans and lower species. In other words, experimental research with animals may demonstrate a much clearer relationship between testosterone and aggressive behavior due to testosterone having a much larger effect on their behavior. Humans have the ability to better control their behavior due to the evolution of the neocortex. Areas of the brain known to regulate hormonal control of aggressive behavior in lower mammals are also smaller in humans. These cumulative factors have allowed our behavior to be more autonomous in the face of hormonal surges (Carré, McCormick, & Hariri, 2011). Of course, the relationship between testosterone and aggression is even more complicated in women than men due to the complicated and variable hormonal profile of women of reproductive age (Giammanco et al., 2005).

Even when relatively higher levels of testosterone are present in those who demonstrate aggressive behavior, until very recently, it was unknown whether this was the cause of the aggression, a product of the aggression, or a secondary product of some other variable (Giammanco et al., 2005). Recent research assessing salivary testosterone levels in conjunction with experimental paradigms designed to provoke aggressive behavior have been able to clarify this. Although somewhat artificial, these experiments have been able to show that provoked increases in testosterone lead to increased aggression (Carré et al., 2011). It should be noted, however, this laboratory model is that of affective aggression—the men were provoked, which led to variable increases in testosterone, correlating with increased retaliative aggression. In models designed to provoke predatory aggression, there was no such relationship between testosterone and aggression (Carré et al., 2011).

Hormones other than testosterone also have an impact on aggressive behavior. Cortisol is the primary glucocorticoid studied in relation to the hypothalamic-pituitary-adrenal (HPA) axis and stress. A number of studies have demonstrated that low basal HPA axis activity is correlated with increased aggressive behavior in both rats and humans (Böhnke, Bertsch, Kruk, & Naumann, 2010). In a recent study where aggression was provoked in an experimental setting, basal cortisol levels showed a strong relationship with aggressive behavior, explaining 67% of the variance. Again, this correlation was strongly negative—as basal cortisol decreases, aggressive behavior increases. That being said, those who were provoked then showed an increase in cortisol as compared to the nonprovoked control group. Prior studies have also shown a correlation between the amount of cortisol increase and aggressive behavior. Also, in the nonprovoked control group, there was a positive correlation between cortisol and aggression. The authors interpret these findings as meaning those with low basal HPA axis activity are more likely to demonstrate reactive aggression when provoked, whereas there is likely to be a relationship between higher basal HPA axis activity and proactive or predatory aggression (Böhnke et al., 2010). These findings highlight both the importance of differentiating affective and predatory aggression as well as basal and acute hormone levels in the research literature.

Of more import than how any single hormone impacts behavior is an understanding of how they act in concert. The triple imbalance hypothesis of reactive aggression explains this nicely. While cortisol is a product of the HPA axis, testosterone is a product of the hypothalamic-pituitary-gonadal (HPG) axis. These two endocrine axes are mutually inhibitory (van Honk, Harmon-Jones, Morgan, & Schutter, 2010). The two hormones are also associated with opposite emotional and behavioral effects; whereas cortisol increases fear and behavioral inhibition, testosterone reduces these predispositions. From this, we can theorize that those with high levels of testosterone and low levels of cortisol are more likely to behave aggressively. Interestingly, however, this hormonal profile is generalized to aggressive behavior—it is not specific to either affective or predatory aggression (van Honk et al., 2010). For that, we must also assess the role of serotonin. Research indicates those with this hormone ratio and low serotonin demonstrate affective aggression, whereas when serotonin is high, predatory aggression is more likely. It is believed that serotonin plays a key role in the frontal cortex to inhibit affective aggression (van Honk et al., 2010).

These hormones play an important role in regulating the neuronal systems responsible for controlling aggressive behavior. Cortical and subcortical structures communicate with various levels of efficiency in each individual. When cortical structures dominate, the information one encounters every day is typically processed in a "top-down" manner, whereas when the subcortical structures dominate, information is processed in a "bottom-up" manner. Testosterone reduces cortical-subcortical communication, predisposing individuals with high testosterone to bottom-up processing, which is inherently more impulsive due to the increased input of the frontal lobes. Cortisol, on the other hand, increases this communication (van Honk et al., 2010). Given this information, one can see how high levels of testosterone and low levels of cortisol—particularly in the presence of low serotonin—can lead to affective violence.

GENETIC CONTRIBUTIONS

Little work has been done to examine the direct genetic contributions to violent behavior. Rather, the existing research has focused on concepts such as aggression and criminality (Rhee & Waldman, 2007). Less yet has attempted to differentiate between predatory and affective aggression. That being said, there is little argument that genetics contribute to aggressive and violent behavior, such as criminal convictions, criminal careers, and violent offending (Frisell, Lichtenstein, & Långström, 2010). Indeed, it is believed genetic background explains 40%–50% of the variance for risk of aggressive behavior (Pavlov, Chistiakov, & Chekhonin, 2012).

One particularly comprehensive study examined the genetic versus environmental etiology of violent behavior through combining a number of national registries in Sweden; this resulted in a longitudinal total population study of 12.5 million people (Frisell et al., 2010). They found genes had a strong effect on violent offending, although shared environment also played some role. For example, the odds ratio (OR) of offending for a biological sibling when the other had been convicted of a violent offense was 4.3; even among full siblings adopted apart, the OR was significant at 1.7. Those convicted of violent offenses who adopted children also had some influence on these children's behavior however; the OR for these children was 1.5. Interestingly, there were even stronger effects for specific violent offenses. Those who had a sibling who committed arson had an OR of 22.4 for committing that same crime. The OR for kidnapping was even higher at 35.7 (Frisell et al., 2010).

Further complicating the topic, much of the genetic research that has been performed has focused on how genes modulate the hormones and neurotransmitter systems of the individuals in question. The genes that are researched can modulate neurotransmitters in one of five ways. First, they can be precursor genes, which affect the rate of production of neurotransmitters from precursor components. Second, they can be receptor genes, which have to do with the regulation of neurotransmitter receptors. Third, they can be transporter genes, which control the reuptake of unused neurotransmitters from the synaptic cleft. Fourth, they can be metabolite genes, which are responsible for the degradation of excess neurotransmitters. Finally, they can be conversion genes, which are involved with the conversion of one neurotransmitter to another (Rhee & Waldman, 2007).

Genetics have an influence on aggression through their programming of androgen receptors. One portion of the androgen receptor gene contains two polymorphic trinucleotide repeats. One of these, CAG, has been extensively linked with aggressive behavior in human men (Pavlov et al., 2012). Essentially, the shorter the repeat, the higher the propensity for verbal and physical aggression. This finding has been confirmed in several European and Asian populations (Pavlov et al., 2012). One study found reduced CAG repeats in this gene among those specifically with violent criminal behavior—rapists, murderers, and those who both raped and murdered (Rajender et al., 2008).

Genes encoding for serotonin transport also play a crucial role in the genetic etiology of aggression. Serotonin transporter (5-HTT) takes serotonin that had been released into the synaptic cleft back into the presynaptic neuron. There are long and short polymorphisms of this gene. The short allele corresponds with reduced 5-HTT and therefore reduced transportation of serotonin (Pavlov et al., 2012). The relationship between this polymorphism and aggression has been well studied in both animals and humans. It is believed that a homogenous genotype for this allele (i.e., short-short as opposed to short-long or long-long) explains 5% of the individual variance in human aggression (Pavlov et al., 2012).

The genetic encoding of monoamine oxidase (MAO), which has an effect on all of the monoamines, has also been implicated in aggressive behavior. MAOA, which preferentially inactivates serotonin, epinephrine, and norepinephrine, has been more strongly implicated than MAOB, which preferentially inactivates dopamine. Specifically, the variable number of tandem repeats of the MAOA promoter has an essentially inverse correlation with aggressive behavior (Pavlov et al., 2012). The most common alleles for this promoter and 3- and 4-repeats, although 2- and 10-repeat alleles also exist. Essentially, the more repeats of this allele, the more activity of MAOA. Those with the 2-repeat allele only have about 25% of the MAOA activity of those with the 4-repeat allele. Several studies have shown those with the 3-repeat variant are more violent than those with the 4-allele repeat; those with the 2-repeat allele are more violent yet. This effect has held true even in women, although to a lesser extent than in men (Pavlov et al., 2012).

This genetic variation has also been demonstrated to affect brain structure and connectivity. Those with fewer MAOA repeats have reduced volume in the cingulate gyrus, bilateral amygdalae, insula, and hypothalamus. The volume reductions averaged about 8% compared to those with more MAOA repeats (Meyer-Lindenberg et al., 2006). It was also associated with reduced orbitofrontal volume and functional connection with the amygdala, although only in men. The authors theorize these differences have important implications for the etiology of impulsive—but not predatory—aggression, predominantly in men, who are hit particularly hard by this allelic variation (Meyer-Lindenberg et al., 2006).

As an extreme example of the relationship between low MAOA and violence, there have been case studies published by Brunner involving a family where the males essentially lack MAOA due to a genetic abnormality (Brunner et al., 1993). All of them have borderline or poorer intellectual functioning and stereotyped behavior. Additionally, they all evidence a variety of aggressive, violent, and deviant sexual behavior. These have included episodes of arson, an attack with a pitchfork, and sexual coercion of siblings (Brunner et al., 1993). A total of 14 men in the family have demonstrated this behavior pattern and genotype.

Genes controlling several aspects of dopamine functioning have been implicated in aggressive behavior. These include genes for dopamine transport, dopamine receptors, and catechol-O-methyl transferase, which degrades dopamine and other catecholamines (Pavlov et al., 2012). These genetic variations in dopamine functioning also seem to impact primarily impulsive aggression.

DIETARY INFLUENCES

Perhaps surprisingly, a number of components of one's diet can strongly influence the functioning of various biological systems implicated in the regulation of violent and aggressive behavior. Here, the discussion shall focus on the roles of various fats, sugar, and alcohol.

Fats

A variety of dietary fats have been implicated in aggressive behavior, including omega-3/omega-6 fats, trans fats, and cholesterol. Omega-3 fats are believed to be necessary both for proper neurodevelopment in early stages of life as well as normal neurological functioning later on. In modern society, omega-3 fats have started to be replaced by increasing amounts of omega-6 fats. Cross-national epidemiological data indicate countries with higher omega-3 intake have lower homicide rates (Hibbeln, Ferguson, & Blasbalg, 2006). Similarly, as omega-6 fats replaced omega-3 fats in five countries, homicide rates went up, and the relationship was very strong ($r = .93$). While these studies are inherently correlational, similar results have been found in rodents, with mice who ingest a diet of 43% soy oil evidencing 3–4 times the aggressive behavior of mice fed 16% soy oil (Hibbeln et al., 2006). Studies involving supplementing a wide variety of populations with omega-3 fatty acids have demonstrated reductions in hostility, verbal aggression, physical aggression, childhood behavioral problems, and felony-level violence (Hibbeln et al., 2006).

Trans fats are another type of fat that began to replace healthier fats in the diets of modernized countries until recently, when legislation was enacted requiring identification of trans fats on nutritional information. They have been identified as having deleterious effects on a wide variety of markers of physical health and are also known to inhibit the production of omega-3 fatty acids (Golomb, Evans, White, & Dimsdale, 2012). In the first study of its kind, Golomb et al. (2012) demonstrated a link between increased intake of dietary trans fats and aggression. The relationship was strong and persevered even after adjusting for sex, age, and ethnicity, and it was present cross-sectionally and prospectively. Unfortunately, the relationship between trans fats and aggression and humans is unlikely to be explored using an experimental paradigm given the known harmful effects of trans fats on health, although further work still remains to be done in this area (Golomb et al., 2012).

Cholesterol levels have been linked to impulsive and violent behavior. Specifically, as cholesterol goes down, impulsive violence toward self or others tends to increase. This link has been found both in those who have naturally lower cholesterol as well as those who take medications to treat hypercholesterolemia (Golomb, Stattin, & Mednick, 2000). It has been demonstrated that those on statin drugs exhibit an increase in impulsivity for approximately the first month after beginning the drugs, with impulsivity scores returning near baseline after 1 year on the medication (Ormiston, Wolkowitz, Reus, & Manfredi, 2003).

The mechanism relating cholesterol levels to impulsive violence is not entirely known, but reduced levels of cholesterol may lead to reductions in serotonin. Indeed, consistent with the aforementioned study showing impulsivity increased within the first month on cholesterol-lowering drugs, other research has demonstrated these drugs increase serotonin transporter (SERT) activity for the first month with it slowly declining after 2 months and returning to baseline around 1 year (Vevera et al., 2005). SERT removes serotonin from the synaptic cleft and returns it to presynaptic neurons, so an increase in its activity would effectively reduce serotonin availability in the synaptic cleft. With the increased prescription of statin drugs to those with hypercholesterolemia in order to reduce deaths by cardiac mechanisms, the concomitant increase in death by other causes—which may be linked to this reduction in serotonin and increase in impulsivity—should be considered, as should the potentially increased propensity for violence toward others (Golomb et al., 2000).

Glucose

Aggressive impulses are common in a large number of people, and resisting these impulses requires self-control. For individuals to be able to do this, a great number of variables must align. As previously discussed, all the key neuroanatomical structures must be intact, and neurotransmitters and hormones must be within key parameters. In addition to these factors however, the basic source of energy the brain uses to perform all of its metabolic functions must also be present—that is, glucose. A shortage of glucose or a metabolic problem that would inhibit the brain from accessing its most important fuel source, such as diabetes, can significantly impair one's ability to control aggressive impulses (de Wall, Deckman, Gailliot, & Bushman, 2011). The relationship between glucose and self-control has been demonstrated on the individual level by giving research participants sugary drinks before the induction of aggression using laboratory paradigms. It has been shown in a small population of those with diabetes, where 4% of the variance in aggressive behavior was explained through their reduced self-control (de Wall et al., 2011). On a larger scale, diabetes rates have been linked with violent crime rates nationally, and an enzyme deficiency that results in difficulties with glucose metabolism has been correlated with violent killings internationally (de Wall et al., 2011).

Hypoglycemia can also be induced by alcohol and leads to increased incidence of aggression. This phenomenon has been verified in studies of alcoholic violent offenders. One study demonstrated that glucose metabolism explained 27% of the variation of recidivism among alcoholic male perpetrators of domestic violence (Virkkunen, Rissanen, Franssila-Kallunki, & Tilhonon, 2009). This may explain the 10% decrease in physical assaults in the United Kingdom after police began giving lollipops to those who were intoxicated on their way home from nightclubs (de Wall et al., 2011).

Alcohol

Alcohol may increase violent behavior through mechanisms other than the obvious direct effects of alcohol as well. At just below the legal limit for intoxication in many locales (blood alcohol level of .08), alcohol affects serum tryptophan concentrations. Specifically, 1.5 to 2 hours after drinking approximately two pints of beer, there were dramatic decreases in the subjects' tryptophan (Badawy, 1998). These started to recover after 3 hours had passed. It appears plausible that alcohol can increase one's propensity to violent behavior through a number of mechanisms over and above the primary disinhibiting effects.

NEUROIMAGING AND NEUROPSYCHOLOGICAL TESTING

Studies assessing the functional neurological systems underlying violence are marred by methodological limitations. Due to the time, labor, and cost involved, they often involve small sample sizes. The other primary limitation of these studies is the heterogeneity of the samples (Hoskins, Roth, & Giancola, 2010). While the definitions of violence and aggression used often vary from study to study, perhaps of more concern is the mix of individuals involved in any one study. In addition to the definition of predatory and affective violence often being ignored (i.e., brain imaging of "murderers" with the circumstances neglected), it has also been suggested there may be a relationship between the type of offense and the location of brain dysfunction. In other words, different systems may be dysfunctional in those who have committed assault as opposed to those who have committed sexual offenses (Hoskins et al., 2010). Additionally, a number of studies have been conducted in those who are highly selected populations, which would not generalize to the average violent offender. For example, violence has been studied in veterans, those with specific personality disorders, schizophrenia, and those with substance abuse disorders. Each of these groups may have associated underlying neuropathology, which has a larger effect on the results of the study than that of violence, obfuscating results if not properly controlled for. Hoskins et al. (2010) provides an excellent review of this research by diagnostic group, and Dolan (2010) provides an in-depth review of the structural and functional neuroimaging of those with personality disorder and comorbid violence. In this chapter, we will focus on criminal offenders in general rather than specific diagnostic groups.

Structural Neuroimaging

Little information is available regarding structural neuroanatomical differences in persistent violent offenders without complicating comorbidities. Structural neuroimaging has also been limited, until recently, to fairly gross measurements of neuroanatomical structures due to technological limitations. One recent study, however, has partially filled this gap (Tiihonen et al., 2008). The persistent violent offenders in this study had no comorbid diagnoses of psychotic spectrum disorders, but they did have very high rates of alcohol dependence and polysubstance abuse. With this limitation in mind, the authors determined the offenders had differences in several brain regions per analysis with voxel-based morphometry and lobar volumetry performed after magnetic resonance imaging (MRI) scanning. In the occipital and parietal lobes, bilaterally, the offenders had significantly greater white matter volume. Alternately, they had more gray matter volume in the cerebellum, although only on the right. Focal, symmetrical areas of atrophy were also found in the frontopolar and orbitofrontal cortex as well as the postcentral gyri. All of these differences were even greater in the subsample of offenders with psychopathy (Tiihonen et al., 2008). The authors noted these differences may due to environmental causes, such as adult substance abuse, or may be due to neurodevelopmental processes. The authors argue the neurodevelopmental hypotheses or an interaction of the two may be the more likely explanation given all the violent offenders in the study would have also met diagnostic criteria for conduct disorder, which generally leads to increased childhood use of substances, head injury, and infection (Tiihonen et al., 2008).

A meta-analysis of structural imaging studies yielded similar, although less specific, results. The analysis of the 12 structural imaging studies available indicated a reduction of the prefrontal cortex, although the low number of studies was not sufficient to conduct more specific region of interest analyses of the prefrontal cortex (Yang & Raine, 2009). Areas outside of the prefrontal cortex have been less studied in violent offenders. There has been evidence, however, that various classes of violent offenders and psychopaths have structural and functional hippocampal abnormalities (Raine et al., 2004). All have shown decreased hippocampal volume or activity in the left hippocampi, and some have demonstrated increased right hippocampi volume and/or functioning. The structural abnormalities were specific to the anterior regions of the hippocampus (Raine et al., 2004). These authors also argue that the finding of atypical brain asymmetry would lead one toward a neurodevelopmental etiology (Raine et al., 2004). Such findings are potentially informative, but they require a great deal of replication before the technology can move from the research laboratory to the clinical and forensic setting.

Functional Neuroimaging

The most commonly used functional imaging for the brain includes positron emission tomography (PET), single-photon emission tomography (SPECT), and functional magnetic resonance imaging (fMRI), all of which can measure brain metabolic activity. Raine et al. (1998) utilized PET methodology to compare the activity of different regions of the brain in affective murderers, predatory murderers, and controls. Murderers who demonstrated both types of aggression in the killings were excluded from the study. They discovered that relative to controls, affective murderers had lower prefrontal glucose metabolism bilaterally. Predatory murderers had prefrontal glucose metabolism similar to controls. Both affective and predatory murderers, however, had higher right subcortical functioning. They interpreted these results as supporting the hypothesis that affective murderers had more difficulty regulating their behavior due to their lower right hemisphere prefrontal to subcortical ratio, whereas the predatory murderers have similar aggressive impulses due to their increased right subcortical activity but retain the ability to control and plan their behavior (Raine et al., 1998).

Other functional imaging studies have also implicated a role in cortical/subcortical coupling. Passamonti et al. (2011) utilized an fMRI paradigm and found that acute tryptophan depletion, which leads to reduced serotonin availability, modulates the activity between the amygdala and both the ventral anterior cingulate cortex and ventrolateral prefrontal cortex. Interestingly, this effect was only significant on the right side. This study highlights the complex interplay between neurotransmitters, distinct brain regions, and communication among those regions in the fine-grained understanding of the etiology of violence. Further emphasizing the complicated nature of this relationship, other fMRI studies have found acute tryptophan depletion actually reduces aggression in those with low trait aggressiveness, whereas no change in aggression was seen in those with high trait aggression (Krämer, Riba, Richter, & Münte, 2011). These apparently conflicting results may be due to features of the studies, such as sampling bias, since functional imaging studies tend to have small samples. The particular research paradigms used (viewing of faces versus the Taylor Aggression Paradigm) may also be implicated in the differential results.

Using SPECT, Amen, Hanks, Prunella, and Green (2007) compared 11 impulsive murderers who were under 30 years old with 11 healthy age-matched controls at rest and during a computerized go/no-go task. They reported finding decreased regional cerebral blood flow during the concentration task for the murderers, largely in the orbital and dorsolateral prefrontal cortices bilaterally, with some involvement of the anterior cingulate, bilateral anterior temporal lobes, and right uncus. The authors suggested these brain areas were implicated with anger management, inhibition, self-censorship, and planning (appreciation of future consequences). A significant weakness of the study was that healthy controls were not matched for history of drug and alcohol abuse.

A meta-analysis of 31 functional imaging studies offered additional insight into brain regions that tend to have abnormal functioning in antisocial, violent, or psychopathic persons (Yang & Raine, 2009). They determined there was a significant decrease in prefrontal functioning, specifically in the right orbitofrontal cortex and anterior cingulate cortex, as well as the left dorsolateral prefrontal cortex. There was no apparent reduction in functioning of the ventrolateral prefrontal cortex, but the medial prefrontal cortex showed a trend toward reduced activity (Yang & Raine, 2009). There appears to be a general consensus that a relationship exists between psychopathy and violent behavior and frontal and temporal lobe functioning; however, methodological flaws and inconsistencies exist in much of the research reflected in this literature (Hoptman, 2003; Wahlund & Kritiansson, 2009).

At this date, metabolic neuroimaging studies are largely used in research settings with specific exceptions. The America Academy of Neurology suggested FDG-PET may have promise as an adjunct for differential diagnosis of dementias (Knopman et al., 2001). The American College of Radiology (ACR) presented Appropriateness Criteria suggesting PET and SPECT were appropriate for differential diagnosis of dementia, movement disorders, and preoperative assessment in seizures and epilepsy (ACR, 2010, 2011b). The ACR indicated PET and SPECT were usually not appropriate in cases of mild to severe head injury or cerebrovascular disease and suggested it would not be a part of routine clinical practice pertaining to general neurobehavioral disorders (ACR, 2011a, 2012).

Neuropsychological Testing

Studies concerning the neuropsychological functioning of various samples of offenders were performed in the 1970s, 1980s, and 1990s, using test batteries such as the Halstead Reitan and the Luria Nebraska (see Fabian, 2010, for a brief review). Less research has been done with violent adults and modern neuropsychological tests. While it has been suggested neuropsychological tests may be insensitive to any deficits present in those with histories of violence due to the propensity for violence being more of a characterological feature than a cognitive feature (Fabian, 2010), a handful of studies have cast some light on the issue.

One study set out to clarify the results of previous studies concerning neuropsychological deficits in violent offenders, which may have been confounded due to failure to control for psychopathy and substance abuse history (Mercer, Selby, & McClung, 2005). Overall, they determined that each group—those that were violent, psychopathic, and had substance abuse history—fared worse on measures of executive functioning than those who did not meet those criteria. Those who met more than one of these criteria performed worse yet (Mercer et al., 2005).

Another study reported in their sample of murderers, the overall neuropsychological profile for the sample was "generally subaverage" (Hanlon, Rubin, Jensen, & Daoust, 2010, p. 8). The average IQ for the group was 85, and memory scores also tended to fall in the low-average range. Executive functioning was significantly worse though, with 55% demonstrating executive dysfunction (Hanlon et al., 2010). Other research has driven home the presence of executive functioning deficits in violent populations. A meta-analysis of classical neuropsychological measures of executive functioning in those with antisocial behavior revealed the antisocial group performed .62 standard deviations worse than comparison groups (Morgan & Lilienfeld, 2000). This finding suggested a moderate relationship between executive functioning and chronic antisocial behavior. This meta-analysis was expanded upon in 2011 (Ogilvie, Stewart, Chan, & Shum) to include 126 studies that used a wider variety of measures of executive functioning. This time, the grand mean effect size was .44. When broken down by type of antisocial behavior, physical aggression had an effect size of .41, indicating a robust relationship between executive functioning and violence.

This meta-analysis (Ogilvie et al., 2011) also calculated effect sizes for specific measures of executive functioning. These ranged from relatively small effect sizes for tasks such as the Wisconsin Card Sorting Test (WCST; .17), to moderate effect sizes for tests such as the Controlled Oral Word Association Test (COWAT; .36), the Trail Making Test Part B (TMTB; .38), and the Booklet Category Test (BCT; .47), to fairly large effect sizes for the Go/No-Go Task (.56) and the Porteus Maze Test (.71).

More recently, the advent of the Delis-Kaplan Executive Function System (D-KEFS; Delis, Kaplan, & Kramer, 2001) has allowed executive functioning to be more finely measured. Broomhall (2005) compared predatory and affectively violent inmates on several subtests of the D-KEFS. The predatory group of offenders was intact on nearly all of the subtests. The affective group, on the other hand, showed impaired performance on one or more scales of each of the subtests. Specifically, it was determined that while predatory offenders were selectively impulsive—in other words, impulsive when they chose to be, depending on their perception of the importance of the task—the affectively violent offenders showed deficits in cognitive flexibility, initiation, verbal inhibition, and maintenance of set (Broomhall, 2005). These differing cognitive skills could have important implications for individualizing treatment plans by offender type.

Another study again used the D-KEFS to measure executive dysfunction in offenders (Hancock, Tapscott, & Hoaken, 2010). These authors determined the D-KEFS scores were related to both the severity and frequency of violent offending. They were able to create a logistic regression that was able to correctly detect 89% of the severely violent offenders while not miscategorizing any of the less violent offenders. The D-KEFS scores did not show a relationship with the frequency of nonviolent offending (Hancock et al., 2010). This implies that executive dysfunction may be specifically related to violent offending. Concerning particular areas of dysfunction, those who performed poorly on measures indicating impulsivity, problems with concept formation and maintenance of set, and difficulty self-monitoring had increasingly large numbers of violent offenses (Hancock et al., 2010). Unfortunately, this sample was too small to differentiate between predatory and affective violence, but it still demonstrates how knowledge about offender executive functioning may be informative to treatment and efforts to prevent recidivism.

One truly unique measure that is often—probably erroneously—grouped in with measures of executive functioning is the Iowa Gambling Task (IGT). The IGT assesses what can best be described as decision-making abilities. In it, the examinee is asked to make selections from four decks of cards with the goal of maximizing his or her winnings. Two decks have bigger wins and losses, with an overall net loss. The other two decks have smaller wins and losses, but with an overall net gain if one keeps choosing from these decks. While it is assumed this is a form of executive functioning, a review of the available literature correlating IGT performance with other measures of executive functioning as well as intelligence demonstrates that IGT performance is, at best, negligibly correlated with other domains of executive functioning (Toplak, Sorge, Benoit, West, & Stanovich, 2010). The IGT was designed to assess decision-making impairment in patients with damage to the ventromedial prefrontal cortex, and its ability to do so has been well supported by neuroimaging research. While performance on the IGT is dependent on some lower order cognitive functions and corresponding brain areas, it does indeed produce activation in the ventromedial prefrontal cortex (Li, Lu, D'Argembeau, Ng, & Bechara, 2010), and performance on the IGT deteriorates—primarily due to an increased focus on recent events as opposed to past experience or future consequences—as the ventromedial prefrontal cortex becomes increasingly damaged or disconnected from the rest of the brain (Hochman, Yechiam, & Bechara, 2010).

Broomhall (2005) included the IGT in his study of instrumental and reactive violent offenders. The reactive violent offenders made significantly more choices from the disadvantageous decks and significantly fewer choices from the advantageous decks on this task when compared to the instrumental violent offenders. When compared to normative data for the IGT, both groups of offenders made poorer decisions overall. The reactive group, however, was most similar to a clinical group with orbitofrontal damage, whereas the instrumental group was intermediate between the orbitofrontal/reactive groups and normal controls (Broomhall, 2005).

Similar results were found in another study (Levi, Nussbaum, & Rich, 2010). This time, inmates who were instrumentally and reactively violent were compared to nonviolent criminals. While all groups initially preferred the disadvantageous decks of the IGT, the nonviolent criminals reversed this preference quickly, whereas both of the violent groups were much slower to begin choosing from the more advantageous decks. Toward the end of the test, those who were instrumentally violent were making somewhat more advantageous choices than those with a history of reactive violence, but both were still far below the nonaggressive controls (Levi et al., 2010). Overall, we are just beginning to accurately assess the neuropsychological functioning of those who are violent. With recent advances in both neuropsychological tests designed to capture differential aspects of executive functioning and the advent of functional neuroimaging, the field is poised to make large strides in this area in the near future, opening important avenues for treatment and preventative efforts.

INCIDENTAL VIOLENCE

In a number of neurological conditions, agitation, aggression, and violence are common sequelae of the disorders. These are often a by-product of brain dysfunction and corresponding confusion and disinhibition, however, rather than any conscious intent to cause harm to others. Therefore, this violence can best be thought of as violence that is incidental to a neurological dysfunction rather than a volitional form of aggression.

Intellectual Disability

Intellectual disability (ID) is often concordant with challenging behavior, of which aggression toward self and others may be the most challenging. In population studies of those with ID, which necessarily included all levels of ID, in all residential settings, 10%–20% of the population could be considered aggressive (Tenneij & Koot, 2008). Some research has demonstrated that aggressive behavior in the ID population is more likely to occur in men, those 20–25 years old, and those with more severe levels of ID. This rate tends to be higher in those who are in treatment for challenging behavior. In one study, 44% of those with mild ID who were in a treatment facility for challenging behavior demonstrated aggression toward others. This aggression was verbal-only in 20% of those clients, while the remaining 80% were physically aggressive (Tenneij & Koot, 2008).

Dementia

A number of excellent studies have examined the rates of aggressive behavior in those diagnosed with dementia. Kunik et al. (2010) examined the rate of development of aggressive behavior in those diagnosed with dementia in a sample of veterans. Participants were diagnosed within the previous 12 months. All participants in the study had to be free of aggression at the onset; the rate of exclusion due to aggressive behavior in the last year was illuminating. Four hundred patients consented to participate, but 19% were screened out due to a report of aggressive behavior by caregivers during a phone interview. Of the remaining 325 patients, an additional 33% were then excluded because of aggression or other exclusion criteria. Of the 215 who were then followed in the study, 41% developed aggressive behavior during the next 24 months. Almost half (46%) of these patients manifested physical aggression and 15% sexual aggression. The unadjusted incidence of aggression was .37 cases per year at risk (Kunik et al., 2010).

In a prospective, 10-year, longitudinal study of those diagnosed with dementia, 61% demonstrated physical aggression, 71% aggressive resistance to care, and 25% destructive behavior (Keene et al., 1999). The pattern of aggressive behavior was also followed; 52% of those who demonstrated physical aggression did so in a single period of behavior that persisted until their death, indicating physical aggression may be indicative of severe, end-stage dementia. This inference is further supported by the MMSE score of the physically aggressive patients at the onset of the aggression, which was 7.5. Overall, 95% of patients evidenced at least one type of severe and persistent aggressive behavior (Keene et al., 1999).

A more recent study discovered a similar rate of physical aggression. Zuidema, de Jonghe, Verhey, and Koopmans (2009) found that 55.9% of nursing home residents demonstrated physically aggressive behavior during a 2-week observation period. There was a higher rate of physical aggression among men (61.3%) than women (54.5%). Dementia severity again correlated with physical aggression; 26.5% of those with moderate cognitive decline were physically aggressive and this increased as cognitive abilities decreased. Over 62% of those with very severe cognitive decline demonstrated physical aggression (Zuidema et al., 2009).

Traumatic Brain Injury

There are several potential relationships between traumatic brain injury (TBI) and violence. In the acute phase of moderate or severe TBI, agitation and aggression are well-documented sequelae. This aggression persists in some cases. In cases of mild TBI, particularly past the acute phase, the evidence is more equivocal as many of these studies have used self-report of TBI and have been conducted with prison inmates (see Williams et al., 2010, for one example). While there are a number of ways to classify the severity of TBI, the use of the Glasgow Coma Scale (GCS) is the most common (Rao et al., 2009). Scores of 13–15 are considered mild TBI, scores of 9–12 are categorized as moderate, and scores of 3–8 are severe. When someone with a TBI has a score on the very low end of this scale, well within the severe range, this is what most people think of as a coma. A score of 14–15 would be comparable to a sports concussion, where the player is hit in the head and dazed, or only unconscious for perhaps a few seconds before regaining consciousness.

ACUTE, MODERATE TO SEVERE TRAUMATIC BRAIN INJURY

For those who have incurred a serious TBI, there are established stages of recovery that are tracked in order to assess their progress. One way of monitoring this progress is using the Rancho Levels of Cognitive Functioning (Hagen, 1998). While some patients do skip levels entirely, most patients will spend at least a brief amount of time in each stage. Level IV of the Rancho Levels is the "Confused/Agitated" level. While the patient is in this stage, he or she may make attempts to remove medical equipment or otherwise resist medical care, scream, and have mood swings with no apparent provocation (Hagen, 1998). This can result in aggressive behavior toward persons or property. Similarly, during Level V, patients have the potential to become agitated in response to external stimulation.

While it is well recognized that this agitation and accompanying aggression are common in those recovering from serious TBI, lack of consistent definitions of agitation and aggression, and other methodological issues, has made it difficult to determine the exact prevalence. Studies assessing the prevalence of agitation in those recovering from TBI have found prevalence rates from 11% to 96% (Nott, Chapparo, & Baguley, 2006). This may be based on when the prevalence of agitation was assessed; it ranges from 86% to 96% of those who are in the acute phase of injury before it abates somewhat to 36%–70% at various points in the rehabilitation process (Nott et al., 2006). Lower estimates are likely due to more stringent definitions of agitation. One study demonstrated those who were in the acute phase of recovery displayed agitated behavior for an average of 32 days, although agitation persisted for longer than 3 months in a few cases (Nott et al., 2006). Agitation is associated with lower levels of cognition, and it usually resolves once the patient is out of posttraumatic amnesia (Nott, Chapparo, Heard, & Baguley, 2010).

Although the definition of agitation does include aggression and violent behavior, this is not always the case. Less research has been conducted examining the prevalence of physical aggression toward persons or property in those recovering from acute TBI. One study (Rao et al., 2009) found the rate of aggression to be 28.4% in the first 3 months of recovery from TBI. It should be noted, however, this was entirely verbal aggression. There was only one incident of violence toward property in their study, and no violence toward self or others. There are those who do become aggressive after TBI, and that violence usually persists for long periods of time, requiring professional management.

POSTACUTE, MODERATE TO SEVERE TRAUMATIC BRAIN INJURY

In one of the few studies specifically monitoring aggressive behavior, the rate was found to be 33.7% in patients with TBI as compared to 11.5% in a control group of trauma patients with no central nervous system involvement (Tateno, Jorge, & Robinson, 2003). These measurements were taken within 6 months of the clearing of posttraumatic amnesia, when aggressive or violent behavior is supposedly reduced compared to the acute phase. There is some question, however, how much of this aggression was due to the TBI; those in the aggressive group were more likely to have a history of mood disorder, substance abuse, and interaction with the legal system due to past aggressive behavior. Alternately, those with frontal lobe lesions were also more likely to be aggressive (Tateno et al., 2003).

Within a neurobehavioral rehabilitation setting, aggression may be even more common. When considering any physical aggression toward self, others, or objects, Alderman (2007) found a rate of nearly one aggressive episode per patient per day. There was a higher rate of verbal aggression with nearly three episodes per patient per day. Over 24% of these episodes had no obvious antecedent (Alderman, 2007). This higher rate is not surprising, however, given the neurobehavioral rehabilitation unit where this data was collected specializes in those with severe and persistent behavior problems due to severe TBI.

Outside of such a specialized setting, there is some evidence aggression following moderate to severe TBI persists for extended periods of time. In one sample, at 6, 24, and 60 months post TBI, approximately 20% of patients demonstrated physical aggression toward others, compared to 4% of controls (Baguley, Cooper, & Felmingham, 2006).

Epilepsy

Epilepsy has sometimes been associated with violence. This is understandable in the context of those who are experiencing or recovering from seizures thrashing or resisting restraint while semiconscious or confused. It is less clear, however, what role seizures play in violence when the perpetrator appears to be conscious and acting seemingly purposefully. This may be the case on rare occasions during a complex partial seizure. Intermittent explosive disorder has also been theorized to involve epileptic activity.

COMPLEX PARTIAL SEIZURES

Epilepsy is a condition that has eluded precise definition through the years, but it can be described as a brain disorder characterized by the excessive neuronal discharge of an area of gray matter. This faulty discharge results in the hallmark symptom of the disorder, a seizure of some type. Seizures can be generalized—affecting the entire brain, resulting in a loss of consciousness and falling down, such as in grand mal seizures—or they can be what are referred to as partial seizures, which affect only a part of the brain. Partial seizures also come in several varieties, the most basic division of which can be described as simple partial seizures and complex partial seizures. In a simple partial seizure, the person remains alert and conscious throughout. These are often motor or sensory seizures; these may consist of phenomena such as one's arm contracting uncontrollably toward the face, or feelings of pins and needles that progress over parts of the body. Complex partial seizures, on the other hand, involve impairment of consciousness and lack of memory for the time of the seizure, although the person may appear alert and conscious. Complex partial seizures have historically been referred to as "temporal lobe epilepsy," although the seizure foci are not necessarily in the temporal lobe; the location must still be confirmed (Moore, 1997).

Complex partial seizures have a wide range of symptoms. They are sometimes precipitated by an "aura," or warning that one is about to have a seizure. The most common aura is the epigastric sensation, which is a feeling of something rising from the stomach, or of "butterflies" in the stomach, so to speak. Unpleasant olfactory hallucinations are another common aura. The seizure itself usually lasts no more than a few minutes; it is sometimes followed by a generalized tonic-clonic seizure. During the seizure the person will appear conscious but will not be acting consciously. The person may continue whatever activity he or she was performing before the seizure began, although this is usually with some impairment in performance (Moore, 1997).

Common symptoms of complex partial seizures include automatisms, which are where the person acts mechanically or repetitively with the environment. Some are reactive to the environment, whereas others appear unrelated and are called "stereotyped" automatisms. The most common stereotyped automatisms are handling nearby objects, chewing or lip smacking, and looking around. They can also include rocking in place, groaning, resisting restraint, and thrashing or kicking. Eye and head turning are also fairly common, as is a motionless stare (Moore, 1997). Reactive automatisms are sometimes in character for the person and sometimes are quite out of character. Out-of-character automatisms may include things such as removing articles of clothing, eating inappropriate objects, or other unacceptable social behavior. If another person attempts to restrain or redirect, or otherwise provokes an individual during a seizure in which he or she is experiencing automatisms, this may result in violent behavior clearly in excess of the provocation (Moore, 1997).

Violence toward persons or property may also occur during complex partial seizures that appear completely senseless. This can be in response to ictal hallucinations or may be spontaneously generated by the seizure but totally undirected. There is a great deal of skepticism, however, at the idea of unprovoked violence directed toward people during a complex partial seizure. Although there have been a number of cases reported, these episodes are rarely captured while the individual is being monitored with an electroencephalogram (EEG; Moore, 1997).

This has not stopped criminal defendants from using epilepsy as a defense during trial, albeit both the defense and its success are exceptional. One study of epilepsy as a defense examined the court records of England and Wales from 1975 to 2001. The authors identified only 13 cases where epilepsy was successfully used in conjunction with a not guilty by reason of insanity (NGRI) defense; this is in a court system that tries over 50,000 cases each year. These 13 cases accounted for 7.3% of all NGRI verdicts during that time period (Reuber & Mackay, 2008). Of note, 12 of these defendants had a confirmed diagnosis of epilepsy prior to the instant offense, and 10 had evidence of neurological or neuropsychological impairment. Perhaps of more import, however, eight of the offenses were committed while the perpetrators were intoxicated with alcohol and three occurred while the perpetrators were withdrawing from alcohol. The authors also state that three of the criminal acts were not directly linked to epileptic seizures. This makes a strong case that it is, indeed, very rare for criminal acts to be committed in association with seizures (Reuber & MacKay, 2008).

Complex partial seizures have also been associated with violence during the postictal period. This phenomena has been deemed subacute postictal aggression (SPA), although it is not yet a widely recognized syndrome (Ito et al., 2007). It is described as occurring shortly after the seizure and lasting approximately 5–30 minutes. It is spontaneous, directed aggressive behavior that can begin anywhere from minutes to hours after the conclusion of the seizure. SPA is believed to be very rare; to date, there are only 12 reported cases in the literature (Ito et al., 2007).

Intermittent Explosive Disorder

Intermittent explosive disorder (IED) is defined by the *DSM-IV-TR* (American Psychiatric Association [APA], 2000) as discrete episodes of aggression resulting in serious violence toward persons or property that are out of proportion to any precipitant. These "attacks" of violence are in many ways reminiscent of complex partial seizures and/or SPA given that the episode is sometimes preceded by a sense of tension or physical symptoms, such as tingling, tremor, or palpitations (APA, 2000), which are known symptoms of sensory and autonomic seizures. These rage attacks are also sometimes followed by feelings of fatigue, which is common in the postictal period. Recent studies have suggested IED is more common than previously thought, with a lifetime prevalence of 5.4%–7.3% (Kessler et al., 2006).

Some clinicians believe that IED is a form of complex partial epilepsy (Moore, 1997). This hypothesis may prove to be correct as nonspecific EEG findings have been reported (APA, 2000; Koelsch, Sammler, Jentschke, & Siebel, 2008), and a number of studies have reported success treating it with anticonvulsive medication (Jones et al., 2011). Others believe it is a distinct clinical entity; they believe that any EEG "abnormalities" found are misleading and can lead to an incorrect diagnosis of epilepsy (McTauge & Appleton, 2010). There are also case studies involving those with clear IED with normal 24-hour EEGs (see Maley, Alvernia, Valle, & Richardson, 2010, for one example). Regardless, violence occurring in the context of complex partial seizures may be distinguishable from nonseizure violence by assessing for the presence of a preseizure aura, simple automatisms during the seizure, secondary generalized seizures, and more specific biomarkers of epilepsy (Moore, 1997). IED is also far more common than epilepsy, which has a lifetime prevalence of .7% (Hirtz et al., 2007), of which complex partial epilepsy necessarily makes up a smaller proportion. It seems most likely that while there may be cases of IED that are undiagnosed epilepsy, the majority of IED is not due to seizure activity.

CONCLUSION

While violence is in no way exclusively a product of neurophysiological mechanisms, there are certainly a number of biological influences that predispose individuals to violence. From genetic code, to neurodevelopmental structural abnormality, to neurotransmitter imbalances, to neurodegenerative diseases, an individual may inherit or acquire any number of biological factors that increase his or her likelihood of violence. With recent advances in technology, particularly the fields of genetics and functional neuroimaging, our understanding of the biological basis of violence has grown immensely in only the past decade. And yet, it is just now that we are beginning to move past the stage of using gross neuroanatomical and biological measurements to understand the complex and nonlinear relationships between these variables and violent behavior. Advances in this field will likely happen at an astonishing pace, given these developments. The biological underpinnings of violence have never shown so much promise for increased understanding and intervention as they do going forward from today.

REFERENCES

Alderman, N. (2007). Prevalence, characteristics and causes of aggressive behavior observed within a neurobehavioural rehabilitation service: Predictors and implications for management. *Brain Injury, 21*(9), 891–911.

Amen, D. G., Hanks, C., Prunella, J. R., & Green, A. (2007). An analysis of regional cerebral blood flow in impulsive murderers using single photon emission computed tomography. *Journal of Neuropsychiatry and Clinical Neuroscience, 19*, 304–309.

American College of Radiology. (2010). ACR appropriateness criteria: Dementia and movement disorders. Retrieved September 2012, from http://www.acr.org/~/media/ACR/Documents/AppCriteria/Diagnostic/DementiaAndMovementDisorders.pdf.

American College of Radiology. (2011a). ACR appropriateness criteria: Cerebrovascular disease. Retrieved September 2012, from http://www.acr.org/~/media/ACR/Documents/AppCriteria/Diagnostic/CerebrovascularDisease.pdf.

American College of Radiology. (2011b). ACR appropriateness criteria: Seizures and epilepsy. Retrieved September 2012, from http://www.acr.org/~/media/ACR/Documents/AppCriteria/Diagnostic/SeizuresAndEpilepsy.pdf.

American College of Radiology. (2012). ACR appropriateness criteria: Head trauma. Retrieved September 2012, from http://www.acr.org/~/media/ACR/Documents/AppCriteria/Diagnostic/HeadTrauma.pdf.

American Psychiatric Association. (2000). *Diagnostic and statistical manual of mental disorders* (4th ed., text rev.). Washington, DC: American Psychiatric Association.

Badawy, A. (1998). Alcohol, aggression and serotonin: Metabolic aspects. *Alcohol and Alcoholism, 33*(1), 66–72.

Baguley, I., Cooper, J., & Felmingham, K. (2006). Aggressive behavior following traumatic brain injury: How common is common? *Journal of Head Trauma Rehabilitation, 21*(1), 45–56.

Beaver, K. (2010). The biochemistry of violent crime. In C. J. Ferguson (Ed.), *Violent crime: Clinical and social implications*. Los Angeles, CA: Sage.

Bechara, A. (2007). *Iowa Gambling Task (IGT) professional manual*. Lutz, FL: Psychological Assessment Resources.

Blair, R., Peschardt, K., Budhani, S., Mitchell, D., & Pine, D. (2006). The development of psychopathy. *Journal of Child Psychology and Psychiatry, 47*(3), 262–275.

Blumenfeld, H. (2002). *Neuroanatomy through clinical cases*. Sunderland, MA: Sinauer Associates.

Böhnke, R., Bertsch, K., Kruk, M., & Naumann, E. (2010). The relationship between basal and acute HPA axis activity and aggressive behavior in adults. *Journal of Neural Transmission, 117*, 629–637.

Booij, L., Tremblay, R., Leyton, M., Séguin, J., Vitaro, F., Gravel, P., ... Benkelfat, C. (2010). Brain serotonin synthesis in adult males characterized by physical aggression during childhood: A 21-year longitudinal study. *PLoS One*, 5(6), e11255. doi: 10.1371/journal.pone.0011255

Broomhall, L. (2005). Acquired sociopathy: A neuropsychological study of executive dysfunction in violent offenders. *Psychiatry, Psychology, and Law*, 12(2), 367–387.

Brunner, H., Nelen, M., van Zandvoort, P., Abeling, N., van Gennip, A., Wolters, E., ... van Oost, B. (1993). X-linked borderline mental retardation with prominent behavioral disturbance: Phenotype, genetic localization, and evidence for disturbed monoamine metabolism. *American Journal of Human Genetics*, 52, 1032–1039.

Butler, T., Schofield, P., Greenberg, D., Allnutt, S., Indig, D., Carr, V., ... Ellis, A. (2010). Reducing impulsivity in repeat violent offenders: An open label trial of a selective serotonin reuptake inhibitor. *Australian and New Zealand Journal of Psychiatry*, 44, 1137–1143.

Carré, J., McCormick, C., & Hariri, A. (2011). The social neuroendocrinology of human aggression. *Psychoneuroendocrinology*, 36(7), 935–944.

Cummings, J., & Miller, B. (2007). Conceptual and clinical aspects of the frontal lobes. In B. Miller & J. Cummings (Eds.), *The human frontal lobes: Functions and disorders* (2nd ed., pp. 12–24). New York, NY: Guilford Press.

De Wall, C., Deckman, T., Gailliot, M., & Bushman, B. (2011). Sweetened blood cools hot tempers: Physiological self-control and aggression. *Aggressive Behavior*, 37, 73–80.

Delis, D., Kaplan, E., & Kramer, J. (2001). *The Delis-Kaplan executive function system*. New York, NY: Psychological Corporation/Harcourt Assessment.

Dolan, M. (2010). What imaging tells us about violence in anti-social men. *Criminal Behaviour and Mental Health*, 20, 199–214.

Fabian, J. (2010). Neuropsychological and neurological correlates in violent and homicidal offenders: A legal and neuroscience perspective. *Aggression and Violent Behavior*, 15, 209–223.

Franzini, A., Marras, C., Ferroli, P., Bugiani, O., & Broggi, G. (2005). Stimulation of the posterior hypothalamus for medically intractable impulsive and violent behavior. *Stereotactic and Functional Neurosurgery*, 83, 63–66.

Frisell, T., Lichtenstein, P., & Långström, N. (2010). Violent crime runs in families: A total population study of 12.5 million individuals. *Psychological Medicine*, 41(1), 97–105.

Giammanco, M., Tabacchi, G., Giammanco, S., Di Majo, D., & La Guardia, M. (2005). Testosterone and aggressiveness. *Medical Science Monitor*, 11(4), RA136–145.

Golomb, B., Evans, M., White, H., & Dimsdale, J. (2012). Trans fat consumption and aggression. *PLoS One*, 7(3), e32175.

Golomb, B., Stattin, H., & Mednick, S. (2000). Low cholesterol and violent crime. *Journal of Psychiatric Research*, 34, 301–309.

Hancock, M., Tapscott, J., & Hoaken, P. (2010). Rose of executive dysfunction in predicting frequency and severity of violence. *Aggressive Behavior*, 36, 338–349.

Hanlon, R., Rubin, L., Jensen, M., & Daoust, S. (2010). Neuropsychological features of indigent murder defendants and death row inmates in relation to homicidal aspects of their crimes. *Archives of Clinical Neuropsychology*, 25, 1–13.

Hernando, V., Pastor, J., Pedrosa, M., Peña, E., & Sola, R. (2008). Low-frequency bilateral hypothalamic stimulation for treatment of drug-resistant aggressiveness in a young man with mental retardation. *Stereotactic and Functional Neurosurgery*, 86, 219–223.

Hibbeln, J., Ferguson, T., & Blasbalg, T. (2006). Omega-3 fatty acid deficiencies in neurodevelopment, aggression and autonomic dysregulation: Opportunities for intervention. *International Review of Psychiatry, 18*(2), 107–118.

Hagen, C. (1998). *The Rancho Levels of Cognitive Functioning* (3rd ed., rev.) Retrieved May 2014, from: http://www.rancho.org/research/cognitive_levels.pdf.

Hirtz, D., Thurman, D., Gwinn-Hardy, K., Mohamed, M., Chaudhuri, A., & Zalutsky, R. (2007). How common are the "common" neurologic disorders? *Neurology, 68,* 326–337.

Hochman, G., Yechiam, E., & Bechara, A. (2010). Recency gets larger as lesions move from anterior to posterior locations within the ventromedial prefrontal cortex. *Behavioural Brain Research, 213,* 27–34.

Hoptman, M. J. (2003). Neuroimaging studies of violence and antisocial behavior. *Journal of Psychiatric Practice, 9,* 265–278.

Hoskins, L., Roth, R., & Giancola, P. (2010). Neuroimaging of aggression: Empirical findings and implications. In A. M. Horton, Jr. & L. Hartlage (Eds.), *Handbook of forensic neuropsychology* (2nd ed., pp. 137–174). New York, NY: Springer.

Ito, M., Okazaki, M., Takahashi, S., Muramatsu, R., Kato, M., & Onuma, T. (2007). Subacute postictal aggression in patients with epilepsy. *Epilepsy and Behavior, 10,* 611–614.

Jones, R., Arlidge, J. Gillham, R., Reagu, S., van den Bree, M., & Taylor, P. (2011). Efficacy of mood stabilizers in the treatment of impulsive or repetitive aggression: Systematic review and meta-analysis. *British Journal of Psychiatry, 198,* 93–98.

Kaufer, D. (2007). The dorsolateral and cingulate cortex. In B. Miller & J. Cummings (Eds.), *The human frontal lobes: Functions and disorders* (2nd ed., pp. 44–58). New York, NY: Guilford Press.

Keene, J., Hope, T., Fairburn, C., Jacoby, R., Gedling, K., & Ware, C. (1999). Natural history of aggressive behaviour in dementia. *International Journal of Geriatric Psychiatry, 14,* 541–548.

Kessler, R., Coccaro, E., Fava, M., Jaeger, S., Jin, R., & Walters, E. (2006). The prevalence and correlates of DSM-IV intermittent explosive disorder in the National Comorbidity Survey replication. *Archives of General Psychiatry, 63*(6), 669–678.

Knopman, D. S., DeKosky, S. T., Cummings, J. L., Chui, H., Corey-Bloom, J., Relkin, N., … Stevens, J. C. (2001). Practice parameter: Diagnosis of dementia (an evidence-based review). Report of the Quality Standards Subcommittee of the American Academy of Neurology. *Neurology, 56*(9), 1143–1153.

Koelsch, S., Sammler, D., Jentschke, S., & Siebel, W. (2008). EEG correlates of moderate intermittent explosive disorder. *Clinical Neurophysiology, 119,* 151–162.

Krämer, U., Riba, J., Richter, S., & Münte, T. (2011). An fMRI study on the role of serotonin in reactive aggression. *PLoS One, 6*(11), e27668.

Kunik, M., Snow, A., Davila, J., Steele, A., Balasubramanyam, V., Doody, R., … Morgan, R. (2010). Causes of aggressive behavior in patients with dementia. *Journal of Clinical Psychiatry, 71*(9), 1145–1152.

Leestma, J. E. (2005). *Forensic neuropathology* (2nd ed.). Boca Raton, FL: CRC/Taylor & Francis.

Levi, M., Nussbaum, D., & Rich, J. (2010). Neuropsychological and personality characteristics of predatory, irritable, and non-violent offenders: Support for a typology of criminal human aggression. *Criminal Justice and Behavior, 37,* 633–655.

Li, X., Lu, Z., D'Argembeau, A., Ng, M., & Bechara, A. (2010). The Iowa Gambling Task in fMRI images. *Human Brain Mapping, 31,* 410–423.

Maley, J., Alvernia, J., Valle, E., & Richardson, D. (2010). Deep brain stimulation of the orbitofrontal projections for the treatment of intermittent explosive disorder. *Neurosurgical Focus, 29*(2), E11, 1–5.

McEllistrem, J. (2004). Affective and predatory violence: A bimodal classification system of human aggression and violence. *Aggression and Violent Behavior, 10*, 1–30.

McTague, A., & Appleton, R. (2010). Episodic dyscontrol syndrome. *Archives of Disease in Childhood, 95*(10), 841–842.

Meloy, J. R. (2006). Empirical basis and forensic application of affective and predatory violence. *Australian and New Zealand Journal of Psychiatry, 40*, 539–547.

Mercer, K., Selby, M., & McClung, J. (2005). The effects of psychopathy, violence, and drug use on neuropsychological functioning. *American Journal of Forensic Psychology, 23*(3), 65–86).

Meyer-Lindenberg, A., Buckholtz, J., Kolachana, B., Hariri, A., Pezawas, L., Blasi, G., … Weinberger, D. (2006). Neural mechanisms of genetic risk for impulsivity and violence in humans. *Proceedings of the National Academy of Sciences USA, 103*(16), 6269–6274.

Moore, D. (1997). *Partial seizures and interictal disorders: The neuropsychiatric elements.* Boston, MA: Butterworth-Heinemann.

Moore, T., Scarpa, A., & Raine, A., (2002). A meta-analysis of serotonin metabolite 5-HIAA and antisocial behavior. *Aggressive Behavior, 28*, 299–316.

Morgan, A. & Lilienfeld, S. (2000). A meta-analytic review of the relation between antisocial behavior and neuropsychological measures of executive function. *Clinical Psychology Review, 20*(1), 113–136.

Mpakopoulou, M., Gatos, H., Brotis, A., Paterakis, K., & Fountas, K. (2008). Stereotactic amygdalotomy in the management of severe aggressive behavioral disorders. *Neurosurgical Focus, 25*(1), 1–6.

Nott, M., Chapparo, C., & Baguley, I. (2006). Agitation following traumatic brain injury: An Australian sample. *Brain Injury, 20*(11), 1175–1182.

Nott, M., Chapparo, C., Heard, R., & Baguley, I. (2010). Patterns of agitated behavior during acute brain injury rehabilitation. *Brain Injury, 24*(10), 1214–1221.

Ogilvie, J., Stewart, A., Chan, R., & Shum, D. (2011). Neuropsychological measures of executive function and antisocial behavior: A meta-analysis. *Criminology, 49*, 1063–1107.

Ormiston, T., Wolkowitz, O., Reus, V., & Manfredi, F. (2003). Behavioral implications of lowering cholesterol levels: A double-blind pilot study. *Psychosomatics, 44*(5), 412–414.

Passamonti, L., Crockett, M., Apergis-Schoute, A., Clark, L., Rowe, J., Calder, A., & Robbins, T. (2011). Effects of acute tryptophan depletion on prefrontal-amygdala connectivity while viewing facial signals of aggression. *Biological Psychiatry.* Advance online publication. doi: 10.1016/j.biopsych.2011.07.033

Pavlov, K., Chistiakov, D., & Chekhonin, V. (2012). Genetic determinants of aggression and impulsivity in humans. *Journal of Applied Genetics, 53*, 61–82.

Raine, A., Ishikawa, S., Arce, E., Lencz, T., Knuth, K., Bihrle, S., … Colletti, P. (2004). Hippocampal structural asymmetry in unsuccessful psychopaths. *Biological Psychiatry, 55*, 185–191.

Raine, A., Meloy, J. Bihrle, S., Stoddard, J., LaCasse, L., & Buchsbaum, M. (1998). Reduced prefrontal and increased subcortical brain functioning assessed using positron emission tomography in predatory and affective murderers. *Behavioral Sciences and the Law, 16*, 319–332.

Rajender, S., Pandu, G., Sharma, J., Gandhi, K., Singh, L., & Thangaraj, K. (2008). Reduced CAG repeats length in androgen receptor gene is associated with violent criminal behavior. *International Journal of Legal Medicine, 122*(5), 367–372.

Rao, V., Rosenberg, P., Bertrand, M., Salehinia, S., Spiro, J., Vaishnavi, S., … Miles, Q. (2009). Aggression after traumatic brain injury: Prevalence and correlates. *Journal of Neuropsychiatry and Clinical Neuroscience, 21*(4), 420–429.

Reuber, M., & Mackay, R. (2008). Epileptic automatisms in the criminal courts: 13 cases tried in England and Wales between 1975 and 2001. *Epilepsia, 49*(1), 138–145.

Rhee, S., & Waldman, I. (2007). Behavior-genetics of criminality and aggression. In D. Flannery, A. Vazsonyi, & I. Waldman (Eds.), *The Cambridge handbook of violent behavior and aggression* (pp. 77–90). New York, NY: Cambridge University Press.

Soderstrom, H., Blennow, K., Forsman, A., Liesivuori, J., Pennanen, S., & Tiihonen, J. (2004). A controlled study of tryptophan and cortisol in violent offenders. *Journal of Neural Transmission, 111*, 1605–1610.

Tateno, A., Jorge, R., & Robinson, R. (2003). Clinical correlates of aggressive behavior after traumatic brain injury. *Journal of Neuropsychiatry and Clinical Neuroscience, 15*(2), 155–160.

Tenneij, N., & Koot, H. (2008). Incidence, types, and characteristics of aggressive behaviour in treatment facilities for adults with mild intellectual disability and severe challenging behaviour. *Journal of Intellectual Disability Research, 52*, 114–124.

Tiihonen, J., Rossi, R., Laakso, M., Hodgins, S., Testa, C., Perez, J., … Frisoni, G. (2008). Brain anatomy of persistent violent offenders: More rather than less. *Psychiatry Research: Neuroimaging, 163*, 201–212.

Tiihonen, J., Virkkunen, M., Räsänen, P., Pennanen, S., Sainio, E., Callaway, J., … Liesivuori, J. (2001). Free l-tryptophan plasma levels in antisocial violent offenders. *Psychopharmacology, 157*, 395–400.

Toplak, M., Sorge, G., Benoit, A., West, R., & Stanovich, K. (2010). Decision-making and cognitive abilities: A review of associations between Iowa Gambling Task performance, executive functions, and intelligence. *Clinical Psychology Review, 30*, 562–581.

Van Honk, J., Harmon-Jones, E., Morgan, B., & Schutter, D. (2010). Socially explosive minds: The triple imbalance hypothesis of reactive aggression. *Journal of Personality, 78*(1), 67–94.

Vevera, J., Fišar, Z., Kvasnička, T., Zdeněk, H., Starkova, L., Česka, R., & Papezova, H. (2005). Cholesterol-lowering therapy evokes time-limited changes in serotonergic transmission. *Psychiatry Research, 133*, 197–203.

Virkkunen, M., Rissanen, A., Franssila-Kallunki, A., & Tilhonen, J. (2009). Low non-oxidative glucose metabolism and violent offending: An 8-year prospective follow-up study. *Psychiatry Research, 168*(1), 26–31.

Wahlund, K., & Kristiansson, M. (2009). Aggression, psychopathy and brain imaging— Review and future recommendations. *International Journal of Law and Psychiatry, 32*, 266–271.

Williams, W., Mewse, A., Tonks, J., Mills, S., Burgess, N., & Cordan, G. (2010). Traumatic brain injury in a prison population: Prevalence and risk for re-offending. *Brain Injury, 24*(10), 1184–1188.

Whitman, C. (1966, July 31). Personal letter. Collection of the Austin History Center, Austin, TX. Retrieved September 2012, from http://alt.cimedia.com/statesman/spe cialreports/whitman/letter.pdf.

Yang, Y., & Raine, A. (2009). Prefrontal structural and functional brain imaging findings in antisocial, violent, and psychopathic individuals: A meta-analysis. *Psychiatry Research, 174*(2), 81–88.

Zuidema, S., de Jonghe, J., Verhey, F., & Koopmans, R. (2009). Predictors of neuropsychiatric symptoms in nursing home patients: Influence of gender and dementia severity. *International Journal of Geriatric Psychiatry, 24*, 1079–1086.

21

Violence

Psychiatric Assessment and Intervention

CHARLES SCOTT, PHILIP J. RESNICK, AND WILLIAM NEWMAN ■

Mental health clinicians are often asked to determine an individual's risk of future violence. Dangerousness assessments are required in a wide variety of situations, including involuntary commitments, emergency psychiatric evaluations, seclusion and restraint release decisions, inpatient care discharges, probation/parole decisions, death penalty evaluations, domestic violence interventions, fitness-for-duty evaluations, and postthreat situations. The term "dangerousness" is not a psychiatric diagnosis; the concept of dangerousness is a legal judgment based on social policy. In other words, dangerousness is a broader concept than either violence or dangerous behavior; it indicates an individual's propensity to commit dangerous acts (Mulvey & Lidz, 1984).

Unfortunately, no psychological test or interview can predict future violence with high accuracy. Relatively infrequent events (e.g., homicide) are more difficult to predict than more common events (e.g., domestic violence) because they have a low base rate of occurrence. The accuracy of a clinician's assessment of future violence is related to many factors, including the circumstances of the evaluation and the length of time over which violence is predicted.

When conducting a violence risk assessment, the clinician may find it helpful to divide the concept of dangerousness into five components. The first component is the magnitude of potential harm that is threatened. Behavior may involve physical harm to persons or property, as well as psychological harm to others. In addition to identifying the likely target of violence, the degree of anticipated harm should be understood. For example, threatening to shoot someone in the head foreshadows a much greater risk of serious harm than threatening to kick someone in the leg.

The second component of dangerousness is the likelihood that a violent act will take place. Here it is important to clarify the seriousness of the person's intent to cause harm. A person's history of acting on violent thoughts is the best predictor that violent intentions will be carried out. The third component is the imminence of the harm. For example, is the person threatening harm in the next 10 hours or the next 10 days? The fourth component examines the frequency of a behavior.

Frequency is defined as the number of times a particular act has occurred over a specified period of time. The greater the frequency of an aggressive act, the higher the risk that the behavior will reoccur in the future. Situational factors constitute the fifth component of potential dangerousness. Situational factors that increase the risk of future violence include association with a criminally offending peer group, lack of financial resources and housing, easy access to weapons, and exposure to alcohol or illicit drugs.

RISK FACTORS ASSOCIATED WITH VIOLENCE

Demographic Factors and Violence Risk

The clinical assessment of dangerousness requires a review of several risk factors that have been associated with an increased likelihood of future violence (Humphreys, Johnstone, MacMillan, & Taylor, 1992; Pearson, Wilmot, & Padi, 1992; Swanson, Holzer, Ganju, & Jono, 1990). For example, data from the Epidemiologic Catchment Area study showed violent behavior generally was associated with younger age groups.

Males perpetrate violent acts approximately 10 times more often than females (Tardiff & Sweillam, 1980). In contrast, among people with mental disorders, men and women do not significantly differ in their base rates of violent behavior. In fact, rates are remarkably similar and in some cases slightly higher for women (Lidz, Mulvey, & Gardner, 1993; Newhill, Mulvey, & Lidz, 1995).

The examiner should also consider the patient's economic status because violence is nearly three times as common among individuals in lower income brackets (Borum, Swartz, & Swanson, 1996). The risk of violence also increases for those with lower intelligence and mild mental retardation (Borum et al., 1996; Quinsey & Maquire, 1986).

Evaluating Violence History

A history of violence is the single best predictor of future violent behavior (Klassen & O'Connor, 1988). It is helpful to ask individuals about the most violent thing that they have ever done. Obtaining a detailed violence history involves determining the type of violent behavior, why violence occurred, who was involved, the presence of intoxication, and the degree of injury. Each prior episode of violence increases the risk of a future violent act (Borum et al., 1996).

Additional sources of information relevant in assessing a person's potential for violence include a military and work history. Persons who are laid off from work are six times more likely to be violent than their employed peers (Catalano, Dooley, Novaco, Wilson, & Hough, 1993).

A person who has used weapons against others in the past may pose a serious risk of future violence. The main difference between assault and homicide is the lethality of the weapon used. Loaded guns have the highest lethality of any weapon. An assault with a gun is five times more likely to result in a fatality than an attack with a knife (Zimring, 1991). Subjects should be asked whether they own or have ever owned a weapon. The recent movement of a weapon, such as transferring a gun from a closet to a nightstand, is particularly ominous in a paranoid person. The greater the psychotic fear, the more likely the paranoid person is to kill someone he or she misperceives as a persecutor in misperceived self-defense.

Substance Use and Violence Risk

Drugs and alcohol are strongly associated with violent behavior (The MacArthur Foundation, 2001; Pulay et al., 2008). The majority of persons involved in violent crimes are under the influence of alcohol at the time of their aggression (Murdoch, Pihl, & Ross, 1990). Stimulants, such as cocaine, crack, amphetamines, and PCP, are of special concern. These drugs typically result in feelings of disinhibition, grandiosity, and paranoia. Among psychiatric patients, a coexisting diagnosis of substance abuse is strongly predictive of violence (The MacArthur Foundation, 2001). The comorbidity of substance abuse and dependence accounts for a significant attributable portion of the violence committed by individuals with mental disorders.

Mental Disorders and Violence Risk

Studies examining whether individuals with mental illness are more violent than the non–mentally ill have yielded mixed results (Steadman et al., 1998; Torrey, 1994). Reported prevalence rates of violence by mentally ill individuals vary according to the sample type studied and the time frame examined (Choe, Teplin, & Abram, 2008). The MacArthur Study of Mental Disorder and Violence provided a specific definition for violence and followed patients prospectively for 1 year. This study involved civilly committed psychiatric patients released into the community. The authors concluded that most mentally ill individuals were not violent (Monahan, 1997). Although a weak relationship between mental illness and violence was noted, violent conduct was greater only during periods in which the person was experiencing acute psychiatric symptoms. In addition, Monahan noted that substance abuse was a much greater risk factor for violence than mental illness (Monahan et al., 2001).

PSYCHOSIS AND VIOLENCE RISK

The presence of psychosis is of particular concern when evaluating a person's risk of future violence. To illustrate, individuals with schizophrenia or another psychotic disorder have a 20 times greater risk of committing homicide compared with the general population (Fazel, Langstrom, Hjern, Grann, & Lichtenstein, 2009).

In paranoid psychotic patients, violence is often well planned and in line with their false beliefs. The violence is usually directed at a specific person who is perceived as a persecutor. Relatives or friends are often the targets of the paranoid individual. In addition, paranoid persons in the community are more likely to be dangerous because they have greater access to weapons (Krakowski, Volavka, & Brizer, 1986).

Do specific delusions increase the risk that a person will behave violently? Research examining the contribution of delusions to violent behavior does not provide a clear answer to this question. Earlier studies suggested that persecutory delusions were associated with an increased risk of aggression (Wessely et al., 1993). Delusions noted to increase the risk of violence were those characterized by threat/control override symptoms. These delusions involve the following beliefs: that the mind is dominated by forces beyond the person's control; that thoughts are being put into the person's head; that people are wishing the person harm; and that the person is being followed (Link & Stueve, 1995).

In contrast, results from the MacArthur Study of Mental Disorder and Violence (The MacArthur Foundation, 2001; Monahan et al., 2001) showed that the presence of delusions did not predict higher rates of violence among recently discharged psychiatric patients. In particular, a relationship between the presence of threat/control override delusions and violent behavior was not found.

The seemingly contradictory findings on the relationship of threat/control override delusions to violent behavior may be explained, in part, by gender. For example, in a reanalysis of the findings from the MacArthur Violence Risk Assessment study, researchers found men and women coped with threat delusions differently. In particular, men were significantly more likely to engage in violent behavior when experiencing threat delusions, in contrast to women, who were actually less likely to behave violently under the same circumstance (Teasdale, Silver, & Monahan, 2006).

Finally, a propensity to act on delusions in general (not including violent actions) is significantly associated with a tendency to commit violent acts (Monahan et al., 2001). Therefore, the clinician should inquire not only about the relationship between prior acts of violence and delusions but also about prior acts that resulted from delusional beliefs.

A careful inquiry about hallucinations is required to determine whether their presence increases the person's risk to commit a violent act. Command hallucinations are those that provide some type of directive to the patient. Command hallucinations are experienced by approximately half of hallucinating psychiatric patients (Shawyer et al., 2003). The majority of command hallucinations are nonviolent in nature and patients are more likely to act on nonviolent versus violent commands (Chadwick & Birchwood, 1994).

The literature on factors associated with a person acting on harmful command hallucinations has been mixed. In a review of seven controlled studies examining the relationship between command hallucinations and violence, no study demonstrated a positive relationship between command hallucinations and violence, and one found an inverse relationship (Rudnick, 1999). In contrast, McNiel, Eisner, and Binder (2000) reported that in a study of 103 civil psychiatric inpatients, 33% reported having had command hallucinations to harm others during the prior year and 22% of the patients reported that they complied with such commands. The authors concluded that patients in their study who experienced command hallucinations to harm others were more than twice as likely to be violent.

Much of the literature examining the relationship of a person's actions to command hallucinations has examined the person's response to all command hallucinations, without delineating factors specific to violent commands. Six factors associated with acting on command hallucinations in general include the following (Shawyer et al., 2008):

1. The presence of coexisting delusions (Mackinnon et al., 2004)
2. Having delusions that relate to the hallucination (Junginger, 1990)
3. Knowing the voice's identity (Junginger, 1990)
4. Believing the voices to be real (Erkwoh et al., 2002)
5. Believing that the voices are benevolent (Beck-Sander, Birchwood, & Chadwick, 1997)
6. Having few coping strategies to deal with the voices (Mackinnon et al., 2004)
7. Not feeling in control over the voices (Beck-Sander et al., 1997)

Factors associated with acting on general command hallucinations as described earlier have also been found to indicate increased compliance with acting on violent command hallucinations (Beck-Sander et al., 1997; Junginger, 1990). Studies that have examined compliance specific to harmful command hallucinations provide additional guidance when evaluating the person's potential risk of harm. Additional aspects relevant to increased compliance to more violent command hallucinations include the following:

1. A belief that the voice is powerful (Fox, Gray, & Lewis, 2004; Shawyer et al., 2008)
2. A sense of personal superiority by the person evaluated (Fox et al., 2004)
3. A belief that command hallucinations are of benefit to the person (Shawyer et al., 2008)
4. Having delusions that were congruent with the action described (Shawyer et al., 2008)
5. Experiencing hallucinations that generate negative emotions such as anger, anxiety, and sadness (Cheung, Schweitzer, Crowley, & Tuckwell, 1997)

In addition to evaluating positive symptoms of psychosis, the clinician should also assess the patient's insight into his or her illness and into the potential legal complications it might have. Buckley et al. (2004) found that violent patients with schizophrenia had more prominent lack of insight regarding their illness and legal complications of their behavior when compared with a nonviolent comparison group. However, a subsequent research study of 209 schizophrenic patients followed for 2 years after hospital discharge found that aggressive behavior was more strongly associated with high scores for psychopathy traits and positive symptoms than with lack of insight (Lincoln & Hodgins, 2008).

Schizophrenia and Violence Risk

Delusions and hallucinations are prominent symptoms of schizophrenia. Although the majority of individuals with schizophrenia do not behave violently (Walsh,

Buchanan, & Fahy, 2002), there is emerging evidence that a diagnosis of schizophrenia is associated with an increase in criminal offending. In a retrospective review of 2,861 Australian patients with schizophrenia followed over a 25-year period, Wallace, Mullen and Burgess (2004) found that patients with schizophrenia accumulated a greater total number of criminal convictions and were significantly more likely to have been convicted of a criminal offense (including violent offenses) relative to matched comparison subjects. These authors noted that the criminal behaviors committed by schizophrenic patients could not be entirely accounted for by comorbid substance use, active symptoms, or characteristics of systems of care (Wallace et al., 2004). In marked contrast to this finding, Fazel et al. (2009) concluded from their study of over 8,000 schizophrenics that the association between schizophrenic and violent crime is minimal unless the patient is also diagnosed as having substance abuse comorbidity.

MOOD DISORDERS AND VIOLENCE RISK

Most studies examining the relationship between mood disorders and violence have not differentiated between bipolar disorder, mania, and depression (Graz, Etschel, Schoech, & Soyka, 2009). To evaluate whether criminal behavior and violent crimes were more common in the diagnosis of depression versus mania, Graz et al. (2009) examined the national crime register for 1,561 patients with an affective disorder who had been released into the community. The rate of criminal behavior and violent crimes was highest in the manic disorder group (15.7%) compared to patients with major depressive disorder (1.4%). The authors concluded that different mood disorders have different risks of subsequent violence. Other studies have examined violence risk factors unique to different mood disorders and these are summarized next.

Depression and Violence Risk

Depression may result in violent behavior, particularly in depressed individuals who strike out against others in despair. After committing a violent act, the depressed person may attempt suicide. Depression is the most common diagnosis in murder-suicides (Marzuk, Tardiff, & Hirsch, 1992). Studies examining mothers who kill their children (filicide) have found that they were often suffering severe depression. High rates of suicide following a filicide have been noted with between 16% and 29% of mothers and 40% and 60% of fathers taking their life after murdering their child (Hatters Friedman, Hrouda, Holden, Noffsinger, & Resnick, 2005; Marzuk et al., 1992; Rodenburg, 1971). In a study of 30 family filicide-suicide files, the most common motive involved an attempt by the perpetrator to relieve real or imagined suffering of the child, an action known as an altruistic filicide. Eighty percent of the parents in this study had evidence of a past or current psychiatric history with nearly 60% suffering from depression, 27% with psychosis, and 20% experiencing delusional beliefs (Hatters Friedman et al., 2005).

In their analysis of 386 individuals from the MacArthur Violence Risk Assessment Study with a categorical diagnosis of depression, Yang, Mulvey, Loughran, and Hanusa (2012) noted two important findings relevant to depression and future violence risk. First, violence that had occurred within the past 10 weeks was a strong predictor of violence by participants with depression, but not by participants with a psychotic disorder. This finding suggests that a past history of *recent* violence may represent a higher risk of future violence in depressed patients than in those with psychosis. Second, this risk of future harm by depressed patients was further increased with alcohol use.

Bipolar Disorder and Violence Risk

Patients with mania show a high percentage of assaultive or threatening behavior, but serious violence itself is rare (Krakowski et al., 1986). Additionally, patients with mania show considerably less criminality of all kinds than patients with schizophrenia. Patients with mania most commonly exhibit violent behavior when they are restrained or have limits set on their behavior (Tardiff & Sweillam, 1980).

Active manic symptoms have been suggested as playing a substantial role in criminal behavior. In particular, Fazel et al. (2010) compared violent crime convictions for over 3,700 individuals diagnosed with bipolar disorder with general population controls and unaffected full siblings. This longitudinal study had two main findings. First, although individuals with bipolar disorder exhibited an increased risk for violent crime compared to the general population, most of the excess violent crime was associated with substance abuse comorbidity. Second, unaffected siblings also had an increased risk for violent crime, highlighting the contribution of genetics or early environmental factors in families with bipolar disorder.

Cognitive Impairment and Violence Risk

Brain injury has been associated with aggressive behavior. After a brain injury, formerly normal individuals may become verbally and physically aggressive (National Institutes of Health, 1998). Characteristic features of aggression resulting from a brain injury include reactive behavior triggered by trivial stimuli, lack of planning or reflection, nonpurposeful action with no clear aims or goals, explosive outbursts without a gradual buildup, an episodic pattern with long periods of relative calm, and feelings of concern and remorse following an episode.

Epilepsy has also been described as having a relationship to violence. However, the evidence for this relationship has focused primarily on small prisoner samples or children with epilepsy (Fazel, Lichtenstein, Grann, & Langstrom, 2011). In their study of 22, 000 individuals with traumatic brain injury and 22,000 individuals with epilepsy, Fazel et al. (2011) evaluated whether persons with either of these disorders were at an increased risk for violent crime compared with the general population or unaffected siblings. The authors reported several important findings. First, individuals with traumatic brain injury had a significantly increased risk of violent crime, particularly in cases involving focal brain injuries or injury after age 16. Second, after adjusting for familiar variables, epilepsy was not associated with an increased risk of violent crime. Therefore, although evaluators should consider traumatic brain injury a risk factor for future violence, such causality does not appear to have been firmly established for epilepsy (Fazel et al., 2011).

Personality Factors and Violence Risk

Violence is also associated with certain personality traits and disorders. While borderline (Meloy, 1992; Tardiff & Sweillam, 1980) and sadistic (Meloy,

1992) personality disorders are associated with increased violence, the most common personality disorder associated with violence is antisocial personality disorder (The MacArthur Foundation, 2001). The violence by those with antisocial personality disorder is often motivated by revenge or occurs during a period of heavy drinking. Violence among these persons is frequently cold and calculated and lacks emotionality (Williamson, Hare, & Wong, 1987). Low IQ and antisocial personality disorder are a particularly ominous combination for increasing the risk of future violence (Heilbrun, 1990).

In addition to *DSM-IV-TR* personality disorders or traits, the clinician should also be familiar with the psychological construct known as psychopathy. The term *psychopath* was described by Cleckley (1976) as an individual who is superficially charming, lacks empathy, lacks close relationships, is impulsive, and is concerned primarily with self-gratification. Hare and colleagues developed the Psychopathy Checklist-Revised (PCL-R) (Hare, 1991) as a validated measure of psychopathy in adults. The concept of psychopathy is important because the presence of psychopathy is a strong predictor of criminal behavior generally and violence among adults (Salekin, Rogers, & Sewell, 1996). Psychopathy is more predictive of violence than a diagnosis of antisocial personality disorder.

ASSESSING CURRENT DANGEROUSNESS

When conducting an assessment of current dangerousness, play close attention to the individual's affect. Individuals who are angry and lack empathy for others are at increased risk for violent behavior (Menzies, Webster, & Sepejak, 1985). When evaluating a patient with persecutory delusions, the clinician should also inquire whether the patient has employed "safety actions." Safety actions are specific behaviors (such as avoidance of a perceived persecutor or an escape from a fearful situation) that the individual has employed with the intention of minimizing a misperceived threat. In one study of 100 patients with current persecutory delusions, over 95% reported using safety behaviors in the past month. In this study, individuals with a prior history of violence reported a greater current use of safety behaviors, and safety behaviors were significantly associated with acting on delusions (Freeman et al., 2007).

When evaluating an individual making a threat, the clinician should take all threats seriously and carefully elucidate the details. An important line of inquiry involves understanding the exact relationship of the person making the threat to his or her intended victim. In regard to written threats, individuals who send threats anonymously are far less likely to pursue an encounter than those who sign their name. Furthermore, the threatener who signs his or her true name is not trying to avoid attention; he or she is probably seeking it.

Understanding how a violent act will be carried out and the expected consequences for the patient helps the clinician in assessing the degree of danger. In addition, fully considering the consequences of an act may help the patient elect an alternative coping strategy. For example, a patient may be focused on revenge against his wife because of her infidelity. When confronted with the likelihood of spending many years in prison, he may decide to divorce his wife instead. Additional information that should be elicited includes potential grudge lists, investigation of the subject's fantasies of violence (The MacArthur Foundation, 2001), and a careful assessment of the future victim if one has been identified. The clinician should also assess the suicide risk in any patient making a homicidal threat. Violent suicide attempts increase the likelihood of future violence toward others (Brizer, 1989; Convit, Jaeger, Lin, Meisner, & Volavka, 1988). One study found that 91% of outpatients who had attempted homicide also had attempted suicide and that 86% of patients with homicidal ideation also reported suicidal ideation (Asnis, Kaplan, Hundorfean, & Saeed, 1997).

Finally, the evaluator should ask the person to rate his or her likelihood of future violence. Roaldset and Bjorkly (2010) asked 489 patients admitted to a psychiatric hospital to rate their risk of future threatening or violent actions toward others. Moderate or high risk scores on self-ratings of future violence remained significant predictors of violence 1 year post discharge. However, persons who rated themselves as "no risk" or refused to answer the question also had a considerable number of violent episodes, indicating that a self-report of low risk of violence may produce false negatives.

When organizing strategies to decrease those risk factors that may contribute to future violence, the clinician should distinguish static from dynamic risk factors. By definition, static factors are not subject to change by intervention. Static factors include such items as demographic information and a history of violence. Dynamic factors are subject to change with intervention and include such factors as access to weapons, acute psychotic symptoms, active substance use, and a person's living setting. The clinician may find it helpful to organize a chart that outlines known risk factors, management and treatment strategies to address dynamic risk factors, and the current status of each risk factor. This approach will assist in the development of a violence prevention plan that addresses the unique combination of risk factors for a particular patient.

STRUCTURED RISK ASSESSMENTS OF VIOLENCE

Clinical risk assessments do not typically incorporate any type of structured or standardized risk evaluation process. Unstructured clinical assessments have been criticized for having less accuracy than structured risk assessments. Structured risk assessments to assess future violence risk are based primarily on actuarial models of risks, referred to as actuarial risk assessment instruments (ARAIs). Over 120 structured instruments have been developed for the purpose of predicting violence in psychiatric or correctional populations (Singh & Fazel, 2010). The goals of these prediction schemes are to assist the clinician in gathering appropriate data and to anchor clinicians' assessments to established research.

PSYCHOPHARMACOLOGIC MANAGEMENT OF AGGRESSION

There is currently no FDA-approved pharmacologic treatment for aggression. Antiepileptic and antipsychotic medications are the classes most commonly used to address long-term aggression. However, research supporting this practice is fairly

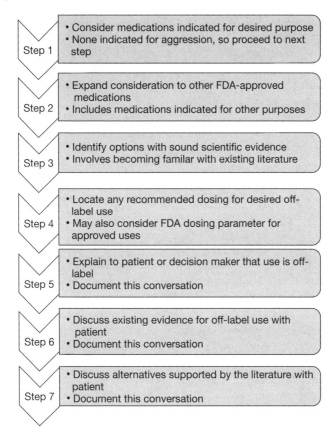

Figure 21.1 Off-label prescribing for treatment of aggression.

limited. Some studies address the benefits of individual agents in all psychiatric patients, while others have focused on patients with particular diagnoses. Based on the published data, no firm conclusions can be drawn about the use of medications to treat aggression. In the absence of FDA-approved interventions, psychiatrists use exclusively off-label interventions to manage aggression.

Prescribing medications off label should be carefully considered. The informed consent process varies somewhat when recommending FDA-approved versus off-label prescriptions. Although manufacturers are prevented from marketing medications for off-label purposes, physicians can legally prescribe FDA-approved medications to any patient for any purpose. As always, evidence-based prescribing is preferred, but physicians are free to prescribe based on their own experience and training. When starting an FDA-approved medication for off-label use, however, physicians should explain to the patient (or his or her substituted decision maker) that the use is off label and document the conversation. Physicians should also discuss FDA-approved alternatives (if they exist) and whether research supports the off-label use of the medication (Wilkes & Johns, 2008). See Figure 21.1 regarding recommended procedures for off-label prescribing, particularly involving the pharmacologic management of aggression.

Most psychiatrists have experience managing acute agitation. In general, long-term strategies for managing recurrent aggression vary from approaches used for acute agitation. Fortunately, clinicians targeting recurrent aggression typically have more extensive information about the individual. This information allows them to craft a focused pharmacologic intervention based on the patient's diagnoses and pattern of aggressive behaviors. For ease of use, this section of the chapter focuses primarily on published data about patients with particular diagnoses most associated with long-term aggression.

Aggression Related to Primary Mental Illness

Patients with a primary mental illness such as major depressive disorder, bipolar disorder, schizophrenia, and schizoaffective disorder can behave aggressively. In their landmark study, Swanson and colleagues (1990) illustrate the link between psychiatric disorders and violence.

The main objective for decreasing the risk of violence in patients with primary mood and psychotic disorders is to treat the underlying mental illness. The American Psychiatric Association's (APA) Treatment Guidelines (n.d.) provide suggestions for treating primary mood and psychotic disorders. Other groups have also published algorithms. After familiarizing themselves with the recommendations, clinicians can incorporate their own treatment preferences based on individual training and experience. However, it is beneficial for clinicians to at least be familiar with standardized treatment guidelines.

Psychiatrists have long debated the degree to which antipsychotic medications independently diminish aggression in patients with a primary mental illness. Typical antipsychotics reduce aggression over the long term, but this effect appears directly related to dose-dependent sedation. Typical antipsychotics can also cause extrapyramidal side effects that indirectly limit the patient's ability to act aggressively. Many clinicians have started using atypical antipsychotics for the long-term management of aggression. Despite this, with the exception of clozapine, the proven benefits of atypical antipsychotics for reducing aggression are equivocal. Clozapine has been shown to reduce long-term aggression in patients with mental disorders in several studies (Citrome et al., 2001; Krakowski, Czobor, Citrome, Bark, & Cooper, 2006; Rabinowitz, Avnon, & Rosenberg, 1996; Spivak et al., 1998; Volavka et al., 2004). These effects are not related strictly to sedation (Chiles, Davidson, & McBride, 1994; Citrome et al., 2001). However, the potential side effects and required laboratory monitoring associated with clozapine limit the number of patients who can tolerate this treatment. With respect to treating aggression, clozapine should primarily be reserved for chronically psychotic, recurrently aggressive patients who have failed other agents. Mood stabilizers such as lithium and lamotrigine can also be combined with clozapine for treating aggressive, refractory patients with schizophrenia (Bender et al., 2004; Pavlovic, 2008).

Mood stabilizers are also an appropriate adjunctive treatment for patients with schizophrenia who display residual aggressive behaviors while taking antipsychotic medications other than clozapine (McEvoy, Scheifler, & Frances, 1999). Dose and colleagues (1998) report valproate to be beneficial in patients with schizophrenia who behave aggressively. In a double blind, placebo-controlled study, carbamazepine was found to decrease agitation and aggression in patients with schizophrenia (Okuma et al., 1989). Lithium has also been used for this purpose, but other than when used in combination with clozapine (as mentioned earlier), the benefits are not well supported (Collins, Larkin, & Shubsachs, 1991; Wilson, 1993).

Benzodiazepines, when used in conjunction with antipsychotic treatment, can also reduce aggressive behaviors in patients with schizophrenia. The long-term use of benzodiazepines is encouraged as a first-line or second-line treatment for patients with schizophrenia who do not have a history of substance abuse (McEvoy, Scheifler, & Frances, 1999).

Aggression Related to Substance Use Disorders

Substance use disorders are often comorbid with mood disorders, psychotic disorders, and certain personality disorders (particularly Cluster B). The presence of substance use disorders complicates the pharmacologic management of aggression, especially when the substance use is unreported or underreported by patients. Alcohol has long been associated with aggression. Alcohol is the substance of abuse most clearly shown to independently increase aggression (Roth, 1994).

Interestingly, the evidence linking other substances of abuse directly to aggression is limited. One potential explanation for this discrepancy is that the aggression involving illicit substance users is often related to violent acts that occur while acquiring drugs, selling drugs, or obtaining money to pay for drugs. Despite the lack of clear evidence supporting direct associations between specific substances of abuse and aggression, it is apparent that substance use can aggravate primary mental illness. Several studies have shown increased aggression among individuals with comorbid substance abuse and primary mental illness (Johns, 1997; Steadman et al., 1998; Swanson, Holzer, Ganzu, & Jono, 1990; Swanson, Borum, Swartz, & Monahan, 1996). Directly addressing a patient's substance use is the primary way to limit his or her risk of aggression. No pharmacologic intervention has been clearly shown to independently decrease aggression in substance users.

Aggression Related to Personality Disorders

Patients diagnosed with personality disorders, particularly antisocial and borderline personality disorders, often behave aggressively. Aggression is so prevalent among these populations that it is an explicit criterion for both antisocial and borderline personality disorders (American Psychiatric Association, 2000). Substance abuse, which is very common in individuals with antisocial and borderline personality disorders, can also exacerbate their aggressive behavior.

There are published reports supporting the use of mood stabilizers, antipsychotics, antidepressants, and beta blockers in patients diagnosed with Cluster B personality disorders. One double-blind, placebo-controlled study addresses the benefits of valproate for impulsive aggression in subjects with Cluster B personality disorders. The Cluster B patients in this study were treated with an average daily dose of approximately 1,400 mg per day, with average valproate trough levels of 65.5 (Hollander et al., 2003). One double-blind, placebo-controlled study shows the beneficial effects of lithium in inmates with "nonpsychotic personality disorders" (Sheard, Marini, Bridges, & Wagner, 1976). The plasma lithium levels of the subjects were generally below 1.0 mEq/L. Another double-blind, placebo-controlled study shows the long-term benefits of treating aggression with fluoxetine in patients with personality disorders (Coccaro & Kavoussi, 1997).

There are numerous studies that have examined the pharmacologic management of borderline personality disorder. Some medications have been demonstrated to significantly decrease anger in this patient population. Aripiprazole is the antipsychotic medication that has proven most effective. A double-blind, placebo-controlled study shows decreased anger in subjects treated with 15 mg per day of aripiprazole (Nickel et al., 2006). Studies showing decreased anger have been published with mood stabilizers, including lamotrigine, topiramate, and valproate as well (Hollander et al., 2001; Loew et al., 2006; Nickel et al., 2004; Stoffers et al., 2010; Tritt et al., 2005). Impulsivity itself contributes to aggressive behaviors. Aripiprazole, lamotrigine, topiramate, and valproate have also been shown to reduce impulsivity in patients with borderline personality disorder (Hollander et al., 2001; Loew et al., 2006; Nickel et al., 2004, 2006; Reich, Zanarini, & Bieri, 2009; Stoffers et al., 2010; Tritt et al., 2005).

No medication has been proven to be beneficial for managing patients with antisocial personality disorder. Some case reports have addressed the pharmacologic management of impulsive aggression in patients with antisocial personality disorder. One report discusses the benefits of quetiapine in four patients with antisocial personality disorder (Walker, Thomas, & Allen, 2003). The authors report improvements in impulsivity, hostility, aggression, and irritability. Since the publication of that study, the abuse of quetiapine has become much more prevalent in correctional settings and psychiatric hospitals. The use of quetiapine for this population and the risk of misuse should therefore be carefully considered. Another case report discusses the benefits of risperidone in one patient diagnosed with antisocial personality disorder (Hirose, 2001). A recently published case report describes the benefits of propranolol to address the impulsive aggression of a patient with antisocial personality disorder (Newman & McDermott, 2011).

Aggression Related to Mental Retardation and Acquired Brain Injury

Patients with mental retardation commonly display impulsive acts of aggression. Some medications have proven useful for managing aggression in this population. Controlled studies have shown the benefits of lithium in individuals with mental retardation (Craft et al., 1987; Spreat, Behar, Reneski, & Miazzo, 1989; Tyrer, Walsh, Edwards, Berney, & Stephens, 1984). The recommended lithium levels in these studies ranges from 0.5 to 1.0 mEq/L. Other controlled studies have shown valproate to decrease aggression in patients with mental retardation (Mattes, 1992). Atypical antipsychotics have demonstrated some benefits in this population as well (Amore, Bertelli, Villani, Tamborini, & Rossi, 2011). Other than clozapine, risperidone is the atypical antipsychotic that has shown the most consistent benefits in treating individuals with mental retardation. Recommended doses of risperidone in the literature range from 0.5 to 4 mg a day (Hassler & Reis, 2010). Beta blockers have also been proposed as a useful intervention for aggressive individuals with mental retardation (Ruedrich, Grush, & Wilson, 1990).

Aggression is often a frustrating component of managing patients with acquired brain injuries. Several medications have been used to target aggression in this population. Beta blockers appear to be most effective for managing aggression in patients with acquired brain injury. Some research has been encouraging, but published results are limited to relatively small studies. One group published three double-blind, placebo-controlled studies describing the beneficial effects of beta blockers in patients with organic brain disease (Greendyke, Berkner, Webster, & Gulya, 1989; Greendyke & Kanter, 1986; Greendyke, Kanter, Schuster, Verstreate, & Wootton, 1986).

Propranolol and pindolol are the beta blockers that have been used in the majority of completed studies. The beta blocker doses used in early studies were actually higher than those commonly used for antihypertensive effects. These higher doses were sometimes associated with adverse effects related primarily to drops in pulse and blood pressure. However, a more recent study using pindolol to target aggression shows promising results with lower doses, specifically 5 mg tid (Caspi et al., 2001). Pindolol is a very good alternative because it is generic, can be easily titrated, and displays partial agonism at the beta-adrenergic receptor. This partial agonism helps prevent problematic drops in pulse and blood pressure.

Other pharmacologic options for patients with acquired brain injuries have been published. There is one report of a patient with acquired brain injury who failed to respond to propranolol and haloperidol but responded to lithium (Haas & Cope, 1985). Lower doses should be used in this population, however, due to increased sensitivity to neurocognitive side effects with lithium (Hornstein & Seliger, 1989). There are other reports of patients with acquired brain injury who benefitted from treatment with valproate (Geracioti, 1994; Horne & Lindley, 1995; Wroblewski, Joseph, Kupfer, & Kalliel, 1997). Azouvi and colleagues (1999) discuss the benefits of carbamazepine in patients with acquired brain injuries.

Aggression Related to Dementia

Patients with dementia sometimes behave aggressively, particularly as their level of functioning declines. If they display primarily psychotic aggression, antipsychotic medications should be prescribed. Antipsychotics also have a role in addressing impulsive aggression in this population. Haloperidol has been used for decades to treat agitation and aggression in patients with dementia. Low-dose haloperidol (1 to 5 mg daily) has been shown to reduce aggression in this population (Allain et al., 2000; De Deyn et al., 1999). Low-dose risperidone (0.5 to 2 mg daily) has also been shown to reduce both aggression and psychosis in this population (De Deyn et al., 1999; Katz et al., 1999). However, the potential associated side effects (mortality, cerebrovascular events, and extrapyramidal side effects) limit the use of risperidone. In 2005, the FDA issued a black box warning regarding the use of atypical antipsychotics in elderly patients with dementia. The warning is specifically for "cerebrovascular events, including stroke." The benefits associated with other atypical antipsychotics in aggressive patients with dementia have been equivocal.

There are several options other than antipsychotics to address primarily impulsive aggression in patients with dementia. Benzodiazepines, given either alone or in combination with antipsychotics, are commonly used to treat aggression in patients with dementia (Yudofsky, Silver, & Hales, 1990). However, it is important to consider that elderly patients are at increased risk for paradoxical agitation, delirium, and side effects of benzodiazepines. Beta blockers, valproate, carbamazepine, and lithium have also been shown to provide some benefits when prescribed to patients with dementia (Kunik, Yudofsky, Silver, & Hales, 1994; Lott, McElroy, & Keys, 1995; Mellow, Solano-Lopez, & Davis, 1993).

Treatment-Resistant Psychiatric Patients

Some patients continue to display aggressive behaviors despite adequate pharmacologic trials. Medication changes can be tried after optimizing the dosing of the initial agent. The next agent should also be selected based on the patient's diagnoses and predominant type of aggression demonstrated. When patients are not improving as expected, the clinician should consider that the patient may not be taking his or her medication as prescribed. When clinically indicated, this issue can be addressed by obtaining serum levels that are easily tracked. Examples of medications with available serum levels include lithium, valproate, and clozapine. Serum levels allow the prescriber to at least have knowledge about the patient's recent adherence and to make a fully informed decision regarding the next course of treatment. Obtaining a serum level that is markedly different from the anticipated level allows treating clinicians to consider potential causes for the discrepancy. Some patients are simply rapid metabolizers and need an increased dose. Other patients do not have a full understanding of their medication regimen and need additional education. Still other patients consciously choose not to take their medications, in which case a frank discussion about their reasoning can benefit both parties.

SUMMARY

The assessment of potential violence is an important area when evaluating psychiatric patients in both outpatient and inpatient settings. The clinician should be familiar with the relationship of various mental health symptoms to a patient's potential aggression. There is unfortunately no "antiviolence" medication. Clinicians should select medication strategies that target the patient's psychiatric symptoms and are consistent with the literature and treatment guidelines.

Despite improvement in the field of risk assessment, the prediction of violence remains an inexact science. Predicting violence has been compared to forecasting the weather. Like a good weather forecaster, the clinician does not state with certainty that an event will occur. Instead, she estimates the likelihood that a future event will occur. Like weather forecasting, predictions of future violence will not always be correct. However, gathering a detailed patient history and using appropriate risk assessment instruments help make the risk assessment as accurate as possible.

REFERENCES

Allain, H., Dautzenberg, P. H., Maurer, K., Schuck, S., Bonhomme, D., & Gérard, D. (2000). Double blind study of tiapride versus haloperidol and placebo in agitation and aggressiveness in elderly patients with cognitive impairment. *Psychopharmacology*, *148*(4), 361–366.

American Psychiatric Association. (n.d.). Clinical practice guidelines. Retrieved August 2012, from http://www.psychiatry.org/practice/clinical-practice-guidelines.

American Psychiatric Association. (2000). *Diagnostic and statistical manual of mental disorders* (4th ed., text rev.). Washington, DC: American Psychiatric Association.

Amore, M., Bertelli, M., Villani, D., Tamborini, S., & Rossi, M. (2011). Olanzapine vs. risperidone in treating aggressive behaviors in adults with intellectual disability: A single blind study. *Journal of Intellectual Disability Research*, *55*(2), 210–218.

Asnis, G. M., Kaplan, M. L., Hundorfean, G., & Saeed, W. (1997). Violence and homicidal behaviors in psychiatric disorders. *Psychiatr Clinics of North America*, *20*(2), 405–425.

Azouvi, P., Jokic, C., Attal, N., Denys, P., Markabi, S., & Bussel, B. (1999). Carbamazepine in agitation and aggressive behavior following severe closed-head injury: results of an open trial. *Brain Injury*, *13*, 797–804.

Beck-Sander, A., Birchwood, M., & Chadwick, P. (1997). Acting on command hallucinations: a cognitive approach. *British Journal of Clinical Psychology*, *36*, 139–148.

Bender, S., Linka, T., Wolstein, J., Gehendges, S., Paulus, H. J., Schall, U., & Gastpar, M. (2004). Safety and efficacy of combined clozapine-lithium pharmacotherapy. *International Journal of Neuropsychopharmacology*, *7*(1), 59–63.

Borum, R., Swartz, M., & Swanson, J. W. (1996). Assessing and managing violence risk in clinical practice. *Journal of Practical Psychiatry and Behavioral Health*, *4*, 205–214.

Brizer, D. A. (1989). Introduction: overview of current approaches in the prediction of violence. In D. A. Brizer & M. Crowner (Eds.), *Current approaches to the prediction of violence* (pp. 1–12). Washington, D.C.: American Psychiatric Press.

Buckley, P. F., Hrouda, D. R., Friedman, L., Noffsinger, S. G., Resnick, P. J., & Camlin-Shingler, K. (2004). Insight and its relationship to violent behavior in patients with schizophrenia. *American Journal of Psychiatry*, *161*(9), 1712–1714.

Caspi, N., Modai, I., Barak, P., Waisbourd, A., Zbarsky, H., Hirschmann, S., . . . Ritsner, M. (2001). Pindolol augmentation in aggressive schizophrenic patients: A double-blind crossover randomized study. *International Clinical Psychopharmacology*, *16*(2), 111–115.

Catalano, R., Dooley, D., Novaco, R. W., Wilson, G., & Hough, R. (1993). Using ECA survey data to examine the effect of job layoffs on violent behavior. *Hospital and Community Psychiatry*, *44*(9), 874–879.

Chadwick, P., & Birchwood, M. (1994). The omnipotence of voices: A cognitive approach to hallucinations. *British Journal of Psychiatry*, *164*, 190–201.

Cheung, P., Schweitzer, I., Crowley, K., & Tuckwell, V. (1997). Violence in schizophrenia: Role of hallucinations and delusions. *Schizophrenia Research*, *26*(2-3), 181–190.

Chiles, J. A., Davidson, P., & McBride, D. (1994). Effects of clozapine on use of seclusion and restraint at a state hospital. *Hospital and Community Psychiatry*, *45*, 269–271.

Citrome, L., Volavka, J., Czobor, P., Sheitman, B., Lindenmayer, J. P., McEvoy, J., . . . Lieberman, J. A. (2001). Effects of clozapine, olanzapine, risperidone, and haloperidol on hostility among patients with schizophrenia. *Psychiatric Services*, *52*, 1510–1514.

Cleckley, H. M. (1976). *The mask of sanity*. St. Louis, MO: Mosby.

Coccaro, E. F., & Kavoussi, R. J. (1997). Fluoxetine and impulsive aggressive behavior in personality-disordered subjects. *Archives of General Psychiatry, 54*, 1081–1088.

Collins, P. J., Larkin, E. P., & Shubsachs, A. P. (1991). Lithium carbonate in chronic schizophrenia -a brief trial of lithium carbonate added to neuroleptics for treatment of resistant schizophrenic patients. *Acta Psychiatrica Scandinavica, 84*, 150–154.

Convit, A., Jaeger, J., Lin, S. P., Meisner, M., & Volavka, J. (1988). Predicting assaultiveness in psychiatric inpatients: a pilot study. *Hospital and Community Psychiatry, 39*(4), 429–434.

Craft, M., Ismail, I. A., Krishnamurti, D., Mathews, J., Regan, A., Seth, R. V., et al. (1987). Lithium in the treatment of aggression in mentally handicapped patients. A double-blind trial. *British Journal of Psychiatry, 150*, 685–689.

De Deyn, P. P., Rabheru, K., Rasmussen, A., Bocksberger, J. P., Dautzenberg, P. L., Eriksson, S., & Lawlor, B. A. (1999). A randomized trial of risperidone, placebo, and haloperidol for behavioral symptoms of dementia. *Neurology, 53*(5), 946–955.

Dose, M., Hellweg, R., Yassouridis, A., Theison, M., & Emrich, H. M. (1998). Combined treatment of schizophrenic psychoses with haloperidol and valproate. *Pharmacopsychiatry, 31*, 122–125.

Erkwoh, R., Willmes, K., Eming-Erdmann, A., & Kunert, H. J. (2002). Command hallucinations: Who obeys and who resists them? *Psychopathology, 35*, 272–279.

Fazel, S., Langstrom, N., Hjern, A., Grann, M., & Lichtenstein, P. (2009). Schizophrenia, substance abuse and violent crime. *Journal of the American Medical Association, 301*(19), 2016–2023.

Fazel, S., Lichtenstein, P., Grann, M., Goodwin, G. M., & Langstrom N. (2010). Bipolar disorder in violent crime. New evidence from population-based longitudinal studies and systematic review. *Archives of General Psychiatry, 67*(9), 931–938.

Fazel, S., Lichtenstein, P., Grann, M., & Langstrom, N. (2011). Risk of violent crime in individuals with epilepsy and traumatic brain injury: A 35-year Swedish population study. *PLOS Medicine, 8*(12), e1001150. doi: 101371/journal.pmed.1001150

Freeman, D., Garety, P. A., Kuipers, E., Fowler, D., Bebbington, P. E., & Dunn, G. (2007). Acting on persecutory delusions: the importance of safety seeking. *Behavior Research and Therapy, 45*(1), 89–99.

Fox, J. R. E., Gray, N. S., & Lewis, H. (2004). Factors determining compliance with command hallucinations with violent content: The role of social rank, perceived power of the voice and voice malevolence. *Journal of Forensic Psychiatry and Psychology, 15*, 511–531.

Geracioti, T.D. (1994). Valproic acid treatment of episodic explosiveness related to brain injury. *Journal of Clinical Psychiatry, 55*, 416–417.

Graz, C., Etschel, E., Schoech, H., & Soyka, M. (2009). Criminal behavior and violent crimes in former inpatients with affective disorder. *Journal of Affective Disorders, 117*, 98–103.

Greendyke, R. M., Berkner, J. P., Webster, J. C., & Gulya, A. (1989). Treatment of behavioral problems with pindolol. *Psychosomatics, 30*(2), 161–165.

Greendyke, R. M., & Kanter, D. R. (1986). Therapeutic effects of pindolol on behavioral disturbances associated with organic brain disease: A double-blind study. *Journal of Clinical Psychiatry, 47*, 423–426.

Greendyke, R.M., Kanter, D. R., Schuster, D. B., Verstreate, S., & Wootton, J. (1986). Propranolol treatment of assaultive patients with organic brain disease. *Journal of Nervous and Mental Disorders, 174*, 290–294.

Haas, J. F., & Cope, D. N. (1985). Neuropharmacologic management of behavior sequelae in head injury: A case report. *Archives of Physical Medicine and Rehabilitation, 66,* 472–474.

Hare, R. (1991). *The Hare Psychopathy Checklist-Revised.* Toronto, ON: Multi-Health Systems.

Hassler, F., & Reis, O. (2010). Pharmacotherapy of disruptive behavior in mentally retarded subjects: A review of the current literature. *Developmental Disabilities Research Reviews, 16*(3), 265–272.

Hatters Friedman, S., Hrouda, D. R., Holden, C. E., Noffsinger, S. G., & Resnick, P. J. (2005). Filicide-suicide: common factors in parents who kill their children and themselves. *Journal of the American Academy of Psychiatry and the Law, 33*(4), 496–504.

Hirose, S. (2001). Effective treatment of aggression and impulsivity in antisocial personality disorder with risperidone. *Psychiatry and Clinical Neuroscience, 55*(2), 161–162.

Hollander, E., Allen, A., Lopez, R. P., Bienstock, C. A., Grossman, R., Siever, L. J., ... Stein, D. J. (2001). A preliminary double-blind, placebo-controlled trial of divalproex sodium in borderline personality disorder. *Journal of Clinical Psychiatry, 62*(3), 199–203.

Hollander, E., Tracy, K. A., Swann, A. C., Coccaro, E. F., McElroy, S. L., Wozniak, P., ... Nemeroff, C. B. (2003). Divalproex in the treatment of impulsive aggression: Efficacy in cluster B personality disorders. *Neuropsychopharmacology, 28*(6), 1186–1197.

Horne, M., & Lindley, S. E. (1995). Divalproex sodium in the treatment of aggressive behavior and dysphoria in patients with organic brain syndromes. *Journal of Clinical Psychiatry, 56,* 430–431.

Hornstein, A., & Seliger, G. (1989). Cognitive side effects of lithium in closed head injury. *Journal of Neuropsychiatry and Clinical Neuroscience, 1,* 446–447.

Humphreys, M. S., Johnstone, E. C., MacMillan, J. F., & Taylor, P. J. (1992). Dangerous behavior preceding first admissions for schizophrenia. *British Journal of Psychiatry, 161,* 501–505.

Johns, A. (1997). Substance misuse: A primary risk and a major problem of comorbidity. *International Review of Psychiatry, 9,* 233–241.

Junginger, J. (1990). Predicting compliance with command hallucinations. *American Journal of Psychiatry, 147*(2), 245–247.

Katz, I. R., Jeste, D. V., Mintzer, J. E., Clyde, C., Napolitano, J., & Brecher, M. (1999). Comparison of risperidone and placebo for psychosis and behavioral disturbances associated with dementia: A randomized, double-blind trial. *Journal of Clinical Psychiatry, 60*(2), 107–115.

Klassen, D., & O'Connor, W. A. (1988). A prospective study of predictors of violence in adult male mental health admissions. *Law and Human Behavior, 12,* 143–158.

Krakowski, M. I., Czobor, P., Citrome, L., Bark, N., & Cooper, T. B. (2006). Atypical antipsychotic agents in the treatment of violent patients with schizophrenia and schizoaffective disorder. *Archives of General Psychiatry, 63*(6), 622–629.

Krakowski, M., Volavka, J., & Brizer, D. (1986). Psychopathology and violence: A review of literature. *Comprehensive Psychiatry, 27*(2), 131–148.

Kunik, M. E., Yudofsky, S. C., Silver, J. M., & Hales, R. E. (1994). Pharmacologic approach to management of agitation associated with dementia. *Journal of Clinical Psychiatry, 55,* S13–7.

Lidz, C. W., Mulvey, E. P., & Gardner, W. (1993). The accuracy of predictions of violence to others. *Journal of the American Medical Association, 269*(8), 1007–1011.

Lincoln, T. M., & Hodgins, S. (2008). Is lack of insight associated with physically aggressive behavior among people with schizophrenia living in the community? *Journal of Nervours and Mental Disorders, 196*(1), 62–66.

Link, B. G., & Stueve, A. (1995). Evidence bearing on mental illness as a possible cause of violent behavior. *Epidemiology Reviews, 17*(1), 172–181.

Loew, T. H., Nickel, M. K., Muehlbacher, M., Kaplan, P., Nickel, C., Kettler, C., … Egger, C. (2006). Topiramate treatment for women with borderline personality disorder: A double-blind, placebo-controlled study. *Journal of Clinical Psychopharmacology, 26*(1), 61–66.

Lott, A. D., McElroy, S. L., & Keys, M. A. (1995). Valproate in the treatment of behavioral agitation in elderly patients with dementia. *Journal of Neuropsychiatry and Clinical Neuroscience, 7,* 314–319.

Mackinnon, A., Copolov, D. L., & Trauer, T. (2004). Factors associated with compliance and resistance to command hallucinations. *Journal of Nervous and Mental Disorders, 192,* 357–362.

Marzuk, P. M., Tardiff, K., & Hirsch, C. S. (1992). The epidemiology of murder-suicide. *Journal of the American Medical Association, 267*(23), 3179–3183.

Mattes, J. A. (1992). Valproic acid for nonaffective aggression in the mentally retarded. *Journal of Nervous and Mental Disorders, 180,* 601–602.

McEvoy, J. P., Scheifler, P. L., & Frances, A. (1999). Treatment of schizophrenia 1999. The expert consensus guideline series. *Journal of Clinical Psychiatry, 60,* S3–80.

McNiel, D. E., Eisner, J. P., & Binder, R. L. (2000). The relationship between command hallucinations and violence. *Psychiatric Services, 51*(10), 1288–1292.

Mellow, A. M., Solano-Lopez, C., & Davis, S. (1993). Sodium valproate in the treatment of behavioral disturbance in dementia. *Journal of Geriatric Psychiatry and Neurology, 6,* 205–209.

Meloy, J. R. (1992). *Violent attachments.* Northvale, NJ: Jason Aronson.

Menzies, J. R., Webster, C. D., & Sepejak, D. S. (1985). The dimensions of dangerousness: Evaluating the accuracy of psychometric predictions of violence among forensic patients. *Law and Human Behavior, 9,* 49–70.

Monahan, J. (1997). Actuarial support for the clinical assessment of violence risk. *International Review of Psychiatry, 9,* 167–170.

Monahan, J., Steadman, H. J., Silver, E., Appelbaum, P. S., Clark-Robbins, P., Mulvey, E. P., … Silver, E. (2001). *Rethinking risk assessment: The MacArthur Study of Mental Disorder and Violence.* New York, NY: Oxford University Press.

Mulvey, E. P., & Lidz, C. W. (1984). Clinical considerations in the prediction of dangerousness in mental patients. *Clinical Psychology Review, 4,* 379–401.

Murdoch, D., Pihl, R. O., & Ross, D. (1990). Alcohol and crimes of violence: Present issues. *International Journal of Addiction, 25*(9), 1065–1081.

National Institutes of Health. (1998). Rehabilitation of persons with traumatic brain injury [Electronic version]. Retrieved March 2008, from http://consensus.nih.gov/19 98/1998TraumaticBrainInjury109html.htm.

Newhill, C. E., Mulvey, E. P., & Lidz, C. W. (1995). Characteristics of violence in the community by female patients seen in a psychiatric emergency service. *Psychiatric Services, 46*(8), 785–789.

Newman, W. J., & McDermott, B. E. (2011). Beta blockers for violence prophylaxis—case reports. *Journal of Clinical Psychopharmacology, 31*(6), 785–787.

Nickel, M. K., Nickel, C., Mitterlehner, F. O., Tritt, K., Lahmann, C., Leiberich, P. K., … Loew, T. H. (2004). Topiramate treatment of aggression in female borderline personality disorder patients: A double-blind, placebo-controlled study. *Journal of Clinical Psychiatry*, 65(11), 1515–1519.

Nickel, M. K., Mühlbacher, M., Nickel, C., Kettler, C., Pedrosa Gil, F., Bachler, E., ... Kaplan, P. (2006). Aripiprazole in the treatment of patients with borderline personality disorder: A double-blind, placebo-controlled study. *American Journal of Psychiatry*, 163, 833–848.

Okuma, T., Yamashita, I., Takahashi, R., Itoh, H., Otsuki, S., Watanabe, S., ... Inanaga, K. (1989). A double-blind study of adjunctive carbamazepine versus placebo on excited states of schizophrenic and schizoaffective disorders. *Acta Psychiatrica Scandinavica*, 80, 250–259.

Pearson, M. E., Wilmot, E., & Padi, M. (1992). A study of violent behavior among in-patients in a psychiatric hospital. *British Journal of Psychiatry*, 149, 232–235.

Pavlovic, Z. M. (2008). Augmentation of clozapine's antiaggressive properties with lamotrigine in a patient with chronic disorganized schizophrenia. *Journal of Clinical Psychopharmacology*, 28(1), 119–120.

Pulay, A. J., Dawson, D. A., Hasin, D. S., Goldstein, R. B., Ruan, W. J., Pickering, R. P., ... Grant, B. F. (2008). Violent behavior and DSM-IV psychiatric disorders: Results from the National Epidemiologic Survey on Alcohol and Related Conditions. *Journal of Clinical Psychiatry*, 69(1), 12–22.

Quinsey, V. L., & Maquire, A. (1986). Maximum security psychiatric patients: Actuarial and clinical predictions of dangerousness. *Journal of Interpersonal Violence*, 1, 143–171.

Rabinowitz, J., Avnon, M., & Rosenberg, V. (1996). Effect of clozapine on physical and verbal aggression. *Schizophrenia Research*, 22, 249–255.

Reich, D. B., Zanarini, M. C., & Bieri, K. A. (2009). A preliminary study of lamotrigine in the treatment of affective instability in borderline personality disorder. *International Clinical Psychopharmacology*, 24(5), 270–275.

Roaldset, J. O., & Bjorkly, S. (2010). Patients' own statements of their future risk for violent and self-harm behavior: A prospective inpatient and post-discharge follow-up study in an acute psychiatric unit. *Psychiatry Research*, 178, 153–159.

Rodenburg, M. (1971). Child murder by depressed parents. *Canadian Psychiatric Association Journal*, 16(1), 41–48.

Roth, J. A. (1994). Psychoactive substances and violence. Retrieved March 2008, from http://www.ncjrs.gov/txtfiles/psycho.txt.

Rudnick, A. (1999). Relation between command hallucinations and dangerous behavior. *Journal of the American Academy of Psychiatry and the Law*, 27(2), 253–257.

Ruedrich, S. L., Grush, L., & Wilson, J. (1990). Beta adrenergic blocking medications for aggressive or self-injurious mentally retarded persons. *American Journal of Mental Retardation*, 95(1), m110–119.

Salekin, R. T., Rogers, R., & Sewell, K. W. (1996). A review of meta-analysis of the Psychopathy Checklist and Psychopathy Checklist-Revised: Predictive validity of dangerousness. *Clinical Psychology: Science and Practice*, 3, 203–213.

Shawyer, F., Mackinnon, A., Farhall, J., Trauer, T., & Copolov, D. (2003). Command hallucinations and violence: Implications for detention and treatment. *Psychiatry, Psychology, and the Law*, 10, 97–107.

Shawyer, F., Mackinnon, A., Farhall, J., Sims, E., Blaney, S., Yardley, P., ... Copolov, D. (2008). Acting on harmful command hallucinations in psychotic disorders. An integrative approach. *Journal of Nervous and Mental Disease*, 196(5), 390–398.

Sheard, M. H., Marini, J. L., Bridges, C. I., & Wagner, E. (1976). The effect of lithium on impulsive aggressive behavior in man. *American Journal of Psychiatry, 133,* 1409–1413.

Singh, J. P., & Fazel, S. (2010). Forensic risk assessment: A metareview. *Criminal Justice Behavior, 37,* 965–988.

Spivak, B., Roitman, S., Vered, Y., Mester, R., Graff, E., Talmon, Y., ... Weizman, A. (1998). Diminished suicidal and aggressive behavior, high plasma norepinephrine levels, and serum triglyceride levels in chronic neuroleptic-resistant schizophrenic patients maintained on clozapine. *Clinical Neuropharmacology, 21,* 245–250.

Spreat, S., Behar, D., Reneski, B., & Miazzo, P. (1989). Lithium carbonate for aggression in mentally retarded persons. *Comprehensive Psychiatry, 30,* 505–511.

Steadman, H. J., Mulvey, E. P., Monahan, J., Robbins, P. C., Appelbaum, P. S., Grisso, T., ... Silver, E. (1998). Violence by people discharged from acute psychiatric inpatient facilities and by others in the same neighborhoods. *Archives of General Psychiatry, 55*(5), 393–401.

Stoffers, J., Völlm, B. A., Rücker, G., Timmer, A., Huband, N., & Lieb, K. (2010). Pharmacological interventions for borderline personality disorder. *Cochrane Database of Systematic Reviews, 6,* CD:005653.

Swanson, J. W., Borum, R., & Swartz, M. (1996). Psychotic symptoms and disorders and risk of violent behavior in the community. *Criminal Behavior and Mental Health, 6,* 317–338.

Swanson, J. W., Holzer, C. E., III, Ganju, V. K., & Jono, R. T. (1990). Violence and psychiatric disorder in the community: Evidence from the Epidemiologic Catchment Area surveys. *Hospital and Community Psychiatry, 41*(7), 761–770.

Tardiff, K., & Sweillam, A. (1980). Assault, suicide, and mental illness. *Archives of General Psychiatry, 37*(2), 164–169.

Teasdale, B., Silver, E., & Monahan, J. (2006). Gender, threat/control-override delusions and violence. *Law and Human Behavior, 30*(6), 649–658.

The MacArthur Foundation. (2001). The MacArthur Violence Risk Assessment Study Executive Summary [Electronic version]. Retrieved March 2008, from http://macar thur.virginia.edu/risk.html.

Torrey, E. F. (1994). Violent behavior by individuals with serious mental illness. *ital.ital and Community Psychiatry, 45*(7), 653–662.

Tyrer, S. P., Walsh, A., Edwards, D. E., Berney, T. P., & Stephens, D. A. (1984). Factors associated with a good response to lithium in aggressive mentally handicapped subjects. *Progress in Neuropsychopharmacology and Biological Psychiatry, 8,* 751–755.

Tritt, K., Nickel, C., Lahmann, C., Leiberich, P. K., Rother, W. K., Loew, T. H., & Nickel, M. K. (2005). Lamotrigine treatment of aggression in female borderline patients: A randomized, double-blind, placebo-controlled study. *Journal of Clinical Psychopharmacology, 9*(3), 287–291.

Volavka, J., Czobor, P., Nolan, K., Sheitman, B., Lindenmayer, J. P., Citrome, L., ... Lieberman, J. A. (2004). Overt aggression and psychotic symptoms in patients with schizophrenia treated with clozapine, olanzapine, risperidone, or haloperidol. *Journal of Clinical Psychopharmacology, 24*(2), 225–228.

Walker, C., Thomas, J., & Allen, T. S. (2003). Treating impulsivity, irritability, and aggression of antisocial personality disorder with quetiapine. *International Journal of Offender Therapy and Comprehensive Criminology, 47*(5), 556–567.

Wallace, C., Mullen, P. E., & Burgess, P. (2004). Criminal offending in schizophrenia over a 25-year period marked by deinstitutionalization and increasing prevalence of comorbid substance use disorders. *American Journal of Psychiatry, 161*(4), 716–727.

Walsh, E., Buchanan, A., & Fahy, T. (2002). Violence and schizophrenia: Examining the evidence. *British Journal of Psychiatry, 180*, 490–495.

Wessely, S., Buchanan, A., Reed, A., Cutting, J., Everitt, B., Garety, P., & Taylor, P. J. (1993). Acting on delusions. I: Prevalence. *Britsh Journal of Psychiatry, 163*, 69–76.

Wilkes, M., & Johns, M. (2008). Informed consent and shared decision-making: a requirement to disclose to patients off-label prescriptions. *PLoS Medicine, 5*(11), 1553–1556.

Williamson, S., Hare, R., & Wong, S. (1987). Violence: Criminal psychopaths and their victims. *Canadian Journal of Behavioral Sciences, 19*, 454–462.

Wilson, W. H. (1993). Addition of lithium to haloperidol in non-affective, antipsychotic non-responsive schizophrenia: A double-blind, placebo-controlled, parallel-design clinical trial. *Psychopharmacology, 111*, 359–366.

Wroblewski, B. A., Joseph, A. B., Kupfer, J., & Kalliel, K. (1997). Effectiveness of valproic acid on destructive and aggressive behaviors in patients with acquired brain injury. *Brain Injury, 11*, 37–47.

Yang, S., Mulvey, E. P., Loughran, T., A., & Hanusa, B., H. (2012). Psychiatric symptoms and alcohol use in community violence by person with a psychotic disorder or depression. *Psychiatric Services, 63*(3), 262–269.

Yudofsky, S. C., Silver, J. M., & Hales, R. E. (1990). Pharmacologic management of aggression in the elderly. *Journal of Clinical Psychiatry, 51*, S22–S28.

Zimring, F. E. (1991). Firearms, violence, and public policy. *Scientific American, 265*, 48–54.

22

Ethical Considerations and Professional Roles in Working With Violent Offenders

KIMBERLY LARSON, ROBERT KINSCHERFF, AND
STACEY GOLDSTEIN ■

Ethical considerations in working with violent offenders are often similar to those that mental health professionals might encounter in general practice. The same principles, codes of ethics, aspirational professional practice guidelines, and legal responsibilities of our profession should guide us in forensic and correctional settings (American Psychological Association, 2002)—unless there is a well-thought-out reason for deviation. Psychologists considering a deviation are strongly advised to first consult with knowledgeable peers, licensing bodies, or other appropriate authorities, and then to document the consultation process and detail the rationale for deviating from established practice.

Multiple professional organizations have developed specialty ethical codes or guidelines applicable to work with violent offender populations. Psychologists engaging in forensic or correctional practice should familiarize themselves with them.[1] Ethical practice helps protect the identified client (which may be a court, correctional system, attorney, or other third party), the direct recipient of professional services (e.g., inmate, defendant, respondent), facility staff and others (e.g., inmates, detainees), and the psychologist.

The challenge to psychologists is the *application* of sources of ethical guidance to specific situations, particularly where there may be multiple competing interests or perspectives on which ethical principles should be weighted more heavily than others. The kinds of tensions[2] that can arise in work with violent offenders often require deliberate analysis. This chapter explores these ethical tensions and ambiguities that can arise in professional practice with violent offenders in forensic and correctional contexts.[3]

FIDELITY, RESPONSIBILITY, AND THE ROLES OF PSYCHOLOGISTS IN FORENSIC AND CORRECTIONAL SETTINGS

Psychologists can take on many roles within forensic and correctional settings. Their ethical duties may change based upon their circumstances and competing rights and interests. This section (1) provides an overview of psychologists' roles within forensic and correctional settings and (2) describes potential conflicts between the ethics of psychologists, their correctional and forensic roles, and system demands.

Of all psychologists, forensic[4] and correctional psychologists[5] are most likely to encounter violent offenders.[6] In *forensic* practice, psychologists are commonly called upon to provide forensic assessment with violent offenders. These include "aid in sentencing" evaluations, "waiver" or "transfer" evaluations for transferring juveniles for trial in adult court, assessments for parole board hearings, or civil commitment proceedings for involuntary psychiatric hospitalization or as dangerous sexual offenders. Forensic psychologists may also provide treatment, assessment, and/or violence risk management planning for persons with histories of violence who are inpatients or in community-based clinical services.

In *correctional* practice, psychologists routinely participate in assessment and risk management during the course of incarceration. In both jails and prisons, correctional psychologists or psychiatrists conduct intake evaluations to assess for safety and help make decisions regarding housing placement. Psychiatrists provide medication management to stabilize symptoms. Psychologists may also provide psychotherapy when resources allow. However, it is often the case that such resources are stretched thin.[7]

To provide adequate professional services in forensic and correctional contexts, psychologists and psychiatrists need specialized knowledge regarding assessment, risk management, and intervention for specific populations of violent offenders (e.g., intimate partner violence, nonsexual violent offenders, violent sexual offenders). Psychologists will also need to be familiar with risk assessment protocols utilized in the settings in which they work and any institutional policies and practices regarding safety. Practice within specific kinds of facilities will also require different skills. For example, psychologists in a forensic inpatient setting will need specialized skills for assessing a defendant who has been found not guilty by reason of insanity (NGRI) for violence risk and treatment needs at the time of NGRI commitment, and later for discharge and community risk management. Similarly, psychologists in prisons need specialized skills to assess the ability of an inmate to tolerate prolonged administrative segregation, adapt to the general population, match an inmate to specific rehabilitation activities, and participate in planning for an inmate's mental health needs in anticipation of parole or discharge.

Dual Roles: Managing Professional Obligations in the Face of Inherent Tensions

Providing psychological services when the primary client (e.g., court, attorney, correctional system) is not the direct recipient of the services provided (e.g., inmate, defendant, involuntarily committed inpatient) creates an inherent tension and potential ethical conflicts. While the work of psychologists in forensic or correctional contexts may often have a therapeutic impact upon the individual directly receiving the services, the services themselves are shaped by the goals of the primary client and may not always be unambiguously helpful to the person receiving services. For example, a defendant charged with a serious violent crime who is found incompetent to stand trial may clinically benefit from treatment—but the primarily goal of the treatment is to render the client competent to stand trial so that prosecution can continue. Similarly, an inmate being treated for a serious mental illness may clinically benefit from treatment, but the primary goal is to maximize the inmate's ability to tolerate incarceration without posing safety risks to himself or others. The tension of providing psychological services under these circumstances raises concerns with potential dual roles or multiple relationships. Dual roles or multiple relationships exist when a psychologist:

> is in a professional relationship with a person and, at the same time, or at a subsequent time, is in a different role with the same person; ... an adverse party; ... a person closely associated with ... the person with whom the forensic practitioner has the professional relationship; ... or offers to enter into such a relationship in the future. (APA, 2013, p. 18)[8]

Forensic and correctional examples include the following:

- *Forensic evaluator versus treatment provider*: One potential dual role is that of forensic evaluator and treatment provider. Psychologists should make clear the difference between the "helper" role, which an individual might expect when he or she encounters a psychologist, and the forensic assessment role in which the psychologist is there not to provide treatment but to assist a court or an attorney, facilitate facility safety, or otherwise support the goals of an entity other than the person directly receiving assessment services. Although not strictly prohibited, it is ethically problematic to blur or move between these two roles unless reasonable efforts to refer the individual to another psychologist are unsuccessful (APA, 2013). Even then, one must carefully consider and seek to minimize any potential harm to the client (APA, 2013, Rule 4.02.01). For example, if a violent individual were to pose an imminent threat, a psychologist might be required to provide emergency psychological services. Following the emergency intervention, the psychologist should consider whether the provision of such services might preclude him or her from continuing in a forensic role, considering such factors as information learned and potentially comprised objectivity.
- *Correctional versus treatment roles*: Psychologists may also encounter tensions between their correctional and treatment roles. Many institutions train mental health staff to consider themselves correctional staff first and mental health providers second. Mental health staff are ordinarily expected to act in a manner that maintains facility security even if that compromises inmate treatment confidentiality, and even to take on correctional staff duties if institutional security is threatened. When

danger is imminent, the psychologist may need to act and attempt to mitigate harms (such as to the therapeutic relationship) afterward. However, psychologists are advised to make ethical conflicts known and resolve them in a manner consistent with the Ethics Code whenever possible. For example, outside of their mental health role, psychology staff may be asked to participate directly in tactical teams (e.g., sometimes called special operations response teams or disturbance control teams) that physically intervene when individuals are not following institutional rules and regulations. Such tactical roles are very different from other roles mental health might play during a disturbance such as de-escalation or more humane management of acutely mentally ill inmates whose institutional infractions are driven by mental illness, which would not be inconsistent with ethical codes and guidelines. While the identity of participants on teams is concealed by tactical gear, it is not advised that clinicians take on this dual role. Ethically, psychologists are obligated to adhere to principles including beneficence and nonmaleficence (avoiding harm). A psychologist identified by inmates as a participant or consultant to a tactical team might be compromised in providing mental health services. For reasons discussed further later in this chapter, it is already difficult to provide treatment in correctional settings, and participation in tactical teams could even further damage the legitimacy of the psychologist as a treatment provider in the eyes of inmates.

Justice, Integrity, and Respect: Rights of Evaluees, Pretrial Detainees, and Inmates

Psychologists working with violent offenders must be familiar with relevant civil and legal rights to make responsible professional practice and ethical decisions. For example, defendants charged with violent crimes are still entitled to the presumption of innocence as well as Fifth and Sixth Amendment protections. Psychologists must take care not to usurp the role of judges or juries by insinuating personal beliefs or implicit findings of fact under the guise of psychological science. Inmates incarcerated following conviction for violent crime are entitled to adequate clinical care and like all inmates have special protections regarding research and experimentation due to their vulnerability to institutional pressures. Psychologists must take care to not intentionally or unwittingly participate in institutional dynamics that degrade basic human regard for inmates or impose targeted additional punishment or humiliation because of the nature of an inmate's crime.

In practice, psychologists working with violent offenders must maintain consistent regard for adequate informed consent, including clear identification of the psychologist's primary client (e.g., court, attorney, correctional authority); transparency regarding the psychologist's role and the goals of the psychological services provided; reasonably foreseeable uses of the psychologist's work; and any limits of confidentiality and/or testimonial privilege. Psychologists must also strive to avoid dual roles that compromise the psychologist's objectivity, competence, or effectiveness, or that risk exploitation or harm to the individual (Standard 3.05 (a), APA, 2002).

Society's Interests, Prisoners' Rights, and the Role of Psychologists: A Delicate Balance

Individuals' rights to privacy, confidentiality, and testimonial privilege differ depending upon context and corresponding expectations.[9] The broadest of the three concepts is *privacy*, or our "right to be let alone" (*Olmstead v. US*, 1928, p. 277), which the US Supreme Court found in the "penumbra" of the Fifth Amendment and other Amendments (*Griswold v. Connecticut*, 1965). *Confidentiality* is a form of *privacy* such as when there are legal and ethical protections for communications that occur in the provision of professional services. These protections give rise to an "expectation of privacy" on the part of the individual directly receiving the professional services that what is communicated is guarded from general disclosure. Communications held in confidence can ordinarily only be disclosed with proper authorization (such as a release of information or a health insurance contract that allows communication between insurer and clinician) or when subject to specific exceptions (such as in emergency circumstances, mandated reporting requirements, or to defend a clinician from license complaint or malpractice action). The obligation to maintain confidentiality exists between the professional and the identified client. When the identified client is not the person(s) directly receiving the professional services, then the person receiving services must be informed that he or she does not have confidentiality (such as when a child protection agency refers parents for an evaluation following allegations of child maltreatment and the agency is the identified client and will receive a report from the mental health professional). Mental health professionals must be familiar with their duties and obligations to protect confidential information and to disclose limits of confidentiality. *Testimonial privilege* is the narrowest of the three concepts. This "privilege" is granted by legislatures to communications made in specific professional or other relationships as a "firewall" against their disclosure in legal proceedings. Ordinarily, the "privilege" belongs to the individual who offered the communications to the professional and only this individual can assert or waive this privilege unless a court rules otherwise. Rules governing testimonial privilege vary across jurisdictions, and psychologists are strongly advised to become familiar with those rules where they practice. Rules regarding privacy, confidentiality, and testimonial privilege in forensic and correctional contexts are often complex and reflect efforts to strike a balance regarding privacy and access to information among individuals directly receiving psychological services, courts and attorneys, correctional systems, and providers of psychological services. The tensions in striking a balance are often especially pronounced in work with violent offenders,

- *Informed consent*: The substance and process of informed consent is especially important in forensic and correctional work where the stakes for individuals, courts and correctional systems, and communities can be especially high—particularly in work with persons accused or convicted of violent offenses. As mentioned earlier, it is critical that persons with whom the clinician works[10] reasonably understand and appreciate all elements of informed consent. This means that the clinician must take measures to assess the extent to which the individual (or his or her legal custodian or guardian) actually understands and can rationally consider the elements of informed consent. This may be done by asking the individual to paraphrase his or her understanding, offering scenarios testing his or her decisional approaches, or other steps. In work with violent offenders it is especially important to be certain the individual appreciates who is the primary identified client; the role of the professional and the primary goals to be served; the reasonably foreseeable uses to which the work of the clinician will be put; any limits on confidentiality or testimonial privilege (such as who will receive oral or written reports of the professional work, possibility of court testimony); and any risks, benefits, or reasonable alternatives to the proposed course of action.[11] In work with defendants or persons convicted of violent offenses, it is crucial to be transparent as to the degree to which the individual's participation is voluntary and the alternative courses of action. For example, in court-ordered evaluations of a defendant, the "court order" ordinarily authorizes the forensic professional to conduct the evaluation on behalf of the court, but it *does not compel* the defendant to participate. In such cases, this should be explained to the defendant, and a reluctant defendant should be directed back to his or her attorney for consultation before proceeding further with direct interview of the defendant. It is also important to be transparent in jurisdictions where there may be ambiguous obligations on the part of the forensic clinician. For example, in many jurisdictions it is not entirely clear whether communications provided by an attorney's client during forensic assessment is protected by attorney-client privilege against a mental health professional's mandated reporting obligations. Where that is unclear, both the attorney and the attorney's client need to be informed about how the forensic clinician would proceed if information ordinarily triggering a mandated reporting obligation is disclosed during forensic assessment.

In treatment with violent offenders, mental health professionals must consider when an individual's potential for violence implicates a mandated or discretionary "duty to warn or protect" third parties.[12] Treating clinicians must be transparent regarding this duty and the circumstances in which it could be triggered in obtaining informed consent and are advised to periodically remind persons with violence histories receiving treatment services of this duty. Disclosures of limits of confidentiality may require more detailed discussion in correctional settings where treating clinicians may be expected to disclose virtually any information reasonably implicating facility security (e.g., presence of weapons, drugs or other contraband; third-party threats to harm others or self-harm, plans to escape or create a disturbance, correctional staff favoritism, improper conduct, or relationships with inmates).

- *Balancing the correctional role with client need for treatment*: Balancing confidentiality and disclosure in treatments provided in correctional settings can be particularly challenging. For example, an inmate with a substance abuse history may disclose a recent relapse while incarcerated. Doing so alerts the treating clinician about recent contraband in the facility and the expectation that the presence of drugs will be reported to correctional staff. Proactive discussions between correctional officials and directors of correctional mental health services may help strike a balance that promotes facility security (reporting the recent presence of contraband) but also supports inmates who are engaging in needed treatment services (perhaps disclosing the unit where drugs had been but not the identity of the specific inmate who disclosed). Issues for discussion and resolution include mandatory and discretionary reports of information that implicate facility security; situations when the specific identify of an inmate disclosing information may be withheld although the information itself is not; who has access to treatment records under what circumstances; steps to protect otherwise protected health information of inmates from general disclosure; protocols for alerting correctional staff of deteriorating mental health status or increased risks to self or others; protocols for monitoring the mental status of inmates in special confinement such as segregation or "difficult to manage" units; and protocols for responding to inmates in special confinement should their mental status deteriorate or alternatives for inmates with identified significant mental health needs. Similarly, inmates should be informed about what must be or might be disclosed to correctional staff under what circumstances, what behavior or disclosures may lead to placement in administrative or disciplinary segregation, and what will be expected in order for them to be released from special confinement.

- *Inmates' rights to treatment and rights to refuse treatment.* Both violent offenders and society have a common interest in effective treatment that reduces the risks of violent reoffense. Knowledge of offenders' rights can also assist psychologists in cases where they might need to fulfill an advocacy role to help ensure fair treatment. This section reviews highlights of Supreme Court jurisprudence in this area.

While most legal cases discuss physical injuries and provision of medical care to inmates (*Estelle v. Gamble*, 1976), one might argue that this case law extends the right to at least minimal psychological intervention for inmates. However, the standard regarding the psychological treatment that must be provided is not high.[13] Staff must only avoid being "deliberately indifferent" to their treatment needs. It is important to note that this is the minimum level established at the federal level. Individual states may provide more but not less protection.

In some limited instances where the penological interest or interest in public safety is high, inmates can be forced into treatment. In *McKune v. Lile* (2002), the Supreme Court said that prisons could use measures, such as threatening transfer or taking away privileges, if the inmate refuses to participate in treatment. Thus, while an inmate can refuse treatment, the prison has a legitimate interest in attempting to prompt the inmate to participate in rehabilitative programming to mitigate future risk to the community.

Prisoners have the right to attempt to block their transfer from a correctional facility to a psychiatric facility *outside of* the correctional system. In *Vitek v. Jones* (1980), the Supreme Court held that because mental health treatment can subject prisoners to stigmatization and denies them the ability to accrue "good time" to shorten their sentence, such a transfer represents a significant deprivation of liberty and prisoners are entitled to due process before transfer can occur. Inmates are entitled to protections such as notice in writing, a hearing at which a burden of proof of clear and convincing evidence must be met that the inmate has a mental illness and that he or she is dangerous as a result of that mental illness. The inmate is also entitled to an independent decision maker, the ability to present testimony, and assistance in preparing his or her case (although representation by a lawyer is not required) (*Vitek v. Jones*, 1980). Similarly, in *Baxtrom v. Herald* (1996), the Supreme Court held it is not double jeopardy to civilly commit an inmate after the completion of his or her sentence, but a showing must first be made that it is necessary.[14]

In some cases, inmates may lose their right to resist or refuse treatment. If an inmate is mentally ill but nonviolent, a hearing must be held to determine whether he or she can be medicated against his or her will. The Supreme Court recognizes that psychotropic medication is a significant bodily intrusion, with potentially permanent and long-lasting effects (*Riggins v. Nevada*, 1992). However, if an inmate becomes violent, this right is abrogated in the interests of maintaining safety. For example, prisoners can be forcibly medicated if they pose a danger within the facility, especially on an emergency basis (*Washington v. Harper*, 1990).

INTEGRITY AND PROFESSIONAL COMPETENCE: ASSESSMENTS OF VIOLENT OFFENDERS

Psychologists must ensure they have the proper education and training to work with violent offenders. Such training should include specialized coursework in areas including the most up-to-date research on violence, its etiology, typologies, assessment, and interventions, as well as information regarding the most recent assessment tools and supervised training in the use of those tools.

A common critique of psychologists in legal arenas is that they overstep the bounds of their science and expertise and enter into the realm of conjecture.[15] Both legal and mental health professionals are often unsure what constitutes sufficient expertise for practice in forensic or correctional contexts as well as what methods of professional practice (assessment or treatment) are sufficiently widely accepted and/or scientifically reliable to be relied upon in making legal determinations or even administrative decisions (such as Parole Board decisions or classification decisions for registries of sexual offenders). Depending upon the jurisdiction, in legal proceedings, the admissibility of mental health testimony is governed by the *Frye* standard or the *Daubert* standard. Each takes a different approach in helping the court determine whether the method(s) relied upon in creating the foundation for expert testimony is sufficiently reliable to support an expert opinion. The older *Frye* test looks to whether the method relied upon in a case has been *accepted in the relevant scientific community*. The newer *Daubert* standard relies upon various indicia of the scientific reliability of the method relied upon to generate the foundation for expert opinion (including but not only acceptance in the relevant scientific community). The *Daubert* standard in particular drives forensic professionals to rely upon empirically based and "best practices" approaches that utilize validated assessment methods that are specifically relevant to the issue before the court about which the expert will offer conclusions or an opinion.

Since the focus is upon the scientific reliability of the methods relied upon in jurisdictions using the *Daubert* test, sophisticated courts, attorneys, and psychologists should be less impressed by a professional curriculum vitae and more focused upon the scientific basis of the methods relied upon and their relevance to the issues before the court in the specific case. Forensic professionals must remain solidly grounded within science and accepted professional practice if their work is to be competent, relevant, and ethical. This means that forensic professionals must increasingly develop specific expertise in assessment methods and tools, relevant research, and professional "best practices" that match specific case demands. For example, different specialized knowledge of relevant law and forensic practice is required for juvenile and adult forensic work, specific forensic issues (e.g., *Miranda* waiver, competency to stand trial, criminal responsibility, involuntary civil commitment), and competent use of assessment tools developed for specific forensic assessment purposes.

Forensic professionals must also appreciate the limits of behavioral and psychological science, including the limits and complexities of prediction and prognostication. Professional practice guidelines also advise disclosure of any relevant limitations of the methods relied upon or of the expert opinion, including disclosure of any reasonably plausible alternative understandings of the information relied upon in rendering an expert opinion.

Psychologists working with violent offenders must be particularly familiar with research and "best practices" approaches to violence risk assessment and management, the limits of prediction, and empirically based treatment interventions, particularly given the high stakes for individuals and communities involved in such cases. It is important that we do not go beyond the limits of what one can legitimately state based upon currently available empirical data.

For example, research established that assessments involving violent offenders relying solely upon "clinical judgment" are likely no better than a "coin toss" (e.g., Monahan, 1981; Webster & Menzies, 1987) and subject to confirmation bias and other distortions in the decision-making process. As a result of the vulnerabilities of "clinical judgment" decision making, the first generation of violence risk assessment research sought to identify specific risk factors associated with violent reoffense. These efforts were based in the belief that if decision making could be guided by research-based factors, it might be possible to determine which individuals with a history of violent offence would reoffend. Specialized tools based upon the identified research-based factors were developed during the second generation of violence risk assessment research. These tools improved upon unstructured clinical judgment regarding recidivism risk but were limited in their usefulness in matching offenders to interventions or risk management strategies because they relied upon "static" (historical) factors that could not be changed by interventions. Additionally, these tools were vulnerable to misuse by psychologists who did not understand the underlying psychometrics of the tools and the fact that they would only assign a probability of reoffense to an individual—they could not indicate at the individual case level whether a specific offender would actually reoffend. More recently, risk research has distinguished between static (historical) factors that can anchor a probability assessment of reoffense, and dynamic (changeable) factors, such as mental status, substance abuse, and affiliation with criminal associates, that can be targets of intervention to reduce and manage risk of violent reoffense. Some of these are factors correlated with criminal reoffense whether or not the individual has a mental illness (criminogenic factors), while others are areas of need that require attention although they are not correlated with violent reoffense. Models of "structured professional judgment" anchored in research-based tools that consider domains of static and dynamic "risk," "needs," and offender "responsivity" (relevant individual offender characteristics) have rendered unstructured clinical judgment of risk assessment and management obsolete. Ethical practice demands that psychologists avoid obsolete methods and practices, rely upon the most up-to-date research-based assessment tools, appreciate the limits of prediction in individual cases, and implement research-based risk assessment and management strategies. This requires psychologists to be adequately informed consumers of research and its application in practice.[16]

EVIDENCE-BASED TREATMENT OF VIOLENT OFFENDERS

The criminogenic needs of violent offenders are perhaps among the most difficult to address effectively. It is important that psychologists stay current on the literature and provide the most up-to-date interventions available for this population.

Evidenced-based treatment has dated back to the 19th century, when medical providers focused all practices toward the use of applied interventions and models that were supported by qualitative and quantitative evidence. In 2005, the American Psychological Association (APA) set forth policy encouraging practicing mental health providers to utilize evidence-based practice in psychology (EBPP). In the official testament, APA (2005) defined EBPP as "the integration of the best available research with clinical expertise in the context of patient characteristics, culture, and preferences" (p. 1). In a correctional context, these specific factors are multiplied to account for the heterogeneous (different and varied) nature of the criminal population, offending behaviors, and competing correctional systems.

Prior to discussing evidence-based interventions, it is first important to explore what specific areas of treatment are deemed pertinent to reducing recidivism. The treatment strategies found to be most effective in reducing recidivism are those that target cognitive distortions (unrealistic offending attitudes and beliefs), emotional dysregulation (inability to cope with, manage, and stabilize various affective states), intimacy deficits (difficulty with interpersonal relationships), negative affect including guilt and shame, coping skills, empathy (the ability to understand and feel another's emotions), anger management (ability to identify and cope with various anger states), attachment (ability to connect emotionally with others), social skills, and relapse prevention (Henggler & Schoenwald, 2011; Klietz, Borduin, & Schaeffer, 2010; Laws & O'Donohue, 2008; Moster, Wnuk & Jeglic, 2008; Stalans, 2004; Timmerman & Emmelkamp, 2005; Wakeling, Webster, Moulden & Marshall, 2007). These treatment targets have been identified as being the most effective in reducing recidivism, essential in addressing the interruption of the cycle of addictive and offending behavior, and are recommended with any correctional approach to treatment.

Among the EBPPs in correctional mental health is the use of cognitive-behavioral therapy (CBT) models. CBT is a therapeutic approach that identifies cognitive distortions and skill deficits, and utilizes restructuring and skill-building techniques to improve upon these areas. Many interventions that have been developed based upon CBT have been molded and shaped to work with the various types of criminal offender populations. These interventions are systemic, relapse prevention, and self-regulation therapies (Ward, Polascek, & Beech, 2006). Systemic therapy is a psychotherapeutic approach to recovery that views the problem as systemic and inclusive of the environment, rather than just seeing it as belonging to just the individual. This particular CBT approach is typically used with the sex offender and juvenile populations, as well as for treating substance abuse (Bahr, Masters, & Taylor, 2012; Brooks-Gordon, Bilby, & Wells, 2006; Craig, Browne, & Stinger, 2003; Levenson, Macgowan, Morin, & Cotter, 2009; Perez, 2009; Ward et al., 2006).

Relapse prevention (RP) models have also been empirically supported as being effective in reducing criminal recidivism (Moster et al., 2008). Relapse prevention planning is not necessarily a component of CBT but rather a stand-alone model that is often incorporated into CBT treatment. According to the RP model, if an offender is to avoid having lapses and full relapses, he or she must devise a concrete intervention for the relapse process. Unlike the RP model, self-regulation therapy is covered under the CBT umbrella and utilized with various criminal populations, yet most frequently with the sex offender population. This particular type of intervention focuses on the cognitive and behavioral aspect of offending goals (i.e., avoiding committing a sexual assault) and the strategies to achieve those goals (Ward et al., 2006). In other words, the provider assists offenders in identifying his or her goals to offend or avoid offending, and then examines the ways in which the offender approaches these goals.

Many of the EBPPs mentioned in this section can be generalized to various populations under correctional care or community supervision (i.e., substance abuse offenders, sex offenders, white and blue collar offenders, felony offenders, domestic violence offenders, and male and female offenders). However, due to the familial and environmental factors involved in adolescent and juvenile offending behavior, many clinical approaches have been tailored to incorporate a familial and systemic focus. One such EBPP strategy is multi-systemic therapy (MST), which is focused on integrating the many systems that affect and impact adolescent and juvenile youth (i.e., family, neighbors, schools, and remaining community) (Henggeler & Schoenwald, 2011; Klietz et al., 2010). MST is a primarily family-based intervention and, as such, not best used with adults who are less affected and impacted by current familial difficulties.

Functional family therapy (FFT) is another EBPP approach (Henggeler & Schoenwald, 2011). FFT views problematic family relationships as the core motivating factor to offending behavior. Using this intervention, the identified patient is the family and the goal of treatment is to replace the problematic interpersonal style of communication among the family with healthier ones (Henggeler & Schonewald, 2011). FFT is grounded in the idea that a child or adolescent develops and adopts antisocial traits and behaviors in response to a troubled family dynamic. If the therapy focuses attentions on reducing or eliminating this dysfunction with healthier methods of communicating and interacting, then the target juvenile would return to a normative way in which to interact with the world and others (Henggeler & Schonewald, 2011).

In summary, the varied etiological factors and backgrounds that influence offending behavior demand a clinical approach that is not uniform. Only through research and examination with different treatments and populations can this be made possible. Additionally, if an approach not based on research is used with the wrong population, the clinical intervention may lead to negative consequences and do serious harm to the patient and/or others; a violation of the ethical principles of psychologists to "do no harm" to his or her patient(s) (APA, 2002). The many EBPP approaches discussed within this section are of the few interventions to pass rigorous investigation and identified as being essential in addressing the interruption of the cycle of offending behavior, and they are recommended with any approach to treatment. However, despite these empirical findings, many therapists and many current intervention programs continue to use a mix of methods that may or may not be linked to credible research evidence.

SPECIAL ETHICAL ISSUES IN JUVENILE VIOLENT OFFENDER CASES

Overview

The first Juvenile Court was established in 1899, and the model spread rapidly across the United States in the early 20th century. These courts were intended to focus upon rehabilitation rather than punishment and based upon recognition that youthful offenders are developmentally different from adult offenders. Then, as now, Juvenile Courts seek to determine "(a) whether an adolescent's antisocial behavior is due to transient immaturity or contextual disadvantage, as opposed to deep-seated criminal character and (b) how best to construct a response to a juvenile's delinquent or criminal acts that will decrease the likelihood of recidivism" (Steinberg, 2009, p. 50).

The history of the Juvenile Court reflects the ambivalence with which adolescents have been regarded in the law. The rehabilitative goal of the early decades of the Juvenile Courts often led to results such as prolonged institutionalization that were far more harsh than consequences imposed on adults for similar misconduct. This was recognized in the US Supreme Court decision of *In re Gault* (1967) and other landmark cases that provided youth in Juvenile Court many of the procedural protections afforded to adults in criminal cases.

The effort to sustain the rehabilitative ideal within a framework of procedural protections would yield to a more punitive approach some 20 years later in the face of a sharp increase in violent crimes by youth between 1987 and 1992 (Snyder & Sickmund, 1999) and highly publicized albeit incorrect predictions of the rise of violent juvenile "superpredators." As a result, despite the significant national declines in violent crime by youth (including homicide) since 1993, between 1992 and 1997 forty-four states amended their laws to allow or require trial and sentencing of youth as adults when they reach certain ages or for certain crimes. Despite differences in procedure and practice among jurisdictions, result was a prompt and sharp increase in the number of youth tried, sentenced, incarcerated, or placed under community supervision (probation, parole) in the adult criminal justice system (Grisso, 1996). Youth charged with even relatively minor crimes against persons were more readily handled as adults (Arya, 2011).

By approximately 2010, the juvenile crime rate had reached a 30-year low. However, research revealed that the punitive reforms of the mid-1990s had not significantly contributed to the decline in the juvenile crime but had generated serious unintended consequences. Most youth convicted as adults are placed on probation, and of those who are incarcerated 80% are released before age 21—suggesting the convictions were not for the most serious charges (Campaign for Youth Justice, 2007). Nonetheless, responding to youth with adult criminal prosecution carries significant direct consequences such as incarceration with adult criminals and collateral consequences such as barriers to jobs, training, education, and housing and participation in civil society such as voting (Legal Action Committee, 2004).

All of these direct and collateral consequences actually *increase* rather than diminish public safety risks over time. The Center for Disease Control and Prevention (CDC) found that "to the extent that transfer policies are implemented to reduce violent or other criminal behavior, available evidence indicates that they do more harm than good," and they recommended "against laws or policies facilitating the transfer of juveniles from the juvenile to the adult judicial system" (CDC, 2007, p. 1). Other research found that the punitive policies also failed to deter youth from engaging in misconduct that would expose them to adult criminal prosecution (Redding, 2008).

Punitive public policies increasingly found to undermine public safety were under scrutiny just as the US Supreme Court began to revisit the jurisprudence of violent juvenile crime. In 2005, the Court in *Roper v. Simmons* found execution of persons convicted of capital offenses under age 18 to be unconstitutional, citing developmental immaturity, emerging brain science, and the substantial scientific limitations in predicting long-term capacities for rehabilitation (*Roper v. Simmons*, 2005). Five years later, the Court in *Graham v. Florida* categorically barred life without possibility of parole (LWOP) for any nonhomicide offense committed under age 18 (*Graham v. Florida*, 2010). Most recently, in *Miller v. Alabama* (2012) the Court barred sentencing schemes imposing *mandatory* LWOP for homicides perpetrated under age 18. The Court left open the possibility of LWOP after an individualized sentencing inquiry finding "evidence of irretrievabl[e] depravity" but commented such an outcome should be "uncommon" (*Miller v. Alabama*, 2012). This line of court cases paralleled movements to limit entrance of youth into the adult criminal justice system, create alternatives to detention and juvenile incarceration, establish specialized courts (e.g., juvenile drug courts), and introduce evidence-based interventions for delinquent youth—all with the goal of maintaining youth safely in their communities whenever possible while avoiding the deleterious effects of criminal justice system involvement.

A PRELIMINARY COMMENT

Professional forensic practice with juveniles who have been accused or found to have engaged in violent or even lethal acts can pose extraordinary ethical challenges. Errors or inadequacies in professional method or judgment have profoundly life-altering consequences for those youth, victims and potential future victims, families, and communities. In short, this professional practice area can be a clinical and ethical quagmire for practitioners who are unfamiliar with juvenile forensic practice, proficient professionals in clinical work with youth and families but naïve to juvenile forensic practice, and proficient adult forensic professionals directed or tempted to take on cases involving youth before adult criminal courts.

Providers of professional services for youth following adjudication on violent offenses have an additional obligation to provide evidence-based or "best practices" intervention approaches and to understand in each case any correlation between a mental health/substance use disorder and risk of violence. Behavioral health treatment may be a necessary but insufficient condition for reducing recidivism. For example, effective treatment of an adolescent who is uncharacteristically but markedly irritable due to depression and is charged with assault may itself substantially reduce the likelihood of future assault by returning him to his nonviolent baseline. By contrast, effective treatment of a depressed adolescent with high frequency of assault when not depressed and whose depression is manifested by low energy, excessive sleep, and social isolation may actually increase risk of violence by restoring him to his high base rate of assaultive behavior. Nonetheless, treatment of his depression is required on humanitarian grounds and also to maximize his potential for the social learning required to address his attitudes, values, and beliefs that justify violent behavior.

Clinical practitioners providing clinical services to court-involved or adjudicated violent youth must be familiar with mental health and substance use disorders commonly found in youth involved with the juvenile justice system, particularly sophisticated regarding trauma presentations, and appreciate the distinction between "rehabilitation" and "treatment" (Kinscherff, 2012). They must also be familiar with empirically based treatments and interventions for youth in the community, in residential treatment of juvenile incarceration facilities, or who are involved in community re-entry.

Context for Ethical Professional Practice With Juveniles With Violence Histories

Controversies and Shifts in Juvenile Justice Policy

The current context for professional practice is shaped by the continuing toll taken by youth violence. National rates of juvenile homicide and crimes against persons have dropped to a 30-year low, but there are "hot spots" in communities where violence is tragically high and its consequences are devastating. Efforts to reform the punitive approaches adopted in the mid-1990s are under way, but in many cases forensic professionals are still operating within old systems. Professional practice within justice systems that currently inadvertently increase public safety risk over time is challenging when working individual cases. However, this only increases the responsibility to provide forensically defensible information to courts, attorneys, and juvenile or criminal justice authorities. The consequences of inadequate practice for the youth, the victims and community of the youth, and potential future victims are extraordinarily high.

Developments in Forensic Practice With Juvenile Offenders

Current professional practice is shaped by relatively recent but critical developments in professional practice. These developments have substantively contributed to establishing the expectations for acceptable ethical practice and include the following:

First, forensic mental health has emerged as a specialty professional practice. Juvenile forensic mental health is an increasingly developed subspecialty of forensic practice. It has long been recognized that standard clinical training does not sufficiently equip practitioners for forensic activities, and it is increasingly recognized that juvenile forensic activities require specialized training and experience. This means that professionals who have been trained as adult forensic professionals must exercise extreme caution in applying those skills to youth who come before adult criminal courts. This is the case when youth may present with familiar forensic issues such as competence to stand trial or criminal responsibility since expertise with adults does not ordinarily translate to sufficient expertise with youth in assessing or remediating these issues. The stakes are even higher when the forensic professional may be asked to examine a youthful defendant involved in a transfer/waiver proceeding that could place the case in criminal court or as an aid in sentencing when risk of violent recidivism is an implicit or explicit element of the referral issue.

Secondly, research has yielded important information with which any practitioner must be sufficiently familiar to work competently with violent youth. These basic competency domains include (a) the heterogeneity of youth for whom one or more violent acts is a common outcome of multiple potential pathways; (b) the variety of developmental trajectories among youth who engage in violence and the pathways of desistance or nondesistance from violent conduct as they mature into young adulthood; (c) the overrepresentation among youth within the juvenile justice system of learning disabilities, psychiatric and substance use disorders, and intellectual and developmental disabilities; (d) the impact of adverse childhood experiences and trauma adaptations upon functioning; (e) the family, peer, community, cultural, and other contexts that may maintain risk of violence or promote positive youth development; (f) the distinction between "rehabilitation" and clinical "treatment" and discerning what, if any, links exist between a clinical diagnosis and violent behavior; and (f) the empirical bases for treatments or other interventions intended to diminish violent misconduct.

Third, there have been significant advances in the development of specific research-based violence risk assessment, risk management, and intervention approaches for youth with histories of violence. For example, practitioners should be familiar with both structured judgment methods of youth violence risk assessment (Borum, 2006a, 2006b) and with applications to youth of targeted threat assessment models (Cornell, Sheras, Gregory & Fan, 2009; Fein et al., 2002). It is beyond the scope of this chapter to detail these advances in assessment, management, and treatment but suffice it to say that for work with violent youth most standard clinical approaches and tools in the absence of specialized tools and guided by relevant research will be insufficient and likely below the standard of ethical professional practice.

Finally, competent professional forensic practice with youth with histories of violence requires sufficient familiarity with law applicable to the jurisdiction in which the case is being heard or serviced, relevant legal cases and controversies, and—since most violent juvenile offenders will return to their communities—the specific capacities of juvenile justice and criminal justice authorities to protect youthful offenders from physical/sexual violence, offer educational and vocational supports, offer developmentally attuned mental health and substance abuse services, and provide re-entry programming and transitional community supervision.

Sources of Ethical Guidance

Sources of ethical guidance in professional practice with youth with histories of perpetrating violence include the following:

- Ethics codes for professional practice promulgated by professional associations such as the American Psychological Association, Academy of Child and Adolescent Psychiatry, and the National Association of Social Workers. Forensic professionals are advised to be familiar in detail with the ethics codes of their own professions and have a working knowledge of the ethics codes of related professions as they bear upon forensic work with youth and families.
- Specialty guidelines for forensic mental health practices, such as the American Psychological Association *Specialty Guidelines for Forensic Psychology* (2011), the *Code of Ethics* of the National Organization of Forensic Social Work (1987), and the *Ethics Guidelines for the Practice of Forensic Psychiatry* of the American Academy of Psychiatry and the Law (2005).
- Specialty guidelines devised by experts or promulgated by professional associations for clinical practice relevant for youth with histories of violent offending, such as practice guidelines or parameters for youth with conduct disorder or substance use disorders.
- Research to support ethically competent professional practice in work with youth with histories of violent misconduct, including specialized assessment; evidence-based treatment and innovative "best practices" interventions; consultation and supervision practices; systems and organizational assessment; and cultural (e.g., ethnic, linguistic, adolescent peer dynamics, gangs and other subcultures, other) and gender factors.
- Consultation and supervision: There is no substitute for securing consultation or supervision from knowledgeable professionals with the requisite special competencies for work with youth with histories of violence. All consultations and supervisions should be documented in the case record.

Consultation is a collegial arrangement in which the professional seeking consultation maintains control and responsibility for the case and may disregard the consultant's *input or advice*. Supervision is an "agency" relationship in which the professional under supervision is acting as the legal and ethical "agent" of the supervisor, who holds full ethical and legal responsibility for the case. The supervised professional *may not disregard and must implement* the *instructions* of the supervisor. Standard 2.05.(3) of the APA Ethics Code (2002) requires that when delegating responsibilities to supervisees, trainees, or others, the psychologist takes "reasonable steps" to "see that such persons perform these services competently" (APA, 2002). This appears to impose a duty upon a psychologist to establish mechanisms independent from solely the self-report of the supervised clinician to assure that competent services are being provided.

Securing consultation or supervision may not only be helpful clinically or forensically, it is also per se evidence of professional prudence and judgment—provided the individual from whom consultation/supervision is obtained is competent to provide those services. The higher the legal, clinical, or risk management stakes involved—as would be the case where violence toward others by a youth is involved—the more a practitioner may wish to consider obtaining consultation/supervision and the more a professional providing those services may wish to affirmatively assure that his or her advice has been understood (consultation) or his or her instructions (supervision) implemented.

AN ETHICAL PRACTICE CHECKLIST FOR FORENSIC SERVICES TO YOUTH WITH HISTORIES OF VIOLENCE

- *The threshold question of professional competency.* The earlier discussion regarding developments in juvenile forensic mental health practice frames the basic question: Do I have sufficient professional competence for professional practice with youth with acknowledged, adjudicated, or alleged violent behavior? The answer to this question will depend upon the nature of the professional involvement (e.g., forensic examination, clinical assessment, case planning, treatment, other), identified client, methods, and other factors. Basic professional competence is a prerequisite for ethical practice, and where there is any doubt it is incumbent upon the professional to secure adequate training, consultation, or supervision.
- *Who is my legal client?* Establish who has the authority to direct, control, and terminate professional services. This will also establish to whom you have primary duties as far as the scope and purpose of professional services, privacy in the form of confidentiality or privilege, control and dissemination of the work product, and the status of mandated reporting obligations. Professionals are strongly advised to clarify in advance relevant law or local practices regarding mandated reporting, especially when retained by attorneys. For example, a May 2013 California appellate decision held that attorney-client privilege trumps the mandated reporting duties of licensed mental health professionals who have been retained by defense counsel (*Elijah W. v. Superior Court of Los Angeles County*, 2013). In most jurisdictions it is not clear whether attorney-client privilege or the mandated reporting obligations of licensed mental health professional prevails. Professionals providing services under attorney-client privilege are strongly advised to specifically address this issue when discussing retainer for services where attorney-client privilege may be implicated.

  Common "legal clients" include judges, defense counsel or prosecutors, juvenile probation or parole officers, juvenile justice service providers, and other participants in the legal process or postdisposition authorities such as juvenile or adult probation, juvenile justice authorities to whose custody they are committed, or adult correctional and parole authorities.

If the youth referrals are made by school authorities after youth have made threats or made a threat or engaged in violent behavior, practitioners are strongly advised to access available professional supports for peer counseling/guidance supports to forestall unwarranted penetration into the juvenile justice system.

- *In addition to my legal client, are there others who are my ethical "clients" to whom I own ethical duties?* Ordinarily, ethical clients would certainly include the youth but may include others to whom the professional has general ethical duties of competent and timely professional services but who are not the identified legal client. These may be family members, school officials and personnel, juvenile justice authorities, child welfare and other governmental authorities, and others.

- *Obtaining informed consent or assent.* Informed consent can only be obtained by the legal client who can authorize, direct and limit, or terminate professional services. Youth under age 18 can ordinarily not be the legal client to offer informed consent. In cases where the identified legal client directs the examination or treatment of a minor after "informed consent" the youth is still entitled to an opportunity to offer "assent."

  Adequate "assent" requires that the youth be advised of the role of the mental health professional in developmentally appropriate language and disclosure of the nature and purpose of the inquiry. Some jurisdictions require specific disclosure that participation in the evaluation or other professional service is voluntary and may be revoked at any time. Efforts to obtain adequate "assent" are required, but if the youth is incapable of offering assent or refuses to offer assent or even agreement to participate in the forensic assessment, treatment or other services may nonetheless proceed if "informed consent" from the legal client has been obtained.

- *What is the scope of professional practice involved?* This will ordinarily be determined by the referral question, so it is critical that the *specific* referral issue be clear before providing professional services. This is particularly the case when the case involves inquiry, assessment, case planning, or treatment regarding violent misconduct given the stakes involved.

- *What are the professional competencies required?* This question can only be addressed if the scope of professional practice being called upon is clear. The broad range of competency domains when providing services in cases involving youth with violence histories was described earlier.

  Specific professional competencies are involved when charged youth with violent misconduct are referred for traditional forensic evaluations focusing upon current functional capacities (competency to stand trial) or mental status at the time of the offense (criminal responsibility). Other competencies are involved with assessing a youth's individual characteristics, developmental trajectory toward violent misconduct, and amenability to rehabilitation (transfer, reverse-transfer, or aid in disposition or sentencing). Still other competencies are required for specific case risk assessment, intervention, or community supervision/reentry planning requested by juvenile or criminal justice authorities.The case-specific competencies required for ethical practice vary widely depending upon the specific demands of the case and/or role of the forensic professional. Broadly speaking, professionals in the first instance should be confident that they have the skills for forensic practice with juveniles in general and with youth with violence histories in particular. General forensic experience with adults is ordinarily insufficient for ethical practice with juveniles even if the juveniles are before adult criminal courts. Beyond that, professionals have an ethical duty to assure themselves and others that they have the specific clinical and forensic skills to bring to bear the necessary professional competencies within the scope of practice required to address the issues identified by the legal client. Professionals providing forensic or clinical assessment/intervention services are strongly advised to seek consultation if they are not certain that they have the professional competencies (clinical, legal, other) required to provide adequate services, recommendations, and/or follow-up services.

- *What are the methods relied upon?* As noted earlier, either the *Daubert* or *Frye* standard will be used to assess methods employed. The *Daubert* standard in particular drives forensic professionals to rely upon empirically based and "best practices" approaches that utilize validated assessment methods specifically aligned to the issue before the court. For example, while the MMPI-A may be a robust clinical tool, if the specific case calls for violence risk assessment, then it may be less relevant than a specialized assessment tool of general violence risk (such as the SAVRY) or an assessment of risk to a potential victim (targeted threat assessment).

The obligation to remain solidly grounded with science and accepted professional practice extends beyond court proceedings to the provision of professional services in juvenile justice contexts. For example, professionals conducting risk and rehabilitation assessments of youth with violence histories are advised to structure them within an individualized risk-needs-assessment framework that considers criminogenic risk and protective factors outside of traditional diagnostic assessments.Similarly, professionals recommending or providing clinical interventions for youth with violence histories must do so with sufficient awareness of research regarding assignment of youth to appropriate levels of juvenile or adult containment (incarceration) or community supervision (probation or parole) and the nature and intensity of preferred clinical intervention. For example, referral for nonspecific individual psychotherapy for higher risk conduct-disordered youth with violent offenses has little to suggest it is effective while intervention with multisystemic therapy, functional family therapy, and other empirically validated treatments have demonstrated efficacy.

Practitioners should also be attentive to cultural competencies required. These include (a) cultures of poverty and the communities in which impoverished families live; (b) cultures of minority ethnicity, language, and immigration status; and (c) cultures of potentially clashing or collaborating groups, including gangs, community leaders, schools, law enforcement, faith communities, social service providers, and state and municipal agencies.

- *Privacy: Confidentiality and testimonial privilege.* Maintaining the privacy of professional communications is a basic ethical responsibility for clinical professionals. The two broad categories of ethically relevant professional privacy are *confidentiality* and *testimonial privilege.* It is incumbent upon the professional providing services to clarify to the legal client, the youth, and any other ethical clients any limitations upon confidentiality and testimonial privilege exist for the professional services provided. For example, parents/guardians and the youth with a violence history must be notified as part of informed consent/assent of the confidentiality/privilege implication if retained by defense counsel or the prosecution to clarify the basic expectations regarding confidentiality and privilege.

Confidentiality refers to the ethically and legally protected privacy offered to behavioral health clients receiving behavioral health services. Parents or legal guardians are ordinarily the "gatekeepers" of the confidentiality of clinical or educational services for children under age 18. For example, parents or legal guardians can ordinarily sign releases of information to disclose clinical or educational information. Emergency exceptions for reporting information, mandated reporter requirements for child abuse or elder abuse, or duty to warn/protect from client/patient violence are common exceptions to confidentiality.

"Testimonial privilege" refers to circumstances in which "professional communications" between an identified patient/client is deemed protected from introduction in legal proceedings. States vary as to whether a parent or legal guardian can waive a psychotherapist "testimonial privilege" on behalf of a minor child with many states allowing a waiver by a parent/guardian and others requiring a court review before a minor's "professional communications" to a licensed mental health professional will be introduced into legal proceedings. Professionals are strongly advised to clarify their legal client, whether they are in a clinical or forensic role, and whether there is an expectation that a specific warning of nonconfidentiality is required before providing professional assessment, treatment, or consultation services.

If in a forensic role, the professional is advised to clarify the identified legal and ethical client(s), the nature and purpose of the evaluation or other professional activity, and any limits upon confidentiality or privilege. Where privilege and mandated reporting obligations may conflict without unambiguous case law or statutory direction, the forensic professional is strongly advised to clarify the issue before engaging in services. For example, if a forensic professional is retained by defense counsel, the clinician is advised to clarify if they should follow mandatory reporting obligations (e.g., duty to warn/protect potential victim, child or elder abuse or neglect) or if attorney-client privilege prevents this. Unless very clear under local statutory or case law, this potential conflict needs to be resolved as a critical element of informed consent with the identified legal client.

Interventions

Interventions provided should not only address clinical needs (psychiatric conditions, substance abuse, learning disabilities, cognitive/intellectual disabilities, developmental disabilities, other) but do so in a manner consistent with broader rehabilitation goals. Interventions should be evidence-based or at least research-informed "best practices," subject to outcome measurement, culturally and gender sensitive, and adapted for the context (community, residential treatment, juvenile justice incarceration) in which they are delivered.

Special Controversies in Behavioral Science Regarding Juveniles

Controversies relevant to the scientific basis and ethical practice with juveniles with alleged or adjudicated violent offenses include the following:

- The behavioral science basis upon which prognostications are made in transfer or reverse-transfer hearings about the likelihood of rehabilitation of a juvenile accused of or adjudicated for a violent crime, especially if the period for prediction extends over months or years
- Forensic professionals are cautioned regarding the very limited behavioral science basis upon which opinions in post-*Miller* hearings about whether juveniles found in these circumstances are amenable to rehabilitation. Professionals are reminded of the important ethical implications of making long-term prognostications that are not supported by current science and which also implicate the obligation to inform courts and other legal actors of the sharp limits of long-term prognostication about rehabilitation of adolescents who have been convicted for homicides prior to age 18.
- Participation of psychologists in any capacity in proceedings where the court may impose a penalty of life without possibility of parole, which would constitute violations of human rights under international law— and thus violations of the Standard 1.03 of the APA Ethics Code (2002) (Kinscherff & Grisso, 2013)
- Persisting evidence of disproportionate minority contact and confinement with the juvenile justice system and subsequently the criminal justice system

SEX OFFENDERS

Perhaps no group of offenders raises the types of concern and fear associated with sexual offenders, especially those who commit violent acts. While a full consideration of the law and policy related to these offenders is beyond the scope of this chapter, numerous ethical issues have arisen in relation to their incarceration and treatment.

Of particular concern for this population are issues such as the ethics of employing controversial treatments such as hormone treatments to suppress sexual drive, intrusive measures such as penile plethysmography, or whether participation in treatment is truly "voluntary" if it is required in order to be released or placed at a lower level of facility security or community supervision. Additionally, if offenders do participate in treatment, they also may risk disclosing information that could be used to eventually civilly commit them from 1 day up to a lifetime as a sexually violent predator. Further, these offenders face multiple challenges upon release, such as difficulties in finding housing or employment due to registration and notification requirements.

Work with juvenile sexual offenders raises an additional issue about the nature and degree of specialized professional competence required for assessment and treatment given the significant differences in sexual offense recidivism rates as compared to adults, the complex developmental context of juvenile problematic sexual behaviors, family and/or caregiver factors, challenges in assessment and treatment matching, and other issues. Competence in work with adult sexual offenders is ordinarily insufficient preparation for work with juvenile sexual offenders.

COMPETENCIES IN CRIMINAL CONTEXTS RAISING ETHICAL ISSUES: COMPETENCE TO BE SENTENCED, IMPRISONED, OR EXECUTED

Most states forbid an individual from being sentenced, imprisoned, or executed if he or she is unable to understand what is occurring and why.[17] The legal system has now largely codified this stance, which originated in the common law, due to concerns over inability to assist counsel, the unethical appearance and actual fairness of conducting such proceedings, and the fact that basic purposes of punishment (e.g., retribution, deterrence) are not met. However, should an evaluation be triggered, the bar for an individual to be competent to be sentenced, imprisoned, or executed is lower than that for other types of criminal competencies, such as competence to stand trial.

Competence to Be Executed and an Overview of Death Penalty Jurisprudence

The death penalty has been the topic of entire books and courses; however, those in the field of correctional and/or forensic psychology considering conducting specialized assessments of competence to be executed should at a minimum be familiar with the basic history of the death penalty in the United States and case law in this area. From its inception, the United States employed this punishment. While the government has imposed some moratoriums,[18] for the most part, the death penalty has been considered legitimate and employed as punishment.

Of particular note to forensic evaluators working with dangerous individuals are a set of cases that began in the early 1980s. In *Estelle v. Smith* (1981), the Court held the admission of expert testimony in that case was unconstitutional because the defendant had not been warned that his statements could be used to determine dangerousness, which could be admissible to support imposition of the death penalty. Thus, such defendants must be advised that they do not have to make any statements to the evaluator and that any information that he or she chooses to provide could be used at capital sentencing.

In *Barefoot v. Estelle* (1983), the Court heard the testimony of two mental health experts regarding future dangerousness in a death penalty case. Despite protestations even from the American Psychiatric Association that the field had not yet advanced to a point where clinicians could accurately predict dangerousness, the Court held that such testimony should be admissible. The Court reasoned that this type of testimony could be challenged, for example, through cross-examination to show that it is unreliable. The court system could determine when such testimony was so undependable that it should either be given less weight or disregarded entirely.

One of the next major challenges to the death penalty came in 1986, when the Court considered whether the execution of the mentally ill was constitutional. In *Ford v. Wainwright* (1986), the Court held that the death penalty could not be applied to those who were currently acutely mentally ill. Since that time, the court has categorically excluded those with intellectual disabilities (*Atkins v. Virginia*, 2002) and juveniles (i.e., those under age 18) (*Roper v. Simmons*, 2005) from the death penalty. Those considering becoming involved in *Atkins* evaluations should be sure that they have sufficient training in conducting forensic assessments and working with intellectually disabled populations.[19]

The Court's most recent pronouncement in the death penalty arena, *Panetti v. Quarterman* (2007), raised the issue of whether Panetti's factual understanding of the reasons for his execution was sufficient for execution if he did not rationally understand the application of that information to his case. Reviewing its earlier decision in *Ford v. Wainwright* (1986), the Court held that allowing the execution of a person who can factually connect the reason the State has provided for his execution with his crime set the bar too low. Just because the prisoner reiterated the link between the crime and the punishment did not mean that he rationally understands the reason for that punishment. Without rational understanding the retributive and deterrent purposes of the death penalty are not met. However, while the Court stated that the bar set in that case was too low, it did not lay out the precise standard for competence for execution.

Competence to Be Executed: Ethics Codes and Conflicts

The American Academy of Psychiatry and the Law (APPL) and the American Medical Association (AMA) forbid participation in executions; however, "participation" has been defined narrowly. Conducting an evaluation of an inmate's competence to be executed does not constitute "participation" in carrying out state-authorized execution. Notably, however, some state ethical boards have taken the position that participation in competence-to-be-executed evaluations constitutes a violation of ethical cannons. Some might argue that it is ethical depending upon the outcome of the evaluation (i.e., it is ethical if the evaluator opines that the inmate is not competent to be executed, and unethical if he or she opines that the individual is competent to be executed).

SELF-ANALYSIS OF ONE'S OWN BIASES IN WORKING WITH VIOLENT OFFENDERS

All mental health professionals must acknowledge and cautiously examine and manage their emotional reactions, rigid preconceptions, and other contributors to bias that might compromise their professional judgment when working with difficult populations. When faced with the evaluation and/or treatment of a violent offender, like anyone, psychologists may experience strong feelings about the offender, the type of offense committed, or the contexts in which this work is undertaken (e.g., courts, prisons). It is important for all individuals working in correctional and forensic settings to think through whether they can truly be unbiased and fair in a given situation. Whether you should take a particular case or work with a particular population is an issue that should be considered prior to it arising. If one has preconceptions about certain difficult issues (e.g., the death penalty) or certain populations (e.g., sex offenders), it is important to recognize and examine these potential sources of personal bias and refer the case to another provider if one is unsure about his or her ability to avoid the intrusion of personal bias and preconception. No individual is impervious to such thoughts, and professional arrogance in assuming so can do a disservice to the contexts and populations with whom one works.

NOTES

1. For example, the American Academy of Psychiatry and the Law, 2005; American Psychology-Law Society, 2011; International Association of Correctional and Forensic Psychology, 2010; United Nations Standard Minimum Rules for the Treatment of Prisoners, 1977; International Covenant on Civil and Political Rights, 1976.

2. "When their responsibilities conflict with law, regulations, or other governing legal authority, forensic practitioners make known their commitment to the EPPCC, and take steps to resolve the conflict.[] ... When the conflict cannot be resolved by such means, forensic practitioners may adhere to the requirements of the law, regulations, or other governing legal authority, but only to the extent required and not in any way that violates a person's human rights. Forensic practitioners are encouraged to consider the appropriateness of complying with court orders when such compliance creates potential conflicts with professional standards of practice" (American Psychological Association, 2011, p. 29).

3. Any source of ethical guidance cannot be used in a cookbook fashion, and often it will not provide answers to the more complicated situations one might encounter, this chapter will review applicable code provisions, legal standards, and other sources of authority on each topic. However, it should be noted that ethical practice dictates that practitioners be familiar with local variations.

4. Forensic psychology encompasses "professional practice by any psychologist working within any sub-discipline of psychology ... when applying the scientific, technical, or specialized knowledge of psychology to the law to assist in addressing legal, contractual, and administrative matters" (APA, 2011, p. 3).

5. Some may conceptualize correctional psychology as a variant of forensic psychology (Bartol & Bartol, 2011), but many correctional psychologists consider themselves part of a specialized practice of psychology that provides services specifically within correctional systems (International Association for Correctional and Forensic Psychology, 2010).

6. Forensic clinicians often assess violence-related issues as part of evaluations conducted for the purpose of court proceedings. In correctional settings, psychologists

both assess and treat violent offenders. Both the setting and role in which a psychologist encounters violent individuals can impact his or her ethical obligations and duties.

7. For example, mental health inmates may be seen weekly or biweekly for a few months in order to help them with current difficulties and assist them in moving through these issues to return to successful adaptation to the general population. By monitoring these inmates, and allowing for quicker intervention before serious issues arise, the facility's safety and security can be better maintained for the protection of both staff and other inmates.

8. Such conflicts are often avoidable if anticipated and planned for ahead of time, even in forensic and correctional settings, perhaps with the exception of imminent threats that can be encountered with violent offenders.

9. While this chapter will provide a general overview of these concepts, it is important that practitioners know the requirements of their particular state or jurisdiction.

10. If the individual is not capable of offering informed consent (such as a legal minor or an adult under legal guardianship), then the person who is the legal custodian or guardian of the individual must offer informed consent for that person. Even so, discussions are had with the person in an effort to secure his or her "informed assent." In situations where the decisional competency of the person is one element at issue (such as competency-to-stand-trial evaluations), psychologists nonetheless try to secure informed consent/assent from the individual and proceed while mindful of the need to resolve the issue of decisional capacity.

11. Note that what information is disclosed to whom and under what circumstances will vary by jurisdiction, type of evaluation, and the procedural posture of the case.

12. As with all legal duties and obligations, there is considerable variation among jurisdictions and among specific agencies and facilities regarding expectations about confidentiality. Professionals working in forensic or correctional contexts are strongly urged to be familiar with these expectations and relevant provisions, and forensic psychologists are specifically required by Standard 2.01 (f) to be "reasonably familiar" with "judicial or administrative rules governing their roles" (APA, 2011).

13. In 1976, inmate Gamble, after refusing to work due to an injury, was sent to disciplinary hearing and placed in solitary. He was then seen by a physician's assistant, who hospitalized him. He sued the prison under the theory that the lack of medical care was a violation of the Eighth Amendment's proscriptions against cruel and unusual punishment because he was not provided with needed medical treatment. The Supreme Court eventually heard the case and laid out a test for whether an inmate's rights had been violated. The Court held that simple negligence was not enough; the facility had to have been deliberately indifferent to the inmate's serious medical needs. In *Farmer v. Brennan* (1994), the Supreme Court expanded upon this decision, stating that a prison official could not be held liable for harm unless the individual knew of a substantial risk to the individual and did not address the risk. In many cases, courts will also find that if an official should have known of a risk, he or she will also be liable. But in *Farmer v. Brennan* (1994), the Court explicitly said it was not cruel and unusual punishment under the Eighth Amendment if the official should have known about the risk but did not know.

14. Inmate Baxtrom was approaching the end of his prison term and prison officials wanted him to be civilly committed. He was then held at Dannemore Hospital, which was used to house correctional inmates with mental illness. At the end of

his sentence, Baxtrom was denied his request to be moved to a civil hospital and remained housed at Dannemore Hospital upon a showing that he continued to need psychiatric care. The US Supreme Court held that his rights to equal protection had been violated because he continued to be held within the Department of Corrections after his prison sentence had ended and he was not transferred to a less restrictive setting. The characteristics of the hospital did not matter to the Court. The legislature had already determined that the two types of facilities were very different because one was housed within the Department of Corrections and the other under the Department of Mental Health. Further, Baxstrom was denied the right to have the same procedure as those similarly situated when they are civilly committed, such as the right to a trial by jury. This does not mean that he could not be held at Dennemore, but instead that there must be a showing that it is necessary.

15. Although the uneasy alliance between the fields of psychology and the law have been well documented and thoroughly discussed, it bears repeating some of the major points of that debate prior to discussing the various roles in which psychologists might interact with the legal system as well as the places in which a reigning in of our opinions might be called for (e.g., Melton, Petrila, Poythress, & Slobogin, 2007; Faust, 2012).

16. *Special considerations with violent offenders:* (1) competence with specialized client populations and/or legal contexts; (2) rigorous attention to the scientific basis of the work including use of appropriate assessment tools and avoiding usurpation of the role of the legal finder of fact; (3) accurate and effective communication of information regarding violence or risk assessment information to legal readers and other non–mental health readers.

17. While competency to be executed is the only issue that applies only to violent offenders, all three will be considered here as they have similar legal and moral underpinnings.

18. While the Supreme Court's decision in *Furhman v. Georgia* began the death penalty moratorium in the United States in 1972, it was relatively short lived. That case held that the statute in Georgia was constitutionally infirm due to the fact that jury discretion was not guided. Thus, in a series of cases following that decision, the states began to tinker with their death penalty statutes to discern a way to reel in jury discretion in a way that the Court would find was constitutional. With safeguards that established guided jury discretion, the United States reinstated the death penalty in 1976 in *Gregg v. Georgia*.

   Despite the fact that the death penalty was reinstated, it has nonetheless been challenged on many fronts since that time, including legitimacy of its use as punishment for crimes other than murder. For example, the death penalty was challenged with regard to whether it was a legitimate punishment for the rape of an adult woman. In *Coker v. Georgia* in 1977, the Court held that this punishment would be disproportionate; however, notably this case left open the question of whether the death penalty could be applied in cases of rape of a child (where the death of the child does not occur). In 2008, the Court decided that issue. In *Kennedy v. Louisiana*, the Court found that the death penalty could not be used in such cases.

19. The legal arguments in these cases often center upon whether the person meets the diagnostic criteria for intellectual disability either due to intelligence testing, or due to functional impairments in major life areas. Developmental disabilities experts are called upon to examine historical information as well as current information

regarding the individual to determine whether the diagnosis is met. If it is not met, the death penalty can be imposed. If it is, the individual is not eligible for a death sentence.

REFERENCES

American Academy of Psychiatry and the Law (AAPL). (2005) *Ethics guidelines for the practice of forensic psychiatry.* Bloomfield, CT: Author. Retrieved May 2014, from http://www.aapl.org/ethics.htm.

American Psychological Association. (2002; amended 2010). *Ethical principles of psychologists and code of conduct.* Washington, DC: American Psychological Association. Retrieved May 2014, from http://www.apa.org/ethics/code/index.aspx.

American Psychological Association. (2005). *Policy statement on evidenced based practice in psychology.* Washington, DC: American Psychological Association Council of Representatives. Retrieved May 2014, from http://www.apa.org/practice/resources/evidence/evidence-based-statement.pdf.

American Psychological Association. (2013). Specialty guidelines for forensic psychology. *American Psychologist, 68,* 7–19.

Arya, N. (2011). *State trends: Legislative victories from 2005 to 2010 removing youth from the adult criminal justice system.* Washington, DC: Campaign for Youth Justice.

Atkins v. Virginia, 536 US 304 (2002).

Bahr, S. J., Masters, A. L., & Taylor, B. M. (2012). What works in substance abuse treatment programs for offenders? *Prison Journal, 92,* 155–174. DOI: 10.1177/0032885512438836.

Barefoot v. Estelle, 463 US 880 (1983).

Bartol, C. R., & Bartol, A. M. (2011). *Criminal behavior: A psychological approach* (10th ed.). Upper Saddle River, N.J.: Pearson Higher Education.

Baxtrom v. Herald, 383 US 107 (1966).

Borum, R. (2006a). Assessing risk for violence among juvenile offenders. In S. N. Sparta & G. P. Koocher (Eds.), *Forensic mental health assessment of children and adolescents* (pp. 190–202). New York, NY: Oxford University Press.

Borum, R. (2006b). *Manual for the structured assessment of violence risk in youth (SAVRY).* Odessa, FL: Psychological Assessment Resources.

Brooks-Gordon, B., Bilby, C., & Wells, H. (2006). A systematic review of psychological interventions for sexual offenders I: Randomized control trials. *Journal of Forensic Psychiatry and Psychology, 17,* 442–466. doi: 10.1136/bmj.333.7557.5

Campaign for Youth Justice. (2007). *Jailing juveniles.* Washington, DC: Campaign for Youth Justice.

Centers for Disease Control and Prevention. (2007). Effects on violence of laws and policies facilitating the transfer of youth from the juvenile to the adult justice system: A report on recommendations of the Task Force on Community Preventive Services. *Morbidity and Mortality Weekly Reports, 56*(No. RR-9). Retrieved May 2014, from http://www.cdc.gov/mmwr/pdf/rr/rr5609.pdf.

Coker v. Georgia, 433 US 584 (1977).

Cornell, D., Sheras, P., Gregory, A., & Fan, X. (2009). A retrospective study of school safety conditions in high schools using the Virginia threat assessment guidelines versus alternative approaches. *School Psychology Quarterly, 24,* 119–129.

Craig, L. A., Browne, K. D., & Stringer, I. (2003). Treatment and sexual offence recidivism. *Trauma, Violence, and Abuse, 4,* 70–89. doi: 10.1177/152483800228946

Elijah W. v. Superior Court of Los Angeles County, No. B241011 (Cal. Ct. App. May 8, 2013).

Estelle v. Gamble, 429 US 97 (1976).

Estelle v. Smith, 451 US 454 (1981).

Farmer v. Brennan, 511 US 825 (1994).

Faust, D. (2012). *Coping with psychiatric and psychological testimony* (6th ed.) New York, NY: Oxford University Press.

Fein, R. A., Vossekuil, B., Pollack, W. S., Borum, R., Modzeleski, W., & Reddy, M. (2002). *Threat assessment in schools: A guide to managing threatening situations and to creating safe school climates.* Washington, DC: US Secret Service and US Department of Education.

Ford v. Wainwright, 477 US 399 (1986).

Furhman v. Georgia, 408 US 238 (1972).

Graham v. Florida, 130 S. Ct. 2011 (2010).

Gregg v. Georgia, 428 US 153 (1976).

Grisso, T. (1996). Society's retributive response to juvenile violence: A developmental perspective. *Law and Human Behavior, 20,* 229–247.

Griswold v. Connecticut, 381 US 479 (1965).

Henggeler, S. W., & Schoenwald, S. K. (2011). Social policy report: Evidenced-based interventions for juvenile offenders and juvenile justice policies that support them. *Sharing Child and Youth Development Knowledge, 25,* 1–20.

In re Gault, 387 US 1, 87 S. Ct. 1428, 18 L. Ed. 2d 527 (1967).

International Association for Correctional and Forensic Psychology. (2010). Standards for psychology services in jails, prisons, correctional facilities, and agencies. *Criminal Justice and Behavior, 37,* 749–808. doi: 10.1177/0093854810368253

Kennedy v. Louisiana, 554 US 407 (2008).

Kinscherff, R. T., & Grisso, T. J. (2013). Human rights violations and standard 1.02: Intersections with human rights law and applications in juvenile capital cases. *Ethics and Behavior, 23,* 71–76. doi: 10.1080/10508422.2013.757963

Klietz, S. J., Borduin, C. M., & Schaeffer, C. M. (2010). Cost-benefit analysis of multi-systemic therapy with serious and violent juvenile offenders. *Journal of Family Psychology, 24,* 657–666. doi: 10.1037/a0020838

Laws, D. R., & O'Donohue, W. T. (2008). *Sexual deviance: Theory, assessment, and treatment.* New York, NY: Guildford Press.

Legal Action Center. (2004). *After prison: Roadblocks to reentry. A report on state legal barriers facing people with criminal records.* New York, NY: A Legal Action Center.

Levenson, J. S., Macgowan, M. J., Morin, J. W., & Cotter, L. P. (2009). Perceptions of sex offenders about treatment: Satisfaction and engagement in group therapy. *Sexual Abuse, 21,* 35–56. doi: 10.117/1079063208326072

McKune v. Lile, 536 US 24 (2002).

Melton, G. B., Petrila, J., Poythress, N. G., & Slobogin, C. (2007). *Psychological evaluations for the courts: A handbook for mental health professionals and lawyers* (3rd ed.). New York, NY: Guilford Press.

Miller v. Alabama, 567 US_(2012).

Monahan, J. (1981). *The clinical prediction of violent behavior.* Rockville, MD: National Institute of Mental Health.

Moster, A., Wnuk, D. W., & Jeglic, E. L. (2008). Cognitive behavioral therapy interventions with sex offenders. *Journal of Correctional Health Care, 14,* 109–121. doi: 10.1177/1078345807313874

National Organization of Forensic Social Work. (1987). *Code of ethics.* Retrieved from, http://nofsw.org/wp-content/uploads/2014/03/NOSFW-Code-of-Ethics-Changes-2-16-12.pdf

Olmstead v. US, 277 US 438 (1928).

Panetti v. Quarterman, 551 US 930 (2007).

Perez, D. M. (2009). Applying evidenced-based practices to community corrections supervision: An evaluation of residential substance abuse treatment for high-risk probationers. *Journal of Contemporary Criminal Justice, 25,* 442–458. doi: 10.1177/1043986209344557

Redding, R. (2008). *Juvenile transfer laws: An effective deterrent to delinquency?* Washington, DC: US Department of Justice, Office of Justice Programs, Office of Juvenile Justice and Delinquency Prevention.

Riggins v. Nevada, 504 US 127 (1992).

Roper v. Simmons, 543 US 551 (2005).

Snyder, H. N., & Sickmund, M. (1999). *Juvenile offenders and victims: 1999 national report.* [NCJ 178257]. Washington, DC: US Department of Justice, Office of Justice Programs, Office of Juvenile Justice and Delinquency Prevention.

Stalans, L. ((2004). Adult sex offenders on community supervision: A review of recent assessment strategies and treatment. *Criminal Justice and Behavior, 31,* 564–608. doi: 10.1177/0093854804267093

Steinberg, L. (2009). Adolescent development and juvenile justice. *Annual Review of Clinical Psychology, 5,* 459–485.

Timmerman, I. G. H., & Emmelkamp, P. M. G. (2005). The effects of cognitive-behavioral treatment for forensic inpatients. *International Journal of Offender Therapy and Comparative Criminology, 49,* 590–606. doi: 10.1177/0306624X05277661

Vitek v. Jones, 445 US 480 (1980).

Wakeling, H. C., Webster, S., Moulden, H. M., & Marshall, W. L. (2007). Decisions to offend in men who sexually abuse their daughters. *Journal of Sexual Aggression, 13,* 81–99. doi: 10.1080/13552600701521330

Ward, T., Polaschek, D. L. L., & Beech, A. R. (2006). *Theories of sexual offending.* West Sussex, UK: Wiley.

Washington v. Harper, 494 US 210 (1990).

Webster, C., & Menzies, R. (1987). The clinical predication of dangerousness. In D. Weisstub (Ed.), *Law and mental health: International perspectives* (Vol. 3, pp. 158–208). New York, NY: Pergamon.

23

Conducting Research With Special Populations

GIANNI PIRELLI AND PATRICIA A. ZAPF ∎

Research on issues relevant to violent offending and violent offenders is an important undertaking that allows for both the development and refinement of risk assessment instruments and treatment programs, as well as an improved understanding of violent offenders and the ways in which to serve these individuals and protect the public. Conducting research in this area can be a daunting task; however, the potential impact of this research can have far-reaching implications for both policy and practice.

In this chapter we will present a broad overview of some of the relevant issues involved in conducting research with special/protected populations from design through implementation and completion. The purpose of this chapter is to delineate areas of consideration for those who wish to conduct research with special, protected populations; namely, violent offenders. Space limitations do not allow for an in-depth consideration of each of the factors discussed; therefore, the interested reader is encouraged to consult other sources of information as appropriate. One particularly relevant resource is the recently published text edited by Barry Rosenfeld and Steven Penrod entitled *Research Methods in Forensic Psychology*, which includes numerous chapters dedicated to a description of the research methods and considerations relevant to specific issues and populations in forensic psychology.

CONCEPTUALIZATION

For research to be technically sound it must be based on the principles of science; however, adherence to the scientific method does not ensure that the findings will be meaningful, relevant, or otherwise informative. Research ideas must make clinical sense before research methods can even be considered. As such, high-quality research is both conceptually and scientifically grounded.

Clinical research questions often develop naturally during the course of a clinician's work. In its purest form, research is conducted to answer questions that are meaningful and can be addressed using empirical methods. Research studies are of most utility when they develop naturally from clinical work or from other programs of research. For example, a clinician may question the utility of an assessment instrument for a population in which normative data are unavailable, thereby prompting him or her to conduct psychometric research on that instrument. Such research is consistent with the scientist-practitioner model in clinical psychology, which is based on the tenet that one's clinical work should inform one's research and vice versa. Overholser (2010) delineated 10 criteria across three domains that, he proposed, should be used to classify a scientist-practitioner. The three domains are scholarship, clinical practice, and the integration of science and practice in psychology, and the 10 criteria are as follows:

1. A scientist-practitioner remains active in scholarship.
2. A scientist-practitioner contributes scholarly works at a national level.
3. Scholarship includes but extends beyond teaching.
4. A scientist-practitioner provides clinical service on a regular basis.
5. A scientist-practitioner provides clinical services that are similar to standard clinical practice.
6. Clinical practice includes but extends beyond supervision.
7. A scientist-practitioner adheres to recommendations for evidence-based practice.
8. A scientist-practitioner in clinical psychology focuses on issues that are central to clinical psychology.
9. A scientist-practitioner in clinical psychology works with medical or psychiatric patients.
10. A scientist-practitioner clinical psychologist uses psychological measures that have adequate psychometric properties and can be easily collected in most mental health treatment centers.

Clinical research, however, is often not conducted by practicing clinicians. Academicians and other research scientists contribute much of the empirical clinical literature. Such researchers typically develop a program of research, which is a coordinated series of research projects intended to result in cumulative knowledge about a particular topic or set of questions. Those engaging in applied clinical research need not be clinicians, but a sophisticated understanding of clinical issues is an essential aspect of conducting applied research.

Although there are many specific considerations to account for when conducting research with violent offenders, such research is based on the same core components as other types of clinical research. First and foremost is the principle of empiricism, which refers to the notion that knowledge is based on objective evidence rather than ideology and, when evidence and ideology conflict, evidence should prevail (Whitley, 2002). That is not to say, however, that ideology or logic is inconsequential in research. In fact, it is what generally underlies theory. Developing or utilizing a theory is an important initial step in the research process, but it is insufficient alone. Theories must be supported or disconfirmed through testable research hypotheses. Hypotheses are statements wherein the researcher predicts a particular finding or set of findings based on an underlying theory or knowledge gleaned from the empirical literature.

Most social science research, including research on violent offenders, includes hypothetical constructs rather than behavioral counts or other types of variables that need not be defined. A hypothetical construct is an abstract concept or term that is created to capture a phenomenon or variable that cannot be directly observed (i.e., an explanatory fiction). Examples of hypothetical constructs are violence and psychopathy. These terms are ambiguous if they are not operationally defined. Thus, a researcher may develop a theory about the relationship between violence and psychopathy, which must then be converted to a research hypothesis. For instance: *Psychopaths will engage in more violence than nonpsychopaths.* This hypothesis needs to be clarified to be testable, however, because it lacks specificity by containing two hypothetical constructs that must be operationally defined (i.e., psychopath, violence). The researcher may decide to classify participants as psychopaths if they receive a score of 30 or above on the Hare Psychopathy Checklist-Revised (PCL-R; Hare, 2003) and define violence as all recorded physical assaults within a 3-year period. The hypothesis would then be testable because the constructs have been operationally defined, making them observable and, therefore, measurable.

Much like clinical work itself, clinical research requires a well-developed conceptualization. Well-designed studies and sophisticated statistical analyses cannot make up for poor theoretical underpinnings at the conceptualization stage. Once a study has been vetted vis-à-vis its conceptualization, its research design can be formulated.

Research Design

There are four commonly noted objectives of science: description, explanation, prediction, and control (Christensen, 2001; Whitley, 2002). The first objective, description, requires one to define the topic being studied and to identify the relevant variables that exist within that topic area. Explanation refers to the determination of why a particular phenomenon exists or what causes the occurrence of the phenomenon. Prediction refers to the ability to anticipate the occurrence of an event. Finally, control refers to the manipulation of the conditions that cause a particular phenomenon. These objectives serve as the underpinnings of specific research designs.

Descriptive research is typically conducted in novel areas of study, as the main goal is to begin to delineate the phenomenon in the context of relevant variables associated with it. Case studies and survey-based studies can be characterized as descriptive research. Strupp (1981) argued that most of what was learned about psychotherapy in the 20th century came from "astute and creative clinical observations" (p. 216) and that scientific knowledge is dependent on the ability of researchers to learn about "clinical realities and stay in touch with clinical phenomena" and practicing therapists' ability to develop "a thorough grasp of basic principles of scientific research" (p. 217). Notable scholars such as Freud, Piaget, Skinner, and von Krafft-Ebing are well known for their case studies. Case studies remain useful today despite receiving less attention and acclaim than studies conducted with large sample sizes. Nevertheless, the only journal currently devoted solely to case studies is *Clinical Case Studies*, which is published bimonthly by Sage Publications.

Case studies or single-case research designs are particularly important to employ when conducting research with violent offenders because they provide an opportunity to delve into the details of a particular case and address meaningful nuances when applicable. Furthermore, such an approach circumvents the limitations associated with data aggregation in this population. It is not uncommon for clinicians working with violent offenders to engage in practices that do not readily lend themselves to empirical investigation with large samples. A clinician may be asked to conduct an evaluation under a very specific set of circumstances for which no empirical research has been conducted, such as administering a neuropsychological test to an inmate who is housed in administrative segregation. There would likely be no empirical literature to draw from in such a case; however, it may be beneficial to publish the case study because much could be learned and generalized from such an evaluation that would not otherwise become part of the empirical literature. Furthermore, offender groups are often heterogeneous, even though researchers often attempt to classify them into groups. For instance, conducting research with a sample of rapists may not ultimately be as informative as conducting a case study or series of case studies with such offenders. In fact, aggregating data from a heterogeneous group can lead to misleading results.

The very strength of case studies or single-case research designs can also be their greatest limitation, however. Larger samples are necessary to utilize because they function more like the population in question as their size increases. The three remaining objectives of science (i.e., explanation, prediction, control) relate to the issue of causality. While it is important to be able to describe a particular phenomenon or the way in which variables appear to relate, in science, it is ultimately most important to discern what is causing a phenomenon to occur. Once causality can be ascertained, phenomenon can be predicted and controlled, or altered. Researchers conducting treatment outcome studies with offenders attempt to determine what is attributable to the variability in particular outcome variables (e.g., recidivism). Thus, recidivism could be prevented or greatly reduced if we could determine what is "causing" it. Although the concept is axiomatic, the constraints that prevent researchers from determining causality are often insurmountable.

In addition to single-case research studies, there are three main types of research designs: experimental, quasi-experimental, and correlational. In an experimental design, or a "true" experiment, the researcher strictly controls which factors are varied and which are kept constant. Control is exercised over the independent variables in the study and experimental and control conditions are included. When all variables other than the main independent variable (i.e., the experimental condition) are essentially equal, or constant, changes in the dependent/outcome variable are attributable to changes in the independent variable. As such, conducting a true experiment is the only way to conclude that there are no other explanations for the results—to determine causality.

It is not always possible to conduct true experiments; in fact, they tend to be conducted relatively infrequently in applied clinical research because of the inability to manipulate independent variables and randomly assign participants to experimental and control conditions. Randomized controlled trials (RCTs) are the exception in clinical research. An RCT is a study in which participants are randomly assigned to treatment groups (see Stolberg, Norman, & Trop, 2004 for a review of RCTs). While experimental methods are advantageous in deducing causality, they can reflect artificiality due to the amount of control set forth by the researcher. As such, experimental designs are often characterized by high internal validity but potentially low external, or ecological, validity, which can limit the generalizability of the findings to the "real world."

While RCTs represent the gold standard research method for treatment outcome studies, most clinical research is not based on RCT or true experimental methods because many clinically relevant variables cannot be subjected to manipulation, or experimental control. In some cases, quasi-experimental designs are conducted, which mimic experimental designs minus the element of random assignment; however, most of the research conducted in the offender arena is correlational in nature, whereby variables are measured or observed, but not manipulated. Correlational research designs are often aimed at investigating group differences on a particular variable or series of variables, or investigating the relationship between or among variables. Examples include comparing defendants found incompetent to stand trial to those found competent on a measure of intelligence, or examining the relationship between scores on an aggression scale with the frequency of violent incidents over a period of time. Correlational designs tend to be the most practical way to conduct applied clinical research; however, causality cannot be determined via such designs.

Issues to Consider in Accessing Special/Protected Populations

Conducting research with offender populations can be a very daunting task for various reasons, including institutional/political barriers and ethical considerations. Most violent offenders are incarcerated or otherwise institutionalized. Consequently, accessing such groups can be difficult or impossible in some cases. Typical research settings include county jails, state and federal prisons, psychiatric centers, and specialized hospitals—none of which tend to be easily accessible to researchers. Outside researchers or academicians must form relationships with administrators in such institutions if they hope to even advocate for their research ideas. While clinicians working in these settings have the advantage of physical access to the facility and the offender population, barriers to conducting research remain. The research culture of an institution is typically a useful indicator of what one can expect in terms of being permitted to conduct research at the facility. One might find that psychiatric centers or hospitals are more amenable to research endeavors as compared to correctional systems because they usually subscribe to a medical model, thereby emphasizing teaching and research. Gaining permission to conduct research at a facility is merely an initial step, however, and ethical concerns may thwart a research study altogether.

ETHICAL CONSIDERATIONS

There are numerous ethical issues to consider when conducting research with offender groups, particularly given the unfavorable history of such research. The inhumane experimentation conducted by Nazi doctors may come to mind in this regard; however, the US government also has a history of promoting unethical research with human participants. The US Public Health Service (USPHS) Syphilis Study at Tuskegee was a 40-year study (1932–1972) in which researchers withheld medical treatment from

African American men infected with syphilis to gain an understanding of the final stage of the disease. Katz and colleagues (2009) characterized the study as "the most infamous example of biomedical research abuse in US history" (p. 468) and, as such, it has often been attributed to the reluctance of ethnic and racial minorities to participate in clinical research. Recent research has demonstrated that many offenders are not aware of the Tuskegee study, and awareness of it likely has a very limited direct impact on the decisions of offenders to participate in research (Poythress, Epstein, Stiles, & Edens, 2011); however, research such as the Tuskegee study resulted in the implementation of strict ethical safeguards for vulnerable populations (e.g., offenders).

The American Psychological Association (APA) clearly addresses "Human Research Protections" under the research heading on their Web site and notes that the National Commission for the Protection of Human Subjects of Biomedical and Behavioral Research was created in the early 1970s in response to "widely publicized cases of research abuse." Legislation, regulations, and educational/training resources are provided on the site in addition to links for various federal offices of research regulation and relevant ethics codes. In addition to federal regulations and ethical guidelines related to conducting research, most institutions have institutional review boards (IRBs). An IRB is a committee tasked with evaluating human participant research with respect to its risks and benefits and, ultimately, its ethicality. IRBs are federally mandated, and federal regulations regarding them are specified in Title 45 Code of Federal Regulations Part 46 (45 CFR 46) and Title 21 Code of Federal Regulations Parts 50 and 56 (21 CFR 50 and 56). The interested reader is referred to a comprehensive article on the matter available on the APA Web site entitled "IRBs and Psychological Science: Ensuring a Collaborative Relationship" (Eissenberg et al., 2004). It is important to note that conducting research at some institutions will require more than one IRB approval. For example, some prisons are affiliated with medical schools; therefore, IRB approval from the Department of Corrections and the medical school may be required.

RESEARCH IMPLEMENTATION

There are several key elements to consider in the implementation stage of research with protected populations. Issues such as obtaining informed consent to participate in research, recruiting participants, obtaining meaningful samples, and a host of additional issues in the data collection phase might arise. This section will delineate some of the relevant considerations in each of these areas of research implementation.

Obtaining Informed Consent

One of the primary areas of consideration is with respect to obtaining informed consent to participate in a research study from the potential participants. Although obtaining informed consent to participate in research can be a relatively straightforward task in most research contexts, there are a few contexts that pose more of a problem in this regard. Two relevant considerations include the type of sample that is being recruited as participants and the type of data that is being collected.

Federal disclosure requirements for informed consent for research require the inclusion of the following eight items in the informed consent procedures: a statement that the study is research, its purpose and procedures; any reasonably foreseeable risks or discomforts; any benefits that may be reasonably expected; any alternative treatments that might be advantageous to the participant; degree of confidentiality expected; compensation, if any, and whether and nature of treatment available is injury occurs; contact information for further questions; and a statement that participation is voluntary ("Protection of Human Subjects," Title 45 Code of Federal Regulations, Pt 46.116a). Beyond these, however, the researcher also needs to consider other relevant elements of the research design, such as the type of sample that is being recruited and whether any special considerations apply.

To give informed consent, potential participants must do so knowingly, willingly, and competently. Full disclosure of the eight required elements and any other relevant considerations must be provided to the potential participant by the researcher. Consent must be given voluntarily; thus, consideration of any inducements is important to ensure that they are not coercive (either because they imply that something negative would happen to the recruit who chooses not to participate or because they are so lucrative that they make it difficult for the recruit to refuse participation). Consent must be given competently; thus, consideration of the type of participant that is being recruited is imperative. If the participant belongs to a special population that has or has the potential for a known vulnerability, consideration of this must come into the informed consent procedures. Known vulnerable populations include individuals diagnosed with mental illnesses, children and adolescents, individuals diagnosed with developmental disabilities and/or cognitive impairments, and the elderly. These special populations may require adapted consent procedures wherein the researcher either needs to specifically consider the competence of the individual to provide consent or needs to come up with an alternative means of obtaining informed consent from a proxy decision maker. In some instances where potential participants are institutionalized, the institution may be able to provide informed consent on behalf of the participant. In other instances, it may be possible for the researcher to negotiate assistance from the institution in obtaining informed consent from the participants in a separate procedure. For example, Zapf and colleagues (2004) were able to elicit the assistance of admitting psychiatrists, who evaluated each patient's competency to consent to research upon admission, thus allowing for an independent assessment of competency that did not involve the researchers. In any instance where adapted consent procedures involve obtaining informed consent from someone other than the participant, the researcher should be careful to also obtain assent from the actual participant.

Another strategy that has been used to circumvent the issue of obtaining informed consent is for the institution to adopt certain procedures as part of institutional practice. For example, a particular risk assessment instrument may be adopted as part of the standard procedures at an institution and used routinely for any risk evaluation. In this situation, it becomes possible for researchers to obtain the results of the risk assessment instrument as archival data, eliminating the necessity of obtaining informed consent from the participant.

The data that will be collected from the participant and the procedures that will be used in the research need to be delineated as part of the informed consent procedures. Researchers who plan to collect sensitive information, such as criminal history or involvement in criminal activity, may wish to obtain a Certificate of Confidentiality as a means of ensuring that these disclosures are protected from subpoena. Certificates of Confidentiality are issued by the National Institutes of Health (NIH) and are provided to prevent the forced disclosure of identifiable research information (see http://grants.nih.gov/grants/policy/coc/index.htm). According to the 2002 NIH notice:

> They allow the investigator and others who have access to research records to refuse to disclose identifying information on research participants in any civil, criminal, administrative, legislative, or other proceeding, whether at the federal, state, or local level. Certificates of Confidentiality may be granted for studies collecting information that if disclosed could have adverse consequences for subjects or damage their financial standing, employability, insurability, or reputation. By protecting researchers and institutions from being compelled to disclose information that would identify research subjects, Certificates of Confidentiality help achieve the research objectives and promote participation in studies by assuring confidentiality and privacy to participants.

If a Certificate of Confidentiality is obtained for a particular research project, this too should be disclosed in the informed consent procedures.

The issue of obtaining informed consent to participate in research is a broad topic well beyond the scope of this chapter. The interested researcher is encouraged to learn more about this topic in resources such as Scott Kim's (2010) book on *Evaluation of Capacity to Consent to Treatment and Research* or other chapters that deal specifically with the issue of informed consent for research (e.g., Stanley & Galietta, 2006).

Participant Recruitment

Participant recruitment is an essential task in research with violent offenders or other protected populations that can have important implications with respect to the validity of results. Recruitment procedures that fail to adequately sample the population of interest can potentially skew results or reduce their generalizability. Inadequate recruitment methods can also be costly in terms of the amount of time and resources expended and have the potential to increase the risk of unintended disclosure of information by participants. A closely associated issue for longitudinal research—retention of research participants over time—can also compromise the scientific quality of research studies as a result of attrition. Thus, recruitment and retention methods are important considerations for research design and implementation.

Studies that have specifically examined recruitment procedures in research have found that face-to-face recruitment tends to produce the highest yield of eligible participants with the lowest attrition rates but has higher associated costs in terms of resources than other methods; media and print advertisements have been found to produce the largest group of potential participants but also the highest rates of attrition and ineligible participants (Gilliss et al., 2001). Direct referral can be reasonably efficient as a means of recruitment that can be implemented in research with violent offenders or protected populations by the creation of partnerships or collaborations with a community or criminal justice agency that serves the population of interest. These partnerships or collaborations are the key to successful recruitment and, ultimately, successful research; however, they can be time consuming to create and build. Using one's network of contacts is a great place to begin to build these relationships with relevant agencies and organizations.

In some instances, such as when conducting research on mandated treatment programs, offenders can be legally compelled to participate. Young and colleagues (2002) found that the use of structured protocols for informing participants about the conditions and legal contingencies of treatment participation and as well as how participation will be monitored and how threatened consequences will be enforced can be an effective means of retention in mandated treatment programs. In most other instances, offenders or protected populations cannot be legally compelled to participate in research and must be given the opportunity to consent to or refuse participation. When participation cannot be legally compelled, retention rates may be dependent upon the therapeutic alliance (in treatment research, e.g., Barber et al., 2001), staff experience (De Leon, Hawke, Jainchill, & Melnick, 2000), or simply the ability to keep the offender engaged in the treatment program. Daly and colleagues (2010) examined the predictors of attrition in treatment programs for batterers and found those participants who completed the fewest treatment sessions were less educated, unemployed at intake, not court ordered, and had a history of alcohol-related problems. Offering support services tailored to the specific needs of the particular offender population being studied may be an effective means of recruiting and retaining research participants.

A primary concern in the recruitment of vulnerable populations, such as violent offenders, relates to the need to avoid coercion or undue influence to participate. This principle is addressed in the American Psychological Association's Ethics Code (APA, 2002) under section 8.06, Offering Inducements for Research Participation. The first part of this principle, part (a), indicates that psychologists must avoid offering excessive or inappropriate financial or other inducements for research participation when such would likely lead to (coerced) participation. Similar to most ethical principles, this principle is context dependent. As such, what constitutes an excessive or inappropriate inducement is largely dependent on the situation in which the research is being conducted. For instance, a $20 inducement may be a reasonable amount of money to give in an outpatient setting, but it may be considered excessive in an inpatient environment. Thus, the researcher and, ultimately, the review board must take into account the relative significance that a particular dollar amount (or other type of inducement) carries in a particular setting.

WORKING WITH AGENCIES OR ORGANIZATIONS

Because much of the research with violent offenders or protected populations will involve community or criminal justice agencies or organizations, forging a relationship with an agency or organization that serves the population of interest can be an effective means of recruiting participants for research. For this to be effective, the researcher must develop a sound working relationship with the leadership of the agency or organization. This can often entail demonstrating that the research team understands and recognizes the needs of the agency and the clientele in which they serve as well as providing concrete evidence of a commitment to conduct research without disturbing or disrupting the day-to-day activities of the agency or organization. Having research staff that will be able to conduct participant recruitment is often an important consideration given that the staff at many community, government, or criminal justice agencies is often overburdened with their own responsibilities. In addition, procedures for conducting the research or recruitment at a time and in a place that is not disruptive to the agency or organization can often be determined through consultation with and observation of the agency staff's daily operating procedures and activities. The more the researcher is able to work around the daily activities of the agency staff, the easier it will be to conduct the research and to maintain a good working relationship with the agency.

Research investigators who maintain an active presence and who consistently nurture the relationship with the agency where data collection will take place tend to form more solid partnerships with the agency and, as a result, have better outcomes in participant recruitment. Relationships with the agency or organization can be fostered through social interaction with the agency staff (e.g., research staff having lunch with the agency staff), the provision of frequent progress reports to the agency staff, and by establishing collaborations with the agency. These actions serve to strengthen the relationship with the agency and, as a result, improve recruitment and retention outcomes.

SAFETY PROTOCOLS

In many instances conducting research with offender or protected populations requires that a safety protocol be implemented. If data collection is to occur at an organization or agency, the research team should be aware of and be able to follow the safety plan of the agency. In longitudinal studies and other research endeavors whereby data are collected in the field, the issue of a safety protocol becomes imperative. Issues such as working in pairs, carrying a cell phone on your person, making someone aware of your destination and expected time of return to the office, wearing sensible attire, and conducting data collection in the field during daylight hours should be included as part of the safety protocol, and everyone on the research team should be familiar with the protocol and procedures to follow in case of a breach. As mentioned earlier, it is important to note that conducting research at some institutions will require more than one IRB approval. For example, some prisons are affiliated with medical schools; therefore, IRB approval from the Department of Corrections and the medical school may be required. In addition, the Bureau of Prisons (BOP) has its own IRB committee, so all research conducted within this setting or with these populations must also be approved by this IRB.

RETENTION IN LONGITUDINAL RESEARCH

One of the biggest issues for longitudinal research designs is the retention of participants over time. At the time of the initial contact, the researcher should obtain relevant information from the participant that will assist in locating the participant again in the future. Collecting the participant's address; home, work, and mobile phone numbers; and the names, addresses, and phone numbers of three individuals who should always know how to find the participant can assist greatly in locating a participant in the future. In addition, maintaining regular contact, such as by mailing or e-mailing the participant to confirm contact information at regular intervals will serve to limit participant attrition in longitudinal research designs. Of course, these same procedures should also be implemented at each point of contact with the participant.

Obtaining Meaningful Samples

One of the primary considerations in the implementation phase (as well as in the conceptualization and design phase) is to ensure that data are being collected from the most meaningful or relevant sample. The goal of all research is to be able to generalize the results to some larger target population. To do so, the research sample must adequately represent the target population. Researchers need to be careful to consider the target population to which they ultimately wish to generalize and then decide how best to create a research sample that will represent that larger population.

Ideally, the research sample will correspond to the target population on the particular characteristic or variable being studied, as well as on other potentially significant variables. The degree of correspondence between the research sample and the target population is especially important when the goal of the research is to determine the proportion of the target population that has a particular characteristic.

Two general approaches to sampling are typically used in social science research: probability sampling and nonprobability sampling. In probability sampling, all members of the target population have some opportunity of being included in the sample, and it is possible to calculate the probability of any one member being selected. In nonprobability sampling, target population members are selected on the basis of their availability or the researcher's belief that they are representative of the target population; thus, by definition, nonprobability sampling results in an unknown portion of the target population being excluded. Researchers who study issues relevant to violent offenders or violent offending tend to use convenience samples, a common type of nonprobability sample, where the researcher recruits/selects participants on the basis of their availability rather than randomly selecting participants from the full target population. One important consequence of using convenience samples is that there is no way to determine the extent to which the convenience sample, regardless of its size, actually represents the target population, thus limiting the generalizability of the results. There are many instances where a convenience sample is simply the most logistical choice; however, researchers should be aware of and take into consideration the trade-off between convenience and generalizability.

RESPONSE RATES AND NONPARTICIPATION

Response rate refers to the extent to which the final data set includes all members of the sample and is calculated by dividing the number of participants who completed the data collection phase by the total number of potential participants in the entire sample, including those who refused to participate or who were unavailable for one reason or another. In general, the lower the response rate, the greater the sample bias. Researchers should be aware of the issue of response rate and nonparticipation and should attempt to collect at least some relevant data on the characteristics of those individuals in the sample who refused or were unavailable to participate. Doing so allows for some determination of the ways in which the research sample differed from the entire sample.

SAMPLE SIZE AND SAMPLING ERROR

Appropriate sampling methods and adequate response rates are necessary, but not sufficient, for a representative sample; sample size must also be considered. As a general rule, smaller samples have greater sampling error than larger samples. Sampling error is a numerical representation of the precision of the sample's estimate of the variable of interest in the population. Simply put, it is the error caused by observing a sample instead of the whole population; every sample will have some degree of sampling error. Sampling error can be exacerbated by using small sample sizes (less than 1,000) or biased samples; it can be controlled by using larger samples (between 1,000 and 2,000 participants) and by using random sampling techniques. In research with violent offenders, it is rare to collect data on samples of 1,000 or more; therefore, researchers should be especially careful to control or minimize bias in their smaller samples as a means of reducing sampling error.

Other Issues in Data Collection

Along with issues related to participant recruitment and meaningful samples, additional issues of relevance deserve mention: statistical power, and the reliability and validity of instrumentation.

STATISTICAL POWER

Related to the issue of obtaining data from meaningful samples is the issue of ensuring that data are being collected from a large enough sample to be able to detect statistical differences in the variable of interest: statistical power. The power of a statistical test is the probability that the test will reject the null hypothesis when the null hypothesis is false (the probability of making a false-negative error). As power increases, the chance of making a Type II error decreases. Statistical power typically depends on three factors: the significance criterion used (typically 0.05), effect size, and sample size. Since the sample size determines the amount of sampling error inherent in a statistical test result, significant effects are more difficult to determine in smaller sample sizes. Increasing the sample size, therefore, is one of the easiest ways to increase the statistical power of a test. Researchers should consider statistical power when making comparisons between statistical tests and in deciding which test to use (e.g., deciding between parametric and nonparametric tests for the same hypothesis). A power analysis should be calculated to determine the minimum sample size necessary to detect the hypothesized effects. The interested researcher is referred to Tabachnick and Fidell (2012).

RELIABILITY AND VALIDITY OF INSTRUMENTATION

Another consideration in data collection is the reliability and validity of the measures or instruments used. Reliability refers to the degree of consistency demonstrated by the instrument in measuring the same thing each time, whereas validity refers to the degree to which the instrument measures what it is intended to measure. Measures or instruments cannot be valid if they are not reliable, but good reliability does not guarantee that a measure is valid. Both reliability and validity are required for an instrument to provide relevant and meaningful information in research.

In research examining issues related to violent offending, especially in risk assessment research, three types of reliability are most relevant: interrater, test-retest, and internal consistency. Interrater reliability describes the degree of consistency between different raters in making ratings of the same information, whereas test-retest reliability describes the degree of consistency obtained on the same instrument at different points in time. Internal consistency describes the degree to which items on an instrument or measure are homogeneous (or measures of the same construct). Researchers should be careful to consider the various types of reliability in the selection of the various measures or instruments used in research.

With respect to validity, in violence risk assessment research, predictive validity is the primary validity consideration, although incremental validity and construct validity are also important considerations. Predictive validity refers to the degree to which scores on an instrument or measure predict scores on some criterion measure. Incremental validity refers to the degree to which one variable (or measure) improves the predictive validity of a second variable (or measure), whereas construct validity refers to the degree to which an instrument correlates with the psychological construct that it purports to measure. Researchers should be careful to consider all relevant aspects of validity in selecting the measures to be used. More information on reliability and validity for research in forensic contexts can be found in Cruise and Pivovarova (2011); Douglas, Skeem, and Nicholson (2011); Rosenfeld, Byars, and Galietta (2011); and Rosenfeld, Edens, and Lowmaster (2011).

COMPLETION AND PUBLICATION OF RESEARCH

There are a number of issues that arise in the completion and publication phase of research that should be considered and planned for at the earlier stages. Issues such as how to analyze the data collected, how and where to publish the results of your research, and maintaining de-identified data sets after the research has been completed are relevant. Of course, each of these topics can, and indeed does, fill an entire textbook; therefore, the interested researcher is referred to the following additional resources: Kazdin (2003); Meyers, Well, and Lorch (2010); Rosenfeld and Penrod (2011); and Tabachnick and Fidell (2012).

Data Analysis

Data analysis and research design go hand in hand; thus, the researcher should make the determination regarding how best to analyze the data collected in the design and conceptualization stage. Changes in data collection procedures, if any, should take into account the original planned analytic strategy. Researchers should consider the nature of the variables of interest (nominal, ordinal, interval, ratio) and be aware of how each of these types of variables affects the choice of data analytic strategy. In addition, the researcher should be careful to collect data in a way that will allow for the most flexibility in statistical analysis. Thus, it is always better to categorize or collapse data at the analytic stage rather than at the collection phase.

There are a number of common data analytic techniques in research with violent offenders, including receiver operating characteristics (ROC) analysis (see

Douglas, Skeem, & Nicholson, 2011), regression analysis (see Groscup, 2011), and structural equation modeling (SEM; see Groscup, 2011), in addition to basic bivariate (chi-square, correlation, and mean differences) and multivariate (MANOVA) statistical tests (see Groscup, 2011, for a review of each of these data analytic techniques within the context of forensic research). Researchers should be familiar with the different data analytic strategies as well as the underlying assumptions and limitations of each. Selection of the data analytic technique should include consideration of the research hypothesis, the type of relationship the researcher wishes to test, and the number and type of variables in the research.

REPORTING RESEARCH RESULTS

The sixth edition of the *Publication Manual of the American Psychological Association* (2010) contains guidelines and examples for data reporting, and researchers should become familiar with many of the new requirements in this regard. The information presented regarding the statistical analyses used and the results of those analyses should allow the reader to understand why those analytic techniques were chosen and to interpret the results. Basic descriptive information, such as means, measures of variability around those means, and cell or sample sizes, is an absolute requirement; additional information will depend upon the analytic techniques used. Multivariate analyses also require that a correlation or covariance matrix for all of the variables be presented as descriptive information. All inferential statistics should be reported in terms of the value and direction of the summary statistic, the degrees of freedom for that statistic, a measure of error for that statistic, and the exact p value for the statistic. In addition, many journals such as *Law and Human Behavior* and any APA-published journal also require the reporting of an effect size and confidence intervals for the statistic. Researchers should become accustomed to presenting their statistical results in tables, with text descriptions of the statistics in the body of the manuscript referring to, but not repeating, the information displayed in the tables. Interested researchers should consult the *Publication Manual of the American Psychological Association*, sixth edition (2010), for more detailed information.

Publication Issues

In deciding where to publish the results of one's research, a primary consideration should be the type of audience one is attempting to reach. Numerous journals and other publication outlets exist; the goal is to determine the outlet that will provide the greatest amount of exposure to your target audience. Research on issues related to violent offenders or violent offending should target those professionals who will be impacted by the results. As a general note, legal professionals and mental health professionals tend to read different journals; thus, the astute researcher might choose to publish the results of his or her work in two different outlets, targeting two different types of professionals for maximal impact.

One issue that might arise at the publication stage, especially when multiple agencies or organizations are involved in the research, is that of *who* will publish the data and *what* data will be published. These issues are best worked out in advance of the research being completed since working these issues out after the fact can be a frustrating endeavor. An agency or organization that allows data collection at their facility might later decide that they do not want the results of the research published (especially if they have the potential to paint the agency or organization in a negative light). Researchers will want to work out issues such as whether the agency or organization is identified as the data collection site, whether relevant individuals at the agency or organization will receive publication credit (authorship or mention in a footnote), and whether there are any limitations that the organization might place on the data that can be published ahead of time so as to avoid any unnecessary frustration or confusion. Having direct conversations about these issues at the start of the research project and maintaining a good working relationship with the agency or organization will serve to alleviate many publication issues later on.

As mentioned earlier in this chapter, researchers should be familiar with latest edition of the APA's *Publication Manual* to ensure that all relevant and necessary information is reported in the published research. In addition, researchers should be familiar with the literature base and the commonly accepted or expected information to be included in published research reports for the particular area or field of study. Statements about research hypotheses, recruitment methods and success (response rate), research design, and data analytic techniques and assumptions should conform to the norm for the particular area of research so that future researchers are able to replicate the research methods and procedures.

Maintaining Deidentified Data Sets

One final topic worth mentioning in the research completion stage is the issue of maintaining data sets and, specifically, maintaining deidentified data sets. An identifier is any piece of data that can, either directly or indirectly, identify an individual or link an individual to his or her identity. The Health Insurance Portability and Accountability Act (HIPAA) regulations provide a list of what is considered an identifier when working with medical records. Information such as name (including any part of an individual's name, his or her initials, and, in some instances, an Internet screen name); street address; phone numbers; e-mail addresses; place of employment; IP address; vehicle ID; personal Web sites; Social Security number; full date of birth (age, year, and/or month of birth would not be considered identifiers); individual account numbers or record numbers; and photos, videos, or audio recordings where the voice and/or image have not been disguised are all considered to be identifiers. Researchers should take care to deidentify their data sets, even when not required by law, as this will reduce the risk that a participant's identity will be linked to his or her data. One benefit of using a deidentified data set in future research is that most IRBs will classify the protocol as exempt since there is no risk that participants' identities will be linked to their data. Another benefit of maintaining a deidentified data set is that the researcher does not have to provide as much security in terms of locked cabinets, password-protected files, secure Internet servers, and secure data encryption as for data sets that include identifiers.

In instances where identifiers must be maintained, it is prudent for the researcher to store the original data set partitioned into two data sets: a deidentified data set and an identity-only data set. The identity-only data set would include any and all personal identity information necessary for future research.

A researcher-assigned identity code, such as a randomly generated number, unique to each participant would then be associated with that participant's data in each of the two data sets. Later on, when the researcher wishes to merge the identity information with the deidentified information, the identity code can be used to link the two data sets.

SPECIAL OFFENDER POPULATIONS

There are additional considerations to take into account when conducting research with particular offender populations, such as sex offenders, juveniles, and those diagnosed with intellectual disabilities (e.g., sample selection, informed consent). Gaining accessibility to these populations can be an especially arduous task because they are typically considered vulnerable populations within an existing vulnerable population (i.e., offenders). Much of the research with these populations is spurred by legal cases and statutory laws, which have burgeoned in recent years among these groups. A brief overview of research considerations for each of the three aforementioned special populations is presented in the sections that follow.

Sex Offenders

Laws regarding sex offenders have been implemented at unprecedented rates over the past two decades, most of which regard the management of sex offenders (Prentky, Lamade, & Coward, 2011). As such, much research has been conducted on the utility of management efforts, such as registration systems (e.g., Megan's Law) and extended civil commitment for those deemed sexually violent predators (SVPs). Prentky and colleagues (2011) proffered that the most salient research questions in the sex offender arena are related to risk assessment, but that at least three other major topic areas exist: classification and diagnosis, etiology, and remediation and management.

Cowburn (2010) outlined some of the ethical dilemmas inherent to conducting research with sex offenders. One major concern pertains to the disclosure of new or intended offenses during the course of a research study, particularly during an interview in a qualitative study. The author stressed the importance of protecting confidentiality and anonymity to conduct successful research, wherein unreported behaviors and attitudes can be elicited. This presents a considerable dilemma for researchers in this area; namely, protecting sex offenders' confidentiality even when a sexual crime has been confessed. The most appropriate and effective way to manage this potential dilemma is through the IRB and informed consent procedures. That is, the researcher must make the review board fully aware of the limits of confidentiality in the research and how such potential challenges to such would be handled. By doing so, the researcher will avoid having to make spontaneous decisions on his or her own during the course of a research project but instead would have a predetermined plan for addressing such issues should they arise—one that was approved by an IRB. This procedure would be relayed to the participants during the informed consent process, and participants would be reminded of this as necessary throughout the course of their participation. Nevertheless, researchers must address all such potential concerns when designing the study and subsequently proposing it to the IRB. As always, it will be necessary to conduct a cost-benefit analysis in advance to determine the appropriate parameters of the study. The decision regarding whether to initiate formal procedures involving law enforcement in the case of an offender who confesses to commission of an unprosecuted sexual crime should be made well in advance of the research implementation and will most often depend upon the context within which the research is being conducted. Thus, protecting confidentiality in such studies is not correct or incorrect per se; it is a context-specific determination initially made by the researchers, but, ultimately, by the IRB.

Blagden and Pemberton (2010) noted that sex offenders are a highly stigmatized group in our society that tend to elicit volatile public reactions and, as a result, are vulnerable in the community as well as in correctional settings and other institutions. Some settings are solely intended for the confinement and/or treatment of sex offenders; however, sex offenders are often housed among general population inmates and psychiatric patients. Given the high level of stigma related to their offenses, sex offenders may be reluctant to discuss offense-related matters or any sex-related issues in environments that include non–sex offender groups. Blagden and Pemberton (2010) also argued that this vulnerability could be transferred to researchers through the discussion of offenses and traumatic histories, which can also bring issues of morality to the forefront. A researcher's sex is also a significant factor that can increase his or her vulnerability depending on the offender-research participant.

Juvenile Offenders

Judicial and societal philosophical shifts between the rehabilitation and punishment of juvenile offenders have influenced the types of research conducted in this area, with the current focus being on rehabilitation (Cruise & Pivovarova, 2011). The relatively recent US Supreme Court case, *Roper v. Simmons* (2005), is an example of such. In *Roper*, the Court held that it was unconstitutional to impose capital punishment upon juveniles. The ruling was largely based on the empirical literature regarding the brain development and associated maturity levels of adolescents in the context of decision making and culpability. The concept of psychosocial/developmental immaturity cuts across other areas, including competence to waive Miranda rights and competence to stand trial (Grisso et al., 2003; Viljoen, Zapf, & Roesch, 2007). Researchers in this area do not simply compare juveniles to adults; specific age ranges are typically delineated and investigated at the subgroup level as well (e.g., 11–13 year olds).

There is a rather extensive body of literature on juvenile offenders; in fact, a PsycInfo search of the term "juvenile offenders" resulted in nearly 3,000 publications. Cruise and Pivovarova (2011) outlined the main areas of research with this population, which has generally included assessment and prediction and treatment-related issues. The authors also highlighted the most relevant ethical issues to consider when conducting research with juveniles. Informed consent procedures with this population generally include attaining consent from the parent or legal guardian (which may be an agent of the state) and assent from the youth. When developing informed consent procedures with juveniles, Cruise and Pivovarova (2011) recommended that researchers consider the length and reading level of forms and the potential waiver or modification of standard written informed parental consent procedures in some cases per federal, state, and/or local laws. In addition to procedural issues related to informed consent, the costs and benefits of the research must be weighed as in all areas of clinical research. In this context, the interests of the juvenile must be considered in the context of the interests of the legal guardian and of the state.

Offenders Diagnosed With Intellectual Disabilities

As was the case with the two aforementioned special populations, legal rulings and legislation has driven much research with offenders diagnosed with intellectual disabilities. In a landmark ruling one decade ago, the US Supreme Court held that it was unconstitutional to execute persons diagnosed with mental retardation (*Atkins v. Virginia*, 2002). Similar to the *Roper* ruling pertaining to capital punishment with juveniles, the Court cited the association between culpability and deficits in the areas of reasoning, judgment, and impulse control of intellectually disabled people. Furthermore, much of the research that has followed the ruling has paralleled that related to juveniles (e.g., competence to waive Miranda rights, competence to stand trial) and sex offenders (e.g., risk assessment). The interested reader is directed to Lindsay, Hastings, and Beech's (2011a, 2011b) editorial introductions to the *Psychology, Crime and Law* journal's two special issues on research with offenders diagnosed with intellectual and developmental disabilities.

Chen, Salekin, Olley, and Fulero (2011) outlined some important issues to account for when conducting research with intellectually disabled offender populations. First, it is essential to utilize appropriate criteria for identifying who is intellectually disabled. The authors recommended using the IQ and adaptive behavior demarcations from the American Psychiatric Association, which consists of mild, moderate, severe, and profound types of intellectual disability. Chen and colleagues also highlighted the importance of obtaining an appropriate sample, including considering comorbid diagnoses, and addressing informed consent–related issues.

Like most diagnostic groups, intellectually disabled offenders are a heterogenous group. A common mistake in clinical practice is to attribute certain behaviors to the fact that someone is diagnosed with mental retardation despite the fact that the diagnosis is related to cognitive functioning rather than personality functioning or other Axis I–related issues. As such, intellectually disabled offenders can differ significantly with respect to their clinical presentations, and researchers must be attuned to this reality when attaining a study sample. Informed consent issues are also salient in this area of research because some intellectually disabled offenders may not be competent to consent to research and, in some cases, formal guardianship may have already been instituted. In such instances, assent should be sought from the offender-participant and informed consent should be sought from the offender-participant's legal guardian.

CONCLUSION

In this chapter we presented an overview of the issues pertinent to conducting research with violent offenders. Considerations for conducting such research are many, and they can be quite complicated and involved; therefore, it is incumbent upon the researcher to develop an understanding of the issues and a framework from which to conduct meaningful research. Conceptual and practical considerations are necessary to consider when conducting research with vulnerable populations, particularly violent offenders. Ethical issues are as important as those related to research design. Thus, a holistic approach whereby the researcher integrates conceptual and practical issues is not only recommended but also necessary. The most technically sound research design will be useless if one cannot gain access to the population of interest. Similarly, having access to such populations and the ability to collect data will ultimately prove to be (clinically) useless if the methods employed are not rooted in the principles of science. Conducting research with violent offender groups is challenging in many respects, but it is important. No research study is perfect or without limitations; however, research is likely to have increased utility if the researcher adheres to relevant clinical, scientific, and ethical principles.

REFERENCES

American Psychological Association. (2002). Ethical principles of psychologists and code of conduct. *American Psychologist, 57,* 1060–1073.

American Psychological Association. (2010). *Publication manual of the American Psychological Association* (6th ed.). Washington, DC: Author.

Atkins v. Virginia, 536 U.S. 304 (2002).

Barber, J. P., Luborsky, L., Gallop, R., Crits-Cristoph, P., Frank, A., Weiss, R. D., ... Sinqueland, L. (2001). Therapeutic alliance as a predictor of outcome and retention in the National Institute on Drug Abuse Collaborative Cocaine Treatment Study. *Journal of Consulting and Clinical Psychology, 69,* 119–124.

Blagden, N., & Pemberton, S. (2010). The challenge in conducting qualitative research with convicted sex offenders. *The Howard Journal, 49,* 269–281.

Chen, D., Salekin, K., Olley, J. G., & Fulero, S. M. (2011). Research with offenders with intellectual disability. In B. Rosenfeld & S. D. Penrod (Eds.), *Research methods in forensic psychology* (pp. 421–432). Hoboken, NJ: Wiley.

Christensen, L. B. (2001). *Experimental methodology* (8th ed.). Boston, MA: Allyn and Bacon.

Cowburn, M. (2010). Principles, virtues and care: Ethical dilemmas in research with male sex offenders. *Psychology, Crime and Law, 16,* 65–74.

Cruise, K. R., & Pivovarova, E. (2011). Special populations: Juvenile offenders. In B. Rosenfeld & S. D. Penrod (Eds.), *Research methods in forensic psychology* (pp. 400–420). Hoboken, NJ: Wiley.

Daly, J. E., Power, T. G., & Gondolf, E. W., (2010). Predictors of batterer program attendance. *Journal of Interpersonal Violence, 16,* 971–991.

De Leon, G., Hawke, J., Jainchill, N., & Melnick, G. (2000). Therapeutic communities: Enhancing retention in treatment using 'senior professor' staff. *Journal of Substance Abuse Treatment, 19,* 375–382.

Douglas, K. S., Skeem, J. L., & Nicholson, E. (2011). Research methods in violence risk assessment. In B. Rosenfeld & S. D. Penrod (Eds.), *Research methods in forensic psychology* (pp. 325–346). Hoboken, NJ: Wiley.

Eissenberg, T., Panicker, S., Berenbaum, S., Epley, N., Fendrich, M., Kelso, R., ... Simmerling, M. (2004). IRBs and psychological science: Ensuring a collaborative relationship. *American Psychological Association*. Retrieved May 2014, from http://www.apa.org/research/responsible/irbs-psych-science.aspx.

Gilliss, C. L., Lee, K. A., Gutierrez, Y., Taylor, D., Beyene, Y., Neuhaus, J., & Murrell, N. (2001). Recruitment and retention or healthy minority women into community-based longitudinal treatment. *Journal of Women's Health and Gender-Based Medicine, 10*, 77–85.

Grisso, T., Steinberg, L., Woolard, J., Cauffman, E., Scott, E., Graham, S., ... Schwartz, R. (2003). Juveniles' competence to stand trial: A comparison of adolescents' and adults' capacities as trial defendants. *Law and Human Behavior, 27*, 333–363.

Groscup, J. (2011). Statistical principles in forensic research. In B. Rosenfeld & S. D. Penrod (Eds.), *Research methods in forensic psychology* (pp. 78–101). Hoboken, NJ: Wiley.

Hare, R. D. (2003). *Manual for the Revised Psychopathy Checklist* (2nd ed.). Toronto, ON: Multi-Health Systems.

Katz, R. V., Jean-Charles, G., Green, B. L., Kressin, N. R., Claudio, C., Wang, M. Q., ... Outlaw, J. (2009). Identifying the Tuskegee Syphilis Study: Implications and results from recall and recognition questions. *BMC Public Health, 9*, 468–476.

Kazdin, A. E. (2003). *Methodological issues and strategies in clinical research* (3rd ed.). Washington, DC: APA.

Kim, S. Y. H. (2010). *Evaluation of capacity to consent to treatment and research*. New York, NY: Oxford University Press.

Lindsay, W. R., Hastings, R. P., & Beech, A. R. (2011a). Forensic research in offenders with intellectual & developmental disabilities 1: Prevalence and risk assessment. *Psychology, Crime and Law, 17*, 3–7.

Lindsay, W. R., Hastings, R. P., & Beech, A. R. (2011b). Forensic research in offenders with intellectual & developmental disabilities 2: Assessment and treatment. *Psychology, Crime and Law, 17*, 97–100.

Meyers, J. L., Well, A. D., & Lorch, R. F., Jr. (2010). *Research design and statistical analysis* (3rd ed.). New York, NY: Routledge.

Overholser, J. C. (2010). Ten criteria to qualify as a scientist-practitioner in clinical psychology: An immodest proposal for objective standards. *Journal of Contemporary Psychotherapy, 40*, 51–59.

Poythress, N., Epstein, M., Stiles, P., & Edens, J. F. (2011). Awareness of the Tuskegee syphilis study: Impact on offenders' decisions to decline research participation. *Behavioral Sciences and the Law, 29*, 821–828.

Prentky, R. A., Lamade, R., & Coward, A. (2011). Sex offender research in a forensic context. In B. Rosenfeld & S. D. Penrod (Eds.), *Research methods in forensic psychology* (pp. 372–399). Hoboken, NJ: Wiley.

Roper v. Simmons, 543 U.S. 551 (2005).

Rosenfeld, B., Byars, K., & Galietta, M. (2011). Conducting psychotherapy outcome research in forensic settings. In B. Rosenfeld & S. D. Penrod (Eds.), *Research methods in forensic psychology* (pp. 309–324). Hoboken, NJ: Wiley.

Rosenfeld, B., Edens, J., & Lowmaster, S. (2011). Measure development in forensic psychology. In B. Rosenfeld & S. D. Penrod (Eds.), *Research methods in forensic psychology* (pp. 26–42). Hoboken, NJ: Wiley.

Rosenfeld, B., & Penrod, S. D. (2011). *Research methods in forensic psychology.* Hoboken, NJ: Wiley.

Stanley, B., & Galietta, M. (2006). Informed consent in treatment and research. In I. B. Weiner & A. K. Hess (Eds.), *The handbook of forensic psychology* (3rd ed., pp. 211–239). Hoboken, NJ: Wiley.

Stolberg, H. O., Norman, G., & Trop, I. (2004). Randomized controlled trials. *American Journal of Roentgenology, 183,* 1539–1544.

Strupp, H. H. (1981). Clinical research, practice, and the crisis of confidence. *Journal of Consulting and Clinical Psychology, 49,* 216–219.

Tabachnick, B. G., & Fidell, L. S. (2012). *Using multivariate statistics* (6th ed.). London, UK: Pearson.

Viljoen, J. L., Zapf, P. A., & Roesch, R. (2007). Adjudicative competence and comprehension of Miranda rights in adolescent defendants: A comparison of legal standards. *Behavioral Sciences and the Law, 25,* 1–19.

Whitley, B. E., Jr. (2002). *Principles of research in behavioral science* (2nd ed.). Boston, MA: McGraw Hill.

Young, D., & Belenko, S. (2002). Program retention and perceived coercion in three models of mandatory drug treatment. *Journal of Drug Issues, 32,* 297–328.